DOMINE EXAUDI
ORATIONEM MEAM

D. DIONYSIVS CARTHVSIEÑ DOCTOR EXTATICVS.

BENEDICTVS DEVS IN SECVLA

Domine Exaudi Orationem Meam

DENIS THE CARTHUSIAN

COMMENTARY
on the
DAVIDIC
Psalms

VOLUME V
[PSALMS 101–125]

Which are most learnedly explained, to the degree able, in their multiple senses, namely LITERAL, ALLEGORICAL, TROPOLOGICAL, & ANAGOGICAL, *with nothing except the most sound Scriptures of both Testaments.*

Translation & Introduction by
ANDREW M. GREENWELL

AROUCA
PRESS

Commentary in Latin taken from
Opera Omnia, Vol. 6
(Montreuil: Typis Cartusiae S. M. de Pratis 1898).
English Translation & Introduction © Andrew M. Greenwell
Copyright © Arouca Press 2025

ISBN: 978-1-998492-05-3 (pbk)
ISBN: 978-1-998492-06-0 (hardcover)

Arouca Press
PO Box 55003
Bridgeport PO
Waterloo, ON N2J3G0
Canada
www.aroucapress.com
Send inquiries to info@aroucapress.com

DEDICATION

To my children,
Elizabeth Grace, Mary Abigail, and Christopher Michael

Ecce haereditas Domini, filii; merces, fructus ventris.
Sicut sagittae in manu potentis, ita filii excussorum.
Beatus vir qui implevit desiderium suum ex ipsis:
non confundetur cum loquetur inimicis suis in porta.
— Psalm 126:3–5

And to my grandchildren,
Piper Feliz, Ryder James, Blaise Francisco, Søren Agnes
(† 6/27/20), Zephyr Amoreena, Roque Telemachus,
Caio Augustus, Fisher Invenio, Rainer Ignatius,
Jesse Radix, and Honor Seraphina († 9/21/23)

Ecce sic benedicetur homo qui timet Dominum . . .
videas filio filorum tuorum.
— Psalm 126:5–6

Materia est universalis: quia cum singuli libri canonicae Scripturae speciales materias habeant, hic liber generalem habet totius theologiae: et hoc est quod dicit Dionysius: divinarum odarum, id est Psalmorum, sacram Scripturam intendere, est, sacras et divinas operationes universas decantare. Unde signatur materia in hoc quod dicit: in omni opere, quia de omni opere Dei tractat.

— St. Thomas Aquinas,
Commentary on the Psalms, pr.

CONTENTS

ABBREVIATIONS

DS Heinrich Denziger, *Enchiridion Symbolorum Definitionum et Declara-tionum de Rebus Fidei et Morum* (*Compendium of Creeds, Definitions, and Déclarations on Matters of Faith and Morals*) (P. Hünerman, ed.) (Robert Fastiggi and Anne Englund Nash, eds., Eng. ed.) (43rd ed.) (San Francisco: Ignatius Press 2012).

PG *Patrologiae cursus completus. Series Graeca.* Ed. J.-P. Migne. Paris: Migne, 1857–1886.

PL *Patrologiae cursus completus. Series Latina.* Ed. J.-P. Migne. Paris: Migne, 1844–1864.

ST St. Thomas Aquinas, *Summa Theologiae* (corpusthomisticum.org)

CCC Catechism of the Catholic Church

INTRODUCTION
to
DENIS THE CARTHUSIAN'S
Commentary on the Psalms

PART 5
[PSALMS 101–125]

Denys entrusts the supernatural wisdom . . . to Thomas Aquinas whom, in various works, he says was "a was a man truly and specially illumined by God," who is "preeminent among Scholastic doctors in sanctity, illumination, and authority," the "most distinguished among modern doctors," and the "most learned of all them," a "remarkable philosopher and profound and outstanding theologian," who moreover was the "most faithful defender of the Roman and Apostolic See."[1]

IN THE INTRODUCTION TO THE FIRST OF six volumes of the translation of Denis the Carthusian's *Commentary on the Davidic Psalms*, I identified four noteworthy aspects of Denis's *Commentary* which make it notable among other commentaries, one of which was its Thomistic quality.[2] For the introduction to this fifth volume, which translates Denis's commentary on Psalms 101 through 125, I would like to elaborate briefly on this particular observation and provide evidence and greater justification for it now that we near completion of the six volumes.

Certainly, in the broadest sense of the term, Denis the Carthusian was Thomistic in education and in spirit. He was a disciple of Thomas from his youth. In the main, he studied the *via Thomae* at the University of Cologne under the instruction of the Thomistic scholar Henry of

---

1 Kent Emery, Jr., *What Does it Mean to be a "Thomist"? Denys the Carthusian and Thomas Aquinas*, in *Widersprüche und Konkordanz: Peter von Bergamo und der Thomismus im Spätmittelalter* (Bill: Leiden, 2020), 265 (herein Emery).
2 Denis the Carthusian, *Commentary on the Davidic Psalms*, Vol. 1 (Beatus Vir), xxx.

Gorkum (*ca.* 1378–1431).[3] Yet Denis's study at Cologne was not exclusively devoted to Thomas, as he appears to have departed Thomas's guidance from time to time, especially in philosophical issues, and flirted with Thomas's master, St. Albert, on some side roads on the *via Alberti*.[4] Also, in the areas of mystical theology, Denis, as is well known, particularly courted the writings of Dionysius the Areopagite. But such departures from St. Thomas were theological peccadilloes at best,[5] and they did not adulterate the main course and focus of his thought which remained decidedly Thomistic. As the Dionysian scholar Kent Emery, Jr. summarized it: Denis the Carthusian's "devotion to the thought of Thomas Aquinas is evident in his first writings after he left Cologne and thereafter until the end of his career."[6] The Dominican theologian Romanus Cessario ranks Denis the Carthusian along with John Capreolus as the two best-known commentators of Thomas in the fifteenth century.[7] The Czech-born Dominican Efrem Jindráček agrees with this assessment: "[T]here can be no doubt that Denys contributed to the diffusion of Aquinas' doctrine in late medieval Germany and France, especially in the monastic environment."[8]

Using the Dionysian scholar Kent Emery's framework of a "threefold order of Wisdom," which emanates down from Wisdom himself, that is, Christ, the *Logos*, Denis's philosophical basis, that is, his "natural wisdom naturally acquired," appears to have been significantly Albertian. On the other hand, Denis's theology, or his "supernatural wisdom naturally acquired," appears to have been firmly Thomist. Finally, Denis's mystical theology, or his "supernatural wisdom supernaturally bestowed," was

---

3 Henry of Gorkum (Henricus de Gorrichem) was a colleague of the Thomist commentator John Capreolus at the University of Paris. He left Paris for Cologne and was director of a *Bursa* he founded (later called the *Bursa Montana* after its second Regent, Gerard de Monte (*ca.* 1400–1480). The *Bursae*, often privately funded, were colleges at universities where students and masters lived in common under the oversight of a regent. *See* Harm Goris, "Thomism in the Fifteenth Century," Aquinas as Authority (Utrecht: Stichting Thomasfonds, 2002), 10–14.

4 Emery, 259–61.

5 One such infrequent divergence is reflected in this *Commentary*, where Denis departs from St. Thomas's view that the existence of God is not self-evident. *See* Volume 1, Article XXXVI (Psalm 13:1), 227 & footnotes 13–35 through 13–39.

6 Emery, 262.

7 Romanus Cessario, O. P., *A Short History of Thomism* (Washington, D. C., Catholic University Press, 2005), 62–63.

8 Efrem Jindráček, O. P., "Western Reception in the Fifteenth Century," *The Oxford Handbook of the Reception of Aquinas* (Oxford: Oxford University Press, 2021), 97–98

clearly Dionysian.[9] Since a scriptural commentary purports to focus on supernatural wisdom revealed in the Word of God, the *Dei Verbum*, it follows that St. Thomas would play a large part in governing the "supernatural wisdom naturally acquired," and so the *Commentary* is properly called Thomistic based upon this central core of Denis's doctrinal commitments.

To be sure, there is some vagueness in the word "Thomistic," particularly when used in reference to Denis the Carthusian's Commentary and relating it to its exact Thomistic analog, Thomas's *Postilla super Psalmos*, more frequently referred to as his *Commentary on the Psalms*. Although St. Thomas began work on a commentary on the Psalms towards the end of his life while at Naples, he never completed it, as death intervened.[10] Moreover, there is no evidence that suggests Denis was aware of Thomas's *Commentary on the Psalms*, so it does not appear to have been publicly available to him in the 1430s. At least as it concerns his *Commentary on the Davidic Psalms*, then, it seems that Denis did not resort to Thomas Aquinas's unfinished *Commentary on the Psalms*. There is no textual evidence that he relied upon, or drew in any way, upon Thomas's commentary. The two cannot be linked. Accordingly, Denis's own commentary on the Psalms cannot be called Thomistic based upon any reliance on St. Thomas's unfinished Commentary on the Psalms. It has to be Thomistic in another sense.

Obviously, the effect of St. Thomas and Denis's credentials as a Thomist could be easily proved were one to review Denis's commentary on Thomas Aquinas's *Summa Theologiae*, a sort of "Summa on the Summa" entitled *Summa Fidei Orthodoxae*.[11] But how do we measure, or at least evidence, the Thomistic footprint specifically in Denis's *Commentary on the Psalms*

---

9 Emery, 269. As is well-known, however, Thomas himself is quite Dionysian; he cites to the Areopagite right up there with St. Augustine and Aristotle. So the Carthusian's reliance on the Areopagite does not necessarily mean a departure from the *via Thomae*.

10 In his *Commentary on the Psalms*, one of St. Thomas's final works authored between 1272 and 1273, St. Thomas comments only on Psalms 1–54. It is believed to be a *reportatio*, or a transcription of his lectures, on the Psalms, which lecture was never completed since its course was untimely ended by the saint's death. Moreover, St. Thomas's commentaries are succinct bullet points, which may be called snippets, apothegms, *pensées*, or vignettes. This is not a sustained commentary in the style of, say, St. Augustine's *Exposition on the Psalms* (*Enarrationes in psalmos*), or *Cassiodorus's* Exposition on the Psalms (*Expositio psalmorum*), or Denis's own *Commentary on the Davidic Psalms* (*Commentarium in Psalmos Omnes Davidicos*).

11 Denis the Carthusian, *Summa Fide Orthodoxae Liber Quatuor*, Opera Omnia, Vols. 17–18 (Montreuil 1899)

where the underlying text is biblical, and Denis in his introduction both disavowed scholastic subtleties and expressed an intent to use scripture to interpret scripture. As Denis put it in his very title, he sought to explain the Psalms "to the degree able ... with nothing except the most sound Scriptures of both Testaments." So by design, the Thomistic influence will not be direct; it must make itself felt obliquely.

Express mentions to Thomas occur sufficiently frequently to provide clear evidence of influence of the *Common Doctor* upon Denis's thoughts. Various examples can be elicited to establish this. One example would be Denis's reference to Thomas in his anagogical exposition of Psalm 20, where he comments on verse 20:4: *You have set on his head a crown.* This verse refers, Denis says, to man's intellect, "which is the supreme power of the soul according to Thomas."[12] Another example of such direct references can be found in Denis's commentary on Psalm 39:7: *Sacrifice and oblation you did not desire; but you have pierced ears for me. Burnt offering and sin offering you did not require.* Denis interprets this verse as foretelling the abrogation of the ceremonial and juridical (but not moral) precepts of the Old Law by Christ, most notably the precepts regarding animal and burnt sacrifices. These were wholly replaced by the sacrifice of Christ, Denis notes, of which they were but a sign or figure.[13] "The three-fold nature of the precepts of the Old Law," Denis states towards the end of his treatment of this issue, "is most elegantly and beautifully addressed by the glorious and holy doctor, blessed Thomas."[14]

There are other instances. In addressing Ps. 49:19: *Your mouth has abounded with evil, and your tongue framed deceits,* Denis has cause to address the issue of scandal. In his discussion of this subject matter, he distinguishes between the "scandal of the little ones" (*scandalum pusillorum*) — which is to be avoided at all costs — and Pharisaic scandal (*scandalum Pharisaeorum*) — which cannot always be avoided and which, in any event, "arises out of malice and blindness of the scandalized, not from the defect of scandalization."[15] Denis notes at the end of his discussion that the perfect neither cause scandal nor, "according to Thomas," are scandalized.[16] This is a clear injection of St. Thomas into his work. In the exposition of Ps. 113:12–15 and discussion of the *idols*

---

12 Vol. 1, 369; *see also* ST Ia, q. 82, art. 3, co.
13 Vol. 2, 295–96.
14 Vol. 2; the reference is to ST IaIIae, qq. 98–103, the so-called "Treatise on Law."
15 Vol. 2, 484–85.
16 Vol. 2; ST IIaIIae, q. 43, art. 5, co.

of the Gentiles referred to in that verse, Denis observes that any sort of power to such idols is entirely rejected by both reason and theological truth, "as St. Thomas beautifully and efficaciously demonstrates in his *Summa Contra Gentiles*."[17]

In Denis's exposition of Psalm 50, one of the six penitential Psalms, Denis addresses the issue of what is meant by Ps. 50:7's statement, *Behold, I was conceived in iniquities*.[18] In his relatively lengthy treatment of this verse, Denis addresses the issue of original sin, which he compares to the "seed of a leper." The "leper generates nothing but lepers," he notes, "and he transfers leprosy with the seed," Denis continues, "but . . . it is not in the seed as in a subject, but as in origin."[19] This leprosy analogy is taken directly from the *Summa*.[20] Here we have a direct contribution, even if not attributed expressly to Thomas.

There are also instances in the *Commentary* where St. Thomas's writings are the probable source of other authorities, for example references to St. Augustine, St. Gregory, St. Jerome, or St. John of Damascus, among others, are frequently uncritically drawn from the *Summa Theologiae*.[21] As an example of this, we might refer to Denis's treatment of Ps. 88:48: *Remember what my substance is. For have you made all children of men in vain?* In discussing this verse, Denis makes reference to the difference between God's antecedent and subsequent will.[22] While Denis refers to "the Damascene" for this distinction, it is likely an indirect reference to St. Thomas's *Summa*, where the same point is made by Thomas by a similar reference to John of Damascus.[23] The same is probably true for Denis's teaching regarding the humanity of Christ as being an instrument of his divinity in interpreting Ps. 88:22: *For my hand shall help him, and*

---

17 Vol. 5, 298 (referring to SCG II, 120).

18 Vol. 2, 494–500.

19 Vol. 2, 499.

20 ST IaIIae, q. 81, art. 1, co.

21 That this is the case in many instances is evidenced by St. Thomas's errors which are imported by Denis's uncritical use of them in his *Commentary*. For example, St. Thomas Aquinas attributes the definition of glory as "brilliant knowledge with praise," *clara cum laude notitia*, to St. Ambrose, although it is actually from St. Augustine. However, Denis attributes (wrongfully along with St. Thomas) to Ambrose in discussing Ps. 94:7. Vol. 4, 424. ST IaIIae, q. 2, art. 3, co. The actual source is to St. Augustine's *Contra Maximinum Arianum*, II, 13, 2. See discussion in Volume 1, footnote 8-22, 152.

22 Vol. 4, 312.

23 ST Ia, q. 19, art. 6, s.c. which cites to St. John of Damascus's *On the Orthodox Faith*, II, 29.

my arm shall strengthen him.[24] While this notion is from St. John of Damascene, it probably comes to Denis through Thomas's treatment in the *Summa contra Gentiles.*[25]

But not all references are direct or express or obvious or certain. There are other references to Thomas which occur *sub silentio*, such as when Denis comments on Psalm 1:4, observing that the wicked are unlike the tree planted beside running waters. This occurs as well in his comments on Psalm 24:21: *The innocent and the upright have adhered to me: because I have waited upon you.* Negatively, in commenting on Ps. 1:4, Denis observes that the wicked who reject Christ are unlike the trees planted beside life-giving waters, and so have neither similarity to, or love for, Christ, for "similarity is the cause of love."[26] Affirmatively, however, those who are innocent and upright and who are referred to in Ps. 24:1 are attracted to the person who waits upon God because "similarity is a cause of love."[27] While this may have been a scholastic maxim derived from Aristotle and so is not unique to Thomas, it is certainly also to be found in the *Summa*,[28] from where it is probable that it came and found itself nestled tacitly in Denis's commentary. Similarly, in discussing Ps 114:11: *Every man is a liar*, Denis refers to a tripartite truth, truth of life, truth of doctrine, and truth of justice.[29] This is probable a reference to ST IIaIIae, q. 109, art. 3, obj. 3 & ad 3, where Thomas — wrongly attributing it to St. Jerome — makes this distinction. It is unlikely that Denis obtained it from another source.

Denis very probably relies heavenly on St. Thomas in discussing the tripartite human knowledge of Jesus, a frequent and core feature of his *Commentary* as explained in the introduction to Volume 2 of the *Commentary*. The evidence of the nexus between Denis and Thomas is found in Denis's position on the *acquired* knowledge of Jesus. Here, commenting on Ps. 26:1 and the statement *The Lord is my illumination* interpreted as referring to Christ, Denis refers to the knowledge of Jesus, the Incarnate Word. In conjunction to the infinite knowledge the person of Christ enjoyed by reason of his divinity, Denis explains that Christ's humanity itself enjoyed a three-fold type of knowledge. In addition to the beatific vision that Christ enjoyed as *comprehensor*, Christ also was

---

24 Vol. 4, 318.
25 SCG, lib. 4, cap. 41, n.11. *See footnote* 195 in Vol. 4, 318 for further elaboration.
26 Vol. 1, 42.
27 Vol. 1, 450.
28 ST IaIIae, q. 26, art. 3, co.
29 Vol. 5, 321.

gifted with a well-night infinite infused knowledge that he could draw from as needed. Yet Denis mentions that Christ also had "an acquired or experimental knowledge," in which he advanced or made progress, "not, however, by learning in any way from others," he makes clear, "but by his own discovery."[30] As man, Jesus would learn by experience what he already knew through his beatific knowledge or his infused knowledge. This experiential or acquired knowledge of Christ is referred to without further elaboration by Denis in his commentary on Ps. 40:12 as referring to Christ: *By this I know that you have had a good will for me.* This knowledge in Christ, Denis explains, does not refer to the divine knowledge, or the beatific or infused human knowledge of Christ, but refers to the knowledge acquired by the humanity of Christ experientially.[31] The case is the same for Ps. 40:17: *You have taught me, O God, from my youth.* In his exposition of this verse, Denis states that "Christ also had (according to some) acquired or experiential knowledge."[32] All these instances would seem to be references to Thomas's later teaching on this subject as found in his *Summa*.[33] As noted in our discussion in the introduction to Volume 2 of the *Commentary*, "Aquinas is generally thought to have been the first thirteenth-century Scholastic doctor to posit the existence of naturally acquired human knowledge in Christ, as opposed to uniquely infused knowledge."[34] It is reasonable, therefore, to infer that the source for Denis's opinions on this issue come directly from St. Thomas and his *Summa Theologiae.*

Denis also relies on St. Thomas for his discussion of virtue. A clear instance of this is found in Denis's commentary on Ps. 40:14, where he closes the tropological commentary on the Psalm with a discussion on the evil of the whisperer (*susurrator*), the detractor, the double-tongued person (*bilinguis*), and the person who is contumacious.[35] Denis's discussion quite clearly and generously draws from Thomas's treatment of the same subject matter in ST IIaIIae, qq. 72–74. Another instance of this borrowing is found in Denis's literal exposition of Ps. 43:14: *You have made us a reproach to our neighbors, a scoff and derision to them that are round about us.* In interpreting this verse, Denis discusses

---

30 Vol. 2, 17.

31 Vol. 2, 315.

32 Vol. 3, 428.

33 ST IIIa, q. 9, art. 4, co., q. 12. Arts. 1–4. Thomas changed his opinion on this issue so as found, *e.g.*, in III Sent. Dist. 14, a. 3, sol. 5 *ad* 3m; d. 18, a. 3, *ad* 5m.

34 Thomas Joseph White, O. P., "The Infused Science of Christ," *Nova et Vetera*, Vol. 16, No. 2 (2018).

35 Vol. 2, 326–27.

how God permitted the Jews "to be mocked with wrinkled nose and derided with mouth open wide" by their enemies.[36] This is a clear, almost verbatim reference St. Thomas.[37] This reliance is also exhibited in Denis's commentary on Ps. 75:12: *Vow and pay to the Lord your God.* In discussing an oath and a vow and their level of bindingness, Denis states: "Thomas affirms that a vow obligates more than an oath."[38] As a final example, Denis refers expressly and specifically to St. Thomas and his *Summa*, specifically IIIa, q. 25, arts. 1–2, in addressing the issue of Christ's humanity and the veneration or adoration owed it when he discusses Ps. 98:5: *Exalt the Lord our God, and adore his footstool, for it is holy.*[39]

Not all references to the Thomasian corpus are to the *Summa Theologiae*, though the vast majority are. With respect to the Davidic authorship of Ps. 89, for example, Denis refers to St. Thomas in discussing Ps. 89:9–10: *For all our days are spent ... The days of our years in them are seventy years.* "Thomas asserts David wrote these verses in reference to his own time." And so," Denis concludes, "according to Thomas, David was the author of this present Psalm."[40] This is most likely a reference to St. Thomas's *De malo*, q. 4, art. 3, ad 11.

Less doctrinally, and at a more personal level, Denis explicitly refers to the *persona* of St. Thomas in his discussion of Ps. 70:9: *Cast me not off in the time of old age: when my strength shall fail, do not forsake me.* Those last words — *do not forsake me, ne derelinquas me* — Denis notes, were particularly dear to St. Thomas. "St. Thomas used to have a singular and special devotion to this verse, and it would reduce him to sweet tears and boundless weeping."[41]

While Denis remains true to his intent to use scripture to interpret scripture in his *Commentary on the Psalms* — his quotations and references to the scriptures to interpret the Psalms are in the thousands — and so the *analogia Scripturae* remains his greatest exegetical and commentarial tool, it still remains true that St. Thomas is behind the scenes providing guidance. Given Denis's Thomistic education under Henry of Gorkum, his public avowal as a disciple of Thomas, his expressed devotion to

---

36 Vol. 2, 366.

37 ST IIaIIae, q. 75, art. 1, ad 1 (the "wrinkled nose" language ultimately is derived from the Gloss); however, it is likely that Denis obtained it directly from Thomas.

38 Vol. 3, 534; ST. IIaIIae, q. 89, art. 8, c.

39 Vol. 4, 452–56.

40 Vol. 4, 335.

41 Vol. 3, 407.

St. Thomas Aquinas, and his direct and indirect references to Thomas, it is clear that the Thomistic synthesis of the *Summa Theologia*, and to a lesser extent Thomas's other works, acts as a sort of theological governor or rudder to Denis, and so behind the *Commentary* we find St. Thomas's steady hand.

ACKNOWLEDGMENTS

As was the case for the last four volumes, there are many people to thank for this one: Certainly, at the top of the list is Alex Barbas, with Arouca Press. Closer to home, there is my wife, Betsy, who has been a quiet, but supporting partner in my venture. I again must include Cindi, my legal assistant, for her dedication to proofreading the text, adding a set of eyes beyond mine to assure as much integrity in the text as humanly possible. Finally, I continue to thank Bishop Daniel Flores, Deacon Keith Fournier, and all the Benedictines who have come out in support of Denis the Carthusian: Dom Hugh Sommerville Knapman, Dom Pius Mary Noonan, Abbot Philip Anderson, and Dom Alcuin Reid. May God bless them all for their support. *Gratias ago vobis.*

— Pentecost Sunday, MMXXIV

PREFACE
to
DENIS THE CARTHUSIAN'S
Commentary on the Psalms

PART 5
[PSALMS 101–125]

David *gave thanks to the Holy One, and to the Most High,* and *with his whole heart he praised the Lord, and loved God that made him.* Ecclus. 47:9, 10.

N THE WORDS ABOVE, THE GLORIOUS PROPHET and holy King David is commended in three ways: for the confession of his own fault wherein he humbly confessed to the most high God, saying, *To you only have I sinned, and had done evil before you.*[1] Second, for his intimate confession of divine praise, for with all his heart, that is, with the fullness of his heart, he praised the Lord with all enthusiasm and readiness, as it says below: *I will sing to the Lord as long as I live; I will sing praise to my God while I have my being.*[2] Third, for the holy love of his own Creator. The entire perfection of the spiritual life consists in these three things.

For since praise is not seemly in the mouth of a sinner,[3] a man must first confess his own evildoings, because all things are washed away in confession. Hence it is written in the seventh chapter of the book of Joshua: *My son, give glory to the Lord God of Israel, and confess . . . what you have done.*[4] Now the soul being cleansed by confession renders a man worthy and fit to praise the Lord, for the confession of one's own sins disposes and makes fit a man for the confession of divine praise in which the pure mind is inflamed with the ardor of divine love to such

---

1 Ps. 50:6a.
2 Ps. 103:33.
3 Ecclus. 15:9.
4 Joshua 7:10.

an extent that he can say: *There came in my heart the word of the Lord like a burning fire shut up in my bones, and I was wearied, not being able to bear it.*[5] Moreover, as the confession of sin is a human act, because it belongs only to man; so praising the Lord is an angelic act, because it belonged to the angels from the beginning of their creation, is continually in them, and will always be in them. But to love God is an act entirely divine: for it belongs to God eternally, perfectly, and infinitely. And so, confessing our sins, let us lead a praiseworthy and human life. For as it is human to sin from weakness, so is it human to rise again by confession. Now we lead an angelic and heavenly life by praising God; but in loving God we become deified, and we are bestowed a deiform life. To attain this, we must direct all our efforts to it. But what especially directs us towards attaining it is constant praise or continual reciting of the Psalms, according to the words of Isaiah: *The Lord . . . will fill your soul with brightness, . . . if you glorify him.*[6]

Since with the help of the Lord, the Savior, two of the books of fifty Psalms have ben exposited, it is now incumbent to bring forth the third part in accordance with the manner and form explained in the beginning, namely, proceeding simply, without ornamentation of style and abstruseness of sense, and to explain these Psalms in a fourfold sense, that is literally, allegorically, tropologically, and anagogically, so long as it is possible and appears expedient, and as much as he, of whom is written: *All wisdom is from the Lord God, and has been always with him, and is before all time*, deigns to give.[7] It is he, whose most merciful enlightenment I most affectionally invoke, through the love, prayers, and merits of our Advocatrix, Salvatrix, and Lady, the holy Virgin, sweet Mary.

---

5   Jer. 7:19.
6   Is. 58:11a, 13b.
7   Ecclus. 1:1.

COMMENTARY
on the
DAVIDIC
Psalms

PART 5
[PSALMS 101–125]

Psalm 101

ARTICLE I

EXPOSITION OF THE ONE HUNDRED AND FIRST PSALM IN THE PERSON OF THE PENITENT: DOMINE, EXAUDI ORATIONEM MEAM. HEAR, O LORD, MY PRAYER.

101{102}[1] *The prayer of the poor man, when he was anxious, and poured out his supplication before the Lord.*

Oratio pauperis, cum anxius fuerit, et in conspectu Domini effuderit precem suam.

THE TITLE OF THE PSALM NOW BEING addressed is: 101{102}[1] *Oratio pauperis, cum anxius fuerit, et in conspectu Domini effuderit precem suam; the prayer of the poor man, when he was anxious, and poured out his supplication before the Lord:* that is, the present Psalm is the prayer of a penitent man, since, in light of his recollection of his sins, he is afflicted with the fear of the future judgment and of the infernal torments, and he pours himself out before the Lord so that he might receive his mercy, namely, a lightening of the present trials, the restitution of innocence, and glory in the future.

101{102}[2] *Hear, O Lord, my prayer: and let my cry come to you.*

Domine, exaudi orationem meam, et clamor meus ad te veniat.

Speaking, therefore, in the person of a man, the holy Prophet [David], recognizing his own weakness, iniquities, and miseries, and deploring his spiritual poverty, says: 101{102}[2] *Domine,* O Lord, almighty God, one and three, totally and by nature merciful, *exaudi,* hear, that is, fulfill by acknowledging, *orationem meam, my prayer,* that is, by my fitting petitions to you; *et clamor meus, and let my cry,* my mental cry, namely, my ardent affection and heavenly desire, or my vocal cry, which is the declaration of great and holy desire, *ad te veniat, come to you,* that is, be accepted by you, be pleasing to you, and be attended to and fulfilled by you in the way that some Scripture says: *The cry of them has entered into the ears of the Lord of Sabaoth.*[1] And the way you yourself have said: *The cry of the children of Israel is come unto me.*[2] For our cry comes unto the Lord, not in terms of place, but in terms of being accepted.

101{102}[3]   *Turn not away your face from me: in the day when I am in trouble, incline your ear to me. In what day soever I shall call upon you, hear me speedily.*

Non avertas faciem tuam a me; in quacumque die tribulor, inclina ad me aurem tuam; in quacumque die invocavero te, velociter exaudi me.

101{102}[3]   *Non avertas faciem tuam, turn not your face,* that is, the aspect of your kindliness, *a me, from me,* a vile and poor, yet penitent sinner. Now the Prophet speaks to God in a human manner, as if there were ears and a face in God, and a fresh or recent turning towards or a turning away from us according to the ongoing state of our merit or demerit. But all these things exist spiritually and immutably in God. For the face of God is the considered intellect of God, and the ear of God is his merciful assistance. The turning away of God is the hatred of evil; but the turning toward God is the approval of the good. *In quacumque die tribulor, in the day when I am in trouble,* that is, when I am afflicted in heart because of committed sins or the trials or perils of the world and the devil, *inclina ad me aurem tuam, incline your ear to me,* that is, apply your mercy to me, declaring the effect of your kindliness in me, that is, consoling my sorrowful soul, strengthening my weakened body, and mitigating or removing the trials which I suffer, so as promptly to renew my soul. *In quacumque die, in what day soever,* indeed, in any hour or moment of the day or the night, *invocavero te, I shall call upon you,* from the intimate affection of mind praying to your goodness, *velociter, speedily,* that is, without delay; in accordance with my need, *exaudi me, hear me,* bestowing upon me the light and the presence of your tender mercies, in the manner that Scripture says regarding the just man: *You shall call, and the Lord shall hear: you shall cry, and he shall say, Here I am.*[3]

See how often the same sense is repeated under other words. For it is customary in Scripture (especially in those things which pertain to the affection) frequently to recapitulate the same statement using other words. This is very salubrious. For as many times as words of affection

---

1 James 5:4b.
2 Ex. 3:9a.
3 Is. 58:9a.

are repeated, the internal affection is renewed, increased, and perfected: because one good affection prepares the mind for other similar ones. And by the repetition of affections the appetite is inflamed: and so it is that a prayer of this kind is calculated to be more heard because the more prayer originates from warmer affection, the more it is pleasing to God. For this reason, it behooves us to recall the same holy desire in prayer, re-urging it in many ways, never ceasing from it because of laziness or indifference. For all of us should be wary never to desist from prayer because of our sluggishness, but all of the divine work should be fervently begun and ended,[4] especially the praise of, and prayer to, God.

Now three things are required for prayer to be heard according to Augustine.[5] The first requirement is that things conducive for salvation must be asked for. For to ask in the name of Jesus or the Savior is to pray for those things which refer to true salvation.[6] It is for this reason that Paul was not heard when he prayed for the removal of the *sting of the flesh*.[7] For that sting in him worked together for his good[8] because, like a man encountering vexation or a soldier the strain of war, it was an occasion for the increasing of merit. Second, we must pray perseveringly, in the manner the Savior says: *We ought always to pray, and not to faint*,[9] and the Apostle, *praying at all times in the spirit; and in the same watching with all instance and supplication.*[10] Third, that we pray for ourselves. We may not always be heard in our prayers for others because of their incapacity.[11] And as blessed Thomas attests, in order that a man might be heard for another, it is necessary in some way that the man praying have a certain

---

4 E. N. By "divine work" or *opus divinum*, Denis is referring to the monastic obligation to recite the Divine Office, the so-called *opus Dei*, the work of God.

5 E. N. It appears that Denis is drawing the Augustinian teaching from St. Thomas Aquinas's treatment of prayer in the *Summa*, though St. Thomas identifies four things as necessary for prayer to be heard: "four conditions, which must exist concurrently, for someone praying always to be heard: namely, that he pray for himself, for things necessary for salvation, piously, and perseveringly." ST IIaIIae, q. 83, art. 15, ad 2.

6 *Cf.* John 15:16.

7 2 Cor. 12:7–9. E. N. Three times St. Paul prayed for the removal of this "sting" of his flesh, to which the Lord answered: "My grace is sufficient for you: for power is made perfect in infirmity."

8 *Cf.* Rom. 8:28a.

9 Luke 18:1b.

10 Eph. 6:18.

11 E. N. Although man is generally by nature *capax Dei or capax gratiae*, that is, capable of receiving God or his grace, ST IaIIae, q. 113, art. 10, c.; IIIa, q. 2, art. 3, c., the particular person we are praying for may not be *capax gratiae*, that is, may not have the capacity of receiving grace because of some obstacle that prevents him from receiving it. *See* ST IIaIIae, q. 83, art. 7, ad 2.

plenitude and abundance of goodness, grace, virtue, and merit, since the other receives clearly from his fullness. Yet we who are imperfect ought not therefore to cease from the aid of mutual prayer, since it is written: *Pray one for another, that you may be saved.*[12] Yet he who assumes the burden of praying for another ought to show himself as living rightly before God so that he might be made worthy of obtaining for others.[13]

101{102}[4]   *For my days are vanished like smoke: and my bones are grown dry like charred remains.*[14]

Quia defecerunt sicut fumus dies mei, et ossa mea sicut cremium aruerunt.

With good reason, then, O Lord, is this prayed for, **101{102}[4]** *Quia defecerunt, for they . . . are vanished,* that is, for they are speedily flowing off, *sicut fumus dies mei, my days . . . like smoke,* that is, the times in which I live. For in the way that smoke rises, and by its rising dissipates, so do our days by growing ascend, and in ascending they approach the end. Whence in Job is contained this: *My days have been swifter than a courier . . . they have passed by as ships carrying fruits.*[15] And James says: *What is your life? It is a vapor which appears for a little while, and afterwards shall vanish away.*[16] Or [alternatively we can understand this verse thus], *my days are vanished like smoke,* that is, they were consumed without bearing fruit or good works, and whatever I have done or have of vanity, passion, and impiety in them has quickly passed away, in accord with this: *What has pride profited us? Or what advantage has the boasting of riches brought us? All those things are passed away like a shadow, and like a courier that runs on.*[17] Here also, the Apostle told converted sinners: *What fruit therefore had you then in those things, of which you are now ashamed? For the end of*

---

12 James 5:16a.

13 E. N. "For the continual prayer of a just man avails much." James 5:16b.

14 E. N. The Douay Rheims translates the Latin *cremium*, a word generally meaning "firewood," with the words "fuel for the fire," but it appears that *cremium* had denotations of charred remains (of wood or even of meat). In some medieval English translations of this Psalm, the word *cremium* was translated as the leavings of meat after its frying or that which remains in the pan after the meat has been fried. It had the connotation, therefore, of charred remains. Since this is plainly how Denis sees it, I have departed from the Douay Rheims as translated *cremium* as "charred remains." See Annie Sutherland, *English Psalms in the Middle Ages 1300–1450* (Oxford: Oxford University Press 2015), 247–48.

15 Job 9:25a, 26a.

16 James 4:15a.

17 Wis. 5:8–9.

them is death.[18] For, according to Ambrose, the days of the depraved are empty and vacuous; but the days of the just are fullness.[19]

Et ossa mea sicut cremium aruerunt; and my bones are grown dry like charred remains. The words charred remains are given to that which remains after flesh is burnt or roasted and the fat has been drawn out. For charred remains (*cremium*) is a word obtained from charring (*cremando*). So in the manner that such flesh is dried, hardened, and dwindled away by fire, so are the bones of the body withered up by abstinence and dried up by the fear of God, according to this: *A sorrowful spirit dries up the bones.*[20] Now the bones of the soul, that is, its virtues and their powers, are like charred remains in a gridiron dried up by heat when, because of one's negligence, the grace of devotion is withdrawn, and the interior food (namely, holy obedience) is abandoned. For Christ says of this food: *My meat is to do the will of my Father.*[21] But sometimes these bones are dried up by temptations and tribulations, especially in those in whom *virtue is* not *made perfect in infirmity,*[22] which was not the case with the Apostle.[23] With respect to the penitent, this verse can be understood in both ways. For before his conversion, the bones of the soul are unhappily dried up; they exist without any spiritual fatness in them. But after conversion and when seized by penitence the bones of the body in some are salubriously dried out, for they develop an aversion to all fleshly delights, all temporal enjoyments, and all bodily nourishment because of their mind's intense preoccupation with God.

101{102}[5]   *I am smitten as grass, and my heart is withered: because I forgot to eat my bread.*

           Percussus sum ut foenum, et aruit cor meum, quia oblitus sum comedere panem meum.

101{102}[6]   *Through the voice of my groaning, my bone has cleaved to my flesh.*

           A voce gemitus mei adhaesit os meum carni meae.

---

18 Rom. 6:21.

19 E. N. The reference is to St. Ambrose's *Commentary on Luke: Plenitudinem iusti vita habet, inanes autem dies sunt impiorum. Super Lucam* II, 29, PL 15, 1562. "The life of the just man has fullness, but the days of wicked men are empty."

20 Prov. 17:22b.

21 John 4:34.

22 2 Cor. 12:9a.

23 E. N. In other words, the "sting of the flesh" of St. Paul that was not taken away despite his prayers allowed his virtue to become perfect by means of this very weakness or infirmity.

101{102}[5] *Percussus sum, I am smitten* with the rod of temptation and tribulation, *ut foenum, as grass,* because as grass is cut with a scythe, so I fall away from grace by temptation and adversity: as the Apostle [Paul] said of some persons: *Because of unbelief they fell away.*[24] *Et aruit cor meum, and my heart is withered* of spiritual graces through my own foment, *quia oblitus sum, because I forgot,* due to my own laziness, *comedere panem meum, to eat my bread* always readied for me by God, provided that I earnestly seek him, saying: *Give us this day our daily bread.*[25] This bread, as Christ said, is the fulfillment of God's commandment: *My meat is to do the will of him that sent me, that I may perfect his work.*[26] Or this bread is the study of sacred Scripture and the meditation upon divine things, of which is written, *With the bread of life and understanding, she shall feed him, and give him the water of wholesome wisdom to drink.*[27] Or this bread is the Sacrament of the Body of Christ, in which there is the plenitude of all heavenly delights and the eternal life of the soul, in the manner that Truth expressed it, *He that eats this bread, shall live forever.*[28] He who neglects spiritually to eat these breads dries up his heart, and he is poor, blind, naked, wretched, and miserable. 101{102}[6] *A voce gemitus mei, through the voice of my groaning,* that is, because of my excessive groaning and pain of my heart which I express through my mouth, *adhaesit os meum carni meae, my bone has cleaved to my flesh,* that is, I am so worn away in the body, that my bones adhere to my skin as it were in the manner that Job describes: *My flesh being consumed, my bone has cleaved to my skin.* For the interior pain conceived from sin, if it is great and continuous, furiously consumes the flesh. And so in this place the word flesh is substituted for the word skin.

101{102}[7]   *I am become like to a pelican of the wilderness: I am like a night raven in the house.*

Similis factus sum pellicano solitudinis; factus sum sicut nycticorax in domicilio.

101{102}[7] *Similis factus sum pellicano solitudinis, I am become like to a pelican of the wilderness:* that is, just like the pelican is a solitary bird that aspires toward solitude and is by nature made to be in a certain way lean, so I, flee from men, remain in solitude, and avoid human solace in order

---

24 Rom. 11:20. *E. N.* The Vulgate has *fracti sunt,* "they were broken off." Denis's quotation departs from the Vulgate: *excisi sunt,* "they fell away."
25 Matt. 6:11; Luke 11:3.
26 John 4:34.
27 Ecclus. 15:3.
28 John 6:59b.

that I might be able freely to lament of my sins.[29] As a Psalm above states, *Lo, I have gone far off flying away; and I abode in the wilderness.*[30] For by a pelican is indicated the first kind of penitence, namely, the order of hermits who punish and macerate their flesh in the wilderness, and they bewail their sins and those of others. For in order to do this, an isolated location is most suitable. Whence, Jeremiah said, *Who will give water to my head, and a fountain of tears to my eyes, and I will weep day and night for the slain of the daughter of my people?*[31] Here, insinuating himself not able to accomplish this very well among people, he desires solitude saying: *Who will give me in the wilderness a lodging place of wayfaring men, and I will leave my people?*[32] *Factus sum sicut nycticorax in domicilio, I am like a night raven in the house*: that is, in the way that an owl or a night crow dwelling in the walls of a home is hateful and abominable to the other birds, and thus does not make an appearance during the day, but seeks food at night, so I, during the nighttime when others are resting, seek food for my soul, persisting in good works and the affliction of penance. But in the day when others roam and are occupied outside, I reside at home; I judge myself unworthy to appear among men because of the abominable life which I have led. By *night raven*, therefore, is signified the second kind of penitence, those, namely, who turn away from human interaction and remain at home with great contrition and humility of soul.

101{102}[8] *I have watched, and am become as a sparrow all alone on the housetop.*

Vigilavi, et factus sum sicut passer solitarius in tecto.

101{102}[8] *Vigilavi, I have watched*: like the Apostle said to the Colossians: *Be instant in prayer, watching in it with thanksgiving.*[33] *I have watched*, that is, I have risen up against sin, according to this same Apostle, *It is now the hour for us to rise from sleep;*[34] and elsewhere, *Rise you that*

---

29 E. N. "It is good to emphasize that we confess to being sinners *both to God and to our brothers and sisters*: this helps us understand the dimension of sin which, while separating us from God, also divides us from our brothers and sisters, and vice versa. Sin severs: sin severs the relationship with God and it severs the relationship with brothers and sisters, relationships within the family, in society and in the community: sin always severs; it separates; it divides." Pope Francis, General Audience, Jan. 3, 2018.
30 Ps. 54:8.
31 Jer. 9:1.
32 Jer. 9:2a.
33 Col. 4:2.
34 Rom. 13:11.

sleep, and arise from the dead.[35] *I have watched*, adhering to holy works, in accordance with what the Apostle admonished, *Watch, stand fast in the faith, do manfully, and be strengthened, and let all your things be done in charity.*[36] And Christ in the Gospel of Matthew said: *Watch, and pray that you enter not into temptation.*[37] So the kingdom of heaven comes to the vigilant, and not to those who sleep. For this reason, Solomon said: *Love not sleep, lest poverty oppress you.*[38] Or [we can understand this verse in this way], *I have watched* during the nighttime and during those hours I may have legitimately used for sleep, so that I might recuperate time that had been uselessly lost, making myself free to praise the Creator and afflicting the body with holy vigils. And it is a great grace when God gives to his devoted and assiduous servant the ability to be content with a small amount of sleep, since sleep is like death, and it is hateful to those who want to engage in many deeds. Whence Solomon asks himself in Proverbs: *How long will you sleep, O sluggard? When will you rise out of your sleep?*[39] Yet just as is true in abstinence, so also it behooves one to keep prudence in view when undertaking vigils, to diligently measure one's strength, lest a man bring about the crime of sacrilege and incur the curse of which Jeremiah speaks: *Because he has done more than he could, therefore they have perished.*[40]

Et factus sum sicut passer solitarius in tecto, I have become as a sparrow all alone on the housetop: that is, in the manner that a sparrow builds his nest in high and safe places, lest it itself be captured or its hatchlings eaten, so have I fled to the nest and protection of the Church or the monastery so as to be separated from the assembly of the wicked so that I may not be entangled by the snares of the devil or despoiled of the fruits of good works, and there be preserved and saved. For the Church is signified by a mountain as when the angels said to Lot: *Look not back, neither stay you in all the country about: but save yourself in the mountain.*[41] But the cloister is signified by the city of which Lot said to the angel: *I beseech you, my Lord, . . . there is this city here at hand, to which I may flee, it is a little one, and I shall be saved in it.*[42] By a sparrow is signified the third kind of penitent, namely, those who enter into the cloister.

---

35 Eph. 5:14a.
36 1 Cor. 16:13–14.
37 Matt. 26:41.
38 Prov. 20:13a.
39 Prov. 6:9.
40 Jer. 48:36. E. N. Denis is using the term "sacrilege" loosely, as meaning a transgression against the virtue of religion.
41 Gen. 19:17b.
42 Gen. 19: 18, 20a.

101{102}[9]   *All the day long my enemies reproached me: and they that praised me did swear against me.*

Tota die exprobrabant mihi inimici mei, et qui laudabant me adversum me iurabant.

101{102}[10]   *For I did eat ashes like bread, and mingled my drink with weeping.*

Quia cinerem tamquam panem manducabam, et potum meum cum fletu miscebam.

While penitent, he then brings to mind his tribulations so that God may be inclined to be merciful. 101{102}[9] *Tota die, all the day long,* that is, every single day and assiduously, *exprobrabant mihi inimici mei, my enemies reproached me,* that is, the lovers of this world, whom I do not hate, but who hate me and scoff at me, as is written, *The simplicity of the just man is laughed to scorn.*[43] And St. John in his epistle states this about certain prideful men: *with malicious words [they are] prating against us.*[44] *Et qui laudabant me, and they that praised me,* either when outside [the Church or other refuge] or when I took a liking to their depraved manner of living, *adversum me iurabant, did swear against me,* that is, now after I abhor, and am repentant of, their manner of life, they firmly set themselves against me to persecute me with words and deeds. 101{102}[10] *Quia cinerem tamquam panem manducabam, for I did eat ashes like bread*: that is, these things were done because I held in contempt the desires of the belly, and I made sparse use of common and harsh food;[45] *et poculum meum cum fletu miscebam, and I mingled my goblet with weeping,*[46] that is, I have drunk bodily drink with tears. Or [alternatively, this might be understood as referring to] the *goblet* of the soul, namely, temporal joy mixed with tears, that is, [it might be understood as saying,] I mixed with good tears as I resolved not to glory in empty things. Spiritually speaking, he who eats ashes like bread is he

---

43 Job. 12:4b.

44 3 John 10.

45 E. N. Some saints have taken this literally. For example, St. Francis often used to sprinkle ashes on his food that he ate, calling, as a cover of his abstinence, "brother ashes to be chaste." *Legenda Trium Sociorum* (Pisauri 1831), 27 (*Et quando comedebat cum fratribus, in cibis, quos edebat, saepe ponebat cinerem, dicens fratribus abstinentiae suae velamen, fratrem cinerem esse castum.*)

46 E. N. Denis's text has *poculum,* "drinking vessel" or "goblet," instead of *potum,* "drink." The editor in the margin suggests that *poculum* should be replaced with *potum,* which accords with the Vulgate. I have stayed with Denis's *poculum,* since the *Commentary* demands it.

who diligently examines the remains of his thoughts and daily deplores even the smallest of his sins, saying to God that which holy Job said: *You have sealed up my offenses as it were in a bag, and you have indeed numbered my steps.*[47]

101{102}[11]   *Because of your anger and indignation: for having lifted me up you have thrown me down.*

A facie irae et indignationis tuae, quia elevans allisisti me.

101{102}[12]   *My days have declined like a shadow, and I am withered like grass.*

Dies mei sicut umbra declinaverunt, et ego sicut foenum arui.

Now this I have done, O Lord, 101{102}[11] *A facie irae indignationis tuae, because of your anger and indignation,* that is, from the consideration of the strictness of your justice and by reason of fear of your just punishments which you have prepared for the ungodly. The soul of the most blessed Job was filled with this fear from this sort of consideration, for he said: *For God is alone, and no man can turn away his thought . . . and therefore I am troubled at his presence, and when I consider him I am made pensive with fear.*[48] *Quia elevans, for having lifted me up,* that is, being adorned with your grace, and sealing me with the image of the most-high Trinity, and preferring me to all sensible things, *allisisti me, you have thrown me down,* that is, you have allowed me to fall and to be subjected to many miseries. God throws us down in this manner lest we boast of ourselves or presume upon our own strength: but while we stand, let us fear the fall; when we do fall, let us strive to rise again. For so does the Apostle [Paul] admonish, that he who stands, *let him take heed lest he fall;*[49] and again, *considering yourself, lest you also be tempted.*[50] And it is written in Ecclesiasticus: *In the day of good things be not unmindful of evils: and in the day of evils be not unmindful of good things.*[51] 101{102}[12] *Dies mei sicut umbra, my days . . . like a shadow,* that is, in a most speedy way, *declinaverunt, have declined* in the way that is expressed in the first book of Chronicles: *Our days upon earth are as a shadow, and there is no stay.*[52] Job also says: *My*

---

47 Job 14, 17a, 16a.
48 Job 23:13a, 15.
49 1 Cor. 10:12b.
50 Gal. 5:1b.
51 Ecclus. 11:27.
52 1 Chr. 29:15b.

days have passed more swiftly than the web is cut by the weaver.[53] Et ego sicut foenum, and I am . . . like grass, which today grows green, and tomorrow is cast into the oven and is dried up;[54] arui, withered in both soul and body: in soul, out of the lack of the grace of God; in body, because of multiple afflictions. Hence we read in Isaiah, Indeed the people is grass;[55] and again, All flesh is grass, and all the glory thereof as a flower of the field.[56]

101{102}[13] But you, O Lord, endure forever: and your memorial to all generations.

Tu autem, Domine, in aeternum permanes, et memoriale tuum in generationem et generationem.

Consequently, all deliverance is founded upon the efficacy of God. 101{102}[13] Tu autem, Domine, in aeternum permanes; but you, O Lord, endure forever, that is, you subsist eternally and without any change, in the way that you assert in Malachi: For I am the Lord and I change not.[57] Et memoriale tuum, and your memorial, that is, the excellent work that you have accomplished in your creature by which your name is preserved in our memory, remains in generationem et generationem, to all generations, that is, because of its greatness it is not permitted for us to forget it or you. Now this remembrance of God is his mercy which he has conferred upon men from the beginning of the world. Whence this is brought to our attention by Isaiah: Your name, and your remembrance are the desire of the soul.[58] For we ought never to be forgetful of the benefits of God.

101{102}[14] You arising shall have mercy on Sion: for it is time to have mercy on it, for the time is come.

Tu exsurgens misereberis Sion, quia tempus miserendi eius, quia venit tempus.

101{102}[15] For its stones thereof have pleased your servants: and they shall have pity on the earth thereof.

Quoniam placuerunt servis tuis lapides eius, et terrae eius miserebuntur.

---

53 Job 7:6.
54 Matt. 6:30.
55 Is. 40:7b.
56 Is. 40:6b.
57 Mal. 3:6a.
58 Is. 26:8b.

101{102}[14] *Tu exsurgens, you arising*, O Lord, that is, powerfully coming to our aid, and, you, in the manner of one having risen up, using your power in a fresh way, *misereberis Sion, shall have mercy on Sion*, that is, upon the Church militant which contemplates upon you faithfully, *quia tempus miserendi eius, for the time to have mercy*—that is, the time of salvation and of grace, of which the Apostle said, *Now is the acceptable time; behold, now is the day of salvation*[59]—comes. This time begins in a particular way through the Incarnation of Christ. *Quia venit tempus, for the time has come*, that is, the time for Christ's advent into the world. Of this time, the Apostle said, *When the fullness of the time was come, God sent his Son.*[60] And truly will he have mercy upon Sion, 101{102} [15] *Quoniam placuerunt servis tui lapide eius, for its stones thereof have pleased your servants*, that is, the persons in the Church—from whom, as if from living stones, is built the holy Church, for which reason in Revelation, the angel says to John: *I am your fellow servant, and of your brethren*[61]—have pleased the angels always ministering unto you. For also *there shall be joy before the angels of God upon one sinner doing penance.*[62] *Et terrae eius miserebuntur, and they shall have pity on the earth thereof*, that is, the goodly angels shall render aid to the Church which is spread throughout the whole world. For they are *all ministering spirits*, offering the prayers of men to God, and bringing back grace to them.[63]

101{102}[16]   *And the Gentiles shall fear your name, O Lord, and all the kings of the earth your glory.*

Et timebunt gentes nomen tuum, Domine, et omnes reges terrae gloriam tuam.

101{102}[16] *Et timebunt gentes, and the Gentiles shall fear*, that is, [the Gentiles] converted from idolatry to the true faith, *nomen tuum, Domine; your name, O Lord*, that is, you yourself. We see this fulfilled in the Christians begotten out of the Gentile peoples. This was also predicted in Malachi: *I am a great King, says the Lord of hosts, and my name is dreadful among the Gentiles.*[64] *Et omnes reges terrae, and all the kings of the earth*, that is, some of all the genus of kings (since [the verse

---

59 2 Cor. 6:2b.
60 Ga. 4:4a.
61 Rev. 19:10a.
62 Luke 15:10.
63 Heb. 1:14a.
64 Mal. 1:14b.

is to be understood] as applying to the kind of each individual, but not to the individual of each kind), shall fear *gloriam tuam, your glory,* O Christ, that is, your majesty, which, by faith, they will acquire knowledge of. For, in the way that Isaiah predicted: *Kings shall see,* he says, *and princes shall rise up, and adore for the Lord's sake.*[65] And he asserts the same thing about Christ: *Kings shall shut their mouth at him.*[66]

101{102}[17] *For the Lord has built up Sion: and he shall be seen in his glory.*

Quia aedificavit Dominus Sion, et videbitur in gloria sua.

101{102}[17] *Quia aedificabit Dominus,* for the Lord has built up, [that is,] Christ [has built up] *Sion,* that is, the holy Church; *et videbitur, and he shall see,* that very same Church *in gloria sua, in his glory,* that is, in great excellence because Christ confirms her against all reprobate and perverse men. Also, he decorates her with great and various graces: To one giving the word of wisdom, and to another a word of knowledge, and to another the working of miracles,[67] and setting some indeed as Apostles, and some as Evangelists, and some as doctors as the Apostle [Paul] more fully sets forth.[68] Or [alternatively we can understand this verse thus], the Lord Christ *shall be seen in his glory* by the sons of the Church as they look upon him with the eyes of faith, as the Apostle testifies: *But we all beholding the glory of the Lord with open face.*[69] And Isaiah: *His eyes shall see the king in his beauty.*[70] Yet in the day of judgment

---

65 Is. 49:7b.

66 Is. 52:15a. *E. N.* As Denis explains this verse in his *Commentary on Isaiah:* "*Kings shall shut their mouth at him,* that is, their mouths shall be restrained lest they speak again against Christ, lest they dare blaspheme him, but they shall venerate him according to that contained in the Psalm: *And all the kings of the earth shall adore him* (Ps. 71:11), and later [in Isaiah] we have: *The Gentiles shall see your just one, and all kings your glorious one* (Is. 62:2)." Doctoris Ecstatici D. Dionysii Cartusiani, *Opera Omnia,* Vol. 8 (Montreuil: 1899), 682.

67 *Cf.* 1 Cor. 12:8–10: *To one indeed, by the Spirit, is given the word of wisdom: and to another, the word of knowledge, according to the same Spirit; to another, faith in the same spirit; to another, the grace of healing in one Spirit; to another, the working of miracles; to another, prophecy; to another, the discerning of spirits; to another, diverse kinds of tongues; to another, interpretation of speeches.*

68 1 Cor. 12:28: *God indeed has set some in the church; first apostles, secondly prophets, thirdly doctors; after that miracles; then the graces of healing, helps, governments, kinds of tongues, interpretations of speeches.*

69 2 Cor. 3:18a.

70 Is. 33:17a.

and also in the heavenly homeland both Christ and the Church of the elect shall be seen in their glory, when that which is stated in Revelation shall be fulfilled: *Behold, he comes with the clouds, and every eye shall see him, and they also that pierced him.*[71] Christ by himself began to build this Church, preaching to the world, and gathering up disciples; and then through the Apostles and other apostolic men he built it up all over the world: as Zechariah predicted, *Behold a man, the Orient is his name,* that is, Christ, *and he shall build a temple to the Lord.*[72]

101{102}[18]   *He has had regard to the prayer of the humble: and he has not despised their petition.*

Respexit in orationem humilium et non sprevit precem eorum.

101{102}[18] *Respexit, he has had regard,* [that is,] the Lord [has had regard] *in orationem humilium, to the prayer of the humble,* praying for the coming of Christ and the building up of the Church; *et non sprevit precem eorum, and he has not despised their petition,* but he has mercifully fulfilled it. For he has heard the Prophets and the other Saints praying for this. For with a kindly eye, the Lord daily is mindful of the prayers of the humble man, as is testified to by Isaiah: *To whom shall I have respect, but to him that is poor and little, and of a contrite spirit, and that trembles at my words?*[73]

101{102}[19]   *Let these things be written unto another generation: and the people that shall be created shall praise the Lord.*

Scribantur haec in generatione altera, et populus qui creabitur laudabit Dominum.

101{102}[20]   *Because he has looked forth from his high sanctuary: from heaven the Lord has looked upon the earth.*

Quia prospexit de excelso sancto suo, Dominus de caelo in terram aspexit.

101{102}[21]   *That he might hear the groans of them that are in fetters: that he might release the children of the slain.*

Ut audiret gemitus compeditorum, ut solveret filios interemptorum.

---

71 Rev. 1:7a.
72 Zech. 6:12.
73 Is. 66:2b.

101{102}[19] *Scribantur haec, let these things be written,* [that is, let] those things that are said regarding God and his benefits [be written], *in generatione altera, unto another generation,* that is, to posterity even until the end of the world, and let none of them be consigned to oblivion; *et populus qui creabitur, and the people that shall be created,* that is the Christian people reborn by water and the Holy Spirit,[74] *laudabit Dominum, shall praise the Lord* because of all his benefits. 101{102}[20] *Quia prospexit, because he has looked forth,* [because] the Lord [has looked forth] *de excelso sancto suo, from his high sanctuary,* that is, from his holy and sublime dwelling he mercifully directs himself to the human race; *Dominus de caelo in terram adspexit, from heaven the Lord has looked upon the earth* with an eye of tenderness. For though God exists everywhere, and he perceives all things everywhere, he is in a particular way said to dwell and to be in heaven, because there he is seen most evidently and most clearly to work; and so he is said to look from heaven particularly, not in the sense that there is some sort of distance between him and that which he is looking at since he penetrates, fills, and fully surrounds all things. He looks therefore from heaven 101{102}[21] *Ut audiret gemitus compeditorum, that he might hear the groans of them that are in fetters,* that is, that he may succor those groaning and who are bound with the chains of vice, forgiving them of their sins, as is told us in the book of Judges: *The Lord was moved to mercy, and heard the groanings of the afflicted, and delivered them from the slaughter of the oppressors.*[75] *Ut solveret, that might release,* that is, that he might absolve from sin, *filios interemptorum, the children of the slain,* that is, men born from sinning parents (for sin is the death of the soul). And we all were killed in the first parent. And *we were also by nature children of wrath;*[76] and so our parents were slain or spiritually destroyed by the devil's fraud.

101{102}[22] *That they may declare the name of the Lord in Sion: and his praise in Jerusalem.*

Ut annuntient in Sion nomen Domini, et laudem eius in Ierusalem.

101{102}[23] *When the people assemble together, and kings, to serve the Lord.*

In conveniendo populos in unum, et reges ut serviant Domino.

---

74 *Cf.* John 3:5.
75 Judges 2:18.
76 Eph. 2:3b.

And so he hears and he unfetters them, 101{102}[22] *Ut annuntient in Sion, that they may declare . . . in Sion,* that is, in the Church, *nomen Domini, the name of the Lord,* gladly preaching Christ and confessing the Catholic faith with their mouth and works, *et laudem eius, and his praise* they will proclaim *in Ierusalem, in Jerusalem,* that is, in that same Church: for it is called Sion because of its contemplation [of God] and Jerusalem because of the quietness of internal peace. Indeed, Sion is interpreted as meaning contemplation; but Jerusalem as meaning the vision of peace. Now this internal peace, which the angels proclaimed when they sang *on earth peace to men of good will,* most greatly exists among the Christian people. Now this annunciation was done 101{102} [23] *in conveniendo populus in unum et reges, when the people assemble together, and kings,* that is, by this means, that the common people, and also their kings and princes, will gather together in the unity of faith, and in Christ they will be made one mystical body through charity, *ut serviant Dominio, to serve the Lord* in the unity of the Church. For Christ condescended to die for the spiritual congregation of the elect, according to this: *Jesus should die [for the nation, and not only for the nation,] but to gather together in one the children of God that were dispersed.*[77]

101{102}[24] *It answered him in the way of its strength: Declare unto me the fewness of my days.*[78]

Respondit ei in via virtutis suae: Paucitatem dierum meorum nuntia mihi.

101{102}[25] *Call me not away in the midst of my days: your years are unto generation and generation.*

Ne revoces me in dimidio dierum meorum, in generationem et generationem anni tui.

101{102}[24] *Respondit, it answered,* [that is,] the faithful people [answered], *ei, him,* namely, their Lord, *in via virtutis suae, in the way of its strength,* through virtuous works. For whenever we respond to some word we do so by deed. And the faithful people respond to Christ by living well, by returning thanks, and by complying with his commands. For regarding such persons, the holy Job says replying to the Lord: *You shall call me, and I will answer you.*[79] For God calls us to a better life through internal

---

77 John 11:51–52. E. N. The part in brackets replace the "etc." in the Latin text.
78 E. N. I have replaced the masculine pronoun "he" and "his" in the Douay Rheims with "it" and "its" since Denis sees this verse as referring to a people.
79 Job 14:15a.

inspiration: and then we respond when we obey. But when we neglect to do so, we remain silent; and when we are disdainful, we oppose him. Of such persons also Jacob has this response: *My justice shall answer for me tomorrow.*[80] And so that this people might respond perfectly to God, he prays: *Paucitatem dierum meorum nuntia mihi, declare unto me the fewness of my days*: that is, grant to me wisely to attend to the brevity of this present life, so that I might despise temporal joys and I might always hurry to await beatitude. 101{102}[25] *Ne revoces me in dimidio dierum meorum, call me not away in the midst of my days*: that is, do not command for me to pass out of this life now, lest I depart from this life unprepared — since, trusting that I will live a long time, I think that I am in the middle of my life; and let me not die at that time while vice reigns greatly in me, which usually is the case in the middle of life. *In generationem et generationem anni tui, your years are unto generation and generation*, that is, the duration or your eternity extends over all generations, and indeed, it never ends. For [in reference to God] he calls the years of creation eternity because he immutably comprehends the long expanse of time or of years.

101{102}[26] *In the beginning, O Lord, you founded the earth: and the heavens are the works of your hands.*

Initio tu, Domine, terram fundasti, et opera manuum tuarum sunt caeli.

101{102}[26] *Initio, in the beginning* of time and together with time *tu, Domine, terram, you, O Lord, ... the earth*, that is, the lowest elements, *fundasti, founded*, that is, firmly in the middle of the universe, so to speak, you placed the center of the world;[81] *et opera manuum tuarum, and the works of your hands*, that is, the creation by your power, *sunt caeli, are the heavens* whole and entirely: in the manner that is contained in Genesis, *In the beginning God created heaven and earth*;[82] And in Job: *Who is ignorant that the hand of the Lord has made all these things?*[83] Whence, the Lord says through Isaiah: *I am the Lord, that make all things, that*

---

80 Gen. 30:33a. E. N. As Denis comments on this verse in his *Commentary on Genesis*: "*And my justice shall answer for me tomorrow*, that is, through God's disposition, I will receive, either soon or in the future, that which I deserve." Doctoris Ecstatici D. Dionysii Cartusiani, *Opera Omnia*, Vol. 1 (Montreuil: 1896), 343.

81 E. N. In the geocentric model of the universe, which was the prevailing scientific view in Denis's time, the earth was perceived as the center of the universe. Denis wrote his *Commentary*, of course, before the Copernican revolution in the 16th century.

82 Gen. 1:1.

83 Job 12:9.

alone stretch out the heavens, that establish the earth, and there is none with me.[84] But all this seems contrary to what we find in Ecclesiasticus: *Wisdom has been created before all things.*[85] The answer is that the wisdom effused over all the works of God or the angelic nature is said to be created before all things, not in terms of time, but in terms of dignity.[86]

101{102}[27]   *They shall perish but you remain: and all of them shall grow old like a garment: And as a vesture you shall change them, and they shall be changed.*

Ipsi peribunt, tu autem permanes; et omnes sicut vestimentum veterascent. Et sicut opertorium mutabis eos, et mutabuntur.

101{102}[28]   *But you are always the selfsame, and your years shall not fail.*

Tu autem idem ipse es, et anni tui non deficient.

101{102}[27] *Ipsi peribunt,* they shall perish. Neither the heaven nor the earth shall perish substantially, but they will perish at the end of the world to the extent of the existence of their accidental forms, because they will exist in another state after the judgment than they do now. For the aerial heaven will perish by means of the fire of conflagration, which will clean the air.[87] But the heavens existing above the sphere of fire will perish by the cessation of the heavenly movement. For when the generation and corruption is completed in the lower [heaven], then the movements of the heavens shall cease. But all generable and corruptible and inferior things are ordered to man as to an end:[88] and so once the

---

84 Is. 44:24.

85 Ecclus. 1:4a. *E. N.* Denis is referring to Gen. 1:1 which suggests that heaven and earth were created in the beginning, but Ecclus. 1:4 says that wisdom was created before all things, which would include heaven and earth; therefore, it would seem that heaven and earth could not have been the first thing created (in the beginning). The wisdom here is created wisdom or rational creation, specifically the angelic nature.

86 *E. N.* As Denis states in his *Commentary on Ecclesiasticus*: "By wisdom which was created before all things, some understand as the angelic nature. For this is said of the angelic intelligence; and since they were simultaneously created at the same time as the heavens, they are still said to be created first, by reason of their dignity, since they are the most noble of all creatures." Doctoris Ecstatici D. Dionysii Cartusiani, *Opera Omnia*, Vol. 8 (Montreuil: 1899), 5.

87 *E. N.* In the Middle Ages, the heavens (following St. John Damascus) were often divided into three layers, the *caelum aereum* (aerial or airy heaven), *caelum sidereum* (sidereal or starry heaven), and *caelum perpetuum* (perpetual heaven) also called the *caelum aetherium* (ethereal heaven) or *caelum empyreum* (empyreal heaven). *See, e.g.,* ST Ia q. 68 art. 4, co.

88 *See* SCG, IV, 97.

number of the elect has been attained, the generation of men shall cease, and, as a consequence, so also the generation and corruption of all other things. And thus movement and time shall cease in the mobile heavens. For this reason, it is written in Revelation: *And the angel... lifted up his hand to heaven, and he swore by him that lives for ever and ever, ... for time shall be no longer.*[89] And so, whoever from his nature has some ordering toward existing forever, he will substantially remain after the day of judgment; but the rest [of creation] shall be destroyed. For this reason, men will remain because, although they are corruptible with respect to their body, yet they are incorruptible according to their soul. Also, the elements will remain: for though they are in part corruptible, yet in themselves they cannot be totally corrupted. But as a whole, the heavens are incorruptible, and so they will not perish, except [they will be changed] as to their manner of existing, as has just been said. And it is in this manner that those places which in holy Scripture affirms the destruction of the heavens—as does this, *the heavens shall be folded together as a book;*[90] and that which the Lord says in Luke, *Heaven and earth shall pass away;*[91] and that in Peter, *The heavens and the earth which are now, ... are reserved unto fire against the day of judgment* (though Peter was speaking of the aerial heaven);[92] also that in Revelation, *I saw a new heaven and a new earth. For the first heaven and the first earth was gone, and the sea is now no more*[93]—are to be understood. Now, by this [teaching in Scripture,] the opinion of the philosophers—who posited that the world and its generation and corruption, and the movement of the heavens as well as time were from eternity and would remain without any end—is destroyed.[94]

Tu autem, but you, O Lord, invariably *permanes, remain*: because your being depends upon nothing, and it truly is eternal, you are completely all at once (*totum simul*) and always equally perfect, in whom no change

---

89 Rev. 10:5–6.
90 Is. 34:4a.
91 Luke 21:33a.
92 2 Pet. 3:7.
93 Rev. 21:1.
94 *E. N. See* St. Thomas Aquinas's short work *On the Eternity of the World* (*De aeternitate mundi*). According to the Catholic faith, the world has a beginning, as it was created by God *ex nihilo*. The world also has an end in the sense that it will be transformed. *See* ST Ia, q. 104, art. 4, co. and ST III (Supp.), q. 74. "The cosmos, exnihilated by God at its beginning, is not brought to an end by a Divine act of annihilation." Mortimer J. Adler, *How to Think About God* (New York: MacMillan Publishing Co. 1980), 37.

can be conceived; *et omnes, and all* of heaven *sicut vestimentum veterascent, shall grow old like a garment* from the state of revolving in orbit to which they are currently assigned. *Et sicut opertorium, and as a vesture,* which according to the demands of time are put on and put off and placed aside, *mutabis eos, you shall change them* from the present state, *et mutabuntur, and they shall be changed* for the better: *for the light of the son shall be sevenfold, and the light of the moon shall be as the light of the sun,* as Isaiah says.[95] The heavenly orbs shall also be dressed with a more clear light, although Scripture does not prescribe the quantity of this change. **101{102}[28]** *Tu autem idem ipse es, but you are always the selfsame,* for you neither substantially nor accidentally suffer any change, but you subsist eternally in a state of highest goodness and simple perfection; *et anni tui non deficient, and your years shall not fail,* that is, your eternity is not able to end.

101{102}[29]   *The children of your servants shall continue: and their seed shall be directed forever.*

Filii servorum tuorum habitabunt; et semen eorum in saeculum dirigetur.

101{102}[29] *Filii servorum tuorum, the children of your servants,* that is, the posterity of your Apostles who are their spiritual children and their imitators, according to the Apostle [Paul]: *My little children, of whom I am in labor again, until Christ be formed in you;*[96] *habitabunt, shall continue,* now in the Church militant by faith and grace even until the consummation of this age; but afterwards in the Church triumphant by glory even for eternity; *et semen eorum, and their seed,* that is their good and fruitful manner of living, *in saeculum, forever,* that is, unceasingly, *dirigetur, shall be directed* [to this good and fruitful life] by your grace, even until the ultimate end or eternal life; or, *shall be directed* by you until they are led to the heavenly fatherland.

Take heed: we have heard the true voice of the penitent man and the form of perfect penitence. Let us therefore learn from this present Psalm what pertains to a true penitent. Let us endeavor also to implement it worthily. For indeed, the first verse of this Psalm declares how ardently and seriously an obligation a penitent has toward God. Thereafter, we are taught to recite sorrowfully the calamity and the misery of our poverty and our insufficiency before God. And then we are instructed on what behooves or what

95 Is. 30:25.
96 Ga. 4:19.

is expedient for us penitents to do, namely, to groan sincerely, profoundly, and sorrowfully so that the bones adhere to the skin out of the maceration of the flesh. We ought also to imitate the pelican by placing ourselves in a solitary place where we may be free to devote ourselves to the affliction of penitence. We ought to be content with common food and to mix it with the drink of lament, and to unceasingly fear the ire of our Judge. Finally, this glorious Psalm teaches us, to mix with the recitation and lamenting of our poverty, or littleness, and our fault the divine declamation of God, praising the majesty, admiring the blessedness, loving the goodness, and imitating the mercy and benevolence of our Creator, so that we might be children of our Father who is in heaven,[97] for he is beneficent and good, causing the sun to rise and the rain to descend upon all, both the grateful and the ungrateful, the good and the evil.[98]

ARTICLE II

ALLEGORICAL EXPLANATION OF THE SAME
ONE HUNDRED AND FIRST PSALM OF CHRIST.

ALTHOUGH, AS ANYONE CAN SEE, THIS PSALM cannot fittingly be explained of Christ, especially since it is one of the penitential Psalms fittingly applying to the sinner (and to the contrary, there is neither fault nor need for penance in Christ);[99] nevertheless, much of the Psalm can still be conveniently referred to Christ. First, because the Apostle applied the words of this Psalm in the letter to the Hebrews beginning from, *In the beginning, O Lord, you founded the earth* up until *and your years shall not fail*,[100] as predictive of Christ, proving from it the Son to be equal to the Father in power and domination.[101] Yet according to Augustine a proof text is of no strength unless it is based upon its literal sense.[102] Therefore, this Psalm must literally deal with the Lord Savior. Second, [it should also be held to refer to Christ] because the Church on the Wednesday before the feast of the Lord's Supper in the

---

97 Luke 6:35; Matt. 4:45.
98 *Cf.* Matt. 5:45.
99 E. N. The Seven Penitential Psalms are Psalms 6, 31 (32), 37 (38), 50 (51), 101 (102), 129 (130), 142 (143).
100 E. N. The epistle to the Hebrews (Heb. 1:10–12) quotes Ps. 101:26–28.
101 Heb. 1:10–12.
102 E. N. The reference is Letter 93 to Vicentius the Donatist. For more on this, *see* footnote 34-54.

office of the Mass takes up in its Gradual the beginning of this Psalm. Whence one must entirely assent that this Psalm can be expounded as referring to Christ in his Passion. For the whole Office of the day, indeed the whole week before the Pasch, relates to the Lord's Passion. Third, moreover, because according to Augustine it is not unfitting for the same Scripture to have multiple literal senses; therefore, it is possible for the same Scripture to have multiple literal senses. Accordingly, though some of what is contained in this Psalm is properly expounded as dealing with the penitent, yet is not unfitting that it be understood as pertaining to Christ according to another understanding of it.

101{102}[1] *The prayer of the poor man, when he was anxious, and poured out his supplication before the Lord.*

Oratio pauperis, cum anxius fuerit, et in conspectu Domini effuderit precem suam.

And so elucidating this Psalm as referring to Christ, the title already discussed is explained as follows: 101{102}[1] *Oratio pauperis, the prayer of the poor man:* that is, the present Psalm befits Christ who became poor for us, for *he did not have where to lay his head,*[103] and about which we have in Zechariah: *Behold your king will come to you, . . . he is poor and riding upon an ass;*[104] *cum anxius fuerit, [et in conspectus Domini effuderit]; when he was anxious [and poured out his supplication before the Lord],* that is, when the Christ felt fear and was sorrowful, when his Passion was imminent, according to Mark: *He began to fear and to be heavy; and before the Lord God Father, he poured out his prayers, saying: Father, if it be possible, let this chalice pass from me.*[105]

101{102}[2] *Hear, O Lord, my prayer: and let my cry come to you.*

Domine, exaudi orationem meam, et clamor meus ad te veniat.

101{102}[3] *Turn not away your face from me: in the day when I am in trouble, incline your ear to me. In what day soever I shall call upon you, hear me speedily.*

Non avertas faciem tuam a me; in quacumque die tribulor, inclina ad me aurem tuam; in quacumque die invocavero te, velociter exaudi me.

103 Matt. 8:20b.
104 Zech. 9:9.
105 Matt. 26:39.

Therefore, Christ as a passible man, the Passion being near, said to God the Father, or to all the superlatively most blessed Trinity, the one true and most simple God: 101{102}[2] *Domine, exaudi orationem meam; hear, O Lord, my prayer* which I pray for the glorification of my body and its quick resurrection, saying to him: *Father, save me from this hour;*[106] *et clamor meus, and ... my cry,* which I pray for my Mystical Body, which is the Church, *ad te veniat, come to you,* so that you might do that which I ask for, as is related in the Gospel of John: *Holy Father, keep them in your name whom you have given me; that they may be one, as we also are.*[107] 101{102}[3] *Non avertas faciem tuam a me, turn not away your face from me,* that is, regarding my prayer for others, do not comport yourself with me as if I were unworthy, so that you cast off my prayers for others or reject them because of the unworthiness of others; but forgive them on account of me. Christ, who was from the very instant of conception in his mother a perfect *comprehensor,* and who was immovably confirmed in the good, did not pray lest the Father withdraw his face, that is, his beatific knowledge or his loving presence from him (for it is plain that this by no means could occur); but he prayed lest, because of the evil deeds of men, the Father turn away from hearing the prayers of Christ poured out for sinners. *In quacumque die tribulor, in the day when I am in trouble,* that is, when I sustain the persecution of the Jews, *inclina ad me aurem tuam, incline your ear to me,* so that you might provide me assistance, and so that you might help me in the suffering I endure for the satisfaction of all the sins of the world. Christ prayed this very thing: *Father, for this I pray ... for them whom you have given me, because they are yours.*[108]

101{102}[4] *For my days are vanished like smoke: and my bones are grown dry like charred remains.*

Quia defecerunt sicut fumus dies mei, et ossa mea sicut cremium aruerunt.

101{102}[4] *Quia defecerunt sicut fumus dies mei, for my days are vanished like smoke,* that is, the days, during which I have abided in the world, have flowed by quickly. For Christ aged or became older, that is, he inclined towards getting older, just as also other men, for his days continually flowed past as is typical of those in time. For indeed,

---

106 John 12:27.
107 John 17:11b.
108 John 17:9.

according to the Damascene he assumed all defects [of men] that are indectractible (*indetrahibiles*).[109] For this reason, the Apostle says to the Hebrews: *It behooved him in all things to be made like unto his brethren.*[110] *Et ossa mea*, [my] bodily [bones], *sicut cremium, like charred remains*, that is, like burnt flesh, *aruerunt, are grown dry* in the Passion: as it states in a Psalm above: *My strength is dried up like a potsherd.*[111] For in the day of preparation before the Passover, because of the extremely great loss of blood of Christ, and the reduction, drying up, and hardening of his flesh, the most sacred bones of his body were dried up, similar to meat in a frying pan cooked up to the removal of all fat. For this reason, Isaiah predicted about Christ: *We have seen him, and there was no sightliness; and we have thought him as it were a leper, and as one struck by God.*[112]

101{102}[5] *I am smitten as grass, and my heart is withered: because I forgot to eat my bread.*

Percussus sum ut foenum, et aruit cor meum, quia oblitus sum comedere panem meum.

Whence, there added: 101{102}[5] *Percussus ut ut foenum, I am smitten as grass*: that is, in the way that grass when it still flourishes, is cut down with a scythe, so was I in my youth snatched away from the society of the living and was killed by the sword of the Passion.[113] [This is like] the way that the ungodly in Jeremiah affirmed: *Let us cut him off from the land of the living;*[114] and also in the book of Wisdom,

---

109 E. N. There are two principles at play here. First, that whatever in human nature Christ did not assume is not cured. St. John of Damascus quotes St. Gregory Nazianzus: "whatever is not assumed [by God] has no share in salvation," *quod assumptum non est, curationis est expers* (Τὸ γὰρ ἀπρόσληπτον ἀθεράπευτον) *Letter* 101, 7.32, PG 37, 181–84. Yet Christ—who was sinless and enjoyed the hypostatic union—cannot be said to have suffered human defects incompatible with that state, the fullness of grace, and the perfection of knowledge. In resolving the tension between these principles, St. Thomas Aquinas notes that Christ suffered those defects that men confront that do not, in and of themselves, detract from his dignity or goodness (such as hunger, thirst, death, propassions). But, the Lord did not, in his human nature, *e.g.*, suffer from sickness, nor concupiscence or other disorders of mind and body. *See* ST IIIa, q. 14, art. 4, co. The reference to Damascus is to *De Fide Orth.*, I, 11; 3, 20.
110 Heb. 2:17a.
111 Ps. 21:16a.
112 Is. 53:2b, 4b.
113 E. N. The *gladius passionis*, the "sword of the Passion," is an oblique reference to Simeon's prophecy that Mary's soul would be pierced by a sword (*et tuam pisus animam pertransibit gladius*) (Luke 2:35).
114 Jer. 11:19b.

Let us condemn him to a most shameful death.[115] *Et aruit cor meum, and my heart is withered,* [my] bodily [heart is withered], from its natural humors, because of the most violent wounding of the body and the loss of blood. For the heart—that is, the mind of Christ—did not dry out by the humor or the plenitude of the grace of God.[116]

Quia oblitus sum comedere panem meum, because I forgot to eat my bread. This would seem not possibly to befit Christ, and yet it most fittingly befits him. For the bread of the soul is its consolation. But in the Passion of Christ, his sensitive appetite in the inferior part of his soul was deprived of its customary overflowing of the divine consolation in it to such an extent that he cried out: *My God, my God, why have you forsaken me?*[117] And so Christ forgot—that is, by effect it was as if he did not remember—to eat the bread of consolation with respect to the inferior powers of his soul. For forgetfulness does not always indicate sloth or negligence, for as is stated in a Psalm above, *Forget your people and your father's house;*[118] and in Genesis, Joseph confesses, *God has made me to forget all my labors, and my father's house.*[119] Hence, sometimes a man is said to have forgotten because he is not working, and so he holds himself out as if no longer knowing: and this is how [this verse] should now be understood. And because Christ withdrew this flowing over or this consolation of the beatitude existing in his superior part from the inferior powers of his soul or his bodily nature, so it was that he was able to suffer and die. Otherwise, he would have been able neither to suffer nor to die: because according to Augustine in his epistle to Dioscorus, there was so much beatitude in the soul of Christ that it flowed into his body, and he was immune from all passibility; indeed much more than the bodies of the elect will be after the day of judgment.[120] But through the use of his dispensatory power, he suspended that flowing over, especially in the hour of the Passion. And so at that time Christ was smitten as grass and his heart was withered.

---

115 Wis. 2:20a.

116 *E. N.* The word "humor" here refers to the body fluids and analogously the fluid of grace, what the anonymous author of the 14th century *Cloud of Unknowing* called the "wetting of grace" or Walter Hilton (*ca.* 1343–96) in is *Ladder of Perfection* called the "liquor of grace."

117 Matt. 27:46b.

118 Ps. 44:11b.

119 Gen. 41:41b.

120 *E. N.* In his *Letter to Dioscorus*, 118, 1, 3, 14, PL 33, 439 St. Augustine speaks of how "God has made the soul with a nature so powerful, that from its most full beatitude

101{102}[6]   *Through the voice of my groaning, my bone has cleaved to my flesh.*

A voce gemitus mei adhaesit os meum carni meae.

101{102}[6]   *A voce gemitus mei, through the voice of my groaning,* that is, through the loud and groaning compassion and sorrow of my heart, by which I suffered for sinners and felt pain from my own wounds, *adhaesit os meum carni meae, my bone has cleaved to my flesh,* that is, to my skin, for from its punishments suffered during the time of my Passion my flesh was distressed and drawn out; and so my bones cleaved to my skin, to such an extent that they could be counted. On account of this, it states: *All my bones are scattered.*[121]

101{102}[7]   *I am become like to a pelican of the wilderness: I am like a night raven in the house.*

Similis factus sum pellicano solitudinis; factus sum sicut nycticorax in domicilio.

101{102}[8]   *I have watched, and am become as a sparrow all alone on the housetop.*

Vigilavi, et factus sum sicut passer solitarius in tecto.

101{102}[7] *Similis factus sum pellicano solitudinis, I am become like to a pelican of the wilderness,* because I have gone forth to the place of the desert avoiding the tumult of the Jews, in the way that is stated in John, *Jesus walked no more openly among the Jews; but he went into a country near the desert.*[122] He was also *led by the Spirit into the desert, to be tempted by the devil;* and he fasted there forty days and nights, not for his moral digressions [for he had none], but for ours. Further, according to Augustine, Christ is compared to a pelican because this bird is said to kill its chicks with its own beak, and to weep for three days, and then finally to shed its blood with its beak over its chicks, so that they might live again.[123] So Christ

which is promised to the saints at the end of time, there flows also into the inferior nature, which is the body, not indeed the beatitude which is proper to enjoyment and the intelligence, but the fullness of health that is the vigor of incorruption." This overflowing, which was in Christ while *in via* because he was also a *comprehensor,* was intentionally suspended by Christ so as to allow his human nature to suffer and die.
121 Ps. 21:15a. *E. N.* Denis could also have cited Ps. 21:18: "They have numbered all my bones."
122 John 11:54.
123 *E. N.* The reference is to St. Augustine's own interpretation of this verse in his own *Commentary. Enarratione in Psalmos,* Ps. 101(2), 8. PL 37, 1299. St. Augustine has doubts

kills our vices in us, and by his own blood he brings us back to life again. *Factus sum sicut nycticorax in domicilio, I am like a night raven in the house,* because during nighttime, when others are idle with sleep, I keep vigil with prayers and with good works. Hence we have in Luke: *Jesus passed the whole night in the prayer of God.*[124] Christ is also said to be similar to a night raven because as this bird is odious to others, so Christ was despised by all, especially, as a Psalm above states: *I am a worm, and no man: the reproach of men, and the outcast of the people.*[125] For this reason Isaiah says of him: *His visage shall be inglorious among men.*[126] **101{102}[8]** *Vigilavi, I have watched* always by doing good works. For bodily sleep did not impede the interior operation and vigilance of the mind in Christ. *Et factus sum sicut passer solitarius in tecto, and I am become as a sparrow all alone on the housetop,* because I have forsaken men and ascended to the mountain to pray, according to this, *He went out into a mountain to pray.*[127]

101{102}[9] *All the day long my enemies reproached me: and they that praised me did swear against me.*

Tota die exprobrabant mihi inimici mei, et qui laudabant me adversum me iurabant.

101{102}[9] *Tota die, all the day long* during my Passion and during the many days of my preaching, *exprobabant mihi inimici mei, my enemies reproached me,* [that is] the Jews [reproached me], saying that which is stated in Matthew, *This man casts not out the devils but by Beelzebub the prince of the devils;*[128] the same thing in John, *He has a devil, and is mad: why hear you him?*[129] *Et qui laudabunt me, and they that praised me,* when I preached to them and when I performed miracles before them, and when I satiated them with five loaves of bread,[130] saying *A great*

---

about the popular reports of the pelican, but acknowledges that it is a symbol of Christ regardless: "Perhaps it is true, perhaps it is false; yet if it is true, see how he who gave us life by his blood agrees with it." In the sixth quatrain of his beautiful Eucharistic hymn *Adoro te devote,* St. Thomas adopts this image: *Pie Pellicane, Iesu Domine, / Me immundum munda tuo sanguine. / Cuius una stilla salvum facere / Totum mundum qut ab omni scelere.* "O true Pelican, Lord Jesus, / Cleanse me who am unclean in your blood, / One drop of which would be enough to wash the whole world of its defilement."

124 Luke 6:12b.
125 Ps. 21:7.
126 Is. 52:14.
127 Luke 6:12.
128 Matt. 12:24.
129 John 10:20.
130 Matt. 14:15–21.

prophet is risen up among us;[131] and, *Never was the like seen in Israel;*[132] *adversum me iurabant, did swear against me,* that is, they unanimously conspired to plot my death, proclaiming in the day of preparation before the Passover, *Away with him; away with him; crucify him,*[133] and *His blood be upon us and our children.*[134] Or [we can understand it in this manner]: *They that praised me* externally through their deception, namely, the Pharisees and the Scribes, saying: *Master, we know that you are a true speaker, and teach the way of God in truth, neither care you for any man;*[135] these took an oath against me and proposed in a hidden manner to have me killed. Whence Scripture says: *Their tongue is a piercing arrow, it has spoken deceit: with his mouth one speaks peace with his friend, and secretly he lies in wait for him.*[136]

101{102}[10] *For I did eat ashes like bread, and mingled my drink with weeping.*

Quia cinerem tamquam panem manducabam, et potum meum cum fletu miscebam.

101{102}[10] *Quia cinerem tamquam panem manducabam, for I did eat ashes like bread.* This applies to Christ according to a dual sense. For it is the case that as he taught sparingness and frugality in food and drink from the time he began to perform deeds and to teach,[137] so he fulfilled it, and so he did eat ashes, that is, he partook in neither delicate nor choice food, but rather simple food. *Et poculum meum, and my goblet,* [that is my] bodily [goblet], *cum fletu, with weeping* of my eyes or of the heart *miscebam, I mingled.*[138] For when Christ ate with publicans and sinners, there is no doubt but that he felt great distress towards them with all his heart; and before the resurrection of Lazarus, *he groaned in spirit, . . . and wept.*[139] But spiritually by ashes is indicated humiliation or affliction: and so Christ ate ashes like bread, that is, in his affliction, derision, and humiliation he feasted with his mind rejoicing in such adversity, in that manner that he taught: *Rejoice* in that hour

---

131 Luke 7:16b.
132 Matt. 9:33b.
133 John 19:15a.
134 Matt. 27:25.
135 Matt. 22:16.
136 Jer. 9:8.
137 Acts 1:1.
138 *E. N. See* footnote 101-46.
139 John 11:33b, 35.

for your reward is very great in heaven.[140] And with respect to himself, he presented himself freely and cheerfully to the Passion, as he himself [speaking through Isaiah] said: *I have given my body to the strikers, and my cheeks to them that plucked them.*[141] *Et potum meum, and my drink,*[142] that is, the joy which I have at the salvation of the elect, *I mingled . . . with weeping,* that is, with the sorrow which I had at the damnation of the reprobate. But in a most special sense this verse can be explained of the bilious food and the bitter drink of Christ on the cross.[143]

101{102}[11] *Because of your anger and indignation: for having lifted me up you have thrown me down.*

A facie irae et indignationis tuae, quia elevans allisisti me.

101{102}[12] *My days have declined like a shadow, and I am withered like grass.*

Dies mei sicut umbra declinaverunt, et ego sicut foenum arui.

But this I did and endured **101{102}[11]** *a facie irae indignationis tuae, because of your anger and indignation,* that is, so as to mitigate your anger and to take away your punishment by which you were angered at the human race because of original and other sin, which [sin] you placed upon me, and for which I willed to make satisfaction to you: as Isaiah said, *The Lord has laid on him the iniquity of us all;*[144] and as we find in Revelation about Christ: *He was clothed with a garment sprinkled with blood; and his name is called, the Word of God.*[145] And he *treads the winepress of the fierceness of the wrath of God the Almighty.*[146] And I endured this, *quia, for* you, Father God, *elevans, having lifted me up,* that is, placing me in command of all creatures, *allisisti me, have thrown me down* in death, that is, you have permitted that I die and be crushed in the manner that is revealed with Isaiah: *For the wickedness of my people have I struck him.*[147] **101{102}[12]** *Dies mei, my days,* [my] temporal, not my eternal [days], *sicut umbra, like a shadow* quickly passing by

---

140 Matt. 5:12a.
141 Is. 50:6a.
142 *E. N.* Here, contrary to the prior *Commentary,* Denis uses *potum* (drink) instead of *poculum* (goblet).
143 Matt. 27:34; John 19:30.
144 Is. 53:6b.
145 Rev. 19:13.
146 Rev. 19:15b; *cf.* Is. 63:3; Lam. 1:15b.
147 Is. 53:8b.

declinaverunt, have declined, that is, they have approached their end and death: because they were ended around thirty-three years. *Et sicut foenum arui, and I am withered like grass* in the Passion, as is not made manifest.

101{102}[14]   *You arising shall have mercy on Sion: for it is time to have mercy on it, for the time is come.*[148]

Tu exsurgens misereberis Sion, quia tempus miserendi eius, quia venit tempus.

101{102}[20]   *...from heaven the Lord has looked upon the earth.*

... Dominus de caelo in terram aspexit.

101{102}[22]   *That they may declare the name of the Lord in Sion: and his praise in Jerusalem.*

Ut annuntient in Sion nomen Domini, et laudem eius in Ierusalem.

101{102}[14] *Tu,* you, God the Father, *exsurgens misereberis Sion, arising shall have mercy upon Sion,* that is, the Church, *quia tempus miserendi eius, for it is time to have mercy on it* with my Incarnation; *quia venit tempus, for the time is come* for deliverance through my Passion. These things are all plainly explained in the preceding article, and they will not receive any kind of special exposition here. **101{102}[20]** *Dominus de caelo in terram aspexit, etc., from heaven the Lord has looked upon the earth, etc.* **101{102}[22]** *ut annuntient, that they may declare* to the faithful *in Sion nomen Domini, et laudem eius in Ierusualem, the name of the Lord in Sion and his praise in Jerusalem.* This can be literally received as referring to the early Church, which after the sending of the Paraclete in a most constant manner announced the name and the glory of Christ in Sion, that is, in the temple built upon mount Sion (as it is written in Acts) in Jerusalem,[149] the holy city, of which Christ in the Gospel stated, *It cannot be that a prophet perish out of Jerusalem.*[150]

101{102}[26]   *In the beginning, O Lord, you founded the earth: and the heavens are the works of your hands.*[151]

---

148 *E. N.* Denis skips verses 101:13, 101:15–19, part of 101:20, 101:21, as inapplicable to Christ.

149 Acts chp. 3.

150 Luke 13:33b.

151 *E. N.* Denis skips verses 101:22 through 101:25, and 101:27 through 101:29 as inapplicable to Christ.

Initio tu, Domine, terram fundasti, et opera manuum tuarum sunt caeli.

101{102}[26] *Initio tu, Domine, terram fundasti,* etc., *in the beginning, O Lord, you founded the earth,* etc. as has been explained. The Apostle asserts that this scripture is written about Christ.[152] For Christ, insofar as he was God, is the Creator of all things, as he himself states in Revelation: *I am the Alpha and the Omega, the beginning and the end.*[153] Indeed, as the Father, and the Son, and the Holy Spirit is one essence,[154] and as their power and action is one, so the three persons are one God, one Creator, one origin, one provider. The remaining things regarding [this Psalm] are clarified in the previous exposition.

ARTICLE III

HOW SOME EXPLAIN THIS
ONE HUNDRED AND FIRST PSALM LITERALLY.

OME CATHOLIC EXPOSITORS ALSO AFFIRM this Psalm as literally written about the Jewish people who were gravely afflicted, either at the time of the Babylonian captivity or during the time of the of Antiochus's persecution of the Jews, who in an exceedingly harsh way oppressed the Jews, as we read about in the book of Maccabees.[155] The commentators also add here that this Psalm speaks of the Jewish people at the time of Christ, namely, because during this time of persecution they desired the coming of the Christ in a great way, and by this they understood that he would perfectly free them, as is stated in Jeremiah: *In those days shall Juda be saved, and Israel*

---

152 Heb. 1:10.

153 Rev. 1:8a, 216a, 22:13a.

154 *E. N.* The singular "is" used by Denis despite the plural subject, giving clear precedent to the one essence shared by all three persons of the Trinity.

155 1 Macc. chp. 1; 2 Mach. chps. 5–7. *E. N.* The Babylonian Captivity refers to captivity or exile of the Jews following the conquest of Judah by King Nebuchadnezzar II (605–562 BC), the destruction of the temple, and the end of the Davidic monarchy in 587/6 BC. The reference to Antiochus is to the Seleucid ruler Antiochus Epiphanes (*ca.* 215–164 BC). This persecution is described by the Jewish historian Josephus in both his *Jewish Antiquities* and his *Jewish War*. It is also the subject matter of the Maccabean books, as Denis notes.

shall dwell confidently.[156] Now, in the manner that they here explain this Psalm as relating to the Jewish people who existed in times past, the contemporary teachers of the Jews explain this Psalm as pertaining to the Jewish people existing in their present state of captivity inflicted upon them by the Romans, in which they daily pray and await the coming of the Messiah, whom we know has already come. Truly, because this above-mentioned exposition brings about little devotion, we shall touch upon it in a cursory manner.

101{102}[2] *Hear, O Lord, my prayer: and let my cry come to you.*

Domine, exaudi orationem meam, et clamor meus ad te veniat.

101{102}[4] *For my days are vanished like smoke: and my bones are grown dry like charred remains.*

Quia defecerunt sicut fumus dies mei, et ossa mea sicut cremium aruerunt.

The holy Prophet [David] speaking, therefore, in the person of the greatly anxious and impoverished Jewish people during the time of Nebuchadnezzar or Antiochus, says: 101{102}[2] *Domine, exaudi orationem meam, etc.; hear, O Lord, my prayer, etc.* And the sentiment of the third verse is obvious from what has been said. Thereafter, this Psalm states: 101{102}[4] *Quia defecerunt sicut fumus dies mei, for my days are vanished like smoke.* For the Chaldeans and the servants of Antiochus in large part killed the Jews.[157] *Et ossa mea sicut cremium aruerunt, and my bones are grown dry like charred remains,* because of hunger, fear, and many forms of oppression. Or this may be said from those persons whom Antiochus caused to be roasted, burned, and fried in the frying pan as we read about in the second book of Maccabees.[158]

101{102}[5] *I am smitten as grass, and my heart is withered: because I forgot to eat my bread.*

Percussus sum ut foenum, et aruit cor meum, quia oblitus sum comedere panem meum.

---

156 Jer. 23:6a.

157 E. N. The Chaldeans is used as a synonym for the Babylonians.

158 2 Macc. 7:3, 5. *The king being angry commanded frying pans, and brazen caldrons to be made hot: which forthwith being heated. . . . And when he was now maimed in all parts, he commanded him, being yet alive, to be brought to the fire, and to be fried in the frying pan.*

101{102}[6] *Through the voice of my groaning, my bone has cleaved to my flesh.*

A voce gemitus mei adhaesit os meum carni meae.

101{102}[5] *Percussus sum,* I am smitten with fervor and the most oppressive fire of tribulations, *ut foenum, as grass* is cut down with the heat of the sun; *et aruit cor meum, and my heart is withered,* by reason of the need and sorrow, according to that stated in Lamentations: *Behold, O Lord, for I am in distress, my bowels are troubled: my heart is turned within me.*[159] Whence again in Lamentations Jeremiah says of these people: *Their face is now made blacker than coals, and they are not known in the streets.*[160] *Quia oblitus sum comedere panem meum, because I forgot to eat my bread,* that is, because I did not observe the commandments of the law: *which if a man do, he shall live in them,* as Moses asserted.[161] Or [we can understand it thus], *I forgot to eat my bread,* [my] material [bread]: because during the time of the persecution of Antiochus many of the Jews quickly fled to the wilderness, where they were not able to partake in bread. For this reason, Scripture says: *Judas Maccabeus . . . had withdrawn himself into a desert place, and there lived amongst wild beasts in the mountains with his company: and they continued feeding on herbs.*[162] 101{102}[6] *A voce gemitus mei adhaesit os meum carni meae; through the voice of my groaning, my bone has cleaved to my flesh,* that is, skin: for the flesh of the Jews wasted away by reason of fear, grief, and lament; and so bones clung to the skin.

101{102}[7] *I am become like to a pelican of the wilderness: I am like a night raven in the house.*

Similis factus sum pellicano solitudinis; factus sum sicut nycticorax in domicilio.

101{102}[8] *I have watched, and am become as a sparrow all alone on the housetop.*

Vigilavi, et factus sum sicut passer solitarius in tecto.

101{102}[7] *Similis factus sum pellicano solitudinis,* I am become like to a pelican of the wilderness fleeing to the wastelands in the face of the fear of my adversaries. *Factus sum sicut nycticorax in domicilio, I am like a night raven in the house,* for I did not dare appear during the day. For during

---

159 Lam. 1:20a.
160 Lam. 4:8a.
161 Lev. 18:5.
162 2 Macc. 5:27.

those times, they hid themselves in various refuges during those times, as is written in the books of Maccabees, Jeremiah, and Kings.[163] 101{102} [8] *Vigilavi, I have watched* also during the night, for I did not have the ability to be at rest on account of the concern and fear of dangers; *et factus sum sicut passer solitarius in tecto, and I am become as a sparrow all alone on the housetop*, that is, I have become divided by myself, scattered here and there, as fugitives do not consort together, but each one of them provides for himself, if he can, and hides himself wherever is possible.

101{102}[9]   *All the day long my enemies reproached me: and they that praised me did swear against me.*

Tota die exprobrabant mihi inimici mei, et qui laudabant me adversum me iurabant.

101{102}[10]   *For I did eat ashes like bread, and mingled my goblet with weeping.*

Quia cinerem tamquam panem manducabam, et poculum meum cum fletu miscebam.

101{102}[11]   *Because of your anger and indignation: for having lifted me up you have thrown me down.*

A facie irae et indignationis tuae, quia elevans allisisti me.

101{102}[9] *Tota die, all the day long*, that is, assiduously, *exprobrabant mihi inimici mei, my enemies reproached me*, the Chaldeans and others blaspheming the God of Israel and the law and his people, in the way that is written in Lamentations: *I am made a derision to all my people, their song all the day long;*[164] *et qui laudabant me, and they that praised me* fraudulently and by feigning, *adversum me iurabant, did swear against me*, proposing to kill me. This occurred in the greatest way to the Jews during the time of the Maccabees by Nicanor and the other ministers of Antiochus, and of the kings that succeeded him.[165] For often they spoke to the Jews words of peace and praise in deceit. The translation of Jerome from the Hebrew has this: *They that exulted me, who swore by me*, that is, the aforesaid enemies were derisive towards me, and rejoiced in my misfortune, swearing by me an oath of execration, putting forward my misery as an example, so that

---

163 2 Macc. 5:27; Jer. 16:15; 2 Kings 13:6.
164 Lam. 3:14.
165 1 Macc. 7:27–30. E. N. This "thrice-accursed Nicanor," 2 Macc. 8:34 (NRCV-CE), refers to one of the generals of King Antiochus IV Epipanes (r. 175–164 BC), Antiochus V Eupator (r. 163–161 BC), and Demetrius I Soter (r. 161–150 BC).

they would say, "Unless I do this or that, it may happen to me as it did the Jews." 101{102}[10] *Quia cinerem tamquam panem manducabam, for I did eat ashes like bread*: for they baked under ashes bread in which there were also ashes mixed. For during the time of the siege of Jerusalem by the Chaldeans the Jewish people suffered a most desperate famishment, so that in Lamentations it is said: *The hands of the pitiful women have sodden their own children;*[166] and again, *They that were brought up in scarlet have embraced the dung.*[167] *Et poculum meum cum fletu miscebam, and I mixed my goblet with weeping,* that is, I cried out while drinking because of the imminent evil. 101{102}[11] *A facie irae indignationis, because of your anger and indignation,* that is, by your just vengeance, for because of my sins you have done this to me, in the manner that is attested by Jeremiah: *I will give them up unto affliction to all the kingdoms of the earth* because you do not hear my word;[168] *quia elevans, for having lifted me,* that is, at one time honoring me, giving me the law, the Prophets, kings, and priests, *allisisti me, you have thrown me down,* during these times of prosecution: as is written in the first book of Maccabees, *There was very great wrath upon the people;*[169] and again, *Her dishonor was increased according to her glory.*[170]

101{102}[13] *But you, O Lord, endure forever....*[171]

    Tu autem, Domine, in aeternum permanes....

101{102}[14] *You arising shall have mercy on Sion: for it is time to have mercy on it, for the time is come.*

    Tu exsurgens misereberis Sion, quia tempus miserendi eius, quia venit tempus.

And so the consolation of the Jews was placed upon the coming of the Christ, who according to his divinity is eternal. Whence regarding him it now says: 101{102}[13] *Tu autem, Domine, in aeternum; but you, O Lord endure forever.* It appears that the Jews who spoke with the Lord Christ recognized this also: *We have heard out of the law, that Christ abides forever.*[172] 101{102}[14] *Tu exsurgens, you arising,* offering assistance or coming by your Incarnation, *misereberis Sion, shall have mercy on Sion,*

---

166 Lam. 4:10a.
167 Lam. 4:5b.
168 Jer. 29:18a.
169 1 Macc. 1:67.
170 1 Macc. 1:42a.
171 E. N. Denis skips verse 12 and the latter part of verse 13.
172 John 12:34a.

that is, the afflicted and captive Jewish people; or [we can look at it this way], *Sion*, that is the temple and the city of Jerusalem demolished by the ungodly Chaldeans; *quia tempus miserendi eius, for it is time to have mercy on it*, namely, the temple and the city, so that they may be rebuilt, which would be accomplished in seventy years as predicted by Jeremiah;[173] or [alternatively understood thus], so that they [Jerusalem and the temple] may be repaired during the time of the Maccabees after the due punishment of the Jewish people. Whence in the second book of Maccabees it states: *The wrath of the Lord was turned into mercy.*[174] Or [one can look at it thus]: *For it is time to have mercy*, that is, the time of your coming into the world, which was predicted in Daniel, has been fulfilled:[175] and so it was fitting for you to come, as you promised in Isaiah: *Therefore my people shall know my name in that day: for I myself that spoke, behold I am here.*[176] *Quia venit tempus, for the time is come*, the predicted [time has come]. This evidently is repeated as emphasis.

101{102}[15] *For its stones thereof have pleased your servants: and they shall have pity on the earth thereof.*

Quoniam placuerunt servis tuis lapides eius, et terrae eius miserebuntur.

101{102}[15] *Quoniam placuerunt servis tuis, for . . . they have pleased your servants*, the Saints and the Prophets, *lapides eius, its stones thereof*, namely, [the stones] of Sion: because they opted to rebuild the temple and the city of Jerusalem with stones; *et terrae eius miserebuntur, and they shall have pity on the earth thereof*, that is, they prayed for the deliverance of the people and the rebuilding of the city of the Jews. And for this reason many prayed — Zechariah, Daniel, Haggai, and other Saints. One can also explain this verse as referring to the building up of the Church, understanding by the stones the persons or the members of the Church; and by servants, the Apostles who first built up the Church after Christ, converting men to the worship of Christ; *et terrae eius, and on the earth thereof*, that is, Judea, *miserabuntur, they shall have pity*, for the Apostles first endeavored to convert the Jews to Christ, as is acknowledged by Paul in the book of Acts: *To you [Jews] it behooved us first to speak the word of God.*[177]

---

173 Jer. 29:10.
174 2 Macc. 8:5b.
175 Dan. 9:23–27.
176 Is. 52:6.
177 Acts 13:46a.

101{102}[24] *It answered him in the way of its strength: Declare unto me the fewness of my days.* [178]

Respondit ei in via virtutis suae: Paucitatem dierum meorum nuntia mihi.

101{102}[25] *Call me not away in the midst of my days: your years are unto generation and generation.*

Ne revoces me in dimidio dierum meorum, in generationem et generationem anni tui.

101{102}[24] *Respondit ei in via virtutis suae,* etc. *It answered him in the way of its strength,* etc. According to some, the Prophet here describes the future tribulation of the Church during the time of the Antichrist, which will be most severe, although it will not be for a long time. Therefore, it says: *Respondit ei, it answered him,* that is, the Church then will respond to Christ then, *in via virtutis suae, in the way of its strength,* that is, in the observation of patience which will then be of the greatest necessity: *Paucitatem dierum meorum, the fewness of my days,* that is, the brevity of my tribulations, *nuntia mihi, declare unto me,* in order that I might be strengthened and find relief in the hope of the closeness of being delivered. For *unless those days had been shortened, no flesh should be saved: but for the sake of the elect those days shall be shortened,* as is written in Matthew. [179] **101{102}[25]** *Ne revoces me, call me not away* from this life, that is, do not permit the Church to be entirely extirpated: do not, I say, call me away *in dimidio dierum meorum, in the midst of my days,* that is, within the first and the second of your comings; but preserve me even until the end of the world, in the way you promised, saying: *Behold I am with you all days, even to the consummation of the world.* [180]

Now because *all these things happened* to the Hebrews *in figure,* according to the Apostle, [181] for this very reason if this exposition were to be taken literally, it is possible [further] to explain this Psalm tropologically of the Christian people when severely afflicted, in a similar manner as was exposited above with respect to any particular penitent. Finally, those things which are now omitted [in this article] are evidently and clearly set forth in the first article [dedicated to this Psalm].

---

178 *E. N.* Denis skips verses 16 through 23 in this Article.
179 Matt. 24:22.
180 Matt. 28:20b.
181 1 Cor. 10:11a.

PRAYER

HEAR, O LORD, OUR PRAYER THAT CRIES out to you, and look down upon this earth from your high sanctuary, and mercifully avert present and future evils from us, so that we might announce your glory in Sion, and your praise in the heavenly Jerusalem.

Ad te clamantium exaudi orationem nostram, Domine, et de excelso sancto tuo in terram adspice, et mala praesentia et futura a nobis propitiatus averte: ut annuntiemus in Sion gloriam tuam, et in Ierusalem caelesti laudem tuam.

Psalm 102

ARTICLE IV

EXPLANATION OF THE
ONE HUNDRED AND SECOND PSALM:
BENEDIC, ANIMA MEA, DOMINO.
BLESS THE LORD, O MY SOUL.

102{103}[1] *For David himself. Bless the Lord, O my soul: and let all that is within me bless his holy name.*

Ipsi David. Benedic, anima mea, Domino, et omnia quae intra me sunt nomini sancto eius.

HIS TITLE IS ASSIGNED TO THE PRESENT Psalm: 102{103}[1] *Psalmus ipsi David, a Psalm for David himself:* that is, this Psalm is sung to Christ who is signified by David. For this Psalm deals with the many benefits of Christ, and the Prophet [David] exhorts himself to give worthy thanks to him. For as the prior Psalm is spoken in the person of the penitent recalling with lamentation and anxiety his misery, so in a similar way [this Psalm] speaks in the person of a fervent lover and a most thankful servant. And this is an appropriate order, for after the humble confession of one's own imperfections and the various afflictions of the troubled spirit, the joyful praise of the divine goodness and cheerful recollection of the benefits of the Creator customarily follows from the infusion of grace. For this reason, it is written in Tobit: *After a storm, O Lord, you make a calm, and after tears and weeping you pour in joyfulness.*[1]

And so it says: *Benedic, anima mea, Domino; bless the Lord, O my soul.* To bless another is to assert good things about him. Now we bless God, and God blesses us. Now, because the speech of God is the cause of things, according to this, *For he spoke, and they were made,*[2] and because our speech is not the cause of things, so the active blessing of God is the cause of our good, and by this we are blessed; but our blessing is not the cause of any goodness in God, and God is not blessed by it [in this way]. And so the blessing by which we bless God is the blessing of

---

1 Tob. 3:22b.
2 Ps. 148:5b.

confession and of praise. Of this [kind of blessing] is written in Luke: Simon *blessed God.*[3] And Tobias: *Bless God,* he said, *at all times.*[4] But the blessing by which God blesses us is the blessing of consecration or actuation. With respect to the first blessing, the lesser being blesses the greater being by praising him; but with respect to the second blessing, the greater being blesses the lesser being, sanctifying or perfecting him in the manner that the Apostle said to the Hebrews: *Without all contradiction, that which is less, is blessed by the better.*[5]

Therefore, *bless the Lord, O my soul,* that is, speak good things about God, rendering praise and giving thanks to him in all things, honoring him in all things and before all things with the mind, with word, and in deed. And not only bless my soul, as far as that which it is, but *et omnia quae intra me sunt, also all that is within me,* that is, with all the power, all the habits, all the acts, all the virtues, all the knowledge, all the thoughts of my soul bless *nomini sancto eius, his holy name,* that is, to the God having a holy name. These [faculties of the soul] bless God occasionally or materially, for clearly, while all these are focused upon God, they provide the occasion or the matter of blessing God; and so we ascribe these to God as first principle in acts of praise and thanksgiving. Or these bless God causally, for by these we know of God and his benefits. Then our soul and all that is within it blesses the most High when the soul honors God for his nature, his power, and his deeds, in the way is contained in Ecclesiasticus: *Magnify his name, and give glory to him with the voice of your lips.*[6]

102{103}[2] *Bless the Lord, O my soul, and never forget all he has done for you.*

Benedic, anima mea, Domino, et noli oblivisci omnes retributiones eius.

102{103}[2] *Benedic, anima mea, Domino; bless the Lord, O my soul:* this I again say to you so that you might be kindled and you might ponder how useful, salvific, and just it is to bless the Creator; *et noli oblivisci, and never forget* by laziness or inadvertence *omnes retributionis eius, all he has done for you,* that is, the gifts of divine goodness which have frequently been bestowed upon you, and no less those gifts restored

---

3 Luke 2 :28.
4 Tob. 4:20a.
5 Heb. 7:7.
6 Ecclus. 39:20a.

and which were given to you once again, for in the first parent we sinned; but the mercy of God through Christ has restored in us that which our first parents were deprived of and lost. For this reason, the Apostle [Paul] says to the Corinthians: *As in Adam all die, so also in Christ all shall be made alive.*[7] We ought not to forget of the tender mercies of our God, but let us consider how often he restores his grace to us. For however often we express sorrow with our hearts, he immediately forgives, and he restores his grace: indeed, he sends us ambassadors, exhorting us and pleading to us by them, so that we may turn back to him, in the manner that is professed by the divine Apostle: *For Christ therefore we are ambassadors, God as it were exhorting by us. For Christ, we beseech you, be reconciled to God.*[8] We ought never to forget, therefore, of the tender compassion of the Savior, for as Seneca asserts, the greatest ingratitude is the forgetting of bestowed benefits.[9] On the other hand, the greatest gratitude and returning of thanks is to receive a benefit gratefully. Isaiah was not forgetful of the benefits of God, when he said: *I will remember the tender mercies of the Lord, the praise of the Lord for all the things that the Lord has bestowed upon us, and . . . which he has given according to his kindness.*[10] Whence it states in Ecclesiasticus: *I remembered your mercy, O Lord, and your works, which are from the beginning of the world.*[11] Moreover, since God has no need of our goods,[12] so he is not in want of anything from us, and we are able to return to him nothing more becoming and nothing more acceptable to him than blessing and praise. For the *sacrifice of praise* honors him.[13]

102{103}[3] *Who forgives all your iniquities: who heals all your diseases.*

Qui propitiatur omnibus iniquitatibus tuis, qui sanat omnes infirmitates tuas.

Some of the benefits of God are appropriately brought to mind, and first of all is the benefit of mercy. **102{103}[3]** *Qui propitiatur omnibus*

---

7 1 Cor. 15:22.

8 2 Cor. 5:20.

9 *E. N.* This is a paraphrase of Seneca's *De Beneficiis*, III, 1, 3. Seneca discusses the different kinds of ingrates, yet of all the kinds of ingrates, *ingratissimus omnium, qui oblitus est*, "the most ungrateful of all is he who has forgotten [a benefit]."

10 Is. 63.7.

11 Ecclus. 51:11.

12 *Cf.* Ps. 15:2: "I have said to the Lord, you are my God, for you have no need of my goods."

13 Ps. 49:23a.

iniquitatibus tuis, who forgives all your iniquities. For when we repent and confess, God directly forgives us all our iniquities with respect to their fault. For one mortal sin is not forgiven, but that another, if it be present is forgiven;[14] but one venial sin can be sometimes forgiven without another.[15] The most beneficent God is merciful to us sinners frequently, namely, in Baptism, in Confession (which is the second plank after shipwreck),[16] and in the entrance or the profession of a religious. *Qui sanat omnes infirmitates tuas, who heals all your diseases,* that is, your inner weakness which are healed by the infusion of grace. Or [we can look at it in this manner]: *Who heals all your diseases,* that is, the fomes or the proneness toward evil, and the four principal wounds of the soul, which are malice, ignorance, concupiscence, and weakness.[17] These God now heals inchoatively, weakening them in Baptism and by daily progress, and by impeding consent [to sin] and [sinful] deeds by grace. But in the future resurrection these wounds will be perfectly healed, when *this mortal must put on immortality,* according to the Apostle.[18] Indeed, at that time Christ will remove from his elect all the punishments inflicted because of original sin both as to

---

14 E. N. *See* ST IIIa, q. 86, art. 3, co. Essentially, true repentance (contrition or attrition with confession) will not take away one mortal sin and not another. There is no such thing as half-repentance and half-forgiveness when it comes to mortal sins. God will not forgive an adulterous murderer unless he repents of both his adultery and his murder. "Every mortal sin is contrary to [sanctifying] grace and excludes it. Hence, it is impossible for one [mortal] sin to be pardoned without another [mortal sin]." This is one reason why it is incumbent upon the penitent to confess all mortal sins. "All mortal sins of which penitents after a diligent self-examination are conscious must be recounted by them in confession, even if they are most secret and have been committed against the last two precepts of the Decalogue." CCC § 1456.
15 E. N. ST IIIa, q. 87, art. 3, ad 2, art. 4, arg. 2 ("one venial sin is able to be forgiven without another venial sin").
16 E. N. The notion of Confession as the "second plank" of sanctifying grace is classic. "Christ instituted the sacrament of Penance for all sinful members of his Church: above all for those who, since Baptism, have fallen into grave sin, and have thus lost their baptismal grace and wounded ecclesial communion. It is to them that the sacrament of Penance offers a new possibility to convert and to recover the grace of justification. The Fathers of the Church present this sacrament as the second plank [of salvation] after the shipwreck which is the loss of grace.'" CCC § 1446. The first mention of it appears to have been in Tertullian's *De paenitentia*, 12, PL 1, 1248, who calls baptism and confession the "like two planks of human salvation" (*duabus humanae salutis quasi plancis*), and likens a man striving for repentance as a shipwrecked man putting his faith on a plank (*ut naufragus alicuius tabulae fidem*). Id. 4, PL 1, 1233. These images were combined by St. Jerome who referred to penance in his epistle to Demetrias as "like a second plank after shipwreck." *Ep.* 130, 9, PL 22, 1115 (*quasi secunda post naufragium miseris tabula sit*). *See also* ST IIIa, q. 84, art. 6.
17 E. N. ST IaIIae, q. 85, art. 3, co.
18 1 Cor. 15:53, 54.

guilt and as to effect; though now he removes them as to guilt, but not as to their effect. For there remains in us even after Baptism the fomes of sin, but these are not imputed to us as fault, for we do not incur the punishment of the damned when dying with these.[19] However, when Christ will perfectly heal all our weaknesses, then we will sing with joy with the Apostle: *O death, where is your victory? O death, where is your sting?*[20]

102{103}[4] *Who redeems your life from destruction: who crowns you with mercy and compassion.*

Qui redimit de interitu vitam tuam, qui coronat te in misericordia et miserationibus.

102{103}[4] *Qui redimit de interitu vitam tuam, who redeems your life from destruction.* Sometimes God redeems our bodily and natural life from unexpected and bodily death, preserving us from various sorts of dangers.[21] But he also redeems the spiritual life of our soul from internal destruction when he conserves us in his charity and grace, preserving us from mortal sin. Or [we can understand it thus], *Who redeems* by the merits of his Passion *de interitu* from destruction, that is the death of hell or eternal damnation, *your life,* that is, the life of grace bestowed or conferred upon you in the present and the life of glory prepared for you in the future. Or [yet another interpretation], *your life,* that is, you the Living One,[22] in the manner that we say: I beseech your love, that is, [I beseech] you, O beloved. Now of this redemption, the Savior says: *I am come that they may have life, and may have it more abundantly;*[23] and

---

19 E. N. That is to say, the wounds of sin (the effects) do not in and of themselves carry any fault or guilt, and so their presence *alone* is immaterial in terms of defining our eternal destiny.

20 1 Cor. 15:55; cf. Hosea 13:14: *I will deliver them out of the hand of death. I will redeem them from death: O death, I will be your death; O hell, I will be your bite: comfort is hidden from my eyes.* E. N. Denis's Latin version has *aculeus* instead of the Sixto-Clementine Vulgate's *stimulus,* but both mean spur, prick, goad, sting.

21 E. N. As we pray in the Litany of the Saints: *A subitanea et improvisa morte, libera nos, Domine.* "From a sudden and unprovided (unforeseen) death, deliver us, O Lord."

22 "Unlike creatures which *possess* life, God *is* Life. It is not imparted to Him from without, but He imparts it to all things, and is the fundamental life, the life of all that lives.... Hence the dictum: God is the life of the soul, as the soul is the life of the body (*Deus vita animae sicut anima corporis*). The Old Testament speaks of the Living God, whereas the New Testament call Him the *Life.* Cf. John xiv.6; 1 John v.20; John I, 4, and v. 26; Acts xvii, 22 sqq." Joseph Wilhelm and Thomas B. Scannell, *A Manual of Catholic Theology Based on Scheeben's 'Dogmatik'* (New York: Benziger Bros., 1906), 214–15.

23 John 10:10b.

again, *I lay down my life for my sheep.*[24] *Qui coronat te in misericordia et miserationibus, who crowns you with mercy and compassion*, that is, who in his mercy and by the various effects of his clemency now crowns you, giving you victory over the world, the flesh, and the devil, as the Apostle says: *Thanks be to God, who always makes us to triumph in Christ Jesus our Lord.*[25] For God crowns us in his mercy, making our souls daughters, brides, and heirs of the eternal kingdom. For this reason, Peter says in his first epistle: *You are a chosen generation, a kingly priesthood.*[26] In the future, he will also crown us with perfect happiness, in the way that Paul affirms: *As to the rest, there is laid up for me a crown of justice, which the Lord . . . will render to me in that day.*[27]

102{103}[5]   *Who satisfies your desire with good things: your youth shall be renewed like the eagle's.*

Qui replet in bonis desiderium tuum: renovabitur ut aquilae iuventus tua.

102{103}[5] *Qui replet in bonis desiderium tuum, who satisfies your desire with good things*, that is, he conducts your reasonable affections and your pious prayers to deeds, giving you what you desire and request. *For everyone that asks, receives.*[28] And it is stated in Psalms above, *The Lord has heard the desire of the poor;*[29] and *There is no want to them that fear him.*[30] And so God fulfils our desires now with grace and with power, not simply nor fully, but according to the measure of the present life. But in the heavenly fatherland, he will simply and perfectly fulfil it, according to that which is written: *I shall be satisfied when your glory shall appear.*[31]

Renovabitur ut aquilae iuventus tuae, your youth shall be renewed like the eagle's: that is, in the way an aged eagle recovers its pristine youth; so you, O my soul, shall return to the pristine and lost condition of spiritual youth, now assuredly by grace, fulfilling that stated by the Apostle, *Be renewed in the spirit of your mind, and put on the new man, who is created according to God;*[32] but in the future by glory, for in the day of

---

24 John 10:15b.
25 2 Cor. 2:14a.
26 1 Pet. 2:9a.
27 2 Tim. 4:8a.
28 Luke 11:10a.
29 Ps. 10:17a.
30 Ps. 33:10b.
31 Ps. 16:15b.
32 Eph. 4:23–24a.

judgment you will be clothed in double garments,[33] that is, with the double stole of immortality, namely, the glory of the soul and the body; and beyond this there will not be old age, but perpetual youth in accordance with Revelation: *Behold, I make all things new.*[34] Moreover, we will be renewed in the day of judgment with the youth of body, for the death shall rise again in a virile age.[35] Now, this eagle, as it is referred to, is nature, which in the time of old age its upper beak grows so long in the form of a hook that he cannot open his mouth, and so is not able to consume food. For this reason, it is aggrieved with hunger and decline, and out of a natural instinct it strikes its beak against a rock, and gets rid of the curved beak which impedes its ability to eat. Once this is done, it returns to its pristine strength by the consumption of meats.[36] So the soul — greatly aggrieved by the burden of the body and earthly habitation and impeded from the contemplation of heavenly things[37] — now sometimes daily insofar as it is possible, withdraws from participating in flesh and occupies itself with leading a heavenly life on earth; and so it renews its interior daily, as the Apostle [Paul] said to the Corinthians: *Though our outward man is corrupted, yet the inward man is renewed day by day.*[38] For the grace of God and of the most-high Trinity is the reformation in us, is the renewal of the youth of our soul. But a vicious manner of life is the old age of the soul. For this reason it is written: *How happens it, O Israel, that . . . you are grown old in a strange country, that you are defiled with the dead, that you are counted with them that go down to hell?*[39] And it adds as the cause: *You have forsaken the fountain of wisdom. For if you had walked in the way of God, you surely would have dwelt in peace* upon the earth.[40]

---

33 *Cf.* Prov. 31:21: *She shall not fear for her house in the cold of snow: for all her domestics are clothed with double garments.*

34 Rev. 21:5a.

35 *E. N. See* ST III (Supp.), q. 81, art. 1, co. ("in the resurrection, human nature will be brought to the state of ultimate perfection, which is in the youthful age (*iuvenili aetate*), at which the movement of increase ends, and when the movement towards decline begins"). "[A]ll men will be raised up with bodies in the perpetual vigour of youth, *in aetate Christi*, at that age at which Christ rose from the grave." John Saward, *The Beauty of Holiness and the Holiness of Beauty* (Brooklyn, NY: Angelico Press, 2021), 66 (citing to St. Thomas Aquinas *Summa contra Gentiles*, 4, 88 and 4 *Sent.*, d. 44, q. 1, a. 3, sol.1 and St. Augustine's *De civitate Dei*, 22, 15–16).

36 *E. N.* This image is taken from Pliny the Elder's *Natural History* (X, 3–6).

37 *Cf.* Wis. 9:15: *For the corruptible body is a load upon the soul, and the earthly habitation presses down the mind that muses upon many things.*

38 2 Cor. 4:16.

39 Baruch 3:10–11.

40 Baruch 3:12–13.

Now those who thus far are led by the literal interpretation can explain this as pertaining to the special benefits bestowed upon holy David: indeed each of us saying these five verses ought especially to think of the excellent benefits given to him, and he ought to ascribe them to God with all manner of thanksgiving, lest it be said on account of the ingratitude of our soul: *You shall be desolate, because you have forgotten God your Savior.*[41]

102{103}[6] *The Lord does mercies, and judgment for all that suffer wrong.*

Faciens misericordias Dominus, et iudicium omnibus iniuriam patientibus.

102{103}[6] *Faciens misericordias Dominus,* the Lord does mercies: that is, God deals with us in a merciful manner, and he communicates to us mercies (that is, the gifts of his kindliness): and not only does he do mercies to us who are merciful, of whom it is said, *Blessed are the merciful, for they shall obtain mercy;* but also to the ungodly and the unworthy, whom he often justifies freely, whom he patiently stands ready for, and to whom he bestows the benefits of natural gifts, namely, the light of the sun, clothing and sustenance, reason and senses, health of body, and many other things. For it is proper to God to have mercy.[42] The Lord also does *iudicium, judgment,* that is, just vengeance, *omnibus iniuriam patientibus, for all that suffer wrong* with equanimity because of justice; in the manner that it elsewhere states, *Revenge is mine, and I will repay them.*[43] God will reserve to himself revenge, as he exhorts in Leviticus: *Seek not revenge, nor be mindful of the injury of your citizens.*[44] And so although someone may bear with impatience the injuries inflicted upon him, yet God, who leaves no evil unkempt or unpunished, avenges. But he especially avenges on behalf of those who are patient and meek [in the face of suffering injuries]. Whence in Proverbs: *Say not, I will return evil: wait for the Lord, and he will deliver you.*[45]

---

41 Is. 17:9b–10a.

42 E. N. Mercy, as Shakespeare states in *The Merchant of Venice* (IV, sc. 1) "is an attribute to God himself, and earthly power doth then show likest God's when mercy seasons justice."

43 Detu. 32:35a. E. N. Denis's version uses the Latin *mihi vindictam* ("vengeance is mine"), which departs from the Sixto-Clementine's *mea est ultio* ("revenge is mine").

44 Lev. 19:18a.

45 Prov. 20:22.

102{103}[7] *He has made his ways known to Moses: his wills to the children of Israel.*

Notas fecit vias suas Moysi, filiis Israel voluntates suas.

102{103}[7] *Notas fecit vias suas, he has made his ways known,* that is, the moral, judicial, and ceremonial precepts, *Moysi, to Moses* the legislator on mount Sinai; and he has made known through Moses *filiis Israel voluntates suas, his wills to the children of Israel,* that is, the signs of his eternal will, namely, the commands of doing good and the prohibitions against doing evil. But that which is signified by the ways of God and his will are the same. And this he now especially made them know. For this reason Baruch in the person of the Israelites says: *We are happy . . . because the things that are pleasing to God are made known to us.*[46] But understanding this from a moral point of view, by Moses is understood to mean anything holy above the waters of pleasure, to which God, by the Holy Spirit, inspires how one ought to live, in the way that is stated in [the first epistle of] John: *his unction teaches you of all things.*[47] Now by the children of Israel is understood all the faithful, to whom God has imparted his precepts.

102{103}[8] *The Lord is compassionate and merciful: longsuffering and plenteous in mercy.*

Miserator et misericors Dominus, longaminis, et multum misericors.

102{103}[8] *Miserator et misericors Dominus, the Lord is compassionate and merciful.* According to the Damascene merciful is asserted as one having a miserable heart, namely, because he suffers greatly with the misery of another.[48] Yet God exists impassibly and immutably; he does not suffer

---

46 Baruch 4:4.

47 John 2:27b. E. N. "above the waters of pleasure" translates *de acquis consupicentiarum sublatus,* "above the waters of concupiscence." In the so-called Psalter of Mary (*Psalterium Marianum*), a compendium of the Psalms composed by St. Bonaventure, Psalm 68 is rendered: *Salvum me fac, Domina, quoniam intraverunt concupiscentiarum aquae usque ad animam meam. Infixus sum in limo peccati: et acquae voluptatis circumdederunt me.* "Save me, O Lady, for the waters of concupiscences have entered even into my very soul. I am stuck fast in the mire of sin: and the waters of pleasure have surrounded me."

48 E. N. See ST IIaIIae, q. 30, art. 1., co. Relying on St. Augustine's *De civitate Dei,* IX, 5, St. Thomas notes "mercy (*misericordia*) is compassion for another's distress in our heart, which impels us, if we are able, to render aid to him. For mercy (*misericordia*) takes its name from the fact that someone has a compassionate heart (*miserum cor*) for over another's misery (*miseria*)." The reference to St. John of Damascus by

pain, nor does he suffer with another. Therefore mercy, to the extent it suggests a suffering with another, does not appear to be compatible with God, but [it does] to the extent it understood to mean freely given aid. And so God is called one who has mercy, one actually showing mercy; but the kind of mercy, according to its natural properties, which is ready to render aid. *Longaminis, longsuffering*, that is, awaiting for a long time the conversion of evil men. Whence in Ecclesiasticus it is written, *The most High is a patient rewarder*;[49] and in the book of Wisdom, *But you have mercy upon all, because you can do all things.*[50] *Et multum misericors, and plenteous in mercy*: indeed, the abundance of his kindliness exceeds the merits and devotion of the supplicant; *and his tender mercies are all over his works.*[51] For this reason, James asserts: *And his mercy exalts itself above judgment.*[52]

102{103}[9] *He will not always be angry: nor will he threaten forever.*

Non in perpetuum irascetur, neque in aeternum comminabitur.

102{103}[10] *He has not dealt with us according to our sins: nor rewarded us according to our iniquities.*

Non secundum peccata nostra fecit nobis, neque secundum iniquitates nostras retribuit nobis.

102{103}[9] *Non in perpetuum irascetur, he will not always be angry* exercising vengeance, *neque in aeternum comminabitur, nor will he threaten forever* readying himself to inflict punishments. These things are not to be understood in an absolute manner, lest we fall into the insanity of those who say that the punishments of hell will eventually end. But [it is to be understood in the manner that] the Lord will not always be angry with his elect, nor will he condemn them forever: for although he may allow them to be scourged or be forsaken for a time, yet at the end he will reconcile himself to them, as it states in Lamentations: *The Lord will not cast off forever, for if he has cast off, he will also have mercy, according to the multitude of his mercies.*[53] **102{103}[10]** *Non secundum peccata nostra fecit nobis, he has not dealt with us according to our sins*: first, because he punishes us less than we deserve; second, because no

---

Denis is to his *De fide orthodoxa*, 2.2, which St. Thomas quotes in his *sed contra* of the same question.
49 Ecclus. 5:4b.
50 Wis. 11:24a.
51 Ps. 144:9b.
52 James 2:13b.
53 Lam. 3:31–32.

sinner who is in mortal sin merits grace by condign merit,[54] and so it is not fitting if he were to restore him to grace because of his sins. Third, because *where sin abounded, grace did more abound.*[55] And so the Apostle said to Timothy: God *has delivered us and called us by his holy calling, not according to our works, but according to his own purpose and grace.*[56] *Neque secundum iniquitates nostras retribuit nobis, nor rewarded us according to our iniquities*: because frequently, by his grace, he commutates eternal punishment through temporal punishments.[57]

102{103}[11] *For according to the height of the heaven above the earth: he has strengthened his mercy towards them that fear him.*

Quoniam secundum altitudinem caeli a terra, corroboravit misericordiam suam super timentes se.

102{103}[12] *As far as the east is from the west, so far has he removed our iniquities from us.*

Quantum distat ortus ab occidente, longe fecit a nobis iniquitates nostras.

102{103}[11] *Quoniam secundum altitudinem caeli a terra, corroboravit misericordiam suam super timentes se; for according to the height of the heaven above the earth, he has strengthened his mercy to those that fear him*: that is, as greatly as heaven is above the earth, so the mercy of God is greatly above our own maliciousness, so that it causes them who fear him with a

---

54 E. N. Condign merit (*meritum de condigno*) means merit in the strict sense of the word, that is, one where there is an equality between the service and the reward, and the reward is therefore a matter *of right.* "Now, man cannot by his own nature set up a *right* towards God, and demand by the law of justice that he be paid for anything he has done." Paul J. Glenn, O. P., *A Tour of the Summa* (St. Louis, MO: Herder Book Co., 1960). "So you also, when you shall have done all these things that are commanded of you, say: We are unprofitable servants; we have done that which we ought to do." Luke 17:10. If being good and doing what we ought to do does not earn a right to a supernatural reward, then certainly being in a state of mortal sin cannot claim any such right.

55 Rom. 5:20b.

56 2 Tim. 1:9.

57 E. N. That is to say, God, by the grace of temporal punishments, might bring a sinner to repentance before the date of his death and his judgment, thereby—by actual and eventually the infusion of sanctifying grace—turning a sinner in mortal sin into a penitent in a state of grace. Perhaps an *in extremis* example of this is the penitent thief—St. Dismas—who through the temporal punishment of his own crucifixion was touched by the grace of the Crucified One, and died in a state of grace to enjoy the fruits of Paradise.

filial and chaste fear to be dealth with in a manner incomparably different than they deserved, just as the Apostle says: *But God commends his charity towards us; because when as yet we were enemies, . . . Christ died for us.*[58] Or [it might be viewed] thus: *For according to the height of the heaven above the earth, etc.,* that is, in the way that heaven covers, makes fruitful, and illumines the earth by reason of its height and of its excellence, so God exists around his people, conserving them in the good, illuminating them inwardly, and busying himself with the fruitfulness of good works, as the Son of God disclosed in John: *My Father is the husbandman.*[59] 102{103}[12] *Quantum distat, as far as* the distance both quantitively and locally, *ortus, the east,* that is, the part of the heaven in the East, *ab occidente,* that is, from the part in the West, which certainly is as great as the distance between the Arctic and the Antarctic poles, since heaven is spherical. Or [looked at another way], *as far* as the distance of condition, *the east,* that is the light or the origin of the day, *is from the west,* that is, from the darkness which spells the end of the day. *Longe fecit a nobis iniquitates nostras, so far has he removed our iniquities from us*: for so far does he make allowance for them with respect to us penitents that they are as if they had never existed. Whence it is attested in Ezechiel: *If the wicked do penance for all his sins, . . . I will not remember all his iniquities that he has done.*[60] And in Micah we have this: *He will put away our iniquities: and he will cast all our sins into the bottom of the sea.*[61]

102{103}[13]   *As a father has compassion on his children, so has the Lord compassion on them that fear him:*

Quomodo miseretur pater filiorum, misertus est Dominus timentibus se.

102{103}[14]   *For he knows our frame. He remembers that we are dust.*

Quoniam ipse cognovit figmentum nostrum; recordatus est quoniam pulvis sumus.

---

58 Rom. 5:8–9a. E. N. In quoting the epistle to the Romans, Denis replaces the Sixto-Clementine's "sinners" (*peccatores*) with "enemies" (*inimici*).

59 John 15:1b. E. N. The notion of God the Father as husbandman or farmer (*agricola*) is quite lovely: "God cultivates us so as to make us better by his work, in that he roots out the evil seeds from our hearts. He opens our hearts with the plow of his words; he plants the seeds of the precepts; he harvests the fruit of piety, as Augustine says." St. Thomas Aquinas, *Super Io.,* cap. 15, l. 1.

60 Ez. 18:21a, 22a.

61 Micah 7:19.

102{103}[15] *Man's days are as grass, as the flower of the field so shall he flourish.*

Homo, sicut foenum dies eius; tamquam flos agri, sic efflorebit.

102{103}[13] *Quomodo miseretur pater,* as a father has compassion [that is,] a father of flesh and one most indulgent, *filiorum* suorum, *on his children, misertus est Dominus timentibus se,* so has the Lord compassion on *them that fear him*: because as a father loves his child, whether by being favorably disposed towards him or whether in threatening or punishing him, so God bestows mercy upon those who fear him, whether he chastises them or whether he fills them with consolation. And this is what he says in Malachi: *I will spare those who fear me, as a man spares his son that serves him.*[62] Whether, therefore adversity or prosperity befalls us, let us give thanks to the Lord, knowing that *to them that love and to them that fear God, all things work together unto good.*[63]

But it reveals to us why it is that the Lord is so clement with us: 102{103}[14] *Quoniam ipse cognovit figmentum nostrum, for he knows our frame,* that is, our substantial weakness and our proclivity to evil because of the fomes and inclination towards vice.[64] Now this weakness of our substance is greatly described, when it adds: *Recordatus est, he remembers,* that is, he lovingly attends to the fact, *quoniam pulvis sumus, that we are dust,* that is, formed, with respect to our body, from the slime of the earth, and we shall return to dust in the way that Scripture states: *And the Lord God formed man of the slime of the earth;*[65] and: *Dust you are and into dust you shall return.*[66] 102{103}[15] *Homo sicut foenum dies eius, man's days are as grass:* for it dries up and is cut down as quickly as if it were grass, as holy Job says: *My days have passed more swiftly than the web is cut by the weaver.*[67] *Tamquam flos agri, as the flower of the field,* which exists today, but tomorrow is not longer to be found, *sic efflorebit, so shall he flourish,* that is, so shall the bloom and vigor of youth depart.

102{103}[16] *For the spirit shall pass in him, and he shall not be: and he shall not know his place any more.*

---

62 Mal. 3:17b.

63 Rom. 8:28.

64 E. N. The *fomes* (meaning "tinder" or "fuel") is an Augustine term which is equivalent to the concupiscence, and it describes the tendency or inclination, inherited from the Fall of Adam and original sin, that we have in us towards sin.

65 Gen. 2:7a.

66 Gen. 3:19b.

67 Job 7:6.

Quoniam spiritus pertransibit in illo, et non subsistet: et non cognoscet amplius locum suum.

102{103}[16] *Quoniam spiritus, for the spirit,* that is, the soul, *pertransibit in illo, shall pass in him,* that is, will have a temporal duration in man, which once completed, will leave; *et non subsistet, and he shall not be,* [that is,] man [shall not be] in this life, his soul having left elsewhere. For this is written: *The days of man are short, and the number of his months is with you: you have appointed his bounds which cannot be passed.*[68] And in the book of Samuel: *We all die, and like waters that return no more, we fall down into the earth.*[69] And this weakness of our nature stirs God into having mercy upon us, in the manner that is expressed in Genesis: *I will no more curse the earth for the sake of man.*[70] For the sensibilities and thoughts of the human heart are prone towards evil from man's youth.[71] *Et non cognoscet, and he shall not know* the soul after its separation [shall not know] *amplius locum suum, his place any more,* that is, the body which it left, until it will dress itself with it again. For the deceased do not know with particularity that which occurs in the present life, unless it be by some special revelation, or because of a special condition towards it which brings them here.[72] For in this way Saints in the heavenly fatherland know the prayers by which they are invoked and the respect by which they are honored. Jerome's translation is this: *And it does not remember its place any more.* But both [translations] share in the truth, because according to Augustine, in the book *On the Care of the Dead,* as the living in this world are ignorant of what occurs in the place of the dead, so the dead do not know what may be occuring in the place of the living: this is to be understood in reference to the present dispensation, and of determinate and natural knowledge.[73] Whence Isaiah says: *You, O Lord, are our Father, our Redeemer, from everlasting is your Name.*[74]

---

68 Job 14:5.

69 2 Sam. 14:14a.

70 Gen. 8:21a.

71 *E. N.* Denis uses the word *adolescentia,* probably referring to that time called the "age of reason," *aetas rationis,* which is that time in human development were a human person becomes morally responsible. Typically, this is considered to be around the age of seven.

72 *E. N.* Denis is drawing from ST Ia, q. 89, arts. 1–8.

73 *E. N.* The way of knowledge in this life (particular, natural, determinate) is through abstraction from the senses and from matter, which is not available to the dead because they do not have bodies until their resurrection. The knowledge of the dead is obtained by the infusion of species by God.

74 Is. 63:16b.

102{103}[17]   *But the mercy of the Lord is from eternity and unto eternity upon them that fear him: And his justice unto children's children.*

Misericordia autem Domini ab aeterno, et usque in aeternum super timentes eum. Et iustitia illius in filios filiorum,

102{103}[18]   *To such as keep his covenant, and are mindful of his commandments to do them.*

His qui servant testamentum eius, et memores sunt mandatorum ipsius ad faciendum ea.

102{103}[17] *Misericordia autem Domini ab aeterno et usque in aeternum,* but the mercy of the Lord is from eternity and unto eternity, that is, without wavering and without end, and from the beginning of the world even until the end it is never-ending, it is imparted *super timentes eum, upon them that fear him* with a holy and filial fear. For now it is present unceasingly by grace, and in the future also by glory. But since neither the world nor sin will be eternal,[75] in what way is the mercy of the Lord upon them that fear him unto eternity? The answer is that the phrase "unto eternity" is in reference to those who received it, and is said by reason of predestination or of preparation,[76] in the manner that is contained in the book of Revelation with respect to Christ: *The Lamb, which was slain from the beginning of the world.*[77] And to Timothy: *Grace . . . was given to us in Christ Jesus before the times of the world,*[78] that is, the giving of it was [eternally] foreseen.

Et iustitia illius, and his justice, that is, the effects of divine justice, namely the just fulfillment of promises and the rewarding of merits will be and is *in filios filiorum, unto children's children,* that is, in all the children of the first parents; this should be understood as applying to the just children.[79] To which is annexed: 102{103}[18] *his qui servant, to such as keep* by faith

---

75 E. N. The elect in heaven will be confirmed in the good, and so there will not be sin in heaven. How then, Denis asks, can mercy be eternal when the elect will be eternally confirmed in the good?

76 E. N. Denis uses the words of predestination (*praedestinationis*) and of preparation (*praeparationis*). This appears to be a reference back to St. Augustine's famous definition of predestination in his *On the Predestination of the Saints* 10, 19. *Inter gratiam porro et praedestinationem hoc tantum interest, quod praedestinatio est gratiae preparatio, gratia vero iam ipsa donatio.* "Furthermore, only this lies between grace and predestination: that predestination is the preparation of grace, but grace is the gift presently bestowed." PL 44, 974.

77 Rev. 13:8b.

78 2 Tim. 1:9b.

79 E. N. Obviously, the children of the first parents that are not justified (who die in a state of mortal sin and therefore not in a state of sanctifying grace) will not enjoy the fulfillment of the promises and any rewards associated with meritorious deeds.

and obedience,[80] *testamentum eius, his covenant*, that is, the divine law that has been given. *Et memores sunt mandatorum ipsius, and are mindful of his commandments*, not in any kind of manner, but *ad faciendum ea, to do them*. For many there are who are mindful of the commandments of the Lord, yet not so that they might fulfill them, but so that they might teach others that which they do not themselves do, which is a mortal sin; or so that they might appear learned, which is vainglory. We ought therefore to be mindful of the divine law and the commandments of the most High, not so that we might merely know them, but so that we might fulfill them. Whence also Aristotle says: Let us scrutinize what virtue is, not so that we might know it, but so that we might do good.[81] Otherwise, we will be counted among college of Pharisees and Scribes, of which the Savior says in Matthew: *Whatsoever they shall say to you, observe and do: but according to their works do not; for they say, and do not. For the bind heavy and insupportable burdens, and lay them on men's shoulders, but with a finger of their own they will not move them.*[82]

102{103}[19] *The Lord has prepared his throne in heaven: and his kingdom shall rule over all.*

Dominus in caelo paravit sedem suam, et regnum ipsius omnibus dominabitur.

102{103}[19] *Dominus in caelo paravit sedem suam*, the Lord has prepared his throne in heaven. This can be received in many ways. The first way is this: *The Lord* God, the holy Trinity, *in* the empyreal *heaven has prepared his throne*, that is, the place of his dwelling. For no corporeal place is as properly fitting to God as is the empyreal heaven. For this reason, Moses said: *His dwelling is above, and underneath are the everlasting arms.*[83] Or [we can understand it this way], *in heaven*, that is, in the city of the kingdom of heaven, and most of all in the angels that pertain to the lowest order

---

80 E. N. "The proper response to God's revelation is 'the obedience of faith' (Rom. 15:25; *cf.* Rom. 1:5; 2 Cor. 10:5–6) by which man freely entrusts his entire self to God, offering 'the full submission of intellect and will to God who reveals,' and freely assenting to the revelation given by him.'. . . The obedience of faith implies acceptance of the truth of Christ's revelation, guaranteed by God, who is Truth itself." Congregation for the Doctrine of the Faith, *Dominus Iesus: Declaration on the Unicity and Salvific Universality of Jesus Christ and the Church*, No. 7 (Aug. 6, 2000) (quoting VII, *Dei Verbum*, 5).
81 E. N. The reference is to Aristotle's *Nicomachean Ethics* II, 2 1103b26–29: "We are not investigating the nature of virtue for the sake of knowing what it is, but in order that we may become good, without which result our investigation would be of no use." (trans., H. Rackham).
82 Matt. 23:3–4.
83 Deut. 33:27a.

of the first hierarchy, which because of the divine indwelling, are called Thrones (that is seats) of God. Or [alternatively], *in heaven*, that is, in in every man on earth having a heavenly manner of living. For such men abide in heaven by grace, according to this: *As in a bride chamber shall he abide all the day long.*[84] Or [as a further alternative], *The Lord* Christ, the man-God, *in heaven*, the empyreal [heaven], *has prepared*, from the beginning of the world *his throne*, that is, lasting mansions both for himself and for his [followers]: about which he said, *I go to prepare a place for you.*[85] For from the beginning of the world he prepared this throne through creation; but after his Ascension, he prepared it for his disciples by interpellation,[86] for according to the Apostle, Jesus *entered into heaven itself, that he may appear now in the presence of God for us.*[87] *Et regnum ipsius, and his kingdom*, that is, the rulership or the regal power of Christ, *omnibus dominabitur, shall rule over all.* For *all things* are subjected *under his feet*, according to the Apostle.[88] For this reason, it is written: *All peoples, tribes and tongues shall serve him.*[89] And in Revelation: *The Lamb shall overcome them, because he is Lord of lords, and King of kings.*[90]

102{103}[20]   *Bless the Lord, all you his angels: you that are mighty in strength, and execute his word, hearkening to the voice of his orders.*

Benedicite Domino, omnes angeli eius, potentes virtute, facientes verbum illius, ad audiendam vocem sermonum eius.

And so the heavenly creation, the angelic minds, the otherworldly intellects, and the deiform souls are invited to the praise of God. **102{103}[20]** *Benedicite Domino, angeli eius; bless the Lord, all you his angels*, that is, the messengers of God, *potentes virtute, you that are mighty in strength*, that is,

---

84 Deut. 33:12b.

85 John 14:2b.

86 *L. per interpellationem.* The difficulty in interpreting this word has left me no recourse but to use its English derivative interpellation. *Interpellatio* can mean "a speaking between," "an interruption in speaking," but it can also mean a "suit," or "appeal to the court." The sense is that Christ, as advocate for humankind, interrupted the process initiated by Adam's sin, interrupted the old dispensation, *the status quo*, and obtained, as part of his plea to the Father after his Ascension, that the Holy Spirit, another advocate, be sent to the Church so that new dispensation could be made manifest among the Jews and the Gentiles, thus making mansions in heaven available to us.

87 Heb. 9:24b.

88 Heb. 2:8a.

89 Dan. 7:14a.

90 Rev. 17:14.

those with special powers, *facientes verbum illius, and execute his word*, that is, implement the divine commission and the commands given to you, *ad audiendam vocem sermonum eius, hearkening to the voice of his orders*, that is, so that men might hear by your execution [of this commission and these commands] that which God orders and announces to them. For God reveals to us his good pleasure by the angels.[91] Now although by angels can be understood as referring to the angelic spirits of the lowest order, those whose place it is to announce lesser things, according to Gregory,[92] nevertheless, by angels we can also understand all the heavenly spirits of which the Apostle says, They are *all ministering spirits*:[93] for, according to the teaching of the great Dionysius, all the angelic minds are called angels.[94] Moreover, the power of the angels is of two kinds. Namely, there is the natural [power], and this power greatly exceeds all the powers of corporeal creation, so that it is written of the devil, *There is no power upon earth that can be compared* to his.[95] For natural qualities of the apostate angels remained in their integrity, according to Dionysius in chapter 4 of *The Divine Names*. By this power it is fitting that angels move the heavens, according to the philosophers. But the other power of the angels is supernatural, which is greater and higher. By this [power] one angel slew in one night all the firstborn in the land of Egypt, as is stated in

---

91 E. N. God's will of good pleasure (*voluntas beneplaciti*) is distinguished from his signified will (*voluntas signi*). "By conformity to the divine will we understand the absolute and loving submission of our will to that of God, whether it be His 'signified will' or His will of 'good pleasure.'" "Conformity to God's *signified will* consists in willing all that God manifests to us of His intentions. 'Christian doctrine clearly proposes unto us the truths which God wills that we should believe, the goods He will have us hope for, the pains He will have us dread, what He will have us love, the commandments He will have us observe and the counsels He desires us to follow. And this is called God's signified will, because He has signified and made manifest unto us that it is His will and intention that all this should be believed, hoped for, feared, loved and practiced.' [Treatise of the Love of God, VIII, 3]." On the other hand, the conformity to God's will of good pleasure "consists in submitting oneself to all providential events willed or allowed by God for our own greater good, and chiefly for our sanctification. It rests upon this basis, that nothing happens without God's order or permission, and that God, being infinite Perfection and infinite Goodness, cannot will or permit anything but for the good of the souls." Adolphe Tanquerey, *The Spiritual Life: A Treatise on Ascetical and Mystical Theology* (Tournai: Desclée & Co. 1932), 233, 236 (2nd ed.) (Herman Branderis, trans.).
92 E. N. The guardianship of mankind belongs generally to the Principalities, the Archangels, and the Angels. The reference is to Pope St. Gregory the Great, specifically, one of his homilies on the Gospels. *In Evang.* II, 34, PL 76, 1251. *See also* ST Ia, q. 113, arts. 2, 3.
93 Heb. 1:14a.
94 E. N. The reference is to chapter 5 of the Areopagite's *The Celestial Hierarchy*.
95 Job 41:24.

Exodus;[96] and in the camp of the Assyrians [an angel by this supernatural power slew] one hundred and eighty five thousand men, as we read in Isaiah.[97]

102{103}[21] *Bless the Lord, all you his hosts: you ministers of his that do his will.*

Benedicite Domino, omnes virtutes eius, ministri eius, qui facitis voluntatem eius.

102{103}[21] *Benedicite, Domino, omnes virtutes eius; bless the Lord, all you his hosts.* By "hosts" we can understand the angels that belong in the middle order of the second hierarchy, which are called by the specific name of Powers, according to Dionysius;[98] or [by "hosts" we can understand] all the angelic minds, because, on the other hand, all angels are called "hosts" from the most excellent efficaciousness of their own powers. But by "hosts" Rabbi Moses understands the natural powers of all the created things.[99] "Hosts," I say, are *ministers of his that do his will,* that is, who obey the command of the divine will.[100]

102{103}[22] *Bless the Lord, all his works: in every place of his dominion, O my soul, bless you the Lord.*

Benedicite Domino, omnia opera eius, in omni loco dominationis eius. Benedic, anima mea, Domino.

102{103}[22] *Benedicite Domino, omnia opera eius; bless the Lord, all his works,* that is, all creatures, *in omni loco dominationis eius, in every place of his dominion,* that is, in heaven, and earth, and everywhere in between. For the Creator is everywhere the ruler. Christ also is given *all power in heaven and earth.*[101] For this reason, it is written: *O Lord, Lord, almighty King, for all things are in your power; you have rulership over all things.*[102] Even irrational creatures materially bless and praise

---

96 Ex. 12:29.
97 Is. 37:36.
98 E. N. The reference is to Chapters 6 and 8 of *The Celestial Hierarchy.*
99 E. N. The Jewish philosopher Moses Maimonides (Moses ben Maimon) (1138–1204) identified the Scriptural angels as equivalent to the Aristotelian intelligences. Serge-Thomas Bonino, O. P., *Angels and Demons: A Catholic Introduction* (Washington, DC: Catholic University of America Press, 2016), 61–62 (Michal J. Miller, trans.).
100 E. N. Denis insists that by angelic "hosts" or powers, we are not to understand natural, impersonal powers, but personal powers who obey the divine will.
101 Matt. 28:18b.
102 Esther 13:9, 11. *O Lord, Lord, almighty king, for all things are in your power, and there is none that can resist your will . . . You are Lord of all, and there is none that can resist your majesty.*

God, for they furnish matter by which the contemplative man can bless the Lord, because in them shines resplendently the wisdom, power, and goodness of the Creator. But because it is to no avail to exhort others and to omit exhortations to one's self—as the Savior said, *What does it profit a man, if he gain the whole world, and suffer the loss of his own soul?*[103]—so does he return back to himself, and says: *Benedic, anima mea, Domino; O my soul, bless you the Lord*: according to the understanding that has been expounded.

Pay heed: we have heard this sweet and delightful Psalm, most noble with all praise and most full with all consolation and suavity, one which especially exhorts us sinners to penance and holy conversion. When singing this Psalm, it behooves us to ignite with the love of God from the recollection of the divine benefits, and to delight with our hearts in his praise. And so that we might find ourselves worthy praisers, let us endeavor to serve Christ with a pure heart, to despise all carnal, worldly, temporal, and vain things, and let us with recollected heart and firmness contemplate, search for, love, and honor—with as much attentiveness and frequency as the many benefits we receive from him—that one thing, the only thing that is necessary.[104] And so Christ asserts in Luke: *Unto whomsoever much is given, of him much shall be required.*[105]

PRAYER

GOD, SAVIOR OF THE LIVING, WHO DO not will the death of sinners, you, O kindly Father, remember our frame, and do not be angry with us sinners in perpetuity, but strengthen us by pouring your mercy over us, and deliver our life from eternal death.

Deus salvator viventium, qui no vis mortem peccantium, tu,
pie Pater, cognosce figmentum nostrum, et peccatoribus
nobis non irascaris in perpetuum; sed corrobora
super nos misericordiam tuam, et redime
de aeterno interitu vitam nostrum.

103 Matt. 16:26.
104 Luke 10:42.
105 Luke 12:48b.

Psalm 103

ARTICLE V

EXPLANATION OF THE ONE HUNDRED AND THIRD PSALM: BENEDIC, ANIMA MEA, DOMINO; DOMINE DEUS MEUS. BLESS THE LORD, O MY SOUL: O LORD MY GOD.

103{104}[1]   *A Psalm of David. Bless the Lord, O my soul: O Lord my God, you are exceedingly great. You have put on praise and beauty.*[1]

Psalmus David. Benedic, anima mea, Domino: Domine Deus meus, magnificatus es vehementer. Confessionem et decorem induisti.

103{104}[2]   *And are clothed with light as with a garment. Who stretches out the heaven like a hide.*[2]

Amictus lumine sicut vestimento. Extendens caelum sicut pellem.

103{104}[3]   *Who cover the higher rooms thereof with water. Who makes the clouds your chariot: who walks upon the wings of the winds.*

Qui tegis aquis superiora eius; qui ponis nubem ascensum tuum, qui ambulas super pennas ventorum.

HE TITLE TO THIS PRESENT PSALM IS BRIEF and simple, since it says: 103{104}[1] *Psalmus David, a Psalm of David.* But the Prophet [David] in this Psalm speaks in the person of a man praising God with a thankful frame of mind. *Benedic, anima mea, Domino; bless the Lord, O my soul.* How this ought to be understood and fulfilled is explained by a lengthy treatment of the matter in the exposition of the preceding Psalm.[3] *Domine Deus meus, magnifiactus es vehementer; O Lord my God, you are exceedingly great:* that is, the great effects from your works and your marvels are powerfully known to us, so that your excellence, magnitude, and majesty have been made clearly

---

1 E. N. The Douay-Rheims, following the Sixto-Clementine Vulgate, has *Ipsi David,* "For David himself." Denis's text, which I have followed, departs from this.

2 E. N. The Douay-Rheims has "pavilion" for *pellem* (skin, hide, pelt) which I have translated as "hide." Whether this taut "hide" was flat or was round like the round dome of a tent played a role in the controversies involving Galileo and Columbus.

3 Ps. 102:1.

known to us by the consideration of your works, though you in yourself are completely immutable and the supremely perfect.[4]

Confessionem et decorem induisti, you have put on praise and beauty: that is, as a man is surrounded by vestments, you are surrounded with the praise of the Saints and their brilliant servitude, for all the Blessed rush toward you from all parts. Or [we can understand it thus], *you have put . . . beauty*, that is, beauty in you yourself, indeed, you are most beautiful, and if beauty were to be regarded as your vestment, you would be everywhere adorned. **103{104}[2]** *Amictus lumine sicut vestimento, you are clothed with light as with a garment*: that is, you are yourself so clear and resplendent, and light is the vestment for you, covering you entirely, so that there is no darkness to be found in you: this accords with this, *God is light, and in him there is no darkness*. And this can be especially understood as pertaining to Christ. For he was clothed with the confession of praise in the way that the Apostle stated to the Philippians: *Every tongue should confess that the Lord Jesus Christ is in the glory of God the Father.*[5] Indeed, the elect everywhere praise Christ. He is also clothed with beauty, especially in his Resurrection, when he, who was not beautiful or appealing during his Passion, rose again in a glorious form. For he rose again with a glorified body, whose splendor transcended incomparably and immeasurably the brightness of the sun: for this reason, it states, *you are clothed with light as with a garment.*

Extendens caelum, who stretches out the heaven where the stars are set or the firmament *sicut pellem, like a hide*: for [the heavens] seem to be like a hide stretched out over a spherical shape, covering and concealing the earth, encircling our hemisphere the way a tent does.[6] Whence Isaiah: *He stretches out the heavens as nothing and spreads them out as a tent to dwell in.*[7] **103{104}[3]** *Qui tegis aquis superiora eius, who cover the higher rooms thereof with water*, that is, the convex stellar heavens. For it is written in Genesis: *Let there be a firmament made amidst the waters: and let it divide the waters from the waters. And God made a firmament,*

---

4 Num. 23:19a: *God is not a man, that he should lie, nor as the son of man, that he should be changed.* Mal. 3:6a: *For I am the Lord, and I change not.*

5 Phil. 2:11. E. N. The tie in between Ps. 103:1 and Phil. 2:11 is not detectable in the English. The "confession of praise" (*confessionem*) of Psalm 103:1 is tied to Phil. 2:11's *confiteatur* ("should confess [in a confession of praise]").

6 E. N. "In line with the cosmology of the time (*cf.* Is 40:22; Ps 19:1–6), the psalm then compares the firmament (*cf.* Gen 1:6) to an enormous tent." *The Navarre Bible: The Psalms* (Dublin: Four Courts Press, 2003), 344. This is why the Douay-Rheims translators clearly opted to translate the Latin *pellem* (hide) with pavilion (*i.e.*, a tent or tabernacle).

7 Is. 40:22b.

and divided the waters that were under the firmament, from those that were above the firmament.[8] Some, therefore, following these words in a literal manner, say that there are waters above the heavens in the form of frozen glaciers and these cover the heavens. But others speaking more philosophically say that by these waters are understood the ninth sphere, which is called the crystalline or aqueous heaven, as the immobile heaven is called empyrean, that is, fiery; this is not, of course, as if the ninth sphere by nature made of water, or that the empyreal heaven by nature made of fire; but because it befits [to describe] the crystalline heaven with the transparency of water; for it appears in the manner that frozen water does. But the empyrean participates with fire in its clarity. That which is said here in this place — *who cover the higher rooms thereof with water* — agrees with that contained in Daniel, *O all you waters that are above the heavens, bless the Lord.*[9] Now by heaven in this place, and the heavens of which Daniel speaks, and by firmament — the word which the book of Genesis uses — Basil understands the aerial heavens, above which the clouds are supported. And this exposition Augustine praises greatly.[10]

Mystically speaking, by heaven is designated the Church, which, because of the pressures and tribulations it suffers, is called in the Song of Songs: *I am black but beautiful, . . . as the hides of Solomon,*[11] that is, the heaven, which is the Solomonic skin of truth, namely, of Christ. Christ, therefore, extends the heaven, that is, the Church, as a hide, since he spreads it through all the parts of the earth, and it exalts through contemplation the sublime nature of the Godhead. Now the higher part of the heaven, that is, the Apostles and the Prophets, and those who are efficacious imitators of them, he covers with the waters of salvation and grace, or the gifts of the Holy Spirit, as we have attested by the Savior: *He that believes in me, . . . out of his belly shall flow rivers of living water.*[12]

Qui ponis nubem ascensum tuum, who makes the clouds your chariot, that is, who causes that the material clouds are things that arise through your command. For by divine rule it occurs that clouds are formed from water vapor and are borne upwards. Whence it is written about God by the Prophet [that he is the one]: *Who calls the waters of the sea and pours them*

---

8 Gen. 1:6–7.
9 Dan. 3:60.
10 *E. N.* Some of the various and competing theories on the firmament of heaven are discussed by St. Thomas in ST Ia, q. 68.
11 Songs 1:4a. *E. N.* I have translated the Latin *pelles* into "hides." The Douay-Rheims has "curtains."
12 John 7:38.

out upon the face of the earth.[13] And in Deuteronomy, *By his magnificence the clouds run here and there.*[14] *Qui ambulas super pennas ventorum, who walks upon the wings of the winds,* that is, who in your operations proceed more quickly than the wind blows. Indeed, the speed of the wind in its movement is signified by wings. For the Lord does something the very instant he wishes it to be done, since his power is simply infinite. And so he does things more quickly than the wind whisks things away. And in Job, in the second chapter, it is said that Lord walks *about the poles of heaven;*[15] and elsewhere it is said about him, *He that is mounted upon the heaven is your helper.*[16] But here it is stated that he *walks upon the wings of the winds.* But all of these things have a similar meaning, for the walking about of God refers to his operations, in the manner that Moses says to the Lord in Exodus: *For how shall we be able to know... that we have found grace in your sight, unless you walk with us?*[17] But it is asserted that the Lord walks over the heavens and the sea on account of the operations of his omnipotence which show forth resplendently in them. And these things also can be literally said of Christ, who made his ascent to the clouds and walked above the wings of the winds when, as we read in Acts, *While they looked on, he was raised up: and a cloud received him out of their sight.*[18]

Now in a mystical sense, the Lord ascended above the clouds, while by his grace he raised the heart of the preachers and ambassadors of the word of God. He also walks upon the wings of the winds, that is, he exceeds in his operations the virtues and contemplation of holy souls. For those virtues and contemplations which raise up the souls into heaven are called wings, the way that Isaiah says: *They that hope in the Lord... shall take wings as eagles.*[19] But the winds are souls, as the Lord bears witness to by Isaiah: *I the Lord give breath to the people* who are upon the earth.[20]

103{104}[4] *Who makes your angels spirits: and your ministers a burning fire.*

Qui facis angelos tuos spiritus, et ministros tuos ignem urentem.

103{104}[4] *Qui facis angelos tuos spiritus, who makes your angels spirits,* that is, who have accomplished this work, so that the holy angels are spiritual

---

13 Amos 9:6b.
14 Deut. 33:26b.
15 Job 22:14b.
16 Deut. 33:26a.
17 Ex. 33:16.
18 Acts 1:9.
19 Is. 40:31a.
20 Is. 42:5b.

and not bodily substances; or [alternatively], who makes that the spirits or spiritual substances become angels, that is, your messengers. For they who are by their creation made spirits are made angels, that is, messengers of God, by divine command and ordination. For "spirit" is the name of their nature, but the "angel" is the name of their office. *Et ministros tuos ignem urentem, and your ministers are a burning fire*: that is, you inflame those zealously serving you with such a love of the Godhead that they can be said to be burning fire or a blaze of fire. For also God (according to the Apostle) *is a consuming fire.*[21] And Daniel left us these words: *The Ancient of Days sat, . . . his throne like flames of fire, the wheels of it like a burning fire.*[22] And what else can we understand the throne and wheels of the eternal God to be other than angelic, deiform, and god-bearing minds? Or [we can understand it thus], *who makes . . . a burning fire*, that is, who makes the highest hierarchy [of created spirits] or the angels of the order of Seraphim who burn with the highest and most ardent divine love, *your ministers*, for by them you illumine others. They themselves are said to be sent and to come to us, though only one is sent by them. For this Isaiah says: *One of the seraphim flew to me.*[23] Or they are called ministers of God or holy angels that become a burning fire, since they frequently appear in the form of fire. Whence Matthew says of the angel: *His countenance was as lightning.*[24] And in Exodus it is written that the angel appeared to Moses in a burning bush.[25] Elijah also was transported in a fiery chariot through the ministry of angels.[26] In addition, God causes his angelic spirits to be among men, when he announces the word of salvation through religious or other devout persons; and his ministers are a burning fire when the hearts of those hearing are set on fire by the Holy Spirit through the exhortation, rebuking, or instruction of preachers or prelates.

103{104}[5] *Who has founded the earth upon its own stability: it shall not be moved for ever and ever.*[27]

Qui fundasti terram super stabilitatem suam, non inclinabitur in saeculum saeculi.

---

21 Heb. 12:29.

22 Dan. 7:9.

23 Is. 6:6a.

24 Matt. 28:3a.

25 Ex. 6:2.

26 2 Kings 2:11.

27 E. N. I have replaced the Douay-Rheims's "bases" with "stability" for the Latin *stablitatem*. I am unsure why the translators would have translated a singular word with a plural one.

103{104}[5] *Qui fundasti, who has founded,* that is, who has firmly founded, *terram super stabilitatem suam, the earth upon its own stability,* that is, upon its immobile foundation, namely upon its own center: because all parts of the earth naturally tend towards its center, according to the Philosopher;[28] *non inclinabitur in saeculum saeculi, it shall not be moved forever and ever,* that is, its location as a whole will never move, in the way that Ecclesiastes attests: *The earth stands for ever.*[29] Whence also Baruch says: You founded *the earth for evermore.*[30] In a spiritual sense, God founded the earth, that is the Church militant, *upon its own stability,* that is, upon Christ as upon an immobile foundation, in which all must strive towards and rest in.[31] *It shall not be moved, etc.,* that is, the Church which shall never, as a whole, depart from the faith.

103{104}[6] *The deep like a garment is its clothing: above the mountains shall the waters stand.*

Abyssus sicut vestimentum amictus eius; super montes stabunt aquae.

103{104}[6] *Abyssus sicut vestimentum amictus, the deep like a garment is its clothing:* that is, the Ocean, which, because of the immeasurability of its depth is called an abyss, circumscribes, surrounds, and contains the earth within it like a cloak, just as a garment surrounds the person who is dressed. For in the manner that the air circumscribes and covers the sea, so does the sea the earth, except that part of the earth, which, by divine disposition, remains uncovered so as to preserve the life of animals. *Super montes stabunt aquae, above the mountains shall the waters stand,* [that is, the] pluvial [waters], which are collected in the clouds. For the clouds are higher than the mountains, and water is preserved in the clouds, as is written in the book of Job about God: *He binds up the waters in his clouds, so that they break not out and fall down together.*[32] Or [alternatively], *above the mountains shall the waters stand,* that is, by the command of God they ascend toward the peaks of the mountains as long as it pleases him, as it did in the universal flood that we know occurred

---

28 *E. N.* Likely a reference to Aristotle's *De caelo* II, 13. 295b20–30.
29 Eccl. 1:4b.
30 Baruch 3:32a.
31 "The Redeemer of man, Jesus Christ, is the center of the universe and of history." "Jesus Christ is the stable principle and fixed center of the mission that God himself has entrusted to man." John Paul II, *Redemptor Hominis,* I, II.
32 Job 26:8.

but once,[33] and in particular floods which occur often. Or [in the further alternative], *above the mountains shall the water stand*, because the waters in the middle of the Ocean are higher than the mountains of the earth. In addressing this, Nicholas of Lyra refers to Rabbi Solomon as having this view on this verse, and he states that it is false for him to assert it.[34] But in any event Rabbi Solomon asserts this in truth, and the reason of the same Nicholas of Lyra does not pass muster when he says: The waters since they are heavy and fluid equally tend to the center, and they are not higher in the middle [of the ocean] than at the shores. First of all, this reasoning is undone in this way: because water is a homogenous body, that is, it has the same nature as a whole and in all of its parts. For this reason, as any part of water, for example, a droplet, tends towards being round, as is plain through simply perceiving drops, so all the water, to the degree it can, tends towards roundness or spherical shape. Finally, the earth is heavier than water: yet parts of the earth do not equally approach toward the center, but the earth in its middle is higher than elsewhere: and much more so than water. Moreover, all who stand by the shore know by their senses that the more a vessel upon the sea departs further, the more it seems to rise up higher: this all great philosophers bear witness to.[35]

---

33 Gen. 7:10–20. *And the waters prevailed beyond measure upon the earth: and all the high mountains under the whole heaven were covered. The water was fifteen cubits higher than the mountains which it covered.*

34 E. N. Nicholas of Lyra (*ca.* 1270-1349) was a Franciscan friar known for his commentary on the Scriptures known as the *Postillae perpetuae in universam Sanctam Scripturam.* Nicholas drew from a variety of sources in crafting his commentary, including Rabbi Solomon. Rabbi Solomon of Isaac (1040-1105), frequently referred to as Rashi, was a medieval Jewish Rabbi, born in Troyes in the north of France, famous for his commentary on the Hebrew Scriptures and the Talmud.

35 E. N. This cosmological excursus by Denis will seem very odd to modern readers. Ultimately, it relates to the relationship of Psalm 103:6 to the various theories of the creation of the earth specifically, what occurred on the third day, when "God . . . said: Let the waters that are under the heaven, be gathered together in one place: and let the dry land appear. And so it was done. And God called the dry land earth; and the gathering together of the water, he called seas." Gen. 1:9–10. Various theories were postulated about how this occurred. In his *Summa Theologiae*, St. Thomas Aquinas briefly refers to them. ST Ia, q. 69, art. 1, ad. 2. St. Thomas opts for St. Basil the Great's theory (found in the fourth homily of his *Hexaemeron*) that the waters were raised to a greater altitude and gathered together, as happened in the Red Sea, so that the sea is actually higher than the land. (*See also* St. Thomas's *De Potentia*, q. 4, art. 1, arg. 17). Nicholas of Lyra rejected the Basililan-Thomistic view. As a disciple of St. Thomas, Denis rejects Nicholas of Lyra's view, siding with both Rabbi Solomon and St. Thomas. *See* Yosi Yisraeli, "When Christian Science and Jewish Providence Collide: Conversion and Biblical Discoveries in the 1390s," 14 *Hispania Judaica* (2019), 130.

Spiritually, by abyss we may understand the inundation of tribulations. The abyss, therefore, that is, great tribulation, is the clothing of the earth, that is, of the Church, because everywhere the Church suffers trials, and it is surrounded by those who are its adversaries as if they were mantles, for *through many tribulations we must enter into the kingdom of God:*[36] this is what the judgment of St. Paul teaches in Acts. For this reason Judith also bore witness: *All that have pleased God, passed through many tribulations, remaining faithful.*[37] But also *above the mountains,* that is, perfect men, *shall the waters* of tribulations *stand,* because *all that will live godly in Christ Jesus shall suffer persecution.*[38] Standing also sometimes above these mountains are the waters of divine consolation, because, according to the Apostle, *as the sufferings of Christ abound in us, so also by Christ does our comfort abound.*[39] For this reason, elsewhere it is said of God: *When you are angry, you will remember mercy.*[40]

103{104}[7] *At your rebuke they shall flee: at the voice of your thunder they shall fear.*

Ab increpatione tua fugient, a voce tonitrui tui formidabunt.

103{104}[8] *The mountains ascend, and the plains descend into the place which you have founded for them.*

Ascendunt montes, et descendunt campi in locum quem fundasti eis.

103{104}[7] *Ab increpatione tua, at your rebuke,* that is, imposed by you by means of a rebuke, *fugient, they shall flee,* [that is,] the waters from the mountains which they covered [shall flee]; or from the place in the air in which there were clouds before; *a voice tonitrui tui, at the voice of your thunder,* that is by your terrible precept, *formidabunt, they shall fear,* that is, they will hold themselves out in the manner of someone in fear, obeying your command. For on this account Job stated: *By his power the seas are suddenly gathered together.*[41] And Ecclesiasticus: *The deep, and all the earth, and the things that are in them, shall be moved in his sight, . . . and when God shall look upon them, they shall be shaken with*

---

36 Acts 14:21b.
37 Judith 8:23.
38 2 Tim. 3:12.
39 2 Cor. 1:5.
40 Hab. 3:2b.
41 Job 26:12a.

trembling.[42] Now mystically speaking, the waters of tribulation, hurled by God against the ungodly, flee and withdraw from the Church, according to this: *When God grants peace, who is there that can condemn?*[43] **103{104} [8]** *Ascendunt montes, et descendunt campi in locum quem fundasti; the mountains ascend, and the plains descend into the place which you have founded for them*: that is, one part of the earth is mountainous and the other part is valleyed; and mountains and the valleys respectively ascend and descend to that level that is predetermined by your wisdom. Spiritually speaking, the mountains ascend when men progress in virtue; and the valleys descend when their inferiors humbly submit to their doctrine, *into the place which you have founded for them*, that is, in the congregation of the Church.

103{104}[9] *You have set a bound which they shall not pass over; neither shall they return to cover the earth.*

Terminum posuisti quem non transgredientur; neque convertentur operire terram.

103{104}[9] *Terminum posuisti, you have set a bound* to the waters of the Ocean, *quem non transgredientur, which they shall not pass over*, nor shall they overflow the banks; *neque convertentur, neither shall they return*, exceeding their channels, *operire terram, to cover the earth* which is to be the dwelling of animals. Whence Solomon said: *With a certain law and compass he enclosed the depths.*[44] Job also stated: *He has set bounds about the waters, until light and darkness come to an end.*[45] And the great power of God, of which one ought to stand in awe of, is reflected in this. For this reason, this is said by Jeremiah: *Hear, O foolish people ... will you not fear me ... who have set the sand a bound for the sea, and everlasting ordinance?*[46] This verse is commonly expounded in this way. But because the preceding verse is not about water, but mention is rather made of mountains, it seems that it might be possibly explained as relating to mountains; and so, it would have this sense: *You have set a bound* to the mountains in both their breadth and their other dimensions, *which they shall not pass over*, so that they do not extend upwards higher or extend outwards more broadly; *neither shall they return to cover the earth*, that is,

---

42 Ecclus. 16:18b–19.
43 Job 34:29a.
44 Prov. 8:27b.
45 Job 26:10.
46 Jer. 5:21–22a.

without your willing, ordering, or permitting (as if it is also often said), they will not fall and destroy by falling upon men and their dwelling places, as is asserted in the book of Job: *He who has removed mountains, and they whom he overthrew...knew it not.*[47] In a spiritual sense, God has *set a bound* to the waters of tribulation, and the mountains of pride, as he will not suffer his elect *to be tempted* or to face tribulations *above that* which they are able, but he makes it (as the Apostle [Paul] says), that *with the temptation* a provision [will be made] so that they might *be able to bear it.*[48] And never *shall* the waters and mountains *return to cover the earth*, that is, to oppress the hearts of good men, extinguishing in them the love of God and neighbor. For this reason, Scripture says: *Many waters cannot quench charity, neither can the floods drown it.*[49]

103{104}[10]   *You send forth springs in the vales: between the midst of the hills the waters shall pass.*

Qui emittis fontes in convallibus; inter medium montium pertransibunt aquae.

103{104}[11]   *All the beasts of the field shall drink: the wild asses shall expect in their thirst.*

Potabunt omnes bestiae agri; expectabunt onagri in siti sua.

103{104}[10] *Qui emittis fontes in convallibus, you send forth springs in the vales*, that is, you cause the streams of water coming forth from their founts in the mountains to descend to the lower places; *inter medium montium, between the midst of the hills*, that is, between the mountains *pertransibunt aquae, the waters shall pass*, that is, they shall flow past, and they shall not stay there, but they shall rest in low places. For water seeks to find a lower place. In a spiritual sense, God emits fountains from the heaven, that is, gifts of grace, *in the vales*, that is, upon humble souls. *Between the midst of the hills the waters shall pass*, that is, grace will not remain among the proud in the manner that James states: *God resists the proud and gives grace to the humble.*[50] And Isaiah: *Every valley shall be exalted, and every mountain and hill shall be made low.*[51] 103{104}[11] *Potabunt omnes bestiae agri, all the beasts of the field shall drink of*

---

47 Job 9:5.
48 1 Cor. 10:13.
49 Songs 8:7a.
50 James 4:6b.
51 Is. 40:4a.

the water coming into the lower places from their sources; *exspectabunt onagri, the wild asses shall expect*, that is, the feral donkeys, growing wild and naturally spirited, *in siti sua, in their thirst* to drink and to be refreshed with this water. Others explain it in this way: *the wild asses shall expect in their thirst*, that is, they will wait for heavenly rain. For the wild asses do not drink from the water flowing from the founts (as they assert here), but they anticipate rain from heaven for a long time so that they might then drink. Mystically understood, *all the beasts of the field* drink from the rivers of water of Christ, that is, all the Gentiles and those converted to the faith; *the wild asses shall* also *expect in their thirst*, that is, the cruel Jews in their thirst, that is, in their desire, for they still await the Christ to come.

103{104}[12] *Over them the birds of the air shall dwell: from the midst of the rocks they shall give forth their voices.*

Super ea volucres caeli habitabunt; de medio petrarum dabunt voces.

103{104}[12] *Super ea, over them*, namely, in the summits of the mountains, and around the waves of the waters, *volucres caeli, the birds of the air*, that is, the birds flying in the air of the sky, *habitabunt, shall dwell*, for in such places they build their nests; *de medio petrarum, from the midst of the rocks*, that is, from rocky places, in which birds nest, *dabunt vocem, shall give forth their voices*, together praising the Lord in their small measure. In a spiritual sense *over* those things already mentioned, namely over the mountains and the waters, the *birds of the air*, that is, holy and contemplative men, *shall dwell*, living according to the commandments of Christ and leading an angelic life upon earth. *From the midst of the rocks, they shall give forth their voices*, that is, they will give things and offer you praise from the most firm places of the Church.

103{104}[13] *You water the hills from your upper rooms: the earth shall be filled with the fruit of your works.*

Rigans montes de superioribus suis; de fructu operum tuorum satiabitur terra.

103{104}[14] *Bringing forth grass for cattle, and herb for the service of men. That you may bring bread out of the earth.*

Producens foenum iumentis, et herbam servituti hominum: ut educas panem de terra.

103{104}[15] *And that wine may cheer the heart of man. That he may make the face cheerful with oil: and that bread may strengthen man's heart.*

Et vinum laetificet cor hominis; ut exhilaret faciem in oleo, et panis cor hominis confirmet.

103{104}[13] *Rigans montes de superioribus suis, you water the hills from your upper rooms*: that is, you, O God, make it that the mountains are wet by the rain-filled clouds which are higher than the mountains, or from the fountains originating at the summits of the mountains, which flowing down moisten as they run down areas of the mountain; *de fructu operum tuorum, with the fruit of your works*, that is, those things produced from the earth, *satiabitur terra, the earth shall be filled*, that is, the inhabitants of the earth [shall be filled]. Spiritually interpreted, God waters the mountains, that is, men that are lofty with grace, *from your upper rooms*, that is, by the heavenly ministry of the angels, and from the *fruit of* God's *works*, that is, by the preaching of such mountain, that is the Church, *the earth shall be filled*. You also, O Lord, are 103{104}[14] *producens foenum iumentis, bringing forth grass for cattle* for their fodder, *et herbam, and herb*, that is, various species and medicinal herbs *servituti hominum, for the service of men*, that is, for the advantage and service of men. For as much as these things are done by secondary causes, yet they are principally also done by the first cause, by God sublime and blessed: whose providence encompasses not only men, but also beasts of burden,[52] as is most clearly made known from this.

You have also brought forth *grass for cattle* for the support of life, *ut educas panem, that you may bring forth bread*, that is, grain, from which bread is made, *de terra, out of the earth*, 103{104}[15] *et vinum laetificet cor hominis, and that wine may cheer the heart of man*. For God created wine so that moderately consumed it disposes the imbiber to good cheer. For this reason it is written in Ecclesiasticus: *Wine was created from the beginning to make men joyful, and not to make them drunk.*[53] But this means to be drunk with great sobriety, in the manner that is written: *How sufficient is a little wine for a man well taught!*[54] For if it is consumed immoderately, it does go in sweetly indeed, but it afflicts the interior as if it were a

---

52 Cf. Judith 9:4–5: *For you have done the things of old and have devised one thing after another: and what you have designed has been done. For all your ways are prepared, and in your providence you have placed your judgments.*

53 Ecclus. 31:35.

54 Ecclus. 31:22a.

serpent.[55] But because men with difficulty and rarity observe moderation in the drinking of wine, therefore Ecclesiasticus warns: *Rebuke not your neighbor in a banquet of wine.*[56] In a spiritual sense, God draws out from the earth the bread of life and of understanding, that is, from the human heart informed by grace, when he causes men to preach to others the good word of salvation and to produce holy works. Also, spiritual wine, namely, the consolation of the strength of the Holy Spirit, gives joy to the soul. *Ut exhilaret, that* man *may make ... cheerful, faciem suam, his face, in oleo, with oil,* that is, from the seasonings of food: for it is not sufficient for him to eat bread without other seasonings; *et panis, and that bread* that is brought forth from the earth *cor hominis confirmet, may strengthen man's heart,* maintaining the natural body. Spiritually, the face (that is the soul) is made cheerful *with oil,* that is, with the unction or the grace of the Holy Spirit, according to that which is written in Revelation: *Anoint your eyes with eyesalve.*[57] But this refers also to that heavenly bread, namely Christ, who is the *power and wisdom* of the Father,[58] who said of himself, *I am the bread of life,* and which most fully strengthens the heart of man, for it converts the one eating into him whom he eats:[59] and so he says, *He that eats my flesh, and drinks my blood, abides in me, and I in him.*[60]

103{104}[16]   *The trees of the field shall be filled, and the cedars of Lebanon which he has planted.*

Saturabuntur ligna campi, et cedri Libani quas plantavit.

103{104}[17]   *There the sparrows shall make their nests. The highest of them is the house of the heron.*

Illic passeres nidificabunt, herodii domus dux est eorum.

103{104}[16] *Saturabuntur ligna campi, et cedri Labani quas plantavit; the trees of the field shall be filled, and the cedars of Lebanon which he has*

---

55 Cf. Prov. 23:31–32: *Look not upon the wine when it is yellow, when the color thereof shines in the glass: it goes in pleasantly, but in the end, it will bite like a snake, and will spread abroad poison like a basilisk.*

56 Ecclus. 31:41a.

57 Rev. 3:18b.

58 1 Cor. 1:24.

59 E. N. This is redolent of St. Augustine's famous sentence in his *Confessions* VII, x, 16 where he relates Christ's words to him: *Cibus sum grandium: cresce et manducabis me. Nec tu me in te mutabis sicut cibum carnis tuae, sed tu mutaberis in me.* "I am the food of the noble. You will not change me into you like the food of your flesh, but you shall be changed into me."

60 John 6:57.

planted [that is, which] God principally and man instrumentally [planted, shall be filled]: that is, shall be fully nourished from the moistness of the earth. For moisture is the nourishment of trees. And Christ in the Gospel declared trees to wither away because they had no moisture.[61] Finally, according to the Philosopher, the roots of trees are similar to the mouths in animals: for they draw in nutrients by the roots.[62] 103{104} [17] *Illic, there,* namely in the cedars, *passers nidificabunt, the sparrows shall make their nests.* For one finds that there are certain kinds of sparrows that customarily nest in cedars; but other kinds of sparrows build nests in the roofs of houses. But mystically, understanding the bread of life and the wine and oil in a spiritual sense, *the trees of the field,* souls, that is, members of the Church or low and humble persons, *shall be filled,* and the *cedars of Lebanon,* that is, perfect men, which God by his grace plants in his Church. *There,* namely, in the Church, *sparrows,* that is, penitents seeking out safe spots like sparrows, *shall make their nests,* that is, shall store the treasure of good works for themselves. Whence it is stated in a Psalm above: *I am become as a sparrow all alone on the housetop.*[63] There also, namely, in the cedars, *herodii domus dux est eorum, the highest of them is the house of the heron,* that is, the nest of the bird that is called the heron, which is a rapacious bird, living through plunder, is larger than other birds, and which also outdoes and eats eagles; and is called the *highest* of the sparrows or of birds, in the sense that a lion is called the king of animals.[64]

103{104}[18] *The high hills are a refuge for the harts, the rock for the irchins.*

Montes excelsi cervis, petra refugium herinaciis.

---

61 Cf. Luke 8:6: *Some seed ... as soon as it was sprung up, it withered away because it had no moisture.*

62 E. N. The reference is to one of the seven short treatises of Aristotle in *Parva Naturali (Little Physical Treatises),* specifically, *De Iuventute et Senectute, De Vita et Morte, De Respiratione (On Youth and Old Age, Life and Death, and Respiration)* 468a7 ("For roots in plants and mouths in animals are analogous organs." *See also* Aristotle's *De Anima* 412b7 ("the roots are analogous to mouths, both being channels of nutrition"). *Aristotle's Psychology: A Treatise on the Principle of Life* (London: Swan Sonnenschein & Co. 1902) (trans., William A. Hammond).

63 Ps. 101:8.

64 E. N. As St. Albert the Great says, "now when the heron is called the king of birds, it is not called king in the sense of truly imitating kingliness, but rather by reason of the violence of its tyranny: for it dominates over all [birds] in that it restrains all and eats all." *De animalibus,* Opera (Lyons: 1651), XXIII, 612.

103{104}[19] *He has made the moon for seasons: the sun knows his going down.*
Fecit lunam in tempora; sol cognovit occasum suum.

103{104}[18] *Montes excelsi,* the high hills or lofty [hills] are a refuge *cervis, for the harts,* who flee towards such places; *petra, the rock* of caverns or subterranean places is *refugium herinaciis, the refuge for the irchins,* that is, the hedgehogs. For the hedgehog is a small and spiney animal which lives in caverns, and feeds on fruit. And whenever it senses some adversity, it contracts itself into a sort of ball, and gathers itself within its arms, so that if you want to touch him, you would first encounter your own blood before you do his small body. By harts fleeing toward the mountains is designated virtuous and contemplative men who when they encounter tribulation hasten toward the contemplation of divine things. But by hedgehog who says, "Do not touch me," is signified sinners, languishing with ailing souls: who reply with murmuring when they are reproved, who express contempt when something is denied them, and for this reason they become more degenerate when they ought to amend themselves.

Consequently, God is praised from the order of times, from change of the bearing of the heavens, from the variation of natural things. God 103{104}[19] *fecit lunam,* has made the moon, which is the lowest of the planets, *in tempora, for seasons,* that by its various movements are distinguished lunar years and months.[65] Whence it is written: *The moon ... is a declaration of times, and a sign of the world; the month is called after her name, increasing wonderfully in her perfection; being an instrument of the armies on high, shining gloriously in the armament of heaven.*[66] *Sol cognovit occasum suum, the sun knows his going down,* that is, it moves itself westward in such an orderly and stable manner as if it were of an intellectual nature, something which, according to Augustine one ought to neither affirm nor to negate, until one knows with certainty.[67] In a mystical sense, God made the moon, that is, the militant Church, a participant in his light through Christ the sun of justice in time, since it

---

65 E. N. A lunar year, based entirely on the motion of the moon, is composed of twelve synodic or lunar months, that is approximately 354 solar days.

66 Ecclus. 43:6, 8–9.

67 E. N. This appears to be a reference to St. Augustine's *Enchiridion on Faith, Hope, and Charity,* 15, 58–59, where, among other questions, Augustine broaches the issue of whether the sun and moon and stars may share some intellectual nexus with the angelic thrones, dominions, principalities, or powers, but then suggests the matter is not worth delving into. *Quid enim opus est ut haec atque huiusmodi vel affirmentur vel negentur vel definiantur cum discrimine, quando sine crimine nesciuntur?* "For what necessity is there that these and such things be either affirmed or be denied, or defined with contention, when they may be blamelessly not known?" PL 40, 260.

now fights, holds on to, and triumphs in time so that it may be crowned and reign eternally. The sun, that is Christ our God enlightening all things,[68] *knows his going down*, that is, he foreknew his own Passion.

103{104}[20]   *You have appointed darkness, and it is night: in it shall all the beasts of the woods go about.*

Posuisti tenebras, et facta est nox; in ipsa pertransibunt omnes bestiae silvae.

103{104}[21]   *The young lions roaring after their prey, and seeking their meat from God.*

Catuli leonum rugientes ut rapiant, et quaerant a Deo escam sibi.

103{104}[20] *Posuisti tenebras, you have appointed darkness* in the hemisphere from which the sun recedes, *et facta est nox, and it is night*, the sun having departed; *in ipsa, in it*, during the night, *pertransibunt omnes bestiae silvae, shall all the beasts of the woods go about* seeking for food. God is said to have appointed darkness, not that the darkness is something positive, but rather that it is a privation, namely, the lack of light; God is therefore said to appoint darkness because he makes the light to recede or he causes it to cease to flow forth. In the same way he is said to blind or to harden some persons. Spiritually speaking, God appointed permissively the darkness of infidelity and fault, the death of Christ, and it became night, that is, deficient of the true faith; in it shall all the beasts of the woods, that is, the devil, go about so as to devour miserable souls. For where faith is absent, there is no power to be good. **103{104}[21]** *Catuli leonum, the young lions* during the nighttime come out of their dens, *rugientes, ut rapiant; roaring after their prey, et, and*, meaning "that is,"[69] *quaerant a Deo escam sibi, seeking their meat from God*: not that they recognize God, but because they move from natural instinct impressed upon them by God, and from God, whose concern is to see all things are fed, for as Christ says of the birds of the air, *Your heavenly Father feeds them.*[70] Spiritually understood, when the sun of eternal light, that is, Christ, goes out in our souls, the young lions, that is, the adherents and supporters of the devil, obstruct us, roaring that they may spiritually devour someone.

---

68 John 1:9.
69 E. N. Denis is saying "et" (and) should not be understood as a conjunction, but attributively, as meaning "that is," so that "roaring after their prey" means they were "seeking their meat from God," and not something different.
70 Matt. 6:26b.

103{104}[22] *The sun rises, and they are gathered together: and they shall lie down in their dens.*

Ortus est sol, et congregati sunt, et in cubilibus suis collocabuntur.

103{104}[23] *Man shall go forth to his work, and to his labor until the evening.*

Exibit homo ad opus suum, et ad operationem suam usque ad vesperum.

103{104}[22] *Ortus est sol, et congregati sunt; the sun rises, and they are gathered together,* that is, these beasts are gathered together by the sun, *et in cubilibus suis, and . . . in their dens,* that is, in their places of refuge, *collocabuntur, they shall lie down:* for they enter into their caves at the first gleams of the light of day. 103{104}[23] *Exibit homo, man shall go forth,* during the day, [man] who is a disciplined and rational animal, *ad opus suum, to his work* carrying on inside his house and his walls, *et ad operationem suam, and to his labor* outside [the home] *usque ad vesperam, until the evening:* for then he ceases so that he may eat and rest and avoid the danger of the night. Also, this is said and done according to the common way of doing things and the customary course of things, since sometimes, because of some special reason, it happens otherwise. In a spiritual sense, when the sun of understanding is rising, Christ is helping us, and the demons gather together and flee. And so man shall go forth aided by Christ to his interior work and will undertake and continue his external labor until the evening, that is, perseveringly, so long as the light of grace shines upon him, even unto death, paying heed to that which the Savior said in Revelation: *Be faithful until death: and I will give you the crown of life.*[71]

103{104}[24] *How great are your works, O Lord! You have made all things in wisdom: the earth is filled with your riches.*

Quam magnificata sunt opera tua, Domine! Omnia in sapientia fecisti; impleta est terra possessione tua.

Because from what has been said the ineffable wisdom of the most high King and prime Artisan is apparent, therefore is admiringly appended the following: 103{104}[24] *Quam magnificata sunt opera tua, Domine! How great are your works, O Lord!* That is, with great magnificence are they performed, they are created, ordered, and preserved very powerfully, wisely, and kindly. For this reason it is stated in Revelation: *Great and wonderful are your works, O Lord God Almighty!*[72] For these are entirely

71 Rev. 2:10b.
72 Rev. 15:3a.

incomprehensible and impenetrable to us, according to that said in Ecclesiasticus: *We shall say much, and yet shall want words.*[73] And again: *There are many things hidden from us that are greater than these: for we have seen but a few of his works.*[74] And Ecclesiastes repeats: *All things are hard: man cannot explain them by word.*[75] For look and pay heed how the unfathomable wisdom of God shines forth in the lowest and most small things: in the way that an ant collects and stores for himself food as winter approaches; and also how the most tiny flea has eyes and a complete set of body parts as we also do. For this reason, Ecclesiasticus sets this forth: *O how desirable are all his works, [and what we can know is but as a spark!] And who shall be filled with beholding his glory?*[76]

Omnia in sapientia fecisti, you have made all things in wisdom, that is, in accordance with the pronouncement of your eternal mind, in accordance with the typical reasons, in accordance with the ineffable glory of the divine artisanship: for you *have ordered all things in measure, and number, and weight,* as the book of Wisdom states. *Impleta est terra posessione tua, the earth is filled with your riches,* that is, men and livestock and all other creatures, which by right of creation are yours.[77] But though these things apply to all the works of creation, yet they are more truly applicable to the works of the re-creation of the human race, and the reparation of the ruin of the heavenly Jerusalem.[78] Now these things were magnificently accomplished by the Incarnation, Passion, Resurrection, Ascension of the Son of God and by the sending of the Holy Spirit; and God the Father made all these things by his begotten Wisdom, that is, by Christ, both God and man. The entire world, that is the human race in the Church, is full with the riches of God, that is, with the sacraments of Christ, the gifts of the Holy Spirit, Catholic men, and diverse bodily and spiritual goods.

---

73 Ecclus. 43:29a.

74 Ecclus. 43:36.

75 Eccl. 1:8a.

76 Ecclus. 23, 26b. *E. N.* I have added the part in brackets. It seemed too fitting to neglect.

77 *E. N.* God has the right of jurisdiction over his creatures by means of the right of creation (*iure creationis*). All men universally are duty-bound by this *ius creationis* to give reasonable worship — the *rationabile obsequium* or λογικὴ λατρεία of Rom. 12:2 — to the one true God, and to do so *as he has revealed*: "[A]ssuredly, of all the duties which man has to fulfill, that, without doubt, is the chiefest and holiest which commands him to worship God with devotion and piety.... And if it be asked which of the many conflicting religions it is necessary to adopt, reason and the natural law unhesitatingly tell us to practice that one which God enjoins." Pope Leo XII, *Libertas*, 20.

78 *E. N.* God also has rights over mankind *iure redemptionis*, by reason of his reparation, repair, or redemption of mankind, but in particular over those who are baptized, where such redemption is beyond potentiality and has ventured into actuality.

ARTICLE VI

CONTINUATION OF THE EXPLANATION OF THIS ONE HUNDRED AND THIRD PSALM.

103{104}[25] *So is this great sea, which stretches wide its arms: there are creeping things without number: creatures little and great.*

Hoc mare magnum et spatiosum manibus; illic reptilia quorum non est numerus, animalia pusilla cum magnis.

103{104}[26] *There the ships shall go. This sea dragon which you have formed to play therein.*

Illic naves pertransibunt; draco iste quem formasti ad illudendum ei.

AND THE HOLY PROPHET CONSEQUENTLY introduces another reason for praise of God, that being from the arrangement and the decorousness of the waters of the oceans. 103{104} [25] *Hoc mare, this sea,* this ocean circumventing the earth, is *magnum, great* in quantity, because it greatly exceeds in weight the earth, *et spatiosum manibus, and it stretches wide its arms,* that is, in breadth and in measure; *illic, there are,* that is, in it there are, *reptilia, creeping things,* that is, wriggling fish swimming, *quorum non est numerus, are without number,* in that their number is not known to us, although something cannot be strictly infinite with respect to creatures. *Animalia pusilla cum magnis, creatures little and great,* that is, small and great fish are found in the sea. In a spiritual sense, *this great sea which stretches wide its arms* is the wretched present age, full of tribulations and bitter trials and vices. *There are the creeping things without number,* that is, the innumerable sinners adhering with all their heart to earthly things, wrapped up in vices, and creeping like cattle in vain and sensible things: of these, some are great in this world, but others are small and are their subordinates. 103{104}[26] *Illic, there,* that is, in the sea, *naves pertransibunt, the ships shall go* with sailors carrying various cargoes from one place and kingdom to another place and kingdom. Viewed spiritually, *ship* refers to the Church, which bears its children to the fatherland of the heavenly kingdom. But *ships* are the particular churches or the worthy prelates who carry those committed to them to Christ. These ships, with Christ leading and navigating, securely pass through this fluctuating world, and at last come to the port of eternal salvation.

Thereafter it especially names one great creature existing in the sea. *Draco iste, this sea dragon*, that is, a sea monster (*cetus*), which is a great fish, whose size (according to Pliny) is four acres of land.[79] Whence Moses said: *And God created the great whales.*[80] *Quem formasti, which you have formed*, that is, created first by yourself, and then produced them after that by secondary causes, *ad illudendum ei, to play therein*, that is, so that the sea dragon might be mocked. And here, the words "so that" are said consecutively, not causally. For it was not finally made so that it might be ridiculed; indeed, it was formed with the purpose of showing the power of God and to complete the order of the universe. But this mockery follows from its formation. For although it is of great bodily size and strength, yet in many ways it is easy (as it is said) to make a mockery of, namely, by the music to which it cheerfully listens to, and because of which it approaches the shore; and also that it will follow a roasted chicken placed upon a pole or stake shown to it until it finds itself out of the water and captured. Finally, since it has a large body, it needs much food, and it devours many fish: for this reason fish that see it by natural instinct flee to the shores, whereupon this sea monster (*cetus*) by following them finds himself beached on land; and because it does not have the ability to swim in shallow water, and, because it is unable to move, it is therefore killed by fishermen: and so, frustrated in his hope [of catching the fish], it is mocked.

Spiritually, this sea dragon (*draco*) is the apostate angel, *that old serpent, . . . the devil and Satan:*[81] called Lucifer by Isaiah,[82] Cherub by Ezechiel,[83] and Leviathan by Job.[84] He was by nature made good in heaven, but out of his own free will was made evil and fell from heaven and was thereafter thrust down into this world so that he might be mocked, for he is mocked by Christ,[85] by the holy angels, and by the strong army of Christ, namely, good men.[86] For when he attempted to

---

79 E. N. The reference is to Pliny's *Historia naturalis*, IX.2, which references "whales (*ballaenae*) covering three acres each." However, the Vulgate has *draco* or "dragon," and not *ballaena* or "whale."

80 E. N. Gen. 1:21. E. N. The Latin has *cete grandia*, "great sea-animal."

81 Rev. 12:9.

82 Is. 14:12.

83 Ez. 28:14: *You a cherub stretched out, and protecting, and I set you in the holy mountain of God, you have walked in the midst of the stones of fire.* E. N. Tertullian tied the Ezechielean cherub to Satan. "This manifestly pertains to the transgression of the angel (*suggillationem angeli*)." *Adv. Marcionem*, II, 10, PL 2, 297.

84 Job 3:8.

85 Matt. 4:1–11; Luke 4:1–13.

86 E. N. "[S]o the devil . . . if he find a man with diligence still seeking to withstand and prevent his temptations he waxeth weary, and at last he utterly forsaketh him,

devour Christ, he was overcome and captured, and he lost those whom he had held in hell.[87] But he was also despoiled of the reign of this world by all those converted to Christ. He is also mocked when the holy angels restrain him from the intent or undertaking evil, as he is by men when they resist his temptation.

103{104}[27]   *All expect of you that you give them food in season.*

Omnia a te expectant ut des illis escam in tempore.

103{104}[28]   *What you give to them they shall gather up: when you open your hand, they shall all be filled with good.*

Dante te illis, colligent; aperiente te manum tuam, omnia implebuntur bonitate.

103{104}[29]   *But if you turn away your face, they shall be troubled: you shall take away their breath, and they shall fail, and shall return to their dust.*

Avertente autem te faciem, turbabuntur; auferes spiritum eorum, et deficient, et in pulverem suum revertentur.

103{104}[27] *Omnia,* all animals and reptiles identified before *a te exspectant ut des illis escam in tempore; expect of you that you give them food in season,* that is, they altogether expect to obtain food from you, because they have nowhere else to turn except to you who are the causal principle of all good. **103{104}[28]** *Dante te illis, what you give to them,* that which they expect from you, *colligent, they shall gather up* the necessary things for their individual preservation and the preservation of their kind; *aperiente te manum tuam, when you open your hand,* that is, when you dispense to them necessities through your power, *omnia implebuntur bonitate, they shall all be filled with good,* that is, with the good that befits them. (Spiritually speaking, this sea dragon, that is, the devil, stands ready to be furnished food by God, that is, the sinning souls which he collects, the Lord having damned them.) **103{104}[29]** *Avertente autem te, but if you turn away* from them, *faciem tuam, your face,* that is, the beneficent and abundant presence of your providence, *turbabuntur, they shall be troubled,* that is, they will meet with the great disorder of

---

being a spirit of so high a pride, that he cannot endure to be mocked." Cresacre More, *The Life of Sir Thomas More* (London: William Pickering, 1828), 106.

87 E. N. This would be limited to those in the "hell of the fathers," and not the hell of the damned.

hunger, thirst, and clamor; *auferes spiritum eorum, you shall take away their breath*, that is, you will take the life from their non-rational souls by the lack of nourishment, *et deficient, and they shall fail*, these animals [shall fail] in their natural life, *et in pulverem suum revertentur, and they shall return to their dust*, that is, they shall dissolve into the matter which they were before, which for the most part may be considered to be earth. For everything will revert back to that of which it is composed.

In a spiritual sense, by the Lord giving us his divine gifts (*charismata*), we together collect his spiritual gifts (*dona*); whenever he opens his hands towards us he fills the entirety of the most interior parts of our souls with the participation of the divine goods, namely, charity, wisdom, and grace. But when he turns away his face, that is, when he suspends the dispensing or justly withdraws his grace, we are troubled, that is, we become interiorly disordered, we become anxious, we become sad, or we fall into many vices, and we experience our own weakness. And when he takes away our spirit, that is, the Holy Spirit given us by divine influence, removing from us his consolation and gifts, we fail and we return to the dust, that is, we miserably cling to, surround ourselves with, and embrace earthly things.

103{104}[30] *You shall send forth your spirit, and they shall be created: and you shall renew the face of the earth.*

Emittes spiritum tuum, et creabuntur; et renovabis faciem terrae.

103{104}[30] *Emittes spiritum tuum, you shall send forth your spirit*, that is, you will exercise your power, *et creabuntur, and they shall be created*, that is, they that were destroyed by death will be returned: for by the power of God they will be made to revert back to the same kind, but not the same number, as the Platonists believed;[88] yet sometimes miraculously they revert to the same number;[89] *et renovabis faciem, and you shall renew,*

---

88 *E. N.* This refers to the Platonic notion that only the species (the form, the *eidos*) would survive, and not the individual instantiations of it.

89 *E. N.* Denis is referring to the natural preservation *of the species*, which preserves the *species*, but not the *individual* of the species. "When substances corrupt, the survival of the species, but not the restoration of the individual, is effected by the action of nature." Thus though the same kind (species) is maintained, not the same individual (there is no numerical identity). *See* St. Thomas Aquinas, *Compendium*, 154. Since nature cannot restore the individual (only the species), "the restoration of all who rise will be effected solely by divine power." By God's miraculous powers, the individual *can* be restored. St. Thomas Aquinas, *Compendium of Theology* (St. Louis, MO: B. Herder Book Co. 1958) (trans., Cyril Vollert, S. J.), 163.

that is, the surface, *terrae, of the earth*, producing in it new beasts of burden, birds, and reptiles. The words *they shall be created* are commonly taken as production or generation. But properly speaking, these brute beasts were not individually created, since, according to the philosophers and theologians, their form is brought forth from the potency of matter.[90]

All this can also be explained as referring to the consummation of the age, the resurrection of men, and the renewal of the world, so that it reads in this sense: *But if you turn away your face*, that is, when you turn it away, namely, at the time of judgment, *they shall be troubled*, [that is,] the non-rational animals [shall be troubled]; *you shall take away* then *their breath* by the fire of conflagration, or before, *and they shall fail* in all things, because they will never be returned to their first state, nor indeed according to kind. *You shall send forth your spirit, and they shall be created*: not indeed these [brute] animals, but men *shall be created*, that is, they will arise anew; *and you shall renew the face of the earth*, that is, you will change the earth to be of a better and more noble quality. For this reason it is written: *We look for new heavens and a new earth according to his promises.*[91]

Spiritually, O Lord, you shall *send forth your spirit*, that is, we hope that you will pour out your gifts of the Holy Spirit upon us; and *they shall be created*, that is, clean hearts shall arise in us; and *you shall renew the face of the earth*, that is, our body, making it to obey the spirit and to do things honestly and soberly.

It is apparent from all this that in sacred Scripture the words "spirit of God" do not always refer to the Holy Spirit, who is the third Person of the holy Trinity; but sometimes the spirit of God is understood as meaning his will, rule, or power.

103{104}[31] *May the glory of the Lord endure forever: the Lord shall rejoice in his works.*

Sit gloria Domini in saeculum; laetabitur Dominus in operibus suis.

Now, because all these things previously stated have been brought to mind in order that we might be roused unto the contemplation of the divine works so as to praise, honor, and love the Creator of all things, so

---

90 E. N. That is, the brute animals are "created" by secondary causes and not directly created by God *ex nihilo*; therefore, the words *they shall be created* are not to be taken in their strict sense.

91 2 Pet. 3:13.

now the Prophet bursts forth in the praise of God with great affection and beauty: **103{104}[31]** *Sit gloria Domini, may the glory of the Lord,* that is, the excellence, renown, honor, and praise of the Creator, *in saeculum, endure forever,* that is, perpetually, so that always and by all he may be exceedingly exalted, praised, and honored. *Laetabitur Dominus in operibus suis, the Lord shall rejoice in his works* both his natural and supernatural works because all things are very well made. Yet this is not to be understood as there being a cause for praising or a reason for exulting outside of God himself, especially since the joy of the divine mind is eternal, uncaused, and not dependent [on anything outside of God]. But the Lord is said to rejoice in his works in that he rejoices in his own power by which he creates all things so gloriously in the manner that he wills.

103{104}[32] *He looks upon the earth, and makes it tremble: he touches the mountains, and they smoke.*

> *Qui respicit terram, et facit eam tremere; qui tangit montes, et fumigant.*

103{104}[32] *Qui respicit terram, he looks upon the earth* with the eyes of his dominion, *et facit eam tremere, and makes it tremble:* as we see when the earth moves; *qui tangit montes, he touches the mountains* by lightning, *et fumigant, and they smoke,* that is, they emit smoke: for a sulfurous fire smokes rather than burns brightly. Whence Job states: [It is God] *who shakes the earth out of her place, and the pillars thereof tremble.*[92] And Ecclesiasticus: *The mountains also, and the hills, and the foundations of the earth: when God shall look upon them, they shall be shaken with trembling.*[93] This does not contradict what was stated earlier—that the earth does not move for ever and ever. For the earth trembles and moves with regard to some parts; but with regard to the whole, it always remains in the same place. Similarly, that which is said above—who has founded the earth upon its own stability—does not contradict that which is said elsewhere, *He hangs the earth upon nothing.*[94] It states that it hangs upon nothing because that which is underneath does not any more support it than if nothing existed. For the natural explanation of why the earth does not move but remains immobile in

---

92 Job 9:6.
93 Ecclus. 16:19.
94 Job 26:7b.

the center of the universe is because all its parts naturally tend towards its center, according to the Philosopher.[95]

Mystically understood, God *looks* with the eye of his kindness *upon the earth*, that is, the human heart, *and makes it tremble*, from the consideration of the strict justice of God and the punishments of hell, as Job states: *I have always feared God as waves swelling over me, and his weight I was not able to bear.*[96] *He touches* moreover *the mountains*, that is, he graciously illuminates great and perfect men, *and they smoke*, that is, they pour out tears with the desire of living with Christ. Or [alternatively], *he touches the mountains*, that is, the proud, *and they smoke*, that is, they pour out tears for the remission of sins. Literally, God looked upon the earth upon which was the early Church, and he caused it to tremble locally. He touched the mountains, that is, the Apostles and others that they had gathered together; and they smoked, that is, from the plenitude of the Holy Spirit they poured forth the smoke of fiery words, when that which is related in the book of Acts occurred: *They were all filled with the Holy Ghost, and they spoke the word of God with confidence.*[97] Similarly, in Acts is related the event of Paul and Silas, who, when they had been captured and imprisoned, a heavenly light appeared in the jail cell that night, and the foundations of the prison were shaken, and the door to the jail cell opened. And Paul and Silas praised the Lord.

103{104}[33] *I will sing to the Lord as long as I live: I will sing praise to my God while I have my being.*

Cantabo Domino in vita mea; psallam Deo meo quamdiu sum.

103{104}[34] *Let my speech be acceptable to him: but I will take delight in the Lord.*

Iucundum sit ei eloquium meum; ego vero delectabor in Domino.

103{104}[33] *Cantabo Domino, I will sing to the Lord*, that is, I will offer a sacrifice of praise to God, *in vita mea, as long as I live*: for *the dead do not praise the Lord.*[98] For this reason it is written: *Praise perishes from the dead as nothing; give thanks while you live . . . and are in health.*[99]

---

95 E. N. See Aristotle, *On the Heavens (De Caelo)*, in particular II, 14 (296b6–24).
96 Job 31:23.
97 Acts 4:31b.
98 Ps. 113:17 (Hebr.). E. N. Cf. Ps. 113:25.
99 Ecclus. 17:26b–27a.

Psallam Deo meo, I will sing praise to my God, indeed, to the God of all men, but in a special sense to my God because of his singular mercy upon me, *quamdiu sum, while I have my being*, that is, unceasingly: for *he that shall persevere unto the end, he shall be saved*.[100] I do not chant and sing praise to my Creator only in the present life, but also in the future life. For to sing praise to him in the life of nature, in the life of grace, in the life of glory, with a prompt and ardent spirit, is the way that Ecclesiasticus admonishes: *Now therefore with the whole heart and mouth praise him, and bless the name of the Lord.*[101] 103{104}[34] *Iucundum sit ei eloquium meum, let my speech be acceptable to him*, that is, may it be pleasing to God, and may it proceed from true charity and holy devotion. For such speech is pleasing to God, regarding which Solomon states: *My delights were to be with the children of men*:[102] not, indeed, with all the children of men, because *the the bloody and deceitful man the Lord will abhor;*[103] but [God delights to be] with humble and simple men, as it says in Proverbs, *His communication is with the simple.*[104] The praise of him who chants and sings praises with spiritual joy is pleasing to God. *Ego vero delectabor in Domino, but I will take delight in the Lord*, from the contemplation and love of his goodness and his benefits. This is a holy and noble pleasure which—if you relish in it—will easily cause you to despise unclean pleasures.

103{104}[35]   *Let sinners be consumed out of the earth, and the unjust, so that they be no more: O my soul, bless you the Lord.*

Deficiant peccatores a terra, et iniqui, ita ut non sint. Benedic, anima mea, Domino.

103{104}[35] *Deficiant peccatores a terra, etc. Let sinners be consumed out of the earth, etc.* This verse can first be explained with respect to evil, as if it were the voice of a man zealous for God, and one who has conformed himself to the divine justice, or who is foretelling of the future;[105] and so, it is to be explained in this sense: *Deficiant peccatores,*

---

100 Matt. 10:22b; 24:13.
101 Ecclus. 39:41.
102 Prov. 8:31.
103 Ps. 5:7b.
104 Prov. 3:32b.
105 E. N. This is a frequent distinction made by Denis on maledictory verses. They are not to be understood in an optative sense (wishing for evil upon the subject, which would be uncharitable), but are understood as being statements that are admonitory or are made in conformity with divine justice (either of which are consonant with

let sinners be consumed, [that is, sinners] obstinate in their vices, *a terra, out of the earth,* that is, the present earth, so that they may die lest they harm the just and the land of the living, and so that they may not enjoy happiness; this is in a manner consonant with that which is written, *May the sight of God's glory be taken away from the ungodly.*[106] *Et iniqui, ita ut non sint; and the unjust, so that they be no more* in the life of grace or glory, but only in the life of nature and punishment. And with this meaning is written, *So let all your enemies perish, O Lord;*[107] and elsewhere, *Let it not be well with the wicked, neither let his days be prolonged.*[108] Secondly, this verse can be explained with reference to the good: *Let sinners be consumed out of the earth* (that is, that they might desist from worldly affections and manner of living), *and the unjust,* so that they might not be what they were, that they not be that which they were by fault and their own free will, but that they might remain that which they were by essence and grace. Whence in Proverbs it is said: *Turn the wicked, and they shall not be.*

Benedic anima mea Domino; O my soul, bless you the Lord, praising God on account of all his splendors which have already been described.

See how we have heard this Psalm, so full of spiritual joy, in which it is manifest that holy David was not only a great theologian, but also an excellent philosopher, for he was both of those as a result of divine inspiration granted to him. We ought therefore to sing this Psalm recalling his benefits with complete thanksgiving and mental joyfulness, and not with sluggish and torpid heart. But this noble Psalm is delightful and powerfully sweet, especially in the beginning and at the end. And it is incumbent upon us to fulfill that which we say in the present Psalm: *I will sing to the Lord as long as I live, I will sing praise to my God while I have my being.* For our soul should advance in the fear of God from the consideration of the divine power which *looks upon the earth and makes it tremble.* And so Scripture says: *You are great, O Lord, and great is your name in might: who shall fear you, O King of nations?*[109]

---

charity). *See, e.g.,* Article LVI (Psalm 24:4) and footnote 24-14 in Volume I.

106 Is. 26:10. *E. N.* The Latin version of Isaiah 26:10 used by Denis — *Tollatur impius ne videat gloriam Dei* — departs from the Sixto-Clementine text which here says: *In terra sanctorum iniqua gessit, et non viedebit gloriam Domini* — "In the land of the saints he has done wicked things, and he shall not see the glory of the Lord."

107 Judges 5:31a.

108 Eccl. 8:13a.

109 Jer. 10:6b–7a.

PRAYER

O GOD, WHO LOOKS UPON THE EARTH AND who makes it tremble, put into our hearts your salutary fear, so that we might abandon the evil by which we have gravely offended you, that we may be renewed by your spirit from any aspect of sin in us, that we might adhere unto you with holy devotion, and consumed in the joyfulness of salvation, we might forever sing praise to you.

Deus, qui respicis terram et facis eam tremere, timorem tuum
salutarem cordibus nostris immitte: ut relictis malis
quibus te graviter offendimus, per spiritum tuum
renovata in nobis facie peccati, sancta tibi
devotione adhaereamus, et in
iucunditate perceptae salutis
semper tibi psallamus.

Psalm 104

ARTICLE VII

**ELUCIDATION OF THE ONE HUNDRED AND FOURTH PSALM:
CONFITEMINI DOMINO, ET INVOCATE NOMEN EIUS.
GIVE GLORY TO THE LORD, AND CALL UPON HIS NAME.**

104{105}[1] *Alleluia. Give glory to the Lord, and call upon his name:
declare his deeds among the Gentiles.*

Alleluia. Confitemini Domino, et invocate nomen eius; annuntiate inter gentes opera eius.

104{105}[2] *Sing to him, and sing praises to him: relate all his wondrous works.*

Cantate ei, et psallite ei; narrate omnia mirabilia eius.

THE TITLE TO THIS PRESENT PSALM IS THIS: 104{105}[1] *Alleluia*, which signifies, "Praise the Lord": and it is composed of two words, because in Hebrew *halelu* signifies "praise," and *yah* signifies God. Now there are twenty Psalms that have this title appended to them, and this is the first of these Psalms.[1] We do not come across any of the holy Saints to have written this whole word before the author of this present Psalm.[2] Now spiritually this powerful and mystical word—Alleluia—describes, better than it is able to express, the ineffable joy of the blessed in heaven. For this reason, no tongue may presume to change this word.[3] So this present Psalm is so entitled because it invites [the speaker] to the praise of God. For it recalls the benefits of God to the Israelite people granted during the times of Abraham, Isaac, Jacob, Moses, and Joshua. And it is not difficult to understand the literal sense of this Psalm; however, there is much within it that can be understood in a spiritual and subtle manner.

And therefore it says: *Confitemini Domino, give glory to the Lord* with a confession of praise, that is, praise God, *et invocate nomen eius, and*

---

1 E. N. 104-106, 110-118, 134-135, 145-150.
2 E. N. This would seem contradicted by Tobit 12:22, where the word is first encountered in Sacred Scripture: *Alleluia shall be sung in [Jerusalem's] streets*; however, the Book of Tobit was written probably in the 2nd century BC, well after the Psalms.
3 E. N. The word tongue (*lingua*) can be used to refer to the physical tongue or, more generally, to language.

call upon his name, that is, pray to him from an intimate affection of the heart and a recollected mind. And this is a most beautiful propriety in a just man.[4] For the just man (because in him the praise of the Creator is beautiful), when he wishes to invoke God, ought first to praise him, and he will be heard. Whence it is stated in an earlier Psalm: *Praising I will call upon the Lord, and I will be saved from my enemies.*[5] But the unjust man must first pray that he may be made worthy to praise God. *Annuntiate inter gentes opera eius, declare his deeds among the Gentiles*, that is, tell of all the marvels of God, being mindful of the salvation of our neighbor according to the demands of fraternal charity. For this reason, we read in Tobit: *Give glory to him in the sight of all that live.*[6] **104{105}** [2] *Cantate ei, sing to him* with a rejoicing voice, *et psallite ei, and sing praises to him* with faithful deeds; *narrate, relate* preaching before all men, singing praises with others, or by oneself before God, *omnia mirabilia eius, all his wondrous works* of those things which are written, or of all things in general, or of some of all things. For, according to Ecclesiasticus, all such things are able to be praised: *Has not the Lord made the saints to declare all his wonderful works?*[7] This also Paul says in Acts: *For I have not spared to declare unto you all the counsel of God.*[8] Not, however, that we have the ability to relate all the marvels of God in detail, for it is stated in Ecclesiasticus: *Who is able to declare his works?*[9]

———————

104{105}[3] *Glory in his holy name: let the heart of them rejoice that seek the Lord.*

Laudamini in nomine sancto eius; laetetur cor quaerentium Dominum.

104{105}[4] *Seek the Lord, and be strengthened: seek his face evermore.*

Quaerite Dominum, et confirmamini; quaerite faciem eius semper.

104{105}[3] *Laudamini in nomine sancto eius, glory in his holy name,* that is, desire to glory, not in yourselves, but in the Lord, seeing that the goods for which you give glory are ascribed not to you, but to the Lord. And live in such a manner that you might be found deserving to

---

4 Cf. Ecclus. 15:9: *Praise is not seemly in the mouth of a sinner.*
5 Ps. 17:4.
6 Tobit 12:6b.
7 Ecclus. 42:17a.
8 Acts 20:27.
9 Ecclus. 18:2.

glory in God. For of those persons who glory and deceptively commend themselves, and who sometimes take delight receiving such praises is written, *O my people, they that call you blessed, the same deceive you.*[10] Let us not, therefore, vainly take delight when we praise, recalling that said in Ecclesiasticus: *Be not exalted in the day of your honor.*[11] It is true that sometimes, for the increase in the honor of God and the edification of one's neighbor, one is at times allowed to praise oneself and to receive praise. For the holy Apostles and Prophets freely described their virtues and graces in this way. This is particularly allowed to the perfect and to prelates, for in this they are ruled by divine instinct; but this is not befitting for others, because it is written, *Justify not yourself before God.*[12]

But one might ask in what way is it allowed to praise a man in this life, since it is stated in Ecclesiasticus: *Praise not any man before death.*[13] And the response to this is that no one ought to praise what is in themselves, but only in the Lord; for commonly it is not fitting to praise any person unless it be to appeal him towards something better or for some similar reason and necessary cause: especially since it seems especially dangerous to praise the imperfect, lest they grow proud [and remain in their imperfections]. We see, moreover, how often the Apostle commends his disciples in his epistles. So the authority of the book of Ecclesiasticus is not to be strictly understood, for this book is not in the canon: unless we are dealing with canonical books, therefore, we are not compelled to assent to it absolutely, as Augustine asserts in his letter to Jerome: and this is what Thomas [Aquinas] states.[14] Nevertheless, the authority of this book should not be slighted or summarily denied.

---

10 Is. 3:12b.

11 Ecclus. 11:4a.

12 Ecclus. 7:5a.

13 Ecclus. 11:30a.

14 *E. N.* It appears that the issue of the canon — specifically, the authority of the deuterocanonical books — was still subject to some uncertainty prior to the Council of Trent, even though it would have appeared to have been definitely settled by the Church's magisterium before that council. DS 1335 (Council of Florence, 1441 AD), DS 350 (*Decretum Gelasianum*), DS 213 (Letter *Consulenti tibi*), 405 AD), DS 179 (*Decretum Damasi*). "In the Latin Church, all through the Middle Ages we find evidence of hesitation about the character of the deuterocanonicals. There is a current friendly to them, another one distinctly unfavourable to their authority and sacredness, while wavering between the two are a number of writers whose veneration for these books is tempered by some perplexity as to their exact standing, and among those we note St. Thomas Aquinas." Catholic Encyclopedia (New York: Robert Appleton, 1908), Vol. 3, 273. The reference to St. Thomas is to *obiter dicta* in ST Ia, q. 89, art. 8, ad 2, where he discusses the knowledge of the departed souls as to what takes place on earth. In addressing the apparition of Samuel to Saul (1 Sam.

Laetetur, let rejoice with a spiritual joy and with the performance of good and salutary deeds in, *cor quaerentium Dominum, the heart of them . . . that seek the Lord* with faith and works so that they might contemplate him more clearly, love him more fervently, and honor him more perfectly. For every good work is to be done with joy. **104{105}[4]** *Quaerite Dominum, seek the Lord* in the just-stated manner, *et confirmamini, and be strengthened,* that is, do not cease, become weary, or faint hearted in searching. For although one cannot attain to God perfectly nor perceive him by sight in this life, yet the more he is sought perseveringly the more he is abundantly found; and one is filled with greater grace; and faith is illuminated, hope is strengthened, and love set afire. For this is what Christ said in the Gospel: *Seek and you shall find.*[15] For all who seek find. And according to the book of Chronicles, Scripture says: *Do you therefore take courage, and let not your hands be weakened: for there shall be a reward for your work.*[16] But what else is it to seek God and to be strengthened in him other than to do that which the Lord orders, *Be converted to me with all your heart?*[17] *Quaerite faciem eius semper, seek his face evermore:* that is, strive incessantly for the knowledge of God, lest that which the most High said to Isaiah should befall you: *My people is led away captive, because they had not knowledge . . . therefore has hell enlarged her soul.*[18] Or [we might understand it this way], *Seek the Lord* and his face always, that is, choose to strive for the presence of God in all your works, and do not live justly for any other reward. For it is fitting that the intention of the heart be always inclined to the last end. For this reason the Savior said: *If your eye be single, your whole body shall be lightsome; but if your eye be evil, your whole body shall be darksome.*[19]

104{105}[5] *Remember his marvelous works which he has done; his wonders, and the judgments of his mouth.*

Mementote mirabilium eius quae fecit, prodigia eius, et iudicia oris eius.

28:11), Thomas states that Samuel appeared "by a special dispensation of God. . . . whence it might also be said of Samuel that he appeared through divine revelation; according to that stated in Ecclesiasticus 46:23, that 'he slept, and told the king the end of his life'. . . . unless, indeed, the authority of Ecclesiasticus be not received since it is not regarded among the canonical Scriptures by the Jews." The letter referred to by Denis is the St. Augustine's Letter 82 to St. Jerome.

15 Luke 11:9, 10.
16 2 Chr. 15:7.
17 Joel 2:12a.
18 Is. 5:13a, 14a.
19 Matt. 6:22b–23a.

104{105}[6] *O you seed of Abraham his servant; you sons of Jacob his chosen.*

Semen Abraham, servi eius; filii Iacob, electi eius.

104{105}[5] *Mementote mirabilium eius quae fecit, remember his marvelous works which he has done* with the Patriarchs of the Old Testament: remember, I say, those marvels which are *prodigia eius, his wonders,* that is, the marvelous works done long ago by his finger,[20] for their cause is the divine will which is unknown to us, *et iudicia oris eius, and the judgments of his mouth,* that is, the effects of divine justice, are announced by God to Moses. Either the works of divine justice or the divine precepts and counsels which God adjudges to be just are called the judgments of God, or the censures or conceptions which the divine mind pronounces within itself regarding things. Remember these things, **104{105}[6]** *O semen Abraham, O you seed of Abraham,* that is, sons of the patriarch Abraham, *servi eius, his servant:* for Abraham was a servant of God; and you, *filii Iacob, O sons of Jacob* the patriarch, *electi eius, his chosen,* that is, who was chosen by God: for as the Lord said, *I have loved Jacob, but Esau have I hated.*[21] This also which is stated — the words servants, and the elect — can also refer to the seed of the sons, for they also were servants and chosen by God. For this reason, Moses said to the children of Israel in Deuteronomy: *Behold heaven is the Lord's, your God, and the heaven of heaven . . . and yet the Lord has been closely joined to your fathers, . . . and chose them, and loved their seed after them.*[22]

104{105}[7] *He is the Lord our God: his judgments are in all the earth.*

Ipse Dominus Deus noster; in universa terra iudicia eius.

104{105}[7] *Ipse Dominus Deus noster, he is the Lord our God.* For other nations have turned toward idolatry, but the faith and the worship of God remained with the Jewish people. Whence it is written: He who made the stars, *this is our God.*[23] *In universa terra iudicia eius, his judgments are in all the earth,* that is, the effects of divine justice extend forth to all the inhabitants of the earth, so that all will be judged by God, receiving that which they deserve, in the manner that is revealed by

---

20 E. N. The "finger of God" is an expression used in Ex. 8:16–20, Ex. 31:18, and Deut. 9:10 to refer to the power of God.

21 Malachi 1:2b, 3a.

22 Deut. 10:14–15a. E. N. Denis's quote varies from the Sixto-Clementine Vulgate; whereas Denis quotes "and he chose them, and he loved their seed after them," the Vulgate says "and he loved them, and chose their seed after them."

23 Baruch 3:36a.

Ezechiel: *I will judge every man according to his ways.*[24] Or [alternatively] the words the "judgments of God in all the earth" are said because the judgments which he employed upon Pharaoh and the Egyptians and the Canaanites have become commonly known throughout the whole world. For this reason, the Lord said to Pharaoh: *For this reason have I raised you, that I may show my power in you, and my name may be spoken of throughout all the earth.*[25]

104{105}[8]   *He has remembered his covenant forever: the word which he commanded to a thousand generations.*

Memor fuit in saeculum testamenti sui; verbi quod mandavit in mille generationes.

104{105}[9]   *Which he made to Abraham; and his oath to Isaac;*

Quod disposuit ad Abraham, et iuramenti sui ad Isaac;

104{105}[10]   *And he appointed the same to Jacob for a law, and to Israel for an everlasting testament;*

Et statuit illud Iacob in praeceptum, et Israel in testamentum aeternum;

104{105}[11]   *Saying: To you will I give the land of Canaan, the lot of your inheritance.*

Dicens: Tibi dabo terram Chanaan, funiculum haereditatis vestrae.

104{105}[8] *Memor fuit, he has remembered* God [has remembered] *in saeculum testamenti sui, his covenant forever,* that is, his promise or compact or law, and *verbi quod mandavit in mille generationes, the word which he commanded to a thousand generations,* that is, all generations. This is the Old Testament given to Abraham, and his precepts to all his posterity.[26] God is said to have remembered his covenant because he frequently confirms and repeats it. For he first commanded it to Abraham, as it states next: 104{105}[9] *Quod disposuit ad Abraham, which he made to Abraham* and confirmed with his son by an oath, affirming him to fulfill that which he had promised to Abraham;[27] and so it adds, *et iuramenti sui ad Isaac, and his oath to Isaac,* which implicitly means it was remembered. 104{105}

---

24 Ez. 18:30a.
25 Ex. 9:16.
26 Gen. 17:2 *et seq.*
27 Gen. 26:3–4.

[10] *Et statuit illud, and he appointed the same* testament or word *Iacob, to Jacob,* the son of Isaac, *in praeceptum, for a law,* instructing him that he might firmly believe it to be fulfilled;[28] *et Israel, and to Israel,* that is, the same Jacob just mentioned, who is called Israel, that is, "seeing God," for he saw an angel of God.[29] It was for this reason that he said, *I have seen God face to face.*[30] *In testamentum aeternum, for an everlasting covenant,* that is, remaining forever with respect to its fruits or with regard to its moral precepts.[31] Regarding the testament that originated with Abraham one finds written in Genesis: *I will bless you, and I will multiply your seed as the stars of heaven . . . and in your seed shall all the nations of the earth be blessed.*[32] And elsewhere he says to Abraham: *In Isaac shall your seed be called.*[33] He also promised Isaac (as is written in Genesis) that he would give the land of Canaan to his seed.[34] **104{105}[11]** The Lord *dicens, saying* to Jacob the patriarch Jacob: *Tibi, to you,* that is, to your seed, *dabo terram Chanaan, will I give the land of Canaan:* in which land dwelt the Canaanites who were descended from Ham, the younger son of Noah;[35] *funiculum, the line,* that is the part or the lot, *hereditatis vestrae, of your inheritance,* so that among all the other parts of the earth, this part I will give to you to possess as your inheritance as if it were specifically bequeathed to you. For this is what he said to Jacob: *I am the Lord God of Abraham your father, and the God of Isaac; the land, wherein you sleep, I will give to you and to your seed.*[36]

104{105}[12] *When they were but a small number: yea very few, and sojourners therein.*

Cum essent numero brevi, paucissimi et incolae eius.

---

28 Gen. 28:13–15.

29 Gen. 32:28.

30 Gen. 32:30.

31 E. N. "By the death of our Redeemer, the New Testament took the place of the Old Law which had been abolished; then the Law of Christ together with its mysteries, enactments, institutions, and sacred rites was ratified for the whole world in the blood of Jesus Christ. . . . [O]n the gibbet of His death Jesus made void the Law with its decrees and fastened the handwriting of the Old Testament to the Cross, establishing the New Testament in His blood shed for the whole human race." Pius XII, *Mystici corporis Christi,* No. 29.

32 Gen. 22:17a, 18a.

33 Gen. 21:12b.

34 Gen. 26:3–4.

35 Gen. 10:6.

36 Gen. 28:13.

104{105}[13] *And they passed from nation to nation, and from one king-dom to another people.*

Et pertransierunt de gente in gentem, et de regno ad popu-lum alterum.

104{105}[12] *Cum essent, when they were,* [when] the previously-mentioned patriarchs [were] *numero brevi, but a small number,* that is, few in number: when, namely, Abraham did not have anyone except his wife, Sarah, and Lot his nephew; and similarly when Isaac had few with him; when also Jacob had not yet begotten anyone, and when he begot all his children, who, in comparison to others, were few in number. Whence there is added, *paucissimi et incolae eius; yea, very few, and sojourners,* that is, since they inhabited the land as if they were pilgrims or guests, being very few in number compared to the other nations. **104{105}[13]** *Et pertransierunt de gente in gentem, et de regno ad populum alterum; and they passed from nation to nation, and from one kingdom to another people.* This is more clearly brought to light in the book of Genesis. For Abraham went forth with Sarah and Lot from the land of Mesopotamia of Syria, entering into the land of Canaan, as we find contained in Genesis.[37] Thereafter he entered into Gerar and Philistine and Egypt.[38] Similarly, Isaac entered into various of these lands.[39] Jacob also first fled from the kingdom of the Canaanites into Syria;[40] and afterwards he entered into the kingdom of Egypt with all his household.[41]

104{105}[14] *He suffered no man to hurt them: and he reproved kings for their sakes.*

Non reliquit hominem nocere eis; et corripuit pro eis reges.

104{105}[15] *Touch not my anointed: and do no evil to my prophets.*

Nolite tangere christos meos, et in prophetis meis nolite malignari.

104{105}[14] *Non reliquit, he suffered,* God [suffered no man] *homi-nem nocere eis, man to hurt them* with deadly harm. Yet frequently the Philistines or their shepherds harassed Isaac and his shepherds in Gerar, plugging up their wells.[42] Similarly, Jacob was for some time controlled

---

37 Gen. 12:4–5.
38 Gen. 20:1; 12:10.
39 Gen. 26:1.
40 Gen. 28:5.
41 Gen. 46:6.
42 Gen. 26:18, 15.

by Laban.[43] *Et corripuit pro eis reges, and he reproved kings for their sakes,* namely, the king of Egypt and Abimelech, the king of Gerar, as both of them caused to have brought to them Sarah, the wife of Abraham. For this reason, God shut up all the wombs of the house [of Abimelech], until Sarah was returned to her husband.[44] He also rebuked the previously-mentioned men and kings, saying by an angel or through inspiration in a dream: **104{105}[15]** *Nolite tangere, do not touch* with violence, *christos meos, my anointed,* that is, the saints just mentioned spiritually anointed by me with the oil and profusion of the Holy Spirit. For they are not called anointed as if they were anointed bodily: for the bodily and exterior anointing was first ordained by God through Moses to be used for kings and priests.[45] *Et in prophetis meis nolite malignari, and do no evil to my prophets,* that is, perform evil works [against them]. For the patriarchs were prophets. Whence of Abraham it is written in the book of Genesis: *He shall pray for you . . . for he is a prophet.*[46] And Isaac many times prophesied to his sons Jacob and Esau and their posterity, as is clearly set forth in Genesis.[47] But also Jacob bound together most excellent prophecies as he was dying, as is described in the book of Genesis.[48]

104{105}[16] *And he called a famine upon the land: and he broke in pieces all the support of bread.*

Et vocavit famem super terram; et omne firmamentum panis contrivit.

104{105}[17] *He sent a man before them: Joseph, who was sold for a slave.*

Misit ante eos virum; in servum venundatus est Ioseph.

104{105}[18] *They humbled his feet in fetters: the iron pierced his soul.*

Humiliaverunt in compedibus pedes eius; ferrum pertransiit animam eius.

104{105}[19] *Until his word came. The word of the Lord inflamed him.*

Donec veniret verbum eius, eloquium Domini inflammavit eum.

---

43 Gen. chps. 29–31.
44 Gen. chps. 12, 20.
45 Ex. 30:25–33; Lev. 8:2, 12.
46 Gen. 20:7a.
47 Gen. 27:28–29; 39–40.
48 Gen. 49.

104{105}[20] *The king sent, and he released him: the ruler of the people, and he set him at liberty.*

Misit rex, et solvit eum; princeps populorum, et dimisit eum.

104{105}[16] *Et vocavit, and he called,* God [called], *famem super terram, a famine upon the land,* that is, he prescribed and bid that there be a famine upon the land, *et omne firmamentum panis contrivit, and he broke in pieces all the support of the bread,* that is, he caused all heart-strengthening bread to perish for the multitude. However, this can also specifically refer to the seven-year famine caused in Egypt and in the land of Canaan during the time of the Pharaoh, because both those lands were severely oppressed with famine as we read in Genesis.[49] This could likewise refer to the famine that occurred in the land of Canaan during the time of Abraham, for which reason he travelled down to Egypt, as is stated in Genesis.[50] But the better understanding is that it refers to the famine that occurred in Egypt and Canaan, because of what follows.

104{105}[17] *Misit, he sent,* God [sent] *ante eos, before them,* namely Jacob and his sons, *virum, a man,* that is, Joseph, courageously virtuous in all things that he did. God is said to have sent him into Egypt, because he permitted him to be sold by his brothers and taken into Egypt, and there to be resold.[51] For he converted the evil which his brothers intended to direct against him into good, both for Joseph himself and his father and brothers. For this reason, Joseph said to his brothers: *For your preservation, . . . God sent me before you into Egypt, . . . that you might be preserved upon the earth. . . . Not by your counsel was I sent here, but by the will of God.*[52] *In servum venundatus est Ioseph, Joseph, who was sold for a slave* by the Ishmaelites to Potiphar, the captain of the army of the king of Egypt, as is stated in Genesis.[53] 104{105}[18] *Humiliaverunt in compedibus pedes eius, they humbled his feet in fetters:* that is, by order of the captain of the army, they bound Joseph in chains and they placed him in prison because of the complaint of the wife of the aforementioned captain,[54] who falsely accused the most chaste Joseph, saying to her husband: *The Hebrew servant, whom you have brought, came to me to abuse me.*[55] Upon hearing this [Potiphar] grew angry, and threw Joseph into jail where the king's prisoners

---

49 Gen. 61:54; 42:5.
50 Gen. 12:10.
51 Gen. 37:28, 36.
52 Gen. 45:5b, 7a, 8a.
53 Gen. 39:1.
54 Gen. 39:20.
55 Gen. 39:17.

were kept.[56] *Ferrum, the iron,* that is, the difficult trial, *pertransiit animam eius, pierced his soul,* that is, vehemently afflicted the spirit of Joseph: not, however, that it made him impatient, but that the fetters on his feet gave rise to sorrow in his soul; **104{105}[19]** *donec venire verbum eius, until his word came,* that is, a divinely-inspired interpretation, which not only explained the dream of the chief butler and the chief baker, but also the [dream] of Pharaoh.[57] This interpretation having been fulfilled, he began to be invigorated, and, a brief time later, to know freedom. But regarding this Joseph said: *Does not the interpretation belong to God?*[58]

Eloquium Domini inflammavit eum, the word of the Lord inflamed him, that is, the aforementioned inspiration and interpretation roused up and taught Joseph: and so **104{105}[20]** *misit, he sent* his servants, [that is], *rex, the king* of Egypt, the Pharaoh, [sent his servants], *et solvit eum, and he released him,* that is, hearing from the chief butler with how assiduously Joseph had explained his dream, he ordered that the holy Joseph be released from prison.[59] *Princeps populorum, the ruler of the people,* that is, the aforementioned king of the Egyptians, sent for [Joseph], *et dimisit eum, and he set him at liberty.* Whence we find contained in Genesis: *Forthwith at the king's command, Joseph was brought out of the prison, and they shaved him, and changing his apparel, brought him in to the king.*[60]

104{105}[21] *He made him master of his house, and ruler of all his possessions.*

Constituit eum dominum domus suae, et principem omnis possessionis suae.

104{105}[22] *That he might instruct his princes as himself, and teach his ancients wisdom.*

Ut erudiret principes eius sicut semetipsum, et senes eius prudentiam doceret.

104{105}[21] *Constituit, he made,* the king of Egypt [made] *eum, him,* namely, Joseph, *dominum domus suae, the master of his house,* that is, of his family and of his people, *et principem omnis possessionis suae, and ruler of all his possessions,* that is, of all the land of Egypt, and of all of

---

56 Gen. 39:19–20.
57 Gen. chps. 40, 41.
58 Gen. 40:8b.
59 Gen. 41:9–14.
60 Gen. 41:14.

his granaries and his harvests. Hence the Pharaoh himself said to Joseph: *You shall be over my house, and at the commandment of your mouth, all the people shall obey; only in the kingly throne will I be above you.*[61] And again: *I am Pharaoh; without your commandment no man shall move hand or foot in all the land of Egypt.*[62] **104{105}[22]** *Ut erudiret, that he might instruct,* [that is, that] Joseph himself [might instruct] *principes eius, his princes,* namely, [the princes] of the Pharaoh, *sicut semetipsum, as himself,* that is, to make them through his instruction to be similar in wisdom, teaching them not only of bodily things and human business, but also of in the manner of doing things. And according to Cassiodorus,[63] Pharaoh figured that Joseph was able to teach the Egyptians the art of the interpretation of the most indecipherable dreams, in the manner understood by the God revealing them. *Et senes eius prudentiam doceret, and teach his ancients wisdom,* instructing them in economic, ethical, and political sciences. Indeed, one teaches economics to run the household,[64] ethics to run one's self, and politics to run the community or the city. One can also piously believe that the holy patriarch, prophet, and worshipper of God taught some Egyptians regarding the worship and the faith of the one true and most-high God.

104{105}[23]   *And Israel went into Egypt: and Jacob was a sojourner in the land of Ham.*

Et intravit Israel in Aegyptum; et Iacob accola fuit in terra Cham.

104{105}[24]   *And he increased his people exceedingly: and strengthened them over their enemies.*

Et auxit populum suum vehementer, et firmavit eum super inimicos eius.

104{105}[23] *Et intravit Israel, and Israel went into,* namely, the father of Joseph with his sons and the children of his sons representing seventy souls,[65] [went into] *Aegyptum, Egypt. Et Iacob, and Jacob,* who was also

---

61 Gen. 41:40.

62 Gen. 41:44.

63 E. N. Cassiodorus (*ca.* 485–*ca.* 585), a Christian Roman statesman who authored a *Commentary on the Psalms.*

64 E. N. The word economics stems from Greek *oikonomia* ([οἶκος] *oikos*=house, dwelling and [νόμος] *nomos*=law, rule, or order), and so originally it had the sense of the proper administration of a household or family.

65 Gen. 46:27.

called Israel,[66] *accola fuit, was a sojourner*, that is, a pilgrim and settler with his seed *in terra Cham, in the land of Ham*, that is, in Egypt, which was the land and the possession of the children of Ham, the son of Noah. Whence Joseph said to his brothers: *You shall tell my father of all my glory, and all things that you have seen in Egypt: make haste and bring him to me.*[67] And regarding Jacob, it is written: *Israel dwelt in Egypt, that is, in the land of Goshen . . . and he lived in it seventeen years.*[68] 104{105}[24] *Et auxit, and he increased*, [that is,] Jacob [increased] in the land of Egypt *populum suum vehementer, his people exceedingly*: not that he himself begot any in Egypt, but he is asserted to have done that which his posterity did. In this manner, the Lord said to him: *I will make a great nation of you there. I will go down with you there, and will bring you back again from there*,[69] not that he would bring back Jacob, for he died in Egypt. *Et firmavit, and he strengthened*, [that is,] Jacob [strengthened] *eum, them*, namely, the people who were born from him, *super inimicos eius, over their enemies*, that is, over the Egyptians. For he strengthened his people in the same manner that he increased them. Or [we might understand it] thus: *And he increased his people*, that is, the Israelites. [This can be said] because of what is said in Exodus: *The children of Israel increased, and sprung up into multitudes, and growing exceedingly strong, they filled the land.*[70] And again, the King of Egypt *said to his people: Behold the people of the children of Israel are numerous and stronger than we.*[71]

104{105}[25]   *He turned their heart to hate his people: and to deal deceitfully with his servants.*

Convertit cor eorum, ut odirent populum eius, et dolum facerent in servos eius.

104{105}[26]   *He sent Moses his servant: Aaron the man whom he had chosen.*

Misit Moysen, servum suum, Aaron quem elegit ipsum.

104{105}[27]   *He gave them power to show his signs, and his wonders in the land of Ham.*

Posuit in eis verba signorum suorum, et prodigiorum in terra Cham.

---

66 Gen. 32:28.
67 Gen. 45:13.
68 Gen. 47:27a, 28a.
69 Gen. 46:3b–4a.
70 Ex. 1:7.
71 Ex. 1:9.

104{105}[25] *Convertit, he turned,* God [turned], not effectively, but permissively, in the way that hardened Pharaoh, *cor eorum, their heart,* that is, [the heart] of the Egyptians, from bad to worse, *ut odirent populum eius, to hate his people,* that is, the Israelite people, *et dolum facerent in servos eius, and to deal deceitfully with his servants,* that is, with this people who had the true faith and worship of God. For of these the book of Exodus states: *The Egyptians hated the children of Israel, and afflicted them and mocked them, and they made their life bitter with hard works in clay, and brick.*[72] And again: *A new king over Egypt arose that knew not Joseph, and he said to his people:.... Come, let us wisely oppress them, lest they multiply.*[73] 104{105}[26] *Misit, he sent,* God [sent], *Moysen servum suum, Moses his servant* to Pharaoh, so that he might release the children of Israel, as is written in Exodus.[74] He also sent *Aaron,* the brother of Moses, *quem elegit ipsum, the man whom he had chosen.* For he chose Aaron, the brother of Moses, to this end: that he might be a helper to Moses in such a great business.[75] God also sent Moses from the Sinai desert, but he sent Aaron who lived in Egypt to meet Moses.[76] And so he sent both at the same time to Pharaoh: Moses so that he might perform signs and Aaron so that he might speak to the king, for he was eloquent. 104{105}[27] *Posuit, he gave,* God [gave] *in eis, in them,* that is, in Moses and in Aaron, *verba signorum suorum, the power to show his signs,* that is, of minor miracles, *et prodigiorum, and his wonders,* that is, of major miracles, *in terra Cham, in the land of Ham,* that is, in Egypt. For by these two God warned Pharaoh what future signs or wonders would occur the next day, as is often recited in Exodus.[77]

104{105}[28] *He sent darkness, and made it obscure: and grieved not his words.*

Misit tenebras, et obscuravit; et non exacerbavit sermones suos.

Thereafter is set forth the plagues of Egypt, not all of them, but seven or eight of them: and they also are not set forth here in the order that they occurred. 104{105}[28] *Misit, he sent,* God [sent], *tenebras, darkness* in the land where the Egyptians dwelled, *et obscuravit, and made it obscure,*

---

72 Ex. 1:13–14a.
73 Ex. 1:8b, 9a, 10a.
74 Ex. 3:10.
75 Ex. 4:14–16.
76 Ex. 3:1–10; 4:27.
77 Ex. chps. 5, 7 *et seq.*

that is, he removed the light of the sun. This was the ninth plague. Of this [plague] is written in Exodus: *Stretch out your hand towards heaven: and may there be darkness upon the land of Egypt, so thick that it may be felt....And there came horrible darkness...for three days, and no man saw his brother, nor moved himself out of the place where he was: but wheresoever the children of Israel dwelt there was light.*[78] Now this darkness was exceedingly marvelous: for it occurred by the subtraction of the rays of the sun from one part of the land of Egypt and not from another part. *Et non exacerbavit, and grieved not,* that is, God did not make bitter, but made sweet *sermones suos, his words,* by which he threatened the Egyptians. For the plague ceased upon Pharaoh promising repentance and appeasing Moses, according to that which Moses said to Pharaoh in Exodus: *As soon as I am gone out of the city, I will stretch forth my hands to the Lord, and the thunders shall cease...that you may know that the earth is the Lord's.*[79] Or [we can understand it thus], *he grieved not,* that is, he did not make his words to be ineffectual, but he fulfilled them.

104{105}[29]   *He turned their waters into blood, and destroyed their fish.*

Convertit aquas eorum in sanguinem, et occidit pisces eorum.

104{105}[30]   *Their land brought forth frogs, in the inner chambers of their kings.*

Edidit terra eorum ranas in penetralibus regum ipsorum.

In addition, God **104{105}[29]** *Convertit aquas eorum, turned their waters,* that is [the waters] of the Egyptians, *in sanguinem, et occidit pisces eorum; into blood, and destroyed their fish* which were in the water and by which they were fed. This was the first plague of the Egyptians. Of this plague is written in Exodus: *The Lord said to Moses: Say to Aaron, Take your rod and stretch forth your hand upon the waters of Egypt,...that they may be turned into blood...and lifting up the rod, he struck the water of the river before Pharaoh, and the fish...died.*[80] **104{105}[30]** *Edidit terra eorum ranas, their land brought forth frogs,* that is, frogs burst forth from the land of Egypt, which frogs entered into the houses of the common people and the household of the Pharaoh, and they were found *in penetralibus, in the inner chambers,* that is, in the most hidden places and in the bedchambers, *regum ipsorum, of their kings,* that is, the nobility of

---

78 Ex. 10:21–23.
79 Ex. 9:29.
80 Ex. 7:19–21a.

the Egyptians. This was the second plague of the Egyptians. Regarding this, the Lord said to Pharaoh: *An abundance of frogs shall come forth and enter in your house, and your bedchamber, and upon your bed, and in the houses of your servants, and to your people.*[81]

104{105}[31]   *He spoke, and there came divers sorts of flies and sciniphs in all their coasts.*

Dixit, et venit coenomyia, et ciniphes in omnibus finibus eorum.

God 104{105}[31] *dixit, spoke,* that is, ordered it to be and it was done, *et, and* by divine command *venit coenomyia, there came diverse sorts of flies* (that is, large and disagreeable dog-flies), that is, a multitude of such flies, with which were mixed other kinds of bothersome flies. This was the fourth plague of Egypt. Regarding this, the Lord said through Moses to the king of Egypt: *I will send upon you, and upon your people all kinds of flies. And the land was corrupted by these kinds of flies.*[82] God also spoke, *et, and* there came *ciniphes, sciniphs,* that is, small flies with an atrocious sting. And these together were the third plague of Egypt: and which the magicians of Pharaoh were found wanting. Regarding this, we find contained in Exodus: *All the dust of the earth was turned into sciniphs.... And the magicians said to Pharaoh: This is the finger of God.*[83] And it came and was *in omnibus finibus eorum, in all their coasts,* that is, and all the ends and all the people of the kingdom of Egypt.

104{105}[32]   *He gave them hail for rain, a burning fire in the land.*

Posuit pluvias eorum grandinem, ignem comburentem in terra ipsorum.

104{105}[33]   *And he destroyed their vineyards and their fig trees: and he broke in pieces the trees of their coasts.*

Et percussit vineas eorum, et ficulneas eorum, et contrivit lignum finium eorum.

104{105}[34]   *He spoke, and the locust came, and the bruchus, of which there was no number.*

Dixit, et venit locusta, et bruchus cujus non erat numerus.

---

81 Ex. 8:3.
82 Ex. 8:21a, 24b.
83 Ex. 8:17, 19.

104{105}[35]   *And they devoured all the grass in their land, and consumed all the fruit of their ground.*

Et comedit omne foenum in terra eorum; et comedit omnem fructum terrae eorum.

104{105}[36]   *And he slew all the firstborn in their land: the firstfruits of all their labor.*

Et percussit omne primogenitum in terra eorum, primitias omnis laboris eorum.

104{105}[32] *Posuit pluvias eorum grandinem, he gave them hail for rain,* that is, instead of rain, God made it that hail should fall; he placed also *ignem comburentum, a burning fire,* that is, lightning storms mixed with ball lightning, *in terra ipsorum, in their land.* 104{105}[33] *Et percussit, and he destroyed,* God [destroyed], with hail, fire, and sulfur *vineas eorum et ficulneas eorum, their vineyards and their fig trees; et contrivit; and he broke,* that is, consumed or destroyed, *lignum finium eorum, the trees of their coasts,* that is, the trees all the way to the ends of Egypt. This was the seventh plague of Egypt. Of this plague, Exodus says: *The Lord sent thunder and hail, and lighting running along the ground; and the hail and fire mixed with it and drove together.*[84] 104{105}[34] *Dixit, he spoke,* God [spoke], *et venit locusta, and the locust came,* that is, a multitude of locusts came into the land of Egypt, *et bruchus cuius non erat numerus, and the bruchus,*[85] *of which there was no number,* that is, there were innumerable bruchuses. These are small animals and have a brief lifespan. 104{105} [35] *Et comedit, and it ate,* the locusts and the bruchuses [ate], *omne foenum, all the grass,* that is, all the plant life, *in terra eorum, et comedit omnem fructum terrae eorum, in their land, and consumed all the fruit of their ground,* that is, the cornfields of the Egyptians. This was the eighth plague of Egypt, in which these pests devoured that which remained after the fire and hail, which so overwhelmed the surface of the earth so that, as we read in Exodus, nothing appeared upon it.[86] 104{105} [36] *Et percussit omne primogentium, and he slew all the firstborn* both with respect to men as well as livestock, *in terra eorum, in their land;*

---

84 Ex. 9:23–24.

85 *E. N.* A bruchus is a kind of beetle or weevil that is considered a pest, and which tends to feed upon legumes such as peas, lentils, and beans.

86 Ex. 10:14–15: *And they covered the whole face of the earth, wasting all things. And the grass of the earth was devoured, and what fruits soever were on the trees, which the hail had left: and there remained not anything that was green on the trees, or in the herbs of the earth in all Egypt.*

he also slew *primitias omnis laboris eorum, the firstfruits of all their labor,* that is, the earliest of the fruits that of all their industry. This was the tenth plague of Egypt. Of this plague we read in Exodus: *It came to pass at midnight, the Lord slew every firstborn in the land of Egypt, from the firstborn of Pharaoh, who sought on his throne, unto the firstborn of the captive woman.*[87]

Now two of the plagues of Egypt are omitted here, namely, the fifth and the sixth. For the fifth [plague] was that all the animals of the Egyptians died of pestilence; the sixth was boils with swelling blains in men and beasts of burden.[88]

104{105}[37]   *And he brought them out with silver and gold: and there was not among their tribes one that was feeble.*

Et eduxit eos cum argento et auro, et non erat in tribubus eorum infirmus.

104{105}[38]   *Egypt was glad when they departed: for the fear of them lay upon them.*

Laetata est Aegyptus in profectione eorum, quia incubuit timor eorum super eos.

104{105}[39]   *He spread a cloud for their protection, and fire to give them light in the night.*

Expandit nubem in protectionem eorum, et ignem ut luceret eis per noctem.

Following this are enumerated the good things bestowed upon the Jews. 104{105}[37] *Et eduxit eos, and he brought them out,* God [brought them out] from Egypt *cum argento et auro, with silver and gold:* for as is written in Exodus, the Lord commanded the Jews to ask for vessels of gold and silver from the Egyptians, and many tapestries, and they despoiled the Egyptians; the fact that this was done, however, was not unjust, for all things are of God,[89] and he will bestow those things upon whom he wills. The Egyptians were ungrateful, and so they held possessions unjustly. But also the children of Israel had not been compensated for their labor of most burdensome servitude. *Et non erat in tribubus eorum, and there was not among their tribes,* namely among the

---

87 Ex. 10:39
88 Ex. 9:6, 10.
89 1 Chr. 29:11–12, 14, 16.

Hebrews, *infirmus, one that was feeble*. For all were kept safe by God who disposes all things so that they could all leave at the same time. 104{105}[38] *Laetata est Aegyptus in profectione eorum, Egypt was glad when they departed*, that is, by the leaving of the Hebrews, *quia incubuit timor eorum super eos, for the fear of them lay upon them*, that is, panic had befallen upon the Egyptians lest all of them be killed as a result of them keeping them from leaving. Whence in Exodus, Pharaoh says: *Arise and go forth from among my people . . . and departing bless me.*[90] And the *Egyptians pressed the people to go forth from the land speedily saying: We shall all die.*[91] 104{105}[39] *Expandit, he spread*, God [spread] *nubem in protectionem eorum, a cloud for their protection*, that is, in refreshment of his people against the heat of the day, *et ignem, and fire*, that is, a column of fire, *ut luceret eis per noctem, to give them light in the night* in the way it says in Scripture: *The Lord went before them to show the way by day in a pillar of a cloud, and by night in a pillar of fire.*[92]

104{105}[40] *They asked, and the quail came: and he filled them with the bread of heaven.*

Petierunt, et venit coturnix, et pane caeli saturavit eos.

104{105}[41] *He opened the rock, and waters flowed: rivers ran down in the dry land.*

Dirupit petram, et fluxerunt aquae, abierunt in sicco flumina.

104{105}[42] *Because he remembered his holy word, which he had spoken to his servant Abraham.*

Quoniam memor fuit verbi sancti sui, quod habuit ad Abraham, puerum suum.

104{105}[43] *And he brought forth his people with joy, and his chosen with gladness.*

Et eduxit populum suum in exsultatione, et electos suos in laetitia.

104{105}[44] *And he gave them the lands of the Gentiles: and they possessed the labors of the people,*

Et dedit illis regiones gentium, et labores populorum possederunt,

---

90 Ex. 12:31–32.
91 Ex. 12:33.
92 Ex. 13:21.

104{105}[45] *That they might observe his justifications and seek after his law.*

Ut custodiant iustificationes eius, et legem eius requirant.

Thereafter is recited the marvels God performed in the desert: **104{105}**
[40] *Petierunt, they asked*, the Hebrews [asked] for pleasing food, *et venit,
and it came*, with the blowing wind of the Lord, *conturnix, quail*, that is,
a multitude of quail, which are birds that fly close to the ground and by
dwellings. Whence in Numbers it states that they burned with desire
for flesh, and they said: *Who shall give us flesh to eat?*[93] And after this
it describes the way the quail flew all around the camp the space of one
day.[94] *Et pane caeli, and with bread of heaven*, namely, manna, *saturavit
eos, he filled them* for forty years, as it states in Exodus.[95] **104{105}[41]**
Dirupit petram he opened the rock, that is, by Moses striking the rock
with the staff, the rock split by a divine miracle, *et fluxerunt aquae, and
waters flowed* from the rock; *abierunt in sicco flumina, rivers ran down in
the dry land*, that is, rivers of water flowed down into the desert from the
rock, so that the people and cattle could drink. Moreover, this splitting
of the rock and the outflowing of water occurred twice. The first at the
rock at Horeb as we read in Exodus;[96] the second is the rock at Zin,
as is written about in Numbers.[97]

Now God bestowed these benefits to the children of Israel not because
of their virtues or their merits, since they were always found to be rebellious, but to fulfill the promises made to Abraham, and also because of
Abraham's merit. For this reason it says: **104{105}[42]** *Quoniam memor
fuit, because [God] remembered* by effect *verbi sancti sui, his holy word*, that
is, the divine promises, *quod habuit ad Abraham puerum suum, which he
had spoken to his servant Abraham*, promising him that he would lead
his seed out of Egypt and give him the land of the Canaanites.[98]

Thereafter the good things given by God to the children of Israel
during the time of Joshua are written about. **104{105}[43]** *Et eduxit, and
he brought forth*, the Lord [brought forth], *populum suum, his people* by
Joshua after the death of Moses from the plains of Moab by the Jordan
into the land of promise, *in exsultatione, with joy*, exterior [joy], *et electos
suos, and his chosen*, that is, the people forechosen by God just described,

---

93 Num. 11:4.
94 Num. 11:31.
95 Ex. 16:35.
96 Ex. 17:6.
97 Num. 20:1–13.
98 Gen. 15:13 *et seq.*

in laetitiae, with gladness, interior [gladness], as is clear in the book of Joshua.[99] **104{105}[44]** *Et dedit illis regiones gentium, and he gave them the land of the Gentiles,* namely, the lands of king Og, and the land of king Sehon, and the lands in which the seven nations dwelt, namely, the Canaanites, the Hittites, the Perizzites, *etc. Et labores populorum, and . . . the labors of the people,* of these people [that is, the labors of those dispossessed of their lands], namely, their cities, towns, and riches built or acquired by labor, the children of Israel *possederunt, possessed.* This we read in many places in the book of Joshua.[100] **104{105}[45]** *Ut custodiant iustificationes eius, that they might observe his justifications,* that is, that they might observe the divine precepts which justify men, *et legem eius, and his law* given by Moses *requirant, they might seek,* that is, they might diligently learn and might strive to understand spiritually.

Now one ought to be warned that the possession of temporal things is neither the principal nor the sufficient reward for the observation of the divine law or the keeping of the commandments: especially since the observation of the law relates to matters of the goods of virtue; but the possession or rewards of temporal goods are the kinds of goods that are useful or delectable.[101] But the good of virtue exceeds in dignity the useful or the delectable good. And so one is not ultimately rewarded by such [useful or delectable] goods, because God is not stingy in his rewards, but he gives much more than one deserves. Eternal beatitude, therefore, is the principal and full reward of a virtuous life; but temporal recompense is a secondary reward, and less than the principal [reward]. This [promise of temporal reward], however, was frequently promised and fulfilled to the Israelite people because of their ignorance, so that from their receiving [rewards] in the present, they might begin to hope for future and spiritual goods. Many things that Moses wrote should be understood in this way, is this in Deuteronomy: The Lord *is your life and the length of your days, that you might dwell in the land* which is given to you;[102] and this, *Honor your father and your mother, that you may be long-lived upon the land.*[103]

---

99 Joshua chps. 1–3.

100 Joshua chps. 12–21.

101 *E. N.* A useful good (*bonum utile*) is a good that is a means to a further end. A delectable good (*bonum delectabile*) is a good which procures pleasure. A virtuous good (or honest or moral good, *bonum honestum*) is a good which is an end in itself. *See* ST Ia, q. 5, art. 6, c.

102 Deut. 30:20.

103 Ex. 20:12.

ARTICLE VIII

MORAL EXPLANATION OF THE SAME ONE HUNDRED AND FOURTH PSALM.

104{105}[1]   *Alleluia. Give glory to the Lord, and call upon his name: declare his deeds among the Gentiles.*

Alleluia. Confitemini Domino, et invocate nomen eius; annuntiate inter gentes opera eius.

104{105}[2]   *Sing to him, and sing praises to him: relate all his wondrous works.*

Cantate ei, et psallite ei; narrate omnia mirabilia eius.

CCORDING TO THE DIVINE AND GREAT DIO-nysius [the Areopagite], the Evangelical law exists in a middle state between the state of the Old Testament and the heavenly fatherland.[104] And just as the state of the Church militant is a figure of the state of the Church triumphant or of the blessed, so is the state of the Old Testament a figure of the New Testament. For this reason, according to the Apostle [Paul], all things are contained in it in figure.[105] Therefore, when the Prophet [David] speaks literally in this Psalm of the Synagogue, so according to its tropological or moral sense, it speaks of the Church, and he says:

104{105}[1] *Confitemini Domino, Give glory to the Lord,* that is, praise to Christ, not only as man, but also as true God, *et invocate nomen eius, and call upon his name. Annuntiate, declare,* O holy Apostles and their successors, *inter gentes, among the Gentiles,* that is, all the pagans, *opera eius, his deeds,* namely, [the deeds] of Christ. Whence in Acts, Paul says: *Behold we turn to the Gentiles; for so the Lord has commanded us.*[106] 104{105}[2] *Narrate omnia mirabilia eius, relate all his wondrous works,*[107] namely, [the wondrous works] of Christ which are written in the Gospel: how [his birth] was announced by an angel, and how he was conceived by and born from a Virgin, was attended to by angels,[108] and his other wondrous works. Regarding his proclamation, Christ states through

---

104 E. N. The reference is to chapter 5 of Pseudo-Dionysius's *Ecclesiastical Hierarchy.*
105 Cf. 1 Cor. 10:11: *Now all these things happened to them [the Israelites] in figure: and they are written for our correction, upon whom the ends of the world are come.*
106 Acts 13:46b–47a.
107 E. N. Denis skips over the first part of 104:2.
108 Luke 1:31–35; 2:7; Matt. 4:11.

Isaiah: *I will send of them that shall be saved to the Gentiles ... afar off, to them that have not heard of me, and have not seen my glory. And they shall declare my glory to the Gentiles.*[109]

104{105}[5]   *Remember his marvelous works which he has done; his wonders, and the judgments of his mouth.*[110]

Mementote mirabilium eius quae fecit, prodigia eius, et iudicia oris eius.

104{105}[6]   *O you seed of Abraham his servant; you sons of Jacob his chosen.*

Semen Abraham, servi eius; filii Iacob, electi eius.

104{105}[5] *Mementote,* remember, O Christ's faithful, *mirabilium eius quae fecit, his marvelous works which he has done,* assuming human nature for you, dwelling in the world, laying down his soul for the ungodly, washing the feet of his disciples, instituting the Sacrament of his Body and Blood, enduring and admonishing sinners with patience, mercifully inviting you to repentance, and graciously justifying you.[111] Recall also *prodigia eius, his wonders*: how he raised the dead by word alone, how he fed five thousand with five loaves of bread and two fish, how he gave sight to the blind, how he looked into the secrets of the heart, how he commanded the wind and the sea, how he rose again on the third day, how he visited his apostles through closed doors, how he rose up to heaven, how he sent the Holy Spirit in visible form.[112] *Et iudicia oris eius, and the judgments of his mouth,* that is, be mindful of his precepts, counsels, examples, and all the discourses of the Gospel of Christ. For these should be always remembered because of what the Savior said: *Blessed are they who hear the word of God and keep it.*[113] Whence also in Deuteronomy we are enjoined: *Forget not the words of the Lord, and let them not go out of thy heart all the days of your life.*[114] And in Proverbs: *Hear, my son, the instruction of your father, and forsake not the law of your mother,* namely of the Church.[115] 104{105}[6] *Semen,* O you seed, [you] spiritual [seed] *Abraham, of Abraham,* that is, the children of

---

109 Is. 66:19.
110 E. N. Denis skips verses three and four in his moral commentary of this Psalm.
111 John 13:5; Matt. 26:26–28.
112 John 11:43; Luke 8:54; 9:14–17; John 9:7; Matt. 9:4; 8:25; Luke 24:5, 7; John 20:19; Acts 1:9; 2:2–4.
113 Luke 11:28.
114 Deut. 4:9.
115 Prov. 1:8.

faith and of obedience,[116] who by believing and obeying follow Abraham, the father of all believers, who obeyed God even to the sacrifice of his son, as Genesis says.[117] We are the children of this Patriarch, believing most fully and most fixedly, and sacrificing ourselves to God through penance and obedience. *Filii, you sons,* [you] spiritual [sons], *Iacob, of Jacob,* who by struggling against vices are sons of Jacob, whose name is interpreted as "supplantor."[118]

104{105}[7] *He is the Lord our God: his judgments are in all the earth.*

Ipse Dominus Deus noster; in universa terra iudicia eius.

104{105}[8] *He has remembered his covenant forever: the word which he commanded to a thousand generations.*

Memor fuit in saeculum testamenti sui; verbi quod mandavit in mille generationes.

104{105}[9] *Which he made to Abraham; and his oath to Isaac;*

Quod disposuit ad Abraham, et iuramenti sui ad Isaac;

104{105}[7] *Ipse, He,* Christ is *Dominus Deus noster, is the Lord our God* to whom Thomas said, *My Lord and my God;*[119] *in universa terra iudicia eius, his judgments are in all the earth,* that is, the precepts, counsels, and just censures of the Lord Savior are preached, written, and divulged

---

116 E. N. "There is no doubt that Christian moral teaching, even in its Biblical roots, acknowledges the specific importance of a fundamental choice which qualifies the moral life and engages freedom on a radical level before God. It is a question of the decision of faith, of the obedience of faith (*cf.* Rom 16:26) 'by which man makes a total and free self-commitment to God, offering the full submission of intellect and will to God as he reveals.'" John Paul II, *Veritatis splendor,* 66 (quoting VII, *Dei Verbum,* 5).

117 Gen. 22:10. E. N. "This is the climax of Abraham's faith. Abraham is tested by that God in whom he had placed his trust, that God from whom he had received the promise about the distant future: 'Through Isaac shall your descendants be named.' (Heb 11: 18) He is called, however, to offer in sacrifice to God precisely that Isaac, his only son, on whom his every hope is based, in accordance moreover with the divine promise.... Through faith Abraham emerges victorious from this test, a dramatic test that challenged his faith directly. 'He considered,' writes the author of the Letter to the Hebrews, 'that God was able to raise men even from the dead.' (11: 9).... Abraham never stopped believing. Indeed, his faith in God's promise reached its climax. He thought that 'God was able to raise men even from the dead.'.... And his faith, his total abandonment to God, did not disappoint him. It is written: 'hence he did receive him back.' (Heb 1: 19) Isaac was given back to him because he believed in God completely and unconditionally." John Paul II, Homily: Commemoration of Abraham, Feb. 23, 2000.

118 E. N. On Jacob as "supplanter," *see* footnote 21-112 in Volume 1.

119 John 20:28.

to the whole world in accordance with that stated by the Apostle [Paul]: Now it is *preached in all creation that is under heaven.*[120]

104{105}[8] *Memor fuit, he has remembered,* Christ himself [has remembered] *in saeculum, forever,* that is, in perpetuity, *testamenti sui, his covenant,* which he instituted in the Last Supper, by which institution the Old Testament was fulfilled and was vacated. Christ remembered this New Testament *in saeculum, forever,* because he commanded it be preached so that it would continue even unto the end of time; and he has approved such preaching by certain miracles, in the way it is written: *But they going forth preached everywhere: the Lord working withal, and confirming the word with signs that followed.*[121] *Verbi quod mandavit in mille, the word which he commanded to a thousand,* that is, to all, *generationes, generations:* for the determinate number is here placed as an indeterminate number.[122] For Christ commanded the word of the Gospel to be preached to all men, and that such [command] be fulfilled even unto the end of the world, in the way that he says in [the Gospel of] Matthew to the Apostles: *Going... teach all nations, ... teaching them to observe all things whatsoever I have commanded you.*[123] For this reason, he says elsewhere: *Why do you call me Lord, Lord, and not do the things which I say?*[124] 104{105} [9] *Quod disposuit ad Abraham, which he made to Abraham,* that is, to his spiritual children, as has just now been stated. *Et iuramenti sui, and his oath,* that is, with a firm promise made *ad Isaac, to Isaac,* that is, to the Christian people, who glory not in themselves, but in the Lord,[125] who were taught by the Apostle always to rejoice,[126] and to heartily exult in all tribulations, happy that they might be conformed to Christ in his Passion and be corrected with the elect while in this world. From these considerations the hope with great certainty to be those children who are described in Revelation: *Such as I love, I rebuke and chastise.*[127] Indeed, Isaac is interpreted as meaning "laughter" or "joy."[128]

---

120 Col. 1:23.

121 Mark 16:20.

122 E. N. The adjective thousand is not to be understood literally (as a determinative number), but loosely, poetically (as indeterminate).

123 Matt. 28:19b–20a. E. N. The verse continues: *And I am with you all days, even to the consummation of the world.*

124 Luke 6:46.

125 *Cf.* 2 Cor. 10:17: *But he that glories, let him glory in the Lord.*

126 *Cf.* Phil. 4:4.

127 Rev. 3:19a.

128 E. N. "And Abraham called the name of his son, whom Sara bore him, Isaac.... And Sara said: God has made a laughter for me: whosoever shall hear of it will laugh with me." Gen. 21:6.

104{105}[10] *And he appointed the same to Jacob for a law, and to Israel for an everlasting testament.*

Et statuit illud Iacob in praeceptum, et Israel in testamentum aeternum.

104{105}[11] *Saying: To you will I give the land of Canaan, the line of your inheritance.*[129]

Dicens: Tibi dabo terram Chanaan, funiculum hereditatis vestrae.

104{105}[10] *Et statuit illud,* and he appointed the same covenant *Iacob,* to Jacob, that is, to the Christian faithful trampling upon vices, *in praeceptum, for a law* faithfully observed; *et Israel, and to Israel,* that is, the people contemplating heavenly things by faith, *in testamentum aeternum, for an everlasting testament,* since they do not expect another law or another future covenant, but they know it to be the last: for this reason it is called "New," because it was given after the law of Moses, and "Eternal," because it will never be replaced by another law. For law of the Antichrist will be a perversity and abuse of law; and it will not be of God, nor will it last long, nor will it wholly extinguish the law of Christ.[130]

104{105}[11] Christ *dicens, saying* to the people believing in him: *Tibi dabo terram Chanaan, To you will I give the land of Canaan,* that is, the land flowing with milk and honey, which, according to the witness of Moses, is the most excellent of all the earth.[131] By this is indicated the land of the living, the fatherland of the blessed, where *they shall be inebriated with the plenty of the house* of God.[132] Whence in John, he says: *I go to prepare a place for you;* and again, *I will come again and will take you to myself, so that where I am you also may be.*[133] *Funiculum hereditatis vestrae, the line of your inheritance,* that is, that part delivered to any just man, or what will occur to any man by a kind of allotment. For Christ gives to the elect the land of the living in this way, that he grants to each person a certain mansion in accordance with the exigencies of

---

129 E. N. I have departed from the Douay-Rheims which translates *funiculum* as "lot," rather than rope or cord or line.

130 E. N. The "law" of the Antichrist clearly will not wholly supplant the law of Christ, since the Church is indefectible. The principle of St. Augustine — that an unjust law is no law at all, *lex iniusta non est lex* — would apply *a fortiori* to the "law" of the Antichrist. On the law of Christ: "If anyone shall say that Christ Jesus has been given by God to men as a Redeemer in whom they should trust, and not also as a legislator, whom they should obey: let him be anathema." DS 1571 (Council of Trent).

131 Deut. 8:7–10.

132 Ps. 35:9a.

133 John 14:2a, 3.

his merits. For this reason, he says: *In my Father's house there are many mansions.*[134] Therefore, as the land of Canaan was distributed to the children of Israel in parts according to the demands of the lots which they cast,[135] so the mansions in the region of the blessed will be divided among the elect in congruity with their merits.[136]

104{105}[12] *When they were but a small number: yea very few, and sojourners therein.*

Cum essent numero brevi, paucissimi et incolae eius.

104{105}[13] *And they passed from nation to nation, and from one kingdom to another people.*

Et pertransierunt de gente in gentem, et de regno ad populum alterum.

104{105}[12] *Cum essent, when they were* Christians in the early Church *numero brevi, but a small number,* namely one hundred and twenty, as is revealed in the Acts of the Apostles,[137] *paucissimi et incolae eius, yea very few, and sojourners therein,* that is, when Christians were exceedingly few, they existed (literally) in the land of Canaan, for the Church first began in Jerusalem and Judea. Or [we can understand it thus], *very few therein,* that is, of the land of the living of the heavenly fatherland: for in the beginning the Church was very small; indeed even now (regrettably!)

---

134 John 14:2a.

135 Joshua 14:2.

136 E. N. "Star differs from star in glory." 1 Cor. 14:41. As St. Thomas puts it in ST Ia, q. 12, art. 6, c., the blessed have greater capacity for happiness than others based upon their charity and the light of glory given them "for where charity is greater, there is greater desire.... Hence, he who possess more charity will see God more perfectly and will be more blessed." That this is the case is dogma. Council of Florence, *Laetentur caeli*, DS 1305 (The blessed "are received immediately into heaven and see clearly God himself, one and three, as he is, though some more perfectly than others, according to the diversity of their merits.") In her autobiography, St. Thérèse of Lisieux describes how her saintly mother explained this truth: "I once told you how astonished I was that God does not give equal glory in heaven to all His chosen. I was afraid they were not at all equally happy. You made me bring Daddy's tumbler and put it by the side of my thimble. You filled them both with water and asked me which was fuller. I told you they were both full to the brim and that it was impossible to put more water in them than they could hold. And so, Mother darling, you made me understand that in heaven God will give His chosen their fitting glory and that the last will have no reason to envy the first. By such means, you made me understand the most sublime mysteries and gave my soul its essential food." St. Thérèse of Lisieux, *The Story of a Soul* (New York: Double Day, 2001), 20.

137 Acts 1:15.

they are few to whom that passage of the Apostle pertains: *Our conversation is in heaven.*[138] 104{105}[13] *Et pertransierunt, and they passed,* the blessed Apostles and the other disciples [passed] *de gente in gentem, et de regno ad populum alterum; from nation to nation, and from kingdom to another people.* This especially is manifested in Paul, who, as he himself testified, travelled through Macedonia, Galatia, Spain, and Italy. So also did Peter first preach in Judea, and thereafter in Antioch, and finally in Italy. *Their sound has gone forth into all the earth.*[139]

104{105}[14]   *He suffered no man to hurt them: and he reproved kings for their sakes.*

Non reliquit hominem nocere eis; et corripuit pro eis reges.

104{105}[15]   *Touch not my anointed: and do no evil to my prophets.*

Nolite tangere christos meos, et in prophetis meis nolite malignari.

104{105}[14] *Non reliquit, he did not suffer,* Christ [abandoned], *hominem, no man* whoever they might be *nocere eis, to hurt them* insofar as interior salvation was concerned; for though some might have been allowed to have been afflicted externally or bodily, yet he conferred great sustenance to the interior of men, as the Apostle stated to the Romans: *We know that to them that love God, all things work together unto good.*[140] For this reason, St. Paul did not regard his persecutors as adversaries, but as proponents, saying: *If God be for us, who is against us?*[141] Regarding this is also written: *And who is he that can hurt you, if you be zealous of good?*[142] Literally speaking, Christ prohibited many corrupt men from harming bodily the Apostles and the rest of the saints, in the manner that we read in the Acts of the Apostles of the freeing of the Apostles from jail through an angel.[143] *Et corripuit pro eis reges, and he reproved kings for their sakes.* For God put to death with an unforeseen and horrible death many kings and princes

---

138 Phil 3:20a. *E. N.* The word *conversatio,* here translated "conversation" in the Douay-Rheims, means manner of living, habit of life, conduct, though it is not frequently used in that manner any longer. Thus 1 Pet. 3:1–2 speaks of "the conversation of the wives," and "your chaste conversation." This sense of the word is preserved in a negative sense in the phrase "criminal conversation" as being equivalent to an unchaste conversation, namely, the act of adultery.
139 Ps. 18:5a.
140 Rom. 8:28a.
141 Rom. 8:31b.
142 1 Pet. 3:13.
143 Acts 5:18–20.

because of their persecution of the Christians, as is contained in the Acts of the Apostles regarding Herod;[144] and this is copiously narrated in the legends of the Saints.[145] He reproved them not only admonishing them, but by scourging them; not with word, but by deed, saying: **104{105} [15]** *Nolite tangere, do not touch* violently *christos meos, my anointed,* that is, Christians anointed by Baptism, and who also are bodily anointed in Confirmation and Ordination, but spiritually anointed by the Holy Spirit, according to that stated by the Apostle to the Galatians: *God has sent the Spirit of his Son into your hearts, crying Abba (Father).*[146] *Et in prophetis meis, and ... to my prophets,* that is, to those preaching the word of God, who sermonize regarding the future age of the Blessed, eternal things, and also the damnation of the reprobate, *nolite malignari, do no evil.* For God will strictly avenge himself to such persons for such injuries, just as he has witnessed by Zechariah: *He that touches you, touches the apple of my eye.*[147]

104{105}[16]   *And he called a famine upon the land: and he broke in pieces all the support of bread.*

      Et vocavit famem super terram; et omne firmamentum panis contrivit.

104{105}[17]   *He sent a man before them: Joseph, who was sold for a slave.*

      Misit ante eos virum; in servum venundatus est Ioseph.

104{105}[16] *Et vocavit, and he called,* God the Trinity [called] *famem super terram, a famine upon the land.* Of this famine it is written: *Behold the days come, says the Lord, and I will send forth a famine into the land: not a famine of bread, nor a thirst of water, but of hearing the word of the Lord.*[148] This famine will precede the coming of Christ, because at

---

144 Acts 12:23: *And forthwith an angel of the Lord struck him [Herod], because he had not given the honor to God: and being eaten up by worms, he gave up the ghost.*
145 E. N. One could start with Lactantius (*ca.* 250–*ca.* 325) and his *Of the Manner in Which the Persecutors Died (De mortibus persecutorum).* "They who insulted over the Divinity, lie low; they who cast down the holy temple, are fallen with more tremendous ruin; and the tormentors of just men have poured out their guilty souls amidst plagues inflicted by Heaven, and amidst deserved tortures. For God delayed to punish them, that, by great and marvelous examples, He might teach posterity that He alone is God, and that with fit vengeance He executes judgment on the proud, the impious, and the persecutors." *The Anti-Nicene Fathers* (New York: Charles Scribner, 1905), Vol. VII, 301.
146 Gal. 4:6.
147 Zech. 2:8b.
148 Amos 8:11.

that time there will have been a long time without there being Prophet other than John the Baptist. And so, at that time the scarcity of spiritual nutrient, namely, the preaching of the word of God which the good always desire, was most great.

Whence, in order to alleviate this famine, 104{105}[17] *misit, he sent,* God the Father [sent], *ante eos, before them.* [that is,] those suffering famine, *virum, a man,* namely, Christ: who from the beginning of his conception was a man, as is stated by the prophet Jeremiah: *A woman shall compass a man.*[149] For, according to that which Christ told the Jews, the Father sent his Son to men so that he might spiritually appease their hunger: *My Father gives you the true bread from heaven;*[150] and again, *Labor not for the meat which perishes, but that which endures unto life everlasting.*[151] For the Father foresigned this. *In servum venundatus est Ioseph; Joseph who was sold for a slave.* That attractive and holy patriarch Joseph, in person, deed, and action was set up as a figure of Christ. For he was sold for thirty pieces of silver, as it states in Genesis,[152] prefiguring the selling out of Christ done for the same quantity of silver, as we read in Matthew.[153] Similarly, the transplanting of Joseph into another region was a sign of the mission of Christ in the world; and the incarceration of Joseph signifies the capture and passion of Christ. And so, *for a slave,* that is, in accordance with the will of the wicked, Joseph, that is Christ signified by Joseph, was sold. For Judas Iscariot sold him to the Jews that they might do to him all things which they wanted to do to him: this they also did, in the manner Christ spoke to them, as Luke states: *This is your hour, and the power of darkness,*[154] that is, I am now allowing you to have dominion over me so that you might do to me what you will.

104{105}[18]   *They humbled his feet in fetters: the iron pierced his soul.*

Humiliaverunt in compedibus pedes eius; ferrum pertransiit animam eius.

104{105}[19]   *Until his word came. The word of the Lord inflamed him.*

Donec veniret verbum eius, eloquium Domini inflammavit eum.

---

149 Jer. 31:22b.
150 John 6:32b.
151 John 6:27a.
152 Gen. 37:28. E. N. The Sixto-Clementine Vulgate reads "twenty pieces of silver." Some versions, however, read "thirty pieces of silver." Others read "twenty gold coins."
153 Matt. 26:14.
154 Luke 22:53b.

104{105}[20] *The king sent, and he released him: the ruler of the people, and he set him at liberty.*

Misit rex, et solvit eum; princeps populorum, et dimisit eum.

104{105}[18] *Humiliaverunt,* the Jews [humbled] *in compedibus, in fetters,* that is, in chains, *pedes eius, his feet,* namely [the feet] of Christ, that is, they bound Christ himself with chains. For the tying up of the entire body is designated through the humiliation of the feet: and especially during the night, when he was in the house of the high priest, were the feet of the most holy Savior bound. The Jews also clamped chains around the neck of Christ when they seized him; afterwards these were shown for a long time in Jerusalem to pilgrims with great devotion. *Ferrum, the iron,* that is, the sensible pain, with great compassion and most vehement sorrow, *petransiit animam eius, pierced his soul,* namely, [the soul] of Christ during the time of the Passion. For this reason, he said, *My soul is sorrowful even unto death;*[155] and, *My God, my God, why have you forsaken me?*[156] 104{105}[19] *Donec veniret verbum eius, until his word came,* that is, until that time his words — *For the things concerning me have an end* — were fulfilled.[157] Or [alternatively], *until his word* where he said: *It is finished;*[158] and, *Father, into your hands I commend my spirit.*[159] Or [in the further alternative], *until his word,* that is, until he fulfilled all the things which were prophesied about the Passion of Christ.

Eloquium Domini inflammavit eum, the word of the Lord inflamed him. For whatever Christ said as man proceeded by divine inspiration. The word of God inflamed Christ because he poured forth preaching most powerful words and fiery words, he was most eloquent, and foretold whatever was to occur in the future to him. For this is written in Matthew, *He was teaching them as one having power, and not as the scribes and Pharisees;*[160] and with John, *Never did man speak like this man.*[161] 104{105}[20] *Misit rex, the king sent,* that is, the sublime God, of whom is said in the book of Esther, *Lord, almighty King;*[162] *et solvit eum, and he released him,* that is, he led Christ forth from death, and from his sepulcher, and from the bonds of suffering, in the manner that is attested in Acts by Peter: *God*

---

155 Matt. 26:38a.
156 Mark 15:34b.
157 Luke 22:37.
158 John 19:30.
159 Luke 22:37.
160 Matt. 7:29.
161 John 7:46.
162 Esther 13:9a.

has raised up Jesus, *having loosed the sorrows of hell.*[163] *Princeps populorum, the ruler of the people,* that is, God, the Lord of all nations, sent, exercising his power, *et dimisit eum, and he set him at liberty,* that is, he led out Christ from the limbo of hell, according to that stated in Acts: *Neither was he left in hell, nor did his flesh see corruption.*[164]

104{105}[21] *He made him master of his house, and ruler of all his possession.*

Constituit eum dominum domus suae, et principem omnis possessionis suae.

104{105}[21] *Constituit eum dominum domus suae, he made him master of his house,* that his head of the Church, *et principem omnis possessionis suae, and ruler of all his possessions,* that is, of all creatures. And for this reason, John says about Christ: *The Father loves the Son: and he has given all things into his hand.*[165] And Christ says in Matthew: *All power is given to me in heaven and in earth.*[166] God the Trinity placed Christ the man in authority not only over the Church militant, but also the Church triumphant, according to that which the Apostle said to the Ephesians: God set him *on his right hand in the heavenly places, and ... above all principality, and power, and virtue, and dominion.*[167] A figure of this is also that Joseph was made the lord of all the lands of Egypt, and he was called the *Savior of the world,* as we read in Genesis.[168] But this seems to contradict that which is seen contained in the book of Job: *What other has he appointed over the earth? Or whom has he set over the world which he made?*[169] It seems [from the words of Job], therefore, that God did not set Christ as ruler of all creatures. In response, this [scriptural] authority intends only to assert that God did not place in command another as provider or ruler in the sense that he would cease from being the provider and ruler of the world: and this is true.[170]

---

163 Acts 2:24a.
164 Acts 2:31.
165 John 3:35.
166 Matt. 28:18.
167 Eph. 1:20b, 21a.
168 Gen. 41:44–45.
169 Job 34:13.
170 E. N. This is a bit cryptic, but what Denis is trying to articulate is what St. Thomas articulates in ST III, q. 59, art. 6, arg. 3 and ad 3 in the context of handling the question of whether Christ is the ruler of the angels. In fact, Thomas cites Job 34:13 in the argument, and answers it succinctly observing that—consistent with

104{105}[22] *That he might instruct his princes as himself, and teach his ancients wisdom.*

Ut erudiret principes eius sicut semetipsum, et senes eius prudentiam doceret.

So, therefore, God placed Christ at the head of the Church, **104{105} [22]** *ut erudiret principes eius, that he might instruct his princes,* that is, the Apostles: of whom is said in a Psalm above, *The princes of the people are gathered together with the God of Abraham;*[171] *sicut semetipsum, as himself,* that is, so faithfully as if they were the same as him. Or [alternatively], *as himself,* that is, regarding divine and heavenly realities by the illumination of the Holy Spirit of those things of which he was informed by the Holy Spirit. And this Christ has done to such an extent, as he stated: *I will not now call you servants, . . . but I have called you friends, because all things whatsoever I have heard of my Father, I have made known to you.*[172] *Et senes eius, and his ancients,* that is, the previously-mentioned rulers and the Apostles and those who imitate them, who all had possessed a manner of life with the seriousness of the ancients, *prudentiam, wisdom,* that is, the knowledge of what to do or of morals, *doceret, he might teach.* This Christ did most copiously in the Gospel, in which he set forth a most moral example, the most outstanding counsels, and the most salubrious commandments.

104{105}[23] *And Israel went into Egypt: and Jacob was a sojourner in the land of Ham.*

Et intravit Israel in Aegyptum; et Iacob accola fuit in terra Cham.

104{105}[24] *And he increased his people exceedingly: and strengthened them over their enemies.*

Et auxit populum suum vehementer, et firmavit eum super inimicos eius.

104{105}[23] *Et intravit Israel, and Israel went,* that is, Christ who saw God by sight [went], *in Aegyptum, into Egypt,* that is, into the world, through the Incarnation, as he asserted in John: *I came forth from the*

Job — God did not set another [person that is a man] as universal provider or ruler "since the Lord Jesus Christ is one [divine person], and he is at the same time God and man." The Incarnation solves the apparent contradiction between Job 34:13 and Ps. 104:21.

171 Ps. 46:10a.

172 John 15:15.

Father and am come into the world.[173] For, as is stated in the book of Revelation, by Egypt is indicated the world: *Their bodies shall lie in the streets of the great city, which is called spiritually, Sodom and Egypt, where their Lord also was crucified.*[174] *Et Iacob, and Jacob,* that is, Christ, the supplanter of all vices, *who did not sin,*[175] as he professed about himself: *The prince of this world comes, and in me he has not anything;*[176] *accola fuit, was a sojourner,* that is, a wayfarer and a pilgrim, *in terra Cham, in the land of Ham,* that is, in Egypt or in the world, as has already been explained. Whence Jeremiah speaking of Christ said: *Why will you be a stranger in the land, and as a wayfaring man turning in to lodge?*[177] **104{105}[24]** *Et auxit, and he increased,* Christ [increased] *populum suum, his people,* the faithful, *vehementer, exceedingly* in both merit and in number—especially in the early Church—through the preaching of the Apostles, converting practically the whole world to the faith. For this reason, Luke affirms in the Acts of the Apostles: *The Lord increased daily together such as should be saved.*[178] *Et firmavit eum, and he strengthened them,* namely, the Christian people, *super inimicos eius, over their enemies,* that is, the world, the flesh, and the devil. For he gave them the power to resist and to prevail over the temptations of demons, the concupiscence of the flesh, and the persecution of ungodly men;[179] and at length he subjected the Roman Empire to the Christian faith during the time of Constantine. Whence it is stated in Micah: *Your hand shall be lifted up over your enemies, and all your enemies shall be cut off.*[180] And elsewhere: *The nation and the kingdom that will not serve you shall perish.*[181]

104{105}[25]   *He turned their heart to hate his people: and to deal deceitfully with his servants.*

Convertit cor eorum, ut odirent populum eius, et dolum facerent in servos eius.

104{105}[26]   *He sent Moses his servant: Aaron the man whom he had chosen.*

Misit Moysen, servum suum, Aaron quem elegit ipsum.

---

173 John 16:28a.
174 Rev. 11:8.
175 1 Pet. 2:22a.
176 John 14:20b.
177 Jer. 14:8b.
178 Acts 2:47b.
179 Matt. 10:1, 8; Mark 16:17–18.
180 Micah 5:9.
181 Is. 60:12a.

104{105}[27] *He gave them power to show his signs, and his wonders in the land of Ham.*

Posuit in eis verba signorum suorum, et prodigiorum in terra Cham.

104{105}[25] *Convertit cor eorum, ut odirent populum eius, he turned their heart to hate his people:* that is, Christ by a just judgment permitted the hearts of the unfaithful and depraved to turn in hatred of the Christians; *et dolum facerent in servos eius, and to deal deceitfully with his servants,* namely, the Christians. The Jews were the first to harbor this hate and this deceit against the early Church, as is frequently displayed in the Acts of the Apostles.[182] Thereafter, the Roman emperors with their supporters acted against the Church of Christ invidiously and deceitfully, killing many thousands of martyrs. Finally, this is also done by heretics and false brethren. **104{105}[26]** *Misit Moysen servum suum, Aaron quem elegit ipsum; he sent Moses his servant: Aaron the man whom he had chosen.* By Moses and Aaron who were sent to the children of Israel in Egypt is designated the Apostles who travelled throughout the world so as to convert the people of the elect. **104{105}[27]** *Posuit, he gave,* Christ [gave], *in eis, them,* that is, in the Apostles and their successors, *verba signorum suorum et prodigiorum, his signs and his wonders* because by those great miracles he caused, *in terra Cham, in the land of Ham,* that is, throughout the whole world signified by the land of Ham. Whence, in the Gospel of Matthew he said to the Apostles: *Heal the sick, raise the dead, cleanse the lepers, cast out devils.*[183]

104{105}[28] *He sent darkness, and made it obscure: and grieved not his words.*

Misit tenebras, et obscuravit; et non exacerbavit sermones suos.

Thereafter is set forth the plagues of Egypt, not all of them, but seven or eight of them: and they also are not set forth here in the order that they occurred. **104{105}[28]** *Misit tenebras, he sent darkness,* that is, the blindness of mind in reprobate souls, *et obscuravit, and made it obscure* [that is,] permissively [made obscure] their intellect; *et non exacerbavit sermones suos, and grieved not his words,* that is, he graciously illumined them to repentance and also made them willing to obtain belief and obedience, and so he abated his threats. This is the first plague of worldly men and from which are born the other six [plagues].

---

182 Acts 13:50; 14:18; 18:12–13.
183 Matt. 10:8a.

104{105}[29]   *He turned their waters into blood, and destroyed their fish.*

Convertit aquas eorum in sanguinem, et occidit pisces eorum.

104{105}[30]   *Their land brought forth frogs, in the inner chambers of their kings.*

Edidit terra eorum ranas in penetralibus regum ipsorum.

104{105}[31]   *He spoke, and there came divers sorts of flies and sciniphs in all their coasts.*

Dixit, et venit coenomyia, et ciniphes in omnibus finibus eorum.

104{105}[29] *Convertit aquas eorum in sanguinem, he turned their waters into blood*: that is, he permitted their wisdom to be carnal, animal-like, and diabolic so that with a proud mind they would disdain the simplicity of faith, and they would expound the sacred Scriptures perversely. This applies especially to heretics. *Et occidit pisces eorum, and he destroyed their fish*: that is, he permitted the souls of the disciples of such expounders and teachers to die or to be without faith and grace. For disciples gather themselves around certain teachers somewhat like fish. **104{105}[30]** *Edidit terra eorum, and their land brought forth*, that is, the hearts of worldly men [brought forth], *ranas, frogs*, that is, garrulous loquacity and the din of sin, as the Apostle said to Timothy: *And their speech spreads like cancer;*[184] *in penetralibus regum ipsorum, in the inner chambers of their king*, that is, in the homes and palace of the rulers of the men just mentioned. For these rulers and potentates lure them with adulatory and fraudulent words, and they labor to have them behave like them. **104{105}[31]** *Dixit, et venit cynomyia et scinifes; he spoke, and there came divers sorts of flies and sciniphs.* Through these frightfully stinging flies and beasts we understand *detractors, hateful to God,*[185] and the remorse of sinful conscience,[186] or the pricks of synderesis[187] which always inclines

---

184 2 Tim. 2:17a.
185 Rom. 1:30a.
186 E. N. "It may seem strange that remorse could ever get us into trouble instead of out of it. On the contrary, nothing is more common. Like every moral impulse, remorse can be displaced. It can refuse the relief of repentance and seek alleviation in another way instead. In the short term, remorse can even be palliated by further wrongdoing." J. Budziszewski, *The Revenge of Conscience: Politics and the Fall of Man* (Eugene, OR: Wipf & Stock 1999), 131.
187 E. N. Synderesis or synteresis (the "spark" of conscience) is a special natural facility, power, or habit in our soul disposing us to know the means which lead to our end, and by which we know the universal principles of natural law or right. It is distinguished from conscience which is an act of judgment or re-assessment applying those principles or natural law to particular situations.

to the good and objects to evil. For this reason, Isaiah says: *Their worm shall not die.*[188]

104{105}[32] *He gave them hail for rain, a burning fire in the land.*

Posuit pluvias eorum grandinem, ignem comburentem in terra ipsorum.

104{105}[34] *He spoke, and the locust came, and the bruchus, of which there was no number.*[189]

Dixit, et venit locusta, et bruchus cujus non erat numerus.

104{105}[36] *And he slew all the firstborn in their land: the firstfruits of all their labor.*

Et percussit omne primogenitum in terra eorum, primitias omnis laboris eorum.

104{105}[32] *Posuit pluvias eorum grandinem, he gave them hail for rain:* that is, God gave the unbeliever great anxiety and many afflictions of heart in place of the dew and refreshment of the grace of God, according to that stated in the book of Job: *Distress shall surround him, as a king that is prepared for the battle.*[190] And again: *The sound of dread is always in his ears: and when there is peace, he always suspects treason.*[191] He also gave *ignem comburentem in terra ipsorum, a burning fire in the land,* that is, evil desires in the body of the wicked, according to that which the Apostle said to the Romans: *God delivered them up to shameful affections, . . . to dishonor their own bodies among themselves.*[192] 104{105}[34] *Dixit, et venit locusta et bruchus, cuius non erat numerus; he spoke, and the locust came, and the bruchus, of which there was no number.* By locusts and bruchus (which are small pests which devour the plants and the fruits of the earth) are understood repeaters of deplorable vices or those with an arrogance of mind or vainglory. For these destroy the freshness and grace in the soul and displace the fruits of an earlier manner of life.[193] 104{105}[36] *Et percussit omne primogenitum in terra; and he slew all the firstborn in the land* of Egypt: that is, God removed faith, the principle of all spiritual edification, from the soul of perverse

---

188 Is. 66:24a.
189 *E. N.* Denis skips over verse 104:33 and 104:35.
190 Job 15:24b.
191 Job 15:21.
192 Rom. 1, 26a, 21b.
193 *E. N.* Denis literally says that the repetition of vices, the pride of the mind, or vainglory — the locusts and weevils of the soul — "destroy the greenness (*virorem*) and grace in the soul (*mentis*)."

men;[194] and so he destroyed *primitias omnis laboris eorum, the firstfruits of all their labor*, because without faith nothing is acceptable to God.[195] For *the unfaithful deals unfaithfully*, as is stated in Isaiah.[196] Also according to the Apostle [Paul], *All that is not of faith is sin.*[197]

104{105}[37]   *And he brought them out with silver and gold: and there was not among their tribes one that was feeble.*

Et eduxit eos cum argento et auro, et non erat in tribubus eorum infirmus.

104{105}[38]   *Egypt was glad when they departed: for the fear of them lay upon them.*

Laetata est Aegyptus in profectione eorum, quia incubuit timor eorum super eos.

104{105}[37] *Et eduxit, and he brought out*, Christ [brought out], *eos, them*, that is the faithful and the elect from spiritual Egypt, and from the communion of the wicked, and the darkness of ignorance, *cum argento, with silver*, that is, with knowledge of created things, *et auro, and gold*, that is wisdom of divine things. Or [we can understand it this way], *with silver*, that is, with faith; *and gold*, that is, with charity: regarding which Revelation states, *I counsel you to buy of me gold fire tried.*[198] Or [alternatively], *with silver and gold*, that is, with natural philosophy and study, which those converted to Christ adapted from the philosophers and brought with them. For it was given to them to philosophize for our sakes, so that we might use natural philosophy to the service of the Christian faith.[199] *Et non erat in tribubus eorum, and there was not*

---

194 E. N. *"Faith is a gift of God, a supernatural virtue infused by him.* 'Before this faith can be exercised, man must have the grace of God to move and assist him; he must have the interior helps of the Holy Spirit, who moves the heart and converts it to God, who opens the eyes of the mind and 'makes it easy for all to accept and believe the truth.'" CCC § 153 (quoting VII, *Dei Verbum*, 5). Since faith is a gift, a grace, it follows that it can be lost.

195 *Cf.* Heb. 11:6a: *Without faith it is impossible to please God.*

196 E. N. The Douay Rheims disguises the difference between belief and fidelity. *Qui incredulus est infideliter agit*, "he who does not believe, acts unfaithfully."

197 Rom. 14:23b.

198 Rev. 3:18a.

199 E. N. Origen famously likened pagan philosophy as one of the *spolia Aegypticaca*, "Egyptian spoils," and recommended to his correspondent, Gregory Thaumaturgus, that he "extract from the philosophy of the Greeks what may serve as a course of study or a preparation for Christianity," so that it should be a "fellow-helper" to Christianity. "Letter to Gregory" in *Translations of the Writings of the Fathers* (Edinburgh: T & T

among their tribes, that is, in the congregation of Christians, *infirmus, one that was feeble*, in soul, because as also Paul says: *When I am weak, then I am powerful. For power is made perfect in infirmity.*[200] **104{105} [38]** *Laetata est Aegyptus in profectione eorum, Egypt was glad when they departed*: that is, secularly-minded men, the ungodly, and the unbelievers were happy by the Christians being separated from them; *quia incubit timor eorum, for the fear of them lay*, that is, fear of the Christians fell, *super eos, upon them*, that is, the unfaithful. This was literally applicable for a period of time, whereby Christ clearly struck the unbelievers because of the persecutions they caused against the Christians, as Ambrose refers to in the legend of St. Agnes:[201] and then that the unbelievers chose to leave the Christians alone, lest they be afflicted even more severely.

104{105}[39] *He spread a cloud for their protection, and fire to give them light in the night.*

Expandit nubem in protectionem eorum, et ignem ut luceret eis per noctem.

104{105}[39] *Expandit, he spread*, Christ [spread], *nubes, a cloud*, that is the grace of the Holy Spirit, *in protectionem eorum, for their protection*, that is, in defense and overshadowing of the souls of the faithful against the heat of temptation and of the desires of the flesh; *et ignem, and fire*, that is, the ray of truth and saving wisdom, or the fervor of charity that expands, indeed, infuses their hearts, *ut luceret eis per noctem, to give them light in the night*, that is, in all adversity as well as danger, so that they may not go astray from the way in their exile, but may be led by the guidance of grace to the heavenly homeland, as the Apostle says: *May God . . . keep your hearts and minds.*[202] *Whence also Christ in the Gospel says: I am come to cast fire on the earth; and what will I, but that it burn?*[203]

Clark 1869), Vol. 10, 888. "[E]very Christian philosophy will be traversed, impregnated, nourished by Christianity as by a blood that circulates in it, or rather, like a life that animates it. One will never be able to say that here the philosophical ends and the Christian begins; it will be integrally Christian and integrally philosophical or it will not be." Étienne Gilson, "The Notion of Christian Philosophy," in Reason Fulfilled by Revelation: The 1930s Christian Philosophy Debates in France (Washington, DC: CUA Press, 2011), 136. (Gregory B. Sadler, trans. and ed.).

200 2 Cor. 12:10b, 9a.

201 *E. N.* The reference is to St. Ambrose's *On Virginity. De virginibus*, I, 2, PL 16, 189–90.

202 Phil. 4:7.

203 Luke 12:49. *E. N.* Denis replaces the Sixto-Clementine's *ut accendatur* ("that it be kindled") to *ut ardeat* "that it burn").

104{105}[40] *They asked, and the quail came: and he filled them with the bread of heaven.*

Petierunt, et venit coturnix, et pane caeli saturavit eos.

104{105}[41] *He opened the rock, and waters flowed: rivers ran down in the dry land.*

Dirupit petram, et fluxerunt aquae, abierunt in sicco flumina.

104{105}[40] *Petierunt, they asked,* the faithful [asked], *et venit, and it came,* God being the one sending, *coturnix, the quail,* that is, humble thinking. For by quail, a bird which flies close to the ground, one can understand the thought of the humble man who is occupied with inner discussions of his own conscience, and not with scrutinizing of useless heavenly objects nor seeking to understand majestic things. *Et pane caeli, and with the bread of heaven,* that is, with the sacrament of the Eucharist, the Savior *saturavit eos, filled them,* as is stated in Matthew: *While they were at supper, Jesus took bread, and blessed, and broke: and gave to his disciples, and said: Take, and eat. This is my body.*[204] **104{105}[41]** *Dirupit petram, he opened the rock,* that is, God, the Father allowed a soldier's lance to perforate Christ in the Passion, *et fluxerunt aquae, and waters flowed: for there came out ... water,* as John said.[205] *Abierunt, there ran down* through the merit of the Passion of Christ *in sicco, in the dry land,* that is, upon the unfruitful and dry peoples of the world, *flumina, rivers* of wisdom and manifold grace. For these rivers of the Holy Spirit fill those who believed by the preaching of the Apostles. Christ says this regarding these streams: *He that believes in me, as the Scripture says, Out of his belly shall flow rivers of living water.*[206] How this is to be understood is immediately added by the Evangelist: *Now this he said of the Spirit which they should receive, who believed in him.*[207]

104{105}[42] *Because he remembered his holy word, which he had spoken to his servant Abraham.*

Quoniam memor fuit verbi sancti sui, quod habuit ad Abraham, puerum suum.

And then God gives all this to the Christian people, **104{105}[42]** *quoniam memor fuit verbi sancti sui, quod habuit ad Abraham puerum suum; because he remembered his holy word which he had spoken to his*

---

204 Matt. 26:26.
205 John 19:34b.
206 John 7:38.
207 John 7:39.

servant Abraham, saying: *In your seed ... shall all the kindred of the earth be blessed.*[208] And so to fulfil this promise, it was necessary that Christ become incarnate and suffer, and convey said gifts to Christians. In a similar manner, the Apostle [Paul] states: *I say that Christ Jesus was minister of the circumcision ... to confirm the promises made unto the fathers.*[209]

104{105}[43] *And he brought forth his people with joy, and his chosen with gladness.*

Et eduxit populum suum in exsultatione, et electos suos in laetitia.

104{105}[44] *And he gave them the lands of the Gentiles: and they possessed the labors of the people,*

Et dedit illis regiones gentium, et labores populorum possederunt,

104{105}[45] *That they might observe his justifications and seek after his law.*

Ut custodiant iustificationes eius, et legem eius requirant.

104{105}[43] *Et eduxit populum suum*, and he brought forth his people, [he brought forth] the Christians from paganism to Christianity, from a way of living that was vicious to an angelic life, to the way to the fatherland, *in exultatio*, with joy. *Et electos suos*, and his chosen he led in this way *in laetita*, with gladness. **104{105}[44]** *Et dedit illis regiones gentium, [et labores populorum possederunt]*; and he gave them the lands of the Gentiles, [and they possessed the labors of the people].[210] For the lands and kingdoms in which pagans once dwelt were after a time inhabited by Christians. Or [alternatively], *he gave them the land of the Gentiles*, that is, the land of the living or the kingdom of heaven, the bountifulness of which is typified by the bountifulness of their regions in the world.

In the present Psalm we are admonished to recall the benefits of God, to think about his providence over the human race, and from this to praise God, to familiarize others with his marvelous works, to

---

208 Gen. 22:18a, 12:3.

209 Rom. 15:8. E. N. In his *Commentary on Romans*, Denis explains the phrase "minister of the circumcision" as follows: "Christ is called the minister of the circumcision, that is, the preacher and the apostle of the Jews, to whom declared he was especially sent, when he said, *I was not sent but to the sheep that are lost of the house of Israel* (Matt. 15:24)." Doctoris Ecstatici D. Dionysii Cartusiani, Opera Omnia, Vol. 13 (Montreuil: 1901), 110.

210 E. N. The part in brackets replaces Denis's "etc."

unceasingly seek the Lord Creator, desiring his presence, to want no other good finally except the eternal, uncreated, superlatively glorious, and immense God, and unceasingly to hunger for the reward of a holy manner of living. And since this Psalm superficially understood in a literal way does not seem so devout in many places, yet according to its mystical exposition just now expounded, it overflows with all kinds of devotion. And those things which are omitted [in this Article] are clear in the prior exposition [in Article VII].

PRAYER

GOD, WHO SHOWS YOURSELF GREATLY offended by our wickedness, pierce our hearts to repentance, we beseech you, so that we might obtain your mercy, and so that, granted forgiveness of our sins, we might confess you and invoke your name with a clean conscience, and, in return for receiving these benefits, let us tirelessly declare your marvelous works.

Deus, qui conspicis te graviter offensum malis nostris, ad impetrandam misericordiam tuam corda nostra, quaesumus, compunge ad poenitentiam: ut concessa delictorum venia, munda conscientia tibi confiteamur, et nomen tuum invocemus, ac pro acceptis beneficiis mirabilia tua indefessi narremus.

Psalm 105

ARTICLE IX

DECLARATION OF THE ONE HUNDRED AND FIFTH PSALM: CONFITEMINI DOMINO ... QUIS LOQUETUR, ETC. GIVE GLORY TO THE LORD ... WHO SHALL DECLARE, ETC.

105{106}[1] *Alleluia. Confess to the Lord, for he is good: for his mercy endures forever.*[1]

Alleluia. Confitemini Domino, quoniam bonus, quoniam in saeculum misericordia eius.

ASSIGNED TO THIS PSALM NOW BEING explained is a repeated or double Alleluia,[2] since it says: *Alleluia, Alleluia*: which is done either to increase the distinctness or certainty, or to designate the double praise of God, namely the praise along the pilgrim path and in the heavenly fatherland. Whence in the Mass an Alleluia is sung at the beginning of the verse, and it is repeated at the end. In a similar manner John says in Revelation: *I heard ... the voice of the angels in heaven saying, Alleluia ... and again they said, Alleluia.*[3] In addition, as Christ in the Gospel sometimes says once, Amen, but other times repeats it, so some Psalms have for their title one Alleluia, but others have two.

Now this Psalm invites us to a twofold confession, namely of the praise of God and of one's own fault, and so it says: **105{106}[1]** *Confitemini Domino, confess to the Lord* who is good and just, praising him and accusing yourselves, sinners wounded with various vices; and do not draw back from such a confession because of your ingratitude and depravity; *quoniam bonus, for he is good,* the Lord is [good]. For he is naturally, totally, and in every way good, and his nature is infinite and pure goodness. For this reason it is written in Mark: *None is good but one, that is God.*[4] One ought not to despair in any event. Whence in the second book of Chronicles, the most pious Hezekiah spoke thus: *The*

---

1 E. N. I have translated *confitemini* with "confess," and have departed from the Douay-Rheims's "give glory," for reasons explained in the *Commentary*.
2 E. N. The Sixto-Clementine Vulgate contains but one Alleluia.
3 Rev. 19:1, 3a.
4 Mark 10:18b.

Lord who is good will show mercy to all them, who with their whole heart, seek him.[5] And again: *For the Lord your God is kind and merciful, and will not turn away his face from you if you return to him.*[6] *Quoniam in saeculum misericordia eius; for his mercy endures forever*: that is, the mercy of God is eternal, in no manner deficient, and from the beginning of the world it has been poured out upon the elect; never will the pouring out of divine kindness cease, because even in hell the miserable [damned] will be afflicted less that they deserve, and in heaven the elect will be rewarded more than they deserve.

105{106}[2] *Who shall declare the powers of the Lord? Who shall set forth all his praises?*

Quis loquetur potentias Domini, auditas faciet omnes laudes eius?

105{106}[2] *Quis loquetur potentias Domini? Who shall declare the powers of the Lord?* That is, who is able to express how powerful God is? And it says *powers* in plural (though, after all, in God there is but one single power) because of the diverse effects of the divine power. Or [we can look at it this way], by *powers* is understood the great works of God powerfully effected. But since God is of infinite power and omnipotent, no creature has the ability to comprehend him perfectly and explain his power. Therefore, those minds who presume to have the ability to measure the divine power, asserting that God cannot to do things supernaturally and that nothing that exceeds the bounds of reason is to be believed are most insane, since God is able to produce infinitely more things than man can comprehend. Indeed, the blessed and holy God cannot do so many and such great things but that, insofar as his powers within him are concerned, he could make them infinitely more and greater. In short, it is impossible for us to understand and express the effects of divine power. For this reason, Wisdom answers: *With difficulty do we guess aright at things that are upon the earth, and with labor do we find the things that are before us. But the things that are in heaven, who shall search out?*[7] And who *auditas faciet omnes laudes eius, shall set forth all his praises?* That is, who is able to bring forth or to announce to others all the proclamations of the Creator, and how he himself is to be praised? It is as if he were saying, "No one." For when

---

5 2 Chr. 30:18b–19a.

6 2 Chr. 30:9b.

7 Wis. 9:16.

God is praised because of his own goodness and because of his works, to the extent we lack in perfect knowledge of his goodness and his works, to that extent we fail in the fullness of divine praises. For this reason it is written in the book of Job: *For we are wrapped up in darkness ... We cannot find him worthily ... and he is ineffable.*[8] And Ecclesiasticus says: *When you exalt him put forth all your strength, and be not weary: for you can never go far enough.*[9] Yet we do not vainly glory when we praise God, when we do this as greatly and as worthily as we can, since neither the Cherubim nor the Seraphim have the sufficient means to praise him; but with great fear and profound humility let us praise him, as it says in an earlier Psalm: *Rejoice unto him with trembling.*[10]

105{106}[3] *Blessed are they that keep judgment, and do justice at all times.*

Beati qui custodiunt iudicium, et faciunt iustitiam in omni tempore.

105{106}[3] *Beati,* blessed are those already in hope, *qui custodiunt iudicium, are they that keep judgment* of discretion and retribution.[11] For prelates and judges, with regard to those under them, ought to keep both kinds of judgments, discerning their causes and inflicting due punishment. But also everyone ought to judge himself, scrutinizing, accusing, and chastising himself, discerning the good and the evil, and the true and the false [in him]: for there is but one thing that is necessary for our salvation, according to this: *Can he be healed that loves not judgment?*[12] And the Apostle Paul says: *But if we would judge ourselves, we should not be judged.*[13] Moreover, this judgment is greatly acceptable to God, as he reveals through Jeremiah: *If you will separate the precious from the vile, you shall be as my mouth.*[14] *Et*

---

8 Job 37:19b, 23

9 Ecclus. 43:34.

10 Ps. 2:11b.

11 E. N. For the judgment of discretion, *see* footnote 1-39. "God hath *Iudicium discretionis,* no mist, no cloud, no darknesse, no disguise keeps him from discerning, and judgment all our actions." God "hath *Iudicium retributionis,* God knows what is evill, he knows when that evill is done, and he knows how to punishment and recompense that evill." John Donne, "Sermon No. 15," *The Sermons of John Donne* (Berkeley: University of California Press, 1955), Vol. II, 316.

12 Job 34:17a.

13 1 Cor. 11:31.

14 Jer. 15:19b. E. N. In his *Commentary on Jeremiah,* Denis elaborates on the meaning of this verse: "*If you will separate the precious from the vile,* that is, if you will suitably discern the just from the impious, virtues from vices, the true from the false, and bring back the good from the fellowship with evil, *you shall be as my mouth,* that is, you will be to me most dear, and in doing this, you will be like my spokesman: for

faciunt iustitiam, and do justice, following and carrying out that which right reason judges,[15] *in omni tempore, at all times,* that is, perseveringly even unto the end, for, according to the Evangelist, Christ our judge affirms, *he who shall persevere unto the end, he shall be saved.*[16]

105{106}[4]   *Remember us, O Lord, in the favor of your people: visit us with your salvation.*

Memento nostri, Domine, in beneplacito populi tui; visita nos in salutari tuo.

105{106}[4] *Memento nostri, Domine, in beneplacito populi tui; remember us, O Lord, in the favor of your people,* that is, in the infusion or by the infusion of your grace, by which your people are pleasing to you, so that we might please you in the manner that they do. Indeed, God is mindful of all men, since the prophet Amos said: *The Lord has sworn . . . surely I will never forget their works.*[17] But the Prophet [David] prays [in this verse] that God might be mindful of us as he is mindful of his elect. Whence Ezra also pleads: *Remember me, O my God, for good.*[18] *Visita nos in salutari tuo, visit us with your salvation,* that is, in the wholesome and bountiful salvation, so that we might be visited by you through your kindly presence to our salvation, and not by a strict sentence to our damnation in the manner that you visit the reprobate. Regarding this, Zephaniah was told by you: *I will visit upon the men that are settled on their lees.*[19] For in this manner also demons will be visited by

---

a person is called another's mouth if he speaks for another person. Hence Bernard calls Augustine the tongue of the Church." See Doctoris Ecstatici D. Dionysii Cartusiani, *Opera Omnia* (Montreuil: 1900), Vol. 9, 139–40.

15 "For there is a true law: right reason. It is in conformity with nature, is diffused among all men, and is immutable and eternal; its orders summon to duty; its prohibitions turn away from offense. . . . To replace it with a contrary law is a sacrilege; failure to apply even one of its provisions is forbidden; no one can abrogate it entirely." CCC § 1956 (quoting Cicero's *Republic*, III, 33).

16 Matt. 10:22b.

17 Amos 8:7.

18 Neh. 5:19.

19 Zeph. 1:12a. E. N. The Douay-Rheims translates *faecibus* (*faex*), literally, grounds, sediment, dregs, wine-lees. The English word *feces* is derived from this Latin word. In his *Commentary on Zephaniah,* Denis states the following in his literal interpretation of this verse: "*I will visit upon the men that are settled on their lees,* that is, the carnal delights and other most foul vices." In his mystical interpretation, he states: "*I will visit upon the men that are settled on their lees,* that is, whose minds are not elevated to supernal things, but are darkened by the most foul desires." Doctoris Ecstatici D. Dionysii Cartusiani, *Opera Omnia* (Montreuil: 1900), Vol. 10, 576, 580.

you, as Isaiah affirms: *The Lord shall visit with his hard, and great, and strong sword Leviathan ... the crooked serpent.*[20] Or [alternatively]: *Visit us with your salvation,* that is, in Christ, sending him to us. For he is your wisdom, eternal and uncreated, which is sent invisibly and daily to your elect, as is prayed for by some in the book of Wisdom: *Give me, O Lord, wisdom, that sits by your throne;* and again, *send her out of your holy heaven, ... that she may be with me, and labor with me.*[21]

105{106}[5] *That we may see the good of your chosen, that we may rejoice in the joy of your nation: that you may be praised with your inheritance.*

Ad videndum in bonitate electorum tuorum, ad laetandum in laetitia gentis tuae, ut lauderis cum haereditate tua.

But this, O Lord, grant me, **105{106}[5]** *ad vivendum, that we may see,* that is, that we may spiritually see and contemplate now by faith and in the future by sight, *in bonitate electorum tuorum, the good of your chosen,* that is, the goods prepared for your elect. Of these, the Apostle says: *Eye has not seen, nor ear heard, neither has it entered into the heart of man, what things God has prepared for them that love him.*[22] These goods are nothing other than the highest good in whom is the immense plenitude of all good and beauty or its vision and enjoyment. What else does the Prophet [David] pray for other than that we might see God, in whose vision consists beatitude, and our full reward, and final prize? Or [we can see it this way], *the good of your chosen,* that is, in the glory of the blessed in heaven or in the supernatural illumination by which the elect are illuminated by you, because without this illumination our vision and our knowledge are empty and without form. *Ad laetandum in laetitia gentis tuae, that we may rejoice in the joy of your nation,* that is, that we might rejoice with the spiritual joy in which your people take delight in you, now in the hope of future goods, but in the heavenly fatherland in the attainment of the heavenly rewards. Or [alternatively], *in the joy of your nation,* that is, that we might rejoice with your people,

---

20 Is. 27:1. *E. N.* In his Commentary on Isaiah, Denis states: "*The Lord shall visit with his sword,* that is, in the rigor of divine justice, *duro, hard,* that is, with a confuting bitterness.... *And great,* that is, piercing all things, ... *and strong,* that is, omnipotent, which nothing can resist, ... *Leviathan ... the crooked serpent,* that is, upon the devil." Doctoris Ecstatici D. Dionysii Cartusiani, *Opera Omnia* (Montreuil: 1899), Vol. 8, 520.

21 Wis. 9:4, 10.

22 1 Cor. 2:9; Is. 64:4.

and not with this world. And all these things are done to the honor of your name, namely, *ut lauderis cum hereditate tua, that you may be praised with your inheritance*, that is, with the Church of your elect, so that if your elect are praised because they are good, you may be praised of the same good, given that you are the principal cause of good. Or [in the further alternative], *so that you may be praised* in all things and before all things which by grace is with your inheritance, that is, the elect. Or [yet again], *that you may be praised with your inheritance*, that is, by your elect, who are your inheritance existing with you.

105{106}[6]   *We have sinned with our fathers: we have acted unjustly, we have wrought iniquity.*

Peccavimus cum patribus nostris; iniuste egimus, iniquitatem fecimus.

105{106}[6] *Peccavimus cum patribus nostris, we have sinned with our fathers*, that is, as our fathers did, or equally with them, not turning away from but imitating their sin. Transgressing the moral precepts, we have also sinned, *iniuste egimus, we have acted unjustly*, transgressing judicial precepts, *iniquitatem fecimus, we have wrought iniquity*, not following the ceremonial precepts.[23] Or [we can understand it in this way], *we have sinned* against God, *we have acted unjustly* against our neighbor, *we have wrought iniquity* against ourselves.

105{106}[7]   *Our fathers understood not your wonders in Egypt: they remembered not the multitude of your mercies: And they provoked to wrath going up to the sea, even the Red Sea.*

Patres nostri in Aegypto non intellexerunt mirabilia tua; non fuerunt memores multitudinis misericordiae tuae. Et irritaverunt ascendentes in mare, mare Rubrum.

105{106}[8]   *And he saved them for his own name's sake: that he might make his power known.*

Et salvavit eos propter nomen suum, ut notam faceret potentiam suam.

---

23 *E. N.* The moral precepts are based upon the natural moral law (unwritten). The judicial precepts refer to positive laws promulgated by human authority dealing with relations between men. The ceremonial precepts relate to laws laid down by God governing men's relationship with him. ST IaIIae, q. 104, art. 1, c.

105{106}[7] *Patres nostri in Aegypto, our fathers ... in Egypt,* that is, who at one time dwelt in Egypt, *non intellexerunt, understood not* spiritually and prudently *mirabilia tua, your wonders,* which you did through Moses in Egypt, in the Red Sea, and in the desert wilderness, because they did not have regard for the omnipotence of God from such marvels and that God had done such things on their behalf in Egypt and thereafter so that he might protect them, and easily fulfill that which he had promised them. They also did not understand what was figured by those wonders. For this reason, we have contained in Deuteronomy: *Moses called all Israel, and said to them: You have seen all the things that the Lord did before you ... And the Lord has not given you a heart to understand, and eyes to see ... unto this present day.*[24] Whence also the Lord again said through Moses: How long will this multitude *not believe me for all the signs that I have wrought before them?*[25] Pay heed here to the first sin of this people, namely the sin of ignorance. It follows from the vice of ingratitude: *non fuerunt memores, they remembered not,* by giving thanks to you for, *multitudinis misericordiae tuae, the multitude of your mercies,* that is, the many and great acts of compassion you bestowed on their behalf, and that because of them you so heavily afflicted the Egyptians with the ten plagues from which you so lovingly spared them.

Et irritaverunt, and they provoked God and his servant Moses, *ascendentes, going up* from the land of Egypt *in mare, mare Rubro, to the sea, even the Red Sea,*[26] for seeing Pharaoh pursuing them before they entered into the channel of the Red Sea, and lacking confidence in the divine power, they said to Moses: *Perhaps there were no graves in Egypt, therefore you have brought us to die in the wilderness. Why would you do this?*[27] But, as we read else-where,[28] they dared not enter into the Red Sea itself, even though divided,

---

24 Deut. 29:2a, 4. *E. N.* In other words, the Jews did not understand the Christological significance of the wonders that they had experienced (*e.g.,* they did not see the crossing of the Red Sea as a figure of baptism, or the bronze serpent representing the healing grace of the Cross). "[T]he crossing of the Red Sea, literally the liberation of Israel from the slavery of Egypt, announces the liberation wrought by Baptism." CCC § 1221. "[A]lready in the Old Testament, God ordained or permitted the making of images that pointed symbolically toward salvation by the incarnate Word: so it was with the bronze serpent." CCC § 2130.

25 Num. 14:11b.

26 *E. N.* The editor notes a likely error in the text (*in mari, mari* instead of *in mare, mare*). I have followed the Vulgate and Douay-Rheims.

27 Ex. 14:11.

28 *E. N.* Denis refers to "Hist. schol." This is presumably an (unnamed) historical scholium. A scholium is an explanatory comment, usually written in the margins, of the text to explain or interpret it, or give some sort of gloss or commentary on the main text. An anthology of these was called a scholia.

without being strongly admonished by Moses for a long time. 105{106} [8] *Et salvavit eos, and he saved them*, the Lord [saved them], though they were ungrateful and incredulous, from the hand of the Egyptians, not because of their virtues or their merits, but *propter nomen suum, for his own name's sake*, that is, for his sake alone and to the glorification of his name. Whence in Ezechiel is written: *It is not for your sake that I will do this, says the Lord, it is not for your sakes, but for my holy name's sake*.[29] *Ut notam faceret, that he might make known* to all men, *potentiam suam, his power*, by which he defeated the Egyptians and saved the Israelites. And so in the book of Exodus, the Lord said: *I will be glorified in Pharaoh, and in all his army, . . . and the Egyptians shall know that I am the Lord*.[30]

105{106}[9]   *And he rebuked the Red Sea, and it was dried up: and he led them through the depths, as in a wilderness.*

Et increpuit mare Rubrum, et exsiccatum est; et deduxit eos in abyssis sicut in deserto.

105{106}[10]   *And he saved them from the hand of them that hated them: and he redeemed them from the hand of the enemy.*

Et salvavit eos de manu odientium, et redemit eos de manu inimici.

105{106}[11]   *And the water covered them that afflicted them: there was not one of them left.*

Et operuit aqua tribulantes eos; unus ex eis non remansit.

105{106}[9] *Et increpuit, and he rebuked*, the Lord [rebuked], that is, he admonished, or by commanding divided *mare Rubrum, the Red Sea*. For the change of the Red Sea from its natural state and movement is called its rebuke. *Et exsiccatum est, and it was dried up*: not the sea, because the remaining water was not dried up: for it is inseparably connatural for water to be wet; but the sea is stated to have been dried up, because the bottom of the ground where it ran was dried up when the water was lifted up. *Et deduxit eos in abyssis, and he led them through the depths*, that is, in the path of the Red Sea, not by water, but by the path in which just a short time before water had flowed, *sicut in deserto, as in a wilderness*, that is, so flat and dry by foot that it was as if they were passing through a desert, and the manner of which is more fully recited in the same place [in the book of Exodus]. 105{106}[10] *Et*

---

29 Ez. 36:22, 32a. *E. N.* Denis highly edits these two verses in combining them.
30 Ex. 14:17a, 18a.

salvavit eos de manu odientium, and he saved them from the hand of them that hated them, namely, of the Egyptians that were pursuing them with six hundred chariots,[31] *et redemit eos de manu inimici, and he redeemed them from the hand of the enemy,* that is, the king of Egypt. Now how that happened is stated next: **105{106}[11]** *Et operuit aqua, and the water covered them,* [the water] of the Red Sea, by reverting back to the place where it was before and where it belonged, *tribulantes eos, that afflicted them,* that is, the Egyptians, who were afflicting the Israelites; *unus ex eis non remansit, there was not one of them left*: for all where submerged [under the waters]. Whence in Exodus we read: *The sea returned at the first break of day to the former place, and as the Egyptians were fleeing away, the waters came upon them, and the Lord shut them up in the middle of the waves . . . neither did there so much as one of them remain.*[32]

105{106}[12] *And they believed his words: and they sang his praises.*

Et crediderunt verbis eius, et laudaverunt laudem eius.

105{106}[12] *Et crediderunt, and they believed,* the children of Israel [believed], *verbis eius, his words,* namely [the words] of God, having seen such a great miracle. For this reason there is added: *The people feared the Lord, and they believed the Lord, and Moses his servant.*[33] *Et laudaverunt laudem eius, and they sang his praises,* that is, [they sang of] his laudable works and the laudable goodness of God that had done these things, according to that which we read in the same place: *Then Moses and the children of Israel sung this canticle to the Lord, and said: Let us sing to the Lord: for he is gloriously magnified, the horse and the rider he has thrown into the sea.*[34] And below that there is written: *So Mary the prophetess, the sister of Aaron, took a timbrel in her hand: and all the women went forth after her with timbrels and with dances: And she began the song to them, saying: Let us sing to the Lord, for he is gloriously magnified, etc.*[35]

105{106}[13] *They had quickly done, they forgot his works: and they waited not for his counsels.*

Cito fecerunt, obliti sunt operum eius; et non sustinuerunt consilium eius.

---

31 Ex. 14:7.
32 Ex. 14:27–28.
33 Ex. 14:31.
34 Ex. 15:1.
35 Ex. 15:20–21.

105{106}[13] *Cito fecerunt,* they had quickly done, that is, they did not persevere long in good works. Or [it can be understood thus], *quickly,* after this act of praise and thanksgiving, they did what is stated thereafter: *obliti sunt operum eius,* they forgot his works, that is, they did not give consideration to the previously mentioned miracles of God with a wise and thankful mind. Whence, in the book of Exodus we have written: *The fifteenth day of the second month, after they came out of the land of Egypt, . . .* they *murmured against Moses and Aaron in the wilderness,* saying: *Would to God we had died . . . in the land of Egypt. . . . Why have you brought us into this desert, that you might destroy all the multitude with famine?*[36] *Non sustinuerunt consilium eius,* they waited not for his counsel: that is, they did not await the time in hope patiently, when God decreed to provide them with food, according with the counsel of his wisdom, by which all things are done in a most orderly way, according to that which the Apostle said to the Ephesians: *All things he works according to the counsel of his will.*[37] This time of counsel they awaited with impatience.

105{106}[14]   *And they coveted their desire in the desert: and they tempted God in the place without water.*

   Et concupierunt concupiscentiam in deserto, et tentaverunt Deum in inaquoso.

105{106}[15]   *And he gave them their request: and sent fulness into their souls.*

   Et dedit eis petitionem ipsorum, et misit saturitatem in animas eorum.

105{106}[14] *Et concupierunt concupiscentiam in deserto,* and they coveted their desire in the desert, that is, the delicate food, namely, meats, according to that which we read elsewhere: *They burned with the desire for the flesh and said: Who shall give us flesh to eat? Our soul is dry, our eyes behold nothing else but manna.*[38] *Et tentaverunt Deum in inaquoso,* and they tempted God in the place without water, that is, in the desert (in which one does not find any or very little water), as is written in the book of Exodus: *They tempted the Lord, saying: Is the Lord amongst us or not?*[39] **105{106}[15]** *Et dedit eis,* and he gave them, God [gave them], *petitionem ipsorum,* their request, that is, the things they demanded, namely, meat and water, *et misit saturitatem in animas eorum,* and he sent fulness into

---

36 Ex. 16:1–3.
37 Eph. 1:11b.
38 Num. 11:4b, 6.
39 Ex. 17:7.

their souls, that is, life into their souls, because for a full month he gave to them quail to eat, until they came out of their nostrils and became loathsome to them, as we read in the book of Numbers.[40]

105{106}[16] *And they provoked Moses in the camp, Aaron the holy one of the Lord.*

Et irritaverunt Moysen in castris, Aaron, sanctum Domini.

105{106}[17] *The earth opened and swallowed up Dathan: and covered the congregation of Abiram.*

Aperta est terra, et deglutivit Dathan, et operuit super congregationem Abiron.

105{106}[18] *And a fire was kindled in their congregation: the flame burned the wicked.*

Et exarsit ignis in synagoga eorum, flamma combussit peccatores.

Following this, the sedition of Korah and his family is recited. **105{106} [16]** *Et irritaverunt, and they provoked,* Korah from the tribe of Levi, and Dathan and Abiram of the tribe of Ruben and another two hundred and fifty leading men of the synagogue, *who in the time of the assembly were called by name*, as it says in the book of Numbers,[41] *Moysen in castris, Moses in the camp*, that is, in the tents, or the people dwelling in tents, *Aaron* also, *sanctum Domini, the holy one of the Lord*, that is, consecrated to the Lord in the high priesthood. For Dathan and Abiram sought to obtain the right to rule because they were born from the first-born of Jacob, namely, from Ruben, or perhaps because they disdained having to be inferior to Moses and Aaron. But Korah and those who were with Korah, who were of the tribe of Levi, as Aaron also was, wanted to be made equal in the priesthood. They therefore provoked Moses and Aaron saying to them that [which is read in the book] of Numbers: *Let it be enough for you, that all the multitude consists of holy ones, and the Lord is among them. Why lift you up yourselves above the people of the Lord?*[42] Because of this rebellion and sedition, therefore, **105{106}[17]** *Aperta est terra, et deglutavit Dathan, et operuit super congregationem; the earth opened up and swallowed up Dathan and covered the congregation*, that is, before all the children of Israel, *Abiron, Abiram*, who was similar to Dathan in fault, when he suffered

---

40 Cf. Num. 11:20: *But even for a month of days, until it come out at your nostrils, and become loathsome to you.*

41 Num. 16:1–2.

42 Num. 16:3.

a similar penalty to him. For the earth covered Korah and On, and also the tents and all the possessions of Dathan and Abiram, as is written in Numbers.[43] It did not, however, devour the sons of Korah, because they had not consented to their father. For this reason it is written: *There was a great miracle wrought, that, when Korah perished, his sons did not perish.*[44] 105{106}[18] *Et exarsit ignis in synagoga eorum, and a fire was kindled in their congregation,* that is, in the congregation of those who supported Korah; *flama, the flame* of that fire *combussit peccatores, burned the wicked,* that is, those who associated with Korah, in the manner that is attested in the book of Numbers: *A fire coming out from the Lord destroyed the two hundred and fifty men that offered the incense.*[45]

105{106}[19] They made also a calf in Horeb: and they adored the sculpted thing.[46]

Et fecerunt vitulum in Horeb, et adoraverunt sculptile.

105{106}[20] And they changed their glory into the likeness of a calf that eats grass.

Et mutaverunt gloriam suam in similitudinem vituli comedentis foenum.

105{106}[21] They forgot God, who saved them, who had done great things in Egypt,

Obliti sunt Deum qui salvavit eos, qui fecit magnalia in Aegypto,

105{106}[22] Wondrous works in the land of Ham: terrible things in the Red Sea.

Mirabilia in terra Cham, terribilia in mari Rubro.

105{106}[19] *Et fecerunt, and they made,* the children of Israel [made] *vitulum in Horeb, a calf in Horeb,* that is, next to the mount of Horeb which is a part, namely at the foot, of mount Sinai: for the peak of that mountain is called Sinai. The making of this calf shortly preceded the just-mentioned sedition. But the children of Israel are said to have made this calf because, as is narrated in the book of Exodus, it was at their insistence that Aaron cast the golden earrings into the fire, and by means

---

43 Num. 16:31–33.
44 Num. 26:10b–11.
45 Num. 16:35.
46 E. N. For the Latin *sculptile,* I have replaced the Douay-Rheims's "graven thing" with "sculpted thing."

of a founders' work a molten calf came forth.[47] *Et adoraverunt sculptile, and they adored the sculpted thing*. Some say that the word "sculpted thing" is placed here for "cast thing" because both names refer to the idol. For the calf was cast, not sculpted. Others say that it was first cast; but because it was not fully formed in the casting, it was afterwards sculpted and more perfectly formed. And therefore, sometimes it is called sculpted and sometimes it is called cast. In any event, they adored this calf. For they offered it victims, saying: *These are your gods, O Israel, that have brought you out of the land of Egypt*, as is written in Exodus.[48] **105{106}[20]** *Et mutaverunt gloriam suam, and they changed their glory*, that is, the honor and the worship of the divine law or God, in whom they alone should have gloried, *in similitudinem vituli comedentis foenum, into the likeness of a calf that eats grass*: because they adored an image of a calf for the true God. **105{106}[21]** *Obliti sunt Deum qui salvavit eos; they forgot God, who saved them* from the Egyptian servitude, *qui fecit magnalia, who had done great things*, that is great works, *in Aegypto, in Egypt*, by defeating the Egyptians with ten main plagues, **105{106}[22]** *mirabilia, wonderous works* through Moses *in terra Cham in the land of Ham*, that is, in Egypt, so-called for the reasons given earlier,[49] *terribilia in mari Rubro, terrible things in the Red Sea*, drowning the king of Egypt with his people.[50]

105{106}[23] *And he said that he would destroy them: had not Moses his chosen stood before him in the breach: To turn away his wrath, lest he should destroy them.*

Et dixit ut disperderet eos, si non Moyses, electus eius, stetisset in confractione in conspectu eius, ut averteret iram eius, ne disperderet eos.

105{106}[23] *Et dixit, and he said*, the Lord [said] to Moses, *ut disperderet eos, that he would destroy them* because of their ingratitude and idolatry in the way that is brought out in the book of Exodus: *The Lord said to Moses: I perceive that this people is stiffnecked; let me alone, that my wrath may be kindled against them and that I may destroy them.*[51] And certainly the Lord would have done this, *si non Moyses electus eius stetisset in confractione, had not Moses his chosen . . . in the breach*, that

---

47 Ex. 32:2–4.
48 Ex. 32:4b.
49 E. N. Article VII (Psalm 104:23) (because it was possessed at one time by the children of Ham, the son of Noah).
50 Ex. chps. 7–12; 14:28.
51 Ex. 32:9–10.

is, before the imminent plague upon the people which was then break-ing, *in conspectu eius, stood before him,* that is before God upon Mount Sinai, praying unceasingly for the people, as is written in Exodus: *But Moses besought the Lord his God.* And following that: *And the Lord was appeased.*[52] This happened because from an ineffable charity he threw himself as an intermediary for the people so that he might say to the Lord: *Either forgive them this trespass, or if you do not, strike me out of the book that you have written.*[53] Moses, therefore, stood in the breach, *ut averteret iram eius, to turn away his wrath,* that is, the vengeance of God from the people, *ne, lest* God *disperderet eos, should destroy them.*

105{106}[24]   *And they set at naught the desirable land. They believed not his word.*

Et pro nihilo habuerunt terram desiderabilem; non crediderunt verbo eius.

105{106}[25]   *And they murmured in their tents: they hearkened not to the voice of the Lord.*

Et murmuraverunt in tabernaculis suis; non exaudierunt vocem Domini.

105{106}[24] *Et pro nihilo habuerunt terram desiderabilem, and they set at naught the desirable land,* that is, by regarding as vile the land of promise, the land flowing with milk and honey,[54] when they were frightened by the words of the spies, and they said, as is contained in Numbers: *Let us appoint a captain, and let us return into Egypt.*[55] *Non crediderunt verbo eius, they believed not his word,* that is, the promises of God made through Moses, which he had told them: that the Lord would fight for them, and he would lead them into the promised land; but they, to the contrary, said: *Would that . . . the Lord may not bring us into this land, lest we fall by the sword.*[56] **105{106}[25]** *Et murmuraverunt in tabernaculis suis, and they murmured in their tents:* in the manner that we read in Numbers: *The whole multitude crying wept that night, and all the children of Israel murmured against Moses and Aaron, saying: Would God that we had died in Egypt, . . . and would that we might die.*[57] *Non*

---

52 Ex. 32:11a, 14a.
53 Ex. 32:31b–32a.
54 Num. 14:8.
55 Num. 14:4.
56 Num. 14:3.
57 Num. 14:1–3.

exaudierunt vocem Domini, they hearkened not to the voice of the Lord, that is, they did not acquiesce to the exhortations of Moses and Caleb and Joshua, who exhorted them to do good, but they desired to stone them.[58]

105{106}[26]   *And he lifted up his hand over them: to overthrow them in the desert.*

Et elevavit manum suam super eos ut prosterneret eos in deserto.

105{106}[27]   *And to cast down their seed among the nations, and to scatter them in the countries.*

Et ut deiiceret semen eorum in nationibus, et dispergeret eos in regionibus.

105{106}[26] *Et elevavit, and he lifted up*, the Lord [lifted up], *manum suam, his hand*, that is, the powers of his vengeance, *super eos, ut prosterneret eos in deserto, to overthrow them in the desert.* For at that time, as is stated in the book of Numbers, God absolutely pronounced that — out of the multitude of them who were first numbered [among the Israelites when they left Egypt] — none of those who had murmured would enter into the land of promise, except that only Caleb and Joshua would enter it.[59] The Lord also lifted up his hand over them because of this sin, so that he might overthrow them, abandoning them all together in the desert, according to that which he said to Moses: *How long will this people detract me? . . . I will strike them therefore with pestilence, and will consume them.*[60] But this punishment was mitigated by the prayer of Moses, so that little by little they would die in the desert. For Moses prayed for them thus: O Lord, *patient and full of mercy, taking away iniquity and wickedness . . . forgive . . . the sins of this people, according to the greatness of your mercy, as you have been merciful to them from their going out of Egypt unto this place. And the Lord said: I have forgiven according to your word.*[61] 105{106}[27] *Et ut deiiceret semen eorum, and to cast down their seed*, that is, their children, *in nationibus, among the nations*, making them to fall in various lands, *et dispergeret eos in regionibus, and to scatter them in the countries.* The Lord threatened this punishment, but through the prayers of Moses it was entirely set aside, because the children of those who had prostrated themselves [before the golden calf] in the desert entered into the land of Canaan.

58 Num. 14:6–9, 10.
59 Num. 14:22–35.
60 Num. 14:11a, 12a.
61 Num. 14:18–20.

105{106}[28] *They also were initiated to Ba'al of Peor: and ate the sacrifices of the dead.*

Et initiati sunt Beelphegor, et comederunt sacrificia mortuorum.

105{106}[29] *And they provoked him with their inventions: and destruction was multiplied among them.*

Et irritaverunt eum in adinventionibus suis, et multiplicata est in eis ruina.

105{106}[28] *Et initiati sunt Beelphegor, they also were initiated to Ba'al of Peor,* that is, they applied themselves to the worship of the idol called by that name. This was close to the death of Moses, when at the suggestion of Balaam, Balak, king of the Moabites, sent beautiful and noble women who brought with them their idols so that they might make the sons of Israel offend their God through idolatry and wantonness, and so to tempt the sons of Israel.[62] For (as is said) they did not allow them to have intercourse with them unless they first adored the idol Ba'al of Peor. And what and how this occurred is fully contained in the book of Numbers.[63] *Et comederunt sacrificia mortuorum, and they ate the sacrifices of the dead,* that is, the flesh of animals that were sacrificed and offered to that idol. 105{106}[29] *Et irritaverunt eum, and they provoked him,* that is, they offended God, *in adinventionibus suis, with their inventions,* that is, by the sins carefully thought out and deliberately performed, *et, and* because of this *multiplicata est in eis ruina, destruction was multiplied among them,* that is, many and great were the plagues inflicted upon them because of this sin. For twenty-four thousand men were struck down.[64] And the princes were ordered to be hung up on gallows.[65]

105{106}[30] *Then Phinehas stood up, and pacified him: and the slaughter ceased.*

Et stetit Phinees, et placavit, et cessavit quassatio.

105{106}[31] *And it was reputed to him unto justice, to generation and generation for evermore.*

Et reputatum est ei in iustitiam, in generationem et generationem usque in sempiternum.

---

62 Num. 31:16.
63 Num. 25:1–3, 18.
64 Num. 25:9.
65 Num. 25:4.

105{106}[30] *Et stetit Phinees, and then Phinehas stood up*, the son of Eleazar who was the son of Aaron the priest, with a constant mind against idolatries, *et placavit, and pacified* the Lord, piercing through the genital parts Zimri, leader of the tribe of Simeon, who was coupling with Cozbi, the daughter of the most noble prince of the Midianites; *et cessavit quassatio, and the slaughter ceased*, that is, the plague of this persecution by the people [ceased], because this was done also by the merit of the zeal of Phinehas. Whence in Numbers we find: *The Lord said to Moses: Phinehas ... has turned away my wrath from the children of Israel, because he was moved with my zeal against them.*[66] **105{106} [31]** *Et reputatum est ei, and it was reputed to him* by God *in iustitiam, in generationem et generationem usque in sempiternum; unto justice, to generation and generation for evermore*: because God approved this work; and he will be called just in eternity for this reason. And he merited to discharge the office of priesthood, both in himself and in his posterity, according to that which the Lord said to Moses: *Say to him: Behold I give you the peace of my covenant; and the covenant of the priesthood forever shall be both to him and his seed, because he has been zealous for his God.*[67]

ARTICLE X

CONTINUATION OF THE EXPOSITION OF THE ONE HUNDRED AND FIFTH PSALM, AND THE MYSTICAL EXPOSITION OF SOME THINGS THAT ARE CONTAINED IN THIS PSALM.

105{106}[32] *They provoked him also at the waters of Contradiction: and Moses was afflicted for their sakes.*

Et irritaverunt eum ad aquas Contradictionis; et vexatus est Moyses propter eos.

105{106}[33] *Because they exasperated his spirit. And he distinguished with his lips.*

Quia exacerbaverunt spiritum eius, et distinxit in labiis suis.

FOLLOWING THIS, THE QUARREL OF THE children of Israel against God, which occurred at the waters of

---

66 Num. 25:10–11a.
67 Num. 25:12–13.

Contradiction because of the sparsity of water,[68] is described. 105{106} [32] *Et irritaverunt eum, and they provoked him*, namely, God, *ad aquas Contradictionis, at the waters of Contradiction*, impatiently speaking according to that which is written: *They came together against Moses and Aaron, and making a sedition, they said: Would God we had perished among our brethren before the Lord.*[69] *Et vexatus, and afflicted*, that is, with perturbation and weariness of spirit, *est Moyses propter eos, was Moses for their sakes*, that is, because of their perversity, 105{106}[33] *quia exacerbaverunt spiritum eius, because they exasperated his spirit*, namely by their ungrateful and injurious words. *Et distinxit, and he distinguished*, Moses [distinguished] *in labiis suis, with his lips*: that is, in the midst of this perturbation, he had another way of speaking in his heart than which he had used before, reciting the words of the Lord and striking the rock. For he was disobedient to God, and by the manner of his speaking he manifestly declared the hesitation of his heart. For as we read in the book of Numbers, when the Lord told to him and Aaron his brother, *Speak to the rock before them, and it shall yield waters*; Moses, striking the rock with his staff, uttered the ambiguous words, *Can we bring you forth water from this rock?*[70] For this reason, he was later reproved by the Lord, and both him and Aaron were prohibited from entering into the land of promise, the Lord saying to them: *Because you have not believed me, to sanctify me before the children of Israel, you shall not bring these people into the land, which I will give them.*[71]

105{106}[34]   *They did not destroy the nations of which the Lord spoke unto them.*

   Non disperdiderunt gentes quas dixit Dominus illis.

105{106}[35]   *And they were mingled among the heathens, and learned their works.*

   Et commisti sunt inter gentes, et didicerunt opera eorum.

105{106}[36]   *And served their idols, and it became a stumbling block to them.*

   Et servierunt sculptilibus eorum, et factum est illis in scandalum.

Then the sins of the children committed after their entry into the land of Canaan is narrated. 105{106}[34] *Non disperdiderunt gentes, they did not destroy the nations*, that is, they did not completely kill those

---

68 *E. N.* The waters of Meribah. *See* Num. 20:13.
69 Num. 20:2–3.
70 Num. 20:8, 10.
71 Num. 20:12.

who dwelt in the land of Canaan, *quas dixit Dominus illis, of which the Lord spoke to them,* that is, of which the Lord ordered them to kill and to overturn their altars, and neither to marry or have familiarity with them. This he frequently commanded to the children of Israel, lest they be brought to idolatry from their cohabitation. But the children of Israel permitted some of the nations around them to dwell among them, and they did this from avarice because of the tribute they were paying them. **105{106}[35]** *Et commixti sunt, and they were mingled* in place, in body, and through work *inter gentes, among the heathens* of the Canaanites, *et didicerunt opera eorum, and they learned their works,* that is, the rituals of the heathens, **105{106}[36]** *Et et servierunt sculptilibus eorum, and they served their idols,* namely, the Ba'als and Ashtaroth, as is clear from the book of Judges;[72] *et factum est illis, and it became … to them,* this sin of idolatry, *in scandalum, a stumbling block,* that is, to their great ruin.

105{106}[37] *And they sacrificed their sons, and their daughters to devils.*

Et immolaverunt filios suos et filias suas daemoniis.

105{106}[38] *And they shed innocent blood: the blood of their sons and of their daughters which they sacrificed to the idols of Canaan. And the land was polluted with blood,*

Et effuderunt sanguinem innocentem, sanguinem filiorum suorum et filiarum suarum, quas sacrificaverunt sculptilibus Chanaan. Et infecta est terra in sanguinibus;

105{106}[39] *And was defiled with their works: and they went aside after their own inventions.*

Et contaminata est in operibus eorum, et fornicati sunt in adinventionibus suis.

105{106}[37] *Et immolaverunt filios suos et filias suas daemoniis, and they sacrificed their sons and their daughters to devils* which they revered through idols. Now in what manner they sacrificed them is added: **105{106}[38]** *Et effuderunt sanguinem innocentem, and they shed innocent blood,* namely, *sanguinem filiorum suorum et filiarum suarum, the blood of their sons and of their daughters,* which, because of their young age, they had not yet sinned, *quas sacrificaverunt, which they sacrificed,* that is, offered, *sculptilibus Chanaan, to the idols of Canaan,* that is, the images of the Canaanites. Although we do not read elsewhere in sacred

---

72 Judges 2:13; 3:7.

history that this was done, still it is to be believed because the Prophet [David] states it here. *Et interfecta est terra, and the land was destroyed of its dwelling places,*[73] that is, the dwellers of that land were killed *in sanguinibus, with blood* so brutally was it shed or so ungodly performed, **105{106}[39]** *et contaminata est in operibus eorum, and was defiled with their works* that were so heinous. Or [we can understand it thus], *the land was destroyed,* that is, the men of this land shedding the blood of innocents were spiritually slain, because the lives of their own souls were despoiled of grace; *and was defiled with their works,* that is, they defiled themselves by their own sins. *Et fornicati sunt, and they went aside,*[74] that is, they withdrew from God by idolatry, *in adinventionibus suis, after their own inventions,* that is, in the sins they committed through their own diligence. For good reason is idolatry called fornication in sacred Scripture, because by it one's soul departs from its true spouse, namely, from God: to whom one is espoused by faith and charity, and by whom one is made fruitful by grace and the gifts of the Holy Spirit, in the way that the Lord says: *I will espouse you to me in faith.*[75] But because Israel committed fornication in this manner, therefore it is stated: *Rejoice not, O Israel, rejoice not . . . for you have committed fornication against your God.*[76]

105{106}[40] *And the Lord was exceedingly angry with his people: and he abhorred his inheritance.*

Et iratus est furore Dominus in populum suum, et abominatus est haereditatem suam.

105{106}[41] *And he delivered them into the hands of the nations: and they that hated them had dominion over them.*

Et tradidit eos in manus gentium; et dominati sunt eorum qui oderunt eos.

105{106}[42] *And their enemies afflicted them: and they were humbled under their hands.*

Et tribulaverunt eos inimici eorum; et humiliati sunt sub manibus eorum.

---

73 E. N. The text has *interfecta est terra,* "the land was destroyed," but the editor notes that other texts have *infecta est terra,* "the land was polluted," which is consistent with the Sixto-Clementine Vulgate and the Douay-Rheims.

74 E. N. The Douay-Rheims uses a euphemism ("went aside") to avoid the literal translation: "they committed whoredom" or "they fornicated."

75 Hosea 2:20a.

76 Hosea 9:1a.

105{106}[40] *Et iratus est furore Dominus, and the Lord was exceedingly angry*, that is, he was vehemently enraged, not by a commotion of the soul, but by the gravity of vengeance, *in populum suum, with his people* in name and not in reality; *et abominatus est hereditatem suam, and he abhorred his inheritance*, that is, the children of Israel whom he had particularly invited and called so that they might be his inheritance; but, not obeying, they became the inheritance of the devil. 105{106}[41] *Et tradidit eos in manus gentium, and he delivered them into the hands of the nations*, that is, he withdrew the divine protection and aid, allowing them to become oppressed by the Philistines, Syrians, and many others; *et dominati sunt eorum qui oderunt eos, and they that hated them had dominion over them*. For as is written in the book of Judges, they served some eighteen years, some longer, and some less.[77] For you see, those whom God abandons, from whom God withdraws help, are subjected to the servitude of their enemies. First of all, by the withdrawal of grace because of the punishment of fault; but secondly, by incursion of malignant domination. 105{106}[42] *Et tribulaverunt eos inimici eorum, and their enemies afflicted them*, placing upon them heavy labors, large tributes, huge indemnities; *et humiliati sunt, and they were humbled*, the children of Israel [were humbled], that is, dejected, oppressed, and vanquished, *sub manibus eorum, under their hands*, that is, under the power and the persecution of their adversaries. Or [we can understand it to mean] they were humbled before God under the hands of their enemies' hand because by the gravity of the persecution they confessed their sins and they pled for their forgiveness, and they promised amendment.

105{106}[43] *Many times did he deliver them. But they provoked him with their counsel: and they were brought low by their iniquities.*

Saepe liberavit eos. Ipsi autem exacerbaverunt eum in consilio suo; et humiliati sunt in iniquitatibus suis.

105{106}[43] *Saepe liberavit eos, many times did he deliver them*, God [delivered them] from the power of faithless people, as is evident from the sequence of events related in the book of Judges where we find written: *And when the Lord raised them up judges, in their days he was moved to mercy, and heard the groanings of the afflicted, and delivered them from the slaughter of the oppressors.*[78] *Ipsi autem exacerbaverunt eum, but they*

---

77 Judges 3:8, 14; 4:3. E. N. The children of Israel served Eglon, the king of Moab, eighteen years, Cushan-rishathaim, the king of Mesopotamia, for eight years, and Jabin, the King of Canaan, for twenty years.

78 Judges 2:18.

provoked him: that is, after their liberation was mercifully accomplished by God, they returned back again to their former evil, and they offended God. Whence it is stated in the book of Judges: *But after the judge was dead, they returned, and did much worse things than their fathers had done, following strange gods.... They left not ... the stubborn way, by which they were accustomed to walk.*[79] And so it was that they provoked God *in consilio suo, with their counsel*, because their evil deeds arose from their evil counsel and most empty inventions; *et humiliati sunt in iniquitatibus suis, and they were brought low by their iniquities*, that is, they were oppressed and vanquished by their enemies because of their sins, and sometimes they were even made humble before God by repentance.

105{106}[44]   *And he saw when they were in tribulation: and he heard their prayer.*

   Et vidit cum tribularentur, et audivit orationem eorum.

105{106}[45]   *And he was mindful of his covenant: and repented according to the multitude of his mercies.*

   Et memor fuit testamenti sui, et poenituit eum secundum multitudinem misericordiae suae.

105{106}[46]   *And he gave them unto mercies, in the sight of all those that had made them captives.*

   Et dedit eos in misericordias, in conspectu omnium qui ceperant eos.

   105{106}[44] *Et vidit cum tribularentur, and he saw when they were in tribulation*, that is, God mercifully beheld them while they were afflicted in such a manner, *et audivit orationem eorum, and he heard their prayer* which pleaded to be freed from the yoke of their adversaries. **105{106}[45]** *Et memor fuit, and he was mindful* by the effect of his mercy, *testamenti sui, of his covenant*, that is, his compact or his promise which he had frequently revealed to them earlier through Moses that he would free them whenever they would wholeheartedly return to the Lord God of their fathers. Whence in Deuteronomy it was told to them by Moses: *If you be driven as far as the poles of heaven, the Lord your God will fetch you back from there, and will take you to himself, and bring you to the land which your fathers possessed.*[80] And in the same book of Deuteronomy it says: *When you shall seek there*

---

79 Judges 2:19.
80 Deut. 30:4–5a.

the Lord your God, you shall find him: yet so, if you seek him with all your heart, and all the affliction of your soul.[81] *Et poenituit eum, and he repented,* that is, he showed himself to them in the manner a penitent man exhibits himself, because he once again kindly rescued them from the plundering and the captivity under which he had placed them, *secundum multitudinem misericordiae suae, according to the multitude of his mercies,* that is, according to the fact that he is greatly merciful, and not because of their virtues. For this reason, Moses says again in Deuteronomy: *Say not in your heart . . . for my justice has the Lord brought me in to possess this land, . . . for you are a very stiffnecked people.*[82] **105{106}[46]** *Et dedit eos in misericordias, and he gave them unto mercies,* that is, he applied the various effects of this divine kindness to them, *in conspectu omnium qui ceperant eos, in the sight of all those that had made them captives:* because he freed the children of Israel while they [their enemies] observed and by their experience of being often relieved from their heavy punishments.

105{106}[47] *Save us, O Lord, our God: and gather us from among nations: That we may confess to your holy name, and may glory in your praise.*[83]

Salvos nos fac, Domine Deus noster, et congrega nos de nationibus; ut confiteamur nomini sancto tuo, et gloriemur in laude tua.

105{106}[48] *Blessed be the Lord the God of Israel, from everlasting to everlasting: and let all the people say: So be it, so be it.*

Benedictus Dominus Deus Israel, a saeculo et usque in saeculum; et dicet omnis populus : Fiat! Fiat!

Finally, the Prophet [David] prays for the liberation and the aid of his people, or their return to the land of their fathers. And this might be regarded as the prayer of the Church for the conversion and spiritual union of the faithful: **105{106}[47]** *Salvos fac nos, Domine Deus noster;* save us, O Lord, our God, from all dangers of mind and body, and from past, present, and future evils, *et congrega nos de nationibus, and gather us from among nations,* that is, separate us from the unbelievers and gather

---

81 Deut. 4:29.
82 Deut. 9:4a, 6b.
83 *E. N.* I have departed from the Douay-Rheims in translating *confiteamur* as "we may confess," rather than "we may give thanks," since Denis sees this verse as incorporating *both* a confession of thanks and praise *and* a confession of fault.

us together, by place or by dedication, since, separated from a perverse generation, we might serve you faithfully, lest we might become perverted with the perverse.[84] *Ut confiteamur nomini sancto tuo, that we may confess to your holy name* both our evil and your good, accusing ourselves and praiseing you, and so venerating you with a twofold confession, namely the confession of your praise and of our iniquity; *et gloriemur, and we may glory* with spiritual joy *in laude tua, in your praise*, so that we may praise you with great delight and with great fervor, not sluggishly and drowsily.

105{106}[48] *Benedictus, blessed* be, that is, may he, *Dominus Deus Israel, the Lord, the God of Israel,* be blessed by all, and may he be always praised, *a saeculo et usque in saeculum, from everlasting to everlasting,* that is, for ever and ever; *et dicet omnis populos, and let all the people say,* all those believing in Christ, not only the Jews: *Fiat! Fiat! So be it! So be it!* That is, Amen, amen. For Christians around the globe of the earth agree in this divine praise, saying: So be it, so be it.

FURTHERMORE, MANY THINGS CONTAINED in this Psalm can be understood spiritually. For that the afore-mentioned fathers did not understand the wonders of God and that they were not mindful of the multitude of his mercies signifies that mindset of many (regrettably!) of the Christians in this age who do not pay attention to the marvels of Christ, neither do they follow in his works, nor do they consider his benefits, nor do they apply themselves to understand the mysteries of the Savior. Also, the leading out of the children of Israel from Egypt prefigures the conversion of the Gentiles to faith and worship of Christ. For this conversion is a spiritual departure from the old life and the fellowship of reprobates, of which the Apostle [Paul] says: *Go out from among them ... and touch not the unclean thing.*[85] It also is a figure of the entry of religious into the cloistered life. For at that time they left completely Egypt, that is, this world, and they completely renounced the works of the devil.

Finally, the Red Sea signifies Baptism consecrated with the blood of Christ. And as the children of Israel were saved from the servitude of Egypt and the hand of Pharaoh by going through the Red Sea, so the faithful are freed from the servitude of sin and the power of the devil by the fount of Baptism. And the Egyptians were drowned by the Red Sea, so also in Baptism: that is, the infidels who do not receive Baptism

---

84 Ps. 17:27b.
85 2 Cor. 6:17.

spiritually perish, for they refuse to be baptized. For unless one is reborn of water and the Holy Spirit, he is unable to see the kingdom of God, as Christ attests in the Gospel.[86] Manna also was a type of the Sacrament of the Body and Blood of Christ. And as the children of Israel after their passage through the Red Sea ate manna,[87] so do Christians after the regeneration of Baptism receive the sacraments of Christ. For the Apostle [Paul] says this: *I would not have you ignorant, brethren, that our fathers were all under the cloud, and all passed through the sea. And all in Moses were baptized, in the cloud, and in the sea, and all did eat the same spiritual food, and all drank the same spiritual drink. And they drank of the spiritual rock that followed them, and the rock was Christ.... Now these things were done in a figure of us.*[88]

In addition, from that which is stated, *The earth opened and swallowed up Dathan* (verse **17**), we are warned to pay attention how enormous the sin of sedition and rebellion and the ambition to dominate is. From such a horrendous punishment of God they who disdain their superiors, they who murmur, they who despise to have to obey, and they who desire to preside over others ought greatly to be terrified. They ought to ponder that which Christ said to his prelates and vicars: *He that hears you, hears me; and he that despises you, despises me.*[89] Whence also Moses in Exodus told those who were rebellious: *Your murmuring is not against us, but against the Lord.*[90] And elsewhere he says: *What is Aaron that you murmur against him?*[91] And pay heed also you priests living carnally and unworthily, who unworthily appropriate the sacerdotal office, how *the flame burned the wicked* (verse **18**).[92] Indeed, as the Apostle says, *Whosoever shall eat this bread or drink the chalice of the Lord unworthily shall be guilty of the Body and the Blood of the Lord.*[93] And so they will be burned with eternal fire, whose figure can be found in that flame sent by God which burnt the followers of Korah. *And they changed their glory into the likeness of a calf that eats grass* (verse **20**). This resembles those persons who are occupied all day with fantasies, not contemplating

---

86 *Cf.* John 3:5.

87 Ex. 16:35.

88 1 Cor. 10:1–4, 6a.

89 Luke 10:16.

90 Ex. 16:8b.

91 Num. 16:11b.

92 Lev. 10:2; Num. 16:35. E. N. In Leviticus, the Lord destroyed the sons of Aaron, Nadab and Abihu for offering "strange fire which was not commanded them." In Numbers, the Lord destroyed by fire 250 men that offered incense.

93 1 Cor. 11:27.

heavenly things nor meditating upon the divine law. Whence John in his first epistle exhorts: *Little children, keep yourselves from idols.*[94]

Also from that which is said, *And he said that he would destroy them, had not Moses his chosen stood before him in the breach, to turn away his wrath* (verse **23**), let them learn from other leaders who are placed as mediators between God and the people, who give themselves by a most insistent, most faithful, and most fervent undertaking to intercede on behalf of the flock; not to be moved by bitterness and indiscrete zeal, but by compassion, against those who are found wanting; yet not to allow them to go unpunished, but that they are strictly corrected and punished in the present, if it is able to be done, and it would be useful to those who might observe it. They ponder like Moses said: *Either forgive them this trespass, or if you do not, strike me from the book that you have written.*[95] These good pastors, therefore, follow after charity, and they show themselves through their lives and prayers to be mediators between God and those committed to their care, lest they become guilty of their damnation; and they consider that which the Lord asserts in Ezechiel: *And I sought among them for a man that might set up a hedge, and stand in the gap before me in favor of the land, that I might not destroy it: and I found none, and I poured out my indignation upon them.*[96]

But also through the example of Phinehas the lovers of God are advised to have zeal for their God against the perverse,[97] in the way that Elijah states in the first book of Kings, *With zeal have I been zealous for the Lord God of hosts.*[98] For it is completely expedient to punish transgressors in this age lest they perish eternally or persevere indefinitely in their vices. And as Chrysostom says, however holy it is to tolerate injury done to oneself, yet it is impious to disregard an injury done to God.[99] Nevertheless, as the Apostle asserted, some have *the zeal of God, but not according to knowledge:*[100] those, namely, who neglect to look at,

---

94 1 John 5:21.

95 Ex. 32:31b–31a.

96 Ez. 22:30–31a. E. N. Denis might also have mentioned Ez. 33:9: *But if you tell the wicked man, that he may be converted from his ways, and he be not converted from his way: he shall die in his iniquity: but you have delivered your soul.*

97 Num. 25:7–8

98 1 Kings 19:10.

99 E. N. The reference is falsely ascribed to Chrysostom. *In propriis iniuriis esse quempiam patientem, laudabile est, iniurias autem Dei dissimulare nimis est impium.* With regard to one's own injuries, it is praiseworthy to be patient, but it is exceedingly impious to disregard the injuries of God. *See, e.g.,* ST IIaIIae, q. 108, art. 1, ad 2.

100 Rom. 10:2.

to bewail, to correct, and to avoid their own vices, yet they adjudge, and without compassion condemn, the sins of others; nor do such persons charitably support the burdens of others. Concerning the deeds of the priest Phinehas, Jerome exhorts every priest of Christ that has rule over others, saying: "The priest to whom souls are commended should diligently pay heed to this. Unsheathe the word of God, slay fornication; *be instant in season, out of season; reprove, entreat, rebuke in all patience and doctrine* so that it might be credited to you as justice."[101] Whence in Leviticus, the Lord says to the priests: *That you may have knowledge to discern between holy and unholy, . . . and may teach the children of Israel all my ordinances.*[102]

In addition, from that which is said, *And they set at naught the desirable land* (verse 24), it is incumbent upon us to take care lest — out of love of this world, temporal honor, the vile delights of the flesh or the complacency of momentary life — we miserably and irreparably lose the promises of Christ, the land of the living, the kingdom of heaven, and eternal beatitude. But with the divine Apostle we ought truly to prefer that which he told the Philippians: *I count all things . . . as dung, that I may gain Christ.*[103] Moreover, from that which is said — *And he saw when they were in tribulation, and he heard their prayer* (verse 44) — we ought to ponder the inestimable depth of the infinite clemency of the most kind God, and we ought always return to him with complete trust, saying: *We have sinned with our fathers: we have acted unjustly, we have wrought iniquity* (verse 6). And then, with certainty, he will repent according to the multitude of his mercies (*cf.* verse 45), and he will be touched (as Scripture says) with our miseries, and he will be merciful.[104]

Now from that which is said — *And they were mingled among the heathens, and learned their works, and served their idols* (verses 35 and 36) — we are admonished to keep in mind how dangerous and noxious it is for the servants of Christ, and especially for the religious or hermits, to converse with worldly men, to inquire about rumors, to think about worldly things. For these things stain the purity of the heart, interrupt

---

101 E. N. Erroneously attributed to Jerome. It comes from *Breviarum in Psalmos,* Ps. 105, PL 26, 1212. The internal scripture quote is to 2 Tim. 4:2.

102 Lev. 10:10–11a.

103 Phil. 3:8.

104 *Cf.* Judges 10:16: *And saying these things, they cast away out of their coasts all the idols of strange gods and served the Lord their God: and he was touched with their miseries. Cf.* Deut. 33:43: *Praise his people, you nations, for he will revenge the blood of his servants: and will render vengeance to their enemies, and he will be merciful to the land of his people.*

the stability of the soul, greatly frustrate divine charity, make solitude a horror or nauseating, and give birth to and feed a false love for the world. Most especially are we Carthusians to avoid these things if we are worthily to live our vocation to which the Holy Spirit has called us.

PRAYER

REMEMBER US WITH YOUR FAVOR, O LORD, and teach us to do justice at all times; and make it that we also glory in your praise, and bless you, O God of Israel, from everlasting to everlasting.

Memento nostri in beneplacito tuo, Domine, et doce nos iustitiam facere in omni tempore; facque nos in laude tua semper gloriari, et a saeculo usque in saeculum, Deus Israel, benedicere tibi.

Psalm 106

ARTICLE XI

ELUCIDATION OF THE ONE HUNDRED AND SIXTH PSALM: CONFITEMINI DOMINO . . . DICANT QUI, ETC. GIVE GLORY TO THE LORD . . . LET THEM SAY, ETC.

106{107}[1] *Alleluia. Confess to the Lord, for he is good: for his mercy endures forever.*[1]

Alleluia. Confitemini Domino, quoniam bonus, quoniam in saeculum misericordia eius.

106{107}[2] *Let them say so that have been redeemed by the Lord, whom he has redeemed from the hand of the enemy: and gathered out of the countries.*

Dicant qui redempti sunt a Domino, quos redemit de manu inimici, et de regionibus congregavit eos.

106{107}[3] *From the rising and the setting of the sun, from the north and from the sea.*

A solis ortu, et occasu, ab aquilone, et mari.

THE TITLE OF THE PSALM NOW BEING TREATED is, in word as well as in sense, identical with the preceding Psalm. For its title is *Alleluia, alleluia.*[2] But the matter of this present Psalm, according to Augustine, is the giving of thanks for the universal redemption of the human race effected by Christ, which the holy David knew by the Spirit revealing it to him. But others proceeding with less sensitivity assert that this Psalm is the giving of thanks, or an invitation to give thanks, of some of the Jews freed from diverse evils and taken away by God to all parts of the world from the place or the danger in which they had found themselves. But because the first exposition is by far more advantageous, more subtle, and more leading to devotion, and is also consonant with its text, therefore it seems that we ought first and principally to dwell upon that, though the other will be perchance also treated.

---

1 E. N. I have translated *confitemini* with "confess," and have departed from the Douay-Rheims's "give glory" in this verse.
2 E. N. The Sixto-Clementine Vulgate contains but one Alleluia.

Therefore, the holy Prophet [David] inviting all men to praise Christ for all his benefits, says: **106{107}[1]** *Confitemini Domino, quoniam bonus, quoniam in saeculum misericordia eius; confess to the Lord, for he is good: for his mercy endures forever.* In the exposition of the previous Psalm, this verse, which begins that Psalm like it does this one, is satisfactorily expounded. **106{107}[2]** *Dicant, let them say so* (to that to which the previous verse exhorts), that is, that they may praise the Lord, *qui redempti sunt a Domino, that they have been redeemed by the Lord,* that is, those whom Christ by his Incarnation and Passion has redeemed according to that contained in [in the epistle] to the Ephesians: *Christ has loved us and has delivered himself up for us, an oblation and a sacrifice to God for an odor of sweetness.*[3] Of whom John says in Revelation: *Christ has loved us, and washed us from our sins in his own blood.*[4] *Quos redemit de manu inimici, whom he has redeemed from the hand of the enemy,* that is, the power and the captivity of the devil. For this reason, the Gospel says, *Now . . . shall the prince of this world be cast out;*[5] and with Hosea, *I will deliver them from the hand of death. I will redeem them from death.*[6] Whence the angel says of Christ with Matthew: *He shall save his people from their sins.*[7]

De regionibus, out of the countries, that is, from all the ends of the world, or from the four corners of the earth, *congregavit eos, he has gathered out:* not by a movement in location, but through spiritual conversion; not into one bodily place, but into one faith, into one Church, and into the same worship. For regarding this spiritual congregation of believers created by the Apostles and their fellow workers, we find written in John: *Jesus should die for the nation; and not only for the nation, but to gather together in one the children of God that were dispersed.*[8] And with the Prophet [Isaiah]: *I will send of them that shall be saved, [to the Gentiles into the sea, into Africa, and Lydia them that draw the bow: into Italy, and Greece, to the islands afar off, to them that have not heard of me, and have not seen my glory. And they shall declare my glory to the Gentiles]. And they shall bring all your brethren . . . to my holy mountain,*[9] that is, to the Church militant. And he will gather them together not only from one side of the world, but *a solis ortu et occasu, from the rising and the setting of the sun,* that is, from the east and the west, *ab aquilone et mari, from the north*

---

3 Eph. 5:2.
4 Rev. 1:5.
5 John 12:31b.
6 Hosea 13:14a.
7 Matt. 1:21b.
8 John 11:51–52.
9 Is. 66:19–20a. *E. N.* The part in brackets replaces the "etc." of Denis.

and from the sea, that is, from the northern and the southern parts. For by the word *sea* is expressed the south wind because it moves towards the Ocean, which is called the sea because of all the other bodies of water it is the greatest. For Christ gathered up believers from all parts of the world. For this reason, he said to his Apostles in the Gospel of Mark: *Go into the whole world and preach the Gospel to every creature.*[10] This is also stated about Christ in Isaiah: *The Gentiles shall see your just one, and all kings your glorious one:*[11] this would not be fulfilled unless the faith of Christ was to be announced in all countries.

106{107}[4] *They wandered in a wilderness, in a place without water: they found not the way of a city for their habitation.*

Erraverunt in solitudine, in inaquoso; viam civitatis habitaculi non invenerunt.

106{107}[4] *Erraverunt, they wandered* in believing before they were converted to the Lord,[12] *in solitudine, in a wilderness*, that is, in this world abandoned by the grace of God: this is to be understood as applying to the world of the damned, and the society of angels deprived [of grace], of those asserting this: *We would have cured Babylon, but she is not healed: let us forsake her;*[13] *in inaquoso, in a place without water*, that is, in infidelity or with a dry heart, one not having the dew of saving grace or the rain of heavenly instruction. *Viam civitatis habitaculi, the way of a city for their habitation*, that is, the right way to come to the supernal Jerusalem, to the dwelling-place of the blessed, to the fatherland of the elect, *non invenerunt, they found not* by human power or natural light. For this way is the Catholic faith, which, according to the Apostle, *He that comes to God must believe.*[14] But man cannot obtain faith or discover it without

---

10 Mark 16:15.

11 Is. 62:2a.

12 E. N. The Latin *erraverunt* can mean "they wandered," as it is translated in the Douay-Rheims, but it can also mean "they erred," or "they went astray." It seems that Denis has this latter connotation in mind.

13 Jer. 51:9a. E. N. In his *Commentary on Jeremiah*, Denis explains: "*We would have cured Babylon, but she is not healed.* From this is intimated that the angels who administer our souls as physicians, realizing the obstinacy and incorrigibility of those over whom they have been given charge, desert them at least in part. This also prelates and preachers are able to say when sinners to whom they propose the words of God and in all possible ways they labor long for their conversion do not appear as desiring at all to convert." Doctor Ecstaticus D. Dionysius Cartusianus, *Opera Omnia* (Montreuil: 1900), Vol. 9, 307.

14 Heb. 11:6.

supernatural aid. He is able also by this means to understand the good manner of living or the observation of the precepts which without grace he is unable to maintain,[15] in the manner that Jeremiah most clearly attests: *I know, O Lord, that the way of a man is not his; neither is it in a man to walk and to direct his steps.*[16] And so this way is always to be sought from God, by the holy angels who are the custodian of our souls, from our teachers, those who are our betters, and our superiors, lest we deviate from it during this exile. For this we again have in Jeremiah: *Ask for the old paths which is the good way, and walk you in it.*[17]

106{107}[5]   *They were hungry and thirsty: their soul fainted in them.*

Esurientes et sitientes, anima eorum in ipsis defecit.

106{107}[5]   *Esurientes et sitientes, they were hungry and thirsty*, that is, striving for happiness which all naturally strive for. Or [alternatively], *they were hungry and thirsty* for natural justice, which many of the nations sought since they exposed themselves to death on account of it. Or [yet another alternative], *they were hungry and thirsty* for satisfaction in earthly, sensible, and perishable goods in which many men regard as the highest good, as Boethius writes.[18] Or [yet again], *they were hungry and thirsty* for the justice of the divine law and the preaching of the Gospel after they received the faith. *Anima eorum in ispsi defecit, their soul fainted in them*: that is, their own power did not suffice to produce the effect of this striving of this hunger and thirst [for the supernatural], but it required grace.[19] Or [yet another interpretation], *their soul fainted in*

---

15 "In the condition of fallen nature it is morally impossible for man without restoring grace (*gratia sanans*) to fulfil the entire moral law and to overcome all serious temptations for any considerable period of time." "[T]here is all the more reason for teaching that the non-justified man without the actual help of grace, cannot avoid all serious sins for any considerable time, even if in virtue of his natural freedom, he is able to avoid individual sins and to fulfil individual commandments." Ludwig Ott, *Fundamentals of Catholic Dogma*, (Rockford, IL, Tan Books 1960), 236 (trans., Patrick Lynch).

16 Jer. 10:23.

17 Jer. 6:16a.

18 *E. N.* A reference to *On the Consolation of Philosophy*, III, pr. 2, by Boethius (*ca.* 466–524).

19 *E. N.* Denis appears to reject that there is a natural desire for union with God, and that such a desire must be elicited by grace for the simple reason that *naturale desiderium ultra naturalem capacitatem se extendere nequit.* Doctor Ecstaticus D. Dionysius Cartusianus, *Opera Omnia* (Tournai: 1911), Vol. 40, 431. This view, of course, was famously challenged by Henri de Lubac in his various works dealing with this issue beginning with *Surnature; études historiques* published in 1946, and elaborated in some of his later works, including the *Mystery of the Supernatural* and *Augustinianism*

them because in a certain way one might concede that they may be led by their hunger and thirst to activity by which they acquire natural justice or an abundance of temporal things, though this would not yet be sufficient to true salvation. For this reason, they remain empty and void.

106{107}[6] *And they cried to the Lord in their tribulation: and he delivered them out of their distresses.*

Et clamaverunt ad Dominum cum tribularentur, et de necessitatibus eorum eripuit eos.

106{107}[7] *And he led them into the right way: that they might go to a city of habitation.*

Et deduxit eos in viam rectam, ut irent in civitatem habitationis.

106{107}[6] *Et clamaverunt ad Dominum,* and they cried to the Lord for the help of his grace, *cum tribularentur,* in their tribulation, that is, when they were afflicted in soul, because they were unable to obtain the desired perfection, or they were overcome by temptations, or also they would succumb to concupiscence: this is a great affliction to the assiduous soul so that the Apostles says of these persons: *I see another law in my members, fighting against the law of my mind, and captivating me in the law of sin, that is in my members. Unhappy man that I am! Who shall deliver me from the body of this death? The grace of God, by Jesus Christ our Lord.*[20] And so it now adds: *et de necessitatibus eorum eripuit eos,* and he delivered them out of their distresses, that is, they were freed by the grace of God, which illuminated them in the faith, from the evil or vices and the dangers of which they were unable by their own power to free themselves. For without [faith] no adult using reason [alone] is able to live without mortal sin, and so according to the Apostle, *whatever is not of faith is sin.*[21] Yet no one is able to have either faith or grace unless it be from God. As long as persons are deprived of the light of faith and lack grace, they unceasingly or exceedingly frequently sin. **106{107}[7]** *Et deduxit eos in viam rectam,* and he led them into the

---

and Modern Theology. "Beginning with Denys the Carthusian (d. 1471) the idea that human nature desires an ultimate end that is beyond human nature's innate ability to obtain came into conflict with an axiom (derived from a certain reading of Aristotle) that 'natural desire cannot extend beyond natural capacity.'" Nicholas J. Healy, "Henri de Lubac on Nature and Grace: A Note on Some Recent Contributions to the Debate," 35 *Communio* 435–64 (2008).

20 Rom. 7:23–25.
21 Rom. 14:23b.

right way: that is, by the preaching of the Apostles and of other teachers, he converted their hearts to the Catholic faith, which is the way to the vision of God by sight. Or [we can look at it this way], *into the right way*, that is, into Christ, who in the Gospel of John says: *I am the way, the truth, and the life; no one comes to the Father but by me.*[22] Or [another interpretation], *into the right way*, that is, into a good manner of living or into the keeping of the precepts, without which no one can be saved, according to that stated in Matthew: *But if you will enter into life, keep the commandments.*[23] *Ut irent in civitatem habitationis, that they might go to a city of habitation*, that is, into the fatherland of the Blessed, which we ought daily to apply ourselves by contemplation and by devotion, so that when this life is completed we might enter into it in reality. Whence the Apostle to the Hebrew says: *Let us hasten into that rest.*[24]

106{107}[8]   *Let the mercies of the Lord confess him: and his wonderful works to the children of men.*[25]

Confiteantur Domino misericordiae eius, et mirabilia eius filiis hominum.

106{107}[8] *Confiteantur Dominio misericordiae eius, let the mercies of the Lord confess him*: that is, let the benefits of the divine kindness or the effects of the mercy of God manifested to men lead them to confess to the Lord with the confession of praise and of thanksgiving; *et mirabilia eius filiis hominum, and his wonderful works to the children of men*, that is, let the [works] shown to men, or done on behalf of men provoke them to confess to the Lord in the manner just stated. For we ought to ascribe all good things to God, and to praise him, love him, and revere him for all things. The mercies of God are that he calls us to faith, he awaits us with great patience, he kindly turns back to us, freely justifies us, makes us advance, and preserves us in good. His wonders are that he became incarnate for us, he *conversed* [with men] in the world,[26] he suffered for mankind, that he rose again, ascended, and sent the Holy Spirit, the Paraclete, and that he condescended to work infinite miracles by himself and through his ministers.

---

22 John 14:6.
23 Matt. 19:17.
24 Heb. 4:11a.
25 E. N. I have departed from the Douay-Rheims's translation, "let the mercies of the Lord give glory to him," to "let the mercies of the Lord confess him." I have done this also in Ps. 106:15, 21, and 31.
26 *Cf.* Baruch 3:38: *He was seen upon earth, and conversed with men.*

106{107}[9] *For he has satisfied the empty soul, and has filled the hungry soul with good things.*

Quia satiavit animam inanem, et animam esurientem satiavit bonis.

106{107}[9] *Quia satiavit animam inanem, et animam esurientem satiavit bonis; for he has satisfied the empty soul, and has filled the hungry soul with good things.* Here he puts the singular for the plural. For Christ satisfies souls that were once given over to idolatry and as a result empty of all grace with its spiritual gifts, namely, faith, hope, charity, the gifts of the Holy Spirit, and multiform grace. So also Christ satisfies the souls of sinners — which are empty, void, and vacuous as long as they are in servitude to vice — when they convert unto penance. And the hungry soul, one vehemently desirous of being joined to God, to be pleasing to God, to live a life that is just he fills with good desires, by giving it daily increase in spiritual riches. *For one that has shall be given, and he shall abound.*[27] Christ satisfies these souls or such men, now inchoatively and according to the manner and state of the present life; he does not yet satisfy them completely. But in heaven, he will satisfy them perfectly, fully, and absolutely as is stated in an earlier Psalm: *I shall be satisfied when your glory shall appear.*[28] This also is written in Matthew: *Blessed are they that hunger and thirst after justice, for they shall have their fill.*[29] For to the extent a soul hungers, desires, or wills — as long as it desires truly, purely, efficaciously, reasonably, and urgently — to that extent it will receive from God both grace in the present and glory in the future. For God fills all men in accordance with how they prepare themselves and make themselves capable to receive. For this preparation or capacity exists in the will, because desire opens up the will to receive that which it loves. And so God fills each man with a pure, efficacious, and stable desire in the amount he desires. Now a desire is pure when it is unmixed with an alien affection, namely, a worldly or carnal love; and it is efficacious when it has the power to obtain the desired good. This, indeed, is set forth in the book of Job: *If a man turn his heart to God, he shall draw his spirit and breath unto himself.*[30] And with Jeremiah: *Who is this that sets his heart to approach to me, says the Lord?*[31] Now that God so satisfies an empty and hungry soul, is acknowledged by Isaiah: *The Lord is the everlasting God, etc., . . . It is he that gives strength to the weary and increases force and might to them that are not.*[32]

---

27 Matt. 25:29a.
28 Ps. 16:15b.
29 Matt. 25:29.
30 Job 34:14.
31 Jer. 30:31b.
32 Is. 40:28–29.

According to Aurelius Augustine,[33] four temptations or four evils from which Christ frees us are addressed in this Psalm. The first evil or the first temptation is straying from God in this world, and spiritual hunger and indigence of mind, from which we are delivered by Christ, so long as we strive toward God by the right way and thence we are spiritually satisfied. The second evil or second temptation is the difficulty of overcoming disordered desires because of bad habits or the assault of passions. Christ helps those who strive [to overcome these disordered desires]. The third is the temptation of tediousness, of spiritual sluggishness or acedia,[34] so long as a man is averse to spiritual labor, and he delays and dreads to apply himself to good works. Through grace, Christ excites and sets on fire this sort of man. The fourth is the difficulty of doing good because of the existence of various impediments which are like storms and tempests and hazards found in this great sea, that is, this world in which the servant of Christ encounters thousands of impediments and periods of disquiet that draw one away from God. Christ saves us from this evil, mitigating the difficulties with grace in this way, namely conferring internal peace and steadfast quiet among all the turbulent business of this present life.

106{107}[10]   *Such as sat in darkness and in the shadow of death: bound in want and in iron.*

Sedentes in tenebris et umbra mortis; vinctos, in mendicitate et ferro.

106{107}[11]   *Because they had exasperated the words of God: and provoked the counsel of the most High.*

Quia exacerbaverunt eloquia Dei, et consilium Altissimi irritaverunt.

---

33 E. N. The reference is to St. Augustine's own *Exposition on the Psalms* dealing with this Psalm, where he speaks of the *quatuor tentationes, quatuor exclamationes, quatuor liberationes, quatuor miserationum dominicarum confessiones. Enarr. in Ps.*, 106, 4–8, PL 36, 1423. The four-fold division of temptations, pleas, deliveries, and confessions of God's mercy is based upon the four-fold repetition of *clamaverunt ad Dominum cum tribularentur*, "they cried to the Lord in their affliction," and *confiteantur Domino misericordiae eius*, "let the mercies of the Lord confess him," or, more literally, "let his mercies confess to the Lord."

34 E. N. Acedia (sometimes accidie or accedie) is considered one of the seven capital sins. The word comes from Greek ἀκηδία (akēdia), which literally means "lack of care," or negligence. It is a "spiritual sloth [that] goes so far as to refuse the joy that comes from God and [is] repelled by divine goodness." CCC § 2093. The spiritual writers understand by [acedia] a form of depression due to lax ascetical practice, decreasing vigilance, carelessness of heart." CCC § 2733.

Thus far, therefore, the Prophet has brought up the first deliverance from the first evil or the first temptation. Now, he addresses the release from the second evil. 106{107}[10] *Sedentes in tenebris et umbra mortis, vinctos in mendicitate et ferro; such as sat in darkness and in the shadow of death: bound in want and in iron.* Christ satisfies and delivers also those who have sat or sit in the darkness of disbelief or ignorance, and in the shadow of death, that is, in evil vice, which is the image of eternal death; those conquered by the yoke of sin and servitude to the devil in want, that is, destitute of all spiritual goods, and an in iron, that is, vicious habit which so forcefully binds men in sin as a chain forcefully binds a man in prison. Now that Christ redeems these is made clear in Isaiah, where God the Father says to Christ: *I the Lord have called you in justice, and taken you by the hand, and preserved you. And I have given you for a covenant of the people, for a light of the Gentiles: That you might open the eyes of the blind, and bring forth the prisoner out of prison, and them that sit in darkness out of the prison house.*[35] Whence in the Gospel, Zacharias exclaims to Christ: *To enlighten them that sit in darkness and in the shadow of death.*[36] Now why men incur such great evil follows: 106{107}[11] *Quia exacerbaverunt, because they had exasperated,* that is, they determined to find bitter and to flee, *eloquia Dei, the words of God,* not desiring to obey them. Or [another explanation is], *because they had exasperated the words of God,* they provoked to anger God speaking to them through the Scriptures, and the preaching of his servants, and the natural law written in the hearts of all men; *et consilium Altissimi, and the counsel of the most High,* that is, the divine exhortation, *irritaverunt, they provoked,* that is, by not willing to relinquish their idolatry and their other sins, they made fruitless and spurned, as the Lord said to Zechariah: *They would not hearken, and they turned away the shoulder to depart . . . and they made their heart as the adamant stone, lest they should hear the law.*[37]

106{107}[12] *And their heart was humbled with labors: they were weakened, and there was none to help them.*

Et humiliatum est in laboribus cor eorum; infirmati sunt, nec fuit qui adiuvaret.

106{107}[13] *Then they cried to the Lord in their affliction: and he delivered them out of their distresses.*

---

35 Is. 42:6–7.
36 Luke 1:79.
37 Zech. 7:11–12a.

Et clamaverunt ad Dominum cum tribularentur; et de neces-
sitatibus eorum liberavit eos.

106{107}[14] *And he brought them out of darkness, and the shadow of*
death; and broke their bonds asunder.

Et eduxit eos de tenebris et umbra mortis, et vincula eorum
dirupit.

106{107}[15] *Let the mercies of the Lord confess him, and his wonderful*
works to the children of men.

Confiteantur Domino misericordiae eius, et mirabilia eius
filiis hominum.

106{107}[12] *Et humiliatum est in laboribus cor eorum, and their heart*
was humbled with labors, that is, through their wicked works, their heart
was made mean, confused, and subject to demons. Whence in the book of
Wisdom they [the wicked] say: *We wearied ourselves in the way of iniquity*
and destruction, and have walked through hard ways.[38] For *God . . . to the*
sinner has given vexation, and superfluous care, as Ecclesiastes acknowledges.[39] *Infirmati sunt, they were weakened* in their hearts and unable to
overcome the snares of the devil through their own power, *nec fuit qui*
adiuvaret, and there was none to help them except for God, who spoke
through Hosea, *There is no God but me, and there is no Savior but me.*[40]
For this reason, 106{107}[13] *Et clamaverunt ad Dominum cum tribu-*
larentur, then they cried to the Lord in their affliction, so that he might
bestow upon them help, which he also did, because *de necessitatibus*
eorum, he delivered them out of their distresses, that is, he delivered them
from their previously-stated dangers as it states in the verse that follows. 106{107}[14] *Et eduxit eos de tenebris, and he brought them out of*
darkness of unbelief and of ignorance, *et umbra mortis, and the shadow*
of death, that is, their former evil manner of life; *et vincula eorum, and*
their bonds, that is, the entangling bonds of vice by which they were
captured by the devil, *dirupit, he broke asunder,* forgiving their sins and
bringing them over to the kingdom and the inheritance of their heavenly
Father. For Christ says this through Isaiah: *I will lead the blind into the*
way which they know not: and in the paths which they were ignorant of
I will make them walk.[41] And in the first epistle of Peter we find: *You*

---

38 Wis. 5:7a.
39 Eccl. 2:26a.
40 Hos. 13:4b.
41 Is. 42:16a.

were redeemed *from your vain conversation of the traditions of your fathers, with the precious blood of Christ.*[42] Christ, however, broke asunder the bonds of the sinners as it is written in the first epistle of John: *For this purpose, the Son of God appeared, that he might destroy the works of the devil.*[43] Therefore, because of all these benefits, **106{107}[15]** *Confiteantur Domino misericordiae eius, et mirabilia eius filiis hominum; let the mercies of the Lord confess him, and his wonderful works to the children of men* in the sense just expounded.

One ought to pay heed also that these two verses — *Then they cried to the Lord in their affliction, etc.* and *Let the mercy of the Lord confess him, etc.* — are repeated four times in succession, in accordance with the four temptations described in this Psalm, and from which we are delivered by God, and for which four deliverances we ought to return thanks to the Lord.

106{107}[16] *Because he has broken gates of brass, and burst the iron bars.*

Quia contrivit portas aereas, et vectes ferreos confregit.

106{107}[17] *He took them out of the way of their iniquity: for they were brought low for their injustices.*

Suscepit eos de via iniquitatis eorum, propter iniustitias enim suas humiliati sunt.

106{107}[16] *Quia contrivit portas aereas, because he has broken gates of brass*: that is, the Lord has extirpated from the heart of the believer bad habits or vices rooted in the soul from vicious customs; *et vectes ferreos, and the iron bars,* by which gates are customarily fortified, that is, excuses regarding our own fault, *confregit, he has burst,* that is, he has removed from the faithful, so that they do not defend themselves, but they humbly recognize their fault. For by this metal is designated the most unyielding sin from which bond the soul is released with great difficulty. Whence, in Isaiah, it is stated to one who is habituated in vice: *For I know that you are stubborn, and your neck is as an iron sinew, and your forehead as brass,* says the Lord.[44] Just as he who is inside cannot get out when the door bolts are shut, so a soul by making excuses from sin, closes its mouth from a saving confession, and sins hidden within are neither uncovered nor are they healed. **106{107}[17]** *Suscepit eos, he*

---

42 1 Pet. 1:18–19a.
43 1 John 3:8b.
44 Is. 43:4.

took *them* to a salutary repentance and pristine friendship *de via iniqui-tatis eorum, out of the way of their iniquity*, that is, from their iniquitous way and life, according to that [which God] promised in return in Jeremiah: *Return . . . and I will not turn my face.*[45] *Propter iniustitias enim suas humiliati sunt, for they were brought low for their injustices*, that is, for their faults they were punished. Or [alternatively], *for their injustices*, that is, from the consideration of their sins, they were humbled before you, confessing themselves worthy of all punishments because of their departures [from the natural and divine law].

106{107}[18]   *Their soul abhorred all manner of meat: and they drew nigh even to the gates of death.*

Omnem escam abominata est anima eorum, et appropin-quaverunt usque ad portas mortis.

106{107}[19]   *And they cried to the Lord in their affliction: and he delivered them out of their distresses.*

Et clamaverunt ad Dominum cum tribularentur; et de neces-sitatibus eorum liberavit eos.

106{107}[20]   *He sent his word and healed them: and delivered them from their destructions.*

Misit verbum suum, et sanavit eos, et eripuit eos de interi-tionibus eorum.

And then he describes the third evil, which is aversion to the good. 106{107}[18] *Omnem escam, all manner of meat*, spiritual [meat], that is, all good work which preserves, nourishes, and perfects the soul in the life of grace, *abominata est anima eorum, their soul abhorred* from the temptation of acedia, from defects in the fervor regarding God, and the sloth of torpor, *et appropinquaverunt usque ad portas mortis, and they drew nigh even to the gates of death*, that is, they nearly gave in to this aversion: and so they drew nigh to mortal sins which are the gates of death and of hell. For if such persons would have neglected the commandments of God out of such disgust for good works, they would have sinned mortally, and they would have entered through the gates of spiritual, eternal, and infernal death; but they were preserved by God, so that they entered not therethrough, for 106{107}[19] *Et clamaverunt ad Dominum, and they cried to the Lord* for the pouring out of holy devotion, *cum tribularentur,*

---

45 Jer. 3:12a.

in their affliction, that is, when they were deeply afflicted by such torpor; *et de neccessitatibus eorum*, *and out of their distresses*, that is, the previously mentioned anxieties, *liberavit eos, he delivered them*, exciting fortitude and charity and fervor in them. 106{107}[20] *Misit, he sent*, God, the Father [sent], *Verbum suum, his Word*, that is, his only begotten Son, of whom is written, *In the beginning was the Word.*[46] He sent him into the world by the Incarnation, according to this: *The Word was made flesh, and dwelt among us.*[47] *Et sanavit eos, and he healed them* from the wounds of the soul, *et eripuit eos de interitionibus eorum, and delivered them from their destructions*, that is, from sins which kill the soul, as is asserted in Ezechiel: *The soul that sins, the same shall die.*[48] Scripture also says this in the first epistle of John: *The Father has sent his Son to be the Savior of the world.*[49] Or [looked at another way], *the word*, that is, the preaching of the heavenly word, by which the infirm soul is healed, in the manner that is stated in the book of Wisdom: *Your word, O Lord, heals all things.*[50]

106{107}[21]   *Let the mercies of the Lord confess him: and his wonderful works to the children of men.*

Confiteantur Domino misericordiae eius; et mirabilia eius filiis hominum.

106{107}[22]   *And let them sacrifice the sacrifice of praise: and declare his works with joy.*

Et sacrificent sacrificium laudis, et annuntient opera eius in exsultatione.

106{107}[21] *Confiteantur Domino misericordia eius*, etc. which has already been spoken about. 106{107}[22] *Et sacrificent, and let them sacrifice*, [let] the sons of men [sacrifice] *sacrificium laudi, the sacrifice of praise* to the Lord who does not need our goods,[51] but who delights in humble praise and spiritual sacrifice rather than all of the holocausts of the Old Law. Whence it states in a Psalm above: *The sacrifice of praise shall glorify me.*[52] *Et annuntient, and let them declare*, that is, [let] all of

---

46 John 1:1.
47 John 1:14.
48 Ez. 18:20a.
49 1 John 4:14.
50 Wis. 16:12b.
51 *Cf.* Ps. 15:2b.
52 Ps. 49:23a.

those already mentioned [declare], or let them recite with them, *opera eius, his works*, that is, the wonders of Christ, his benefits, namely, and his mercies, *in exsultatione, with joy*, that is, with spiritual happiness arising out of divine charity. For he who loves God glories in his heart by the proclamation of his works, as it states in a Psalm above: *My lips shall greatly rejoice when I shall sing to you.*[53]

106{107}[23] *They that go down to the sea in ships, doing business in the great waters,*

Qui descendunt mare in navibus, facientes operationem in aquis multis,

106{107}[24] *These have seen the works of the Lord, and his wonders in the deep.*

Ipsi viderunt opera Domini, et mirabilia eius in profundo.

106{107}[23] *Qui descendunt mare in navibus, they that go down to the sea in ships*, that is, they who from the exercise of a contemplative life set themselves down to the active life, having regard for the welfare of their neighbor, and going down toward the sea, that is, the world, or drawing near to men, *facientes operationem, doing business*, that is, pious exhortations, diligent questioning, just correction, *in aquis multis, in the great waters*, that is, among many peoples. For the many waters are many people, according to John in Revelation.[54] For good pastors and those who have care of others, engage in many activities with those subject to them, since they purify them, enlighten them, and perfect them. 106{107}[24] *Ipsi, these* prelates and contemplatives that descend in this manner, *viderunt, have seen* with the eye of faith, *opera Domini, the works of the Lord*, that is, the deeds of Christ clearly set forth in the Gospel, or all the works of the Creator expressed in sacred Scripture; *et mirabilia eius, and his wonders* they spiritually have seen *in profundo, in the deep*, that is, in the high intellect, by which historical things are understood mystically: as that the marriage of Solomon with the daughter of Pharaoh signifies the espousal of the Church gathered together from the nations with Christ; and the sale of Joseph, the sale of Christ; and also Jonah remaining three days in the belly of the whale prefigures Christ's sepulture. Or [we can understand it thus], *they have seen ... the marvels of God in the deep*, that is, in the secret of the human heart, which is

---

53 Ps. 70:23a.
54 Rev. 17:1, 15: *The waters which you saw ... are peoples, and nations, and tongues.*

called deep because it is inscrutable, just like that said in Jeremiah, *The heart is perverse above all things, and inscrutable.*[55] And pastors look into the deep wonders of God when, by their exhortations, they dissolve a hard heart into tears, they raise the spiritually dead soul to the life of grace, they turn hardened sinners towards repentance; [when by their exhortations they persuade] the incontinent, and those who only for a short time are able to be continent, to preserve continence their whole life; when they make the proud humble, they make the angry meek. These are the wonders of God, for, according to Augustine, to justify someone who is ungodly is a greater thing than the creation of the whole world.[56]

106{107}[25] *He said [the word], and there arose a stormy wind: and the waves thereof were lifted up.*[57]

Dixit, et stetit spiritus procellae, et exaltati sunt fluctus eius.

Following this, the danger or temptation of storms is described. 106{107}[25] *Dixit,* he said, God, for whom saying is doing, [said] *et stetit, and there arose,* that is, it was steady and strong, *spiritus procellae, a stormy wind,* that is, the tyrannical persecution against the faithful or grave temptations. God says, that is, he permits them to be, for the greater merit of his elect. *Et exaltati sunt fluctus eius, and the waves thereof were lifted up,* that is, the disturbances associated with these persecutions were strengthened and augmented, because as long as God permits it, the tribulations of the just increase, and the cruelty of the perverse becomes strong.

---

55 Jer. 17:9.

56 E. N. That is to bring someone outside of a state of grace and in a state of mortal sin into a state of grace, and therefore justified — a supernatural reality — is greater than the creation out of the world from nothing. The reference is to St. Augustine's Tract 72 of his Tractates on the Gospel of John. In asking whether it is a greater thing to create a just man than to justify a sinner, St. Augustine responds that mercy used to justify a sinner is greater than the creative power to create a just man. PL 35, 1823. St. Thomas paraphrases St. Augustine's teaching thus: "It is a greater thing to make a man just from being a sinner than it is to create heaven and earth" (*maius opus est ut ex impio iustus fiat, quam creare caelum et terram*). As St. Thomas summarizes it: "The good of grace in one person is greater than the good of nature of the entire universe." ST IaIIae, q. 113, art. 9, c. & ad 2.

57 E. N. The Latin text does not support the words "the word" which is found in the Douay Rheims, so I have put them in brackets; they have gone unmentioned in Denis's *Commentary* since they are not in the Latin text. I have also replaced "a storm of wind" with "a stormy wind."

106{107}[26] *They mount up to the heavens, and they go down to the depths: their soul pined away with evils.*

Ascendunt usque ad caelos, et descendunt usque ad abyssos; anima eorum in malis tabescebat.

106{107}[26] *Ascendunt usque ad caelos, they mount up to the heavens:* that is, the persecutors and tempters in the deep are aroused against almighty God, and, because of their magnitude, their cruelty, and perversity they penetrate heaven, and thus they provoke God to a vehement vengeance. Whence in the second book of Chronicles it is said to the children of Israel: *Your cruelty has reached to heaven.*[58] *Et descendunt usque ad abyssos, and they go down to the depths,* that is, they live repulsive and carnal lives, and finally are forsaken, and they slide into hell. Or [another view is], *they go down to the depths,* that is, to the degree they exalt themselves against God, to that degree they are humiliated by God and perish, according to that in Job: *If his pride mounts up even to heaven, and his head touches the clouds, in the end he shall be destroyed like a dunghill.*[59] Whence in Isaiah it is said to the proud man who has contrived to exalt himself above the stars of heaven and his [God's] sun: *But yet you shall be brought down to hell, into the depth of the pit.*[60] *Anima eorum in malis tabescebat, their soul pined away with evils,* that is, in his own sins he languishes, withers, and falls into ruin, in the manner that is acknowledged by Jeremiah: *Everyone shall die for his own iniquity;* and again, *Every man that shall eat the sour grape, his teeth shall be set on edge.*[61] For he who strives to cause injury, first causes injury to himself, and any evil done redounds to one's self. For this reason in the book of Proverbs, Solomon confessed: *His own iniquities catch the wicked, and he is fast bound with the ropes of his own sins.*[62]

---

58 2 Chr. 28:9b. E. N. The context is the prophet Oded who met the Israelite army which had been victorious over Judah in Samaria, and he reproached them because of the unnecessary brutality of their victory.

59 Job. 20:6–7a.

60 Is. 14:15.

61 Jer. 31:30. E. N. Denis elaborates on the latter part of Jeremiah: "*Every man that shall eat the sour grape,* that is, who has committed iniquity, *his teeth shall be set on edge,* that is, he will pay for what he did, and he will carry the debt of punishment.... Rightly is sin called the sour grape because it takes one toward eternal bitterness, and it inhibits the taste for divine sweetness, it gives birth to the remorse of conscience, and the soul disordered by sin is, in itself, its own most burdensome punishment." Doctor Ecstaticus D. Dionysius Cartusianus, *Opera Omnia* (Montreuil: 1900), Vol. 9, 226.

62 Prov. 5:22.

Or [we might understand it this way]: *They mount up to the heavens*: that is, the faithful that are so direly afflicted, by praying and contemplating ascend to the heavens, even to Christ, since by the consideration of heavenly rewards, they more easily suffer all things. For the consideration of reward lessens the force of the whip.[63] *And they go down to the depths*: that is, after so much contemplation acquired from grace, they fall again to useless fantasies and to unworthy occupations from human weakness and carnal thoughts. For even Paul after the rapture suffered the sting of the flesh.[64] But God permits this so that man may consider what he has from himself and also what he has from God. Or [another way is understanding it is], *And they go down to the depths*, considering the storms of hell: and all the punishments of this world become tolerable in consideration of these. *Their soul*, [the souls] of those afflicted in this way, *in malis, with evils*, that is, in punishment and fault, which surround men everywhere in this miserable life in which the *just man* falls *seven times a day*,[65] *tabescebat, pined away*, that is, [their soul] is affected with tedium and sorrow which causes languishing, as Jeremiah says in Lamentations: *Therefore our heart is sorrowful with sadness; therefore are our eyes become dim.*[66]

106{107}[27] *They were troubled, and staggered like a drunken man; and all their wisdom was swallowed up.*[67]

Turbati sunt et moti sunt sicut ebrius; et omnis sapientia eorum devorata est.

106{107}[27] *Turbati sunt, they were troubled* in soul *et moti sunt, and staggered* away from the right judgment of reason *sicut ebrius, like a drunken man*, following the impulses of passion and irrational movements; *et omnis sapientia eorum, and all their wisdom*, which they appeared to have during the time of tranquility, *devorata est, was swallowed up* during the time of persecution or temptation, so that the act of reason succumbed to passion, and their foolishness inhibited the act of wisdom. For many appear to be virtuous and wise during times of peace, quiet, prosperity, and joy; but reason falls, sensuality dominates, and virtues collapse and vices prevail

---

63 E. N. *Consideratio praemii minuit vim flagelli.* This appears to be a common proverb whose exact lineage is difficult to trace.

64 2 Cor. 12:2, 7.

65 Prov. 24:16.

66 Lam. 5:17.

67 E. N. I replaced the word "reeled" found in the Douay-Rheims with "staggered."

when adversity, disquiet, and tribulation interfere and overcome them. Whence also Christ speaks of some people in the Gospel, saying: *These have no roots, for they believe for a while, and in time of temptation, they fall away.*[68] And again in another place he says regarding those people who do not do what they know they ought to do, but from passion or persecution they fall from the mean of reason: *He will be similar to a foolish man that built his house upon the sand; and the rain fell, and the floods came, and the winds blew, and they beat upon that house, and it fell, and great was the fall thereof.*[69] All this just said is especially pertinent to those who rule others, who — giving in to movements of anger or impatience from various occasions, employments, or the imperfection of those under their care — tend to fall from the fortitude of mind and the right judgment of reason. For such persons especially, indeed for all of us, we ought to pray that God may confirm our heart daily in him, and that it not be dashed by the adversity and the storms of others: for as the Apostle says to the Hebrews, *It is best that the heart be established with grace.*[70] For dishonest and shameful is a learned man, and especially the teacher of others, who falls in adversity. For this reason in the book of Job it is stated to him who appeared disturbed because of adversity: *Where is your fear, your fortitude, your patience, and the perfection of your ways?*[71]

106{107}[28] *And they cried to the Lord in their affliction: and he brought them out of their distresses.*

Et clamaverunt ad Dominum cum tribularentur; et de necessitatibus eorum eduxit eos.

106{107}[29] *And he turned the storm into a breeze: and its waves were still.*

Et statuit procellam eius in auram, et siluerunt fluctus eius.

106{107}[28] *Et clamaverunt ad Dominum,* and they cried to the Lord: who, as the Prophet Nahum attests, *He rebukes the sea and dries it up;*[72] *cum tribularentur, in their affliction* in such adversity, saying with Peter, *Lord, save us, we perish.*[73] And not in vain: for *et de necessitatibus eorum,*

---

68 Luke 8:13.
69 Matt. 8:26–27.
70 Heb. 13:9. *E. N.* For "established" (*stabilari*) we might substitute "confirmed," "supported," or "made secure."
71 Job 4:6.
72 Nahum 1:4a.
73 Matt. 8:25b.

and ... out of their distresses, that is, from the previously-mentioned dangers, *eduxit eos, he brought them out*: for he will not let us to be tempted above that which we are able.[74] **106{107}[29]** *Et statuit procellam eius, and he turned the storm*, that is, he removed the din of persecution, the harshness of adversity, and the motions of temptation, *in auram, into a breeze*, that is, into a softly-flowing wind, so that he might mitigate adversity and fill the mind with the serenity of tranquility. Not, however, that he takes away temptation completely: for, as Augustine says, "Persevere even unto the end, because temptation perseveres even unto the end."[75] Therefore, if we ask one to be taken away from us, we should expect another. *Et siluerunt fluctus eius, and its waves were still*, that is, the attacks of temptation ceased for a time.

106{107}[30] *And they rejoiced because they were still: and he brought them to the haven which they wished for.*

Et laetati sunt quia siluerunt; et deduxit eos in portum voluntatis eorum.

106{107}[30] *Et laetati sunt, and they rejoiced*, men unburdened from the yoke of temptation [rejoiced] in the Lord. Hence it is written in the book of Tobit: *You are not delighted, O Lord, in our being lost, because after a storm you make a calm, and after tears and after ... weeping, you pour in joyfulness.*[76] And they rejoiced, glorying in the Lord for their liberation, *quia siluerunt, because they were still* of the flow of persecution of these things. For here Tobias after he was healed said: *I will bless you, O Lord, because you have chastised me, and you have saved me.*[77] And the Apostle also: *Blessed be the God ... who comforts us in all our tribulation.*[78] *Et deduxit eos in portum voluntatis eorum, and he brought them to the haven which they wished for*, that is, into the peace desired by all mortals, into the desired perfection, into the security of conscience, and into the most sweet tranquility, and, after the course of this life, into the heavenly homeland of the elect. For he who endures adversities

---

74 *Cf.* 1 Cor. 10:13.

75 *E. N.* The reference is to *In Ioannis Evangelium Tractatus*, 45, 13, although Denis does not quote it precisely: *Temptatio accidit; persevera usque in finem: quia tentatio non perseverat usque in finem.* "A temptation befalls you; persevere unto the end, for temptation will not persist until the end." PL 35, 1726.

76 Tob. 3:22.

77 Tob. 11:17a.

78 1 Cor.1:3a, 4a.

strongly and remains firmly faithful to Christ even during sorrowful conditions is deserving of this haven of peace and worthy to be led to this consolation. For this reason the Savior says to his disciples: *Amen, amen I say to you, that you shall lament and weep, but the world shall rejoice; and you shall be made sorrowful, but your sorrow shall be turned into joy.*[79] And the Apostle [Paul] says to the Corinthians: Know that *as you are partakers of the sufferings, so shall you be also of the consolation.*[80] And again: *As the sufferings of Christ abound in us, so also by Christ does our comfort abound.*[81]

106{107}[31]   *Let the mercies of the Lord confess him, and his wonderful works to the children of men.*

Confiteantur Domino misericordiae eius; et mirabilia eius filiis hominum.

106{107}[32]   *And let them exalt him in the church of the people: and praise him in the chair of the ancients.*

Et exaltent eum in ecclesia plebis, et in cathedra seniorum laudent eum.

106{107}[31] *Confiteantur Domino misericordiae eius,* etc. *Let the mercies of the Lord confess him,* because after so much persecution, such a peace has been bestowed. 106{107}[32] *Et exaltent eum, and let them exalt him,* that is, let them pay him honor with magnificent word and deed, *in ecclesia plebis, in the church of the people,* that is, in the congregation of the faithful; *et in cathedra seniorum, and in the chair of the ancients,* that is, in the place and the seat of the those who are superior, *laudent eum, let them praise him,* [that is, let them] who sit in such chairs, [praise him]. The Prophet [David] wishes, therefore, that all men unanimously praise God, both the great and the small, the superior and the inferior, in the manner that is stated in Revelation: *Give praise to our God, all you his servants; and you that fear him, little and great.*[82] And the Apostle to the Romans said: *The God of patience and of comfort grant you to be of one mind one towards another, according to Jesus Christ, so that with one mind, and with one mouth, you may glorify God.*[83]

---

79 John 15:20.
80 1 Cor. 1:7.
81 1 Cor. 1:5.
82 Rev. 19:5.
83 Rom. 15:5–6.

106{107}[33] *He has turned rivers into a wilderness: and the sources of water into dry ground.*

Posuit flumina in desertum, et exitus aquarum in sitim.

106{107}[33] *Posuit flumina in desertum, he has turned rivers into a wilderness,* that is, God diverted the flow of grace and of doctrine into the hearts of the Gentiles. For the Gentiles are called the wilderness, according to this in Isaiah: *The land that was desolate and impassible shall be glad, and the wilderness shall rejoice.*[84] In short, while God pours out his grace from heaven upon our soul, he turns waters in the wilderness. *Et exitus aquarum, and the sources of water,* that is, the Synagogue of the Jews, whose rain of preaching used to flow into others, he turned *in sitim, into dry ground,* because they were deprived of the true wisdom of Christ due to their disbelief. And in this they are similar to that which Christ attested to: *For judgment I am come into this world; that they who see not, may see; and they who see, may become blind.*[85] For the Jews, who before could see, began to be blind at the coming Christ, but the Gentiles, who before lived in darkness, began to see. For he whom the Jews believed would come, they did not recognize when he was present before them; but the Gentiles by the preaching of Christ and of the Apostles were enlightened by a ray of wisdom. And so we have in Isaiah: *They to whom it was not told of him, have seen; and they that heard not, have beheld.*[86]

106{107}[34] *A fruitful land into barrenness, for the wickedness of them that dwell therein.*

Terram fructiferam in salsuginem, a malitia inhabitantium in ea.

God also turned **106{107}[34]** *Terram fructiferam in salsuginem, a fruitful land into barrenness:* that is, he made dry and sterile the Jews or the Synagogue that had been once fruitful with doctrine and life, withdrawing from the Jewish people the infusion of grace in the manner that is prophesized in the book of Hosea: *Their root is dried up, they shall yield no fruit.*[87] Now this he did *a malitia inhabitantium in ea, for the wickedness of them that dwell therein,* that is, because of the sins of that people, according to that which again is attested to in Hosea: *My Lord my God will cast them away,*

---

84 Is. 35:1.
85 John 9:39.
86 Is. 52.15b.
87 Hosea 9:16a.

because they hearkened not to him.[88] And the Lord said through Jeremiah: *I will make the pride* of this wicked people, *that will not hear my words, and that walk in the perverseness of their heart to rot.*[89]

106{107}[35]   *He has turned a wilderness into pools of water, and a dry land into water springs.*

Posuit desertum in stagna aquarum, et terram sine aqua in exitus aquarum.

106{107}[36]   *And has placed there the hungry; and they made a city for their habitation.*

Et collocavit illic esurientes, et constituerunt civitatem habitationis.

106{107}[35] *Posuit desertum, he has turned into wilderness,* that is, the Gentile nations, *in stagna aquarium, into pools of water,* that is, into an unwavering superabundance of spiritual graces and of heavenly doctrine: *for where sin abounded, grace did more abound;*[90] *et terram sine aqua, and a dry land,* that is, peoples once existing without divine illumination and grace, he turned *in exitus aquarum, into water springs,* that is, he poured forth such abundant grace into them by the Apostolic preaching that they were also able to teach and to covert others. Whence the Apostle [Paul] said to the Ephesians: *It is now revealed to his holy apostles and prophets in the Spirit, that the Gentiles should be fellow heirs, and of the same body, and copartners of his promise in Christ Jesus.*[91] 106{107}[36] *Et collocavit, and he has placed,* God [has placed], *illic, there,* that is, within the previously-stated affluence of grace and heavenly doctrine, *esurientes, the hungry* for justice, by which they eagerly received the Catholic faith and the preaching of the heavenly words, in the way that in the Acts of the Apostles is written about the Thessalonians: *The more noble of them... received the word with all eagerness, daily searching the Scriptures.*[92] *Et constituerunt civitatem habitationis, and they made a city for their habitation,* that is, [they made] the Church militant — which is the city of God and the household of Christ collected and constructed from the faithful — [to be their dwelling].

---

88 Hosea 9:17a.
89 Jer. 13:9–10.
90 Rom. 5:20b.
91 Eph. 3:5b–6.
92 Acts 17:11.

106{107}[37] *And they sowed fields, and planted vineyards: and they yielded fruit of birth.*

Et seminaverunt agros et plantaverunt vineas, et fecerunt fructum nativitatis.

106{107}[37] *Et, and* these Apostles, and their successors and followers, *seminaverunt agros, sowed fields,* that is, they made fruitful and filled men dwelling in the world with the word of God, sending into their heart the Gospel of the Savior. For as Christ in the Gospel of Matthew asserts, *The seed is the word of God, and the field is the world.*[93] And the Apostles filled the world with this seed, in the way that is stated in Isaiah: *They shall blossom and bud, and they shall fill the face of the world with seed.*[94] This seed did not bring forth fruit from the Jews, but [it did] from the Gentiles: and so Christ said to them [as stated] in Matthew: *The kingdom of God shall be taken from you and shall be given to a nation yielding the fruits thereof.*[95] *Et plantaverunt vineas, and they planted vineyards,* that is, they founded particular churches in Christ. For Peter planted a vineyard of Christ in Italy, John in Asia, Thomas in India. Now that the Church is called a vineyard arises from that which we have in the prophecy of Isaiah: *For the vineyard of the Lord of hosts is the house of Israel.*[96] *Et fecerunt fructum nativitatis, and they yield fruit of birth,* that is, they generated many in Christ, in the manner that the Apostle said: *In Christ Jesus, by the Gospel, I have begotten you.*[97] For they spiritually generated all those that they converted to Christ.

106{107}[38] *And he blessed them, and they were multiplied exceedingly: and their cattle he suffered not to decrease.*

Et benedixit eis, et multiplicati sunt nimis; et iumenta eorum non minoravit.

106{107}[38] *Et benedixit eis, and he blessed them,* God [blessed them], that is, he bestowed abundant grace upon them, as is read in the Acts of the Apostles: *And the disciples were filled with joy and with the Holy*

---

93 Luke 8:11; Matt. 13:38. *E. N.* Actually, it is a combination of phrases in both the Gospel of Luke and the Gospel of Matthew, and not the Gospel of Matthew alone.
94 Is. 27:6.
95 Matt. 21:43.
96 Is. 5:7a.
97 1 Cor. 4:15b.

Spirit;[98] *et multiplicati sunt nimis,* and they were multiplied exceedingly in both merit and number, according to that which Luke says in Acts: *The Lord increased daily together such as should be saved.*[99] *Et iumenta eorum,* and their cattle, that is, the uneducated and the simple humbly carrying the yoke of the Lord above them, *non minoravit,* he suffered not to decrease: for many of such persons are chosen by God compared to those who are more noble and more wise. Whence the Apostle says to the Corinthians: *See your vocation, brethren, that there are not many wise according to the flesh, not many mighty, not many noble among you, but the foolish things of the world has God chosen, that he may confound the wise.*[100]

106{107}[39]   Then they were brought to be few: and they were afflicted through the trouble of evils and sorrow.

Et pauci facti sunt et vexati sunt, a tribulatione malorum et dolore.

106{107}[40]   Contempt was poured forth upon their princes: and he caused them to wander in an impassible place, and out of the way.[101]

Effusa est contemptio super principes; et errare fecit eos in invio, et non in via.

106{107}[41]   And he helped the poor out of poverty: and made him families like a flock of sheep.

Et adiuvit pauperem de inopia, et posuit sicut oves familias.

106{107}[39] *Et pauci facti sunt,* then they were brought to be few faithful in some places and some churches because of their death by tyrants and ungodly men; *et vexati sunt a tribulatione malorum,* and they were afflicted through the trouble of evils, which the ungodly afflicted them with, *dolore,* sorrow inflicted upon them by tyrants and perfidious men. For often, cities and towns with unbelievers devastated and destroyed Christian lands and churches and killed the faithful. 106{107}[40] *Effusa est contentio super principes,* contempt was poured forth upon their princes: that is, the greater number of those persecuting Christians

---

98 Acts 13:52.
99 Acts 2:47b.
100 1 Cor. 1:26–27.
101 E. N. I departed from the Douay-Rheims's "where there was no passing" to "an impassible place."

were in contention: either against one another, or against the truth of the Christian faith, or against the Christian leader; *et errari fecit eos, and he caused them to wander*, that is, God permitted them [to wander] *in invio, in an impassible place*, that is, in infidelity, where there is no way to come to the ultimate end, *et non in via, and out of the way*, that is, [out of] the true faith, because they did not have faith. **106{107}[41]** *Et adiuvit pauperem de inopia, and he helped the poor out of poverty*: that is, he raised the Gentile people, destitute of spiritual riches, from this penury, enriching them with spiritual goods; *et posuit, and he made* them *sicut oves familias, families like a flock of sheep*: that is, he placed them, fed them, and took care of them in his home (which is the Church) just like a shepherd keeps, finds pasture for, and feeds his sheep. Whence Christ says in the Gospel of John: *Other sheep I have, that are not of this fold, them also I must bring.*[102] Or [an alternative explanation is], *he helped the poor*, that is, the humble,[103] *out of poverty*, as it says in the Gospel: *Blessed are the poor in spirit, because theirs is the kingdom of heaven.*[104] Who, therefore, can possibly be richer than this poor man to whom has been promised the possession of the kingdom of heaven? With merit, therefore, Tobias says: *Fear not, my son: we lead indeed a poor life, but we shall have many good things if we fear God.*[105] And the Apostle to the Corinthians: *Their very deep poverty has abounded unto the riches of their simplicity.*[106]

106{107}[42] *The just shall see, and shall rejoice, and all iniquity shall stop their mouth.*

Videbunt recti, et laetabuntur; et omnis iniquitas oppilabit os suum.

106{107}[42] *Videbunt recti, the just shall see*, that is, the just will understand the previously-mentioned mercies of God, *et laetabuntur, and shall rejoice* in God because of his benefits that are so bountiful; *et omnis iniquitas, and all iniquity*, that is, all the iniquitous—namely, a demon, tyrant, false brother, or heretic—impudently and insolently prating against the truth and against the just, *oppilabit, shall stop*, that

---

102 John 10:16a.
103 James 4:6: *God resists the proud, and gives grace to the humble.*
104 Matt. 5:3.
105 Tobit 4:23a.
106 2 Cor. 8:2. *E. N.* St. Paul is informing the Corinthians of the churches in Macedonia.

is, will close, *os suum, their mouth*, because they will be overcome and confounded by that truth, and at length they will be rejected and condemned by Christ. For this reason, the Lord says to the proud in Isaiah: *I will put a ring in your nose, and a bit between your lips.*[107] Also the ungodly, who often disparage the just while they observe their holy manner of life, do not speak evil, and sometimes even commend those that they have disparaged. Therefore, the prince of the Apostle says: *This is the will of God, that by doing well you may put to silence the ignorance of foolish men.*[108]

106{107}[43] *Who is wise, and will keep these things? And who will understand the mercies of the Lord?*

Quis sapiens et custodiet haec? Et intelliget misericordias Domini?

106{107}[43] *Quis sapiens, et custodiet haec? Who is wise and will keep these things?* That is, he who is truly wise will retain this in his memory, will spiritually take a hold of it, and will reckon himself needy; *et [quis] intelliget misericordias Domini, and who will understand the mercies of the Lord?* That is, [who] will diligently think of the manifold graces bestowed to him and to others, and will know by experience how kind and clement is the Lord,[109] *the Father of mercies, and the God of all comfort?*[110] And this is similar to that which Hosea says: *Who is wise, and he shall understand these things? Who is prudent, and he shall know these things?*[111] But this appears contrary to what Truth affirms in the Gospel when he says: *I confess to you, O Father, Lord of heaven and earth, because you have hid these things from the wise and prudent.*[112] The response [to this apparent inconsistency] is that Christ speaks there of the wise of this world, whose wisdom God makes foolish.[113] But here it speaks of those truly wise, those illuminated by the Holy Spirit.

---

107 Is. 37:29a.

108 1 Pet. 2:15.

109 *Cf.* 2 Chr. 30:9: *For if you turn again to the Lord: your brethren, and children shall find mercy before their masters, that have led them away captive, and they shall return into this land: for the Lord your God is merciful, and will not turn away his face from you, if you return to him.*

110 2 Cor. 1:3.

111 Hosea 14:10a.

112 Matt. 11:25; *cf.* Luke 10:21.

113 *Cf.* 1 Cor. 1:20b: *Has not God made foolish the wisdom of this world?*

ARTICLE XII

LITERAL EXPOSITION OF THE SAME
ONE HUNDRED AND SIXTH PSALM.

OW SOME EXPOUND UPON THIS PSALM IN a literal sense as pertaining to the Jews only, and the bodily dangers from which they were delivered by God: and this exposition is not sufficiently fruitful, nor is it, in certain respects, consonant with its words.[114] It says, therefore: **106{107}[1]** *Confitemini Domino, etc. Confess to the Lord*, etc. as it has [already] been expounded. **106{107}[2]** *Dicant qui redempti sunt, let them say so that they have been redeemed* from diverse dangers, *a Domino, by the Lord*, the God of Israel, *quos redemit de manu inimici, whom he has redeemed from the hand of the enemy* and of the tyrant, however it might be that they are afflicted. *De regionibus, from out of the countries* in which they were dispersed, *congregavit eos, he gathered them*, leading them back to the lands of their fathers, as is stated by Ezechiel: *I will take you from among the Gentiles, and will gather you together out of all the countries, and will bring you into your own land.*[115] **106{107}[3]** *A solis ortu et occasu, ab aquilone et mari; from the rising and setting of the sun, from the north and from the sea*, that is, from the land neighboring Judah on every one of its sides, inasmuch as some of the land with respect to it was eastward, and some westward, etc. to which some of the Jews were dispersed, and from which they were returned.

106{107}[4] *Erraverunt in solitudine, they wandered in the wilderness*, that is, in the desert, *in inaquoso, in a place without water*, that is, in a dry place, because in the desert there will be found no or very little water. *Viam civitatis habitaculi, the way of a city for their habitation*, that is, a well-worn and fixed road leading to some city, in which they might obtain secure habitation, *non invenerunt, they found not*, because in place of the desert they did not come upon paved roads. And because with such straying [in the desert] comes hunger and thirst, therefore it continues: **106{107} [5]** *Esurientes et sitientes, they were hungry and thirsty* for bodily bread and drink, *anima eorum in ipsis defecit, their soul fainted in them* from its natural vigor. **106{107}[6]** *Et clamaverunt ad Dominum, and they cried to*

---

114 E. N. Because of the format of Denis's treatment of the literal meaning of this Psalm, the complete verses of the Psalm will not be incorporated into the *Commentary* as in the other Psalms.
115 Ez. 36:24.

the Lord for a straight path. 106{107}[7] *Et deduxit eos in viam rectam, ut irent in civitatem habitationis; and he led them into the right way, that they might go to a city of habitation,* in which they might dwell safely. For this reason 106{107}[8] *Confiteantur Domino misericordia eius,* etc. *Let the mercies of the Lord confess him,* etc. 106{107}[9] *Quia satiavit animam inanem, for he has satisfied the empty soul,* that is, men who have empty bellies, *et animam, and the soul,* that is, men, *esurientem satiavit bonis, he has filled the hungry with good* food and drink.

Thereafter the liberation from captivity is set forth: 106{107}[10] *Sedentes in tenebri, such as sat in darkness,* that is, in dark prisons, *et umbra mortis, and in the shadow of death:* because of the heavy afflictions [suffered in prisons], such places are similar to death; *vinctos in mendicitate, bound in want,* that is, with sparse provisions, *et ferro, and iron,* that is, in chains: for a captive is given little food. He therefore redeemed those who had been captured, 106{107}[11] *Quia exacerbaverunt eloquia Dei,* etc. *Because they had exasperated the words of God,* etc. 106{107}[14] *Et educit eos de tenebris, and he brought them out of darkness,* that is, from the previously-mentioned dungeons, *et umbra mortis, and the shadow of death,* that is, the miserable life in captivity, which is similar to death, *et vincula eorum, and their bonds,* by which they were tied, *dirupit, he broke asunder,* 106{107}[16] *quia contrivit portas aereas, because he has broken gates of brass,* behind which they were locked.

106{107}[18] *Omnem escam, all manner of meat* fit for the body *abominata est anima eorum, their soul abhorred,* from their grave bodily weakness, *et appropinquaverunt usque ad portas mortis, and they drew nigh even to the gates of death,* that is, to agony, because they despaired themselves of being made healthy. 106{107}[20] *Misit verbum suum, he sent his word,* that is, by saying he commanded, *et sanavit eos, et eripuit eos de interitionibus eorum, and he healed them and delivered them from their destructions,* that is, from the diseases which lead to death.

Following this, it directs its attention on the liberation from the tempests and the dangers of the seas. 106{107}[23] *Qui descendunt mare in navibus, they that go down to the sea in ships,* to sail upon them, *facientes operationem in aquis multis, doing business in the great waters,* that is, exerting labor in the various seas. 106{107}[24] *Ipsi viderunt opera Domini, these have seen the works of the Lord,* of those things that swim in the sea, namely, fish and some other unusual things that frequently appear in the sea. Whence it continues, *et mirabilia eius, and his wonders,* they have seen, *in profundo, in the deep* of the sea, namely marine monsters and whales. 106{107}[25] *Dixit, he said,* God [said], *et stetit, and there arose,* that is, there rose up and grew powerful, *spiritus procellae, a stormy wind*, that is, tempestuous wind and disturbance, *et exultati sunt fluctus eius, and the waves thereof were lifted up*, that is, they ascended up high, and they swirling waters of the sea swelled up. 106{107}[26] *Ascendunt usque ad caelos, they mount up to the heavens*, that is, through the sea swelled-up in such a fashion, the ships and the seamen that dwelt within them rose unto the air at great heights, *et descendunt usque ad abyssos, and they go down to the depths*, that is, the great depth of the sea as they follow the descending waters; *anima eorum, their soul*, that is, that of the seamen, *in malis, with evils* of punishment *tabescebat, pined away*, because of the imminent dangers. 106{107}[27] *Turbati sunt, they were troubled* of heart, *et moti sunt, and they staggered* in their body, and they trembled with fear, *sicut ebrius, like a drunken man* who cannot stand and use his reason perfectly; *et omnis sapientia eorum devorata est, and all their wisdom is swallowed up*, because they do not know how to deliberate when faced with such dangers: because great passions impede the act of reason, because the strength of the imagination disorients many. 106{107}[29] *Et statuit procellam eius, and he turned the storm*, that is, God changed the tempest of the sea, *in auram, into a breeze*, that is, into an agreeable breeze and a quiet state;[116] *et siluerunt fluctus eius, and its waves were still*, that is, the waves of the sea ceased from their crashing. 106{107} [30] *Et laetati sunt, and they rejoiced*, the seamen [rejoiced], *quia siluerunt, because they were still*, [that is,] the waves [were still]; *et deduxit eos, and he brought them*, God [brought them] *in portum voluntatis eorum, to the haven which they wished for*, that is, into the chosen port.

106{107}[33] *Posuit, he has turned*, God [turned] *flumina in desertum, rivers into a wilderness*, that is, he made the waters of rivers to cease so that the land which before was irrigated is as dry as the desert; *et exitus aquarum in sitim, and the sources of the water into dry ground*, that is, the land flowing with water he has made parched and barren. 106{107} [34] *Terram frucitferam, a fruitful land* he has changed *in salsuginem, into barrenness*, that is, he has made unfruitful, *a malitia inhabitantium in ea, for the wickedness of them that dwell therein*, that is, because of the sin of its inhabitants. 106{107}[35] *Posuit desertum in stagna aquarum, he has turned a wilderness into pools of water*, that is, an arid land he has made abounding in water. All these things the Providence of God does according to the demands of divine justice and of the merits of human lives.

---

116 E. N. The editor suggests an alternative reading *flatum*, a breeze, instead of *statum*, a state or fixed condition.

106{107}[36] *Et collocavit illic, and has placed there,* that is, in the land abounding in water and fertile, *esurientes, the hungry,* that is, those who are in need of the fruits of the earth; *et constituerunt civitatem habitionis, and they made a city for their habitation,* that is, they built dwellings by the land so fertile, since they could cultivate it, and would be able to obtain its fruits. 106{107}[37] *Et seminaverunt agros, and they sowed fields* so as to obtain food, *et plantaverunt vineas, and they planted vineyards,* so as to have drink, *et fecerunt fructum nativitatis, and they yielded fruit of birth,* that is, they cultivated the land and the vineyards in such a manner that they produced suitable fruit. 106{107}[38] *Et benedixit eis, and he blessed them,* that is, he gave to men the gifts of his goodness; *et multiplicati sunt nimis, and they were multiplied exceedingly,* in the land that was so good from the divine blessing; *et iumenta eorum non minoravit, and their cattle he suffered not to decrease,* that is, he multiplied their cattle.

106{107}[38] *Et, and* — again because of their recent sins, *pauci facti sunt, they were brought to be few* in number, because part were killed, others perished, because they did not revere God; *et vexati sunt a tribulatione malorum et dolore, and they were afflcted through the trouble of evils and sorrow,* from the punishment inflicted upon them by wicked men, and because of the inward pains which they conceived from the death of those close to them: by which ruin they were made few. 106{107}[40] *Effusa est contemptio super principes, contempt was poured forth upon their princes,* that is, the princes had discord among themselves; *et errare fecit eos in invio, and he caused them to wander in an impassible place,* that is, God, by just judgment, permitted them to abandon the right way, *et non in via, and out of the way,* because they did not deserve to be directed in the way of good. 106{107}[41] *Et adiuvit pauperem de inopia, and he helped the poor out of poverty,* enriching them, *et posuit sicut oves familias, and made him families like a flock of sheep,* that is, he multiplied the subjects of the princes who were at odds with each other. The rest is clear from the prior article.

Now if this was the intended sense by the Prophet, I do not know why at the end of the present Psalm he would say in both a special and novel way, *Who is wise and will keep these things?* By this, of course, he suggests something singularly mystical, fruitful, and profound is contained in this present Psalm. And so I do not think this sense which is so superficial and rude was finally and principally the intent of the holy Prophet; but in the way Augustine asserts, the exposition of the preceding article is the one which truly expresses the literal sense of the present Psalm.

PRAYER

AT YOUR COMMAND, O LORD, MAY THE billows of the tempests of our lives be silenced, and turn our storms into a breeze of tranquility and joy, so that, with you as our helmsman, we may be led into the port of salvation, so that we might confess to you the works of your mercy.

Te, Domine, praecipiente, sileant fluctus tempestatum vitae nostrae, et statue procellam nostram in auram tranquillitatis et laetitiae : ut in portum salutis te gubernatore deducti, nos misericordiae tuae opera confiteamur tibi.

Psalm 107

ARTICLE XIII

EXPOSITION OF CHRIST OF THE
ONE HUNDRED AND SEVENTH PSALM:
PARATUM COR MEUM, DEUS.
MY HEART IS READY, O GOD.

107{108}[1] *Canticum, psalmus ipsi David.*

A canticle, a Psalm for David himself.

HE TITLE OF THE PRESENT PSALM IS: 107{108} [1] *Canticum, psalmus ipsi David; a canticle, a Psalm for David himself*: that is, this scripture or this tractate is a canticle, because it contains spiritual joy; and [it is] a psalm because it admonishes us to good deeds: and it refers to David himself in a threefold way. For it befits the holy prophet David as its author; and because, as indicated by its literal circumstances, this Psalm is the exultation of king David glorying in the Lord and giving thanks to him for his benefits, namely for the victory conceded to him by God and the restitution of the reign of Israel in a good state. It is also applicable to David, that is, Christ signified by David: and this, according to an allegorical understanding. For many things occurred to holy David in the figure of the Lord Savior. Also, it relates to David, that is, the Church or any one Christian who is inwardly beautiful and strong of hand in the Lord.[1] But because that exposition of Christ is more sweet, more fruitful, and leads to more devotion, so it is expedient to introduce it first.

107{108}[2] *My heart is ready, O God, my heart is ready: I will sing and will give praise, with my glory.*

Paratum cor meum, Deus, paratum cor meum; cantabo, et psallam in gloria mea.

Christ, therefore, as man obedient in all things to God the Father, says to the Father or to the whole superlative most blessed

---

1 *E. N.* The name David was interpreted by St. Jerome, among others, as meaning *manu fortis,* "strong of hand." *See De nominibus Hebraicis,* PL 23, 813.

Trinity,[2] 107{108}[2] *Paratum cor meum, my heart is ready*, that is, my will is ready to submit to you, *Deus, O God*, Father. And it repeats it so as to confirm it, so he says: *paratum cor meum, my heart is ready*: ready, I say, to do what is pleasing to you, ready to endure the necessary things for the redemption of humankind, ready to praise, and ready to work. For Christ acknowledges this in John: *I came down from heaven, not to do my own will, but the will of him that sent me.*[3] And in Matthew, he said to the Father: *Not as I will, but as you will.*[4] *Cantabo et psallam, I will sing and will give praise*, that is, I will praise you with words and with deeds, and I will give you thanks, *in gloria mea, with my glory*, that is, in clear knowledge mixed with praise:[5] which knowledge you gave me from your goodness and majesty. For unless one knows God, one has no means to praise him. For this reason, as the man Christ, or the soul of Christ, knew most excellently God in this life, so he most perfectly sang and gave praise to God. Or [an alternative reading is], *I will give praise with my glory*, that is, with all the dignity of the grace infused in me, so that with all the goods blended in with my humanity, I will occupy myself in proclaiming you, I will never ever cease in honoring you in accordance to that professed by the Evangelist, *I do always the things that please him;*[6] and, *I seek not my own glory, but I honor the Father.*[7] Or [we can look at it thus], *with my glory*, that is, in the beatitude of my soul and the glorification of my body.

107{108}[3]   *Arise, my glory; arise, psaltery and harp: I will arise in the morning early.*

Exsurge, gloria mea; exsurge, psalterium et cithara; exsurgam diluculo.

107{108}[3] *Exsurge, arise*, to become known by men and to the act of the divine veneration, *psalterium, the psaltery*, that is, the Gospel or my evangelical doctrine, in which I sang about the sublime things of the divine

---

2 E. N. This (*superbeatissimam*) is an instance of a super-superlative that is so common to Denis. For more on this feature of his writing and its source in Denis the Areopagite, *see* footnote 17-128 in Volume 1 (*Beatus Vir*). It could be translated (cataphatically) as eminently most blessed or (apophatically) as beyond the most blessed.
3 John 6:38.
4 Matt. 26:39b.
5 E. N. This definition comes from Augustine. *See* footnote 28-15 in Volume 2 (*Deus Illuminatio Mea*).
6 John 8:29b.
7 John 8:50a, 49b.

majesty, or I taught (which doctrine, like the psaltery, sounds sweet in the ears of God), *et cithara, and harp,* that is, my moral doctrine, exemplary life, and the passion of my death. In this way *arise* since men do not know these things and lead them to imitate it. *Exsurgam, I will arise in* the place of burial *diluculo, in the morning early,* that is, very early in the morning, according to the scripture Luke handed down: *One the first day of the week very early in the morning,* women *came ... and they found the stone rolled back from* the mouth of the sepulcher; *and going in, they found not the body of the Lord Jesus.*[8] And also Mark repeats: Jesus *rising early in the first day of the week.*[9]

107{108}[4] *I will confess you, O Lord, among the people: and I will sing unto you among the populations.*[10]

Confitebor tibi in populis, Domine, et psallam tibi in nationibus.

107{108}[5] *For your mercy is great above the heavens: and your truth even unto the clouds.*

Quia magna est super caelos misericordia tua, et usque ad nubes veritas tua.

107{108}[4] *Confitebor tibi, I will confess you,* that is, I will praise you, *in populis, among the people* of the Jews, *Domine, O Lord,* Father: to whom I proclaimed myself, and among them I have always praised you, especially among my disciples, who were Jews; *et psallam tibi, and I will sing* through the Apostles and my other ministers *in nationibus, among the populations,* that is, among the Gentiles converted to the faith by their preaching. Christ sang to God among the Gentiles when he sent Apostles to preach the Gospel of the Kingdom amount the Gentiles.[11] For God is most highly praised in the Gospel. For this (reports John) the only-begotten Son said to the Father: *I have glorified you on the earth; I have finished the work which you gave me to do,* and I have made known *your name to men.*[12] 107{108}[5] *Quia magna est super caelos misericordia tua, for your mercy is great above the heavens,* that is, the mercy of your goodness is copiously poured forth over the heavenly citizens. And in them shines forth your goodness, because they are preserved from evil

---

8 Luke 24:1–3.

9 Mark 16:9a.

10 *E. N.* I have translated *confitebor* as "I will confess," and not "I will praise," since, as Denis clarifies in the *Commentary,* the confession here is one of praise, not one of fault.

11 Matt. 28:19–20.

12 John 17:4, 6a.

and confirmed in the good only by your grace. *Et usque ad nubes veritas tua, and your truth even unto the clouds,* that is, the enlightenment of the evangelical truth or the infusion of saving wisdom was impressed upon the holy Apostles and the good preachers (which are called the heavens), in the way that you promised in the Gospel, saying: *When he, the Spirit of truth, is come, he will teach you all truth.*[13]

107{108}[6]   *Be exalted, O God, above the heavens, and your glory over all the earth.*

Exaltare super caelos, Deus, et super omnem terram gloria tua.

107{108}[7]   *That your beloved may be delivered. Save with your right hand and hear me.*

Ut liberentur dilecti tui, salvum fac dextera tua, et exaudi me.

And then the Prophet [David] addresses Christ 107{108}[6] *Exaltare super caelos, Deus; be exalted, O God, above the heavens*: that is, you, O Christ, the true God, who are so downtrodden and humiliated in your Passion, ascend above all the heavens, and return from where you came; *et super omnem terram gloria tua, and your glory over all the earth*: that is, your excellence is made known throughout all the world, your divinity is proclaimed, and your glory acknowledged in the ways predicted in Isaiah: *Behold my servant . . . shall be exalted, and extolled, and shall be exceedingly high.*[14] Hence also Isaiah says again: *They shall give glory to the Lord, and shall declare his praise in the islands.*[15] This also Christ committed to fulfil after his Resurrection, saying to his Apostles: *You shall be witnesses unto me in Jerusalem, and in all Judea, and Samaria, and even to the uttermost part of the earth.*[16] 107{108}[7] *Ut liberentur dilecti tui, that your beloved may be delivered,* that is, that all those elected by you from eternity [may be delivered] by faith and the observance of your law. And so Christ sent the Apostles to preach everywhere so that all the elect might be saved.[17] *Salvum fac, save me dextera tua, with your right hand,* that is, those on your right hand, so that I might abide in heaven on your right, in your highest and heavenly good, *et exaudi me, and hear me* praying for these things.

---

13 John 16:13.
14 Is. 52:13.
15 Is. 42:12.
16 Acts 1:8b.
17 2 Tim. 2:10: *Therefore, I endure all things for the sake of the elect, that they also may obtain the salvation, which is in Christ Jesus, with heavenly glory.*

107{108}[8] *God has spoken in his holiness. I will rejoice, and I will divide Shechem, and I will mete out the vale of tabernacles.*

Deus locutus est in sancto suo: exsultabo, et dividam Sichimam; et convallem tabernaculorum dimetiar.

107{108}[8] *Deus locutus est in sancto suo, God has spoken in his holiness:* that is, the Father *has spoken to us by his Son* who is the Saint of Saints.[18] Now that which follows can be understood as being the words of Christ or of God the Father, or of the entire superlatively most happy Trinity. *Exultabo, I will rejoice,* that is, I will take joy in my elect, *for the Lord is well pleased with his people.*[19] And with Jeremiah he acknowledged: *I will rejoice over them, when I shall do them good.*[20] *Et dividam Sichimam, and I will divide Shechem,* that is, the pagans, by mercifully converting some pagans to the faith, and others by justly abandoning them. *For all men have not the faith.*[21] And in the Acts of the Apostles we read that Paul was prohibited from speaking the word of God in Asia.[22] *Et convallem Tabernaculorum dimetiar, and I will mete out the vale of Tabernacles,* that is, I will divide the people of the Jews, converting some of them, and deserting the others. For *a remnant is saved* by election,[23] according to the Apostle. And Christ says in John: *I speak not of you all: I know whom I have chosen.*[24] Now by Shechem is understood the Gentiles, for pagans dwelt in the land of Shechem, but by the vale of Tabernacles is designated the Jews, because (as we read in Genesis), Jacob, when returning from Syria, fixed tents in this place, for which reason he called it Succoth, that is tabernacles.[25]

107{108}[9] *Gilead is mine, and Manasseh is mine and Ephraim the protection of my head. Judah is my king.*

Meus est Galaad, et meus est Manasses; et Ephraim susceptio capitis mei. Iuda rex meus.

18 Heb. 1:2a.
19 Ps. 149:4a.
20 Jer. 32:41a.
21 2 Thess. 3:2.
22 Acts 16:6. E. N. "The vision of St. Paul, who saw the roads to Asia barred and in a dream saw a Macedonian man plead with him: 'Come over to Macedonia and help us!' (*cf.* Acts 16:6–10) — this vision can be interpreted as a 'distillation' of the intrinsic necessity of a rapprochement between biblical faith and Greek inquiry." Benedict XVI, Regensburg Lecture, Sept. 12, 2006.
23 Rom. 11:5.
24 John 13:18a.
25 Gen. 33:17.

107{108}[10]   *Moab the pot of my hope. Over Edom I will stretch out my shoe: the aliens are become my friends.*

Moab lebes spei meae; in Idumaeam extendam calceamentum meum; mihi alienigenae amici facti sunt.

107{108}[9] *Meus est Galaad, Gilead is mine,* that is, the congregation of martyrs, who by their own effusion of blood exhibit testimony of the Christian faith. Indeed, Gilead is interpreted to mean "hill of testimony." *Et meus est Manasses, and Manasseh is mine:* that is, the people oblivious of temporal and carnal things, contemplative of divine things, and desirous of heavenly things belong to the flock of my elect. For Manasseh is interpreted to mean "causing to forget." And the Apostle [Paul] states that *forgetting those things that are behind, I extend myself to those things that are ahead.*[26] *Et Ephraim, and Ephraim,* that is, the people fertile with good works, is *susceptio capitis mei, the protection of my head,* that is, received by me because it is acceptable to me. For Ephraim is interpreted to mean "fertility." *Iuda rex meus, Judah is my king:* that is, the people of the confessors, are the guides of Mystical Body, namely, the Church. For others are governed by confessors, who profess and praise the Lord by life and word. For this reason, the Lord speaking through Jeremiah says: *I will give you pastors according to my own heart, and they shall feed you with knowledge and doctrine.*[27] **107{108}[10]** *Moab lebes spei meae, Moab is the pot of my hope.* Moab is interpreted to mean, "from the father." By this is understood the elect, of whom the Evangelist says they *were born not of blood, nor of the will of the flesh, nor of the will of man, but of God.*[28] Whence also Christ says: *Every plant which my heavenly Father has not planted, shall be rooted up.*[29] These, therefore, are the pot or jar of hope of Christ himself, because they are filled up by him, for it is on their account that he shed his own blood. For these are the saved, and so by them Christ repairs the glory and the glorification of the Father lost by the fall of our first parents.

In Idumaeam, over Edom, that is, the land of the Gentiles, *extendam calceamentum meum, I will stretch out my shoe,* that is, my human nature, which was, as it were, the shoe of divinity. Christ extended this foot over Edom, since he is preached throughout the whole world, and he has made himself to be known by others, as is said of Paul in Acts: *This*

---

26 *Cf.* Phil. 3:13.
27 Jer. 3:15.
28 John 1:13.
29 Matt. 15:13.

man is to me a vessel of election, to carry my name before the Gentiles and kings.[30] *Mihi alienigenae, the aliens . . . to me,* that is the Gentiles in the past alienated from God and the faith, who at one time were not a people [in good standing with God], *amici facti sunt, are become my friends,* by believing in me through the preaching of the Apostles. For this reason the Apostle writes to such person in Ephesians: *Now therefore you are no more strangers and foreigners; but you are fellow citizens with the saints, and the domestics of God.*[31] And again he says: *You who some time were afar off, are made nigh by the blood of Christ.*[32] Whence also Balaam in the book of Numbers predicted: *He shall possess Edom.*[33]

107{108}[11]   *Who will bring me into the strong city? Who will lead me into Edom?*

               Quis deducet me in civitatem munitam? Quis deducet me usque in Idumaeam?

107{108}[12]   *Will not you, O God, who has cast us off? And will not you, O God, go forth with our armies?*

               Nonne tu, Deus, qui repulisti nos? Et non exibis, Deus, in virtutibus nostris ?

But because these things have been done, not by human or natural power, but by divine and supernatural [power], so Christ as man adds: 107{108}[11] *Quis deducet me in civitatem munitam? Who will bring me into the strong city?* That is, into the city of Rome (which was the head and mistress of the world, and of which was predicted through Isaiah, *The high city he shall lay low*).[34] It is as if her were saying: "This — that this city be converted to me — cannot be done through human power." But this was done by the divine power through the preaching of Peter and Paul, as Isaiah asserts: *The foot of the poor man,* that is, of Peter the fisherman, the *steps of the needy,* that is, the coming of Peter and Paul *shall tread it down.*[35] *Quis deducet me usque in Idumaeam, who will lead me into Edom* so that the whole earth takes upon itself my yoke and believes in me? 107{108}[12] *Nonne tu, Deus; will not you, O God* do these things,

30 Acts 9:15.
31 Eph. 2:19.
32 Eph. 2:13.
33 Num. 24:18.
34 Is. 25:5a.
35 Is. 26:6.

qui repulisti nos, who has cast us off? Who permitted my Mystical Body assembled together from the Gentiles to stray for a long time before they were converted — when they were not yet the Mystical Body actually, but [only] by predestination, in the manner that Paul asserts in the Acts of the Apostles: God disdained the former time of ignorance.[36] Or [another exposition], *you have cast us off,* that is, during the Passion, you in a way forsook my Body and Soul with respect to its inferior powers, so that I would proclaim: *My God, my God, why have you forsaken me?*[37] *Et non exibis, Deus, in virtutibus nostris; and will not you, O God, go forth with our armies?* That is, these things you will not do by our power, or by the power of creation, but by divine power. For God is said to go forth, not in terms of movement or place, but by operation.

107{108}[13]   *O grant us help from trouble: for vain is the help of man.*

   Da nobis auxilium de tribulatione, quia vana salus hominis.

107{108}[14]   *Through God we shall do mightily: and he will bring our enemies to nothing.*

   In Deo faciemus virtutem; et ipse ad nihilum deducet inimicos nostros.

Then Christ prays, to the degree he was passible, for the reunion of his body and soul. **107{108}[13]** *Da nobis auxilium de tribulatio, O grant us help from trouble,* that is, resuscitate me from my death brought upon me by my Passion: which I ought to ask from you alone, *quia vana salus hominis, for vain is the help of man,* that is, pure man is is unable to confer salvation, nor is he able to deliver anyone.[38] Indeed, he who hopes in him [in pure man] acts vainly and is a fool.[39] **107{108}[14]** *In Deo faciemus virtutem, through God we shall do mightily,* that is, we will be united again

---

36 *Cf.* Acts 17:30: *And God indeed having winked at the times of this ignorance, now declares unto men, that all should everywhere do penance.*

37 Matt. 27:46.

38 *E. N.* In saying "pure man," *homo purus,* Denis means a man who is also a human person, he does not mean a man who is a divine person: *Christus non fuit purus homo, sed homo et Deus. Ergo quod philosophus dicit, oculum hominis mortui esse aequivoce oculum, non habet locum in Christo.* "Christ was not pure man, but man and God. Therefore, that which the Philosopher [Aristotle] says about the eye of a dead man [that the eye of a dead man, like the eye of a portrait or of a statue, is called an eye equivocally] does not have a place in Christ." St. Thomas Aquinas, *Quodlibet* III, q. 2 a. 2 arg. 2.

39 *Cf.* Jer. 17:5: *Cursed be the man that trusts in man, and makes flesh his arm, and whose heart departs from the Lord.*

through divine power, and we will come out from the sepulcher, and we will ascend unto heaven, O my soul and my body; *et ipse, and he*, God, *ad nihilum deducet inimicos nostros, will bring our enemies to nothing*, that is, the people of the Jews, depriving them of grace in the present, and glory in the future, and destroying them in large part by the Romans.

ARTICLE XIV

TROPOLOGICAL EXPOSITION OF THE SAME ONE HUNDRED AND SEVENTH PSALM, IN WHICH ITS LITERAL EXPOSITION IS BRIEFLY ADDRESSED.

107{108}[2] *My heart is ready, O God, my heart is ready: I will sing and will give praise, with my glory.*

Paratum cor meum, Deus, paratum cor meum; cantabo, et psallam in gloria mea.

THIS PSALM IS WOVEN FROM TWO INDIVID-ual Psalms. For the first part of the Psalm up until it says, *Save with your right hand* [*i.e.*, Ps. 107:1–7] is taken from the fifty-sixth Psalm, which begins with *Have mercy on me, O God, have mercy on me.* But the rest of it is obtained from the fifty-ninth Psalm, whose beginning is: *O God, you have cast us off.*

Now viewed from a moral point of view, this Psalm refers to the Church or to any devout, thankful, and fervent lover, who, by the fervor of holy charity and fully confident of his beloved, yet not knowing the manner [of expressing it] says to the Lord: 107{108}[2] *Paratum cor meum, Deus, paratum cor meum; my heart is ready, O God, my heart is ready*, so that I might do and suffer all things pleasing to you. I pray that you do your will in me:[40] that whatever it is that might be pleasing to you will be for me my good all of my days of my life. I commend myself to you, I relinquish and offer myself completely to your will. Take heed: the totality of our perfection consists in this. For the more our heart is ready to please God in all things, that much more are we similar to and dear to God, and we will easily acquire all that which we desire.[41]

---

40 *Cf.* Matt. 6:10.
41 *E. N.* This brings to mind St. Augustine's famous saying in his sermon on 1 John 4:4–12: "Love [God] and do what you will: whether you are silent, be silent through

For this promptitude of the heart proceeds from fervent love, and, the more our interior and exterior works are born out of a more ready heart or a greater promptitude, the more strongly meritorious they are; and the less our self-love is, the greater is this readiness and the greater is this divine love. Hence the Apostle says to the Corinthians: *not with sadness or of necessity: for God loves a cheerful giver.* And in the book of Chronicles, David said: *And you, my son, . . . know the God of your father, and serve him with a perfect heart and a willing mind.*[42] *Cantabo, I will sing,* bringing forth divine words of proclamation; *et psallam, and I will give praise,* performing holy works, *in gloria mea, with my glory,* that is, with spiritual joy. Or [alternatively], *with my glory,* that is, with a pure conscience. *For our glory is this: the testimony of our conscience,* according to the Apostle.[43] In a literal sense, this applies to the holy David, who gave thanks to God for the benefit of the restitution of his reign in a good state, offering himself as ready to accept all things from God.[44]

107{108}[3]   *Arise, my glory; arise, psaltery and harp: I will arise in the morning early.*

Exsurge, gloria mea; exsurge, psalterium et cithara; exsurgam diluculo.

107{108}[3] *Exsurge psalterium et cithara, arise psaltery and harp.*[45] For by these musical instruments he praised God. *Exsurgam diluculo, I will arise in the morning early,* that is, in the morning I will arise from my bed so that I might praise and submit to the Lord. But spiritually [understood], by a psaltery, which has ten strings and renders sound from its upper part, is understood the keeping of the ten precepts of the Decalogue, which were given and imposed upon us by heaven, and the keeping of which, indeed, sounds more sweetly to the ears of God than does all musical instruments. Now by harp — which has six or seven strings, and renders sound from its bottom part — is understood

---

love; whether you cry out, cry out through love; whether you amend yourself, amend yourself through love; whether you spare, spare through love; let the root within you be love, for from this root nothing can exist but good." *Dilige, et quod vis fac: sive taceas, dilectione taceas; sive clames, dilectione clames; sive emendes, dilectione emendes; sive parcas, dilectione parcas: radix sit intus dilectionis, non potest de ista radice nisi bonum existere. In epist. Ioannis,* 10, 8, PL 35, 2033.

42 1 Chr. 28:9a.
43 2 Cor. 1:12a.
44 2 Samuel chp. 22.
45 *E. N.* Denis skips the first two works of this verse.

the works of mercy which are occupied by attending to bodily needs, and they look to the active life. And so [we should understand this verse] in this sense, therefore: *Arise, psaltery*, that is, may the keeping of the precepts of the most High be roused up and be in me, so that by you I might praise God. And in the same way also arise, *harp*, that is, the doing of works of mercy. *For a merciful man does good to his own soul;*[46] and, *Blessed are the merciful, for they shall obtain mercy.*[47] And so in the book of Tobit we have: *According to your ability, be merciful;*[48] and in the book of Job, *From my infancy mercy grew up with me.*[49] *I will arise* from the bed, from sin, from slothfulness, *in the morning early*, that is, in the beginning of the sunrise, by the infusion of divine illumination. For this is brought forth in the book of Ecclesiasticus: *He will give his heart to keep watch early in the morning to the Lord.*[50] Isaiah also says: *Early in the morning, I will watch for you.*[51]

107{108}[4] *I will confess you, O Lord, among the people: and I will sing unto you among the populations.*[52]

Confitebor tibi in populis, Domine, et psallam tibi in nationibus.

107{108}[5] *For your mercy is great above the heavens: and your truth even unto the clouds.*

Quia magna est super caelos misericordia tua, et usque ad nubes veritas tua.

107{108}[4] *Confitebor tit in populis, Domine; I will confess you, O Lord, among the people*, that is, I will praise you before all men, *et psallam tibi in nationibus, and I will sing unto you among the populations*, that is, I will honor among all men present. I will not be ashamed of your name before men, because you said: He who *shall confess me before men, I will also confess before my Father.*[53] And in Matthew: *So let your light shine before men that they may see your good works and glorify your Father*

---

46 Prov. 11:17a.
47 Matt. 5:7.
48 Tobit 4:8.
49 Job 31:18a.
50 Ecclus. 39:6a. *E. N.* I have modified the Douay-Rheims's translation somewhat to accord it better to Denis's text without altering its meaning.
51 Is. 26:9a.
52 *E. N.* I have translated *confitebor* as "I will confess," and not "I will praise," since, as Denis clarifies in the *Commentary*, the confession here is one of praise, not one of fault.
53 Matt. 10:32; *cf.* Luke 12:8.

who is in heaven.[54] We must also sometimes confess our sins among the people, when, namely, sins are manifest. 107{108}[5] *Quia magna est super caelos, for great above the heavens,* that is, above all who lead a heavenly and angelic life on earth, whose *conversation is in heaven,*[55] *misericordia tua, is your mercy*: for whatever good that is in them emanates from, depends upon, and is preserved by your ordination and your goodness. Or [alternatively], *above the heavens,* that is, the blessed in the heavenly homeland, because they have attained blessedness through your mercy. *Et usque ad nubes, and even unto the clouds,* that is, the holy angels, *veritas tua, your truth,* that is, attain your illumination. For according to chapter 15 of the *Heavenly Hierarchy* of Dionysius [the Areopagite], sacred Scripture understands by the term clouds angels, because they first and immediately and copiously receive the rays of highest light, and transfuse it to others.

107{108}[6]   *Be exalted, O God, above the heavens, and your glory over all the earth.*

Exaltare super caelos, Deus, et super omnem terram gloria tua.

107{108}[7]   *That your beloved may be delivered. Save with your right hand and hear me.*

Ut liberentur dilecti tui, salvum fac dextera tua, et exaudi me.

107{108}[6] *Exaltare super caelos, Deus; be exalted, O God, above the heavens,* that is, you will be adored, magnified, and praised by all the citizens of the heavenly fatherland, *et super omnem terram, and over all the earth,* that is, in the whole militant Church, *gloria tua, your glory,* that is, clear knowledge of your name, glorious praise, and excellent veneration will increase and will always exist as long as men convert toward you, and obey you, and render you glory; 107{108}[7] *ut liberentur dilecti tui, that your beloved may be delivered* from all danger. *Salvum fac, save* me *dextera tua, with your right hand,* that is, through your abundant help and gracious presence, *et exaudi me, and hear me* praying for these things.

107{108}[8]   *God has spoken in his holiness. I will rejoice, and I will divide Shechem and I will mete out the vale of tabernacles.*

Deus locutus est in sancto suo: exsultabo, et dividam Sichimam; et convallem tabernaculorum dimetiar.

---

54 Matt. 5:16.
55 Phil. 3:20a.

107{108}[9] *Gilead is mine, and Manasseh is mine and Ephraim the protection of my head. Judah is my king.*

Meus est Galaad, et meus est Manasses; et Ephraim susceptio capitis mei. Iuda rex meus.

107{108}[10] *Moab the pot of my hope. Over Edom I will stretch out my shoe: the aliens are become my friends.*

Moab lebes spei meae; in Idumaeam extendam calceamentum meum; mihi alienigenae amici facti sunt.

107{108}[8] *Deus locutus est, God has spoken* by internal inspiration or angelic revelation, *in sancto suo, in his holiness* the Prophet [David], that is to say, me or any other devout person that which follows: *Exsultabo, et dividam Sichimam, etc. I will divide Shechem, etc.* whose exposition may be found in the preceding article [and will not be addressed at length here]. For God has divided and measured Shechem and the vale of the tabernacles by the preaching of the early Church, and so, at length, he will cause the division of the elect and the reprobate, according to the sense explained. Something similar can be said with respect to: 107{108} [9] *Meus est Galaad, et meus est Manasses, et Ephraim susceptio capitis mei; Gilead is mine, and Manasseh is mine and Ephraim the protection of my head*: because holy people and Christians are designated by Gilead and Manasseh, as is stated in the preceding article, and they belong together in unity and in the Mystical Body of the Church, namely, the martyrs signified by Gilead, the forgetters of temporal things are figured by Manasseh, and the suitable doers of deeds are denoted by Ephraim. And of Ephraim he means the Church, which is supported by its head, that is, its people are supported in their fruitful good works by Christ the head. *Iuda, Judah,* that is, the people confessing the Lord by word and deed, is *rex meus, my king,* that is, the leader of the members of the Church, for by such men are those below them ruled. 107{108}[10] *Moab,* that is, the people born from the Father, namely the children of the highest Father, are *lebes spei meae, the pot of my hope*: for the Church trusts that these sorts of men will be saved because in the first epistle of Jonh is written: *Whosever is born of God, commits not sin, for his seed abides in him.*[56]

And so the Church says: *In Idumaeam extendam calceamentum meum, over Edom I will stretch out my shoe,* that is, I will stretch out my feet out to the Gentiles, preaching throughout all the earth, in the manner

---

56 1 John 3:9.

that the Apostle states: *Behold we turn to the Gentiles.*[57] *Mihi alienigenae amici facti sunt, the aliens are become my friends*, that is, the Gentiles have become one with me in Christ through charity. For all the faithful are brought into union by charity in God, for (as the Apostle says) Christ *is our peace, who has made both one.*[58] Whence in Zechariah is predicted: *The counsel of peace shall be between them both.*[59] Indeed, in the Church of Christ these two people, namely the Gentile and Jew, are unified by charity. And see how amicably and lovingly those Gentiles who converted to the early Church which consisted of Jews were. For Paul writing to the Philippians said: *My dearly beloved brethren, and most desired, my joy and my crown;*[60] and elsewhere, *I most gladly will spend and be spent myself for your souls; although loving you more, I be loved less;*[61] and again, we then live, *if you stand in the Lord.*[62]

107{108}[11]   *Who will bring me into the strong city?...*[63]

Quis deducet me in civitatem munitam?...

107{108}[13]   *O grant us help from trouble....*[64]

Da nobis auxilium de tribulation....

107{108}[14]   *Through God we shall do mightily: and he will bring our enemies to nothing.*

In Deo faciemus virtutem; et ipse ad nihilum deducet inimicos nostros.

But because this progression and preaching of the Church throughout the world is accomplished not by human power, but by divine power, so it adds the Church in the person of those of its preachers: **107{108}[11]** *Quis deducet me in civitatem munitam, who will bring me into the strong city?* And this sentence is clear from what is stated above. **107{108} [13]** *Da nobis auxilium de tribulatione, O grant us help from trouble*, that is, against all the persecutions and adversities, so that we might not be oppressed by the wicked, but we might preserve patience, and by it we

---

57 Acts 13:46b.
58 Eph. 2:14a.
59 Zech. 6:13.
60 Phil. 4:1.
61 2 Cor. 12:15.
62 1 Thess. 3:8.
63 *E. N.* Denis does not address the second half of this verse in the *Commentary*.
64 *E. N.* Denis skips over verse 12 in this part of the *Commentary*. He also only addresses the first part of verse 13.

might overcome all difficulties. 107{108}[14] *In Deo, through God*, that is, by the grace of God, *faciemus virtutem, we shall do mightily*, resisting the world, the flesh, and the devil, and keeping the divine commandments. *Et ipse ad nihilum deducet, and he will bring... to nothing*, that is, he will destroy and cause to fail, *inimicos nostros, our enemies* both visible and invisible: according to that which is written to the Romans, *God ... will crush Satan under your feet speedily.*[65]

Finally, up to the verse *God has spoken in his holiness*, all these things fittingly apply to holy David, as it does to other Saints, according to the sense already explained. These things, therefore, can be literally explained as referring to David.

107{108}[8] *God has spoken in his holiness. I will rejoice, and I will divide Shechem and I will mete out the vale of tabernacles.*

Deus locutus est in sancto suo: exsultabo, et dividam Sichimam; et convallem tabernaculorum dimetiar.

107{108}[9] *Gilead is mine, and Manasseh is mine and Ephraim the protection of my head. Judah is my king.*

Meus est Galaad, et meus est Manasses; et Ephraim susceptio capitis mei. Iuda rex meus.

107{108}[10] *Moab the pot of my hope. Over Edom I will stretch out my shoe: the aliens are become my friends.*

Moab lebes spei meae; in Idumaeam extendam calceamentum meum; mihi alienigenae amici facti sunt.

107{108}[11] *Who will bring me into the strong city? Who will lead me into Edom?*

Quis deducet me in civitatem munitam? Quis deducet me usque in Idumaeam?

107{108}[12] *Will not you, O God, who has cast us off? And will not you, O God, go forth with our armies?*

Nonne tu, Deus, qui repulisti nos? Et non exibis, Deus, in virtutibus nostris ?

And so he says: 107{108}[8] *Deus locutus est in sancto suo, God has spoken in his holiness*: that is, through Samuel and the prophet Nathan.

----

65 Rom. 16:20a.

He said and he promised me that I, David, *exultabo et dividam, will rejoice, and will divide,* that is, will measure out with joy *Sichiman, Shechem,* that is, the spoils of the land of Shechem, to my servants and adjutants fighting along me against them; *et convallem tabernaculorum, and . . . the vale of tabernacles,* that is, the place which is called Succoth beside the Jordan, *dimetiar, I will mete out,* that is, I will restore to the children of Israel, giving all of them their due part. For David drove out from this valley the Philistines who had taken possession of this land unjustly.[66] But because David did this with the help of his people — especially of those who were more bellicose and stronger — so he named those tribes which furnished their help to him. 107{108}[9] *Meus est Galaad, Gilead is mine,* that is, the people having possession of the land of Gilead beyond the Jordan, who were renowned for their strength because they came from the land of Jair and Jephthah;[67] *et meus est Manasses, and Manasseh is mine,* that is, the progeny of the son of Joseph named Manasseh,[68] which people were famous because Gideon came from that tribe.[69] *Et Ephraim susceptio capitis mei, and Ephraim the protection of my head:* that is, the people begotten of Ephraim, who were principally received by me: because they were numerous and most strong, and Joshua was from this tribe, and Jacob preferred Ephraim to Manasseh himself.[70] *Iuda rex meus, Judah is my king:* because the princes were from Judah; 107{108}[10] *Moab lebes spei meae, Moab the pot of my hope:* that is I trust to conquer and possess the Moabites with the help of God in the manner that a pot is possessed by the father of a family. This actually occurred: for the Moabites served David under tribute.[71] *In Idumaeam, over Edom,* that is, in the land of Edom, in which Esau had dwelt,[72] *extendam calceamentum meum, I will stretch out my shoe,* that is, I will enter it and shodden I will pass through it, subjecting it to my rule. *Mihi alienigenae, the aliens . . . to me,* that is, the people remaining around Judah, *amici facti sunt, are become . . . friends,* that is, confederates, proposing to make peace with me.

---

66 2 Sam. 8:1.

67 Judges 10:3, 11:1.

68 Gen. 41:51.

69 Judges 6:15. E. N. Gideon was the son of Joash, a member of the Abiezrite clan which was part of the greater tribe of Manasseh. He was famous for his defeat of the Midianite army, though he was vastly outnumbered. *See* chapter 7 of the book of Judges.

70 Num. 13:9, 17.

71 2 Sam. 8:2.

72 Gen. 36:8.

107{108}[11]   *Who will bring me into the strong city? Who will lead me into Edom?*

Quis deducet me in civitatem munitam? Quis deducet me usque in Idumaeam?

107{108}[12]   *Will not you, O God, who has cast us off? And will not you, O God, go forth with our armies?*

Nonne tu, Deus, qui repulisti nos? Et non exibis, Deus, in virtutibus nostris ?

But because David recognized this was to be fulfilled not through his own power, but by the power of God, therefore he adds: 107{108}[11] *Quis deducet me in civitatem munitam, who will bring me into the strong city,* [fortified] by walls and doors? *Quis deducet me usque in Idumaeam, who will lead me into Edom,* so that it might be made subject to me? 107{108}[12] *Nonne tu, Deus, qui repulisti nos; will not you, O God, who has cast us off,* that is, who in times past permitted the people of Israel to be heavily and in many ways afflicted? The rest [of this Psalm] is clear from what has been said before.

See, we have heard this Psalm full of spiritual joy in its opening and sweet with the fervor of a lover. And it endeavors in this way to make us grow in every way in the love of God, so that we might truly say: *My heart is ready, God, my heart is ready.* For it befits the rational creature to be perfectly subject to his Creator, and to be quick in pleasing him with all desire. Each one of us ought also to exhort, excite, and inflame himself to proclaim and to subject himself to God, saying: *Arise, psaltery and harp.* Whence the Apostle said to the Hebrews: *Exhort one another every day, . . . so that none of you be hardened through the deceitfulness of sin.*[73] We ought in addition every hour to have a firm purpose unceasingly to praise and to revere the most High, saying within ourselves: *I will arise in the morning early,* and *I will praise you, O Lord, among the people.* But in all things and above all things we ought, indeed, it behooves us, to attend to the honor of God, and to exult in his praises, to rejoice in his blessedness, in accordance with what divine charity demands.

Finally, so that we might belong to the Lord's flock, we should endeavor to be spiritually, Gilead, Manasseh, Ephraim, and Judah. For we become Gilead when we attest to our faith with our works, to the extent that no one can possibly say but that such a faith — which suggests and requires such a way of life — is good. Now we become Manasseh by forgetting

73 Heb. 3:13.

temporal goods, and remembering heavenly goods with affection, since as the Apostle exhorts, we behold *the glory of the Lord with open face,*[74] and now we are daily illumined in Christian wisdom, which the Apostle desired so greatly, so that he said to the Philippians: *I count all things to be but loss for the excellent knowledge of Jesus Christ my Lord.*[75] And it is altogether fitting that, *having food and something wherewith to be covered,*[76] we relinquish our solicitude for temporal things, and occupy ourselves completely with heavenly things. Now we also become Ephraim by being fruitful in spiritual works, and efficaciously employing works of the spirit. And we become Judah by confessing to the Lord with mouth and deed.

Lastly, it is to be kept in mind with respect to this verse — *Through God we shall do mightily* — our most holy Jerome says: Let us not have hope except in God alone. Let us not say: If this or that should befall me, what shall I have to live on? If I grow old, if I were to be become ill, how shall I live? You possess Christ, yet you fear? If he feeds the birds, you doubt it possible for him to feed you?[77] Let us, therefore, cast off all cares from our hearts, and let us say, *Through God we shall do mightily*: and he will be our might, and our guide.

PRAYER

O GOD, WHO LOVE ALL THAT ARE SINCERE and pure, and who dwell in the chaste souls of the faithful, purify us through the munificence of your kindness from all contagion: so that we might also have a heart always ready for you, and we might be found worthy to sing and to praise you in glory.

Deus, qui omne quod sincerum et mundum est amas, et castas
fidelium mentes inhabitas, benignitatis munificentia ab
omni nos contagione expurga: ut et in te semper
paratum cor habemus, et digni in gloria
tua tibi cantemus et psalamus.

---

74 2 Cor. 3:18a.
75 Phil. 3:8a.
76 1 Tim. 6 :8.
77 *E. N.* This appears to be a loose quotation from St. Jerome's Homily 34 on the Psalms. *See* Homilies of St. Jerome (Washington, DC: Catholic University of America Press, 1964), Vol. 1, 253.

Psalm 108

ARTICLE XV

LITERAL EXPLANATION OF THE
ONE HUNDRED AND EIGHTH PSALM:
DEUS, LAUDEM MEAM NE TACUERIS.
O GOD, BE NOT SILENT IN MY PRAISE.

108{109}[1]   *Unto the end, a Psalm for David.*

In finem. Psalmus David.

NOW THE TITLE OF THIS PRESENT PSALM IS: 108{109}[1] *In finem, Psalmus David; unto the end, a Psalm for David:* that is, this Psalm elevates us unto the end, which is Christ, because it is written about him, and David is its author. For that this Psalm literally speaks of Christ is established by Apostolic authority. For Peter, from the report of Luke in Acts, asserts that verses of this Psalm speak of the traitor Judas and the punishment inflicted upon him because of the sin of betraying Christ. For this is what he states in Acts: *Peter rising up in the midst of his brethren, said: Men, brethren, the scripture must needs be fulfilled, which the Holy Spirit spoke before by the mouth of David concerning Judas, who was the leader of them that apprehended Jesus.*[1] And a little later: For it is written in the book of Psalms: *Let their habitation become desolate, and let there be none to dwell therein. And his bishopric let another take.*[2] The first part of this authority deals with the sixty-eighth Psalm;[3] but the other part it contains is the present Psalm. Now Peter joins both scriptures together because both Psalms speak of the Passion of Christ. Also, the first part of this authority explains the punishment of the Jews, who were moved by envy to buy and to kill Christ;[4] but the second part of it expresses the punishment of Judas, which was moved by avarice to sell Christ.[5] And as the words of buying and the selling were mixed in the narrative and the description, so in this Psalm the words of the traitor Judas and the buying of the Jews are referred to simultaneously and made to run together.

1 Acts 1:15a, 16.
2 Acts 1:20 (quoting Ps. 68:26 and 108:8).
3 Ps. 68:26.
4 Matt. 27:18.
5 Matt. 26:15.

108{109}[2] *O God, be not silent in my praise: for the mouth of the wicked and the mouth of the deceitful man is opened against me.*

Deus, laudem meam ne tacueris, quia os peccatoris et os dolosi super me apertum est.

Christ, therefore, inasmuch as he was in a certain way a wayfarer and was passible, prayed to the Father, saying 108{109}[2] *Deus, laudem meam ne tacueris; O God, be not silent in my praise*, that is, do not hide from it, and do not permit it to be for naught; but you who see me being reproached and killed, seeking not my own glory,[6] but referring all things to your honor, do to me as I do to you, so that you might manifest my glory and praise and justice to others, and you might convert them to praise me. This is what Christ prayed for: *Father, the hour is come, glorify your Son, that your Son may glorify you.*[7] And this, O Father, I ask for, *quia os peccatoris, for the mouth of the wicked*, that is, the priestly caste, *et os dolosi, and the mouth of the deceitful man*, that is, the traitor Judas, *super me apertum est, is opened against me*, that is, is opposed to me. For the priests agitated the people against Christ, and they along with their partisans spoke many blasphemies against Christ, saying: *He is mad, why do you hear him?*[8] And elsewhere we have with the same Evangelist: *Do we not say well that you are a Samaritan, and have a devil?*[9] Judas also opened his mouth against Jesus, saying: *What will you give me, and I will deliver him unto you?*[10] And that which Mark reports: *Whomsoever I shall kiss, that is he; lay hold on him, and lead him away carefully.*[11]

108{109}[3] *They have spoken against me with deceitful tongues; and they have compassed me about with words of hatred; and have fought against me without cause.*

Locuti sunt adversum me lingua dolosa, et sermonibus odii circumdederunt me, et expugnaverunt me gratis.

108{109}[3] *Locuti sunt, they have spoken*, the Jews and the priests [have spoken] *adversum me lingua dolosa, against me with a deceitful tongue*, bringing forth praises so that they might catch me with words. For as

---

6 John 8:50.
7 John 17:1b.
8 John 10:20.
9 John 8:48b.
10 Matt. 22:16a.
11 Mark 14:44.

stated in Matthew, they said just this: *Master, we know that you are a true speaker, and teach the way of God in truth, neither care you for any man.*[12] *Et sermonibus odii circumdederunt me, and they have compassed me about with words of hatred*, saying to me in the day of Palms: *Hear you what these say?*[13] And by another Evangelist: *You give testimony of yourself: your testimony is not true.*[14] And elsewhere: *We know that this man is a sinner.*[15] Whence the Savior says through Hosea: *They have transgressed against me: and I redeemed them: and they have spoken lies against me.*[16] And in Jeremiah: *I heard the reproaches of many, and terror on every side: Persecute him, and let us persecute him.*[17] *Et expugnaverunt, and they have fought against me*, that is, they have persecuted me even unto death, *me gratis, without cause*, that is, without a reasonable cause. For this reason Pilate said to the Jews: *I found no cause in this man.... No, nor Herod either.*[18]

108{109}[4] *Instead of making me a return of love, they detracted me: but I gave myself to prayer.*

Pro eo ut me diligerent, detrahebant mihi; ego autem orabam.

108{109}[5] *And they repaid me evil for good: and hatred for my love.*

Et posuerunt adversum me mala pro bonis, et odium pro dilectione mea.

108{109}[4] *Pro eo ut me diligerent*, instead of making me a return of love, that is, [instead of] being brought together by me for my benefits, for which they were bound to love me, *detrahebant mihi, they detracted me*, saying, *He seduces the crowds;*[19] and *Behold a man that is a glutton and a wine drinker, a friend of publicans and sinners;*[20] and, *This man is not of God, who keeps not the sabbath.*[21] *Ego autem orabam, but I gave myself to prayer* for their conversion. For suspended on the Cross, I said: *Father, forgive them, for they know not what they do.*[22] Whence in Isaiah is written: *He has prayed*

---

12 Matt. 22:16.
13 Matt. 21:16. *E. N.* The scribes and chief priests were indignant with the cries of the people, "Hosanna to the son of David," and chastised Jesus for receiving such acclaim.
14 John 8:13.
15 John 9:24b.
16 Hosea 7:13.
17 Jer. 20:10a.
18 Luke 23:14b, 15a.
19 John 7:12b.
20 Matt. 11:19.
21 John 9:16a.
22 Luke 18:34.

for the transgressors.[23] For Christ fulfilled that which he taught, because *he began to do and to teach.*[24] And he taught that prayer ought to be said for one's adversaries, saying: *Pray for them that persecute and calumniate you.*[25] **108{109}[5]** *Et posuerunt adversum me mala pro bonis, and they repaid me evil for good,* that is, for informing them that I was announcing the kingdom of God, and for the many miracles that I performed before them so that they might convert to the faith, they unleashed injuries by words and by scourging. Whence I said to them: *Many good works I have showed you from my Father; for which of these works do you stone me?*[26] And through Jeremiah: *Shall evil be rendered for good, because they have dug a pit for my soul?*[27] *Et odium pro dilectione mea, and hatred for my love,* that is, they responded to my love with rancor, the way we read in Hosea, *I have chastised them, and strengthened their arms: and they have imagined evil against me.*[28] Here also Christ says in Matthew: *Jerusalem, Jerusalem . . . how often would I have gathered together your children, as the hen gathers her chickens under her wings, and you would not?*[29]

108{109}[6] *Set the sinner over him: and may the devil stand at his right hand.*

   Constitue super eum peccatorem; et diabolus stet a dextris eius.

108{109}[6] *Constitue super eum, set . . . over him,* that is, over the Jewish people, *peccatorem, the sinner,* that is, an evil prince, because of the just deserts of that people: in the manner that is contained in the book of Job: *Who makes a man that is a hypocrite to reign for the sins of the people?*[30] This was fulfilled when Caiaphas was the high priest in that year; he deserves to be called a sinner because he provided the final counsel in the killing of Christ, saying: *It is expedient for you that one man should die for the people.*[31] As a result of this, therefore, *from that day therefore they devised to put him to death,* as John says.[32] Or [an alternative explanation is], *Set . . . over him,* that is, this people, and also

---

23 Is. 53:12b.
24 Acts 1:1a.
25 Matt. 5:44b.
26 John 10:32.
27 Jer. 18:20a.
28 Hosea 7:15.
29 Matt. 23:37.
30 Job 34:30.
31 John 11:50.
32 John 11:53.

upon the traitor Judas, *the sinner*, that is, the devil, whose will those who persevere in evil serve. Here Christ asserts in John: *You are of your father the devil, and the desires of your father you do.*[33] For those who do not desire to find repose with the Savior deserve to be subject to the devil. Whence in Luke we have this regarding Judas: *Satan entered into Judas, who was surnamed Iscariot. Et diabolus stet a dextris eius, and may the devil stand at his right hand*, that is, both with the traitor and with the people, he will work together with and assist in evil by hidden suggestions. For the suggestions inciting persecution against Christ were suggestions from the devil. These things are said, not wishing for it, but predicting it, and expressing that they are deserving of this. For they deserved to be possessed in such a manner by the devil.

108{109}[7] *When he is judged, may he go out condemned; and may his prayer be turned to sin.*

Cum iudicatur, exeat condemnatus; et oratio eius fiat in peccatum.

108{109}[7] *Cum iudicatur, when he is judged*, [when] Judas [is judged] by Christ, *exeat condemnatus, may he go out condemned*. This was fulfilled in the Last Supper. For Christ carried out judgment against Judas when he told him at the Last Supper: *Woe to that man by whom the Son of man shall be betrayed: it were better for him, if that man had not been born.*[34] This judgment was extended when Christ gave to Judas a morsel, which he ate, and *Satan entered into him*; and *he went out immediately* from the most happy college of Christ and the Apostles to the children of darkness, and then the judgment of Christ was damnation.[35] Or [we can understand it] thus: *When he is judged* [referring to] the Jewish people or the traitor in the particular judgment at the time of death, *exeat, may he go out* from the sight of the judge, *condemnatus, condemned* to the eternal fire. *Et oratio eius, and may his prayer*, that is, the word of Judas, for prayer (*oratio*) is said to be like the mouth's reason (*oris ratio*),[36] *fiat in peccatum, be turned to sin*, that is, may be imputed him

---

33 John 8:44.
34 Matt. 26:24.
35 John 13:26–27, 30.
36 E. N. This etymology or maxim was a commonplace. *E.g.*, referring to Cassiodorus's *Expositio in Psalmum*, 85.1, 2 PL, 70, 610 (*Oratio nomen homonymum est, cuius etymologia est oris ratio*), St. Thomas also states this. ST IIaIIae, q. 83, art. 1, co. (*secundum Cassiodorum, oratio dicitur quasi oris ratio*). Jerome also uses it in Letter 140 to the priest Cyprian, CXL, 4, PL 22, 1168 (*oratio est oris ratio*).

as fault, as when he said, *Hail Rabbi,* and *Whomsoever I shall kiss, that is he.*[37] Indeed, his repentance turned against him as the sin of despair. For since he said, *I have sinned in betraying innocent blood,* he despaired, and *he hanged himself with a halter,*[38] and this was a sin against the Holy Spirit. For, according to Jerome, the sin of despair and of self-slaughter was greater than the sin of betraying Christ.[39] Or [alternatively], *prayer* (that is petition offered to God) *be turned into sin,* that is, is disapproved by God and appears vicious — or at least becomes the occasion for greater fault — because he prayed against the forms prescribed by Christ. For Christ, in the prayer which he taught, said: *Forgive us our debts, as we also forgive our debtors.*[40] But Judas did not do this: and so, according to Cassiodorus, he sinned in saying, *Forgive us our debts, as we also forgive our debtors* because he had nursed brotherly hatred.[41]

108{109}[8]   *May his days be few: and his bishopric let another take.*
Fiant dies eius pauci, et episcopatum eius accipiat alter.

108{109}[9]   *May his children be fatherless, and his wife a widow.*
Fiant filii eius orphani, et uxor eius vidua.

108{109}[8] *Fiant dies eius, may his days,* namely, those of Judas, *pauci, be few.* For after Christ had been judged, he immediately killed himself out of despair. For he hung himself with a halter, as is said in Matthew;[42] and *being hanged, burst asunder in the midst, and all his bowels gushed out,* as is stated in the book of Acts.[43] *Et episcopatum eius, and his bishopric,* that is, his position as apostle, *accipiat alter, let another take,* namely Matthias, who was elected by the Apostles to replace him, as is clearly

---

37 Matt. 26:49b, 48b.
38 Matt. 27:4a, 5b.
39 E. N. The reference is to St. Jerome's Homily 34 on Psalm 108. PL 26, 1157.
40 Matt. 6:12.
41 E. N. The reference to Cassiodorus is to his *Explanation of the Psalms,* namely that commentary dealing with this verse. The brotherly hatred nursed by Judas was the specific brotherly hatred *of Christ,* and the broader brotherly hatred shown by his *giving scandal* and bad example to others. Judas's prayer, says Cassiodorus, "is seen to have become for him the most serious sin, for in it are contained the words: *And forgive us our debts, as we too forgive our debtors.* But what could he forgive his debtors for, when he betrayed the Author of all kindnesses *[beneficiorum]*? So it was right that His holy prayer should be turned into sin for Judas, because he sinned and set an execrable precedent *[detestabili peccavit exemplo].*" Cassiodorus, *Explanation of the Psalms* (Mahwah, NJ: Paulist Press, 1999), Vol. 3, 105; *see also Expositio in Psalterium,* 108, 5, PL 70, 784.
42 Matt. 27:5.
43 Acts 1:18.

recited in the Acts of the Apostles.[44] Whence the bishops are said to be the successors to the Apostles.[45] **108{109}[9]** *Fiant filii eius orphani, et uxor eius vidua; may his children be fatherless, and his wife a widow.* Both of these things occurred simultaneously when he hung himself—and rightly so. For as is reported, he had pilfered that which had been given to Christ for supporting children and widows, and of which he himself was the custodian. And this we see to be consonant with what is written in John, where after the words of Judas where he stated, *Why was not this ointment sold for three hundred pence, and given to the poor?* the Evangelist adds: *He said this, not because he cared for the poor; but because he was a thief, and having the purse, carried the things that were put therein.*[46]

108{109}[10] *Let his children be carried about vagabonds, and beg; and let them be cast out of their dwellings.*

Nutantes transferantur filii eius et mendicent, et eiiciantur de habitationibus suis.

108{109}[11] *May the usurer search all his substance: and let strangers plunder his labors.*

Scrutetur foenerator omnem substantiam eius, et diripiant alieni labores eius.

Then is described the penalty of the Jewish people, who can also be called the children of Judas because they imitated his malice. Of these is stated: **108{109}[10]** *Nutantes, vagabonds,* that is, those staggering in their steps and ignorant of the precise place to which they ought to venture, *transferantur, let . . . be carried about,* from their own land, *filii eius, his children,* that is, the Jews, *et mendicant, and [let them] beg,* since they were despoiled from the real and personal property by their enemies, that is, the Romans; *et eiiciantur de habitationibus suis, and let them be cast out of their dwellings* unto alien lands. All these things were done by Titus and the Roman army, in the manner that Christ speaking through Hosea predicted: *I hated them: for the wickedness of their devices I will cast them forth out of my house . . . and they shall be wanderers among the nations.*[47] **108{109}[11]**

---

44 Acts 1:23–26.

45 E. N. "'In order that the full and living Gospel might always be preserved in the Church the apostles left bishops as their successors. They gave them their own position of teaching authority.'" CCC § 77 (citing VII, DV 7 § 2; St. Irenaeus, *Adv. haeres.* 3,3,1, PG 7, 1,848; Harvey, 2, 9).

46 John 12:5–6.

47 Hosea 9:15a, 17b.

Scrutetur foenerator, may the usurer search, that is, [may] he who expels them, namely Titus [search], *omnem substantiam eius, all his riches,* that is, all the riches of the Jewish people. For Titus diligently inquired about and took the substance of the Jews. *Et diripiant alieni, and let the strangers plunder,* that is let the the Roman officials under Titus [plunder], *labores eius, their labors,* that is, the riches of the Jews gained by their labor.

108{109}[12]   May there be none to help him: nor none to pity his fatherless offspring.

Non sit illi adiutor; nec sit qui misereatur pupillis eius.

108{109}[13]   May his posterity be cut off; in one generation may his name be blotted out.

Fiant nati eius in interitum; in generatione una deleatur nomen eius.

108{109}[12] *Non sit illi adiutor, may there be none to help him,* [to help] the Jews against the Romans. For there was no one who dared to help them; indeed, as Josephus wrote, although the king of the Jews, Agrippa, sided with the Romans.[48] *Nec sit qui misereatur pupillis eius, nor none to pity his fatherless offspring,* that is, the children of the Jews who were killed. For the Romans either killed them, or sold them into slavery, or greatly afflicted them without mercy. 108{109}[13] *Fiant nati eius in interitum, may his posterity be cut off,* that is, may the children of these people perish by sword, hunger, and pestilence: this occurred during the siege of Jerusalem by the Romans. *In generatione una deleatur nomen eius, in one generation may his name be blotted out,* that is, may this people with their children within the time of one generation be overwhelmed. This clearly was fulfilled because Jerusalem was destroyed around forty years from the Passion of Christ, and its people were destroyed by the head and army of the Romans, in the manner that we know through Daniel the prophet: *After sixty-two weeks Christ shall be slain: and the people that shall deny him shall not be his. And a people with their leader that shall come, shall destroy the city and the sanctuary.*[49]

---

48 *E. N.* Titus Flavius Josephus (37–*ca.* 100) was a Romano-Jewish historian famous for his Jewish histories, most notably *The Jewish War.* The reference to Agrippa is to Agrippa II (27/28–*ca.* 92 or 100), who sided with the Romans against the Jews. Denis cites to *De Bello Iud.*, book 2, c. 16.

49 Dan. 9:26.

108{109}[14] *May the iniquity of his fathers be remembered in the sight of the Lord: and let not the sin of his mother be blotted out.*

In memoriam redeat iniquitas patrum eius in conspectu Domini, et peccatum matris eius non deleatur.

108{109}[14] *In memoriam redeat iniquitas patrum eius, may the iniquity of his fathers be remembered,* that is, the sin committed against Christ by the fathers of the Jews who existed during the time of Titus, was recalled *in conspectus Domini, in the sight of the Lord,* that is, before God: so that not only were the fathers who killed Christ punished and in large part killed during the time of Titus, but also their children who followed in the infidelity and fault of their fathers, since they fulfilled that which the fathers of the children had exclaimed before Pilate: *His blood be upon us and our children.*[50] *Et peccatum matris eius, and the sin of his mother,* that is, of the unfaithful Synagogue, *non deleatur, let it not be blotted out.* For she was not penitent, and therefore in the present life she is punished temporally, and in hell eternally. Whence Christ said of them through Hosea: *I will love them no more.*[51]

But the Lord says in Ezechiel, that there will be among you this *as a proverb: The fathers have eaten sour grapes, and the teeth of the children are set on edge;*[52] and again, *The soul that sins, the same shall die: the son shall not bear the iniquity of the father, and the father shall not bear the iniquity of the son.* Therefore, one might ask in what way are the sins of the Jews avenged upon their children. The response to this is that punishment is twofold, namely, temporal and eternal. Again, some punishment is imposed that injures spiritual goods, but other [punishment] injures bodily [goods]. Now if the children do not imitate the sins of their parents, they are not punished for their sins by the infliction of eternal punishment or spiritual harm, namely, by the removal of grace in the present and glory in the future; but if they follow in the sins of their parents, such are also punished like them and with them, and sometimes even more heavily. Moreover, if the children do not imitate the sins of their parents, they are sometimes punished for the sins of their parents with temporal punishments and the infliction of corporal harm because

---

50 Matt. 27:25

51 Hosea 9:15b.

52 Ez. 18: 2b–3a. E. N. Denis elaborates on this verse in his *Commentary on Ezechiel*: "*The fathers have eaten sour grapes,* that is, they committed the fault which brings forth the bitterness of punishment, *and the teeth of the children are set on edge,* that is, the children suffer the punishment due their parents." Doctoris Ecstatici D. Dionysii Cartusiani, *Opera Omnia*, Vol. 9 (Montreuil: 1900), 496.

a child is in a way a part of his parents, seeing that he is born of their substance in the manner that a fruit hanging from a tree is a part of the tree. This is not to be regarded as unjust, especially since according to human laws one may be punished like this for the fault of another: as when because of the crime of *lèse-majesté* committed by the father, his son is deprived of inheritance.[53] And from this one knows how to understand that which the Lord says in the book of Exodus: *I am the Lord your God, mighty, jealous, visiting the iniquity of the fathers upon the children, unto the third and fourth generation of them that hate me.*[54] This is more clearly said by Moses in the same book, when speaking to the Lord, he said: *O the Lord, the Lord God ... no man of himself is innocent before you, who render the iniquity of the fathers to the children, and to the grandchildren, unto the third and fourth generation.*[55] Whence also in Jeremiah it is stated: *O Lord God ... you return the iniquity of the fathers into the bosom of their children after them.*[56]

108{109}[15]   *May they be before the Lord continually, and let the memory of them perish from the earth.*

Fiant contra Dominum semper, et dispereat de terra memoria eorum.

108{109}[16]   *Because he remembered not to show mercy.*

Pro eo quod non est recordatus facere misericordiam.

108{109}[15] *Fiant contra Dominum semper,* may they be before the Lord continually, that is, may the Jews at all times be proud and remain unfaithful against Christ, the King of kings and the Lord of lords. We see this fulfilled because nearly all remain obstinate [in their disbelief]. For this reason the Prophet [Amos] attests: *The house of Israel is fallen, and it shall rise no more.*[57] *Et dispereat de terra,* and let ... *perish from the earth* of the Church militant and triumphant *memoria eorum, the memory of them,* namely, of the Jews, in the same way that sacred Scripture many times testifies that the memory of evil men will perish as far as good and usefulness. For in such a manner the memory of the ungodly perishes,

---

53 E. N. The crime of *lèse-majesté* (Fr. "injured majesty," sometimes Anglicized as lese majesty) is a crime against the crown (*e.g.,* treason) that resulted in the loss of inheritance (disherison). Thus the children be punished for the fault of their parents.
54 Ex. 20:5.
55 Ex. 24:6–7.
56 Jer. 32:17–18a.
57 Amos 5:1.

because there is not a recollection that can be brought to mind of their good. Nevertheless, sometimes he makes notorious their singular and great evil, as he did the Jews who killed Christ. But the memory of the just remains in the good. Whence in the book of Proverbs it is written: *The memory of the just is with praises: and the name of the wicked shall rot.*[58] **108{109}[16]** *Pro eo quod non est recordatus*, because he remembered not, [because] this people and Judas [remembered not], *facere misericordiam*, to show mercy to the Lord Savior: indeed, they showed the greatest cruelty to him, according that which follows.

108{109}[17] *But persecuted the poor man and the beggar; and the broken in heart, to put him to death.*

Et persecutus est hominem inopem et mendicum, et compunctum corde mortificare.

108{109}[17] *Et persecutus est hominem inopem et mendicum*, but *persecuted the poor man and the beggar*, that is, Christ who led in this world a life of great poverty in accordance with what he himself said in Matthew: *The foxes have holes, and the birds of the air nests: but the Son of Man has not where to lay his head.*[59] And as Luke attests, certain religiously-minded women *ministered unto him of their substance.*[60] Whence upon the Holy Spirit revealing that Christ in his first coming would come in complete poverty, Jeremiah greatly marveled speaking to him these words: *Why will you be a stranger in the land, and as a wayfaring man turning in to lodge?*[61] So also does Zechariah describe how he would come in his first coming sometime in the future, saying: *Rejoice greatly, O daughter of Sion, . . . your King will come to you, the just and Savior: he is poor, and riding upon an ass, and upon a colt the foal of an ass.*[62] Greatly, therefore, did the Jews err who awaited for a Messiah to come in his first coming with such great majesty that he would obtain monarchical power over all the world and would subject all things under his reign. *Et compunctum corde mortificare, and the broken in heart, to put him to death*: that is, the Jewish people persecuting Christ, for whose salvation he had especially been sent,[63] attempting to kill him from an errant compassion as one

---

58 Prov. 10:7.
59 Matt. 8:20.
60 Luke 8:3b.
61 Jer. 14:8.
62 Zech. 9:9.
63 Matt. 15:24.

being afflicted in mind, and because the ingratitude of the Jews.[64] Whence they said in John: *We have a law; and according to the law he ought to die, because he made himself the Son of God.*[65]

108{109}[18]   *And he loved cursing, and it shall come unto him: and he would not have blessing, and it shall be far from him. And he put on cursing, like a garment: and it went in like water into his entrails, and like oil in his bones.*

Et dilexit maledictionem, et veniet ei; et noluit benedictionem, et elongabitur ab eo. Et induit maledictionem sicut vestimentum; et intravit sicut aqua in interiora eius, et sicut oleum in ossibus eius.

108{109}[19]   *May it be unto him like a garment which covers him; and like a girdle with which he is girded continually.*

Fiat ei sicut vestimentum quo operitur, et sicut zona qua semper praecingitur.

108{109}[18]   *Et dilexit, and they* loved,[66] both Judas and the people aligned with him [loved], *maledictionem, cursing,* not under the aspect of cursing—for, according to Dionysius [the Areopagite] no one looks to the doing of evil works nor does anyone desire evil under the aspect of evil.[67] But *they loved cursing,* that is, the cause for which the curse was put upon them, namely their fault, and by their deed they show themselves to love that which is either a curse or the origin of a curse. *Et veniet ei, and it shall come to them,* the desired curse [shall come to them]: for they will be atrociously oppressed by the Romans.[68] *Et noluit,*

---

64 E. N. That is Jesus was the one "broken in heart" because of the Jewish response to, and rejection of, his mission. Thus the Jews put to death the "broken in heart."
65 John 19:7.
66 E. N. Judas and the Jewish people are considered singular nouns here. In both the verb and the pronoun, there is no distinction between "he" (referent to Judas) and "it" (referent to the Jewish people). I have tried to indicate this ambiguity (which does not exist in English) by using the pronoun "their" so it refers to both Judas and the Jewish people. Thus, the English will not follow the Douay-Rheims, which has assumed a singular masculine pronoun.
67 *De Divinis nom.* cap. 4. E. N. "'Evil does nothing except in virtue of good,' as Dionysius says." ST IaIIae, q. 29, art. 3, s. c. "Every agent acts for an end under the aspect of good." ST IIaIIae, q. 94, art. 2, co. "Evil is never loved except under the aspect of good." ST IaIIae, q. 27, ad 1, and ST Ia. 1. 100, art. 2, co.
68 E. N. In other words, the desire to harm Christ would turn out to actually turn back upon them, and both Judas and those Jews who persecuted Christ would suffer: Judas by his violent death and the Jews by the destruction of Jerusalem by Titus.

and they would not have, that is, this people and Judas [would not have] *benedictionem, a blessing,* that is, the faith, doctrine, and grace of Christ,[69] *et elongabitur ab eo, and they shall be far from him,* because he will not fill their hearts [with faith, doctrine, and grace]. *Et induit maledictionem sicut vestimentum, and they put on cursing, like a garment:* that is, the sin for which cursing was inflicted, surrounded this people and Judas, and covered them, as clothing surrounds and covers the man who is clothed. For this reason, Hosea says: *Their own devices now have surrounded them, they have been done before my face.*[70] *Et intravit sicut acqua in interiora eius, and it went in like water into their entrails:* that is, by consenting to this sin, this sin entered into the heart of this people; or this cursing, namely, the inflicted pain, entered *like water,* that is, copiously and easily, *into their entrails,* for they were afflicted not only in body, but also in mind by their rivals [the Romans]; *et sicut oleum in ossibus eius, and like oil in their bones:* that is, like oil refreshes, soothes, and delights the bones of the body; so did these glory in their sin, and in this manner they were nourished by their malignancy. 108{109}[19] *Fiat ei sicut vestimentum quo operitur, may it be unto them like a garment which covers them:* that is, may a mighty persecution fall all around them, and may their sin turn back upon them in most heavy punishments; *et sicut zona qua semper praecingitur, and like a girdle with which they are girded continually:* that is, may this people be taken captive in their cursing, and may they be bound in captivity even until the end of the age.

108{109}[20] *This is the work of them who detract me before the Lord; and who speak evils against my soul.*

Hoc opus eorum qui detrahunt mihi apud Dominum, et qui loquuntur mala adversus animam meam.

108{109}[20] *Hoc opus eorum, this is the work of them,* that is, this is the punishment and the cursing of the Jews, *qui detrahunt mihi apud Dominum, who detract me before the Lord,* that is, before the knowing and attentive God, from whom nothing is hidden; *et qui loquuntur mala adversus animam meam, and who speak evils against my soul,* that is, who

---

69 E. N. The "faith . . . of Christ," is "faith . . . in Christ." In other words the genitive is an objective genitive (as it is in Gal. 2:16), where Christ is the object of faith, not a subjective genitive (because Christ strictly speaking had no "faith," since Jesus, in his human nature, enjoyed the beatific vision of God and saw him face to face even while he was on earth.

70 Hosea 7:2.

impose the evil of fault upon me and demand that the evil of punishment be inflicted upon me, saying that in Luke: *We have found this man perverting our nation, and forbidding to give tribute to Caesar, and saying that he is Christ the king;*[71] and that also which they cried out in John, *Away with him; away with him; crucify him.*[72]

108{109}[21]   *But you, O Lord, O Lord, do with me for your name's sake: because your mercy is sweet. Deliver me.*

Et tu, Domine, Domine, fac mecum propter nomen tuum, quia suavis est misericordia tua. Libera me,

108{109}[22]   *For I am needy and poor, and my heart is troubled within me.*

Quia egenus et pauper ego sum, et cor meum conturbatum est intra me.

Then Christ prays to the Father: 108{109}[21] *Et tu, Domine, Domine fac mecum; but you, O Lord, O Lord, do with me,* that is, give to me that which I request, *propter nomen tuum, for your name's sake,* that is, for you yourself and for the honor of your name, raising me up from the dead; *quia suavis est misericordia tua, because your mercy is sweet,* that is, to the elect your mercy, which has done so many and so great things for the salvation of men, tastes sweet. See how sweet, decorous, conscientious, and full of meaning this verse is, [this verse] in which the name of the Lord is repeated, so as to ignite one's affection, [this verse] in which God is beseeched so that he might do for himself that which he is requested to do, and not because of any merit whatsoever [of the one beseeching]. And to this it adds the reason: *because your mercy is sweet.* For his justice is dreadful.[73] *Libera me, deliver me* by the blessed resurrection from all passibility of body and persecution, 108{109}[22] *quia egenus, for I am needy,* that is, inasmuch as I am man, in the condition of requiring aid from you, *et pauper ego sum, and I am poor:* as is now readily apparent. Whence the Apostle says: *You know the grace of our Lord Jesus Christ, that being rich he became poor, for our sakes; that through his poverty we might be rich.*[74] *Et cor meum, and my heart,* [my] human [heart], but not

---

71 Luke 23:2.

72 John 19:15a.

73 2 Macc. 1:24.

74 2 Cor. 8:9. *E. N.* Denis changes the verse from second person plural to first person plural.

my divine mind, *conturbatum est intra me, is troubled within me*, that is, is vehemently affected with pain, fear, sorrow, so that I would say: *My soul is sorrowful even unto death.*[75] For here, as we find with John, he said: *Now is my soul troubled. And what shall I say?*[76] Now one can ask the question as to how it was fitting for Christ to suffer this trouble, since he himself according to this same Evangelist told the Apostles, *Let not your heart be troubled, nor let it be afraid.*[77] In response [one should consider] that sometimes being troubled means disorientation or an immoderate affection of the heart: and this did not exist in Christ; and so it was rejected by him. But sometimes being troubled means a strong affection of the soul arising from some particular consideration or cause: and this did exist in Christ, since, as explained previously, he freely took this upon himself as we see in John: *Jesus . . . groaned in spirit, and troubled himself.*[78]

108{109}[23] *I am taken away like the shadow when it declines: and I am shaken off as locusts.*

Sicut umbra cum declinat ablatus sum, et excussus sum sicut locustae.

108{109}[23] *Sicut umbra cum declinat*, like the shadow when it declines at sunset and the approach of darkness, and quickly becomes faint and disappears; so *ablatus sum, I am taken away* from corporal life and the fellowship of the disciples, affixed to the cross, quickly dying upon it: as is written in Mark, *Pilate wondered that he should be already dead.*[79] *Et excussus sum, and I am shaken* from the hand of the persecuting Jews in the day of my Resurrection: for then I rose again in an immortal body and I shed myself free from all penalties; *sicut locustae, as locusts*, who fly off and are not detained by anyone. Or [we can see it thus], *I am shaken*, fleeing from place to place because of the persecutions of my adversaries. For in infancy I had to flee to Egypt in the face of Herod,[80] and from time to time I turned away from the persecution of the Jews,[81] *as locusts* who move from place to place.

---

75 Matt. 26:38.
76 John 12:27a.
77 John 14:27b.
78 John 11:33.
79 Mark 15:44a.
80 Matt. 2:13–15.
81 John 8:59; 11:54; 12:36.

108{109}[24] *My knees are weakened through fasting: and my flesh is changed for oil.*

Genua mea infirmata sunt a ieiunio; et caro mea immutata est propter oleum.

108{109}[24] *Genua mea infirmata sunt a ieiunio, my knees are weakened through fasting.* However much some may think that this does not literally befit Christ, and so it should be expounded to refer to his members in this way, *my knees,* that is, the Apostles who ought to have supported others through their example, *are weakened* during the time of my Passion, *through fasting,* that is, by a deficiency of spiritual refreshment, because they did not yet fully taste or receive the gift of fortitude, but all (as the Evangelist narrates) were dispersed and fled;[82] but it seems not to be absurd if we assert Christ to be weakened and debilitated in his own bodily knees through fasting. For he fasted continuously for forty days and nights, and afterwards he was hungry from the dwindling of the body. Now hunger causes weakness in the body, and most commonly it is readily felt in the knees. And so why is it unfitting to say that Christ was weakened in the knees from fasting when he was wearied from other bodily labors? He was wearied from bodily labors according to this: *Jesus . . . being wearied with his journey, sat thus on the well.*[83] For he assumed undetractive defects according to the Damascene, which are hunger, thirst, weariness, fear, natural sufferings and ones similar to these.[84] *Et caro mea immutata est, and my flesh is changed* from its natural vigor by the defect of hunger or a certain leanness, *propter oleum, for oil,* that is, from the lack of savory food. Whence the translation of Jerome is this: *My flesh is lean, without oil.* But various Hebrew texts have it rendered thus: *My flesh is lean from fat,* that is, from the absence of fat. For Christ had in his youth a fitting fleshly and full body, because his complexion was ruddy and perfect inasmuch as he had assumed a body from the most pure blood of the Virgin and formed by the Holy Spirit; but afterwards because of the various labors of vigils, of fasts, and of travel he was worn out so much that he seemed older than he was. For this reason the Jews said to him: *You are not yet fifty years old.*[85]

---

82 Matt. 26:56.

83 John 4:6.

84 *E. N. See, e.g.,* Chapter 20 of Book III St. John of Damascus's *An Exposition of the Orthodox Faith (De Fide Orthodoxa).* These are defects that do not detract from the dignity of Christ. Denis uses the word *indetrahibiles,* while St. John of Damascus describes them as "innocent" or "inculpable" defects that are not voluntary (*inculpatae passiones* or ἀδιάβλητα πάθη [*adiáblēta pathē*]). PG 94, 1081–82.

85 John 8:57.

For although he was not more than thirty-three years old, he seemed nevertheless to appear to be older. These statements are not asserted pertinaciously [by me], but as pious opinions.

108{109}[25] *And I am become a reproach to them: they saw me and they shook their heads.*

Et ego factus sum opprobrium illis; viderunt me, et moverunt capita sua.

108{109}[25] *Et ego factus sum opprobrium illis, and I am become a reproach to them.* For the Jews often derided Christ, especially during the Passion, according to what is said in a Psalm above: *I am a worm, and no man: the reproach of men, and the outcast of the people.*[86] *Viderunt me, they saw me* hanging upon the cross, *et moverunt capita sua, and they shook their heads,* expressing their joy in my misery, as it is written: *They that passed by, blasphemed him, wagging their heads, and saying: Vah, you that destroy the temple of God.*[87]

108{109}[26] *Help me, O Lord my God; save me according to your mercy.*

Adiuva me, Domine Deus meus; salvum me fac secundum misericordiam tuam.

108{109}[27] *And let them know that this is your hand: and that you, O Lord, have done it.*

Et sciant quia manus tua haec, et tu, Domine, fecisti eam.

108{109}[26] *Adiuva me, help me:* during the Passion, according as I am man, and assist my humanity, and cooperate with it in all things. For the man Christ asked to be helped by God, not that he feared that it was possible for him to sin, but so that he might prevail in the battle through divine power. For this reason, he said: *The Lord God is my helper;*[88] and also, *The Lord is with me as a strong warrior.*[89] *Salvum me fac, save me* from death and from mortality, *secundum misericordiam tuam, according to your mercy.* Why does he not say, "According to your justice?" Indeed, he could say both things: but so that he might teach us by his example never to presume on our own perfection, but rather to

---

86 Ps. 21:7.
87 Matt. 27:39, 40a.
88 Is. 50:7a.
89 Jer. 20:11a.

hope incessantly on the goodness of God, so he says, *save me according to your mercy*; and also, because in all the works of God one finds the mercy of God mixed in; and also because all the virtue and grace of Christ is granted to his soul only by the mercy of God. 108{109}[27] *Et sciant, and let them know*, [that is, let] my adversaries [know] through experience of their damnation and the good through the proclamation of the Gospel of truth, *quia manus tuae haec, that this is your hand*, that is, that this salvation and resurrection of mine, is the effect of your divine power, which alone is able to resuscitate the dead, *et tu, Domine fecisti eam; and you, O Lord have done it*, that is, the aforesaid effect, namely my resuscitation.

108{109}[28]   *They will curse and you will bless: let them that rise up against me be confounded: but your servant shall rejoice.*

Maledicent illi, et tu benedices; qui insurgunt in me confundantur, servus autem tuus laetabitur.

108{109}[28] *Maledicent illi, et tu benedices; they will curse and you will bless*. For the unbelieving Jews blasphemed Christ before the Passion, during the Passion, and after the Passion. But God blessed the man Christ both with respect to his accidental rewards and with respect to his Mystical Body.[90] *Qui insurgunt in me, they that rise up against me*, that is, my persecutors, *confundantur, let them be confounded*, either with temporal confusion, embarrassing them with their sins, or eternal confusion, undergoing torments if they do not repent. Whence through Jeremiah the Savior says: *Let them be confounded that persecute me, and let not me be confounded.*[91] *Servus autem tuus laetabitur, but your servant shall rejoice*: that is, I, your Son, who took on the form of a servant,[92] and am your servant as man, shall rejoice in you before those who are embarrassed and who perish.

108{109}[29]   *Let them that detract me be clothed with shame: and let them be covered with their confusion as with a double cloak.*

Induantur qui detrahunt mihi pudore, et operiantur sicut diploide confusione sua.

---

90 *E. N.* On the topic of Christ's accidental rewards, *see* Arts. XII (Psalm 2:5), XXIV (Psalm 7:13), and footnote 1-48 in Volume I.
91 Jer. 17:18a.
92 *Cf.* Phil. 2:7.

108{109}[29] *Induantur qui detrahunt mihi, pudore; let them that detract me be clothed with shame,* that is, let them be covered on all sides so that they may be ashamed of their detraction, with the end either toward saving repentance or toward eternal damnation; *et operiantur sicut diploide, and let them be covered . . . as with a double cloak,* that is, as if dressed twice, *confusione sua, with their confusion:* so that before God and man they might be ashamed; indeed, so that their confusion and punishment might begin now and in the future last for eternity. For with some people the punishments begin at the present and continue in the future age without end; but the chastisement of the elect only begins [at the present], but afterwards it comes to an end. These things were also manifestly fulfilled in the Jews. For they were wanderers and in exile from the time of the destruction and their expulsion during the time of Titus even unto the present day; and they are under the dominion of their adversaries and afflicted with various punishments and confusions. And yet they do not amend themselves on this account, but their punishment now begins and afterwards will last for eternity. For this reason, this is written about them: *With a double destruction, destroy them,* O Lord our God.[93] Finally, this prophecy regarding the confusion of the Jews will be completely fulfilled at that time when they will see him whom they have pierced, namely, in the day of judgment.[94] For then they will be judged by Christ whom they have judged, and they will behold him whom they put to death.

108{109}[30] *I will give great thanks to the Lord with my mouth: and in the midst of many I will praise him.*

Confitebor Domino nimis in ore meo, et in medio multorum laudabo eum.

108{109}[31] *Because he has stood at the right hand of the poor, to save my soul from persecutors.*

Quia astitit a dextris pauperis, ut salvam faceret a persequentibus animam meam.

108{109}[30] *Confitebor Domino nimis, I will give great thanks to the Lord,* that is, with utmost devotion, *in ore meo, with my mouth,* praising him for all the good things that he has bestowed upon me; *et in medio multorum, and in the midst of many,* that is, among the faithful or in the Church, *laudabo eum, I will praise him* for his goodness and the perfection

93 Jer. 17:18b.
94 *Cf.* Rev. 1:7.

that he is in himself. This Christ accomplished after his resurrection, when he appeared before his disciples and stood in the midst of them and said: *Peace be unto you; as the* living *Father has sent me, so I also send you.*[95] And: *It is not for you to know the times or moments, which the Father has put in his own power.*[96] But [it refers] also Christ in himself as man, where he now, in the empyrean heaven, unceasingly praises God, or the holy Trinity, with incomprehensible reverence of heart. In the Church militant also he praises God through his ministers whom he leads in the divine praise. **108{109}[31]** *Quia adstitit a dextris pauperis,* because he has stood at the right hand of the poor, that is, in all tribulation he was a fatherly help to me in my poverty, and he has never forsaken me, as I spoke in the Gospel of John: *He has not left me alone: for I do always the things that please him;*[97] *ut salvam faceret a persequentibus animam meam,* to save my soul from persecutors, that is, as far as myself or my bodily life, he will save me from the hands of the Jews and of my crucifixion, raising me on the third day from death.

In the exposition of the present Psalm, St. Jerome argues against the Jews thus: "Respond to me, O Jews. You were in Babylon, you had there the Prophets, Daniel, Ezechiel; seventy years you were captive there, and afterwards you came back home. See now that there are four hundred years (computing the years from Christ up to Jerome): why has not a Prophet been sent to you, and why has the Lord abandoned you? Back then you abandoned the Lord, and you worshiped idols, and you were miserable. Now when you do not worship idols, why does the Lord abandon you?"[98] Thus says Jerome.

But see now that much more than one thousand four hundred years have passed from the time that they were in [the Babylonian] captivity. There has not appeared to them a Prophet that has been sent to them, nor have they been given any certain and evident divine sign by which they might be able to know that they belong to the people of God: indeed, notwithstanding the fact that we most clearly point out to them by evident demonstration (*ad oculum*) that this is their final captivity because of their sin committed against Christ,[99] in the manner that

---

95 John 20:21.

96 Acts 1:7.

97 John 8:29b.

98 *E. N.* This is taken from the commentary to Psalm 108 in the so-called *Breviarum in Psalmos* wrongly attributed to St. Jerome. PL 26, 1159.

99 *E. N.* An *demonstratio ad oculum,* a "demonstration to the eye," was a demonstration of some present corporeal thing (*e.g.,* historical fact); whereas a *demonstratio ad intellectum,* a "demonstration to the intellect," involved an incorporeal matter.

is brought forth by Daniel: *The people that shall deny him shall not be his ... and the end thereof shall be waste ... and the desolation shall continue even ... unto the end.*[100] And by Hosea: *The children of Israel shall sit many days without king, and without prince, and without sacrifice, and without altar, and without ephod, and without theraphim; and after this the children of Israel shall return, and shall seek the Lord their God, and David their king* (that is, the Messiah, as all understand it): *and they shall fear the Lord, and his goodness in the last days.*[101] Now in this which the holy Hosea testifies regarding them returning back later to God and seeking the Messiah, he gives us plainly to understand that these of whom he speaks [in the interim] will sit without God and without Christ, that is without true faith and without worthy worship of God and of the Messiah. Or therefore, by these many days of which Hosea speaks we can understand them to be the days of this captivity or not. If so [and it refers to the days of captivity], it follows that for a time they sit without God and Christ as both infidels and reprobates; if it is not so [and does not refer to the days of captivity], then it still follows that [they are undergoing] another longer captivity which they did not expect. However this may be, yet they do not want to be informed, to believe, or to be converted, inasmuch as the holy Prophets predicted their blindness and obstinacy, regarding which they also have been found to be true. For truly *the wrath of God is come upon them to the end,*[102] and this is verified by that which Solomon says: He whom God *has despised no man can correct.*[103] Also most of all, our most noble Cassiodorus states: "The Virgin gave birth, the Messiah came, the immaculate Lamb was slain, the Redeemer rose again from the dead, the world heard and believed: and yet the Jew still pretends not to know what the entire world knows. Grant, O Lord, conversion to the obstinate, light to the darkened, faith to the unbelieving, so that you might deign to come to the aid of those who are in peril and for whom you prayed when upon the Cross.[104] For rightly do we pray to you for them, O Lord, whom we are unable to persuade to be just."[105]

---

100 Dan. 9:26–27.
101 Hosea 3:4–5.
102 1 Thess. 2:16b.
103 Eccl. 7:14b.
104 *Cf.* Luke 23:34: *Father, forgive them, for they know not what they do.*
105 E. N. The reference is to the peroration of Cassiodorus's commentary on Psalm 108, which exhibits a great love for the Jew and a heartfelt prayer for their conversion to Christ, and that they might find themselves justified. PL 70, 792.

ARTICLE XVI

MORAL OR TROPOLOGICAL EXPOSITION OF THE SAME ONE HUNDRED AND EIGHTH PSALM.

108{109}[2]   *O God, be not silent in my praise: for the mouth of the wicked and the mouth of the deceitful man is opened against me.*

Deus, laudem meam ne tacueris, quia os peccatoris et os dolosi super me apertum est.

SINCE CHRIST SAID, *IF ANY MAN WILL COME after me, let him deny himself, and take up his cross daily, and follow me,*[106] it is no surprise, then, that this Psalm which speaks literally about the Passion of Christ, can be morally expounded as relating to his Church or any member of the faithful. The Church, therefore, or any man worthy of following the footsteps of Christ, spurning human praises and enduring diverse persecutions in his own person is able to say to the Lord: 108{109}[2] *Deus, laudem meam ne tacueris, O God be not silent in my praise:* that is, you—for whom I disdain temporal honors and praises and endure diverse things—approve, praise, and save me in judgment, saying: *Well done, good and faithful servant, . . . enter into the joy of your Lord.*[107] Do not permit my praise to be silent from others when it is for the edification of my neighbor and to the glory of your name. *Quia os peccatoris et os dolosi super me apertum est, for the mouth of the wicked and the mouth of the deceitful man is opened against me,* that is, proud and deceitful words are said against me.

108{109}[3]   *They have spoken against me with deceitful tongues; and they have compassed me about with words of hatred; and have fought against me without cause.*

Locuti sunt adversum me lingua dolosa, et sermonibus odii circumdederunt me, et expugnaverunt me gratis.

108{109}[3] *Locuti sunt, they have spoken,* depraved men [have spoken] *adversum me linguam dolosa, against me with deceitful tongues,* proposing evil under the guise of good, for, as they are not able to deceive with manifest evil, they deceive by covering it with kindness: which is

---

106 Luke 9:23.
107 Matt. 25:21, 23.

greatly iniquitous, according to that stated by Isaiah: *The vessels* (that is, the words) *of the deceitful are most wicked; for he has framed devices to destroy the meek, with lying words.*[108] And Malachi says: *Cursed is the deceitful man.*[109] And yet this vice — sadly! — is exceedingly common. For this reason, Jeremiah says: *Let every man take heed of his neighbor, and let him not trust in any brother of his: for every brother will utterly supplant, and every friend will walk deceitfully, and a man shall mock his brother.*[110] Here also it is written: *Every one hunts his brother to death. Keep the doors of your mouth from her that sleeps in your bosom, for ... a man's enemies are they of his own household.*[111] Since, therefore, things are so, with good reason Scripture says: *Open not your heart to every man;*[112] and, *Blessed is he that finds a true friend.*[113] *Et sermonibus odii circumdederunt me, and they have compassed me about with words of hatred,* seeking to distract me from the highest good, which is a most grievous hatred. But this should not be a cause for us to fear, because Christ has said: *Blessed shall you be when men shall hate you, and when they shall separate you, and shall reproach you, and cast out your name as evil, for the Son of man's sake.*[114] *Et expugnaverunt me gratis, and have fought against me without cause.* This most fittingly applies to the martyrs of Christ, who were found worthy to be killed for justice: but also all men who, without cause, suffer or are oppressed because of justice, that is, are attacked without having deserved it.

108{109}[4] *Instead of making me a return of love, they detracted me: but I gave myself to prayer.*

Pro eo ut me diligerent, detrahebant mihi; ego autem orabam.

108{109}[4] *Pro eo ut me diligerent, detrahebant mihi; instead of making me a return of love, they detracted me.* This fittingly applies to good prelates and brethren who charitably reprove those who are committed to them or their neighbors: because they ought to be loved in the manner that is written, *Rebuke a wise man, and he will love you.*[115] But these sorts of

---

108 Is. 32:7a.
109 Mal. 1:14a.
110 Jer. 9:4–5a.
111 Micah 7:2b, 5b, 6b.
112 Ecclus. 8:22a.
113 Ecclus. 225:12a.
114 Luke 6:22.
115 Prov. 9:8b.

men are completely contrary to those that harbor hate, and suffer contradiction, as Scripture says: *They have hated him that rebukes, ... and have abhorred him that speaks perfectly.*[116] *Ego autem orabam, but I gave myself to prayer* for the ungrateful and the malicious. This is what the Apostle says: *We are reviled, and we bless, ... we are blasphemed, and we suffer it.*[117] Whence also he elsewhere admonishes: *Be not overcome by evil, but overcome evil by good.*[118] This is the shield of patience of the servants of Christ: to take recourse in prayer when faced with any wrongdoing, first praying for oneself, lest our minds might be overcome and we might be moved to impatience, and in the face of all adversity we might remain constant; and second praying for adversaries, so that God may forgive them and infuse grace for a better life. Of such patience, Peter says: *Let them also that suffer according to the will of God, commend their souls in good deeds to the faithful Creator.*[119] Whence also Christ says: *If you love them that love you, what reward shall you have? Do not even the publicans this? And if you salute your brethren only, what do you more? Do not also the heathens* (that is, the Gentiles and the unbelievers) *this?*[120]

108{109}[6]   *Set the sinner over them: and may the devil stand at their right hand.*[121]

Constitue super eum peccatorem; et diabolus stet a dextris eius.

108{109}[7]   *When they are judged, may he go out condemned; and may their prayer be turned to sin.*

Cum iudicatur, exeat condemnatus; et oratio eius fiat in peccatum.

108{109}[8]   *May their days be few: and their bishopric let another take.*

Fiant dies eius pauci, et episcopatum eius accipiat alter.

108{109}[9]   *May their children be fatherless, and their wife a widow.*

Fiant filii eius orphani, et uxor eius vidua.

---

116 Amos 5:10.
117 1 Cor. 4:12b, 13a.
118 Rom. 12:21.
119 1 Pet 4:19.
120 Matt. 5:46, 47.
121 *E. N.* In this part of the *Commentary*, Denis skips over verse 108:5. From this point forward, I have translated the third person pronoun from "he" or "him" to "they" or "them." Denis refers it to a people and to an individual person, and rather than wrestle with "he" or "it," I have decided to use the third person plural.

108{109}[6] *Constitute super eum peccatorem, et diabolus stet a dextris eius. Set the sinner over them: and may the devil stand at their right hand.* 108{109}[7] *Cum iudicatur, exeat condemnatus, etc. When they are judged, may they go out condemned, etc.* It may seem wondrous how now so much imprecation is inveighed against the adversary of the just man, by the same just man who immediately before prayed for his rival. One should know, therefore, that these and similar words, by which one appears to be wishing for evil upon the enemy, are to be understood in three ways: First, in the manner of prophetic pronouncements, not in the manner of the imprecation of harm upon someone. Second, in the manner of demonstration of that which the ungodly deserve. Third, in the manner of zeal, that a man might conform himself to the divine justice, calling down evil upon ungodly men according to the order of divine justice unless they repent. In this way, Jeremiah says, *O Lord ... forgive not their iniquity, and let not their sin be blotted out from your sight.*[122]

He says to the Church or to any one member of the faithful: *Constitue super eum, set ... over them,* that is, you will set over and fittingly set over an unfaithful people — and I pray that you set up for the praise of your justice, unless they repent — *peccatorem, the sinner,* that is, the devil or the unworthy prelate, seeing that as the servants are, so are so the masters;[123] *et diabolus stet a dextris eius, and may the devil stand at their right hand,* inducing them to all evil deeds. 108{109}[8] *Fiant dies eius pauci, may their days be few,* that is, may they not persist in the life of grace, or may the days of their natural life be cut short because of their sins, in the manner that Ecclesiastes says: *Let it not be well with the wicked, neither let his days be prolonged.*[124] *Et episcopatum eius accipiat alter, and their bishopric let another take.* This is asserted against unworthy prelates — would that they be deprived of their office! For as nothing is more useful than a good prelate, so nothing is more harmful than an unworthy prelate. 108{109}[9] *Fiant filii eius orphani, may their children be fatherless:* that is, let the imitators of such evil people be deprived of a heavenly Father, for they are not adopted children of the eternal Father, but are servants of the devil to whose will they have consented; *et uxor eius, and may their wife,* that is, the church of the wicked,[125] with whom

---

122 Jer. 18:23a.

123 *E. N. Quales servi, tales sint domini.* This brings to mind Joseph de Maistre's famous saying: *Toute nation a le gouvernement qu'elle mérite,* every nation has the government it deserves. Joseph de Maistre, *Lettres et Opuscules Inédits* (Paris: A Vaton, 1861) (Letter, June 1810), Vol. 2, 281–82.

124 Eccl. 8:13a.

125 *E. N.* Denis uses the term *ecclesia malignantium,* a sort of anti-Church of which Satan is the head, and is opposed to the authentic Church, the *ecclesia sanctorum,*

he himself fornicates spiritually or bodily, become *vidua, a widow*, that is, cease to be the spouse of Christ, because they have fornicated with *many lovers*;[126] and they are not made fecund with the light and the grace of the Holy Spirit, but they are made sterile in all good works.

108{109}[10]   *Let their children be carried about vagabonds, and beg; and let them be cast out of their dwellings.*

Nutantes transferantur filii eius et mendicent, et eiiciantur de habitationibus suis.

108{109}[11]   *May the usurer search all their substance: and let strangers plunder their labors.*

Scrutetur foenerator omnem substantiam eius, et diripiant alieni labores eius.

108{109}[12]   *May there be none to help him: nor none to pity his fatherless offspring.*

Non sit illi adiutor; nec sit qui misereatur pupillis eius.

108{109}[13]   *May his posterity be cut off....*

Fiant nati eius in interitum....

108{109}[10] *Nutantes transferantur filii eius, let their children be carried about vagabonds*: that is, let the imitators of the perverse people be carried about from the reign of Christ to the power of the devil, from the state of salvation to the state of damnation, from temporal death to the perpetual death of hell; and these are vagabonds, that is, have become homeless, wandering, and dissolute, as it states in a Psalm above: *Strange children have faded away, and have halted from their paths.*[127] *For the wicked makes an unsteady work*, as is written.[128] *Et mendicent, and let them beg*, inasmuch as they are deprived from all spiritual goods in the manner that the foolish virgins begged, saying to the wise ones: *Give us of your oil.*[129] *Eiiciantur de habitationibus suis, let them be cast out of their dwellings*, that is, from the place of the Church as its unworthy and putrid members; or [alternatively] *from their dwellings*, that is, from their

---

the Church of the Saints, of which Christ is the head. The term is from Ps. 25:5: "I have hated the assembly of the malignant (*ecclesiam malignantium*)."

126 Jer. 3:1.
127 Ps. 17:46b.
128 Prov. 11:18a.
129 Matt. 25:8b.

celestial mansions prepared for them (had they lived well). **108{109}[11]** *Scrutetur foenerator, may the usurer search*, that is, the extortioner, namely the tempter, the devil, from whom the sinner borrows sin when he satisfies his desires by suggestion and cooperation as if borrowing money, *omnem substantiam eius, all their substance*, that is, all the interior riches from the ungodly, namely, the gifts of nature and of grace bestowed upon them; and he subjects, removes, and corrupts them under his dominion. *Et diripiant alieni, and let the strangers plunder*, that is, the demons tempting of particular vices [plunder], *labores eius, their labors*, that is, their virtues and merits, robbing them of the gifts of God. For in the way that an extortioner enters the home of a debtor unable to pay the debt and takes his goods, so, God permitting, a demon comes into the heart of the sinner who persists in vice and robs him of his goods, and so falls under his dominion. **108{109}[12]** *Non sit illi adiutor; may there be none to help him*. For he who is deprived of the help of God justly, cannot be saved or obtain beneficial help from anyone else. *Nec sit qui misereatur pupillis eius, nor none to pity his fatherless offspring*, that is, those who follow his depraved works but are punished with just punishment, either in this world, or in the future, as is written: *So let all your enemies perish, O Lord: but let them that love you shine, as the sun shines in its rising*.[130] **108{109}[13]** *Fiant nati eius in interitum, may his posterity be cut off* spiritually, losing the life of the soul, namely, charity and grace.

108{109}[15] *May they be before the Lord continually, and let the memory of them perish from the earth*.[131]

Fiant contra Dominum semper, et dispereat de terra memoria eorum.

108{109}[16] *Because they remembered not to show mercy.*

Pro eo quod non est recordatus facere misericordiam.

108{109}[17] *But persecuted the poor man and the beggar; and the broken in heart, to put him to death.*

Et persecutus est hominem inopem et mendicum, et compunctum corde mortificare.

108{109}[15] *Fiant contra Dominum semper, may they be before the Lord continually*, that is, may they displease God the whole time, as is

---

130 Judges 5:31.
131 *E. N.* Denis skips over verse 14.

written: *But to God the wicked and his wickedness are hateful alike;*[132] *et dispereat de terra,* and let . . . *perish from the earth* of the wayfarer and of the comprehensor [in heaven], that is, from the Church at the present and the land of the living or the heavenly fatherland, *memoria eorum, the memory of them,* as it relates to the good, so that they are not known by God by approbation;[133] **108{109}[16]** *Pro eo quod non est recordatus, because they remembered not* their covenant or themselves, *facere misericordiae, to show mercy* to their neighbor; **108{109}[17]** *Et persecutus est hominem inopem et mendicum, but they persecuted the poor and the beggar:* which is a sin crying out before God; *et compunctum corde, and the broken in heart* from contrition of their own sin and the sin of others, the wicked endeavored *mortificare, to put to death.* Rightly, therefore, are such cruel people consigned to eternal oblivion, where they will receive no mercy, as Job says: *Let mercy forget him: may worms be his sweetness.*[134] Whence also Christ says: *With the same measure that you shall mete withal, it shall be measured to you again.*[135] And elsewhere we read: *Man . . . has no mercy on a man like himself; and does he entreat for his own sins* to the most High? . . . *Who shall obtain pardon for his sins?*[136] It is as if he were saying, "this is absolutely unpardonable."

108{109}[18]   *And he loved cursing, and it shall come unto him: and he would not have blessing, and it shall be far from him. And he put on cursing, like a garment: and it went in like water into his entrails, and like oil in his bones.*

Et dilexit maledictionem, et veniet ei; et noluit benedictionem, et elongabitur ab eo. Et induit maledictionem sicut vestimentum; et intravit sicut aqua in interiora eius, et sicut oleum in ossibus eius.

---

132 Wis. 14:9.
133 E. N. God lacks knowledge of no thing, including sinners. Accordingly, Scholastic theologians distinguished between God's absolute knowledge and his knowledge of approbation (*notitia approbrationis*). Because of the sinner's spiritual state, a condition of disapprobation or reprobation, he is *as if* unknown by God. *Nescio vos,* "I know you not," (Matt. 25:12; Luke 13:25, 27). Orestes Brownson: "*Nescio vos,* it is just as if [the Lord] would have said: 'You have thrown yourselves out of my life!' And St. Chrysostom remarks, that this expression, *nescio vos,* is worse than hell itself, and is identical with the sentence: *Discedite a me; ite in ignem aeternum!* [Depart from me; go into everlasting fire!] It is the sentence of reprobation." Brownson's Quarterly Review (New York: D & J Sadlier 1862), "The Punishment of the Reprobate," Vol. II, 88.
134 Job 24:20.
135 Luke 6:38b.
136 Ecclus. 28:3a, 4, 5b.

108{109}[19] *May it be unto him like a garment which covers him; and like a girdle with which he is girded continually.*

Fiat ei sicut vestimentum quo operitur, et sicut zona qua semper praecingitur.

108{109}[18] *Et dilexit maledictionem, et veniet ei; and he loved cursing, and it shall come unto him.* The man who loves cursing is he who loves the works for which Christ says in the end to the reprobate: *Depart from me, you cursed, into everlasting fire.*[137] He who loves that which is not [morally] profitable for him, *who is glad when he has done evil, and rejoices in most wicked things* is the man who loves cursing.[138] It refers to those of whom Job asserts: *They have said to God, Depart from us, we desire not the knowledge of your ways* and Isaiah: *Say to the seers: See not: and to them that behold: Behold not for us those things that are right* they who love cursing.[139] *Et noluit, and he would not have,* the reprobate people [would not have], *benedictionem, blessing,* that is, the grace of God, because they spurned the law of the most High, *et elongabitur ab eo, and it shall be far from them* because he will not give it to them. *Et induit maledictionem sicut vestimentum, and he put on cursing like a garment,* that is, they filled up with sin. For here Wisdom says: *Because I called, and you refused: I stretched out my hand, and there was none that regarded; you have despised all my counsel and have neglected my reprehensions; I also will laugh in your destruction and will mock when that shall come to you which you feared, when sudden calamity shall fall on you.*[140] **108{109}[19]** *Fiat ei sicut vestimentum quo operitur, may it be unto him like a garment which covers him,* that is, he covers the ungodly with cursing, namely, with fault and due punishment, as a garment covers a man who is clothed with a garment. This occurs to the impenitent in the manner that Isaiah says: *Evil shall come upon you, . . . and calamity shall fall violently upon you, and . . . misery shall come upon you suddenly.*[141] *Et sicut zona qua semper praecingitur, and like a girdle with which he is girded continually:* that is, like a body that is bound with a girdle, so the perverse is bound up with cursing and is unable to free himself from the net of the devil. This is what Solomon has confessed: *His own iniquities catch the wicked, and he is fast bound with the ropes of his own sins.*[142]

---

137 Matt. 25:41.
138 Prov. 2:14. *E. N.* Denis has changed the proverb from third person plural to third person singular.
139 Job 21:14; Is. 30:10a.
140 Prov. 1:24–27a.
141 Is. 47:11.
142 Prov. 5:22.

108{109}[20]   *This is the work of them who detract me before the Lord; and who speak evils against my soul.*

Hoc opus eorum qui detrahunt mihi apud Dominum, et qui loquuntur mala adversus animam meam.

108{109}[21]   *But you, O Lord, O Lord, do with me for your name's sake: because your mercy is sweet. Deliver me.*

Et tu, Domine, Domine, fac mecum propter nomen tuum, quia suavis est misericordia tua. Libera me.

108{109}[22]   *For I am needy and poor, and my heart is troubled within me.*

Quia egenus et pauper ego sum, et cor meum conturbatum est intra me.

108{109}[23]   *I am taken away like the shadow when it declines: and I am shaken off as locusts.*

Sicut umbra cum declinat ablatus sum, et excussus sum sicut locustae.

Then the Church, or any member of the faithful, adds: 108{109}[20] *Hoc opus eorum, this is the work of them,* that is, this will be their reward, *qui detrahunt mihi apud Dominum, of them who detract me before the Lord.* It is terrible, therefore, to detract the just. 108{109}[21] *Et tu, Domine, Domine, fac mecum; but you, O Lord, O Lord, do with me* [in accordance with] your mercy *propter nomen tuum, for your name's sake,* that is, for your own goodness and glory, not because of any righteousness of mine. In this way God forgives us our sins and bestows the gift of grace for his own sake. For he says through Isaiah: *I am he who blots out your iniquities for my own sake;*[143] and elsewhere, *For my own sake will I do it, that I may not be blasphemed.*[144] *Quia suavis est misericordia tua, for sweet is your mercy* towards us. *For your mercy is better than lives.*[145] *Libera me, deliver me* from all danger and the evil of punishment and of fault, 108{109}[22] *quia egenus, for... needy,* because of the imperfections of nature, *et pauper, and poor,* because of the lack of grace, *ego sum, I am. Et cor meum conturbatum est intra me, and my heart is troubled within me* from the recollection of the divine judgment, of eternal torments, and also because of my own sins, and because of diverse dangers to

143 Is. 43:25a.
144 Is. 48:11a.
145 Ps. 62:4a.

which I am exposed, so that with holy Job I can say: *Before I eat I sigh: and as overflowing waters, so is my roaring.*[146] **108{109}[23]** *Sicut umbra cum declinate, ablatus sum; I am taken away like the shadow when it declines*: that is, in the manner that a shadow lengthens as the sun sets and quickly disappears and leaves, so I suddenly grew faint and fell, either from the former grace, or from the flower of youth, or from the strength of the body. *Et excussus sum, and I am shaken* from the state of perfection, and the stability of mind, from contemplation falling toward useless phantasms, *sicut locustae, as locusts* drive forth from their place. Now there is a taking away that is good, such as when a man takes leave from the world so that he might serve Christ, or when he takes leave of the devil so that he might live with virtues. In a similar manner also there is a certain good shaking, of which Isaiah says, *Shake yourself from the dust,*[147] that is, ascend from worldly things to heavenly things by contemplation and love.

108{109}[24] *My knees are weakened through fasting: and my flesh is changed for oil.*

Genua mea infirmata sunt a ieiunio; et caro mea immutata est propter oleum.

108{109}[24] *Genua mea infirmata sunt a ieiunio, my knees are weakened through fasting.* According to the previously held sense, this agrees with that where the Apostle says, *I chastise my body, and bring it into subjection.*[148] There are also certain knees of the heart; of which Manasseh in his prayer says: *And now I bend the knees of my heart.*[149] There is also a certain spiritual and evil fasting, when the soul of man fasts from spiritual food, namely, when he is deprived of the refreshment of the grace of God. By this fast, therefore, the knees of the heart (that is the virtues) are weakened, because they proceed to action weakly and without fervor. For as long as grace increases, all the virtues are strengthened, and they operate more strongly and fervently; but when grace decreases, the virtues weaken. *Et caro mea immutata est, and my flesh is changed*, that is, made joyful and strengthened, *propter oleum, for oil*, that is, because of

---

146 Job 3:24. E. N. As Denis explains in his *Commentary on Job*, sighs are a sign of moderate sorrow, but roaring is a sign of overwhelming sorrow. Doctoris Ecstatici D. Dionysii Cartusiani, Opera Omnia, Vol. 4 (Montreuil: 1897), 359.

147 Is. 52:2a.

148 1 Cor. 9:27a.

149 Prayer of Manasseh.

internal consolations and from the promptitude of our soul cheerfully to do and to endure all things. For in fasting we ought to avoid the exterior appearance of hypocrites. For this reason, Christ said: *But you, when you fast, anoint your head, and wash your face, that you appear not to men to fast.*[150]

108{109}[25] *And I am become a reproach to them: they saw me and they shook their heads.*

Et ego factus sum opprobrium illis; viderunt me, et moverunt capita sua.

108{109}[25] *Et ego factus sum opprobrium illis,* and I am become a reproach to them. For the just are derided and despised by the impious. For this reason, the Savior says: *If they have persecuted me, they will also persecute you* for *the servant is not greater than his master. Viderunt me, et moverunt capita sua; they saw me, and they shook their heads,* insulting and ridiculing me, in the manner that the Apostle said, *We are made as the refuse of this world, the offscouring of all even until now;*[151] and again, *We are made a spectacle to the world, and to angels, and to men, and we are fools for Christ's sake.*[152]

108{109}[26] *Help me, O Lord my God; save me according to your mercy.*

Adiuva me, Domine Deus meus; salvum me fac secundum misericordiam tuam.

108{109}[27] *And let them know that this is your hand: and that you, O Lord, have done it.*

Et sciant quia manus tua haec, et tu, Domine, fecisti eam.

108{109}[28] *They will curse and you will bless: let them that rise up against me be confounded: but your servant shall rejoice.*

Maledicent illi, et tu benedices; qui insurgunt in me confundantur, servus autem tuus laetabitur.

108{109}[26] *Adiuva me, Domine Deus meus;* help me, O Lord my God, lest by impatience I be vanquished by such adversities. Help me, so that I might endure all things strongly for your love. *Salvum me fac,* save

---

150 Matt. 6:17–18a.
151 1 Cor. 4:13.
152 1 Cor. 4:9b–10a.

me, now with hope and the multiplication of graces, and in the future in reality and the infusion of glory, *secundum misericordiam tuam, according to your mercy*, that is, speedily and abundantly, as you are abundant, full, and quick in mercy. 108{109}[27] *Et sciant, and let them know*, that is, may my enemies both invisible and visible see through experience, *quia manus tua haec, that this is your hand*, that is, that this comfort and salvation is the effect or the work of your divine power; *et tu, Domine, fecisti eam; and you, O Lord, have done it*, that is, these [enemies of mine] should also recognize that these operations in me are from your power, so that my soul is saved by you. 108{109}[28] *Maledicent illi, they will curse* me from their wickedness; *et tu benedices, and you will bless*, that is, you will provide me with great grace for that injury which I suffer with equanimity. For the more God has sight of his faithful enduring great disgraces and scourgings, the more abundantly he renders aid, as it says in a Psalm above: *I am with him in tribulation.*[153] *Qui insurgunt in me, confundantur, let them that rise up against me be confounded*, that is, let them be ashamed of their maliciousness, and let them find themselves vanquished; *servus autem tuus laetabitur, but your servant shall rejoice* in you: as the Apostle admonishes, *He that glories, let him glory in the Lord.*[154]

108{109}[30] *I will give great thanks to the Lord with my mouth: and in the midst of many I will praise him.*[155]

Confitebor Domino nimis in ore meo, et in medio multorum laudabo eum.

108{109}[31] *Because he has stood at the right hand of the poor, to save my soul from persecutors.*

Quia astitit a dextris pauperis, ut salvam faceret a persequentibus animam meam.

Then the voice referring thanks to the Lord follows: 108{109}[30] *Confitebor Domino, I will give thanks to the Lord*, my benefactor *nimis, greatly*, that is, with all affection, with particular devotion, and above the power of natural virtue, *in ore meo, with my mouth*, praising him; according to this: *I will bless the Lord at all times;*[156] that is, among others and in the Church *laudabo eum, I will praise him*, because of his goodness and

---

153 Ps. 90:15b.
154 2 Cor. 10:17.
155 *E. N.* Denis skips over verse 29.
156 Ps. 33:2a.

the benefits that he has bestowed upon me. **108{109}[31]** *Quia adstitit a dextris pauperis, because he has stood at the right hand of the poor,* that is, he was favorably present to his poor: for being there is to help; *ut salvam faceret a persequentibus, to save ... from persecutors,* that is, the wicked and cruel men and demons, *animam meam, my soul,* preserving it from the wound of sin, and conserving it in the state of salvation.

See how we have heard this Psalm so full of mystery: in which we regard the dire persecutions and the admirable patience of our Head. We are taught, therefore, by the example of Christ, to pray with sincere heart for adversaries and persecutors, to requite those who hate us with affections of holy love, and in all things to imitate the steps of Christ.

PRAYER

OU, O LORD, WHO ARE SWEET IN MERCY, with your benevolent spirit give joy to our heart disturbed within us by the torments of sin, mercifully help us and save us: may your servants rejoice in you, and make us to give great thanks to you Lord in eternity.

Tu, Domine, qui suavis in misericordia, cor nostrum peccatis exigentibus perturbatum intra nos, spiritu tuo bono laetificas, adiuva nos misericorditer et salva: laetentur in te servi tui, et fac nos in perpetuum tibi Domino nimis confiteri.

Psalm 109

ARTICLE XVII

LITERAL ELUCIDATION OF THE
ONE HUNDRED AND NINTH PSALM:
DIXIT DOMINUS DOMINO MEO.
THE LORD SAID TO MY LORD.

109{110}[1]   *A Psalm of David. The Lord said to my Lord: Sit at my right hand: Until I make your enemies your footstool.*

Psalmus David. Dixit Dominus Domino meo: Sede a dextris meis, donec ponam inimicos tuos scabellum pedum tuorum.

NOW THE TITLE TO THE PSALM CURRRENTLY being addressed is: 109{110}[1] *Psalmus David; a Psalm of David.* It befits this Psalm because David the prophet is its author, and also because by David is signified Christ both as its matter or subject: for it literally speaks of Christ, in the manner that Christ himself in Matthew attested. For speaking to the Pharisees, he said: *What think you of Christ? Whose son is he?* To which when they responded, *David*, he added: *How then does David in spirit call him Lord, saying, The Lord said to my Lord, Sit on my right hand, until I make your enemies your footstool?*[1] Also, the Apostle showed from this scripture how Christ was greater than the angels and equal to the Father. *To which of the angels said he at any time: Sit on my right hand, until I make your enemies your footstool?*[2] And so this Psalm speaks of Christ according to both of his natures, and of his magnificence in the Ascension, of his coeternity, and of his substantial identity with the Father, of the universality of his dominion, and of his eternal priesthood, and the final judgment.

And therefore the most blessed David, to whom God revealed his inscrutable and hidden wisdom, says: *Dixit Dominus Domino meo, the Lord said to my Lord*: that is, God the Father spoke to his only-begotten Son, true God and my Lord, who is my Lord according to his divinity, and is my son according to his human nature, which he received from my seed.

---

1 Matt. 22:42–44.
2 Heb. 1:13. *E. N.* Recall that Denis the Carthusian held to the opinion that St. Paul was the author of the Epistle to the Hebrews. *See* footnote 8-34 in Volume 1.

Yet he says this not by an externally-sounding or transient word, but he makes it known intellectually; indeed, it has been stated so from eternity. And for this reason, he adds: *Sede a dextris meis, sit at my right hand*: that is, you, my most dear Son, who for my honor and the salvation of men humbled yourself below all creatures, and became *the reproach of men*,[3] yet in your Ascension you will be exalted above all other creatures,[4] and you will be raised up even unto the throne of my majesty and glory, and you will reside, dwell, and rest at my right hand eternality.

Donec ponam inimicos tuos, until I make your enemies, that is, all the unbelievers and the wicked, especially the Jews, *scabellum pedum tuorum, your footstool*, that is, so subject to your power and domination as a footstool sits beneath seated feet. In a certain way, this subjection has already been fulfilled. For Christ after his Resurrection said: *All power is given to me in heaven and in earth.*[5] Indeed, before his Passion regarding himself he said to the Father: *You have given him power over all flesh.*[6] And so they who at one time resisted Christ were made subject to him after their conversion to the faith. But this subjection will appear most completely and will be totally fulfilled in the day of the final judgment, for then Christ will overthrow and condemn all his adversaries. For that which is predicted of Christ in Isaiah will also then be fulfilled: *They shall come to him, and all that resist him shall be confounded.*[7]

In the meantime, therefore, Christ sits at the right hand of the Father. But will he not sit afterwards [*i.e.*, after the final judgment] on the right hand? Indeed, he will sit [at the right hand] afterwards. For in divine Scripture, it is customary that this saying — *until* — in affirmative speech posits and includes all time, as when it says also in a later Psalm: *Our eyes* [are affixed] *unto the Lord our God, until he have mercy on us.*[8] And so here in this place it should be held that Christ will sit eternally at the right hand of the Father. But in negative sentences [the word "until"] negates and denies for all time, as when it is asserted in Matthew about Joseph and the blessed Virgin: *He knew her not until she brought forth her firstborn son.*[9] And this is reasonable. For when Scripture affirms or denies something when it least appears to be so, then it is certain that

---

3 Ps. 21:7: *But I am a worm, and no man: the reproach of men, and the outcast of the people.*
4 Heb. 2:7–8.
5 Matt. 28:18.
6 John 17:2a.
7 Is. 45:25b.
8 Ps. 122:2b.
9 Matt. 1:25.

it wants to imply it to have it at other times: so that when Matthew affirms St. Joseph not to have known Mary until she gave birth to Christ, it is certain that after [the birth] he did not know her. For how could he attempt to approach the Mother of the only-begotten Son of God when he knew himself to be unworthy to live with her?[10] In a similar way, when the Prophet [David] asserts Christ will set at the right hand of God until he subjects to himself all his adversaries, it is certain that he will sit [at the right hand of God] after they are subject.

But now it should be kept in mind that the seating of Christ at the right hand of the Father can be understood in two ways. One way is according to his divine nature: and so by the right hand of the Father is indicated his equality, so that it reads in this sense: *Sit at my right hand,* that is, residing with me, be equal to me. And in this way the Father says to the Son from eternity, that he sit at his right hand: indeed, begetting him, he says and confers this to him, since that begetting is nothing else but the [eternal] enunciation of the Word. For the Father is said to demonstrate or to speak the Son according to his divinity, because in generating the Son, he gives to him the divine essence, which is that very Wisdom which, being received by the Son, he is said to hear and to know from the Father. There is not, therefore, a bodily right hand with the Father, nor is there with the Son, inasmuch as he is God, a localized place of sitting. But by the right hand of God is designated his equality, so that by the sitting of the Son is expressed his most high domination. For it is befitting for kings and judges to sit. In the second way [of understanding Christ sitting at the right hand of the Father] Christ is understood to sit according to his human nature, that is, to be and to remain at the right hand of the Father, that is, at the highest and most important good of his Creator, namely in the highest summit of the empyreal heaven and in the perfect participation of the uncreated beatitude of God the Father. The soul of Christ receives more of the beatitude of God than all the elect added together. Viewed in this way, the Father says to the man Christ, *Sit at my right hand,* from beginning of the creation of the soul of Christ as regards to intellectual revelation. For he revealed himself to him at the instant of his creation, that he with his body would be raised above all heavens; but as regards

10 E. N. Denis is referring to the view that St. Joseph, upon learning that the child that Mary had miraculously conceived by the Holy Spirit, thought himself unworthy even to dwell with her, *approximare sese indignum aestimabat,* "he thought himself unworthy to approach her," as a sermon attributed to Origen states it. PL 95, 1164. Among others such as St. Basil, the bishop Eusebius also held this view, as can be found in his book *Questions and Solutions to Stephen,* PL 22, 883. *See generally,* "The Doubt of St. Joseph," The Catholic Biblical Quarterly, Vol. 10, No. 3 (July 1948), 296–309.

to its execution and fulfillment, the Father says to Christ, *Sit at my right hand,* at the Ascension. For saying it then, that is intellectually and causally commanding, he will exalt Christ, and he will give him *a name which is above all names.*[11] And of this sitting of Christ the Evangelist says: *The Lord Jesus, after he had spoken to them, was taken up into heaven, and sits on the right hand of God.*[12] Whence it is also written: *I beheld therefore in the vision of the night, and lo, one like the Son of Man came . . . and he came even to the Ancient of days: and they presented him before him.*[13]

109{110}[2] *The Lord will send forth the scepter of your power out of Sion: rule in the midst of you enemies.*

Virgam virtutis tuae emittet Dominus ex Sion: dominare in medio inimicorum tuorum.

Consequently, the Prophet addresses Christ: 109{110}[2] *Virgam virtutis tuae, the scepter of your power,* that is, the doctrine of the evangelical law by which the unjust are corrected, or the power of your domination and the dignity of your reign, O Christ, *emittet Dominus, the Lord will send forth,* the Father or God the Trinity [will send forth] by his servants, the Apostles, *ex Sion, out of Sion,* that is, from this just-stated place located in Jerusalem. For Sion is a mountain that was in Jerusalem in which the temple was constructed; and also the chamber or cenacle in which Christ celebrated his Last Supper,[14] in which he appeared after his Resurrection to this disciples,[15] and in which the Apostle and others gathered together with them received the Holy Spirit [was located there].[16] From this cenacle and from this temple placed in mount Sion and out of Jerusalem God sent through his Apostles the scepter of the power of Christ, that is, the evangelical law and the magnificence of Christ, throughout all the world. For when the Apostles received the Holy Spirit in the day of Pentecost,[17] they all with their colleagues immediately, like a swarm of bees, broke out of the upper room in which a short time before they had dwelt with door shut for fear of the Jews, entered into the temple, and began to preach Christ.[18] And after that followed their preaching

---

11 Phil. 2:9b.
12 Mark 16:19.
13 Dan. 7:13.
14 Mark 14:15.
15 John 20:19, 26.
16 Acts 2:1–14.
17 *Ibid.*
18 John 20:19.

throughout all the world, according to what Christ had previously told them: *You shall be witnesses unto me in Jerusalem, and in all Judea and Samaria, and even to the uttermost part of the earth.*[19] This also Isaiah prophesied, saying: *The law shall come forth from Sion, and the word of the Lord from Jerusalem.*[20] And from this going forth and preaching followed the conversion of the world to Christ. Hence, it adds:

Dominare, rule O Christ, *in medio inimicorum tuorum, in the midst of your enemies,* that is, in among the infidel kingdoms and peoples, which during the time of their disbelief were your enemies, but which were made friends following their conversion to the faith; and you rule in them by yourself and your vicars, the prelates of the Church. They are subject to you by faith and by the keeping of the divine law, because they observe that which you have commanded them to do. Of this dominion of Christ is said by Micah: *Now shall he be magnified even to the ends of the earth.*[21] And also Zechariah: *His power shall be from sea to sea, and from the rivers even to the end of the earth.*[22] Whence also in Daniel is written: *And he gave* the Ancient of Days *power, and glory, and a kingdom: and all peoples, tribes and tongues shall serve him.*[23]

109{110}[3] *With you is the principality in the day of your strength: in the brightness of the saints: from the womb before the day star I begot you.*

Tecum principium in die virtutis tuae in splendoribus sanctorum; ex utero, ante luciferum, genui te.

Now that which follows can be understood as the words of the Prophet to Christ: **109{110}[3]** *Tecum principium, with you is the principality,* that is, with you, O Christ, is the Father existing as your principle,[24] of which you say in the Gospel of John: *All my things . . . are from you.*[25] For the Father is with the Son, and the Son is with the Father, for they are

---

19 Acts 1:8.
20 Is. 2:3b.
21 Micah 5:4b.
22 Zech. 9:10b.
23 Dan. 7:14.
24 E. N. "The Father is the principle of the Son, and the Son the principle of the Holy Spirit." St. Thomas Aquinas, *Contra errores Graecorum*, pars 2 cap. 8. "The word 'principle' signifies only that whence another proceeds: since anything whence something proceeds in any way we call a principle; and conversely. As the Father then is the one whence another proceeds, it follows that the Father is a principle." ST Ia, q. 33, art. 1, co.
25 John 17:7.

inseparably Father and Son. For they must be distinguished in person, yet they are identical in essence. For this reason, John says: *In the beginning was the Word, . . . and the Word was with God.*[26] With you, therefore, O Son, is the principle, that is, God the Father, *in die virtutis tuae, in the day of your strength,* that is, in the day of eternity, which is itself eternity. The Father is with you in this day, for he is eternally with you, and you are co-eternally with him: and in this, none is before or after. For this reason it is stated in Micah: *His going forth is from the beginning, from the days of eternity.*[27] And in Proverbs, the Wisdom of God, which is the Lord Christ, asserts: *I was set up from eternity; . . . the depths were not as yet, and I was already conceived; . . . before the hills I was brought forth.*[28] In this manner, the principle of the day of your strength is with you, *in splendoribus Sanctorum, in the brightness of the Saints,* that is, in the splendid understanding of the Blessed in the heavenly fatherland, because your co-existence and co-eternity with the Father is known to them from the beginning of the world: for indeed, they *always see the face of the Father,*[29] and therefore also the Son, for the Son (as is stated in John) says: *He who sees me, sees the Father also.*[30] But the day of power, that is the power of Christ, is said to be eternal because it subsists in him without change and omnipotently. And this eternity, properly understood, is nothing other than the eternal God; eternity has no measure or days of divine duration except according to [human] reason.[31]

Others expound on this in another manner, so that they understand them to be words of the Father to the Son: *With you is the principality,* that is, one and the same authority of rulership exists with me and with you, because you and I are one in essence, one as Founder of all things, and as the one Creator of all things. For here Christ states himself to be the principle, responding to the Jews: [I am] *the beginning [principle] who also speak unto you.*[32] But this is thus known to be *in the day of your strength,* that is, the brightness of the heavenly fatherland, where the Blessed will see in your light how the authority of creating and governing is one in you and in me; *in the brightness of the Saints,* that is,

---

26 John 1:1.
27 Micah 5:2b.
28 Prov. 8:23–25.
29 Matt. 18:10.
30 John 14:9.
31 *E. N.* "Eternity is nothing else but God Himself. Hence God is not called eternal, as if he were in any way measurable; but the idea of measurement (*ratio mensurae*) is understood according to our apprehension alone." ST Ia, q. 10, art. 2, ad 3.
32 John 8:25.

in the full view of the elect in the heavenly homeland. For at that time the Saint shall perceive this when they are awash in the divine light, so that *they shall shine as the son in the kingdom of their Father.*[33] For now, according to the Apostle, we see *through a glass in a dark manner — for we walk by faith and not by sight.*[34] But then we will know as we are known. Whence John in his epistle says: *We shall be like to him: because we shall see him as he is.*[35]

In this passage, therefore, is declared the co-eternity and the co-equality of the Father and the Son.

Ex utero, from the womb, that is, from my own heart, *ante luciferum, before the day star,* that is, before the production of any created light, and before the production of the stars, which are designated by the name day star, *genui te, I begot you* with an eternal, intellectual, pure, and most actual generation. For the Son is begotten from the substance of the Father, so that he proceeds from the substance of the Father immediately by natural intellectual emanation, as brightness proceeds from light. This generation of the Son from the Father is also nothing else except the processing of light from light, of act from act, and of God from God. In the Father, essence, power, and operation are really one and the same. And so the Father understanding himself brings forth the Word within himself which is most similar to him, and in this alone is it distinguishable: that it proceeds from him. And as the Father beholds himself with one gaze, and fully knows all things to be created, all things created, and all things creatable, so he eternally and with one internal conception begets within himself the one Word in which all of his nature and perfection is completely and most fully contained and shines forth, and by which he comprehends and enlightens all other things. And so this Word is the image of the Father, and the exemplar of all creatures, and he proceeds immediately from the intellect of the Father, according to Thomas [as he states] in various places.[36] And so Christ, insofar as he is God, is begotten from eternity: as if the sun would have been from eternity, and the bright splendor would have flowed from it and would have arisen eternally with it. For this reason, it is attested in Ecclesiasticus: *I came out of the mouth of the most High, the firstborn before all creatures.*[37] And in the book of Wisdom it says: *Your wisdom, O Lord, which knows your works,*

---

33 Matt. 13:43.
34 1 Cor. 13:12; 2 Cor. 5:7.
35 1 John 3:2b.
36 *E. N. See, e.g.,* ST Ia, q. 34, arts. 1–3.
37 Ecclus. 24:5.

which then also was present when you made the world, and knew what was agreeable to your eyes.[38] In these words, the wisdom of God is evidently expressed to be of two kinds, namely, the begotten and the unbegotten.

109{110}[4]   *The Lord has sworn, and he will not repent: You are a priest forever according to the order of Melchisedech.*

Iuravit Dominus, et non paenitebit eum: Tu es sacerdos in aeternum secundum ordinem Melchisedech.

In addition, the Prophet deals with the priesthood of Christ: 109{110} [4] *Iuravit Dominus, the Lord has sworn,* that is, he has irretractably affirmed and has firmly promised, *et non paenitebit eum, and he will not repent* so he swears what follows: *Tu,* you O Christ, as man, *es sacerdos in aeternum secundum ordinem Melchisedech, are a priest forever according to the order of Melchisedech.* Christ did not offer the sacrifices of the law, which it was incumbent upon the priests who were the sons of Aaron to offer; but he was a priest offering himself to God and reconciling the world to his eternal Father, dissolving *the enmities in himself,* according to the Apostle [in his epistle] to the Ephesians.[39] He repeats this: Christ *has delivered himself for us, an oblation and a sacrifice to God for an odor of sweetness;*[40] and to the Hebrews: *Christ, being come an high priest of the good things to come, . . . by his own blood, entered once into the holies, having obtained eternal redemption.*[41] And of the excellence of this priesthood of Christ the Apostle says: *It was fitting that we should have such a high priest, holy, innocent, undefiled, separated from sinners, and made higher than the heavens.*[42] Whence in Zechariah it is stated: *He shall bear the glory, and shall sit, and rule upon his throne: and he shall be a priest upon his throne.*[43] And how Christ is said to be a priest in eternity the Apostle declares to the Hebrews, saying: Christ *for that he continues for ever, has an everlasting priesthood. Whereby he is able also to save forever them that come to God by him, always living to make intercession for us.*[44] Indeed, the office of priesthood is to act as a mediator and advocate between God and the people, to offer prayers for the people of God, to placate God, and to bless the people. But all

---

38 Wis. 9:9.
39 Cf. Eph. 2:16: *And might reconcile both to God in one body by the cross, killing the enmities in himself.*
40 Eph. 5:2.
41 Heb. 9:11–12.
42 Heb. 7:26.
43 Zech. 6:13.
44 Heb. 7:24–24.

these things coincide in Christ. For this reason, in the epistle of John it is stated: *If any man sin, we have an advocate with the Father, Jesus Christ the just; and he is the propitiation for our sins.*[45]

Christ is also said to be a priest in eternity according to the order of Melchisedech: First, because as Melchisedech offered bread and wine to God, as we read in Genesis,[46] so Christ under the form of bread and wine offered his Body and Blood and gave it to his disciples, converting the bread into flesh and the wine into blood. Second, because as Melchisedech is asserted to have been *without father, without mother, without genealogy* — not because he did not have them, but because Scripture kept silent about it because of its mystery — so Christ was born outside of the order of natural human generation; and he truly was eternal. For this the Apostle says: *The forerunner Jesus has entered for us, made a high priest forever according to the order of Melchisedech.*[47] And again: *Melchisedech was king of Salem ... that is, the king of peace, ... without father, without mother, ... likened unto the Son of God.*[48]

Therefore, God swore this to Christ as man. For at that very moment when he created his soul, he revealed this to him. And he did not repent it. For repentance, properly speaking, has no place in God, as is written in the book of Samuel: *But the triumpher in Israel will not spare, and will not be moved to repentance: for he is not a man that he should repent.*[49] Yet in the same chapter the Lord says to Samuel: *It repents me that I have made Saul king.*[50] But this is said because of the similarity of the work, not for the truth of the emotion. For God is frequently spoken of in holy Scripture in a human way.

109{110}[5] *The Lord at your right hand has broken kings in the day of his wrath.*

Dominus a dextris tuis; confregit in die irae suae reges.

109{110}[5] *Dominus a dextris tuis,* the Lord at your right hand. This can be understood two ways. The first this way: *The Lord* Father or the triune God, existing *at your right hand,* O Christ, as you said of yourself in the preceding Psalm, *I will give great thanks to the Lord with my mouth ... because*

---

45 1 John 2:1–2a.
46 Gen. 14:18.
47 Heb. 6:20.
48 Heb. 7:1–3.
49 1 Sam. 15:29.
50 1 Sam. 15:11a.

he has stood at the right hand of the poor (which is expounded upon there);[51] also [in a Psalm] above, *I set the Lord always in my sight: for he is at my right hand, that I be not moved.*[52] Or [the second way is] thus: *The Lord* Christ who is the *Lord of all*,[53] existing and present at your right hand, O God the Father, as you said a short while ago, *Sit at my right hand. Confregit in die irae suae, has broken . . . in the day of his wrath,* that is, in the name of his vengeance: of which is said through Isaiah, *The day of vengeance is in my heart;*[54] *reges, kings* infidel [kings], depriving them in this life of the life of grace, or also of bodily life, and shortly thereafter damning them eternally. Now we can most assuredly say this of those kings who are recalcitrant, of which are said in a Psalm above: *The kings of the earth stood up, and the princes met together, against the Lord and against his Christ.*[55] For these kings (assuming the name of king to be commonly understood as being one who presides), namely, Herod, Pilate, the leaders of the Jews were in the manner stated destroyed by divine vengeance: which destruction can be attributed to any of the Persons in the Godhead, because the effects of the most superlative glorious Trinity are indivisible. Whence, by Isaiah Christ has declared: *I have trampled on them in my indignation, and have trodden them down in my wrath.*[56]

109{110}[6]   *He shall judge among nations, he shall fill ruins: he shall crush the heads in the land of the many.*

Iudicabit in nationibus; implebit ruinas, conquassabit capita in terra multorum.

109{110}[6] *Iudicabit in nationibus, implebit ruinas; he shall judge among the nations, he shall fill ruins.* The advent of Christ is twofold. The first [coming is] that he would be judged, the second [coming] will be that he may judge. For this reason, the Apostle says: *Christ was offered once to exhaust the sins of many; the second time he shall appear without sin to them that expect him unto salvation.*[57] This second judgment is twofold, namely, the judgment of discretion and the judgment of retribution. The first judgment Christ did during his first coming, and he

---

51 Ps. 108:30–31a.
52 Ps. 15:8.
53 Acts 10:36.
54 Is. 63:4a.
55 Ps. 2:2.
56 Is. 63:3.
57 Heb. 9:28.

will do it up until the end of the world, calling some to faith and grace, but secretly abandoning others, but with just judgment. Of these [latter] he said before his Passion, *Now is the judgment of this world: now shall the prince of this world be cast out.* Christ, therefore, in his first coming and even unto the present, *shall judge the nations,* that is, exercising among those nations the judgment of discretion, some mercifully helping, others justly abandoning. But in the second coming he will judge the nations, saving the just ones and damning the ungodly in the manner that is stated in John: *The hour comes, wherein all that are in the graves shall hear the voice of the Son of God, and they that have done good things, shall come forth unto the resurrection of life; but they that have done evil, unto the resurrection of judgment,* that is, damnation.[58] Now in the first coming and in the judgment which he now performs, Christ fills the ruins, that is, human defects, filling empty hearts with grace, enriching empty minds with spiritual goods. But in the future judgment, he will fill the ruins of the angels with those whom he has saved, restoring the heavenly mansions that the fall of the angels caused to be emptied.[59]

Conquassabit capita, he shall crush the heads, that is, he will humiliate the hearts, *in terra multorum, in the land of the many,* that is, in many places and many dwellings of men. For in all the lands of the faithful he has humbled some of the proud. But in the final judgment he shall crush, that is, eternally condemn, the heads in the land of the many, that is, those ruling in many lands reigning with self-exaltation. Whence in Isaiah it is written: *The Lord of hosts has designed it, to pull down the pride of all glory, and bring to disgrace all the glorious ones of the earth.*[60] Moreover, Christ insofar as he is God, fittingly has the judicial power authoritatively; but as man, it is fitting to have it instrumentally, as he merited this through his humiliation and his Passion. For this reason he said, speaking both of the Father and of himself: *He has given him power to do judgment, because he is the Son of man.*[61]

109{110}[7] *He shall drink of the torrent in the way: therefore shall he lift up the head.*

De torrente in via bibet; propterea exaltabit caput.

---

58 John 5:28–29.
59 *E. N.* It was a pious opinion, apparently held by Denis, that the number of the saved (elect) would replace, and therefore in number equate to, the number of fallen angels. *See* footnote 16-22 in Volume I. *See also* ST Ia, q. 23, art. 7, co.
60 Is. 23:9.
61 John 5:27.

109{110}[7] *De torrente in via bibet, he shall drink of the torrent in the way*: that is, Christ in this world would suffer punishments, tribulations, and a most bitter death, and so he would drink from the torrent of tribulations, tasting adversity. Of this drinking, of this torrent, he told John and James: *Can you drink the chalice that I shall drink?*[62] Now that the word torrent designates the magnitude of tribulations is clear by that stated in Isaiah: *His breath as a torrent overflowing... to destroy the nations unto nothing.*[63] *Propterea, therefore*, that is, through the merits of this drinking, *exaltabit, he shall lift up*, Christ [shall lift up], his *caput, head*, that is, he will glorify and raise himself, rising in a glorious body and ascending to the Father in order that he may sit with him, both as the judge of all the universe and the Lord. For Christ, as God, resuscitated, exalted, and glorified himself insofar as he was man. And so he professes in John: *I have power to lay my life down: and I have power to take it up again.*[64] And because the works of the holy Trinity are indivisible, hence this exaltation can be attributed to any one of the divine Persons. For Christ said with the same Evangelist: *For what things soever the Father does, these the Son also does in like manner.*[65] And the Apostle says of the Holy Spirit: *All these things one and the same Spirit works.*[66]

Finally, in the exposition of this Psalm, Hugo[67] says concerning that verse *the Lord has sworn*, that we read God has sworn in three places: namely, in Genesis, saying to Abraham, *By my own self have I sworn;*[68] also in this place; and also in the one hundred thirty-first Psalm below, where it is written, *The Lord has sworn truth to David.*[69] But this [statement of Hugo] is not to be understood in a precise way, for in Scripture we read God to swear many more times than merely three. For in Isaiah, the Father says: *I have sworn by myself, the word of justice shall go out of my mouth.*[70] And in the prophet Amos is written: *The Lord God has sworn by his own soul, ... I detest the pride of Jacob.*[71] Also above in the eighty-eighth Psalm which begins with the words *The mercies of the*

---

62 Matt. 20:22b.

63 Is. 30:28.

64 John 10:18b.

65 John 5:19b.

66 1 Cor. 12:11.

67 *E. N.* Probably a reference to the Dominican Hugo de Sancto Charo (Hugh of Saint-Cher) (*ca.* 1200–1263), but I was unable to discover the reference.

68 Gen. 22:16a.

69 Ps. 131:11a.

70 Is. 45:23.

71 Amos 6:8a.

Lord, the Lord says: *I have sworn to David my servant: your seed will I settle for ever.*[72] And in Luke, Zacharias says: *The oath, which he swore to Abraham our father.*[73] And the Apostle to the Hebrews says: God *interposed an oath.*[74] And also in other places we read God to have sworn.

See how this Psalm of few words has such an infinite meaning. For in it is expressed the twofold nature of Christ and his simple and one person. It describes within it the begetting of Christ from the Father, the destruction of his enemies, the promulgation of the Christian faith, and also the co-eternity and co-substantiality of the Father and the Son. And also in the present Psalm one finds declared the priesthood of Christ, and his judicial power, and the final judgment. And so it is becoming for us to utter it forth with great reverence, with special devotion, and with profound contemplation because of the dignity, sweetness, and highness of its meaning.

PRAYER

O JESUS, SAVIOR OF THE WORLD, IN eternity made king and priest according to the order of Melchisedech, at the time of your judgment place us, through your ineffable mercy, at your right hand, and, numbered among the blessed of your Father, make us to possess the heavenly kingdom, who the same Father, etc.

Iesu, salvator saeculorum, secundum ordinem Melchisedech
rex et sacerdos factus in aeternum, ineffabili tua
miseratione, a dextris tuis in iudicio nos constitue;
atque inter benedictos Patris tui deputatos,
regnum caeleste fac possidere: qui
cum eodem Patre, etc.

---

72 Ps. 88:4–5.
73 Luke 1:73.
74 Heb. 6:17b.

Psalm 110

ARTICLE XVIII

DECLARATION OF THE
ONE HUNDRED AND TENTH PSALM:
CONFITEBOR TIBI, DOMINE.
I WILL PRAISE YOU, O LORD.

110{111}[1] *Alleluia: I will confess you, O Lord, with my whole heart;
in the council of the just: and in the congregation.*[1]

*Alleluia. Confitebor tibi, Domine, in toto corde meo, in consilio
iustorum, et congregatione.*

NOW THE TITLE TO THE PSALM CURRENTLY
being addressed is: 110{111}[1] *Alleluia*, which signifies, Praise God,
of whose acclamation this Psalm very beautifully and delightfully relates,
especially with regards to the most admirable works of God in the consecration of the Body and Blood of Christ, so that it treats of the institution
of this Sacrifice and the efficaciousness of the Sacrament of the Altar.

And so, the holy Prophet [David] speaking in his own person, and
in the person of the Church or any one member of the faithful, says:
Confitebor tibi, I will confess you, that is, I will praise you, *Domine, in toto
corde meo; O Lord, with my whole heart*, that is, with all of my intellect and
affection, with a mind both recollected and fixed. The heart [is mentioned]
here not as an organ of the body, but it is used to refer to the soul. But
the soul is immaterial, and it does not have parts: so how is it, therefore,
that it testifies to confess to the Lord with the whole heart, as if it would
be possible to confess with but part of the heart? The response to this
is that the soul does not have quantitative parts, since it is incorporeal;
nor essential [parts], since it is a simple form; but it has potestative parts,
that is, distinct powers. Now these powers or potestative parts of the
rational soul, insofar as it is rational, are three; the image of the most
high Trinity is found in the soul in these three powers, namely intellect,
memory, and will.[2] Knowledge relates to the understanding, love to the

---

1 E. N. I have translated *confitebor* by "I will confess" [a confession of praise], and
so have departed from the Douay-Rheims translation, "I will praise."
2 E. N. This refers to St. Augustine's *De Trinitate*, VIII, 6. "Augustine reflected on the
three powers of the human soul — memory, intellect, and will — and suggested that

257

will, and a firm indwelling in both to the memory. Therefore, one who praises together with the intellect, will, and memory confesses to the Lord with his whole heart, so that he directs himself with the intellect, he loves with the will, and he retains the divine word with the memory, and by these he sacrifices the confession of praise to the Lord. For he who praises God with the mouth but loves or thinks upon illicit things with the mind does not confess to the Lord with a whole heart. Whence it is written of some wandering and unsettled souls: *Their heart is divided, now they shall perish.*[3] And the Lord says through Jeremiah: *If you will return, ... return to me,* that is, if you, O man, desire to return to God with your heart, convert to him with your whole heart, adhering to him perfectly, serving him completely with all your powers, not tepidly or in a divided fashion.[4] I will also confess you, O Lord, not ill-advisedly, indiscreetly, or with vain intention, but *in consilio iustorum, in the council of the just,* that is, I will praise you in a way that conforms with the council of the just. For the council of the just is to praise you with a heart entirely cleansed from vice, since *Praise is not seemly in the mouth of a sinner;*[5] and because of the love and the honor of your name, and not because of temporal advantage or human praise.[6] *Et congregatione, and in the congregation* of the just, that is, I will praise you not in the conventicles of heretics,[7] but in the Church of the faithful.

110{111}[2]   *Great are the works of the Lord: sought out according to all his wills.*

   Magna opera Domini, exquisita in omnes voluntates eius.

Why one ought to confess to the Lord is addressed next: **110{111}[2]** *Magna opera Domini, great are the works of the Lord,* that is, magnificently

---

these three powers are, in a very limited way, like the three Persons of the Holy Trinity: our memory being like the Father, our intellect like the Son, and our will like the Holy Spirit." Scott Hahn and Leon J. Suprenant, eds., *Catholic for a Reason: Scripture and the Mystery of the Family of God* (Steubenville, OH: Emmaus Road Publishing, 1998) 158.

3 Hosea 10:2.

4 *Cf.* Rev. 3:16: *Because you are lukewarm, and neither cold, nor hot, I will begin to vomit you out of my mouth.*

5 Ecclus. 15:9.

6 *E. N.* In other words, not in the spirit of Henry III of Navarre's (Henry IV of France's) apocryphal: *Paris vaut bien une messe,* Paris is well worth a Mass!

7 St Alphonsus Liguori in his *Theologia Moralis* (Lib.5, Tract. 1, Cap. 3) writes: *Infidelium et haereticorum sacris non licet ita interesse, ut eis communicare censearis,* "It is not permitted to be present at the sacred rites of infidels and heretics in such a way that you would be judged to be in communion with them."

performed, or worthy of praise and admiration: as is manifestly clear of the creation of the heaven and earth, the governance of the universe, of the work of restoration, glorification, and the other effects of God. Indeed, the effects are proportionate to and correspond with their cause. Therefore, since God sublime and blessed is of infinite magnitude, wisdom, and dignity, it is fitting that the works done by him are great. *Exquisita, sought out,* that is, produced with studied care, *in omnes voluntates eius, according to all his wills,* that is, according to every desire or good pleasure of the Creator. For he produced each thing there and then, in such a manner, and therefore, where and according to however he wished. For this reason it is attested through Isaiah: *My counsel shall stand, and all my will shall be done.*[8] And the Apostle [Paul] says: *God works all things according to the counsel of his will.*[9] But since there is not in God but one, eternal, simple, and invariable will, why does it now say, *according to all his wills?* The response to this is that as we say that in God there are many ideas or many knowledges with respect to created things, so we say there are many wills according to our reason, by reference to created things which are willed and which are many.

110{111}[3] *His work is confession and magnificence: and his justice continues for ever and ever.*[10]

Confessio et magnificentia opus eius; et iustitia eius manet in saeculum saeculi.

110{111}[3] *Confessio, confession,* that is, the praise of God or the mention of one's own fault, *et magnificentia, and magnificence,* that is the magnificent words shown to the honor of God, are *opus eius, his work,* that is, the works pleasing to God that are granted to us by him. For all good proceeds from him, and these two works especially please God; and they do not belong to us except by the grace of God, and so they are attributed to God rather than to ourselves. *Et iustitia eius manet in saeculum saeculi, and his justice continues for ever and ever.* For the justice existing in God, which is God himself, is eternal, just like his divine essence, from which it is distinguished only by reason. Also, justice — which is the effect of divine equity — will persevere in perpetuity because the glory of the elect and the misery of the impious will never cease.

---

8 Is. 46:10b.
9 Eph. 1:11b.
10 E. N. Denis understands the Latin *confessio* in a broader sense than just praise; hence, I have departed from the Douay-Rheims's "praise," and replaced it with "confession."

110{111}[4]   *He has made a remembrance of his wonderful works, being a merciful and gracious Lord.*

Memoriam fecit mirabilium suorum, misericors et miserator Dominus.

110{111}[5]   *He has given food to them that fear him. He will be mindful forever of his covenant.*

Escam dedit timentibus se; memor erit in saeculum testamenti sui.

110{111}[6]   *He will show forth to his people the power of his works.*

Virtutem operum suorum annuntiabit populo suo.

110{111}[4] *Memoriam fecit mirabilium suorum misericors et miserator Dominus. He has made a remembrance of his wonderful works, being a merciful and gracious Lord.* This verse can neither be better nor more literally explained than as referring to the institution and provision of the Sacrament of the Altar, so that it reads in this sense: The Lord Christ who is *merciful* by nature and *gracious* in act, *made a remembrance*, that is, instituted a memorial, of his *wonderful works*, that is, his Incarnation, his love, his manner of life, and his Passion. For at the Last Supper, imminently to depart in his bodily presence, desiring to have us always remember the extraordinariness of his love and his most bitter Passion — indeed, all those things which he so graciously assumed, did, and endured for our salvation — instituted the Sacrament of his Body and Blood, converting bread into his Body and wine into his Blood. And so, under the species of bread and wine, 110{111}[5] *escam dedit timentibus se, he has given food to them that fear him,* that is, he has given his Body and Blood to his Apostles, entrusting them and their successors to give it to all the faithful: for this reason he said, *Do this in memory of me.*[11] Whence the Apostle said: *For as often as you shall eat this bread, and drink the chalice, you shall show the death of the Lord, until he come.*[12] Christ also spoke of this food in John: *For my flesh is meat indeed: and my blood is drink indeed.*[13]

Memor erit, he will be mindful, Christ himself [will be mindful] *in saeculum, forever,* that is unceasingly, *testamenti sui, of his covenant,* that is, of this Sacrament, which is called a covenant according to that stated

---

11 Luke 22:19.
12 1 Cor. 11:26.
13 John 6:56.

by the Apostle: *This chalice is the new covenant in my blood.*[14] By the fact that this Sacrament confers grace in the present and eternal life in the future upon all who devoutly and faithfully consume it, as he promised — *He that eats my flesh, and drinks my blood, abides in me, and I in him*: and again, *He that eats this bread, shall live forever* — Christ will be remembered in this covenant or Sacrament in perpetuity.[15] Or Christ is said to be always mindful of this covenant because he makes us recall it and because he will preserve the faith in this Sacrament in the hearts of men even until the consummation of the world. 110{111} [6] *Virtutem operum suorum, the power of his works*, that is, the fruits and the efficacity of this Sacrament, namely, his Body and Blood, which are works of the Creator; or [alternatively], *power of his works*, that is, the sacramental power effected by his Body and Blood; *annuntiabit, he will show forth*, Christ [will show forth], saying: *This is the bread which comes down from heaven; so that if any man eat of it, he may not die* in eternity; and *He that eats me, the same also shall live by me.*[16]

This can also be explained in a more general way, and it would be in this sense: *He has made a remembrance of his wonderful works*: because he taught the holy Prophets and Apostles through the Holy Spirit to write about and proclaim his wonderful works, which, of course, are copiously narrated in the Old and New Testaments and kept in mind by the faithful. *He has given* spiritual *food to them that fear him*, refreshing their souls with the *bread of life and understanding*,[17] and the word and grace of the Holy Spirit. God also provides his servants with the bodily food, about which he says in Matthew: *Seek therefore first the kingdom of God, and his justice, and all these things shall be added unto you.*[18] For this reason, he says again: *Be not solicitous for your life, what you shall eat, nor for your body, what you shall put on . . . for your Father knows that you have need of all these things.*[19] *He will be mindful forever of his covenant*, that is, the new and evangelical law, strengthening and preserving it even until the end of the world. He will be mindful also of his covenant, that is, his promises made in the New Testament, because he will fulfill

---

14 1 Cor. 11:25. E. N. I have changed the Douay-Rheims's "testament" to "covenant" so as to retain the parallelism between the Psalm and the Pauline epistle. In both the Psalm and 1st Corinthians, the word *testamentum* is used, though the Douay-Rheims uses "covenant" to translate the one and "testament" to translate the other.

15 John 6:57, 59.

16 John 6:50, 58.

17 Ecclus. 15:3a.

18 Matt. 6:33.

19 Matt. 6:25a, 32b.

them, provided we make ourselves to be that which he commands us to be. The promise of the New Testament is: *The just shine as the sun, in the kingdom of their Father;*[20] and, in the future age *they shall neither marry nor be married, but they shall be as the angels of God in heaven.*[21] That also which Christ most clearly stated: *Father, those you have given me, I will also that where I am, they also may be with me, so that they may see my glory which you have given me.*[22] All these things are fulfilled in us if we carry out that which the Apostle says to the Corinthians: *Having...these promises, dearly beloved, let us cleanse ourselves from all defilement of the flesh and of the spirit, perfecting sanctification in the fear of God.*[23] *The power of his works,* that is, the power of his miracles or his virtuous and holy works, *he will show forth to his people.* For Christ of himself preached the words of God the Father, and from time to time he proclaimed to the Jews the innocence of his manner of life and the excellence of his miracles: as he did in John: *Which of you shall convict me of sin?* And, *I seek not my own glory;* and elsewhere, *The works which the Father has given me to perfect; the works themselves, which I do, give testimony of me.*[24] Moreover, these works, that is, the life and the signs of Christ, were announced to us by the Apostles, indeed, they daily announce it to us in the canonical Scriptures of the New Testament, especially in the Gospels.

110{111}[7]   *That he may give them the inheritance of the Gentiles: the works of his hands are truth and judgment.*

     Ut det illis haereditatem gentium. Opera manuum eius veritas et iudicium.

Now all these things God did for his faithful, 110{111}[7] *Ut det illis haereditatem gentium,* that he may give them the inheritance of the Gentiles, that is, the kingdom of heaven and eternal life, prepared for men from the beginning of the world, in the manner that the Savior said in Matthew: *Come, you blessed of my Father, possess the kingdom prepared for you from the foundation of the world.*[25] In a special way, the kingdom of heaven is called the *inheritance of the Gentiles* because it has

---

20   Matt. 13:43a.
21   Matt. 22:30.
22   *Cf.* John 17:24.
23   2 Cor. 7:1.
24   John 8:46a, 50a; 5:36.
25   Matt. 25:34.

been justly taken away from Jews because of their unbelief and given to the humbly-believing Gentiles. For this reason, Christ said: *The kingdom of God shall be taken from you, and shall be given to a nation yielding the fruits thereof.*[26] And again he said: *Many shall come from the east and the west, and shall sit down with Abraham, and Isaac, and Jacob in the kingdom of heaven: but the children of the kingdom shall be cast out into the exterior darkness.*[27] And so rightly the kingdom of heaven is called the inheritance of the Gentiles, about which the Apostle says: *You are fellow citizens with the saints, and the domestics of God.*[28]

Opera manuum eius, the works of his hands, that is, the effects of divine power, are *veritas et iudicium, truth and judgment,* that is, salvation and damnation. For truth is called the true fulfillment of divine promises, drawn from the heavenly inheritance bequeathed to the elect to whom it is also given. This fulfilment is their salvation, and this is the work of Christ. But judgment frequently is received as meaning the disapproval of the evil. Whence it is stated in John: *He that believes* in the Son of God *is not judged; but he that does not believe is already judged,* that is, he is a reprobate.[29] And the Apostle says: *If we would judge ourselves, we should not be judged.*[30] Christ also speaking clearly about this in John said: *He who hears my word, and believes him that sent me, has life everlasting; and comes not into judgment.*[31] Judgment, that is, the just damnation of the damned, therefore, is the work of God. Or [an alternative explanation is] thus: *Truth and judgment,* that is, each truth and each judgment, is the work of God. For there is a truth of nature, a truth of life, and a truth of prayer. And there is a judgment of discretion and a judgment of remuneration. And all of these works are of the hand of God. Or [yet another way of looking at it is] thus: *The works of his hands are truth and judgment,* that is, true and just or set apart. For while something befits a thing excellently, it is pronounced of him not only concretely but also in the abstract: as Christ said to his Apostles, *You are the light of the world;*[32] and the Apostle [Paul] [said], *You were heretofore darkness, but now light in the Lord,* that is, you were at one time in the darkness of vice, but now by grace you are full of light.[33] Whence we say of a man

---

26 Matt. 21:43.
27 Matt. 8:11–12.
28 Eph. 2:19.
29 John 3:18.
30 1 Cor. 11:31.
31 John 5:24.
32 Matt. 5:14.
33 Eph. 5:8.

that is much loved and very dear: This is my love, and my sweetness or consolation. Because all the works of God are exceedingly just, true, and set apart, therefore, it is not only called true and just, but truth and judgment.[34] This can also refer to the Sacrament of the Altar, in which works of God contained in the consecration are *truth*, because in this Sacrament Christ is contained not only figuratively, but truly and substantially, and the *judgment* of death to he who consumes unworthily: for he who eats unworthily, *eats judgment to himself.*[35]

110{111}[8]   *All his commandments are faithful: confirmed for ever and ever, made in truth and equity.*

Fidelia omnia mandata eius, confirmata in saeculum saeculi, facta in veritate et aequitate.

110{111}[8] *Fidelia omnia mandata eius, all his commandments are faithful*: that is, the divine precepts are without deceit, but firm and certain, so that those who observe them receive trustworthy and true reward; *confirmata in saeculum saeculi, confirmed for ever and ever*, that is, by divine miracles and other things upon which faith rests,[36] are strengthened in eternity, so that it is certain that these commandments are from God, and as a consequence holy and salutary; *facta, made,* that is, commanded and promulgated to us, *in veritate et aequitate, in truth and equity*, so that they are true and equitable. Or [we can understand it in this way], *in truth*, that is, in wisdom, *and equity*, that is, the justice of the God who commands them, who according to his wisdom and justice, or in his wisdom and justice, designed and bestowed these commandments to us. Or they are said to be *made* or given in the truth of angelic illustration, and the equity of angelic administration. For the legal precepts were given to Moses through the ministry of the angels, as Stephen said to the Jews: *You have received the law by the disposition of angels.*[37]

---

34 E. N. In other words the adjectives "true" and "just" can be made substantives or nouns, "truth" and "judgment," just like a person who is sweet is called sweetness.
35 1 Cor. 11:29.
36 E. N. Denis is referring to the so-called "motives of faith" or "motives of credibility." These are the rational grounds. They include miracles, prophecy, the proofs of the existence of God based upon reason. "[T]he miracles of Christ and the saints, prophecies, the Church's growth and holiness, and her fruitfulness and stability 'are the most certain signs of divine Revelation, adapted to the intelligence of all'; they are 'motives of credibility" (*motiva credibilitatis*), which show that the assent of faith is 'by no means a blind impulse of the mind.'" CCC § 156 (quoting Vatican I, DS 3009, 3013).
37 Acts 7:53.

110{111}[9] *He has sent redemption to his people: he has commanded his covenant forever. Holy and terrible is his name.*

Redemptionem misit populo suo; mandavit in aeternum testamentum suum. Sanctum et terribile nomen eius.

110{111}[10] *The fear of the Lord is the beginning of wisdom. A good understanding to all that do it: his praise continues for ever and ever.*

Initium sapientiae timor Domini; intellectus bonus omnibus facientibus eum, laudatio ejus manet in saeculum saeculi.

110{111}[9] *Redemptionem,* redemption, that is, salvation and the Savior, namely, Christ, *misit, he has sent,* [that is,] the Father [has sent], *populo suo, to his people,* that is, the elect, sending Christ into this world. *For God sent not his Son into the world, to judge the world, but that the world may be saved by him,* as is written in John.[38] Whence in Isaiah, the Father says to Christ: *I have given you to be the light of the Gentiles, that you may be my salvation even to the farthest part of the earth.*[39] Or Christ himself *has sent,* that is, by the preaching of the Apostles has announced, the *redemption,* that is, the salvation of the human race acquired by his Passion, *to his people,* that is, to all the faithful, according to what he told them to do in Mark: *Go into the whole world, and preach the gospel to every creature.*[40] *Mandavit in aeternum testamentum suum, he has commanded his covenant forever,* that is, he has ordered the evangelical law to be kept even until the end of time; he did not command from the old covenant because it was succeeded by the new covenant which was prefigured by it. But the new covenant will not be succeeded by another; accordingly, he ordered that it be kept even unto the end of time. What is said now is particularly applicable to the Sacrament of the Altar, because this is to be repeated frequently even until the end of the world. *Sanctum et terribile nomen eius, holy and terrible is his name:* that is, God is holy in himself, because he is substantially pure and perfect; and he is terrible by reason of his effects.[41] But God is terrible to all men, he is to be feared with filial and chaste fear: for so even the blessed in the heavenly fatherland fear God. But to the ungodly, who fear God not from the love that exists within them, but from the terror of having to endure torments, he is

---

38 John 3:17.
39 Is. 49:6b.
40 Mark 16:15.
41 *Cf.* Deut. 10:17, 21.

terrible with servile fear. 110{111}[10] *Initium sapientiae timor Domini, the fear of the Lord is the beginning of wisdom.* For servile fear, inasmuch as it makes evil lose ground, starts to prepare the soul for the receiving of wisdom. And initial fear disposes one to be approach closely to the infusion of wisdom or an increase in perfection: for one cannot have initial fear without charity and wisdom. Now this that is stated — *the fear of the Lord is the beginning of wisdom* — is said in Ecclesiasticus and elsewhere.[42] But this seems to be contradictory to what is also stated in Ecclesiasticus: *To fear God is the fullness of reason.*[43] And Job states: *Behold the fear of the Lord, that is wisdom.*[44] The answer [to this seeming contradiction] is that these [latter verses] are to be understood as dealing not with servile fear, but with chaste and filial fear, which perfect charity does not expel, but brings in, and pours forth or causes. For Christ fully lived with this fear, according to that stated in Isaiah: *He shall be filled with the spirit of the fear of the Lord.*[45] Now this fear is not wisdom, or is not essentially the fullness of wisdom, for it is really distinguishable from it; but it is called wisdom according to a certain resplendency, for someone who fears God with chaste fear most brilliantly manifests himself to be truly wise. And in this same way, wisdom is predicated of the many virtuous acts of virtuous men, such as in these statements: not to command, but to will to be subject, is wisdom; to flee men is wisdom; to wish to be despised on account of Christ is wisdom.[46]

Intellectus bonus omnibus facientibus eum, a good understanding to all that do it: that is, knowledge is fruitful and useful to those who do what they know they ought to do. For, as it states in the second epistle of Peter, *It had been better for them not to know the way of justice, than, after they have known it, to turn back.*[47] And James affirms: *To him ... who knows ... the good, and does it not, to him it is sin.*[48] Whence also in the Gospel, Christ says: *That servant who knew the will of his lord, and prepared not himself, and did not according to his will, shall be beaten with many stripes.*[49] He, therefore, who puts himself forward as being erudite, who exults in his being illuminated by God, and yet trusts himself to be

---

42 Ecclus. 1:16; Prov. 1:7; 9:10.
43 Ecclus. 1:20.
44 Job 28:28a.
45 Is. 11:3. *E. N.* In distinguishing between initial fear, servile fear, and filial and chaste fear, Denis is drawing from ST IIaIIae, q. 19.
46 *Cf.* Acts 5:41.
47 2 Pet. 2:21a.
48 James 4:17.
49 Luke 12:47.

wise should take heed and implement that which James enjoins: *Who is a wise man, and endued with knowledge among you? Let him show, by a good conversation, his work in the meekness of wisdom.*[50] Otherwise, he will hear from Christ that which is stated in Isaiah: *Your wisdom, and your knowledge, this has deceived you.*[51] Or [we can understand it] thus: *A good understanding,* that is, intellectual power, the intellectual habit and the intellective operation, are healthy and worthy of praise *to all that do it,* namely, the timorous, or they who fear God, who, that is, live according to that which fear suggests, with that which Ecclesiasticus puts forth: *The fear of the Lord drives out sin;*[52] and elsewhere, *He that fears God neglects nothing.*[53] *His praise* which he so understands, and fulfills that which is understood, *continues for ever and ever:* for he will praise God without end, and he will receive praise from God as a reward, and with the Saints he will praise, as Ecclesiasticus attests: *Many shall praise his wisdom, and it shall never be forgotten.*[54]

RIEFLY, THIS PSALM CAN BE EXPLAINED ANA-gogically: for the blessed in the heavenly fatherland agree to that which is said in it. The Church triumphant, therefore, or any one member of the blessed, can say **110{111}[1]** *I will confess you, O Lord, with my whole heart.* For the saints in the heavenly homeland unceasingly praise God without any interruption: and this they do with their whole heart, that is, with all of their strength. For as they most perfectly fulfill the precept of charity loving God with all their heart, with all their strength, and with all their power, for they totally, actually, and unceasingly are taken up into God; so they confess to the Lord the confession of praise with the entire heart, in the manner that the Lord bears witness in Isaiah: *Behold my servants ... shall praise for joyfulness of heart.*[55] *In the council of the just,* that is, according to the act of the prudence of the elect in the heavenly fatherland. For the saints in the kingdom of God praise together in the manner that the gift of counsel poured into them by the Holy Spirit suggests and persuades. *And in the congregation,* that is, in union with the blessed or the Church triumphant. For the blessed with one heart and in general praise God, glorifying his name in himself.

---

50 James 3:13.
51 Is. 47:10a.
52 Ecclus. 1:27.
53 Eccl. 7:19b.
54 Ecclus. 39:12.
55 Is. 65:14a.

110{111}[2] *Great are the works of the Lord*, especially those which he does in the empyrean heaven around the blessed: whom he blesses by the face-to-face vision, and in whom he effects the most marvelous works which are totally hidden from us. 110{111}[3] *Confession*, by which they most unceasingly praise God, *and magnificence* by which they reverently obey and appear before him, is *his work*, that is, are the words of God, pleasing to God. 110{111}[4] *He has made a remembrance of his marvelous works*. God has made in the hearts of the blessed a remembrance of his marvelous works, admitting them to the blessed vision of his essence, in which they splendidly contemplate how many and great things God did for their salvation. 110{111}[5] *He has given food to them that fear him*: that is, to us blessed, who fear him with a chaste fear, from reverential subjection, and not from the concern of punishment, he provides the excellence of his divine fruitfulness, by which we are happily and joyfully refreshed within. *He will be mindful forever of his covenant*, that is, he will verify his promises in eternity, for he promised us the prize of his vision,[56] so that we will never fall back to our earlier misery, but we will remain with God without end. 110{111}[6] *He will show forth to this people the power of his works*. For in the heavenly fatherland, God reveals his Godhead and powerful effects, and by the superior angels he illuminates the inferior ones with such works. The rest can easily be brought to light from what has been said earlier.

Finally, who has the strength worthily to praise the present Psalm, most sweetly redolent of the praise of the Creator, marvelously inflammatory of the affection of singing, perfuse with spiritual joyfulness? In it the faithful man begins with so trusting and affectionate words; in it God so clearly is extolled for his effects, is commended for his divine justice; in it is prophetically revealed the institution of the Eucharist, is announced the perpetuity of the new covenant, is brought to mind the reward of eternal life; and it is comprised of other many beautiful things. If, therefore, we truly love God, we will never sing this so greatly mystery-filled and meaningful Psalm without the fervor of pious devotion. For he who truly loves God, to the extent he embraces him with more ardent affection, to that extent he will more vehemently take delight in his praise of him and in obedience to him. So that it may befit us, let us struggle always to stand before the Lord with a pure heart,[57] to

---

56 Cf. 1 John 3:2b: *We know, that, when he shall appear, we shall be like to him: because we shall see him as he is.*
57 Cf. 2 Chr. 19: 3, 9: *You have… prepared your heart to seek the Lord the God of your fathers. Thus shall you do in the fear of the Lord faithfully, and with a perfect*

grow daily in his grace, and to fulfill the duties of our Office, with all ordered diligence. For if we try not to be negligent with the work of God, but rather discharge it reverently, we might then be able to abound in spiritual graces.

PRAYER

MERCIFUL AND COMPASSIONATE LORD, who in your customary goodness continually spare sinners, fill us at long last with good understanding, and pour forth into our minds your fear, which is the beginning of your wisdom; and make us to please you by living sober and just lives.

Misericors et miserator Domine, qui diu nobis peccantibus
solita pepercisti bonitate, intellectu tandem bono nos
reple, et initium sapientiae timorem tuum
mentibus nostris infunde; atque deinceps
fac nos sobrie et iuste vivendo
tibi placere.

heart. 2 Tim. 2:22: Pursue justice, faith, charity, and peace, with them that call on the Lord out of a pure heart.

Psalm 111

ARTICLE XIX

DECLARATION OF THE
ONE HUNDRED AND ELEVENTH PSALM:
BEATUS VIR QUI TIMET DOMINUM.
BLESSED IS THE MAN THAT FEARS THE LORD.

111{112}[1] *Alleluia, a turning back to Haggai and Zechariah. Blessed is the man that fears the Lord: he shall delight exceedingly in his commandments.*

Alleluia, reversionis Aggaei et Zachariae. Beatus vir qui timet Dominum, in mandatis eius volet nimis.

THIS PSALM HAS FOR ITS TITLE: *ALLELUIA.* But what is added to it, *reversionis Aggai et Zachariae, a turning back to Haggai and Zechariah,* is not found in the Hebrew nor in the translation of Jerome based upon the Hebrew text; this ought not to be understood as meaning this Psalm was edited by these prophets or during their time. But this is added, then, because as Haggai and Zechariah prophesied of the building of the material temple in Jerusalem after the return from the Babylonian captivity.[1] So this present Psalm handles the virtues by which the faithful build up Christ in the immaterial temple of their hearts, after their return away from the miserable servitude of sin or their captivity by the devil. But this Psalm especially speaks of the works of mercy, regarding which Christ in a specific way testifies about being how he would render judgments in the last day.[2]

And so it says: 111{112}[1] *Beatus vir, blessed is the man,* that is, happy the man now in hope and after a time happy he will be in reality, *qui timet Dominum, that fears the Lord,* with a chaste and filial fear, or at least initial [fear]. For servile fear is not meritorious, because it does not proceed from charity, without which nothing is meritorious toward eternal life. For this is borne witness to in Ecclesiasticus: *With him that fears the Lord, it shall go well in the latter end, and in the day of his death he shall be blessed.*[3] And so, since nothing separates us from God except sin, and

---

1 Haggai chps. 1, 2; Zech. chp. 2.
2 Matt. 25:34–45.
3 Ecclus. 1:13.

271

because *fear drives out sin*[4] and disposes one to all good, so it is in a way the cause of all good. *In mandatis eius volet nimis, he shall delight exceedingly in his commandments*, that is, he who fears God will strongly choose to fulfill the divine commandments. For filial fear, because it fears offense to the beloved and separation from him, greatly strives to avoid that which offends the beloved and causes him to withdraw — namely sins of omission and commission; and as a consequence he exceedingly desires to do that which pleases the beloved, which is to obey the precepts with a prompt and fervent spirit. For this word — *nimis, exceedingly* — is not indicative of a vice by excess, but of a fervent affection.[5] In addition, this fear makes us to will exceedingly the fulfillment of the precepts of God, because *it shall delight the heart, and shall give joy, and gladness, and length of days.*[6]

111{112}[2]   *His seed shall be mighty upon earth: the generation of the righteous shall be blessed.*

Potens in terra erit semen eius; generatio rectorum benedicetur.

111{112}[3]   *Glory and wealth shall be in his house: and his justice remains for ever and ever.*

Gloria et divitiae in domo eius, et iustitia eius manet in saeculum saeculi.

111{112}[2] *Potens in terra erit semen eius, his seed shall be mighty upon earth*: that is, the fruits of the good manner of life of fearing men will be strong and stable in the Church militant as it will in the Church triumphant. For this fruit is attached with an eternal prize, according to this: *For the fruit of good labors is glorious.*[7] *Generatio rectorum, the generation of the righteous*, that is, of just people, *benedicetur, shall be blessed* by God by receiving his grace, and from men the goods they pray for. For it is written: *The blessing of the Lord is upon the head of the just;*[8] and, *They that are upright shall dwell in the earth, and the simple shall continue in it.*[9] 111{112}[3] *Gloria, glory*, that is, spiritual joy, a good

---

4 Ecclus. 1:27.
5 E. N. In one sense, there is no "excess" or "defect" or "golden mean" that governs the theological virtues of faith, hope, and charity. "Man is unable to love God as much as he ought to be loved, nor to believe and hope in him, as much as he ought." And yet, because of our condition, it may be that our faith, hope, and love is limited. ST IaIIae, q. 64, art. 4
6 Ecclus. 1:12.
7 Wis. 3:15a.
8 Prov. 10:6a.
9 Prov. 2:21.

name, and excellence of life, *et divitiae, and wealth,* that is, affluence of spiritual goods, shall be *in domo eius, in his house,* that is, in the heart of the man fearing God: as we read in Ecclesiasticus, *There is none greater than he that fears God.*[10] *Et iustitia, and justice,* that is, a just manner of life, *eius manet in saeculum saeculi, remains for ever and ever.* For the fearing man perseveres even unto the end, and then he will be crowned for eternity. Whence again it is stated in Ecclesiasticus: *No evils shall happen to him that fears the Lord, but in temptation God will keep him, and deliver him from evils.*[11] Solomon also said: *Be in the fear of the Lord all the day long, and you shall have hope in the latter day.*[12]

111{112}[4] *To the righteous a light is risen up in darkness: he is merciful, and compassionate, and just.*

Exortum est in tenebris lumen rectis, misericors, et miserator, et iustus.

111{112}[4] *Exortum est in tenebris, [there is] risen up in darkness,* that is, among sinners, or in this age of the darkness of ignorance and the gloom made up of vices, *lumen, a light,* a divine [light], eternal and uncreated, *rectis, to the righteous* heart, that is, to the just men. And what this light consists in is stated in what follows: *Misericors et miserator et iustus, merciful, and compassionate, and just,* that is, God who is said to be merciful by nature, compassionate in operation, and just in retribution. God is also said to rise up in justice by this: that they receive from him the light of grace, by which they contemplate and love their Creator. For this reason he says through Malachi: *Unto you that fear my name, the Sun of justice shall arise.*[13] This verse can also be understood as referring to the coming of Christ, so that it reads in this sense: *A light is risen up in darkness,* namely, Christ, *to the righteous* of heart. For by the Incarnation the invisible righteous light appeared visibly, and he rose up to them for their salvation, as Scripture says in Isaiah: *The people that walked in darkness have seen a great light; to them that dwelt in the region of the shadow of death, light is risen.*[14] And in John, Christ himself says: *I am the light of the world: he that follows me, walks not in darkness, but shall have the light of life.*[15]

---

10 Ecclus. 10:27b.
11 Ecclus. 33:1.
12 Prov. 23:17b–18a.
13 Malachi 4:2a.
14 Is. 9:2.
15 John 8:12.

111{112}[5]   *Acceptable is the man that shows mercy and lends: he shall order his words with judgment.*

Iucundus homo qui miseretur et commodat, disponet sermones suos in iudicio.

111{112}[6]   *Because he shall not be moved forever.*

Quia in aeternum non commovebitur.

111{112}[5] *Iucundus homo, acceptable is the man,* that is, spiritually rejoicing in the Lord, and providing the cause of joy to others, *qui miseretur, that shows mercy,* that is, that employs the works of mercy to his neighbor. This is understood to include not only bodily alms, but also the spiritual works of piety, such as to instruct the ignorant, to forgive the sinner, to correct the erring, etc.[16] *Et commodat, and lends,* that is, he lends from his goods to others without usury. Or [we can understand it thus], *and lends,* that is, he gives to others temporal goods, so that he might receive eternal goods from God. Whence in the book of Proverbs it states: *He that has mercy on the poor, lends to the Lord.*[17] *Disponit sermones suos, he shall order his words,* that is, he shall reveal his words, *in iudicio, with judgment* of discretion, not in excessive words, but in the manner that the Apostle admonishes the Colossians: *Let your speech be always in grace seasoned with salt* (that is to say, discretion).[18] For, as is written in Ecclesiasticus, *He that uses many words shall hurt his own soul;*[19] and elsewhere, *He that has no guard on his speech shall meet with evils.*[20] And also in Proverbs, Solomon says: *He that keeps his mouth and his tongue, keeps his soul from distress.*[21] Now a person orders his words with judgment by the use of right reason, so that he knows that it will not be possible for him to fulfil it without the specific and great aid of the grace of God. For, as James attests, *If any man offend not in word,*

---

16 "The works of mercy are charitable actions by which we come to the aid of our neighbor in his spiritual and bodily necessities." CCC § 2447. The corporal works of mercy are traditionally numbered at seven: Feed the hungry, give drink to the thirsty, clothe the naked, shelter the homeless, visit the sick, visit the imprisoned, and bury the dead. The spiritual works of mercy are also traditionally listed as seven: Counsel the doubtful, instruct the ignorant, admonish sinners, comfort the afflicted, forgive offenses, bear wrongs patiently, and pray for the living and the dead. See Appendix, *Compendium of the Catechism of the Catholic Church.*

17 Prov. 19:17a.

18 Col. 4:6a.

19 Ecclus. 20:8a.

20 Prov. 13:3b.

21 Prov. 21:23.

the same is a perfect man.[22] For this reason Solomon again says: *It is the part of man to prepare the soul: and of the Lord to govern the tongue.*[23] 111{112}[6] *Quia in aeternum non commovebitur, because he shall not be moved forever* from the state of salvation and grace, for as it states [only a few verses below] *his justice remains forever and ever.* Whence it is written in the book of Proverbs: *The way of the just is without offense.*[24]

111{112}[7] *The just shall be in everlasting remembrance: he shall not fear the evil hearing. His heart is ready to hope in the Lord.*

In memoria aeterna erit iustus; ab auditione mala non timebit. Paratum cor eius sperare in Domino.

111{112}[8] *His heart is strengthened, he shall not be moved until he look over his enemies.*

Confirmatum est cor eius; non commovebitur donec despiciat inimicos suos.

111{112}[7] *In memoria aeterna erit iustus, the just shall be in everlasting rememberance*: that is, God by the effect of his kindness and grace will be eternally mindful of him: for he is written in the book of life, and God knows him by approbation; and he will be in the sight of the divine majesty in the kingdom of eternal happiness without end. *Ab auditione mala, from the evil hearing,* [that is hearing] the evil of punishment (not of fault), namely from those most hopeless words, *Depart from me, you cursed, into everlasting fire,*[25] *non timebit, he shall not fear* in the day of judgment, although now he may be very afraid of it. For they who are now fearful will then be secure; and they who now have no fear will then be struck with terror. Indeed, as much as the perverse will be in terror at the day of judgment and harsh sentence of the judge, so will the elect have reason for exulting. For this reason, Christ said: *When these things begin to come to pass, look up, and lift up your heads, because your redemption is at hand.*[26]

Paratum cor eius sperare in Domino, his heart is ready to hope in the Lord: for through the hope that exists in him, which is a virtuous habit, it is prompt and easy to hope actually in God, and not in any other created, transient, and vain good. Whence in Ecclesiasticus we have: *They that fear the Lord, will prepare their hearts, and in his sight will sanctify their*

---

22 James 3:2a.
23 Prov. 16:1.
24 Prov. 15:9b.
25 Matt. 25:41.
26 Luke 21:28.

souls.[27] 111{112}[8] *Confirmatum est cor eius, his heart is strengthened* in God by grace, in the way which the Apostle says to the Hebrews: *For it is best that the heart be established with grace.*[28] And in Proverbs it is written: *The just is as an everlasting foundation.*[29] *Non commovebitur, he shall not be moved* from the stable foundation of justice, *donec despiciat inimicos suos, until he look over his enemies,* that is, until the life or the way of this exile ends, and he exists secure in beatitude. For when the just arrive before God, all his visible and invisible adversaries will be accounted as nothing—not out of pride, but from true justice, because he will disdain their vices; and to the degree they are sinful he will regard them [his adversaries] as nothing, as a Psalm above asserts of the just man: *In his sight the malignant is brought to nothing.*[30]

111{112}[9]   *He has distributed, he has given to the poor: his justice remains for ever and ever: his horn shall be exalted in glory.*

Dispersit, dedit pauperibus; iustitia eius manet in saeculum saeculi; cornu eius exaltabitur in gloria.

111{112}[9] *Dispersit, he has distributed,* that is, he has dispersed, and *dedit pauperibus, he has given to the poor* their temporal benefits, or their spiritual gifts, as Peter asserts in the first of his epistles: *As every man has received grace, ministering the same one to another. Iustitia eius manet in saeculum saeculi, his justice remains for ever and ever.*[31] This [verse] in this Psalm has already been explained. *Cornu eius, his horn,* that is, the dignity or the sublimity of grace, which he possesses at present, *exaltabitur, shall be exalted,* that is, will be made perfect and will be consummated, *in gloria, in glory* of the blessed, for then he will receive his prize in full, and the light of grace will be elevated to the light of glory. For this reason, Solomon says: *He that shows mercy to the poor shall be blessed.*[32]

111{112}[10]   *The wicked shall see, and shall be angry, he shall gnash with his teeth and pine away: the desire of the wicked shall perish.*

Peccator videbit, et irascetur, dentibus suis fremet et tabescet; desiderium peccatorum peribit.

27 Ecclus. 2:20.
28 Heb. 13:9a.
29 Prov. 10:25b.
30 Ps. 14:4a.
31 1 Pet. 4:10.
32 Prov. 14:21a.

111{112}[10] *Peccator, the wicked* man who is impenitent *videbit, shall see* the happiness of the just, which they have for a time in an inchoate manner and which in the future they will have perfectly, *et irascetur, and he shall be angry* against them as a result of impatience or against himself in that he has earned such great torments; *dentibus suis fremet, he shall gnash with his teeth*: for his body will shake as out of its interior fury, and the shaking from his anger will show itself in a grinding of the teeth; or [we can interpret it this way], *he shall gnash with this teeth* in hell, where there will be *weeping and gnashing of teeth;*[33] *et tabescet, and he shall pine away* in himself from envy. *Desiderium peccatorum peribit, the desire of the wicked shall perish*, that is, he will be deprived of its effect or the thing he desires. For in the manner that the just desiring God eternally enjoy him, and in this life enrich themselves with spiritual goods, so the ungodly desire temporal things and always take delight in transient things, because they cling to these things as their end. But such a desire completely perishes at death, for then there can be no more enjoyment of temporal things, but in exchange for these delights, they are compelled to suffer eternal torments. But the desire of the just after this life is fulfilled. For this reason, it is written in Proverbs: *To the just their desire shall be given; as a tempest that passes, so the wicked shall be no more.*[34]

ARTICLE XX

ALLEGORICAL EXPLANATION OF THE SAME ONE HUNDRED AND ELEVENTH PSALM OF CHRIST.

111{112}[1] *Blessed is the man that fears the Lord: he shall delight exceedingly in his commandments.*

Beatus vir qui timet Dominum, in mandatis eius volet nimis.

NOW THIS PSALM IS MOST FITTINGLY explained of the person of Christ; and so it will be [understood] in this sense: 111{112}[1] *Beatus vir, blessed is the man*, namely, Christ, who from the beginning of his conception in the Virgin, was both *blessed*, seeing God by sight, and a *man*, because the perfection of all virtues and wisdom. For the soul of Christ saw God by sight from the first

---

33 Matt. 8:12; 13:42, 50, etc.
34 Prov. 10:24b–25a.

instant of its creation, and it was full of all virtues (there being no imperfection included in his reason) and knowledge. Whence, though yet unborn, but even while subsisting as a tiny infant in the womb of his mother, it is written by Jeremiah: *A new thing the Lord has created upon earth: a woman shall compass a man.*[35] Therefore, blessed is the man *qui timet, that fears,* insofar as he is man, *Dominum, the Lord* with a filial fear, especially given that it is one of the seven gifts of the Holy Spirit, as is stated by Isaiah: *And he shall be filled with the spirit of the fear of the Lord.*[36] *In mandatis eius volet nimis, he shall delight exceedingly in his commandments.* For to the degree Christ most fervently loved God above all things, to that degree he willed most fully to carry out his commandments, because with a most ardent appetite he willed to be obedient to God in all things. And not only did he so wish, but also he most completely carried out his wish, for he perfectly fulfilled the moral precepts and the two commandments of love. For this reason, he states in John: *As the Father has given me commandment, so do I;*[37] and within the same [Gospel], *I do always the things that please him.*[38] Indeed, so desirable, and so agreeable was it to Christ the man to serve the precepts of the Father that he said: *My meat is to do the will of him that sent me, that I may perfect his work.*[39]

111{112}[2] *His seed shall be mighty upon earth: the generation of the righteous shall be blessed.*

Potens in terra erit semen eius; generatio rectorum benedicetur.

111{112}[3] *Glory and wealth shall be in his house: and his justice remains for ever and ever.*

Gloria et divitiae in domo eius, et iustitia eius manet in saeculum saeculi.

111{112}[4] *To the righteous a light is risen up in darkness: he is merciful, and compassionate, and just.*

Exortum est in tenebris lumen rectis, misericors, et miserator, et iustus.

---

35 Jer. 31:22b.
36 Is. 11:3a.
37 John 14:31.
38 John 8:29b.
39 John 4:34.

111{112}[2] *Potens in terra erit semen eius, his seed shall be mighty upon earth.* The seed of Christ is the Christian people, of which is stated in Isaiah: *If he shall lay down his life for sin, he shall see a long-lived seed.*[40] This seed is powerful in the land of this exile, because the Christian people are great, many, and powerful in spiritual and corporal goods. This seed is also powerful in the heavenly fatherland of the blessed, where they are made equal to the angels of God. Also, by the seed of Christ one can understand the preaching of the evangelical law, in the manner that Christ said: *The seed is the word of God.*[41] Now this seed of Christ is powerful, for as Mark said, *He was teaching them as one having power, and not as the scribes.*[42] *Generatio rectorum, the generation of the righteous,* that is, the congregation of Christians, born again from water and the Holy Spirit,[43] *benedicetur, shall be blessed* by God, according to that stated by the Apostle [Paul]: *Blessed be God ... who has blessed us with spiritual blessings in heavenly places, in Christ Jesus.*[44] And Luke says of Christ: *Lifting up his hands, he blessed them, ... and was carried up to heaven.*[45] Whence the Lord declares through Isaiah: *My elect shall not labor in vain, nor bring forth in trouble; for they are the seed of the blessed of the Lord.*[46] 111{112}[3] *Gloria, glory,* that is, eternal happiness, *et divitiae, and wealth,* that is, the sufficiency of all goods, *in domo eius, shall be in his house,* that is, in the kingdom of heaven, in the Church triumphant, in the fatherland of the blessed, which is the house of Christ. Especially in the Church militant, glory and wealth are to be found according to the sense brought out in the preceding article; and this Church is the house of Christ according to that contained in the epistle to Timothy: *You may know how you ought to behave yourself in the house of God, which is the Church of the living God, the pillar and ground of the truth.*[47] *Et iustitia eius manet in saeculum saeculi, and his justice remains for ever and ever:* for the divine and uncreated justice of Christ is eternal; but his created justice is in no way deficient. 111{112}[4] *Exortum est in tenebris lumen rectis, etc. To the righteous a light is risen up in darkness, etc.* This verse is expounded upon in the previous article.

---

40 Is. 53:10a.
41 Luke 8:11.
42 Mark 1:22.
43 John 3:5.
44 Eph. 1:3.
45 Luke 24:50–51.
46 Is. 65:23.
47 1 Tim. 3:15.

111{112}[5]   *Agreeable is the man that shows mercy and lends: he shall order his words with judgment.*[48]

Iucundus homo qui miseretur et commodat, disponet sermones suos in iudicio.

111{112}[6]   *Because he shall not be moved forever.*

Quia in aeternum non commovebitur.

111{112}[5] *Iucundus homo, agreeable is the man,* namely, Christ, regarding whom Isaiah asserted: *He shall not be sad, nor troublesome.*[49] For the soul of Christ was always remained in the joy of the fruition of heavenly bliss. *Qui miseretur, that shows mercy.* For he had so much compassion and was so merciful to us that he gave his life for us, and he delivered us with his own blood: for he shows mercy upon all those who cry to him, providing forgiveness and grace. *Et commodat, and he lends*: all things that we receive from Christ he in a certain way lends to us, because he will require an accounting of them and will require they bear fruit, the way he states in the parable of the talents in Luke.[50] *Disponit sermones suos in iudicio, he shall order his words with judgment* of true prudence. For in Christ nothing inordinate or indiscrete was present: indeed, as Luke testifies, *They wondered at the words of grace that proceeded from his mouth.*[51] 111{112}[6] *Quia in aeternum non commovebitur, because he shall not be moved forever,* for the soul of Christ from the beginning of its creation was confirmed in the good.

111{112}[7][52] *Paratum cor eius sperare in Domino, his heart is ready to hope in the Lord.* In Christ there was no hope, which is a theological virtue, because it is an expectation of future blessedness, which is something that Christ never expected, but rather from the beginning he was as perfect a comprehensor as he is now.[53] Yet he hoped in God

---

48 E. N. I have departed from the Douay-Rheim's rather neutral "acceptable" as a translation to *iucundus* to "agreeable."

49 Is. 42:4a.

50 Luke 19:15 *et seq.*

51 Luke 4:22.

52 E. N. I have not recited verses 7–10 separately since Denis does not use the entirety of the verses, but only select phrases in them. What verses these phrases are taken from are indicated in the text.

53 E. N. In other words, Christ as man, had the vision of God — the beatific vision — which is the reward of the elect; and Christ had it in its perfection at the instant of his conception; accordingly, it was not subject to increase and was the same at the moment of conception as it is now when he is at the right hand of God the Father in glory.

by means of a kind of trust, by which he most certainly trusted that he would receive all the good that he desired from God. $111\{112\}[8]$ *Confirmatum est cor eius, his heart is strengthened* by consummated grace, so that he never had the power to sin, just like the Saints in the heavenly homeland do not. $111\{112\}[9]$ *Dispersit, he has distributed* the spiritual gifts of the Holy Spirit, and *dedit, he has given* them *pauperibus, to the poor,* that is, to the humble. For this reason the Evangelist confesses: *Of his fulness we have all received, and grace for grace.*[54] For he sent the Holy Spirit to the Apostles; and as it says in the first epistle of John, *Whatsoever we shall ask, we shall receive of him.*[55] *Cornu eius, his horn,* that is, the regal power of Christ, which he kept hidden when he lived among men, *exaltabitur in gloria, shall be exalted in the glory* of the Resurrection, Ascension, and the brightness of heaven. For in the Resurrection all power in heaven and on earth was given him, both as to its manifestation and its use; and in the heavenly fatherland he sits at the right hand of the Father, both as the King of kings and as the Lord of Lords.

$111\{112\}[10]$ *Peccator, the wicked,* that is, all heretics, pagans, Jews, and reprobate Christians, and most especially the Antichrist, *videbit, shall see* the majesty and glory of Christ in the day of judgment, *et irascetur, and shall be angry,* that is, his heart shall be troubled, in accordance with this: *These seeing it, shall be troubled with terrible fear;*[56] *dentibus suis fremet, he shall gnash with his teeth* against himself, for he will not be able to avoid the place. The rest of the matters [in this Psalm] are clearly set forth in the preceding article.

Be attentive to this doctrinal and beautiful Psalm we have heard, in which we are invited especially to the works of mercy, to which Scripture frequently invites us. Whence in the Proverbs of Solomon it says: *Let not mercy and truth leave you, . . . and you shall find grace and good understanding before God and men.*[57] And our Judge says in Matthew: *Blessed are the merciful, for they shall obtain mercy.*[58] And Ecclesiasticus: *Lend to your neighbor in the time of his need;* and again, *Lose your money for your brother and your friend.*[59] Now Gregory says that mercy can be more aptly described as justice, for when we distribute something

---

54 John 1:16
55 1 John 3:22a.
56 Wis. 5:2a.
57 Prov. 3:3–4.
58 Matt. 5:7.
59 Ecclus. 29:2a, 13a.

to the poor, we do not give something from our own, but something we have borrowed from them.[60] And so also St. Ambrose and that excellent Basil: They say that the bread of the hungry is what you hold, the clothing of the naked is what you display, and the money for ransoming captives is that which you had buried underground.[61] This also Augustine argued: Scrutinize that which God has given you, and from that take what suffices for you; the superfluous remainder is for the poor. When someone possess superfluous wealth, he is in possession of the things of others. God wants you to expend from that which he has given you. For what do you have that he has not given?[62] And so superfluous possessions ought not to be retained either by the rich or those have enough, but they are to be expended upon the poor: otherwise, in both retaining and receiving, let them be fearful of engaging in robbery.

---

60 *E. N.* St. Gregory the Great, *Regula Pastoralis*, 3, 21, PL 77, 87. "For, when we minister necessaries of any kind to the indigent, we return what is theirs, and we do not give from what is ours; we rather pay a debt of justice than carry out works of mercy."

61 *E. N.* See ST IIaIIae, q. 32, art. 5, ad 2. The reference to St. Basil is from a homily on Luke, Homily 6, 12:18, PG 31, 276. But Denis seems to paraphrase a sermon (Sermon 81) attributed to St. Ambrose which is not in his works. St. Thomas appears to draw it from the Decretals, c. 8, dist. XLVII, where a Basilian homily, PG 31, 1744, is erroneously ascribed to St. Ambrose. It *Esurientium panis est, quem tu (tenes) detines, nudorum (vestis) indumentum est quod (quam recludis) tu recludis, miserorum (captivorum) redemptio est pecunia quam tu in (sub) terram defodis (fodis)*. See Ermenegildo Lio, *Osservazioni Critico-Letterarie e Dotrinali sul Famoso Testo: "Proprium Nemo Dicta ... " E Testi Connessi*, Franciscan Studies, Vol. 21, No. 2 (June 1952), 214–31.

62 1 Cor. 4:7: *What have you that you have not received? And if you have received, why do you glory, as if you had not received it?* E. N. The reference to St. Augustine is to his commentary on Psalm 147, Enarr. in Ps., 147, 12, 13, PL 36, 1921, 1922. It is not an exact quotation, but the paraphrase is close in intent to the original: *Quaere quantum tibi dederit, et ex eo tollo quod sufficit: caetera quae superflua iacent, aliorum sunt necessaria. Superflua divitum, necessaria sunt pauperum. Res alienae possidentur, cum superflua possidentur. ... Erogari sibi vult Deus ex illo quod dedit. Quid enim das quod ille non dedit?* "Scrutinize how much he has given to you, and take from that which suffices for you, the superfluous rest which remains are the necessaries of others. The superfluity of the rich are the necessities of the poor. When one is in possession of superfluous wealth, he is in possession of the things of others. ... God wants you to expend from that which he has given you. For what do you give which he has not given?"

PRAYER

MAKE US, O LORD, MIGHTY UPON THE earth, with works that are pleasing to you, and may our soul live preserved in your justice by you: grant to us, we beseech you, that we may always run in your commandments, from whose grace, we receive all that we ask.

Operatione tibi placita effice nos, Domine, potentes in terra, et vivat te praestante in iustitia tua anima nostra: tribue nobis, quaesumus, ut in mandatis tuis semper curramus, cuius gratia totum quod rogamus, impetremus.

Psalm 112

ARTICLE XXI

ELUCIDATION OF THE
ONE HUNDRED AND TWELFTH PSALM:
LAUDATE, PUERI, DOMINUM.
PRAISE THE LORD, YOU CHILDREN.

112{113}[1] *Alleluia. Praise the Lord, you children: praise the name of the Lord.*

Alleluia. Laudate, pueri, Dominum, laudate nomen Domini.

NOW TO THIS PRESENT PSALM IS ASSIGNED the title, *Alleluia*, because praise is offered to God throughout the whole Psalm, the participation in which the holy Prophet [David] invites us: 112{113}[1] *Laudate, pueri, Praise . . . you children*, that is, the pure and innocent, *Dominum, the Lord*: for such children are worthy to praise God. We are invited to this childhood by the Apostle [Paul]: *Brethren, do not become children in sense: but in malice be children, and in sense be perfect.*[1] And in Matthew, Christ says: *Unless you be converted, and become as little children, you shall not enter into the kingdom of heaven.*[2] But some of these are children not by age, but in sensibility, such as is found in Isaiah: *The child shall die a hundred years old.*[3] *Laudate nomen Domini, praise the name of the Lord.* Sacred Scripture frequently exhorts us to praise and to bless the name of the Lord; but this is understood to refer to the one named by the name, namely of the reality signified by the name, and not of the name of the one named. Now we always ought to praise God because this is precisely the work of the angels, and by this man becomes a friend and son of God. Whence also through Isaiah, the Lord says: *Every one that calls upon my name, I have created him for my glory.*[4] And the Apostle says to the Ephesians: *Be filled with the Holy Spirit, speaking to yourselves in psalms, and hymns, and spiritual canticles, singing and making melody in your hearts to the Lord, giving thanks always for things.*[5]

---

1 1 Cor. 14:20.
2 Matt. 18:3.
3 Is. 65:20b.
4 Is. 43:7a.
5 Eph. 5:18b–20a.

112{113}[2]   *Blessed be the name of the Lord, from henceforth now and forever.*

Sit nomen Domini benedictum ex hoc nunc et usque in saeculum.

112{113}[3]   *From the rising of the sun unto the going down of the same, the name of the Lord is worthy of praise.*

A solis ortu usque ad occasum laudabile nomen Domini.

So as to praise in this manner, say: 112{113}[2] *Sit nomen Domini benedictum, blessed be the name of the Lord,* that is, God himself is to be praised and blessed by all, *ex hoc nunc et usque in saeculum, from henceforth now and forever,* that is, unceasingly, continually, and perpetually. He who fervently loves God is frequently set alight with zeal of the divine honor, and he longs that God be praised, blessed, and honored in every possible way by all. 112{113}[3] *A solis ortu usque ad occasum, from the rising of the sun unto the going down of the same,* that is, from the morning until the evening. Or [we can understand it thus], *from the rising of the sun,* that is, from the lands and the people in the East, *unto the going down of the same,* that is even until the lands and the people of the West, *laudabile nomen Domini, the name of the Lord is worthy of praise:* for in all parts of the world it is evident that the goodness of God is operating and is encountered. For this reason, he is to be praised everywhere and always, as is stated by Malachi: *From the rising of the sun [even to the going down] my name is great among the Gentiles.*[6]

112{113}[4]   *The Lord is high above all nations; and his glory above the heavens.*

Excelsus super omnes gentes Dominus, et super caelos gloria eius.

112{113}[4] *Excelsus super omnes gentes Dominus, the Lord is high above all nations,* that is, he is more worthy and more sublime than all men, as is stated in Isaiah: *All nations are before him as if they had no being at all, and are counted to him as nothing, and vanity.*[7] And in the book of Job: *I will not accept the person of man, and I will not level God with man.*[8] Also, Wisdom states: *The whole world before you is as the least grain of the balance, and as a drop of the morning dew, that falls down upon the*

---

6 Mal. 1:11a. *E. N.* I have added the part in brackets because it seems so appropriate to Denis's argument and matches the verse of the Psalm. It is unclear to me why Denis would not have included it.

7 Is. 40:17.

8 Job 32:1.

earth.[9] *Et super caelos gloria eius, and his glory is above the heavens*: that is, the joy of the blessed [in heaven], which they receive from God as a reward, is above all the circles of heaven, namely in the empyrean heaven, which is the place of the glory of God and of the elect.[10] Or [we can also interpret it thus], *above the heavens*, that is, above all citizens and dwellers of the heavenly court, is *his glory*, that is, the excellence of God the creator, because God is superior to the angelic spirits, according to that set forth in the book of Job: *The pillars of heaven tremble, and dread at his beck;*[11] and elsewhere, *Behold they that serve him are not steadfast, and in his angels he found wickedness.*[12]

112{113}[5] *Who is as the Lord our God, who dwells on high:*

  Quis sicut Dominus Deus noster, qui in altis habitat,

112{113}[6] *And looks down on the low things in heaven and in earth?*

  Et humilia respicit in caelo et in terra?

112{113}[5] *Quis sicut Dominus Deus noster, who is as the Lord our God*, namely, the blessed Trinity? It is as if he were saying: "No one is similar to him with the similitude of equality, although many are similar to him with the similitude of imitation." Whence with Jeremiah we have: *Who is like to me? And who shall abide me?* says the Lord.[13] *Qui in altis habitat, who dwells on high*, that is, in heaven, about which we daily say, *Our Father who art in heaven*: where by heaven we understand the holy and contemplative souls (or the empyrean heaven, which is often called the plural "heavens," because the word "heaven" lacks singular number in Hebrew, according to Chrysostom). In this dwelling, God is circum-scribed by grace, 112{113}[6] *et humilia, and the low things*, [the low, humble] hearts, *respicit, he looks down on* with approval and preservation, *in caelo et in terra, in heaven and on earth*, indeed in every place and at every time. *For he gives grace to the humble.*[14] And the book of Isaiah, according to another translation, says: *To whom shall I have respect, but to him that is at peace and humble, . . . and who trembles at my words?*[15]

---

9 Wis. 11:23

10 E. N. The empyrean or empyreal heaven is the highest heaven in the Medieval cosmology. *See* footnote 19-11.

11 Job 26:11.

12 Job 4:18.

13 Jer. 49:19b.

14 James 4:6b.

15 Is. 66:2b. E. N. The version quoted by Denis states: *Ad quem respiciam, nisi ad quietum et humilem* (at peace and humble). . . . This departs from the Sixto-Clem-entine which reads *Ad quem respiciam, nisi ad pauperculum* (poor and little). . . . "

He, therefore, who desires to be regarded by God should humble his spirit, keeping in mind the glorious Virgin: *He has regarded the humility of his handmaid.*[16] For the more profoundly a man depreciates himself, the higher is judged to be by God.

112{113}[7]   *Raising up the needy from the earth, and lifting up the poor out of the dunghill:*

Suscitans a terra inopem, et de stercore erigens pauperem,

112{113}[8]   *That he may place him with princes, with the princes of his people.*

Ut collocet eum cum principibus, cum principibus populi sui.

112{113}[7] *Suscitans, raising,* God [raising] by his grace *a terra, from the earth,* that is, from the carnal life, from the love of earthly things, from the thoughts of temporal things, *inopem, the needy,* that is, those in spiritual emptiness and in need, enriching them with divine gifts, heavenly love, and the contemplation of divine things; *et de stercore, and . . . out of the dunghill,* that is, from the dwelling of this corruptible body, *erigens, lifting up* to the dwelling of the heavenly kingdom,[17] *pauperem, the poor* in spirit, namely, the humble, for *he that humbles himself shall be exalted,*[18] according to this, *He that has been humbled shall be in glory.*[19] **112{113} [8]** *Ut collocet eum, that he may place him* in the heavenly homeland *cum principibus, with princes,* that is, with the holy angels, *cum principibus populi sui, with the princes of his people,* that is, with the majority of the elect, namely, with the Apostles and the Prophets. For the Church triumphant is one, united out of good men and holy angels.[20] Or [we can understand it in this way], *that he may place him* in the day of judgment at his right hand,[21] *with princes,* of which is written by Isaiah: *The Lord will enter into judgment with the ancients of his people, and its princes.*[22] These judgments are contained in those two verses of the canticle of Anna contained in the first book of Samuel, where we read this about

---

16 Luke 1:48a.

17 *E. N.* Denis's text has *elevans,* which the editor corrects in the margin to *erigens.*

18 Luke 14:11b.

19 Job 22:29a.

20 *E. N.* ST IIIa, q. 8, art. 4, co. "Now it is manifest that both men and angels are ordained to one end, which is the glory of the divine fruition. Hence the mystical body of the Church does not only consist of men, but also of angels."

21 *Cf.* Matt. 25:33.

22 Is. 3:14a.

God: *He raises up the needy from the dust, and lifts up the poor from the dunghill: that he may sit with princes, and hold the throne of glory.*[23]

112{113}[9] *Who makes a barren woman to dwell in a house, the joyful mother of children.*

Qui habitare facit sterilem in domo, matrem filiorum laetantem.

112{113}[9] *Qui habitare facit sterilem, who makes a barren woman to dwell,* that is, the congregation of the Gentiles, once lacking in all spiritual fecundity, *in domo, in a house,* that is, in the Church militant by grace, and afterwards in the Church triumphant by glory. He makes, I say, her dwell, *matrem filiorum laetantem, the joyful mother of children,* that is, in such a way that the dwelling is a mother rejoicing in the spiritual children who are reborn of water and the Holy Spirit, since the Synagogue of the Jews, which was at one time fertile has become barren. And it is in this sense that the Apostle asserts what is contained in Isaiah: *Rejoice, you barren, that bear not: break forth and cry, you that travail not: for many are the children of the desolate, more than of her that has a husband,*[24] that is, the Synagogue, whose spouse and husband was God, but who has abandoned her because of her disbelief in the manner that is confessed by Jeremiah: *I have forsaken my house, I have left my inheritance.... My inheritance is become to me as a lion in the wood.*[25] Now the Prophet [David] calls the Gentiles or the people of the Gentile nations sterile and barren because for a long time they were deserted by God because of their idolatry, so that they produced no fruit of the Holy Spirit, nor did they generate any children of Christ. Whence, in the first book of Samuel, the prophetess Anna spoke: *The barren has borne many: and she that had many children is weakened.*[26]

Take note: it befits us to sing this delightful and brief Psalm with extraordinary joy because all our praise encompasses the Lord God and Creator. And it is entirely incumbent upon us to be as children, that is, pure, innocent, and humble, so that we might worthily praise God and be found deserving of being regarded by his goodness, because *praise is not seemly in the mouth of a sinner.*[27]

---

23 1 Sam. 2:8.
24 Gal. 4:27; Is. 54:1.
25 Jer. 12:7a, 8a.
26 1 Sam. 2:5.
27 Ecclus. 15:9.

PRAYER

OUR GOD, O YOU WHO DWELL IN THE heights, and who raise the needy from the dunghill, look mercifully upon us your humble servants on earth; and lift us up to the sublime heights of virtue in which we might make progress day by day and persevere in so as to never to be found wanting.

Deus noster, qui in altis habitas, et de stercore inopem suscitas,
nos humiles tuos in terra clementer respice; atque
ad sublimia virtutum attolle, in quibus in
dies proficientes, in his perseveremus
non deficientes.

Psalm 113

ARTICLE XXII

LITERAL EXPOSITION OF THE
ONE HUNDRED AND THIRTEENTH PSALM:
IN EXITU ISRAEL.
WHEN ISRAEL WENT OUT.

113{114}[1] *Alleluia. When Israel went out of Egypt, the house of Jacob from a barbarous people:*

Alleluia. In exitu Israel de Aegypto, domus Iacob de populo barbaro,

THE TITLE OF THIS PSALM IS: *ALLELUIA.* FOR God is praised in this present Psalm literally in consideration of the marvels which he effected for the Jewish people in Egypt, in the Red Sea, and the desert.

Therefore, it says: 113{114}[1] *In exitu Israel, when Israel went out,* that is, when Israel, that is, the Israelite people, had gone out *de Aegypto, domus Iacob; of Egypt, the house of Jacob,* that is, at the leaving of his family or people, which is called the house of the patriarch Jacob inasmuch as they arose from his seed, *de populo barbaro, from a barbarous people,* because they possessed a barbarous language. For all languages — except for Hebrew, Greek, and Latin — are called barbarous:[1] and so all peoples are said to be barbarous except for the Hebrews, the Greeks, and the Latins.

113{114}[2] *Judea was made his sanctuary, Israel his dominion.*

Facta est Iudaea sanctificatio eius, Israel potestas eius.

Therefore, while this people were going out of Egypt, according to

---

1 *E. N. See, e.g.,* St. Isidore of Seville, *Etymologies* 9.3: "The sacred languages are three in number: Hebrew, Greek, and Latin, which are the most excellent in all the world. For the case of the Lord was written atop the Cross by Pilate in these three languages. For this reason (and also on account of the obscurity of Sacred Scriptures), it is necessary to have an understanding of these three languages, so that you may have recourse to one or the other on the occasion when some doubt arises in a word or in the interpretation of a phrase in one of the languages." PL 82, 326.

that which is recited in Exodus,[2] **113{114}[2]** *Facta es Iudaea, Judea was made*, that is, the people of the Jews [were made] *sanctificatio eius, his sanctuary* (namely, [the sanctuary] of God), that is, a sanctified thing, or a people consecrated to God, because they were chosen and deputed to give worship to the one God. Also, often in Exodus and elsewhere the Lord says to Moses: *Sanctify unto me every firstborn . . . among the children of Israel.*[3] Also *Israel was made*, that is, the people born of Jacob, whose other name is Israel, were made *potestas eius, his dominion*, that is, that [people] to which God showed his power, by freeing them from Egypt with his mighty hand.[4] Now although in the preceding verse the name of God is not expressed, it is still fitting to use the relative pronoun "his" to refer to God because in the divine Scriptures pronouns often designate and refer to that to which is not expressed, but which is granted to be obviously known: in the manner that the angel in Luke says in speaking about John, *He shall go before him in the spirit and power of Elias,*[5] where Christ is indicated by the "him." Others explain this verse thus: *Judea was made his sanctuary*, that is, the people in Judea, namely the land of promise, are sanctified; *Israel his dominion*, that is, he has caused this people to be powerful in the previously mentioned land. But because this sanctuary came to exist forty years after the departure from Egypt,[6] it may be more apt to say [in verse 113:1]: *After (post)* the departure of Egypt [Israel his dominion, and not *when (in)*.[7] Finally, as the word Gentile means the gentile people, so Judea means the people of the Jews.

113{114}[3]   *The sea saw and fled: Jordan was turned back.*

Mare vidit, et fugit; Iordanis conversus est retrorsum.

113{114}[4]   *The mountains skipped like rams, and the hills like the lambs of the flock.*

Montes exsultaverunt ut arietes, et colles sicut agni ovium.

113{114}[3] *Mare vidit et fugit, the sea saw and fled*, that is, the Red Sea, by the command of God, was divided in such manner, and so obeyed God

---

2 Ex. 12:41 *et seq.*; chp. 13, *etc.*
3 Ex. 13:2; 22:29; Num. 3:13, *etc.*
4 Gen. 32:28; 35:10. Ex. 32:11.
5 Luke 1:17.
6 Num. 14:24.
7 E. N. In other words, the Ps. 113:2 presupposes the passage of forty years, since the people were not strong in Israel until they entered the promised land, so "when (*in*)" is used loosely.

as if it were something with an intellectual nature. For it was as between one wall and another that the children of Israel walked with dry feet until they got to the other side, as we read in Exodus.[8] *Iordanis conversus est retrorsum, Jordan was turned back,* that is, some parts of the Jordan's waters turned back against their origins, for they did not descend, but they swelled up in the manner of a mountain, as the book of Joshua states: *As soon as the children of Israel came into the Jordan, . . . the waters that came down from above stood in one place, and swelling like a mountain, were seen afar off . . . but those that were beneath ran down into the sea of the wilderness, until they wholly failed . . . And all the people passed through the channel that was dried up.*[9] 113{114}[4] *Montes exsultaverunt ut arietes, et colles sicut agni ovium; the mountains skipped like rams, and the hills like lambs of the flock.*

113{114}[5]   *What ailed you, O sea, that you did flee: and you, O Jordan, that you were turned back?*

Quid est tibi, mare, quod fugisti? Et tu, Iordanis, quia conversus es retrorsum?

113{114}[6]   *The mountains skipped like rams, and the hills like the lambs of the flock.*

Montes, exsultastis sicut arietes? Et colles sicut agni ovium?

Then, the holy Prophet [David] rejoicing in the Lord because of his miracles, speaks and asks questions of inanimate objects, not supposing that they might understand and respond, but so that men might be aroused in admiration and the proclamation of God: For he says: 113{114}[5] *Quid est tibi, mare, quod fugistis? What ailed you, O sea, that you did flee?* This is said in the manner just stated. *Et tu, Iordanis; and you, O Jordan,* what happened to you, *quia conversus es retrorsum, that you were turned back?* It is as if he were saying: "Whence and by which power was the miracle done?" What also has occurred to you, O 113{114}[6] *montes, mountains,* for *exsultastis sicut arietes, for you have skipped like rams,* who jump out of joy? *Et, and* what happened to you, O *colles, hills* for you have exulted *sicut agni ovium, like the lambs of the flock,* who run with great happiness to the udders of their mothers? Now this verse can be read and expounded upon in an assertive sense, and not in an interrogative sense. And so the same verse can be understood to say, the mountains [in their exultation] skipped like rams. Now the

---

8 Ex. 14:12–22.
9 Joshua 3:15–17.

mountains are said to skip like rams [in their exultation] in the way that the earth is said to bless the Lord, namely, metaphorically, materially, and occasionally in that they gave to the children of Israel cause to rejoice. Some explain this exultation of the mountains of the rocky crags, that is, the steep cliffs, which were by the Arnon River,[10] and which (as they assert) were bowed down each side toward the other, preventing the children of Israel from traveling by this river. Whence we find contained in the book of Numbers: *As he did in the Red Sea, so will he do in the streams of Arnon: the rocks of the torrents were bowed down.*[11]

113{114}[7]   *At the presence of the Lord the earth was moved, at the presence of the God of Jacob.*

A facie Domini mota est terra, a facie Dei Jacob.

113{114}[8]   *Who turned the rock into pools of water, and the stony hill into fountains of waters.*

Qui convertit petram in stagna aquarum, et rupem in fontes aquarum.

Following this, he responds to the questions made regarding the exultation of the earth: **113{114}[7]** *A facie Domini mota est terra; at the presence of the Lord, the earth was moved,* that is, at the sight of the divine command these miracles happened: as the earth swallowed Dathan and Abiram,[12] so the cliffs of the mountains were bowed down; *a facie Dei Iacob, at the presence of the God of Jacob,* the patriarch, [the God] to whom, as the almighty Creator, all animate and inanimate nature are most immediately ready to move at his mere nod. For this reason it states in Ecclesiasticus: *Behold the heaven, and the heavens of heavens, the deep, and all the earth, and the things that are in them, shall be moved in his sight ... when God shall look upon them, they shall be taken with trembling.*[13] **113{114}[8]** *Qui convertit petram in stagna aquarum, who turned the rock into pools of water,* that is, who made water flow out of rock, as still rivers of water burst forth into motion. This was the rock at Horeb which when Moses struck there flowed out a great quantity of water, as is written in the book of Exodus.[14]

---

10 E. N. This is a river (probably the modern Wadi Mujib) in Jordan which empties the Dead Sea. It is a narrow river in many parts, and is bordered by canyon and rocky limestone cliffs.

11 Num. 21:14b–15a.

12 Num. 15:23–33; 21:15.

13 Ecclus. 16:18, 19b.

14 Ex. 17:6.

He also turned *rupem, the stony hill,* that is, hard rock, *in fontes aquarum, into fountains of waters*: for, as we read in the book of Numbers, when Moses struck rock twice with his rod, water flowed out copiously.[15]

113{114}[9]   *Not to us, O Lord, not to us; but to your name give glory.*

Non nobis, Domine, non nobis; sed nomini tuo da gloriam.

113{114}[10]   *For your mercy, and for your truth's sake: lest the Gentiles should say: Where is their God?*

Super misericordia tua et veritate tua; nequando dicant gentes: Ubi est Deus eorum?

113{114}[11]   *But our God is in heaven: he has done all things whatsoever he would.*

Deus autem noster in caelo; omnia quaecumque voluit fecit.

Because these things are not accomplished through our merits or our powers, but by the divine power and mercy, therefore: **113{114}[9]** *Non nobis, Domine, non nobis, sed nomini tuo da gloriam; not to us, O Lord, not to us; but to your name give glory*: that is, make it that all men know this, that they may praise not us, but may gloriously praise you. **113{114}[10]** *Super misericordia tua et veritate tua; for your mercy, and for your truth's sake,* that is, for these effects produced by your goodness and equity. For these prodigies are mercifully done because they are done without the previous merits of men. Yet they are done justly insofar as God promised to the holy patriarchs that their seed would be led out of Egypt and that he would protect them by his divine power.[16] When we pray these things, let us conform our affection to the divine will, because God has declared through Isaiah: *I the Lord, this is my name: I will not give my glory to another.*[17] And the Apostle said: *To the only God be honor and glory.*[18] Those who, therefore, request these things from their heart deserve to be glorified by God, who in the book of Samuel said: *Whosoever shall glorify me, him will I glorify: but they that despise me, shall be despised.*[19] Since, therefore, to God alone ought glory be given for good works, it is not to be wondered at that true and humble

---

15 Num. 20:11.
16 Gen. 1:23; Ex. 3:7 *et seq.* and elsewhere.
17 Is. 42:8.
18 1 Tim. 1:17.
19 1 Sam. 2:30b.

servants of Christ are greatly bothered when they perceive glory is being attributed to them by men: for they dare not usurp that which is God's.

Therefore, do this, O Lord, *nequando, lest,* that is, so that at no time, *dicant gentes, the Gentiles,* who are given to idolatry, *should say: Ubi est Deus eorum, where is their God,* namely, [the God] of the Hebrews? That is to say, lest it appear now that he is not the true and almighty God because he does not glorify his name by demonstrating his power and fulfilling that which he promised. This is the reason Moses often recalls and asserts in his pleas, speaking to God in this manner: *Let not the Egyptians say, I beseech you: He craftily brought them out that he might kill them in the mountains.*[20] Joshua also said: *My Lord God, what shall I say, seeing Israel turning their backs to their enemies? . . . What will you do to your great name?*[21] For the Lord bears witness that he will hear our prayers for this reason, saying: *For my own sake will I do it, that I may not be blasphemed.*[22] **113{114}[11]** *Deus autem noster in caelo, but our God is in heaven,* that is, in the heart of the devout man, which is the incorporeal heaven; or, in the empyrean heaven, in which he is in a special sense said to be, because there he most excellently performs his works and is most clearly seen. *Omnia quaecumque voluit, fecit; he has done all things whatsoever he would,* since he is omnipotent. And so, in the book of Job we read: *Whatsoever his soul has desired, that has he done.*[23]

113{114}[12]   *The idols of the Gentiles are silver and gold, the works of the hands of men.*

   Simulacra gentium argentum et aurum, opera manuum hominum.

113{114}[13]   *They have mouths and speak not: they have eyes and see not.*

   Os habent, et non loquentur; oculos habent, et non videbunt.

113{114}[14]   *They have ears and hear not: they have noses and smell not.*

   Aures habent, et non audient; nares habent, et non odorabunt.

113{114}[15]   *They have hands and feel not: they have feet and walk not: neither shall they cry out through their throat.*

   Manus habent, et non palpabunt; pedes habent, et non ambulabunt; non clamabunt in gutture suo.

---

20 Ex. 32:12; cf. Num. 14:13–16.
21 Joshua 7:8, 9b.
22 Is. 48:11.
23 Job 23:13b.

113{114}[12] *Simulacra gentium, the idols of the Gentiles,* that is, the idols of the pagans, are not substantially different from *argentum et aurum, silver and gold:* which is understood to apply to those idols that are made from the more precious materials. For they have idols whose entire substance is copper, bronze, or wood, for, according to the Philosopher, in artificial things the entire substance is in the matter.[24] Now these idols are artificial things as it states further, *opera manuum hominum, the works of the hands of men.* For they are formed by human hands and human art. 113{114}[13] *Os habent, they have mouths,* neither truly nor univocally, but only by similitude, in the manner that a dead man is said to have feet or eyes; *et non loquentur, and speak not,* for they have no life nor understanding in them. *Oculos habent, they have eyes,* in the same manner that they have mouths, *et no videbunt, and they see not* through them. And in similar manner the two following verses state that they [the idols] have organs without function, namely ears without hearing, noses without smell, hands without feeling, feet without the ability to walk about, and throats without sound.

But this seems to be contradicted: for the idols of the Gentiles are said to respond to their worshippers, indeed, to have predicted the future. It should be noted, therefore, that as Valerius Maximus relates, certain of the Romans, and especially the ancient Romans, did not worship the idols in themselves, as if they were true or animated, but in honor of those things which they represented. But other Romans worshipped them, insofar as they honored them as if they were live, animated, and rational things, and this madness originated from the error of Hermes.[25] For as St. Augustine describes in the eighth book of the *City of God,* Hermes Trismegistus asserted that as the most high God is the maker of the heavenly gods, so man is the maker of gods that are worshiped in the temples and are pleased with the proximity to humans. For the statues are said to be full of sense and spirit, prescient of the future, foreknowing of dreams and many other things, rendering men weak and curing them, giving them joy or sadness in accordance with their merit.[26]

---

24 E. N. The reference is to book II.1 of Aristotle's *Physics* 192b30–33 where he distinguishes between artificial things or artifacts (*e.g.,* beds or pots) and natural things (*e.g.,* trees). In contradistinction to natural things, where "the source is in the thing, but not in the thing itself," artificial things do not have a source or form of their making within them; rather "the source is in something else and external." *Aristotle Physics: Books I and II* (Oxford: Clarendon Press, 1992), 23 (trans., William Charlton).

25 E. N. Valerius Maximus (*fl.* 30 AD) was a Roman moralist and historian best known for his *Memorable Deeds and Sayings* (*Facta et dicta memorabilia*).

26 E. N. St. Augustine, *City of God,* VIII, 23.

This position is not only at odds with theological truth, but also with natural reason, as St. Thomas beautifully and efficaciously demonstrates in his *Summa Contra Gentiles*.[27] Against this error the book of Wisdom also most amply takes issue.[28] Whence Seneca also says that idols are not animated, and that they ought not to be worshipped, even though he himself appeared externally to worship them. Of this dissimulation, St. Augustine strongly excoriates Seneca.[29]

113{114}[16] *Let them that make them become like unto them: and all such as trust in them.*

Similes illis fiant qui faciunt ea, et omnes qui confidunt in eis.

113{114}[16] *Similes illis fiant qui faciunt ea, let them that make them become like unto them*: that is, let all those who fashion or procure idols become like their idols, seeing that as they are bodily blind, deaf, mute, and existing without any natural life, so these — lacking the life of grace — will be spiritually blind, deaf, mute, and dead; *et omnes qui confidunt in eis, and all such as trust in them*, not in the true God, will become like to them. This is said not wishing it, but foreannouncing it, and to show that they deserve that which is asserted unless they come to comprehend their obstinacy.

113{114}[17] *The house of Israel has hoped in the Lord: he is their helper and their protector.*

Domus Israel speravit in Domino; adiutor eorum et protector eorum est.

113{114}[18] *The house of Aaron has hoped in the Lord: he is their helper and their protector.*

Domus Aaron speravit in Domino; adiutor eorum et protector eorum est.

113{114}[19] *They that fear the Lord have hoped in the Lord: he is their helper and their protector.*

Qui timent Dominum speraverunt in Domino; adiutor eorum et protector eorum est.

---

27 *E. N.* SCG II, 120.
28 Wis. 13:10–19; Is. 44:9–20.
29 *E. N.* St. Augustine's *On the City of God*, VI, 10.

113{114}[17] *Domus Israel, the house of Israel,* that is, the faithful people originating from Jacob, *speravit in Domino, has hoped in the Lord,* not in idols. For this reason Balaam said: *There is no idol in Jacob, neither is there an image god (simulacrum) to be seen in Israel. The Lord his God is with him, and the sound of the victory of the king in him.*[30] And this is what is added: *adiutor eorum et protector eorum est, he is their helper and their protector,* that is, God helps them in the good and he protects them in adversity. For he drowned the Egyptians and put to death the Canaanites on their behalf.[31] 113{114}[18] *Domus Aaron, the house of Aaron,* that is, his posterity, namely the priests of the Old Testament, *speravit in Domino, has hoped in the Lord.* And since the house of Aaron is included in the house of Jacob, as part of a whole, yet special mention is made of it because of the priestly dignity. *Adiutor eorum et protector eorum est, he is their helper and their protector* — and was [their helper] — as is clear in the books of the Law and the Prophets. 113{114}[19] *Qui timent Dominum, they that fear the Lord* with a filial fear, or at least initial fear, *speraverunt in Domino, have hoped in the Lord*: otherwise they are to be despaired of. For they have hoped in the Lord that he would give them virtue and grace to avoid all evil, and to attain all good: and they will not be frustrated because *adiutor eorum et protectorum eorum est, he is their helper and their protector.* Whence it is written: *Behold . . . and know that no one has hoped in the Lord and has been confounded.*[32] And consequently Scripture admonishes this: *You that fear the Lord, hope in him: and mercy shall come to you for your delight.*[33]

113{114}[20]   *The Lord has been mindful of us, and has blessed us. He has blessed the house of Israel: he has blessed the house of Aaron.*

Dominus memor fuit nostri, et benedixit nobis. Benedixit domui Israel; benedixit domui Aaron.

113{114}[21]   *He has blessed all that fear the Lord, both little and great.*

Benedixit omnibus qui timent Dominum, pusillis cum maioribus.

113{114}[20][34] *Dominus memor fuit nostri, the Lord has been mindful of us,* namely, of the Israelite people, by showing to us through his effects

---

30 Num. 23:21.

31 Ex. 14:24–28; Deut. 1:30; Joshua 3:10; chp. 12.

32 Ecclus. 2:11.

33 Ecclus. 2:9.

34 E. N. Denis's numbering of his verses departs slightly from the Douay Rheims from here to the end. I have retained the division of the Douay Rheims and adapted Denis's text to it.

the care and love that he has concerning us; *et benedixit nobis, and he has blessed us*, giving us an abundance of spiritual and temporal goods, so long as we remain in his service. This is very clearly stated next: *Benedixit domui, he has blessed the house*, that is, the families, *Israel; benedixit domui Aaron; of Israel, he has blessed the house of Aaron*, that is, the priests. **113{114}[21]** *Benedixit omnibus que timent Dominum, he has blessed all that fear the Lord*, namely, *pusillis, the little*, that is, the simple and the subordinate, *cum maioribus, and the great*, that is, the prelates. *For God is not a respecter of persons, but in every nation, he that fears him and works justice is acceptable to him.*[35]

113{114}[22]   *May the Lord add blessings upon you: upon you, and upon your children.*

Adiiciat Dominus super vos, super vos et super filios vestros.

113{114}[23]   *Blessed be you of the Lord, who made heaven and earth.*

Benedicti vos a Domino, qui fecit caelum et terram.

113{114}[24]   *The heaven of heaven is the Lord's: but the earth he has given to the children of men.*

Caelum caeli Domino; terram autem dedit filiis hominum.

113{114}[22] *Adiiciat Dominus super vos*, may the Lord add blessing *upon you*, [the blessing of] the greater goods, so that you might unfailingly advance in the spiritual life: for not to go forwards is to go backwards.[36] This the Apostle prays for us in his letter to the Thessalonians: *God direct your way . . . and make you abound in charity towards one another, and towards all men.*[37] And elsewhere: *I pray that you may abound the more.*[38]

---

35 Acts 10:34b–35.

36 E. N. *Non proficere, est deficere.* This is a classic formulation of the spiritual life, central, for example, in the thought of St. Bernard of Clairvaux. *Ep.* 254, 4: *Nolle proficere deficere est. See also Ep.* 385, 1. "[T]he great St. Austin . . . says we cannot possibly prevent ourselves from descending, but by always striving to ascend; for as soon as we begin to stop, we descend, and not to advance, is to go back; so that if we wish not to go back, we must always run forward without stopping. St. Gregory, St. Chrysostom, St. Leo Pope, and many other saints, say the same, and express themselves almost in the same terms." Alphonsus Rodriguez, S. J., *The Practice of Christian & Religious Perfection* (Dublin: James Duffy & Sons, 1882), Vol. I, 22. "It is the sign of a Saint to *grow*." St. John Henry Newman, Letter to Miss Holmes (July 31, 1850). *Letters and Diaries of John Henry Newman: July 1850–1851* (Oxford: Oxford University Press, 1963), Vol. 14, 29.

37 1 Thess. 3:11–12.

38 1 Thess. 4:1b.

Super vos et super filios vestros, upon you and upon your children both carnal and spiritual, giving to you and to them daily progress that you might go *from virtue to virtue.*[39] 113{114}[23] *Benedicti esti vos, blessed be you,* O fathers and children, *a Domino, of the Lord,* that is, by the Lord, or to the honor and glory of God, who bestows upon you all exterior and interior goods, all temporal and eternal goods, *qui fecit caelum et terram, who made heaven and earth,* along with everything in between. And he also created 113{114}[24] *Caelum, caeli, the heaven of heaven,* the supreme and empyrean [heaven], *Domino, is the Lord's,* that is, is itself his palace for himself, so that they might eternally dwell with him with the blessed: not indeed that they lack a place, but that he has prepared for them this home to the glory of his elect. *Terram autem dedit filiis hominum, but the earth he has given to the children of men* so that it may be dwelt upon and cultivated as is necessary for human life, as is attested by Jeremiah: *I made the earth . . . and I have given it to whom it seemed good in my eyes.*[40]

113{114}[25] *The dead shall not praise you, O Lord: nor any of them that go down to hell.*

Non mortui laudabunt te, Domine; neque omnes qui descendunt in infernum.

113{114}[26] *But we that live bless the Lord: from this time now and forever.*

Sed nos qui vivimus, benedicimus Domino, ex hoc nunc et usque in saeculum.

113{114}[25] *Non mortui, the dead shall not,* [that is,] those in mortal sin [shall not] *laudabunt te, Domine; praise you, O Lord,* with meritorious praise, because with charity and grace no one is worthy of the divine good, *neque omnes qui descendunt in infernum, nor any of them that go down to hell* of the damned: for such persons blaspheme God. Whence Ecclesiastes exhorts: *Whatsoever your hand is able to do, do it earnestly: for neither work, nor reason, nor wisdom, nor knowledge shall be in hell.*[41] Baruch also states: *The dead that are in hell, whose spirit is taken away from their bowels, shall not give glory . . . to the Lord.*[42] 113{114}[26] *Sed nos qui vivimus, but we that live* spiritually having charity which is the

---

39 Ps. 83:8b.
40 Jer. 27:5.
41 Eccl. 9:10.
42 Baruch 2:17.

life of the soul, *benedicimus Domino, bless the Lord*, that is, we praise God, *ex hoc nunc, from this time now*, that is, at the present instant, *et usque in saeculum, and forever*, that is, without end. For now this praise begins, and it continues even unto death, and when the soul is separated from the body, and it remains with [the soul] in the kingdom of heaven for eternity, according to that which the Lord said through Isaiah: *You shall be glad and rejoice even for eternity.*[43]

ARTICLE XXIII

TROPOLOGICAL OR MORAL EXPOSITION OF THE SAME ONE HUNDRED AND THIRTEENTH PSALM.

N THE MANNER THAT THE APOSTLE SAID to the Corinthians—*All these things happened to them in figure: and they are written for our correction, upon whom the ends of the world are come*—we ought therefore to draw moral instruction from the previous words.[44] And so, as it has been touched upon on occasion, by Egypt is understood this present time or world, of which (according to John in his epistle) *the whole is seated in wickedness.*[45] For this reason, James says: *Whosoever therefore will be a friend of this world, becomes an enemy of God.*[46] Here, by the term "world" is not meant the world structure,[47] made from the elements and the other irrational components, but worldly people, living for the present world, of which the Apostle says, *If I pleased men, I should not be the servant of Christ:*[48] for, as James has written, *A friend of this world, becomes an enemy of God.*[49] Also, by Israel, which is interpreted to mean "man seeing God," is understood a faithful people contemplating God by faith. But by Jacob, which means "supplanter," is understood any person fighting against vice. Now the departure of the children of Israel from Egypt signifies the departure of the Christians from this world, or,

---

43 Is. 65:18a.
44 1 Cor. 10:11.
45 1 John 5:19.
46 James 4:4.
47 *E. N.* Denis speaks of the *machina mundialis*, the "machine of the world," that is the whole of the created world, which, of course, is good. Gen. 1:4, 10, 12, 18, 21, 25, 31.
48 Gal. 1:10b.
49 James 4:4b.

rather, from the worldly and vicious life, because we leave the world, not by movement or by place, but by manner of living and merit.

113{114}[1] *When Israel went out of Egypt, the house of Jacob from a barbarous people:*

In exitu Israel de Aegypto, domus Iacob de populo barbaro,

113{114}[2] *Judea was made his sanctuary, Israel his dominion.*

Facta est Iudaea sanctificatio eius, Israel potestas eius.

Therefore, it says: 113{114}[1] *In exitu Israel, when Israel went out,* that is, [when] the Christian people [went out], *de Aegypto, out of Egypt,* that is, from a worldly manner of living, *domus Iacob, the house of Jacob,* that is, the same people, *de populo barbaro, from a barbarous people,* that is, from the congregation of the reprobate—who are called barbarians because, as Augustine says, it is not our language, but a barbarous one, which does not know how to praise God.[50] In this departure, 113{114}[2] *Facta est Iudaea, Judea was made,* that is, a people confessing God (for Judea is interpreted as meaning "confession"), *sanctificatio eius, his sanctuary,* that is, a thing or a people sanctified by the Lord. For when we leave the world, changing our life, the grace of God, by which we are sanctified, is bestowed upon us. *Israel potestas eius, Israel is his dominion:* that is, in this departure—which is nothing other than an aversion of the mind from illicit things and its conversion to God—a contemplative man or people are made a mirror of the divine power, because the divine power is reflected in them, as if in a mirror, since it is a greater thing to justify a sinner than it is to create heaven. And so Israel is made his dominion, that is, the effect of the power of God. Or [we can understand it] thus: *Judea was made his sanctuary,* that is, one is sanctified by that confession through which one is cleansed. *Israel,* that is, in knowing God, contemplating the divine judgments by faith, and in every respect placing and examining oneself before God, one is made *his dominion,* that is, powerful in God, for by this he is made powerful to withstand all temptations.

113{114}[3] *The sea saw and fled: Jordan was turned back.*

Mare vidit, et fugit; Iordanis conversus est retrorsum.

---

50 *E. N.* The reference is to Augustine's *Commentary on the Psalms,* Psalm 113, 5, PL 37, 1478.

113{114}[4]   *The mountains exulted like rams, and the hills like the lambs of the flock.*[51]

Montes exsultaverunt ut arietes, et colles sicut agni ovium.

113{114}[3] *Mare, the sea,* that is, the restless, turbulent man, bitter with vice, of which is written in Isaiah: *The wicked are like the raging sea, which cannot rest.*[52] Therefore, this sea *vidit, saw* the foretold leaving of the elect from the darkness of vices, *et fugit, and fled,* that is, he did not wish to imitate them. For those who disdained conversion also departed from God. For this reason, the Lord said through Jeremiah: *They are gone far from me, and have walked after vanity, and are become vain.*[53] Also, in Proverbs is stated: *They leave the right way and walk by dark ways.*[54] The Jordan, that is, the humble man who judges himself — indeed, Jordan is interpreted to mean a descent or downflow of judgment, and so by it is designated a man who has descended from the height of pride to the depth of humility and regards himself as nothing. Here, therefore, the Jordan is seen as it is also the sea, but it does not flee, indeed *conversus est retrorsum, it was turned back,* that is, it has turned back from its beginning down an evil path, it has come back from its depraved habits, and it has turned toward the source of its salvation, namely, God. Pay heed in what way some persons become worse and flee from the good works of others, yet other persons are edified and make progress. And so the Apostle [Paul] says something similar about himself and his own [disciples]: *We are the good odor of Christ unto God, . . . to some indeed to odor unto life, but to others the odor unto death.*[55] And from this Jordan-like manner of living, 113{114}[4] *Montes, the mountains,* that is, the holy Apostles, elevated above the rest by their holiness, their wisdom, and their miraculous works, *exsultaverunt, exulted* in the Lord, giving him all thanks, *ut arietes, like rams* leading sheep into the sheepfold. And so John in his epistle professes: *I have no greater grace than this, to hear that my children walk in truth.*[56] And often Paul in his epistles asserts himself to glory indescribably in the conversion of the Gentiles.[57] Certainly as to a

---

51 E. N. I departed from the Douay Rheims's "skipped," and replaced it with "exulted." As will be seen in the subsequent *Commentary,* I could not envision, even metaphorically, the apostles "skipping."

52 Is. 57:20a.

53 Jer. 2:5b.

54 Prov. 2:13.

55 2 Cor. 2:15–16. E. N. Denis takes liberty with the quoted verse and rearranges it.

56 3 John 4.

57 Rom. 15:15–19; 2 Cor. 1:14; 1 Thess. 2:19–20.

good prelate nothing weighs so heavily as perversity and incorrigibility in his flock; so nothing gives him greater joy than when those under him make progress and amend their lives. *Et colles, and the hills,* that is, the inferior prelates, successors and imitators of the Apostles, exult for this reason in the Lord, not attributing anything to their own strength, *sicut agni ovium, like lambs of the flock.*

113{114}[5]   *What ailed you, O sea, that you did flee: and you, O Jordan, that you were turned back?*

Quid est tibi, mare, quod fugisti? Et tu, Iordanis, quia conversus es retrorsum?

113{114}[6]   *The mountains skipped like rams, and the hills like the lambs of the flock.*

Montes, exsultastis sicut arietes? Et colles sicut agni ovium?

113{114}[5] *Quid est tibi, mare; what ailed you, O sea,* that is, you worldly people, *quod fugisti, that you did flee* from God, not willing to convert? *Et tu, Iordanis; and you, O Jordan,* that is, the humble people, what ailed you, *quia conversus es retrorsum, that you were turned back,* ceasing from the evil in which you began? Of this, namely, that some have rightly converted, you, 113{114}[6] *O montes, exsultatis sicut arietes,* etc., *the mountains skipped like rams,* etc. It is as if it were saying: "What is the cause of this distinction: that one person is corrected but the other person becomes hardened?"

113{114}[7]   *At the presence of the Lord the earth was moved, at the presence of the God of Jacob.*

A facie Domini mota est terra, a facie Dei Jacob.

113{114}[8]   *Who turned the rock into pools of water, and the stony hill into fountains of waters.*

Qui convertit petram in stagna aquarum, et rupem in fontes aquarum.

And he responds: 113{114}[7] *A facie Domini mota est terra, at the presence of the Lord the earth was moved:* that is, this [distinction between those who convert to, and those who harden themselves against, God] occurs as a result of this divine presence: that one is mercifully touched by the Holy Spirit and makes amendment, and another is justly refused and made obstinate. For this reason, the Apostle cries out: *O the depth of the riches of the wisdom and of the knowledge of God! How incompre-hensible are his judgments, and how unsearchable his ways!*[58] And again: *See then the goodness and the severity of God: towards them indeed that are fallen, the severity; but towards you, the goodness of God, if you abide in goodness.*[59] **113{114}[8]** *Qui convertit petram, who turned the rock,* that is, hardened minds, *in stagna aquarum, into pools of water,* that is, bountiful tears, in that they weep for their own sins and those of others; and he who converts *et rupem, and the stony hill,* that is, the heart habituated in evil, *in fontes aquarum, into fountains of waters,* so that they copiously weep holy tears because of it. For as the Apostle [Paul] says, *Where sin abounded,* grace abounds more.[60] This can also be explained as referring to the Savior, of which we read: *The rock was Christ.*[61] He [Christ] is also called *the stony hill* because of the constancy of his mind in God. God converted this *rock,* and this *stony hill,* into *pools* and *fountains of water* when he delivered him over for all of us, so that *they have dug* his hands, feet, and side, from which flowed five most limpid fountains of sacred Blood, which are called water [here], not in a substantial sense, but because of their effect, because as water cleanses the body, so the Blood of Christ cleans the heart, according to that John states in Revelation: *He who has loved us, and washed us from our sins in his own blood.*[62]

113{114}[9]   *Not to us, O Lord, not to us; but to your name give glory.*

Non nobis, Domine, non nobis; sed nomini tuo da gloriam.

113{114}[10]   *For your mercy, and for your truth's sake: lest the Gentiles should say: Where is their God?*

Super misericordia tua et veritate tua; nequando dicant gentes: Ubi est Deus eorum?

Now of these your benefits, or our advancements [in virtue], which are the gifts of your goodness, **113{114}[9]** *Non nobis, Domine, non nobis, sed nomini tuo da gloriam; not to us, O Lord, not to us, but to your name give glory.* **113{114}[10]** *Super misericordia tua, for your mercy,* that is, for the grace by which we are kindly favored, *et veritate tua, and for your truth's sake* by which you kindly inform us, truly correct us, and teach us of your

---

58 Rom. 11:33.
59 Rom. 11:22.
60 *Cf.* Rom. 5:20b.
61 1 Cor. 10:4b.
62 Rev. 1:5.

law. *Nequando dicant gentes: Ubi est Deus eorum? Lest the Gentiles should say: Where is their God?* That is, that you might mercifully glorify your name in us, and magnificently save us, lest you be blasphemed by the ungodly saying that you either do not will to save or are unable to save.

113{114}[12][63] *The idols of the Gentiles are silver and gold, the works of the hands of men.*

Simulacra gentium argentum et aurum, opera manuum hominum.

113{114}[13] *They have mouths and speak not: they have eyes and see not.*

Os habent, et non loquentur; oculos habent, et non videbunt.

113{114}[14] *They have ears and hear not: they have noses and smell not.*

Aures habent, et non audient; nares habent, et non odorabunt.

113{114}[15] *They have hands and feel not: they have feet and walk not: neither shall they cry out through their throat.*

Manus habent, et non palpabunt; pedes habent, et non ambulabunt; non clamabunt in gutture suo.

113{114}[16] *Let them that make them become like unto them: and all such as trust in them.*

Similes illis fiant qui faciunt ea, et omnes qui confidunt in eis.

113{114}[12] *Simulacra, the idols,* that is, the gods and graven images, *gentium, of the Gentiles,* that is, those living bestial or criminal lives are *argentum et aurum, opera manuum hominum; silver and gold, the works of the hands of men,* that is, they are produced through human artifice. For avaricious men worship money as god. For this reason, the Apostle [Paul] says that *covetousness is the service of idols.*[64] Indeed, according to Augustine, every man's god is that which he most thinks about, loves, and cultivates. And therefore, the god and idol of the lustful man is a woman; of the gluttonous, the belly. But such men as these are far from those who are able to say with the holy Job: *If I have thought gold my strength, and have said to fine gold: My confidence.*[65] Whence the Apostle

---

63 *E. N.* Denis skips over Ps. 113:11.

64 Col. 3:5b.

65 Job 31:24. *E. N.* This is Job's scrutiny in his defense; in other words, he is responding to his friends that he might be justly judged guilty for his predicament had he

in his first epistle to Timothy says: *Charge the rich of this world not to be high-minded, nor to trust in the uncertainty of riches, but in the living God, who gives us abundantly all things to enjoy.*[66] But some, preoccupied in their imaginations and in their most vain fantasies, forsake God. And these men, whose idols, gods, and works are these, 113{114}[13] *os habent, et non loquentur, have mouths and speak not* saving things by praising God and confessing their own vices; *oculos habent, they have eyes* open to vain and worldly things, *et non videbunt, and see not* eternal and heavenly goods. 113{114}[14] *Aures habent, they have ears* focused on useless words, *et non audient, and hear not* the divine words through obedience; *nares habent, they have noses* to distinguish, *et non odorabunt, and smell not* the fragrance of a good life and the sweetness of virtue. 113{114}[15] *Manus habent, they have hands* stretching out towards doing vicious works, *et non palpabunt, and feel not*, that is, their fingers do not touch those things they proclaim so that they might perform the good that they teach and know; *pedes habent, they have feet* running towards evil things, *et non ambulabunt, and walk not* in the way of the commandments of God; *non clamabunt in gutture suo, neither shall they cry out through their throat*, resounding devoutly praises to the Creator. 113{114}[16] *Similis illis fiant qui faciunt ea, let them that make them become like unto them*: that is, let those who make idols or lead others to venerate them become like them in the evil of fault and punishment: *for not only they that do them, but they also that consent to*, or cooperate with, *them that do them ... are worthy of death*, according to the Apostle.[67]

Take heed how impious and ungrateful sinners misuse all the gifts of God, namely, the members of the body and the powers of the soul. For they use for the works of darkness those things that they ought to use in the service of God; they not only hide the talents that have been committed to them, but they iniquitously squander them.[68] For this reason, the Apostle exhorts the Romans: *As you have yielded your members to serve uncleanness and iniquity, unto iniquity; so now yield your members to serve justice, unto sanctification.*[69]

---

been guilty of making money the god in which he put his trust. The question is a rhetorical question which — in Job's case — demands a no.

66 1 Tim. 6:17.

67 Rom. 1:32. *E. N.* "[W]e have a responsibility for the sins committed by others when *we cooperate in them*: by participating directly and voluntarily in them; by ordering, advising, praising, or approving them; by not disclosing or not hindering them when we have an obligation to do so; and by protecting evil-doers." CCC § 1868.

68 *Cf.* Matt. 25:18.

69 Rom. 6:19.

113{114}[17] *The house of Israel has hoped in the Lord: he is their helper and their protector.*

Domus Israel speravit in Domino; adiutor eorum et protector eorum est.

113{114}[18] *The house of Aaron has hoped in the Lord: he is their helper and their protector.*

Domus Aaron speravit in Domino; adiutor eorum et protector eorum est.

113{114}[17] *Domus Israel, the house of Israel,* that is, the Church of Christ, lovingly contemplating God by faith, of which house the Apostle says to the Hebrews: *Christ as the Son in his own house: which house are we;*[70] *speravit in Domino, has hoped in the Lord,* knowing that it is written, *Blessed be the man that trusts in the Lord.*[71] Regarding this house, Christ says in Luke: *Fear not, little flock, for it has pleased your Father to give you a kingdom.*[72] *Adiutor eorum et protector eorum est, he is their helper and their protector.* For as we read in Matthew, Christ promised the Church: *I am with you all days, even to the consummation of the world.*[73] 113{114}[18] *Domus Aaron, the house of Aaron,* that is, the congregation of faithful priests: of which the Apostle states, *The priests that rule well, are worthy of double honor.*[74] And of these Isaiah says: *You shall be called the priests of the Lord: to you it shall be said: You are ministers of our God.*[75] *Speravit in Domino, has hoped in the Lord,* that with his help [the congregation of faithful priests] might live in a priestly way, and worthily preside over others. For the more they are bound to a more perfect life and are subject to graver danger if they find themselves unworthy, the more need they have to hope more firmly and completely in the Lord. But — most unfortunately! — we nowadays find many priests neither trusting in the Lord nor living priestly lives, but instead *hoarding up silver and gold, wherein men trust* and devoting themselves to venery. Of these, that which Jeremiah says is fitting: *The priests did not say: Where is the Lord? And they that held the law knew me not, and the pastors transgressed against me.*[76] Here also Ezechiel:

---

70 Heb. 3:6a.
71 Jer. 17:7a.
72 Luke 12:32.
73 Matt. 28:20b.
74 1 Tim. 5:17a.
75 Is. 61:6a.
76 Jer. 2:8.

The priests . . . have not distinguished between the polluted and the clean.[77] And we have seen fulfilled that which has been foretold by Isaiah and Hosea: *And it shall be as with the people, so with the priest.*[78] The rest of this Psalm is clear from the preceding article.

And so let us spiritually depart out of Egypt, making haste toward the heavenly fatherland, hating (according to the admonishment of the apostle Jude) *the spotted garment which is carnal.*[79] For, as Paul wrote to the Corinthians, *What fellowship has light with darkness? What concord has Christ with Belial? Or what part has the faithful with the unbeliever?* And so let us not join our souls together with idols of sensible things or images of transitory goods; but with a clean heart and mind adorned with speculative contemplation, let us strive to serve, to please, and to stand by the Lord, fulfilling that which is stated in Jude: *Build yourselves upon your most holy faith, praying in the Holy Ghost, keeping yourselves in the love of God, waiting for the mercy of our Lord Jesus Christ, unto live everlasting.*[80]

PRAYER

MOST POWERFUL GOD OF ALL CREATURES, who turns rock into pools of water, may the earth of our body be moved to repentance by your face, so that your name may be given glory for having mercifully saved us unto perpetual blessedness.

Fortissime Deus creaturarum, qui convertis petram in stagna
aquarum, a facie tua ad poenitentiam moveatur
corporis nostri terra, unde sit nomini tuo gloria
pro nobis misericorditer salvandis in
beatudine perpetua.

---

77 Ez. 22:26a.
78 Is. 24:2a; *cf.* Hosea 4:9a. E. N. "After God, the priest is everything! Leave a parish twenty years without a priest, and it will worship beasts." *Après Dieu, le prêtre, c'est tout! . . . Laissez une paroisse vingt ans sans prêtre, on y adorera les bêtes. Esprit du Curé d'Ars* (Paris: Ch. Douniol 1875), 120.
79 Jude 23.
80 Jude 20–21.

Psalm 114

ARTICLE XXIV

ELUCIDATION OF THE
ONE HUNDRED AND FOURTEENTH PSALM:
DILEXI, QUONIAM EXAUDIET DOMINUS.
I HAVE LOVED, BECAUSE THE LORD WILL HEAR.

114{115}[1] *Alleluia. I have loved, because the Lord will hear the voice of my prayer.*

Alleluia. Dilexi, quoniam exaudiet Dominus vocem orationis meae,

114{115}[2] *Because he has inclined his ear unto me: and in my days I will call upon him.*

Quia inclinavit aurem suam mihi, et in diebus meis invocabo.

HE TITLE OF THIS PSALM IS: *ALLELUIA*. BUT the Prophet [David] speaks in this Psalm in the person of any member of the faithful *sojourning to the Lord* in this evil age, which is the region of vices.[1] Such a man, therefore, giving thanks to God for his deliverance, in part already accomplished or beginning but ultimately to be completed, so begins: 114{115}[1] *Dilexi, I have loved* the highest Good, who alone is to be loved most fully in himself and because of himself. And he does not say what about him is to be loved, suggesting that God alone is to be loved for himself, and other things only in him. *Quoniam exaudiet Dominus vocem orationis meae, because the Lord will hear the voice of my prayer.* This is a word of good hope. For we ought to hope that God will not regard our prayers vain in all things, as long as we ask for that which we ought to seek; otherwise, that which James says applies to us: *You ask, and receive not; because you ask amiss.*[2] Now such a [wrong] petition neither truly nor properly is able to be called prayer, because prayer (according to the Damascene) is the petition to God for something befitting.[3] Now here he states himself to love God

---

1 2 Cor. 5:6.
2 James 4:3a.
3 E. N. A reference to St. John of Damascus's classic definition found in *De Fide Orthodoxa*, III, 24.

311

because of the benefit of being heard. For God is to be loved because of his benefits, and more than all other things the more we receive from him better and greater gifts. Indeed, God is to be loved more because of himself and his own goodness, which is truly pure and infinite. We ought therefore to love God greatly for both reasons together: and this conforms with that written in the epistle of John, *Let us therefore love God, because God first has loved us.*[4] Hence I trust that the Lord will hear me: 114{115}[2] *Quia inclinavit aurem suam mihi, because he has inclined his ear unto me,* that is, he has bestowed his mercy upon me asserting himself to be ready to aid those in need, to hear the miserable, and to save those that are imperiled. For this reason, *et in diebus meis, and in my days,* that is, all the days in which I subsist, and not only for an hour or for a short time, *invocabo, I will call upon,* that is, from an intimate affection of the heart I will pray to God: according to that which Christ stated in Luke, *We ought always to pray, and not to faint.*[5]

114{115}[3] *The sorrows of death have encompassed me: and the perils of hell have found me. I met with trouble and sorrow:*

Circumdederunt me dolores mortis; et pericula inferni invenerunt me. Tribulationem et dolorem inveni,

114{115}[4] *And I called upon the name of the Lord. O Lord, deliver my soul.*

Et nomen Domini invocavi: O Domine, libera animam meam.

114{115}[5] *The Lord is merciful and just, and our God shows mercy.*

Misericors Dominus et iustus, et Deus noster miseretur.

114{115}[6] *The Lord is the keeper of little ones: I was little and he delivered me.*

Custodiens parvulos Dominus; humiliatus sum, et liberavit me.

114{115}[3] *Circumdederunt me, they have encompassed me,* that is, they have completely and upon all sides attacked when placed in the middle of a snare, *dolores morti, the sorrows of death,* that is, the mortal punishments, the impetuous temptations, the inordinate affections which bring perpetual death to the soul unless the kindness of God saves it; *et pericula inferni, and the perils of hell,* that is, mortal sin, or at least an

---

4 1 John 4:19.
5 Luke 18:1b.

easy way towards it, *invenerunt me, have found me* when I have lost grace, consenting to malicious desires. Now mortal sin is here called the *perils of hell* because by it the soul is flung into hell and perishes in eternity. We can also understand the *sorrows of death* to mean the punishments that follow from original sin and are inflicted upon us because of it, such as the unavoidableness of sickness and death, the rebellion of the senses, and the other wounds of the soul. But the *perils of hell* are all those things which drag men down to spiritual destruction. These sorrows and these dangers were not unknown to blessed Job, who said: *The arrows of the Lord are in me, the rage whereof drinks up my spirit, and the terrors of the Lord war against me.*[6]

Tribulationem, trouble in the body *et dolorem, and sorrow* in the soul *inveni, I met with* by experience the same in the manner that the Apostle said: *Our flesh had no rest, but we suffered all tribulation; combats without, fears within;*[7] and: *We were pressed out of measure.*[8] Take stock how the elect of the living God are cleansed, hewn, and refined by the scourges of the present life, so that they might be fitting stones from which to build the walls of Jerusalem. And so in Proverbs it is written: *My son, reject not the correction of the Lord: and do not faint when you are chastised by him: for whom the Lord loves, he chastises, and as a father in the son, he pleases himself.*[9] Here the angel Raphael also told Tobias: *Because you were acceptable to God, it was necessary that temptation should prove you.*[10] Let us not, therefore, be broken by adversity; but the more evils that surround us, the more confidently and more fully can we hope to belong to the number of the elect and of his children. But let us pray unceasingly with unshakeable patience for grace, as it states next: **114{115}[4]** *et nomen Domini invocavi, and I called upon the name of the Lord,* that he might be with me by grace, and he might deliver me, if it is useful for my soul. Whence it is written: *I cried out of my affliction to the Lord, and he heard me. When my* spirit *was in distress, I remembered the Lord.*[11]

O Domine, libera animam meam; O Lord deliver my soul from all danger, for **114{115}[5]** *misericors Dominus, the Lord is merciful,* because you immediately forgive the penitent sinner; *et iustus, and just,* because you do not leave untouched any evil unpunished, and you have struck me

---

6 Job 6:4.
7 2 Cor. 7:5.
8 2 Cor. 1:8b.
9 Prov. 3:11–12.
10 Tob. 12:13.
11 Jonah2:3a, 8

with such punishments because of my sins. Whence Job said: *God does not suffer it to pass unrevenged.*[12] *Et Deus noster miseretur, and our God shows mercy*: as the book of Wisdom attests: *You have mercy upon all, because you can do all things, and overlook the sins of men for the sake of repentance.*[13] And in Joel: *Turn to the Lord your God: for he is gracious and merciful, patient and rich in mercy, and ready to repent of the evil.*[14] 114{115}[6] *Custodiens parvulos, the Lord is the keeper of the little ones,* that is, you graciously preserve the humble from sin. For he *resists the proud, but he gives grace to the humble.*[15] Hence we read in Proverbs: Wisdom *protects them that walk in simplicity,*[16] that is, humbly; and in Isaiah: The Lord is *high and sublime, inhabiting eternity, and his name is holy, who dwells in the high and holy place, and with a contrite and humble spirit, to revive the spirit of the humble, and to revive the heart of the contrite.*[17] *Humiliatus sum, I was little,* having descended from the mountain of pride, and doing that which Ecclesiasticus counsels: *The greater you are, the more humble yourself in all things;*[18] *et liberavit, and he delivered me* from the evil of many punishments and a variety of vices. For this reason, the divine word warns us in the first epistle of Peter: *Be you humbled therefore under the mighty hand of God, that he may exalt you in the time of visitation.*[19]

114{115}[7] *Turn, O my soul, into your rest: for the Lord has been bountiful to you.*

Convertere, anima mea, in requiem tuam, quia Dominus benefecit tibi.

114{115}[7] *Convertere, anima mea; turn, O my soul,* from turbulent thoughts, from superfluous concerns, from impetuous and disordered movements of passion and misdeeds, *in requiem tuam, into your rest,* that is, into internal peace, to contemplative repose, to mental steadfastness, to your own emptying-out, to security of conscience. And because no one has the power to do this unless it be in God, so, *turn, O my soul,* from these many things *into your rest,* namely, to the *one thing* that

---

12 Job 24:12b.
13 Wis. 11:24.
14 Joel 2:13.
15 James 4:6b.
16 Prov. 2:7b.
17 Is. 57:15.
18 Ecclus. 3:20a. E. N. The verse continues: *and you shall find grace before God.*
19 1 Pet. 5:6.

alone *is necessary*,[20] from creatures to the Creator, of which is written in Isaiah: *The Lord will give you rest continually, and will fill your soul with brightness*.[21] *Quia Dominus benefecit tibi, for the Lord has been bountiful to you*: that is, you ought rightly to convert to God, resting in him as the ultimate end and the highest good because of his kindness, who rescued you from evil, preserved you from danger, and filled you with grace. So that these benefits may be specified, there is added:

114{115}[8]   *For he has delivered my soul from death: my eyes from tears, my feet from falling.*

Quia eripuit animam meam de morte, oculos meos a lacrimis, pedes meos a lapsu.

114{115}[8] *Quia eripuit animam meam de morte, for he has delivered my soul from the death* of sin, in which it wallowed; and also of the death of hell, in which — but for the mercy of God — it would have found itself; *oculos meos a lacrimis, my eyes from tears*, that is, from the cause of weeping: for because he delivered it from sin, he removed the cause of weeping. Or [we might understand it thus], *from tears* which I pour out due to sins, and which give me the internal consolation of the hope of remission, and so reduce in me the sorrow and tears.[22] Or it may be seen better this way: *He has delivered . . . my eyes from tears*, which are wont to arise from cowardice, or inordinate sorrow, or from any irrational cause. It is expedient that these sorts of tears be taken away — but not those tears (unless it be for a time) that come from our recollection of sins or which arise from our desire for God and the heavenly fatherland, since these are a great gift of the Holy Spirit.[23] Now regarding the ceasing of these tears, Lord says through Jeremiah: *Let your voice cease from weeping, and your eyes from tears: for there is a*

---

20 Luke 10:42a.

21 Is. 58:11a.

22 *E. N.* The sequence *Veni Sancte Spiritus* speaks of *in fletu solatium*, of the solace in tears.

23 *E. N.* St. Julian of Norwich's advice to Margery Kempe: "[W]hen God visits a creature with tears of contrition, devotion, or compassion, he may and ought to believe that the Holy Ghost is in his soul. Saint Paul says that the Holy Ghost asks for us with mournings and weepings unspeakable; that is to say, He makes us ask and pray with mournings and weepings so plenteously that the tears may not be numbered. There may no evil spirit give these tokens, for Jerome says that tears torment the devil more than do the pains of hell." *The Book of Margery Kempe* (New York: Image, 1998).

reward for your work.[24] And of these tears, the Lord says in Matthew: *Blessed are they that mourn: for they shall be comforted.*[25] *Pedes meos, my feet,* that is, my affections, thoughts, and works, he has delivered *a lapsu, from falling,* that is, by the ruin of sin.

114{115}[9] *I will please the Lord in the land of the living.*

Placebo Domino in regione vivorum.

Here, therefore, so that I might hope: 114{115}[9] *Placebo Domino, I will please the Lord* fully and perfectly, *in regione vivorum, in the land of the living,* that is in the fatherland of the blessed who truly live in such a fashion that our life — when compared to theirs — can be called death rather than life. In this life — wherein the just man falls seven times a day,[26] in which *all our justices are as the rag of a menstruous woman*[27] — we are unable to please God perfectly, because he sees in us venial evils which by no means are pleasing to him, and in some cases are displeasing to him. But in the heavenly fatherland we shall please him perfectly, because no impurity will be in us, but we will be similar to him, by reason of perfect purity.[28]

N A SPECIAL WAY THREE [PORTIONS] OF these verses [Psalm 114:7–8] are fittingly used by a devout man at the point of death (*in extremis*), who, seeing death to be already close by, can speak to his own soul saying: 114{115}[7] *Turn, O my soul, from the body of this death,*[29] from the pressures of the present, from the burden of this exile, *into your rest,* that is, into the heavenly paradise, into eternal life, *quia Dominus benefecit tibi, for the Lord has been bountiful to you* in this life by grace. And so return to your Creator by your fervent love, so that he might bestow the benefit of glory. For regarding this rest, one can obtain what the Lord has attested through Isaiah: It will be *security for ever; and my people shall sit in the beauty of peace, and in the tabernacles of confidence, and in wealthy rest.*[30] 114{115}[8] *For he has delivered my soul from death:* as has already been explained. Or this is

---

24 Jer. 31:16a.
25 Matt. 5:5.
26 *Cf.* Prov. 24:16a.
27 Is. 64:6a.
28 *Cf.* 1 John 3:2.
29 Rom. 7:24b.
30 Is. 32:17b–18.

said because Christ by his blood delivered our souls from eternal death, about which is written in Revelation: *He that shall overcome, shall not be hurt by the second death.*[31] *[He has delivered] my eyes from tears* which I would have had in hell, in which there *will be weeping and gnashing of teeth,* had not Christ delivered me; *[he has delivered] my feet from falling,* because he confirmed my promises and works in him.

See this Psalm of brief sentences is decorated with great fullness. In it we are beautifully instructed on what we ought to do when confronting adversity, where we ought to fasten our intention and desires, reflecting succinctly upon the benefits of God while in it. For good reason, this Psalm is at the head of the Office of the Dead, for many things are said in it which are said in the person of the dead or may be said for the dead themselves. For the dead (for whom we pray) who are in Purgatory love God, and they know they will be delivered from their torment, yet for which deliverance they are not able to pray with meritorious prayers, even though they inestimably desire it.[32] And so they are certain they will never be damned — a matter of which (sadly!) we are not certain [as to ourselves].[33] For this reason it is necessary for us *to walk solicitous with* our *God with fear,*[34] and to fulfill that which the Apostle states: with apprehension and *with fear and trembling to work out* our *salvation.*[35] For this reason, the holy Job says: *I have always feared God as waves swelling over me.*[36] And this is nothing to be marveled at, since none of us knows, whether *he be worthy of love or hatred.*[37]

---

31 Rev. 2:11b.

32 "It is at least probable that the souls in purgatory cannot pray for themselves or for us." Joseph C. Fenton, *The Theology of Prayer* (Milwaukee: Bruce Publishing, 1939), 145. "Those who are in purgatory even though they are superior to us because of impeccability, yet they are inferior to us as to the punishments which they suffer. And according to this, they are not in a state to pray, but rather a state where we must pray for them." ST IIaIIae, q. 83, art. 11, ad 3.

33 "[O]f the gift of perseverance, . . . [l]et no one promise himself any security about this gift with absolute certitude, although all should place their firmest hope in God's help. . . . Yet let anyone who thinks that he stands take heed lest he fall, and let him work out his salvation with fear and trembling in labors, in vigils, in almsgiving, in prayers and offerings, in fastings and chastity. Knowing that they are reborn unto the hope of glory and not yet unto glory, they should be dread about the battle they still have to wage with the flesh, the world, and the devil." DS 1541 (Council of Trent, Decree on Justification).

34 Micah 6:8b.

35 Phil. 2:12.

36 Job 31:23a.

37 Eccl. 9:1b.

PRAYER

O GOD OF HEAVEN AND EARTH, KINDLY receive the voice of the prayers of those who love you, incline the ear of your mercy to the prayers of those who call upon you: deliver us from all tribulation and sorrow, and grant us eternal goods when we pass out of this life.

Deus caeli et terrae, vocem orationis te diligentium benignus admitte, aurem clementiae precibus te invocantium inclina: ab omni tribulatione et dolore nos libera, et ab hac transeuntibus vita, redde nobis bona sempiterna.

Psalm 115

ARTICLE XXV

ELUCIDATION OF THE
ONE HUNDRED AND FIFTEENTH PSALM:
CREDIDI, PROPTER QUOD.
I HAVE BELIEVED, THEREFORE.

115{116}[10] *Alleluia. I have believed, therefore have I spoken; but I have been humbled exceedingly.*

Alleluia. Credidi, propter quod locutus sum; ego autem humiliatus sum nimis.

THIS PSALM, LIKE THE LAST ONE, ALSO HAS the title: **115{116}[10]** *Alleluia.* And just like some expound the preceding Psalm literally of David confronting the persecution of Saul, so that in that Psalm he pleads to be delivered from this unjust persecution, so in the present Psalm they expound it literally of David facing the persecution of Absalom, his son, so that the first verse is understood in this sense: *Credidi, I have believed* Ziba telling me the lying words of his lord, Mephibosheth: *propter quod locutus sum, therefore have I spoken* to Ziba: All that belonged to your lord, are yours;[1] *ego autem humiliatus sum, but I have been humbled,* that is, disdained and reproached, *nimis, exceedingly,* for on account of Absalom I have had to entertain fleeing. In accordance with this exposition, David speaks here of his evil, hasty, and deceptive credulity (for he believed a great detractor without due questioning), and from these unjust words, which he believed, he bestowed to Ziba all the goods of a godly man, namely Mephibosheth. But this exposition does not seem to be consonant with the exposition or the assertions of the apostle Paul, who full of the Holy Spirit, and knowing fully the mind of David, asserts these words in the second epistle to the Corinthians, as words of a sound belief in the holy faith and the holy confession of truth to be believed, of which he says to the Romans: *With the heart, we believe unto justice, but with the mouth, confession is made unto salvation.*[2] For he asserts this present verse in

---

1 2 Sam. 16:3–4.
2 Rom. 10:10.

319

this manner: *As it is written: I believed, for which cause I have spoken; we also believe, for which cause we speak also.*[3] Whence, it is certain that the Apostle intimates this scripture to speak literally of a good belief and a salutary speaking. And so David did not write this Psalm of himself in the previously-mentioned sense. It must be said, therefore, that the topic of this Psalm is the constancy of the faithful, and especially of the holy martyrs, in faith and the public profession of the faith. Speaking in those persons, the Prophet [David] says: *Credidi, I have believed* all those things that the Catholic Faith asserts must be believed; *propter quod locutus sum, therefore have I spoken* publicly confessing before the infidel and the tyrant, or any other person whatsoever, those things that I believe. Now first something must be believed, and then it must be followed by a true confession, which originates from faith. For in certain cases, one does not suffice without the other. For it is certain that speech or confession without faith is insufficient, since *the just man lives by faith.*[4] But it is also necessary to confess the faith before men when there is a reasonable cause to do so, namely, so that another person not be scandalized, or so that God not be blasphemed, as is clear from what Christ said: *He that is ashamed of me and my words, of him the Son of Man shall be ashamed* when he comes into his kingdom.[5] And the Apostle [Paul] says to Timothy: *Be not ashamed of the testimony of our Lord* Jesus Christ.[6] The martyrs fulfilled this most eminently. But we also believe in the peace of the Church, and we speak and confess the things we believe to our neighbors. *Ego autem, but I* because of the true faith and the holy confession of it, *humiliatus sum, have been humbled,* that is, vexed, disdained, and endured suffering, *nimis, exceedingly* by the adversaries of truth: in the manner Christ stated in the Gospel, *In the world you shall have distress;*[7] and again, *You shall be hated by all men for my name's sake.*[8] Or [an alternative exposition], *I have been humbled exceedingly,* that is, I have not become haughty from the true faith and constant confession, nor have I ascribed to myself any strength to do good, but I have humbled myself most profoundly before God, and therefore I have deserved to be preserved by him.

---

3 2 Cor. 4:13.
4 Rom. 1:17b.
5 Luke 9:26a.
6 2 Tim. 1:8a.
7 John 16:33a.
8 Matt. 10:22a.

115{116}[11] *I said in my excess: Every man is a liar.*

Ego dixi in excessu meo: Omnis homo mendax.

115{116}[11] *Ego dixi in excessu meo, I said in my excess,* that is, in consideration of sublime or in ecstatic contemplation, wherein I examined the difference between the divine essence and human nature: *Omnis homo mendax, every man is a liar,* that is, in comparing himself to God and in considering himself every man *is a liar,* in word and or in deed, or in patience, or by comparison: so that as God is being and truth, so man is nothing and a liar—if one refers back to the truth and the divine essence. Therefore, every man is said to be a liar not out of the habit of falsity, but because sometimes he lies in word or in act, speaking or acting in a manner that is not right, not just, not true, and as a consequence in a lying and crooked way. Whence the Apostle writes to the Romans: *But God is true; and every man a liar.*[9] And in Jeremiah it is stated to God: To you the Gentiles shall come from the ends of the earth and shall say: *Surely our fathers have possessed lies, a vanity which has not profited them.*[10] For one thing is the truth of life, and another thing is the truth of being, and yet another thing is the truth of a proposition. Again, the truth of life is one thing, the truth of doctrine another thing, and the truth of justice yet another thing.[11] Similarly, the lie of life—which it seems might be called simulation or injustice—is one thing; and the lie of being, such as when we say, "This is false and counterfeit gold," is another thing; and the lie of speech is yet another thing. And this is certain: that every man in pilgrimage is in one of these ways *a liar,* since *there is no . . . man upon earth that does good and does not sin,* as Ecclesiastes states.[12] Indeed, James testifies, *In many things we all offend.*[13] Or [alternatively], it is said that every man to the degree he is a liar, in other words, is unstable, weak, and disposed to sins.

---

9 Rom. 3:4a.

10 Jer. 16:19b.

11 E. N. This tripartite division is attributed by St. Thomas to St. Jerome, though its origin is unknown. *See* ST IIaIIae, q. 109, art. 3, obj. 3 & ad 3. The *veritas vitae,* the truth of life, arises when one lives or attains its rule or measure (the natural law or the divine law). The *veritas iustitiae,* the truth of justice, refers to the truth of living by the natural or divine law as it relates to relationship with other men (giving them their due). The *veritas doctrinae,* the truth of doctrine or teaching, consists of truths related to knowledge (*scientia*).

12 Eccl. 7:21.

13 James 3:2a.

115{116}[12]   *What shall I render to the Lord, for all the things he has rendered unto me?*

Quid retribuam Domino pro omnibus quae retribuit mihi?

Since, therefore, every man in himself is a liar, but I am true by the grace of God, so **115{116}[12]** *Quid retribuam Domino, what shall I render to the Lord*, that is, with what worthy thing shall I repay him, what recompense shall I return to him, *pro omnibus quae retribuit mihi, for all the things he has rendered unto me*, that is, for all the gifts of his grace, which he has so often bestowed upon me? For he gave these to me in the first parents, and by their sin I have lost them. Again he gave them to me in Baptism, but sinning once more, I lost the gifts of the grace of God; but he in the Sacrament of Penance restored them to me. Who, therefore, can number or express all the general and special, natural and gratuitous benefits of God? He created all things because of us, and then deputed and dispatched the holy angels to guard us. At length, he himself came to us, and *he was seen upon earth, and conversed with men*, he nourished with his Body and Blood, and he deigned to die for us.[14] This verse should be said with great devotion so that we might pray with all our soul to be thankful to God, bringing to mind and frequently recalling his benefits, and humbly praising the Lord for these, fervently loving and reverently worship him for them.

115{116}[13]   *I will take the chalice of salvation; and I will call upon the name of the Lord.*

Calicem salutaris accipiam, et nomen Domini invocabo.

But because God has no need for our goods,[15] as Scripture affirms in the first book of Chronicles, *All things are yours, O Lord, and we have given to you what we received of your hand*,[16] therefore, I am not able to repay him with anything more worthy than to follow his path, and to offer myself to him, accepting suffering and death or other difficult things willingly for the sake of his love — as it states in what follows: **115{116}[13]** *Calicem salutaris, the chalice of salvation*, that is, salvific suffering, persecution, or death, that is, [the chalice] by which I attain salvation — for through the chalice [of suffering] we come to glory; *accipiam, I will take*, that is, I will carry with equanimity. Or [an alternative

---

14 Baruch 3:38.
15 *Cf.* Ps. 15:2b.
16 1 Chr. 29:14.

interpretation is]: *the chalice of salvation*, that is, carrying daily my cross, and following Christ, I will take up a penitential life, apply strict chastisements upon myself, and undertake daily mortification. For, as the Apostle said to the Romans, *If by the Spirit you mortify the deeds of the flesh, you shall live.*[17] *Et nomen Domini invocabo, and I will call upon the name of the Lord*, lest I be found wanting in adversity or begin to hope in my own merits, or attribute anything to myself.

115{116}[14] *I will pay my vows to the Lord before all his people.*

Vota mea Domino reddam coram omni populo eius.

115{116}[14] *Vota mea*, my vows, that is, my desires, *Domino reddam, I will pay . . . to the Lord*, desiring nothing disordered or contrary to God, but acquiring heavenly goods and praying for them, *coram omni opulo eius, before all his people*, his faithful people present, so that they also may pay to the Lord their desires, and that they might desire heavenlty things through my example. Or [alternatively]: *I will pay my vows to the Lord*, that is I will fulfill my promises to the praise of the Lord, according to this in Ecclesiastes: *If you have vowed anything to God, defer not to pay it: for an unfaithful and foolish promise displeases him.*[18] And Jonah said: *I will pay whatsoever I have vowed for my salvation to the Lord.*[19] In Baptism we promised to renounce all the pomps and deeds of Satan; in our religious profession we promised poverty, chastity, and obedience; and if only we would resolve to pay both these vows to the Lord! Pay to the Lord, therefore, these vows not only secretly, but before all the people, not for vainglory, but to the honor of God and the edification of one's neighbor, as I apply that stated in Matthew: *So let your light shine before men, that they may see your good works, and glorify your Father who is in heaven.*[20]

115{116}[15] *Precious in the sight of the Lord is the death of his saints.*

Pretiosa in conspectu Domini mors sanctorum eius.

115{116}[15] *Pretiosa in conspectu Domini mors sanctorum eius, precious in the sight of the Lord is the death of his saints*: that is, the leaving of the perfect man [from this earthly life] is worthy and approved before

17 Rom. 8:13b.
18 Eccl. 5:3.
19 Jonah 2:10.
20 Matt. 5:16.

God because this death is the threshold of eternal life. But [worldly] men regard lightly the death or killing of the Saints; but God judges them worthy of receiving the eternal reward. Indeed, this is stated by Isaiah: *The just perishes, and no man lays it to heart, and men of mercy are taken away, because there is none that understands.*[21] And in the book of Wisdom: *The just man, if he be prevented with death, shall be in rest.*[22]

115{116}[16]   *O Lord, for I am your servant: I am your servant, and the son of your handmaid. You have broken my bonds.*

O Domine, quia ego servus tuus; ego servus tuus, et filius ancillae tuae. Dirupisti vincula mea.

115{116}[16] *O Domine, O Lord,* rightly do I call you Lord, *quia ego servus tuus, for I am your servant,* being obedient and believing in you, *ego servus tuus, I am your servant* in all my doings, *et filius ancillae tuae, and the son of your handmaid,* that is, born of a faithful mother who worshipped you; or the son of your handmaid, that is, of the Church ministering to you. *Dirupisti vincula mea, you have broken my bonds,* that is, the evil customs and the vicious works which restrain a man so that he cannot freely advance toward the service of God. For these things bind and hold captive the sinner under the power of the devil. God breaks these fetters that are within us when he forgives sins, pours forth his grace, and makes us adopted sons out of the servants of sin. For this reason, the Apostle says: *God has sent the Spirit of his Son into your hearts, crying: Abba, Father.*[23] Or [alternatively], *You have broken my bonds,* that is, all impediments which impede from your contemplation, namely, the penalties and the ensnaring nature of sin. God does not accomplish this perfectly, unless it be in the death of the perfect man who departs to heaven, especially if they are martyrs. For although others are holy, and effect great miracles, yet they do not go to the Lord as securely, but their consciences tremble according to Jerome; and this can be taken as a general rule.[24] Yet some, even though

---

21 Is. 57:1.

22 Wis. 4:7. *E. N.* In this context word "prevented," which translates *praeoccupatus,* means to die sooner than expected or anticipated.

23 Gal. 4:6.

24 *E. N.* Denis refers here to a tractate on Psalm 115, attributed to St. Jerome, which observes that any saint — regardless of the good works, miracles, and exorcisms he might effect — does not go to the Lord upon death with an absolutely secure conscience: *horrescit eius conscientia quando videt Dominum* — he is horrified by his conscience when he sees the Lord. But a martyr — even one who has sinned after

they were not martyrs, through a special revelation given to them, were assured of their salvation, indeed even of their flying [past purgatory and straight into heaven].

115{116}[17]   *I will sacrifice to you the sacrifice of praise, and I will call upon the name of the Lord.*

Tibi sacrificabo hostiam laudis, et nomen Domini invocabo.

115{116}[18]   *I will pay my vows to the Lord in the sight of all his people.*

Vota mea Domino reddam in conspectu omnis populi eius.

115{116}[19]   *In the courts of the house of the Lord, in the midst of you, O Jerusalem.*

In atriis domus Domini, in medio tui, Ierusalem.

115{116}[17] *Tibi sacrificabo hostiam laudis, I will sacrifice to you the sacrifice of praise:* that is, I will praise you for these benefits, and I will offer to you myself or all things whatsoever that I have received from you in your praise, in the way that is written: *But I with the voice of praise will sacrifice to you;*[25] and again: *What shall I offer to the Lord that is worthy? I shall kneel before the high God.*[26] *Et nomen Domini invocabo, and I will call upon the name of the Lord,* that is, for the preservation of, or the advance in, all good. O how great is the power of this verse! 115{116}[18] *Vota mea Domino reddam in conspectus omnis populi eius, I will pay my vows to the Lord in the sight of all his people:* as will now be expounded upon; 115{116}[19], *in atriis domus Domini* that is, in the place of the Church, which is the *house of prayer,*[27] *in medio tui, Ierusalem, in the midst of you, O Jerusalem,* that is, in the midst of the universal Church, spread throughout the whole world, so that I might persevere in ecclesiastical unity and the Catholic faith, avoiding the scissures of heretics, for sometimes by Jerusalem is signified the faithful soul and the Church militant.

---

his baptism — goes to the Lord with all security of conscience. *Anecdota Maredsolana: Sancti Hieronymi Commentarioli in Psalmos* (Mardesoli: J. Parker, 1895), Vol, III, part 1, 218.

25 Jonah 2:10a.

26 Malachi 6:6.

27 Matt. 21:13.

ARTICLE XXVI

EXPOSITION OF THE SAME
ONE HUNDRED AND FIFTEENTH PSALM OF CHRIST,
AND HOW IT IS TO BE SAID BY
THE CELEBRATING PRIEST.

115{116}[10]   *I have believed, therefore have I spoken; but I have been humbled exceedingly.*

Credidi, propter quod locutus sum; ego autem humiliatus sum nimis.

115{116}[11]   *I said in my excess: Every man is a liar.*

Ego dixi in excessu meo: Omnis homo mendax.

LL THE WORDS OF THIS PSALM STATED ABOVE can be satisfactorily and fittingly understood as applying to Christ, except for the first word, which says, *Credidi, I have believed.* For since Christ from the beginning of the creation of his soul was a comprehensor, it was not fitting for him to have faith, which is a theological virtue: but in the same manner that earlier Christ is said to hope or have hope—not hope as a theological virtue, but insofar as he expected to receive some future good—so the act of belief can be attributed to Christ by taking this act as some knowledge of the faith. For as sometimes Scripture understands "to know" to mean "to believe," as when holy Job says, *I know that my Redeemer lives, and in the last day I shall rise out of the earth* (for the future resurrection is not known except by faith); so also sometimes to the contrary, Scripture takes "to believe" to mean "I know." And so [understood in this manner], it is fittingly applied to Christ, of whom this Psalm can be expounded in this way:

115{116}[10] *Credidi, I have believed,* that is, I have harbored no doubt of those truths which God has revealed to me (as man); *propter quod locutus sum, therefore I have spoken* the doctrine of the evangelical law, asserting myself to be the Christ, and expressing the testimony of the truth: as I stated in the Gospel: *For this came I into the world; that I should give testimony to the truth.*[28] *Ego autem humiliatus sum nimis, but I have been humbled exceedingly* by the Jews, who held me in contempt, blasphemed me, and killed me in a most disgraceful and most bitter death. Whence it is written in Isaiah: *We have thought him as it were a*

---

28 John 18:37b.

leper, and as one struck by God and afflicted.[29] Or [we can understand it thus], *I have been humbled exceedingly*, that is, in accord with what I said in Matthew — *Learn of me, because I am meek, and humble of heart* — I was humbled in my own body;[30] and elsewhere, *I seek not my own glory.*[31] **115{116}[11]** *Ego dixi in excessu meo, I said in my excess,* that is, in the contemplation wherein I saw God by sight: *Omnis homo, every man,* other than me, *mendax, is a liar:* as has been fully discussed in the preceding article. And because I said this, I knew that all men needed to be delivered by me, as the Apostle confessed: *For all have sinned, and do need the glory of God.*[32] It is stated in Micah in this way: *The holy man is perished out of the earth, and there is none upright among men.*[33]

115{116}[12]   *What shall I render to the Lord, for all the things he has rendered unto me?*

         Quid retribuam Domino pro omnibus quae retribuit mihi?

115{116}[13]   *I will take the chalice of salvation; and I will call upon the name of the Lord.*

         Calicem salutaris accipiam, et nomen Domini invocabo.

115{116}[14]   *I will pay my vows to the Lord before all his people.*

         Vota mea Domino reddam coram omni populo eius.

    115{116}[12] *Quid retribuam Domino pro omnibus quae retribuit mihi, what shall I render to the Lord, for all the things he has rendered to me,* that is, for the incomparable graces that he has bestowed upon me? *For God does not give the Spirit by measure,*[34] and without any previous merit he assumed my humanity unto his divine being, the Word of God, indeed he gave more to me than the entirety of the universe. As Christ was most grateful to God, so he said this in a most affectionate way. And he responded: **115{116}[13]** *Calicem salutaris accipiam, I will take the chalice of salvation:* that is, I will endure the saving Passion and the death which would give life to the world, so that I might recover the honor of God, dying for all men, so that they may be brought back to God. This is what Christ said at the beginning of his Passion: *The chalice which my Father has given me,*

---

29 Is. 53:4b.
30 Matt. 11:29.
31 John 8:50a.
32 Rom. 3:23.
33 Micah 7:2.
34 John 3:34b.

shall I not drink it?[35] And elsewhere: *My Father, if this chalice may not pass away, but I must drink it, your will be done.*[36] And to the sons of Zebedee: *Can you drink the chalice that I shall drink?*[37] *Et nomen Domini invocabo, and I will call upon the name of the Lord.* Christ frequently called upon the Father. Whence it is written: Jesus *passed the whole night in the prayer of God.*[38] He prayed at the instance of his Passion in the manner that the Apostle stated to the Hebrews: Jesus *with a strong cry and tears offered up prayers and supplications to him that was able to save him from death, and he was heard for his reverence.*[39] **115{116}[14]** *Vota mea Domino reddam, I will pay my vows to the Lord,* that is, I will offer to God my desires, by praying and teaching for his honor and the salvation of the world, *coram omni populo eius, before all his people* that were present. For Christ said before his disciples and the Jews in John: *I honor my Father.*[40] And suspended upon the Cross, he prayed: *Father forgive them.*[41]

115{116}[15]   *Precious in the sight of the Lord is the death of his saints.*

Pretiosa in conspectu Domini mors sanctorum eius.

115{116}[15] *Pretiosa in conspectu Domini mors sanctorum eius; precious in the sight of the Lord is the death of his saints.* This is what Christ said in the Gospel: *A hair of your head shall not perish;*[42] and again, *Fear not them that kill the body.*[43] It is as if it were saying: Your death shall be as precious to the Lord to the extent that you suffer for his name, so that you ought rightly to desire it.

115{116}[16]   *O Lord, for I am your servant: I am your servant, and the son of your handmaid. You have broken my bonds.*

O Domine, quia ego servus tuus; ego servus tuus, et filius ancillae tuae. Dirupisti vincula mea.

115{116}[17]   *I will sacrifice to you the sacrifice of praise, and I will call upon the name of the Lord.*

Tibi sacrificabo hostiam laudis, et nomen Domini invocabo.

---

35 John 18:11b.
36 Matt. 26:42b.
37 Matt. 20:22.
38 Luke 6:12b.
39 Heb. 5:7.
40 John 8:49b.
41 Luke 23:34. E. N. Denis's text states *Pater, ignosce illis,* whereas the Sixto-Clementine Vulgate has *Pater, dimitte illis.*
42 Luke 21:18.
43 Matt. 10:28a.

115{116}[18] *I will pay my vows to the Lord in the sight of all his people.*

Vota mea Domino reddam in conspectu omnis populi eius.

115{116}[19] *In the courts of the house of the Lord, in the midst of you, O Jerusalem.*

In atriis domus Domini, in medio tui, Ierusalem.

115{116}[16] *O Domine, quia ego servus tuus; O Lord, for I am your servant,* as man. Whence I said: *The Father is greater than I*; and: *As the Father has given me commandment, so do I*;[44] and also in Isaiah: *The Lord, that formed me from the womb to be his servant.*[45] And the Lord said of me: *Behold, I will bring my servant the Orient.*[46] *Ego servus tuus et filius ancillae tuae, I am your servant, and the son of your handmaid,* namely, of the blessed Virgin, who said: *Behold the handmaid of the Lord.*[47] *Dirupisti vincula mea, you have broken my bonds*: that is, you have removed from me passibility and all natural defects which I had assumed, resurrecting me in a glorious body. Or [we can look at it thus], *you have broken my bonds*: that is, you have permitted my body and my bodily members during the time of the Passion to be torn, wounded, and lacerated, so that *from the sole of the foot unto the top of the head there was no soundness in me.*[48] **115{116}[17]** *Tibi sacrificabo hostiam laudis, I will sacrifice to you the sacrifice of praise,* that is, I will offer myself upon the Cross to your glory for human redemption: in the way that the Apostle stated to the Hebrews: Christ *by the Holy Spirit offered himself unspotted unto God.*[49] **115{116}[18]** *Vota mea Domino reddam in conspectus omnis populi eius; I will pay my vows to the Lord in the sight of all his people*: as has already been made clear; **115{116}[19]** *in atriis domus Domini, in medio tui, Ierusalem; in the courts of the house of the Lord, in the midst of you, O Jerusalem.* Christ literally prayed and preached in the temple of

---

44 John 14:28, 31.

45 Is. 49:5a.

46 Zech. 3:8. E. N. Denis expounds on this verse in his *Commentary on Zechariah*: "*Behold, I will bring my servant the Orient,* that is, Christ, who is the *brightness of his glory* [Heb. 1:3], the *brightness of eternal light* [Wis. 7:26]: of whom the Gospel states, *the Orient from on high has visited us* [Luke 1:78]. For this Orient is the fountain of universal light, begotten in eternity by the superlatively most splendid Father, in the manner that is revealed in Ecclesiasticus: *I came out of the mouth of the most High, the first born of all creatures; I made that in the heavens there should rise light that never fails.* [Ecclus. 24:5–6]." Doctoris Ecstatici D. Dionysii Cartusiani, *Opera Omnia*, Vol. 10 (Montreuil: 1900), 632.

47 Luke 1:38a.

48 Is. 1:6a.

49 Heb. 9:14a.

God which was in Jerusalem, as was predicted in Malachi: *And presently the Lord, whom you seek, and the angel of the testament, whom you desire, shall come to his temple.*[50]

INALLY, SINCE THIS PSALM IS ONE OF THOSE that the priest customarily recites before the celebration of Mass, how the sense of this Psalm should be understood as it relates to the holy office of the Mass and the Sacrament of the Altar ought to be briefly touched upon. The faithful and most devout priest of Christ says, therefore:

115{116}[10] *Credidi, I have believed,* that is, I have most firmly held and will hold and presently hold, that Christ is fully in this Sacrament, in the way that he himself attested and is professed by the Church; *propter quod locutus sum, thefore I have spoken* my confession and my sermon to the people, or done other good things that pertain to this faith, and I have prepared myself for this great office [of offering Mass]. *Ego autem humiliatus sum nimis, but I have been humbled exceedingly,* that is, I account and hold myself to be entirely unworthy to approach the altar of Christ, and to offer such a divine sacrifice, which worthiness, in consideration of the dignity of the Sacrament, I would not possess even if I had all the virtues and merits possible in the world. **115{116}[11]** *Ego dixi in excessu meo, I said in my excess,* that is, deeply considering those things that ought to be weighed regarding this Sacrament: *Omnis homo mendax, every man is a liar,* that is, no man is truly worthy to consecrate or to consume it, because all are weak and fallen.

115{116}[12] *Quid retribuam Domino pro omnibus quae retribuit mihi; what shall I render to the Lord for all the things he has rendered to me,* especially for the Holy Communion of his Body and Blood? **115{116}[13]** *Calicem salutaris, the chalice of salvation,* that is, the chalice of the Savior, in which his Blood is consecrated and is contained, *accipiam, I*

---

50 Mal. 3:1. *E. N.* In his *Commentary on Malachi,* Denis points out that the "angel" who "shall prepare the way before my face" (which precedes the quoted verses) refers to Christ's precursor, St. John the Baptist. With respect to Christ: "*And presently after the birth of John, the Lord (Dominator), whom you seek,* that is, Christ, the King of kings and the Lord of all, whose coming all devout and good enlightened men desired from the beginning of the world." "*And the angel of the testament (angelus testamenti), who you desire,* that is, Christ, the Angel of great counsel [Is. 9:6 (LXX)], to whom, insofar as he is mediator of God and man, God the Father or the most blessed Trinity gave and bestowed a New Testament." Doctoris Ecstatici D. Dionysii Cartusiani, *Opera Omnia,* Vol. 10 (Montreuil: 1900), 704–05.

will take into my hands at the altar; *et nomen Domini invocabo, and I will call upon the name of the Lord,* praying for myself and for others, for the living and the dead, and for all the reasons the Church has established or which are incumbent upon me. **115{116}[14]** *Vota mea, my vows,* that is, my desires, *Domino reddam coram omni populo eius, I will pay . . . to the Lord before all his people,* that is, before all those surrounding me, offering, for all those present, my vows and prayers to God. **115{116} [16]** *Dirupisti vincula mea, you have broken my bonds,* O Christ, that is, you have washed away my sins with your most precious Blood: indeed, daily you rent asunder the shackles of my vices through the most saving sacrifice of your Body and Blood.[51] **115{116}[17]** *Tibi, to you,* O God the Father or the superlatively blessed Trinity, *sacrificabo hostiam laudis, I will sacrifice to you the sacrifice of praise,* offering the Body and the Blood of the Savior to your praise, by which oblation praise, honor, and glory is rendered to you. The rest [of the Psalm] is clear.

Now we have heard this worthy Psalm filled with truly ineffable praise, at whose beginning the devout man and unconquerable martyr acknowledges the true faith and holy confession; and then, with respect to the divine truth, it considers all men to be liars; above all, it is concerned lest one ever find himself ungrateful to God, and in bringing forth many good works to the glory of the Creator, lest one be found ungrateful. It befits us, therefore, to sing with special devotion this Psalm that is so sweet, so decorous, and so full of meaning so that we might deserve to partake in its virtue.

PRAYER

RECEIVE, O LORD, THE PRAYERS OF THE people who believe in you, and grant us always to offer to you the sacrifice of praise: break the bonds of our sins so that we might worthily pay to you the vows of the Christian faith.

Preces populi in te credentis, Domine, suscipe, et concede nos
sacrificium laudis tibi semper offerre: dirumpe peccatorum
nostrorum vincula, ut tibi digne reddamus fidei
christianae vota.

---

51 E. N. Denis skips verse 15, and a portion of verse 16.

Psalm 116

ARTICLE XXVII

DECLARATION OF THE
ONE HUNDRED AND SIXTEENTH PSALM:
LAUDATE DOMINUM, OMNES.
O PRAISE THE LORD, ALL.

116{117}[1] *Alleluia. O praise the Lord, all you nations: praise him, all you people.*

Alleluia. Laudate Dominum, omnes gentes, laudate eum, omnes populi.

116{117}[2] *For his mercy is confirmed upon us: and the truth of the Lord remains forever.*

Quoniam confirmata est super nos misericordia eius, et veritas Domini manet in aeternum.

NOW THE TITLE OF THIS PRESENT PSALM IS: 116{117}[1] *Alleluia* because the Prophet [David] invites all nations and peoples, that is, all men, namely both Jew and Gentile, to praise God for the benefit of the incarnation of Christ, and for the fulfillment of those things that were prophesied about Christ and of the conversion of the Gentiles. And that this is the literal sense of this Psalm arises from the fact that the Apostle asserts the words of this Psalm to the Romans as a foretelling of the conversion of the Gentiles, since he says: *I say that Christ Jesus was a minister of the circumcision . . . but that the Gentiles are to glorify God for his mercy, as it is written: Therefore will I confess to you, O Lord, among the Gentiles . . . and again, Praise the Lord, all you all you nations, praise him all you people.*[1] For Christ is the *corner stone* upon which the Gentiles and the Jews are joined,[2] forming out

---

1 Rom. 15:8a, 9, 11a; Ps. 17:50a; Ps. 116:1.

2 Is. 28:16; Eph. 2:20. E. N. The image of Jew and Gentile forming one wall with Christ as the cornerstone appears in St. Irenaeus, where Jesus, as the chief cornerstone is said to have "gathered into one and united those who were far off and those who were near, that is, the circumcision and the uncircumcision, enlarging Japheth and placing him in the dwelling of Shem." *Adv. Haer.* III, 5, 3 in *Anti-Nicene Fathers* (New York: Charles Scribner's Sons, 1905) Vol. 1, 418 (eds. Alexander Roberts and James Donaldson).

of both one Church in which there is *no distinction between the Jew and the Greek*.[3] For, as the Apostle said, *In Christ Jesus neither circumcision avails anything nor uncircumcision, but a new creature*.[4]

But because many more Gentiles than Jews converted to Christ, so the Prophet (foreseeing this) first invites the Gentiles, saying: *Laudate Dominum, omnes gentes; O praise the Lord, all you nations* called to faith. Of these Christ said: *It behooved Christ to suffer and to rise again from the dead, and that penance and remission of sins should be preached in his name*.[5] *Laudate eum, omnes populi; praise him, all you people,* converted from Judaism. The reason for this invitation is added: **116{117} [2]** *Quoniam confirmata est super nos misericordia eius, for his mercy is confirmed upon us*: that is, the effects of divine kindness, or the grace of God, has been copiously and more fully poured out upon the human race than before: "namely, upon all peoples." When, assuredly if not at the coming of Christ? For at that time (as John testifies) *grace . . . came by Jesus Christ*.[6] Because of the certainty of this prophecy, therefore, the Prophet [David] speaks of the future by means of the past. Of this confirmation of the mercy of God over us, which came in the coming of Christ, and not before, as the Apostle [Paul] says: *God indeed having winked at the times of this ignorance, now declares unto men, that all should everywhere do penance*.[7] *Et veritas Domini, and the truth of the Lord*, that is, the fulfillment of the divine promises and of the mysteries of Christ *manet in aeternum, remains forever*, both as to its fruit and those things obtained from it, which is the deliverance of the human race. Of this truth we find contained in John: *Truth came by [Jesus] Christ*.[8] For he fulfilled all that was foretold about him. Whence, hanging on the Cross, he said: *It is finished*.[9] Or [we can understand it thus], *the truth of the Lord*, that is, the doctrine and the preaching of Christ and the evangelical law, *remains forever*, in the way that Christ attested: Heaven and earth shall pass away, but my words shall not pass away.[10] Or [another alternative understanding is], *the truth of the Lord*, that is, Christ, the Son of God, who said, *I am the way, the truth, and the life,*[11]

---

3 Rom. 10:12.
4 Gal. 5:6; 6:15.
5 Luke 24:46–47a.
6 John 1:17b.
7 Acts 17:30.
8 John 1:17b.
9 John 19:30.
10 Luke 21:33.
11 John 14:6.

remains forever: the Jews also confessed this, saying to the Savior, *We have heard out of the law, that Christ abides forever.*[12]

The holy doctors strongly commend this Psalm of very few words but full and great with meaning. For it contains in summary form that which is dispersedly treated in other Psalms. And so, what can a desperate people say that is more joyful, and those who are miserable, blind, and lost say more sweetly than that mercy of God is confirmed upon them, and they ought to praise God for this? Therefore, let this Psalm be pronounced by us with a kind of flame of holy devotion.

PRAYER

LORD, ALMIGHTY FATHER, MAKE US always to offer praises fitting to your majesty, confirm your mercy upon us, lest some corruption of sin stain our soul, so that your Truth, which is consubstantial with you, might remain with us for eternity.

Omnipotens Pater Domine, condignas maiestati tuae laudes
fac nos tibi semper offerre; confirma super nos
misericordiam tuam, ne aliqua corruptela
criminum inficiat animam nostram: ut
Veritas tua tibi consubstantialis,
nobiscum maneat in
aeternum.

12 John 12:34a.

Psalm 117

ARTICLE XXVIII

ELUCIDATION OF THE
ONE HUNDRED AND SEVENTEENTH PSALM:
CONFITEMINI DOMINO QUONIAM BONUS.
GIVE PRAISE TO THE LORD, FOR HE IS GOOD.

117{118}[1] *Alleluia. Confess the Lord, for he is good: for his mercy endures forever.*[1]

Alleluia. Confitemini Domino, quoniam bonus, quoniam in saeculum misericordia eius.

117{118}[1] *Alleluia* is the title assigned to this Psalm. For in this Psalm the chosen people are invited to the divine praise. According to Jerome, this Psalm is manifestly written about the first coming of Christ, which will be shown as we proceed further. That [verse] which is stated below [Ps. 117:22] — *the stone which the builders rejected, etc.* — Christ states foretold of him when speaking to the Jews: *Have you never read in the Scriptures*, he says, *The stone which the builders rejected, the same is become the head of the corner, etc.?*[2] Also, Peter speaking to the chief priests of Christ and informing them of the glorification of Christ, says: *This is the stone which was rejected by you the builders; which is become the head of the corner; neither is there salvation in any other.*[3] But [a verse] is not valid proof unless it is in the literal sense, especially to the Jews who (as is reported) do not accept anything but the literal sense. Many, therefore, say that this Psalm in that place [117:19] — *Open to me the gates of justice*, even up to the end — speaks of Christ. But others say it speaks of the invitation to the Jews to the praise of God because of the deliverance of David from many dangers, so that at all times David speaks in his own person of his own dangers in this part. But this does not seem to be a suitable explanation. For Peter in the Acts of the Apostles asserts the verse [Ps. 117:16] — *The right hand of the Lord has*

---

1 E. N. I have translated *confitemini* as "confess," rather than the Douay-Rheims's "give praise," because as Denis states in his text, the confession here is not one of sin, but a confession of praise.

2 Matt. 21:42.

3 Acts 4:11–12a.

exulted me, the right hand of the Lord has wrought strength — as referring to the exaltation of Christ performed by God: even though that verse precedes the verse — *Open to me the gates of justice.*[4] Therefore, we will expound the entirety of this Psalm as referring to Christ, to the extent it can be done.

The holy David speaking in the person of Christ or the Church says: *Confitemini Domino, confess the Lord* with the confession of praise; praise God, *quoniam bonus, for he is good*, that is, because of himself, for he is naturally in every way and uncircumscribably and superessentially good, so that as Christ affirms in Mark, *None is good but one, that is God.*[5] This also is addressed by Luke, *None is good but God alone.*[6] And not only ought the Lord to be confessed [in the confession of praise] because the good that he himself is, but also because he is good in comparison to you, as it states subsequently: *quoniam in saeculum misericordia eius, for his mercy endures forever*, that is, he is always ready to have mercy upon you, and his mercy is eternal, as he himself is, since it is the same for him *to be* as it is for him *to be merciful.* Now, the effects of the divine mercy remain in the world, because he unceasingly gives grace at least to some in the present, and mercy is always mixed in with all the works of God: indeed, *His tender mercies are over all his works.*[7] For this reason, it is written in James: *Mercy exalts itself above judgment.*[8] But it seems to be inconsistent that in the same place [in James] it states, *Judgment without mercy to him that has not done mercy,*[9] which conforms with that in Job, *Let mercy forget him.*[10] The response to this is that in some of the works of God justice preponderates and shines forth brightly, as in the eternal damnation of evil men. And so it is said that justice is done to them without mercy, and that the mercy of God does not remember them — not as if the employment of mercy is entirely absent, since they suffer less than they deserve; but because it is not evident that they receive mercy in that they are eternally punished.[11]

---

4 *E. N.* In other words, St. Peter's reference (inspired by the Holy Spirit) establishes that the Psalm refers to Christ from 117:19 forwards, even though the proof text (Psalm 117:16) comes before Psalm 117:19.
5 Mark 10:18b.
6 Luke 18:19b.
7 Ps. 144:9b.
8 James 2:13b.
9 James 2:13a.
10 Job 24:20a.
11 *E. N.* See ST Ia, q. 21, art. 4, c. & ad 1.

117{118}[2]   *Let Israel now say that he is good: that his mercy endures forever.*

Dicat nunc Israel: Quoniam bonus, quoniam in saeculum misericordia eius.

117{118}[3]   *Let the house of Aaron now say, that his mercy endures forever.*

Dicat nunc domus Aaron: Quoniam in saeculum misericordia eius.

117{118}[4]   *Let them that fear the Lord now say, that his mercy endures forever.*

Dicant nunc qui timent Dominum: Quoniam in saeculum misericordia eius.

117{118}[2] *Dicat nunc Israel, let Israel now say,* that is, especially at the coming of Christ, [let Israel say], *quoniam bonus, that he is good,* [that is, that] God [is good] *quoniam in saeculum misericodia eius, that his mercy endures forever:* for he gives grace in the present and eternal glory in the future. **117{118}[3]** *Dicat nunc domus Aaron: Quoniam in saeculum misericordia eius; let the house of Aaron now say, that his mercy endures forever.* This can be understood equally of the Israelite people stemming from the patriarch Jacob and the priests born from the seed of Aaron as well as the Christian people and the priests of Christ signified by them. For the Christian people are called Israel, that is, those contemplating God by faith working through love. But the house or family of Aaron figuratively is the congregation of the priests of the Church, who are the sons of the great Priest, namely of Christ, who is our priest and indeed our supreme priest, in the manner that Peter asserts in his epistle: At one time *you were as sheep going astray, but you are now converted to the shepherd and bishop of your souls.*[12] **117{118}[4]** *Dicat nunc qui timent Dominum, let them that fear the Lord now say,* as also the blessed Virgin said, *And his mercy is from generation unto generations to those that fear him.*[13] Whence in Exodus the Lord said: *I am the Lord your God, . . . showing mercy unto thousands to them that love me and keep my commandments.*[14]

117{118}[5]   *In my trouble I called upon the Lord: and the Lord heard me, and enlarged me.*

De tribulatione invocavi Dominum; et exaudivit me in latitudine Dominus.

12 1 Pet. 2:25.
13 Luke 1:50.
14 Ex. 20:5a, 6.

117{118}[6]   *The Lord is my helper, I will not fear what man can do unto me.*

Dominus mihi adiutor; non timebo quid faciat mihi homo.

117{118}[7]   *The Lord is my helper: and I will look over my enemies.*

Dominus mihi adiutor; et ego despiciam inimicos meos.

117{118}[8]   *It is good to confide in the Lord, rather than to have confidence in man.*

Bonum est confidere in Domino, quam confidere in homine.

117{118}[9]   *It is good to trust in the Lord, rather than to trust in princes.*

Bonum est sperare in Domino, quam sperare in principibus.

117{118}[5] *De tribulatione invocavi Dominum, in my trouble I called upon the Lord.* This is what is now is mentioned in the words of the Apostle, for Christ, at the time of his Passion, *with a strong cry and tears* offered prayer to God.[15] For this reason, Luke said, that *being in agony, he prayed the longer.*[16] *Et exaudivit me in latitudine Dominus, and the Lord heard me and enlarged me,* the Almighty Father, [heard me] out of his love and his kindness. And so the Apostle adds that he *was heard for his reverence.*[17] And he said to the Father: *I give you thanks that you have heard me; and I knew that you hear me always.*[18] 117{118}[6] *Dominus mihi, the Lord to me,* according as I am man, was and is *adiutor, a helper,* cooperating with me and always protecting me while I was on the way, in the manner that Jeremiah said of me in divine writ: *The Lord is with me as a strong warrior.*[19] And so *non timebo, I will not fear* with an inordinate fear, *quid faciat mihi homo, what man can do to me,* [that is, what a] perverse man [can do to me], whosoever he might be: as is written of me in Isaiah: *Who is my adversary? Let him come near to me.*[20] 117{118}[7] *Dominus mihi adiutor, the Lord is my helper:* this in the manner Isaiah says: *The Lord God is my helper;*[21] *et ego despiciam inimicos meos, and I will look over my enemies* persecuting me, not despising their nature, but their malice, so that I do not fear their evil intent, nor do I consider them to be anything to the degree that they are evil.[22]

---

15 Heb. 5:7.

16 Luke 22:43b.

17 Heb. 5:7b.

18 John 11:41b–42a.

19 Jer. 20:11a.

20 Is. 50:8b.

21 Is. 50:9a.

22 E. N. This brings to mind St. Augustine's thought often (mis)stated as "love the sinner, but hate the sin." The source for this is one of St. Augustine's epistles to a convent of

Additionally, any Christian can say this with respect to himself. For we ought to cry out to the Lord in our tribulations, as it states in a Psalm above: *Call upon me in the day of trouble.*[23] And certainly, if we cry out perseveringly during such times, our God with largesse, that is, generously and copiously, will hear us: as he is kind and good, and exceeds our merits. For *who has called upon God and God despised him?*[24] The Lord is the helper of every member of the faithful, for we are not *sufficient to think anything of ourselves, as of ourselves: but our sufficiency is from God.*[25] And so the Christian truly does not fear what a perverse man might do to him: indeed, he rejoices in adversity, and he is ready to die for the love of Christ and for heavenly reward, because it is written: *Fear not the reproach of men, and be not afraid of their blasphemies.... Who are you that you should be afraid of mortal man, and the son of man, who shall wither away like grass?*[26] For this reason, Solomon declares: *He that fears man shall quickly fall; but he that trusts the Lord shall be set on high.*[27] The Lord is my helper by his grace preserving me in prosperity and adversity; and I regard my enemies, both visible and invisible, trusting in the help of God, and not relying upon my strength. For it is certain that those adhering unto the Lord are not able to be harmed. From this it follows that 117{118}[8] *Bonum est, it is good,* that is, it is better, *confidere in Domino, quam confidere in homine; to confide in the Lord, rather than to have confidence in man.* For *blessed is the man that trusts in the Lord;*[28] but *cursed be the man that trusts in man, and makes flesh his arm, and whose heart departs from the Lord.*[29] 117{118}[9] *Bonum est, it is good,* that is, it is better, *sperare in Domino, to trust in the Lord,* who alone is able to save, *quam sperare in principibus, than to trust in princes,* who have no power either to save themselves or others.

---

nuns discussing the care needed to guard the "frowardness of the eyes," advising that the prioress, in diligently surveying those under her care for sin that could destroy the peace of the community, ought to look upon her sister in religion *cum dilectione hominum et odio vitiorum,* "with love for the man, but hate for the vice," in "discovering, prohibiting, reporting, exposing, and punishing sins." *Epist.* 211, 11, PL 37, 962. Another Augustinian notion is that evil is the privation of good, and not a positive substance, and so to the degree a man lapses into evil, he is lapsing into nothingness.

23 Ps. 49:15a.

24 Ecclus. 2:12b. *E. N.* I replaced the personal pronouns in the Douay-Rheims's translation with "God" for clarity's sake.

25 2 Cor. 3:5.

26 Is. 51:7b, 12b.

27 Prov. 29:25.

28 Jer. 17:7a.

29 Jer. 17:5a.

117{118}[10]   *All nations compassed me about; and in the name of the Lord I have been revenged on them.*

Omnes gentes circuierunt me; et in nomine Domini quia ultus sum in eos.

In addition, Christ says: 117{118}[10] *Omnes gentes, all nations*, that is, some of all kinds of men, namely, men and women, superiors and subordinates, old and young, Jews and Gentiles, *circuierunt me, compassed me about*, during the time of the Passion, in approval of my death. It is not to be marveled that Christ said *all nations* in a universal sense, since Luke wrote: *There were dwelling at Jerusalem... devout men out of every nation under heaven.*[30] And elsewhere we read: *And the whole people answering, said: His blood be upon us and our children.*[31] Pay heed how all nations compassed Christ about in evil. Though on occasion, all nations compassed him about in good, in the manner that the Pharisees and the Jewish leaders said: *Do you see that we prevail nothing? Behold, the whole world is gone after him.*[32] *Et in nomine Domini, and in the name of the Lord*, that is, this has been done to the glory of God, *quia ultus sum in eos, for I have been revenged on them* out of the zeal of justice, and not from any sort of impatience. Whence Christ says: *The day of vengeance is in my heart.*[33] Christ's vengeance is upon the Jews, blinding their heart, withdrawing from them grace in the present and glory in the future, handing them over to the hands of the Romans, and keeping them in this most burdensome captivity. Christ as God performed this vengeance, but as man he prayed for it, saying as stated in Jeremiah: *But you, O Lord of Sabaoth, who judges justly, and tries the reins and hearts, let me see your revenge on them: for to you I have revealed my cause.*[34]

117{118}[11]   *Surrounding me they compassed me about: and in the name of the Lord I have been revenged on them.*

Circumdantes circumdederunt me, et in nomine Domini quia ultus sum in eos.

117{118}[12]   *They surrounded me like bees, and they burned like fire among thorns: and in the name of the Lord I was revenged on them.*

---

30 Acts 2:5.
31 Matt. 27:25.
32 John 12:19b.
33 Is. 63:4a.
34 Jer. 11:20.

Circumdederunt me sicut apes, et exarserunt sicut ignis in spinis; et in nomine Domini, quia ultus sum in eo.

117{118}[11] *Circumdantes circumdederunt me, surrounding me they compassed me about,* that is, with affections of great malignity they canvassed against me, crying out before Pilate, *Away with him; away with him; crucify him.*[35] *Et in nomine Domini, qui ultus sum in eos; and in the name of the Lord, I have been revenged on them.* What is in this verse is a repetition of what was in the prior verse and which has been explained, for the meaning is the same. And these words will be asserted three times so as to designate the magnitude of the zeal for justice which Christ had, for he always was united and conformed to the divine justice. 117{118}[12] *Circumdederunt me sicut apes, they surrounded me like bees,* which puncture you with stingers: so did the words and the blows of the Jews sting me as they spoke words full of blasphemy against me.[36] Whence it is written: *They will see him whom they have pierced.*[37] *Et exarserunt sicut ignis in spinis, etc.; and they burned like fire among thorns, etc.,* that is, with the fire of furor and the most vehement flame of anger they became inflamed against me, just like fire lights up quickly among thorns. Of these those sorts of persons it is therefore written: *Let us therefore lie in wait for the just, because...he is contrary to our doings, and...he is grievous unto us, even to behold.*[38]

117{118}[13] *Being pushed I was overturned that I might fall: but the Lord supported me.*

Impulsus eversus sum, ut caderem; et Dominus suscepit me.

117{118}[13] *Impulsus, being pushed,* that is, being captured by the Jews, and being led to the place of Calvary carrying the cross,[39] *eversus sum, I was overturned* from corporeal life, *ut caderem, that I might fall,* that is, that I might remain entirely dead, that there might no longer be any memory of my name on earth, as is written what my adversaries said regarding me: *Let us...cut him off from the land of the living, and let his name be remembered no more.*[40] *Et Dominus suscepit me, but the Lord supported me:* that is, he preserved me from this sort of ruin; indeed, he

---

35 John 19:15a.
36 John 19:37.
37 *Cf.* Zech. 12:10; Rev. 1:7.
38 Wis. 2:12a, 15a.
39 John 19:17.
40 Jer. 11:19b.

did exactly the opposite, because they [my adversaries] completely perished, and I rose again and am glorified everywhere. For this reason, the Father said of me: *Behold my servant, I will uphold him.*[41] This can also be understood as referring to that pushing against Christ of which Luke said: *They brought him to the brow of the hill . . . that they might cast him down headlong; but he passing through the midst of them, went his way.*[42]

117{118}[14]   *The Lord is my strength and my praise: and he is become my salvation.*

Fortitudo mea et laus mea Dominus; et factus est mihi in salutem.

117{118}[15]   *The voice of rejoicing and of salvation is in the tabernacles of the just.*

Vox exsultationis et salutis in tabernaculis iustorum.

Because the Lord so supported me, therefore 117{118}[14] *Fortitudo mea, my strength,* that is, the cause of all my created strength, *et laus mea, and my praise,* that is, he whom I praise, namely the thing praised by me, is *Dominus, the Lord,* the Father or God the Trinity. For with respect to this, the Savior said: *The son cannot do anything of himself;*[43] and elsewhere, *I seek not my own glory, but I honor my Father.*[44] *Et factus est mihi in salute, and he is become my salvation,* that is, he is the source of all the well-being of my soul and body, for my glorification in mind and body comes from him. 117{118}[15] *Vox exsultationis, the voice of rejoicing,* that is, the praise of spiritual joy, *et salutis, and of salvation,* that is, blessed praise and of salvation, namely, agreeable and wholesome praise proceeding from an interior joy and salvation, is *in tabernaculis iustorum, is in the tabernacles of the just,* that is, in the heavenly fatherland of the blessed, in the hearts of the elect, in the Church of Christian faithful in accordance with this, *Joy and gladness shall be found therein, thanksgiving, and the voice of praise.*[45] Whence it states in a Psalm above: *Blessed are they that dwell in your house, O Lord: they shall praise you for ever and ever.*[46]

---

41 Is. 42:1a.
42 Luke 4:29b–30.
43 John 5:19a.
44 John 8:50a, 49a.
45 Is. 51:3b.
46 Ps. 83:5.

117{118}[16] *The right hand of the Lord has wrought strength: the right hand of the Lord has exulted me: the right hand of the Lord has wrought strength.*

Dextera Domini fecit virtutem, dextera Domini exaltavit me; dextera Domini fecit virtutem.

117{118}[16] *Dextera Domini, the right hand of the Lord,* that is, the kindly and gracious assistance or the great power of the eternal Father, *fecit virtutem, has wrought strength* in me, preserving me during the time of Passion, and doing the miracles which then occurred in the sun and the moon, and the earth and temple, whose veil was rent; and raising me as well as many others from the dead on the third day, as Matthew narrates.[47] *Dextera Domini exaltavit me, the right hand of the Lord has exulted me* in the day my ascension above all heavens; he has also exalted me, glorifying me throughout the whole world by the doctrines and signs of the Apostles, as I prayed for during my Passion: *Father, the hour is come, glorify your Son.*[48] God foretold of this exaltation: *Behold my servant shall understand, he shall be exalted, and extolled, and shall be exceeding high.*[49] *Dextera Domini fecit virtutem, the right hand of the Lord has wrought strength* in my Mystical Body, which is the Church, sending to them the Holy Spirit in the day of Pentecost, and giving the grace of miracles to my disciples. Whence we read: *God wrought by the hand of Paul more than common miracles.*[50]

117{118}[17] *I shall not die, but live: and shall declare the works of the Lord.*

Non moriar, sed vivam; et narrabo opera Domini.

117{118}[18] *The Lord chastising has chastised me: but he has not delivered me over to death.*

Castigans castigavit me Dominus, et morti non tradidit me.

117{118}[17] *Non moriar, I shall not die* in that manner that you, O Jews, thought, for I will not spiritually die, as would a blasphemer or ungodly man, nor would I be subject to the empire of bodily death: indeed, to the contrary, I would shortly be raised to the immortal life,

---

47 Matt. 27:45, 51–53; 28:6.
48 John 17:1.
49 Is. 52:13.
50 Acts 19:11.

as the Gospel often foretold. And so the verse continues: *sed vivam, but I shall live*, and be made impassible, *et narrabo opera Domini, and I shall declare the works of the Lord*. For, as is narrated in the Acts of the Apostles and in all the Gospels, Christ after his Passion and Resurrection for forty days frequently appeared to his disciples, entering and leaving and eating with them, and discussing the kingdom of God.[51] For during this time he spoke to them of the works of the Lord, namely, his Resurrection, the future judgment, and the prediction of the Prophets, and many other things which were not written, for, as is stated in the Gospel of John, *There are also many other things which Jesus did; which, if they were written every one, the world itself, I think, would not be able to contain the books that should be written.*[52] **117{118}[18]** *Castigans castigavit me Dominus, the Lord chastising has chastised me*, not because of my own faults, but for the sins of those for whom I willed to die, as is written: *The Lord has laid on him the iniquity of us all; he was bruised for our sins... and by his bruises we are healed.*[53] And elsewhere: *The breath of our mouth, Christ the Lord, is taken in our sins.*[54] *Et morti non tradidit me, but he has not delivered me over to death*, so that I would be subject to the empire of death, but he would quickly return bodily life to me, as is stated in an earlier Psalm: *Because you will not leave my soul in hell; nor will you give your holy one to see corruption.*[55]

117{118}[19] *Open to me the gates of justice: I will go into them, and confess to the Lord.*[56]

Aperite mihi portas iustitiae: ingressus in eas confitebor Domino.

117{118}[20] *This is the gate of the Lord, the just shall enter into it.*

Haec porta Domini, iusti intrabunt in eam.

117{118}[19] *Aperite mihi portas iustitiae, open to me the gates of justice.* These are the words of Christ has he ascends to heaven commanding the holy angels: *Open to me the gates* to those ascending and coming with me, *the gates of justice*, that is, that provide access to the heavenly kingdom.

---

51 Acts 1:3; Matt. 28:17–18; Mark 15:9 *et seq.*; Luke chp. 24; John chps. 20, 21.
52 John 21:25.
53 Is. 53:6b, 5.
54 Lam. 4:20a.
55 Ps. 15:10.
56 E. N. I have, as is now customary, replaced the Douay-Rheims's "praise," with the more generic "confess." As Denis makes clear in his *Commentary*, the confession here is one of praise, not of sin.

The holy angels are said to open these gates for two reasons. The first is because they remove impediments from those entering into the heavenly kingdom by the fact that it is part of their duty to restrain the aerial powers which are always striving to impede those who are ascending. The second is from the fact that they dispose themselves to receive those who are devoutly ascending to the angelic society. And so Christ at that time [that he ascended into heaven] commanded that they dispose themselves to greet reverently those coming with him, and so that they might introduce them into the heavenly reign with due service, praise, and veneration. *Ingressus in eas, I will go into them,* namely, the gates and the mansions of the heavenly kingdom, and *confitebor Domino, confess to the Lord* with the confession of perfect praise. For Christ sitting at the right hand of the Father—for himself and for others whom he has led there—unceasingly praises the Lord as man. **117{118}[20]** *Haec porta Domini, iusti itrabunt in eam; this is the gate of the Lord, the just shall enter into it.* Before it stated the plural, *gates;* now, it has the singular *this gate* because since there are as many gates of justice as there are virtues, yet no one to go through the gates unless it be by charity; and so charity is the gate which virtually contains all other gates. The just shall enter through it in the manner that the Apostle admonishes: *Walk in love, as Christ also has loved us.*[57]

117{118}[21] *I will give glory to you because you have heard me and are become my salvation.*

Confitebor tibi quoniam exaudisti me, et factus es mihi in salutem.

117{118}[21] *Confitebor tibi, I will give glory to you,* that is, I will praise you, O Lord Father, *quoniam exaudisti me, et factus es mihi in salutem; because you have heard me and are become my salvation:* as is presently to be stated [in verses **22** forwards].

In addition to all this expounded regarding Christ, we can also expound it as applying to the Church or the faithful—those who follow the path of Christ. *All nations compassed me about:* that is, some of all kinds of men have persecuted me, or have tempted me with blandishments or intimidation, and this for no other reason than to cause a fall. Whence also Christ said: *If they have persecuted me, they will also persecute you* because *the servant is not greater than his master;*[58] and elsewhere, *You shall be hated by all men*

---

57 Eph. 5:2a.
58 John 15:20. *E. N.* Denis has re-arranged the verse somewhat.

because of me.[59] *And in the name of the Lord, I have been revenged on them,* according to the order of justice. Or [alternatively] *I have been revenged on them,* by the Lord, who said: *Vengeance belongs to me, and I will repay.*[60] This is presented to us in Deuteronomy: *He will revenge the blood of his servants: and will render vengeance to their enemies.*[61] *Surrounding me they compassed me about,* in order that their sins might infect and kill my soul. *They surrounded me like bees,* which hold honey in their mouths, but a sting in their tail. Such are those who offer blandishments to defraud, in the manner that is written: *Their tongue is a piercing arrow . . . with his mouth one speaks peace with his friend, and secretly he lies in wait for him.*[62] *And they burned* with the fire of desire, with the flame of rancor, with the fervor of smoking anger by which they subvert me in every possible way, *like* material *fire* is commonly found to burn *among dry thorns,* which are easily ignited.

Being pushed by temptation or persecution, *I was overturned* from the rectitude of perfection, *that I might fall,* that is, that I might in all things fail, consenting to mortal sin or persevering in evil; *but the Lord supported me* with the arms of his mercy, not allowing me to be tempted beyond my power,[63] but providing with such temptation the means to prosper over it. For since the holy and blessed God — whose judgments are altogether inscrutable — sometimes permits the elect to be gravely troubled, to be direly struck, and venially, or even mortally, to sin, yet he does not allow them to fall entirely. Whence it states in an earlier Psalm: *When he shall fall he shall not be bruised, for the Lord puts his hand under him.*[64] And with Micah: *Rejoice not, you, my enemy, over me, because I am fallen: I shall arise, when I sit in darkness, the Lord is my light.*[65] So that we might be able to resist temptation, that we might rise up again after sin, that we may not entirely be undone, let us say with a sincere heart that which follows: *My strength,* that is, the cause and giver of all my firmness and victory, *and my praise is the Lord,* whom in all things I give thanks, and to whom I ascribe all good. Whence it is written: *The Lord is my might, and my strength, and my refuge in the day of tribulation.*[66] *And he is become my salvation,* that is, you have become for me a Savior, giving me constancy in adversity and

---

59 Matt. 10:22a.
60 Heb. 10:30a.
61 Deut. 32:43.
62 Jer. 9:8.
63 *Cf.* 1 Cor. 10:13.
64 Ps. 36:24.
65 Micah 7:8.
66 Jer. 16:19a.

humility in prosperity. For this reason, Moses said: Do not say in your heart: *My own might, and the strength of my own hand have achieved all these things for me; but remember the Lord your God, that he has given you strength.*[67] Whoever places all his hope in God in this way, calling him his strength and his praise, to him God becomes salvation.

The right hand of the Lord, that is, Christ the Son of God, who is called an arm, the right hand or power of God the Father, as is written of him: *To whom is the arm of the Lord revealed?*[68] And this is more clearly said again: *The Lord has prepared his holy arm in the sight of all the Gentiles.*[69] And this is in concord with what Simeon discerned: *My eyes have seen your salvation, which you have prepared before the face of all peoples.*[70] Or *the right hand*, that is, the power, *of the Lord has wrought strength*, making a just man out of a sinner, which is greater than the creation of man. *The right hand of the Lord has exulted me* from an ignoble, vicious, carnal life unto a noble, virtuous, spiritual, and humble life; *the right hand of the Lord has wrought strength*, preserving me in the good, fighting and subduing my adversaries for me. This concurs with that which we read in Exodus: *Your right hand, O Lord, is magnified in strength; your right hand, O Lord, has slain the enemy; and in the multitude of your glory you have put down your adversaries.*[71]

Therefore, because the Creator is so bountiful with so many goods to me, I can confidently say to him: *I shall not die* through mortal sin and eternal damnation, *but I will live* in the life of grace in the present, and the life of glory in the future. And in just this sense Christ said: *If any man keep my word, he shall not see death forever.*[72] *And I shall declare the works of the Lord*, that is, I will recall to myself, and I will announce to others the benefits of God bestowed upon me to the glory of the One who gives the gifts, as Christ in the Gospel says to someone: *Tell what great things God has done to you.*[73] *The Lord chastising has chastised me*, that is, he has paternally corrected me and afflicted me during this time because of my sin, lest I perish in eternity. And so there is added: *he has not delivered me over to eternal death.* Whence the Apostle says: *For what son is there whom the father does not correct? But if you be without*

---

67 Deut. 8:17b–18a.
68 Is. 53:1.
69 Is. 52:10a.
70 Luke 2:30–31.
71 Ex. 15:6–7.
72 John 8:51a.
73 Luke 8:39a.

chastisement ... then you are bastards, and not sons.[74] And Solomon said: *My son, reject not the correction of the Lord: and do not faint when you are chastised by him; for whom the Lord loves, he chastises.*[75] We can ascribe to our own demerits whatever adversity and punishment might befall us, therefore, and we might patiently — indeed, joyfully — endure them, thinking that which Judith thought: *Let us not revenge ourselves for these things we suffer; but esteeming these very punishments to be less than our sins deserve, let us believe that these scourges of the Lord, with which like servants we are chastised, have happened for our amendment, and not for our destruction.*[76] For this is written: *My children, suffer patiently the wrath that is come upon you, etc. For he that has brought evils upon you, shall bring you everlasting joy again with your salvation.*[77]

And so David in the person of the Church or any one member of the faithful says: *Open to me the gates of justice:* that is, O you Apostles of Christ and holy preachers, show me through your teaching the commandments of Christ, the Sacraments of the New Law, the Evangelical counsels, the works of virtue, which are all called the gates of justice, for by them the righteous life is entered into. *I will go into them and give praise to the Lord.* For he who has entered these gates has a praiseworthy manner of life, and so he is rendered worthy to praise God. For the Lord has said to a person who has not entered through these gates: *Why do you call me, Lord, Lord, and not do the things which I say?*[78] *This*, that is, this confession [of praise], is *the gate of the Lord*, for by it one goes toward God; *the just shall enter into it*, that is, those who assume this confession of praise.[79]

117{118}[22] *The stone which the builders rejected; the same is become the head of the corner.*

Lapidem quem reprobaverunt aedificantes, hic factus est in caput anguli.

117{118}[22] *Lapidem*, the stone, that is, Christ, of whom is written: [he is] *the stone cut out of the mountain without hands.*[80] Peter stated of him: *Behold, I lay in Sion a chief corner stone, elect, precious, founded*

---

74 Heb. 12:7b–8a.
75 Prov. 3:11–12a.
76 Judith 8:26–27.
77 Baruch 4:25a, 29.
78 Luke 6:46.
79 Cf. Jer. 7:16: *Therefore, do not pray for this [sinful] people, nor take to praise and supplication for them; and do not withstand me, for I will not hear you.*
80 Dan. 2:45a.

in the foundation; and he that believes in him shall not be confounded.[81] Therefore, this stone, namely, Christ *quem reprobaverunt aedificantes, which the builders rejected,* that is, the chiefs of the priests, the Scribes, and the Pharisees whose [duty] it was to edify others in faith and morals, by preaching and living well, *hic factus est in caput anguli, the same is become the head of the corner*: so that in him was joined two people, such as two walls are joined in a cornerstone. For Christ established one Church from the Jews and Gentiles, of which he is the Head, causing to flow into it movements of virtue and the life of grace. For this reason, Christ said: *Other sheep I have, that are not of this fold: them also I must bring, and they shall hear my voice, and there shall be one fold and one shepherd.*[82]

117{118}[23] *This is the Lord's doing: and it is wonderful in our eyes.*

A Domino factum est istud, et est mirabile in oculis nostris.

117{118}[23] *A Domino factum est istud, this is the Lord's doing*: that is, this joinder by the cornerstone or Christ, and this making of two people into one in Christ is accomplished not by human or natural power, but by divine and supernatural power. For the whole Church of Christ is united by the Head through faith, charity, and grace, which are supernatural gifts of God. Whence, the Apostle [Paul] said: *God, who is rich in mercy, for his exceeding charity wherewith he has loved us, when we are dead in sins, has quickened us together in Christ, by whose grace you are saved.*[83] *Et est mirabile in oculis nostris, and it is wonderful in our eyes*: that is, from the vantage point of faith, this conversion and joinder of men into Christ is a marvelous thing. For no one can sufficiently marvel at the ineffable mercy of the Creator, by which he had mercy upon the world, sending his only begotten Son, delivering him up for us, and making us all one with him.[84] Whence elsewhere, the Apostle [Paul] states: *In other generations it was not known to the sons of men, as it is not revealed to his holy apostles and prophets in the Spirit, that the Gentiles should be fellow heirs, and of the same body, and co-partners of his promise in Christ Jesus.*[85] And elsewhere he says: *Thanks be to God for his unspeakable gift.*[86]

---

81 1 Pet. 2:6; Is. 28:16. *E. N.* The quote is a patchwork of Peter's epistle (who partially quotes Isaiah 28:16) and Isaiah.
82 John 10:16.
83 Eph. 2:4–5.
84 *Cf.* Rom. 8:32.
85 Eph. 3:5–6.
86 2 Cor. 9:15.

But especially marvelous was this conversion of the Gentiles to the early Church that was composed of Jews, according to this: *The faithful of the circumcision, who came with Peter, were astonished, for that the grace of the Holy Spirit was poured out upon the Gentiles also.*[87] Or [an alternative exposition is] thus: *This is the Lord's doing,* that is, [this is the doing of] the three Persons in one nature, namely, which made the cornerstone out of the stone which the builder's rejected; *and it is wonderful in our eyes,* [that is], in our mental [eyes]. For it is a powerful and marvelous thing that he who was so humiliated during the time of his Passion was, but a short time later, so glorified by God, so that he might convert all kinds of men to himself: among whom were some who had consented to his death and had procured it, to whom he said before his Passion: *When you shall have lifted up the Son of man, then shall you know, that I am he.*[88]

117{118}[24]   *This is the day which the Lord has made: let us be glad and rejoice therein.*

Haec est dies quam fecit Dominus; exsultemus, et laetemur in ea.

117{118}[24] *Haec dies, this is the day,* in which God did this, this is the day *quam fecit Dominus, which the Lord has made:* that is, the time of Christ, the time of the evangelical law and of grace, in which, of course, the one Church was constituted from both people in Christ, was a time especially made by God. For though granted that God has made all of the days of time, yet of all those days and times God is said to specially make those days in which he performed important and special works. Because, therefore, in the coming of Christ and thereafter there is bestowed more benignity and grace to men than before, with good reason is the time or the day of Christ said to be made by God. For often in sacred Scripture, the time of the New Testament is called day because the clear revelation of those figures hidden in the Old Testament was known, and because in the New Testament the splendor of the grace of God shone forth more clearly and bountifully upon men than in the times of the Old Law. *Exultemus, et laetemur in ea; let us be glad and rejoice therein,* that is, let us with both body and soul rejoice in the Lord for this time, and the benefits and graces being done by it. Whence the Apostle said, *Now is the acceptable time; behold, now is the day of*

---

87 Acts 10:45.
88 John 8:28.

salvation, and he added: *As sorrowful, yet always rejoicing.*[89] With good cause is this verse sung in the time of Easter frequently, because Christ, the Son of justice, the *brightness of eternal light*, the light of light and the fountain of brightness,[90] who the day before the Passover was obscured by the darkness of the Passion, and was hidden in the stone tomb as if behind a most dense cloud, in the day of Passover was glorified in the sepulcher, and came forth from it *white and ruddy* illuminating the whole world, and casting off the night of infidelity and the darkness of ignorance from the hearts of his disciples.

117{118}[25] *O Lord, save me: O Lord, give good success.*

O Domine, salvum me fac; o Domine, bene prosperare.

117{118}[26] *Blessed be he that comes in the name Lord. We have blessed you out of the house of the Lord.*

Benedictus qui venit in nomine Domini: benediximus vobis de domo Domini.

117{118}[27] *The Lord is God, and he has shone upon us. Appoint a solemn day, in the crowd, even to the horn of the altar.*[91]

Deus Dominus, et illuxit nobis. Constituite diem solemnem in condensis, usque ad cornu altaris.

117{118}[25] *O Domine, salvum me fac; O Lord, save me* from the punishments and the vices of this present life; *O Domine, bene prosperare; O Lord, give success*: that is, grant prosperous gifts to us, increasing the Church both in number and merit, and by leading us through the guidance of your grace to your beatific vision. As it states in a Psalm above, *The God of our salvation will make our journey prosperous to us.*[92] **117{118} [26]** *Benedictus, blessed is qui venit in nomine Domini, he who comes in the name of the Lord*, that is, Christ, who said: *I come in the name of my Father.* According to Jerome,[93] the song of the children who sang to

---

89 2 Cor. 6:2, 10a.

90 Wis. 7:26.

91 E. N. I have changed the Douay-Rheims from "with the shady bows," which translated *in condensis*, to "in the crowd." The Septuagint has the term πυκάζουσιν, making close, thick, covered, shut. The Hebrew word (בעבתים), however, appears to be closer in meaning to the Douay-Rheims: "with branches," "with cords," or with foliage."

92 Ps. 67:20b.

93 E. N. See St. Jerome, *Commentary on Matthew*, 23.39, PL 26, 175 (*"Blessed is he who comes in the name of the Lord, Hosanna in the highest is taken from the one hundred*

Christ in the day of Palms—*Hosanna to the Son of David: Blessed is he that comes in the name of the Lord: Hosanna in the highest*—was derived from these verses.[94] And so David prophesied in this place of that praise.

Thereafter, speaking in the person of the Apostles and their successors, namely of the pastors and the priests of the Church, he adds: *Benediximus, we have blessed*, we bishops and prelates [have blessed], *vobis, you*, O you who are under our care, *de domo Domini, out of the house of the Lord*, that is, of the Church of Christ, preaching to you the word of salvation, administering to you the sacraments of the New Law, and also praying for you, and communicating to you (as charity obliges) the grace of God given to us. Properly speaking a blessing is said to be a granting of the grace of God. Yet grace is not conferred by anyone except God. In what manner, therefore, is one of us able to bless another or to communicate grace other than instrumentally, and not principally? For this reason, he adds: **117{118}[27]** *Deus Dominus, et illuxit nobis; the Lord is God, and he has shone upon us*: that is, God, who is *our Lord*,[95] he both shines upon us, illuminating our heart with the Holy Spirit, and pours into our soul splendid grace, giving to us also, the authority of binding and loosing, administering the Sacraments, preaching the words of the Gospel, consecrating, and blessing, from which we are qualified to bless you. For this reason, John attests: *Of his fullness we have all received.*[96]

Constituite, appoint, O you bishops of Christ, *diem solemnem, a solemn day*, that is, a feast of celebration, or festival days, in commemoration of the Incarnation, the Resurrection, and the Ascension of Christ, namely, the feast of the Nativity, the solemnity of the Resurrection, *etc*. And regard this, do it *in condensis, in the crowd* of the unified people, so that the Christian faithful in great solidity and abundance assemble together for these feasts. Other translations have, "in the congregations," but others, "in those crowding together," from which is clear that this is to be taken in a literal sense.[97] That this is so is also clear from that which follows: *usque ad cornu altaris, even to the horn of the altar*, that is, perseveringly, until you reach to the sublime altar of God prepared in heaven, where all the blessed unceasingly offer to God hymns of praise.

---

and seventeenth Psalm which is manifestly written about the coming of the Lord."
94 Matt. 21:9b.
95 Ps. 8:2a.
96 John 1:16a.
97 E. N. The different Latin words are *in condensis, in congregationibus*, and *in frequentationibus. See also* footnote 117-90.

117{118}[28] *You are my God, and I will confess you: you are my God, and I will exalt you. I will confess you, because you have heard me, and are become my salvation.*[98]

Deus meus es tu, et confitebor tibi; Deus meus es tu, et exaltabo te. Confitebor tibi quoniam exaudisti me, et factus es mihi in salutem.

Finally, referencing the predicted benefits to the Church or the faithful, it gives thanks: 117{118}[28] *Deus meus es tu, you are my God,* O Lord Christ, of whom Thomas said, *My Lord, and my God;*[99] *et confitebor tibi, and I will confess you,* that is, I will praise you. *Deus meus es tu, you are my God,* O Jesus, Son of the most high God, as is written of you: *This is the true God and life eternal;*[100] *et exaltabo te, and I will exalt you:* not that I will make you higher, but because I will declare and I will preach with words and with deeds your dignity and height; and by these, you — who are in yourself always high and great — will become high and great in my heart and in my neighbor to whom I will recite your marvelous works. *Confitebor tibi quoniam exaudisti me, I will confess you, because you have heard me,* that is, I will give you thanks because you have heard me, *et, and* because *factus es mihi in salutem, you are become by salvation,* as has already been explained.

117{118}[29] *O confess the Lord, for he is good: for his mercy endures forever.*

Confitemini Domino, quoniam bonus, quoniam in saeculum misericordia eius.

117{118}[29] *Confitemini Domino quoniam bonus, quoniam in saeculum misericordia eius; O confess the Lord, for he is good: for his mercy endures forever.* See this verse, which has already been addressed in the beginning of this Psalm, is again repeated so as to suggest that all the efforts of the perfect begin with the praise of God and end in such praise in the manner that the divine Apostle teaches: *Whether you eat or drink, or whatsoever else you do, do all to the glory of God.*[101]

We have heard in this sweet and beautiful Psalm such great meaning

---

98 E. N. I have replaced "I will praise" in the Douay-Rheims (twice in this verse) with the more generic "I will confess," for the Latin *confitebor.*
99 John 20:28.
100 1 John 5:20a.
101 1 Cor. 10:31.

and mystery. In its beginning we are invited over and over again to praise God publicly. In it we are taught morally to cry out to the Lord in our tribulation, securely hoping that he will answer us expansively, and not to be broken, to be sorrowful, or to despair, as we are elsewhere persuaded: *Be of good comfort, my children, cry to the Lord, and he will deliver you out of the hand of...your enemies.*[102] Let us learn above all from this present Psalm to place our confidence in God alone, and always to lean on his grace. The benefits of God are also described in this light-filled Psalm, and the mysteries of Christ are recited in it. Therefore, let us sing this most splendid Psalm with much devotion and special joyfulness — indeed, if we sing it with an intent and pure heart, we shall most copiously experience its sweetness. For the wandering, fearful, carnal, or worldly soul will not have the ability to experience the power of this Psalm.

PRAYER

O GOD, STRENGTH AND PRAISE OF THE faithful, and hope of all who confide in you, cause us to make progress in salvation through your goodness, exalt us in good through your right hand, so that we might enter through the gates of justice to see you unveiled, and let us confess you forever with the just.

Deus, fortitudo et laus fidelium, spesque cunctorum in te
confidentium, da nobis in salute tua pietatis profectum,
dextera tua in bonis nos exalta: ut te aperiente,
portas iustitiae ingress, perenniter cum
iustis confiteamur tibi.

102 Baruch 4:21.

Psalm 118

ARTICLE XXIX
EXPLANATION OF THE
ONE HUNDRED AND EIGHTEENTH PSALM:
BEATI IMMACULATI.
BLESSED ARE THE IMMACULATE.

THIS PSALM BEING NOW EXPLAINED HAS THE title Alleluia. This is not surprising since this Psalm is full of the praises of God. In it we are taught to praise God by words and good works. And this present Psalm is alphabetical, having groups of eight verses that are arranged under the Hebrew alphabet, namely, twenty-two [such eight-verse sections]. Each eight-versed section begins with a letter in the order of the Hebrew alphabet, so that each individual verse of such eight-versed section begins by the letter preceding that section; thus each eight-verse group is prescribed by that one single letter. Now at its surface, this Psalm is satisfactorily clear, but upon close examination one uncovers a profound excellence. For it speaks of blessedness and the means by which one can arrive at that blessedness. But blessedness is of two kinds, namely, of the way (*viae*) and of the heavenly fatherland (*patriae*). For of the present time, it speaks of the way of beatitude of the way (*viae*), and this Psalm is conspicuous, dazzling, and supreme due to all of its moral doctrine. In it, the holy Prophet [David] familiarly and sweetly addresses God from a heart burning and exuberant with his divine love, and he frequently repeats the same sentence, though using various words, so as to avoid tedium. For it is customary for one possessing a fervent and impatient desire to repeat frequently the same thing, for he does not become tired when he speaks to his beloved. According to those who do not accept that all the Psalms are composed by David, the author of the present Psalm is not known because the author is not revealed in the title. But according to nearly all the holy and great Catholic doctors, David edited it, for, having confidence in God, he so greatly loved the Lord that he proceeded through this whole Psalm and declared his admirable fervor of charity and devotion of holy discipline. In it, all the faithful are most fully instructed as to what to do, what to avoid, and what to desire. And the doctors eminently and marvelously praise this present Psalm.

Regarding the happiness, therefore, which we all naturally desire, the writer of the Psalm begins to speak, saying:

357

ALEPH
(PART I)

118{119}[1]   *Blessed are the immaculate in the way, who walk in the law*
of the Lord.[1]

Beati immaculati in via, qui ambulant in lege Domini.

118{119}[1] *Beati, blessed* are those now in hope, and, after due time,
made to be blessed in reality, *immaculati, the immaculate*, that is, those
without the stain of mortal sin, *in via, in the way*, that is, in the present
life, which is the way to the future, true, and eternal life; *qui ambulant in
lege Domini, who walk in the law of the Lord*, that is, who live their life
in observation of the divine law or the precepts of the Decalogue. For
it is not sufficient to turn aside from evil, unless that which is good is
also done. For this reason, Christ says: *Every branch in me, that bears not
fruit, he will take away.*[2] And elsewhere he says: *Every tree therefore that
does not yield good fruit, shall be cut down, and cast into the fire.*[3] But the
state of being undefiled does not only concern the sins of commission,
but also the sins of omission. Scripture frequently attests to this, that
no one can call himself spotless, according to this: *Who can say: My
heart is clean, I am pure from sin?*[4] And elsewhere: *No one is clean from
sin, not even the infant who has lived but one day of life on earth.*[5]

And so one might reflect upon the fact that something can be said to
be immaculate in various ways. First, because he could never be subject
to sin, neither original, nor mortal, nor venial: and in this manner Christ
as man is considered immaculate. Second, because one is not darkened
by either mortal or venial sin: and in this way the blessed Virgin is
immaculate. As far as adults go, this [second way] applies only to her,
for before the years of discretion or the use of reason, others may also be
immaculate in this way; yet still, these people are said to be blemished
and infected with stain because of the original sin, which they have or
have had — from which the blessed Virgin, by the preemptive grace of

---

1 E. N. The Douay-Rheims has "undefiled" for *immaculate*, which literally means
"stainless" or "spotless." Because Denis uses the word in different senses (for Christ,
for the Blessed Virgin Mary, and for the person in sanctifying grace) I decided to
use the word immaculate as better suited to understand Denis's exposition.

2 John 15:2a.

3 Matt. 3:10b.

4 Prov. 20:9.

5 Job 14:4–5 (according to the LXX).

her Son is believed to have been preserved. Third, [one is immaculate] because one is not polluted with mortal sin, or, if he has been, it has been cleansed through penance: and in this [third] manner, many live immaculate lives by the grace of God, yet no wayfarer is able certainly to know without a special revelation whether he is immaculate in this manner. However, one is able to know conjecturally or with probability: and so it is written, *Although I should be simple, even this my soul shall be ignorant of.*[6] The divine word exhorts us to this sort of immaculateness: *Show yourselves holy and immaculate, and blameless before him.*[7] Now this immaculateness is the blessedness of the way, which is nothing other than the observation of the precepts of the most High; here we are speaking of the blessedness of the active life (*vitae activae*), of which Christ speaks about in Matthew,[8] and David in this verse. For this blessedness is the act of virtues which are ordained to works. Moreover, the blessedness of the contemplative life (*vitae contemplativae*) — which is an act of wisdom to which the former blessedness [of the active life] which consists in acts of the moral virtues, disposes one to — is another thing. For since the ordering of the sensitive appetite or the curbing of passions is required for contemplation, it is necessary that the blessedness of the active life precede the blessedness of the contemplative life, because the moral virtues brake and order the passions lest they impede the reason in its consideration of truth or the will in the desire for good.

———————

118{119}[2] *Blessed are they who search his testimonies: that seek him with their whole heart.*

Beati qui scrutantur testimonia eius, in toto corde exquirunt eum.

———————

6 Job 9:21. *E. N.* As Denis elaborates on this verse in his *Commentary on Job*: "*Although I should be simple,* that is, virtuous, *this my soul shall be ignorant of,* until it is certified by God. For we are not able to know with certainty whether we are in charity and grace without [special] divine revelation." Certain signals provide us with conjectural or probable knowledge: if we listen to the word of God; if we find sin offensive, not only because of punishment, but because it is offensive to God; if we are solicitous to the worship of God; if we are obedient to the life of charity and grace; if we are obedient to the precepts of God; if we do good works; finally, if we find that we hold the world in contempt, if we try to curb our passions, if we have a heartfelt affection toward God, a zeal to glorify him in all things, and to bring others to love and worship him, and that we might obtain eternal life." Doctoris Ecstatici D. Dionysii Cartusiani, *Opera Omnia*, Vol. 4 (Montreuil: 1897), 443.

7 Col. 1:22b. *E. N.* The Douay-Rheims uses the word "unspotted" to translated *immaculatos*. For consistency's sake, I have translated *immaculatos* as "immaculate."

8 Matt. 5:3–12. *E. N.* The reference is to the Sermon on the Mount and the Beatitudes.

And so the Psalm proceeds to the blessedness of the contemplative life: **118{119}[2]** *Beati, blessed* are now in hope *qui scrutantur, they who search*, not out of presumption or out of curiosity, but diligently and with humility, *testimonia eius, his testimonies*, that is, the assertions of holy Scripture or those divine Scriptures in which God asserts that which we ought to believe. The parts of the divine law are two, namely, commandments and testimonies. Commandments pertain to the things to be done, testimonies to those things to be believed. And so the blessedness of the active life is to be found in the observation of the commandments; but the blessedness of the contemplative life is the contemplation of the testimonies. For this reason the Savior speaking to the Father said: *This is eternal life: That they may know you, the only true God, and Jesus Christ, whom you have sent.*[9] And the Apostle [Paul] says: *I count all things to be but loss for the excellent knowledge of Jesus Christ my Lord.*[10] If we really want true blessedness, we must, therefore, search the sacred Scriptures and apply ourselves in the continuous study of the divine books and to view, with great reverence, the sacred words as letters sent to us by the Holy Spirit. For the Holy Spirit speaks to us when we study. And as that most studious Jerome confessed, he who loves the study of the Scriptures, abhors the gluttony and delights of the belly.[11] For this is stated in Ecclesiasticus: *The wise men will seek out the wisdom of all the ancients, and will be occupied in the prophets.*[12] Indeed, this occupation is exceedingly delightful and salutary, as we read: *We . . . having for our comfort the holy books that are in our hands.*[13]

But one must be watchful always lest we occupy our intellect in the consideration of truth to so great an extent that our affections in the delight of the greatest goodness and the light of holy devotion grows cool or tepid. Indeed, we ought more frequently, and more principally, and if it be possible, daily to spend time in the exercising and in fanning the flames of the affections than in mere intellectual studies. Many (most sadly!) do the opposite: for this reason, they never reach true perfection. And so there is added: *in toto corde exquirunt eum, that seek him with their whole heart:* that is, that undertake this searching of the testimonies of God related totally to God so

---

9 John 17:3.

10 Phil. 3:8a.

11 E. N. This is a loose paraphrase. The statement is found in St. Jerome's letter (125) to the monk Rusticus: *Ama scientiam scripturarum et carnis vitia non amabis,* "Love the study of the Scriptures and you will not love the vices of the flesh." *Epist.* 125.11, PG 22, 1078.

12 Ecclus. 39:1.

13 1 Macc. 12:9.

that the they might advance in his love from sincere contemplation and they might honor him in all respect in their intellect and their affection. And in this regard the contemplation of holy things differs from the contemplation of vanities, as does the contemplation of the philosophers from that of the theologians — in that the saintly and true theologians are not carried off by empty speculation, but they refer [their contemplation] to the actual and fervent love of God; but the philosophers and vain believers do nothing in response to such consideration, or, what is worse, sometimes mix with it a desire for vain glory, or money, or some temporal good.

118{119}[3] *For they that work iniquity, have not walked in his ways.*

Non enim qui operantur iniquitatem in viis eius ambulaverunt.

These, then, immaculate and studious persons are blessed; but this is not so for the vicious and lazy, the condition or rather sign of which is [is then addressed]: **118{119}[3]** *Non enim qui operantur iniquitatem, in viis eius ambulaverunt; for they that work iniquity, have not walked in his ways,* that is, [those in] mortal sin which no one can commit without the consent of reason,[14] have not lived a manner of life following the divine precepts during the time that they did iniquitous things: indeed, such persons walk in the ways of the devil. About these persons is written: *We wearied ourselves in the way of iniquity and destruction, and have walked through hard ways, but the way of the Lord we have not known.*[15] This is the broad and wide way which leads to death in which many walk.[16] For regarding this we read: *The ways of the Lord are right, and the just shall walk in them: but the transgressors shall fall in them.*[17] They do not walk in the ways of the Lord of which are said: *His ways are beautiful ways, and all his paths are peaceable.*[18] Now of the beauty of the ways of the just by which they serve God in holiness is written: *The path of the just, as a shining light, goes forwards and increases even to the perfect day.*[19]

---

14 *E. N.* "For a sin to be mortal, three conditions must together be met: 'Mortal sin is sin whose object is a grave matter and which is also committed with full knowledge and deliberate consent.'" CCC § 1857 (quoting St. John Paul II's *Reconciliatio et Paenitentia*, 17 § 12).

15 Wis. 5:7.

16 *Cf.* Matt. 7:13.

17 Hosea 14:10b.

18 Prov. 3:17a. *E. N.* The original text in the Douay-Rheims uses feminine pronouns (referring to personified "Wisdom," *Sapientia*, a noun of feminine gender in Latin). I have changed them to masculine pronouns so that it fits with the subject, Lord.

19 Prov. 4:18.

118{119}[4] *You have commanded your commandments to be kept most diligently.*

Tu mandasti mandata tua custodiri nimis.

118{119}[4] *Tu, you,* O Lord, *mandasti mandata tua custodiri nimis, have commanded your commandments to be kept most diligently,* that is, very carefully. For the service due to the great, high, and infinite Lord must be performed with incomparable reverence, love, and fear. And therefore this is made known to us in Jeremiah: *Cursed be he that does the work of the Lord deceitfully.*[20] And elsewhere: Now *because you are lukewarm, . . . I will begin to vomit you out of my mouth.*[21] This Moses wrote also: *Keep yourself, therefore, and your soul carefully; and do not forget the words of the Lord . . . and let them not go out of your heart all the days of your life.*[22] Now if we want to know how diligently Christ instructed us to keep his commandments, let us hear that which he asserts regarding the precept of charity: *Love the Lord your God, with your whole heart, and with your whole soul, and with your whole mind, and with your whole strength.*[23] See, he ordered such great diligence that no one in this life can possibly fulfill it. We ought to walk with fear, therefore, and great solicitude before the Lord our God,[24] keeping this in mind: *The time is that judgment should begin at the house of God. And if first at us, what shall be the end of them that believe not the gospel of God? And if the just man shall scarcely be saved, where shall the ungodly and the sinner appear?*[25]

118{119}[5] *O that my ways may be directed to keep your justifications!*

Utinam dirigantur viae meae ad custodiendas iustificationes tuas!

118{119}[5] *Utinam dirigantur viae meae, O that my ways may be directed,* O Lord, that my ways, that is, the desires, words, and work which direct a man to the heavenly homeland, [be directed] by you and the holy angel through your grace, *ad custodiendas iustificationes tuas, to keep your justifications,* that is, in such a way and so directly that your

---

20 Jer. 48:10a.
21 Rev. 3:16.
22 Deut. 4:9.
23 Mark 12:30.
24 *Cf.* Micah 6:8.
25 1 Pet. 4:17–18.

just commandments and justifications might be observed by me. That this be done by you, O Lord, I vehemently desire, because I am unable to fulfill this by my natural power, since (as the Apostle attests) it is not he who wills, nor he who runs, but the mercifulness of God [that provides such supernatural virtue].[26] Whence also the holy Jeremiah said: *I know, O Lord, that the way of a man is not his: neither is it in a man to walk, and to direct his steps.*[27] And Solomon: *The heart of a man disposes his way: but the Lord must direct his steps.*[28] This ought to shame Pelagius, the enemy of the grace of God, who said that man was able to merit, to become justified, and also to be saved without grace, notwithstanding what the Apostle said: We are not *sufficient to think anything of ourselves, as of ourselves.*[29] And Christ professes: *As the branch cannot bear fruit of itself, unless it abide in the vine, so neither can you, unless you abide in me.*[30]

118{119}[6] *Then shall I not be confounded, when I shall look into all your commandments.*

Tunc non confundar, cum perspexero in omnibus mandatis tuis.

118{119}[6] *Tunc non confundar,* then shall I not be confounded out of negligence, *cum perspexero in omnibus mandatis tuis,* when I shall look into all your commandments, that is, when I shall thoroughly examine, profoundly think upon, and efficaciously fulfill all the divine precepts: for, as James testifies in his epistle, *He that has looked into the perfect law of liberty ... shall be blessed in his deed.*[31] And this applies to all the commandments, for he says: *Whosoever shall keep the whole law, but offend in one point, is become guilty of all.*[32] And that this is the case is seen by that contained in Ecclesiastes: *He that shall offend in one, shall lose many good things.*[33] And from this it is determined that he who offends one [commandment] becomes guilty of all [commandments] as it relates to the punishment of the damned.

---

26 Cf. Rom. 9:16: *So then it is not of him that wills, nor of him that runs, but of God that shows mercy.*
27 Jer. 10:23.
28 Prov. 16:9.
29 2 Cor. 3:5. E. N. St. Paul continues: *but our sufficiency is from God.*
30 John 15:4.
31 James 1:25.
32 James 2:10.
33 Eccl. 9:18b.

118{119}[7] *I will confess you with uprightness of heart, when I shall have learned the judgments of your justice.*[34]

Confitebor tibi in directione cordis, in eo quod didici iudicia iustitiae tuae.

118{119}[8] *I will keep your justifications: O do not utterly forsake me!*

Iustificationes tuas custodiam; non me derelinquas usquequaque!

118{119}[7] *Confitebor tibi, I will confess you,* that is, I will praise you, and I will accuse myself, by a twin confession to you, namely, of praise and of fault, offering, *in directione cordis, with uprightness of heart,* that is, as long as you direct my heart to yourself, or I direct it to you by grace, *in eo quod didici, when I shall have learned,* that through divine revelation, human explanation, or appropriate considerations, *iudicia iustitiae tuae, the judgments of your justice,* that is, the just determinations contained in Scripture by which you judge the good and the evil, returning to every person those things which he deserves. These are judgments: Go, *you cursed, into everlasting fire;*[35] and, *Come, you blessed of my Father;*[36] and *Woe to the world because of scandals.*[37] Now when saying these things, we ought to give thanks to God for the benefits of his illumination; we ought also to be troubled by and also fear our excesses: and so confess to God, not only with the confession of praise, but also the confession or our own sinfulness. But because both confessions require obedience to the heavenly commandments, so I fixedly propose that: **118{119}[8]** *Iustificationes tuas, your justifications,* that is, your precepts, *custodiam, I will keep:* as is written: *He that keeps the commandment, keeps his own soul.*[38] And so that I might have the power to do this, *non me derelinquas usquequaque, do not utterly forsake me,* that is, do not withdraw the support of your grace completely from me, nor suspend your usual kindliness from me. Indeed, we ought to pray that God never removes from us the habit of charity and of grace for any moment, for in such a case we would be in a state of damnation. But sometimes, as it regards some acts of grace, it is better for us that God abandons us for a time, namely by withdrawing or suspending internal consolations and feelings of devotion in order that

---

34 E. N. Again, I have replaced the Douay-Rheim's translation "I will praise" with "I will confess." Clearly, in this part of the *Commentary*, Denis considers the confession both one of praise and one of fault.

35 Matt. 25:41.

36 Matt. 25:34.

37 Matt. 18:7a.

38 Prov. 19:16a.

he might test our virtue, increase or merits through patience, preserve the souls from all pride, so that a man might learn of his weakness by experience; and so one ought to have recourse to God and to be more cautious in the future. For without the help of God, we are never able to do acts that are meritorious or to persevere in the good.

PRAYER

LORD, ON OUR WAY THROUGH THIS world, make us to walk holy and immaculate in your law, and diligently to keep your commandments; and do not ever abandon us from the keeping of your justifications.

In huius, Domine, saeculi via fac nos sanctos et immaculatos ambulare in lege tua, mandata tua nimis custodire, et in iustificationum tuarum custodia non nos derelinquas usquequaque.

BETH
(PART II)

118{119}[9] *By what does a young man correct his way? By observing your words.*

In quo corrigit adolescentior viam suam? In custodiendo sermones tuos.

118{119}[9] *In quo corrigit adolescentior viam suam? By what does a young man correct his way?* That is, through what means does a young man who is prone to passions refrain from the impulses of his passions towards those things to which they naturally incline him? For young men are particularly inclined to anger and disordered desire. And he responds: *In custodiendo sermones tuos, by observing your words,* that is, in obeying sacred Scripture which prohibits, condemns, and punishes evil doing; but it rejoices in praises, and rewards the doing of good. For truly, the young man who ponders the Savior well is healed from the concupiscence of the flesh: *Whosoever shall look on a woman to lust after her, has already committed adultery with her in his heart;*[39] *He who hates not his father, and*

---

39 Matt. 5:28.

mother, and wife, etc. cannot be my disciple;[40] and again, *Take heed lest perhaps your hearts be overcharged with surfeiting and drunkenness.*[41] He also who hears and follows that said by holy Job, *I made a covenant with my eyes, that I would not so much as think upon a virgin,* as a corrective against concupiscence.[42] Similarly, the word of Christ restrains one from anger, when he says: *Whosoever is angry with his brother, shall be in danger of the judgment;*[43] and, *Learn of me, because I am meek.*[44] This Peter also says in his epistle, *I beseech you as strangers and pilgrims, to refrain yourselves from carnal desires which war against the soul.*[45] Now he who does not fulfill these things, cannot hold himself to belong to Christ, since Paul says: *They that are Christ's have crucified their flesh, with the vices and concupiscences.*[46] And in Ecclesiasticus this is written: *If you give to your soul her desires, she will make you a joy to your enemies.*[47]

118{119}[10] *With my whole heart have I sought after you: let me not stray from your commandments.*

In toto corde meo exquisivi te; ne repellas me a mandatis tuis.

Since this is so, in order that I might have any possibility of correcting my way through the observing of your words, **118{119}[10]** *In toto corde meo, with my whole heart,* that is, with the intellect and the will; or, *with my whole heart,* that is, with a heart totally turned toward you so that it is absolutely averse to unlawful things; *exquisivi te, I have sought after you* as the highest good, to whom I in the end intend and desire to cling to. We ought not to seek after God with a divided or duplicitous heart, for to the extent we seek something else, to that degree we do not seek God. Whence of these sorts of persons it is written: *Their heart is divided: now they shall perish;*[48] and, *Come not to God with a double heart.*[49] *Ne repellas me a mandatis tuis, let me not stray from your commandments,* that is, do not allow me to be overcome by my own vices and passions and because of this to distance myself from the keeping

---

40 Luke 14:26.
41 Luke 21:34.
42 Job 31:1.
43 Matt. 5:22a.
44 Natt. 11:29a.
45 1 Pet. 2:11.
46 Gal. 5:24.
47 Ecclus. 18:31.
48 Hosea 10:2a.
49 Ecclus. 1:36b.

of your commandments; but accept my prayers, and grant that I might fulfill the divine commands. This is what we pray: O Lord, *cast me not off from among your children;*[50] and, *O Lord, father, and sovereign ruler of my life, leave me not to the counsel* of evil men.[51]

118{119}[11] *Your words have I hidden in my heart, that I may not sin against you.*

In corde meo abscondi eloquia tua, ut non peccem tibi.

118{119}[12] *Blessed are you, O Lord: teach me your justifications.*

Benedictus es, Domine; doce me iustificationes tuas.

118{119}[11] *In corde meo abscondi,* I have hidden in my heart, that is, I have retained in my memory, *eloquia tua, ut non peccem tibi, your words . . . that I may not sin against you,* that is, cause you offense. For sacred words teach what ought to be done and what ought to be omitted lest the Lord be offended. And so Christ said: *Blessed are they who hear the word of God, and keep it.*[52] But this seems to contradict that which was said earlier: *I have not concealed your mercy and your truth from a great council.*[53] The answer is that there is a twofold hiding of sacred words. One is the kind by which we do not communicate to our neighbor fraternal instruction: and this kind is vicious, according to this: *Wisdom that is hid, and treasure that is not seen: what profit is there in them both?*[54] The second kind, therefore, is a hiding which does not include forgetfulness: and it is of this hiding which we now speak. **118{119}[12]** *Benedictus es, Domine; blessed are you, O Lord,* in yourself because of the sanctity of your nature, *doce me iustificationes tuas, teach me your justifications,* that is, your divine commandments: so that I know and fulfill them not only habitually, but also actually.[55]

---

50 Wis. 9:4.

51 Ecclus. 23:1.

52 Luke 11:28.

53 Ps. 39:11b.

54 Ecclus. 20:32.

55 E. N. To understand this distinction between fulfilling the commandments "habitually" versus "actually," we might refer to the *Summa* of St. Thomas, specifically ST IIaIIae, q. 44, art. 4, ad 2: "To love God with all one's heart can be taken in a twofold way," St. Thomas says. "The first way is in act (*in actu*), that is, that the whole heart of man is always actually directed to God. And this is the perfection of the heavenly fatherland (*perfectio patriae*). The second way is the whole heart of man is directed to God habitually (*habitualiter*), so that the heart of man accepts nothing that is against the love of God. And this is the perfection of the way (*perfectio*

118{119}[13]   *With my lips I have pronounced all the judgments of your mouth.*

In labiis meis pronuntiavi omnia iudicia oris tui.

118{119}[14]   *I have been delighted in the way of your testimonies, as in all riches.*

In via testimoniorum tuorum delectatus sum, sicut in omnibus divitiis.

118{119}[13] *In labiis meis pronuntiavi, with my lips I have pronounced,* preaching or making known to others who are in my presence, *omnia iudicia oris tui, all the judgments of your mouth,* that is, all the words of your justice contained in the Scriptures: all, I say, both generally and specifically, bringing to mind your judgments by which the ungodly are condemned and the good are saved. And although (according to the Apostle [Paul]) the judgments of God are incomprehensible,[56] especially that [judgment providing that] some are among the elect for eternity and others are reprobate, yet they can still be proclaimed, as when we proclaim that wondrous written judgment of God: *Jacob I have loved, but Esau I have hated.*[57] 118{119}[14] *In via, in the way,* that is, by the keeping and contemplation, *testimoniorum tuorum, of your testimonies,* that is, of the words of sacred Scripture, *delectatus sum, sicut in omnibus divitiis, I have been delighted . . . as in all riches,* that is, [I have been] so heartily and exuberantly [delighted] as the avaricious rejoice in temporal goods, so that I read, hear, and carry out the words of sacred Scripture — such as, *Blessed are the poor in spirit, Blessed are the merciful, Blessed are the meek, Blessed are they who mourn;* and *He that humbles himself shall be exalted* — with a joyful and loving heart.[58]

118{119}[15]   *I will meditate on your commandments: and I will consider your ways.*

In mandatis tuis exercebor, et considerabo vias tuas.

---

viae)." "*In via* this love for God is normally oscillating between its being a *habitus* and its actualization. Although the human creature is completely capable to realize this *habitus* [*in via*], it may be difficult to do so, because of obstacles." Jan G. J. van den Eijnden, *Poverty on the Way to God: Thomas Aquinas on Evangelical Poverty* (Nijmegen: Peeters Publishers, 1994), 83.

56 *Cf.* Rom. 11:33.
57 Mal. 1:2, 3.
58 Matt. 5:3, 7, 4, 5; Luke 14:11.

118{119}[16] *I will meditate upon your justifications: I will not forget your words.*[59]

In iustificationibus tuis meditabor: non obliviscar sermones tuos.

118{119}[15] *In mandatis tuis exercebor, I will meditate on your commandments*, frequently recalling them, and faithfully following them; *et considerabo vias tuas, and I will consider your ways*, that is, the works and examples of those who pleased you, by which one comes to you; or, *your ways*, that is, your operations which you carry out in us, seeing that as you rain upon the just and the unjust,[60] so I ought to learn to do good to my enemies; or, *your ways*, that is, your fairness and clemency, of which was stated in an earlier Psalm: *All the ways of the Lord are mercy and truth.*[61] **118{119}[16]** *In iustificationibus tuis, in your justifications*, that is, in observing your preceptive justifications, *meditabor, I will meditate*: as is contained the beginning of the book of Psalms: *His will is in the law of the Lord, and on his law he shall meditate day and night;*[62] *non obliviscar sermones tuos, I will not forget your words*, but I will endeavor to fulfill that which Moses stated: *These words* of the Lord *shall be in your heart, and you shall tell them to your children, and you shall meditate upon them sitting in your house, and walking on your journey, sleeping and rising; and you shall bind them as a sign on your hand, and they shall be and shall move between your eyes; and you shall write them in the entry and on the doors of your house.*[63] Therefore, so that the children of Israel might recall the divine precepts unceasingly, God commanded that they should make for themselves four fringes in the four corners of their garments, *putting in them ribands of blue, so that when* they might see them they might remember *all the commandments of* God, lest they follow their thoughts and eyes, *fornicating after divers things.*[64]

---

59 *E. N.* I departed from the Douay-Rheims by replacing "I will think of your justifications" with "I will meditate upon your justifications."

60 Matt. 5:45.

61 Ps. 24:10.

62 Ps. 1:2.

63 Deut. 6:6–9.

64 Num. 15:38–39. *E. N.* I have replaced the Douay-Rheims's "going astray" (which translates *fornicantes*) to "fornicating," which is more literal. We ought recall St. Augustine's famous words in his *Confessions*: "I did not love you, and I committed fornication against you, and all about me those fornicating echoed 'Well done! Well done!' For the friendship of this world is fornication against you, and 'Well done! well done!' echoes on until one is ashamed not to be thus a man. *Conf.* I, 13.

PRAYER

AKE US WHO ARE MADE FOR YOUR SER-
vice, O Lord, to seek you diligently with our whole heart,
and to follow your commandments courageously so that, with our
understanding taught by you and considering your ways, we might
always take delight in them as in all riches.

*In servitio tuo constitutos, Domine, fac nos te toto cordo exquirere,
et in mandatis tuis viriliter exerceri: ut consideratis viis tuis, et te
docenter intellectis, semper sicut in omnibus divitiis delectemur in illis.*

GHIMEL
(PART III)

118{119}[17]   *Give bountifully to your servant, enliven me: and I shall
keep your words.*

Retribue servo tuo, vivifica me, et custodiam sermones tuos.

118{119}[18]   *Open my eyes: and I will consider the wondrous things of
your law.*

Revela oculos meos, et considerabo mirabilia de lege tua.

118{119}[17] *Retribue servo tuo, give bountifully to your servant,* give
grace, namely, to me and to all of the assemblage of Christians lost by
sinning or neglecting to obtain merit by omission; *vivifica me, enliven
me* spiritually with the life of grace: for as the soul gives life to the
flesh, so grace gives life to the soul; *et custodiam sermones tuos, and I
shall keep your words,* that is, strengthened with the aid and the light
of grace—without which grace I am unable to accomplish anything
meritoriously—I will fulfill your commands. **118{119}[18]** *Revela oculos
meo, open my eyes* (unquestionably the interior [eyes]), that is, teach
and enlighten by the gifts of wisdom, knowledge, understanding, and
counsel, and also by angelic illumination and human instruction, my
speculative and practical intellect, my superior and inferior reason;[65] *et*

---

65 "Practical reason is distinct from speculative reason because it is ordered to some work
or end. The difference between the practical and speculative intellects is that the speculative is concerned only with the truth, whereas the practical apprehends the truth for the
sake of some further end." *The Oxford Handbook of Aquinas* (Oxford: Oxford University

considerabo, and I will consider, so illumined by you, *mirabilia de lege tua, the wondrous things of your law,* that is, the incomprehensible testimonies, the supernatural articles of faith, and all the other mysteries contained in both Testaments — which, without divine enlightenment, cannot be sincerely considered; indeed, many unhappy heretics presuming to consider and to measure such things by natural light have led sects into eternal perdition. The Apostle [Paul] wished to open these eyes of his disciples, when he said: *May the Father of glory give unto you the spirit of wisdom and of revelation of him, the eyes of your heart enlightened, so that you may know the hope of your calling.*[66]

118{119}[19] *I am a sojourner on the earth: hide not your commandments from me.*

Incola ego sum in terra, non abscondas a me mandata tua.

I need, O Lord, this just-mentioned revelation: for **118{119}[19]** *Incola ego sum in terra, I am a sojourner on the earth,* that is, a wayfarer, not a comprehensor as are the inhabitants of heaven, but I am a pilgrim and stranger. And so I walk by faith and not by sight: because (as the Apostle attests) *while we are in the body, were are absent from the Lord;*[67] and *we see through a glass in a dark manner, . . .* knowing *in part.*[68] For this reason I unceasingly need the divine illumination, for *the corruptible body is a load upon the soul,* and *the thoughts of mortal men are fearful, and our counsels uncertain.*[69] *Non abscondas a me mandata tua, hide not your commandments from me,* but teach them to me, removing from me the fog of vices, the obscure knowledge of your commandments and thereby increasing the light of grace in my soul so that no occupation impede it from the memory of the divine commandments.

118{119}[20] *My soul has craved to long for your justifications, at all times.*

Concupivit anima mea desiderare iustificationes tuas in omni tempore.

Press, 2012) (eds. Brian Davis and Eleonore Stump). "[H]uman acts are directed both by superior reason and inferior reason, and the first follows divine and eternal reasons and considerations, the second those which are human and temporal." Jacques Maritain, *Science and Wisdom* (London: Geoffrey Bles, 1940), 158–60 (trans., Bernard Wall).

66 Eph. 1:17–18.
67 2 Cor. 5:6b.
68 1 Cor. 13:12.
69 Wis. 9:15a, 14.

118{119}[20] *Concupivit anima mea desiderare iustificationes tuas, my soul has craved to long for your justifications*: that is, my soul, which still imperfectly and tepidly craves your commandments or the acts of your commandments, longs to crave them ardently and perfectly. For as the intellect, so also the will is reflective of its own acts. Therefore, as the soul recognizes itself to understand through the intellect and it knows the imperfection of its acts and craves more perfect knowledge, so also the soul by its will craves and wants intellectual desire, and it experiences its lack of completeness, and it strives to obtain a more complete desire. This is so because both the intellect and the will make progress from the imperfect to the more perfect. My soul therefore craves to desire the divine justifications, that is, the just works by which it may be justified, and not just in some manner, but *in omni tempore, at all times*, so that it may persevere in the holy affection: not that it can desire in this way actually every hour of the day, but that it desire this at due, certain, and fitting hours of time: according to that way the Apostle said: *Pray without ceasing.*[70] We ought at least unceasingly to desire this good in act or habit.[71]

118{119}[21] *You have rebuked the proud: they are cursed who decline from your commandments.*

Increpasti superbos; maledicti qui declinant a mandatis tuis.

118{119}[21] *Increpasti superbos, you have rebuked the proud.* Frequently in sacred Scripture all the proud are reprehended. An instance of this is when Ecclesiasticus says: *Why is earth and ashes proud?* And elsewhere: *Every one that exalts himself, shall be humbled;*[72] and, *God resists the proud, and gives grace to the humble.*[73] For this reason God soundly rebuked the proud angels in heaven when he cast them from heaven into the gloomy airs of hell, as is written: *The angels who kept not their principality, but forsook their own habitation, he has reserved under darkness in everlasting chains, unto the judgment of the great day.*[74] And Peter said: *God spared not the angels that sinned, but delivered them, drawn down by infernal ropes to the lower hell, unto torments, to be reserved unto judgment.*[75] Also, God

---

70 1 Thess. 5:17.
71 E. N. For the distinction between possession of a quality (say a virtue) *habitually* versus *actually*, see footnote 118-55.
72 Luke 18:14b.
73 James 4:6.
74 Jude 6.
75 2 Pet. 2:4.

rebuked and expelled from paradise our first parents who grew proud.[76] *Maledicti, they are cursed,* that is, they are censured and eternally damned by God, *qui declinant, who decline* until their end *a mandatis tuis, from your commandments,* not observing them: for no man can be saved or blessed except by keeping the precepts of the most-high God. The proud angels are cursed for eternity, as the Lord said to their prince: *Your inner parts were filled with iniquity, and you have sinned: and I cast you out from the mountain of God, and destroyed you, O covering cherub, out of the midst of the stones of fire.*[77] Our first parents were temporarily cursed when they were assessed certain punishments and miseries in the present life, as we read in Genesis.[78]

118{119}[22] *Remove from me reproach and contempt: because I have sought after your testimonies.*

Aufer a me opprobrium et contemptum, quia testimonia tua exquisivi.

118{119}[22] *Aufer a me opproprium et contemptum,* remove from me reproach and contempt. This can be understood in three ways. The first, as active reproach and contempt, so it is [to be understood] in this sense: Grant that I do not reproach anyone or spurn someone, because this is a great evil, and it warrants eternal damnation according to this: *Woe to you that spoils, shall you not yourself also be spoiled? And you that despise, shall you not yourself also be despised? When you shall have made an end of spoiling, you shall be spoiled: when being wearied you shall cease to despise, you shall be despised.*[79] And: *Have we not all one Father? Has not one God created us? Why then does every one of us despise his brother, violating the covenant of our fathers?*[80] The second, is understood as referring to passive reproach and contempt, from which we pray we might be delivered: [not, to be sure,] that we might not be reproached and contemned by anyone, especially when we might obtain merit from it, or suffer it for reasons of justice, since the holy Peter says, *If you be reproached for the name of Christ, you shall be blessed;*[81] in such cases we ought not to be overcome with impatience. For if we endure

---

76 Gen. 3:9–24.
77 Ez. 28:16.
78 Gen. 3:16–19.
79 Is. 33:1.
80 Mal. 2:10.
81 1 Pet. 4:14a.

such patiently, they will be removed from us to the extent that they are harmful, and then indeed they will greatly profit us in obtaining the crown. The third is this: *Remove from me the reproach of the curse,* the curse of the proud and disobedient, *and the contempt* of transgressors, lest that which was said to David be said to me, *Why have you despised the word of the Lord?*[82] *Quia testimonia tua, because...your testimonies,* that is, the sacred words testified to and in many ways confirmed by you, *exquisivi, I have sought* to know them and to perform them. And therefore it is fitting that you hear me.

118{119}[23]   *For princes sat, and spoke against me: but your servant was employed in your justifications.*

Etenim sederunt principes, et adversum me loquebantur; servus autem tuus exercebatur in iustificationibus tuis.

118{119}[23] *Etenim sederunt principes, et adversum me loquebantur; for princes sat and spoke against me.* The princes of the world and ungodly men frequently have sat, and sit, against the martyrs of Christ and other just men, speaking against them in councils or judgments, and seeking their death or their persecution. Against all of us, however, the princes, that is, the demons, remain always ready [to speak against us]. Of this the Apostle said: *Our wrestling is not against flesh and blood; but against principalities and powers, against the rulers of the world of this darkness, against the spirits of wickedness in the high places.*[83] *Et adversum me loquebantur, and spoke against me.* For they discuss things among themselves, and they speak in this way about what sort of temptation can trip up someone. For they explore the manners and interests of every person, and they seek to introduce harm where they see someone studiously occupied; they also endeavor to tempt every person of that vice that they see him to be prone. It is therefore not to be suprising that such [demons] set and machinate against us, when Christ has professed as to one of these: *For the prince of this world comes, and in me he has not anything.*[84] *Servus autem tuus, but your servant* undergoing such an attack *exercebatur, was employed,* that is occupied in both mind and deed, *in iustificationibus tuis, in your justifications,* that is, in your divine precepts. For one occupation expels or reduces another, especially if it is done with great intensity. And so when we see ourselves to be greatly tempted, we

---

82 2 Sam. 12:9a.
83 Eph. 6:12.
84 John 14:30.

ought all the more vehemently to occupy ourselves with divine things: meditating, praying, singing hymns, writing, or performing other good works: for in this manner we feel the temptation less. For idleness greatly increases the power of the adversary.[85]

118{119}[24] *For your testimonies are my meditation: and your justifica-tions my counsel.*

Nam et testimonia tua meditatio mea est; et consilium meum iustificationes tuae.

118{119}[24] *Nam et testimonia tua meditatio mea est; for your testi-monies are my meditation,* not essentially, but materially, for I meditate continuously on your testimonies, and I detest to think on other things; *et consilium meum, and my counsel* are *iustificationes tuae, your justifications,* that is, commandments, so that my whole counsel is turned toward, and is ordered to, this: that I might observe your precepts. So did the venerable Sarah do, as she said: *Never have I joined myself with them that play: neither have I made myself partaker with them that walk in lightness.*[86]

PRAYER

LORD, BESTOWER OF EVERY GOOD, MAKE us to crave your justifications at all time and to persevere doing good in them; remove from us the reproach and contempt of our enemies, and grant that we might perpetually receive from your hand the kingdom of beauty and honor.

Bonorum omnium largitor, Domine, fac nos desiderare iustificationes tuas in omni tempore, et in eis bene operando perseverare; aufer a nobis opprobrium inimici et contemptum, et da nos perpetim de manu tua accipere decoris et honoris regnum.

---

85 E. N. "Idleness is school of vice: *Idleness hath taught much evil* (Eccl. xxxiii. 29). As long as the mind is occupied, it hardly thinks of anything else except the object that occupies it. But as soon as the mind is inactive, it is filled with thousands of phantoms and shameful thoughts. Idleness is like a stagnant water which conceals the most hideous reptiles.... Hence, if you wish to avoid the vice of impurity, fly idleness. Let the devil find you always occupied." *The Catechism of Rodez* (St. Louis, MO: B. Herder, 1899), 319. (trans., Rev. John Thein).

86 Tob. 3:17.

DALETH
(PART IV)

118{119}[25]   *My soul has cleaved to the pavement: quicken me according to your word.*

Adhaesit pavimento anima mea; vivifica me secundum verbum tuum.

118{119}[25] *Adhaesit pavimento anima mea, my soul has cleaved to the pavement,* that is, my soul is joined with this troublesome, earthly, and corruptible body both as a substantial and intrinsic form: and so it is frequently impeded from doing good works, because *the earthly habitation presses down the mind that muses upon many things.*[87] Frequently also my soul cleaves to this pavement by the illicit consent in the following of its desires. Against this it states in Ecclesiasticus: *Go not after your lusts, but turn away from your own will.*[88] And so the soul is held captive by the law of sin which reigns in my members. Regarding this, the Apostle says: *I see another law in my members, fighting against the law of my mind.*[89] Whence, along with the holy Apostle I am compelled to cry out: *Unhappy man that I am! Who shall deliver me from the body of this death,*[90] that is, from the vice, defects, disordered desires, or impediments of this mortal body? And he responds: *The grace of God, by Jesus Christ our Lord.*[91] For now the previously described ills which befall souls from their union with the body are diminished or alleviated by grace. But in the future resurrection, they will be completely removed, for then the bodies of the saints will be fully subject, proportionate, and assimilated to their souls, according to that which is expressed in Romans: *The creature also itself shall be delivered from the servitude of corruption, into the liberty of the glory of the children of God.*[92] And for this reason it now adds: *vivifica me, quicken me* by the infusion of grace, to the prompt and lively execution of good works, so that I might not adhere to the inferior things, but be completely preoccupied with heavenly things, and that I might *live* in the flesh, not that I might *walk* according to the flesh, but so that with the Apostle I am able to confess: *Our conversation is in*

---

87 Wis. 9:15b.
88 Ecclus. 18:30.
89 Rom. 7:23a.
90 Rom. 7:24.
91 Rom. 7:25a.
92 Rom. 8:21.

heaven.[93] And *quicken* me *secundum verbum tuum, according to your word,* for in sacred Scripture you promise to hear those who pray to you, and to bestow upon them all the grace they pray for, as it is written: *All things, whatsoever you ask when you pray, believe that you shall receive; and they shall come unto you.*[94] Or [we can understand it thus], *according to your word,* that is written in Deuteronomy where it says: *Not in bread alone does man live, but in every word that proceeds from the mouth of God.*[95]

118{119}[26] *I have declared my ways, and you have heard me: teach me your justifications.*

Vias meas enuntiavi, et exaudisti me; doce me iustificationes tuas.

118{119}[26] *Vias meas,* my ways, that is, my internal and exterior activities, *enuntiavi,* I have declared to you who know all things, or to your priestly representative, humbly confessing my imperfections and my faults, and ascribing all good totally to you, *et exaudisti me, and you have heard me,* bestowing merciful indulgence and showing forth grace. Whence Job said: *I will reprove my ways in his sight, and he shall be my Savior.*[96] Also, in a Psalm above: *Commit your way to the Lord, and trust in him, and he will do it.*[97] *Doce me iustificationes tuas, teach me your justifications,* that is, commandments, so that I might know them and fulfill them not uselessly, but so as to lead to salvation.

---

93 *Cf.* 2 Cor. 10:2–3; Phil. 3:20. E. N. Here one should recall that the Latin word *conversatio,* here translated by the word "conversation," has the implication of "manner of life," or "lifestyle." St. Paul does not have in mind here a dialogue or a *tête-à-tête.*
94 Mark 11:24. E. N. Rightly disposed prayers for those things necessary for our salvation are always granted: "Understand this beloved: Every believer having the word of God in his heart, fearing with dread the future judgment, living commend-ably so that no one may blaspheme the name of the Lord because of him, prays for many things according to the world and is not heard; but he will always be heard to obtain eternal life. For who does not pray for health when he is sick? And yet it may be that remaining sick is for his benefit. It may be that in this instance you would not be heard—though you are heard as to your will, you are not heard because it is useful [that you remain sick]. But be assured of this: when you ask God to give you eternal life, that he give you the kingdom of heaven, and that he grant that you might stand at the right hand of his Son when he comes to judge the earth, you will receive it; if for a time you do not receive it, it is because the time has not yet come for you to receive it. You are heard, though you do not know it: that which you ask for will be done, even if you do not know how it will be done. The reality is in the root, though not yet in the fruit." *Enarr. in Psalmos,* 59, 7, PL 36, 718.
95 Deut. 8:3; Matt. 4:4.
96 Job 13:15b–16a.
97 Ps. 36:5.

118{119}[27]   *Make me to understand the way of your justifications: and I shall be exercised in your wondrous works.*

Viam iustificationum tuarum instrue me, et exercebor in mirabilibus tuis.

118{119}[27] *Viam, the way,* that is, the process and order, *iustificationum tuarum instrue me, of your justifications . . . make me to understand,* so that I might know which commandments are first and most important, which are necessary first and principally to fulfill. For two in number are these precepts of charity in which all others are virtually contained. *Et exercebor in mirabilibus tuis, and I shall be exercised in your wondrous works.* This refers to what a short time earlier was stated [in verse 18]: *I will consider the wondrous things of your law.* And so what does it mean to be exercised in the wondrous works of God? [It means] nothing other than to contemplate with an enlightened eye the incomprehensible testimonies of the Christian faith humbly and profoundly, namely, how the holy and glorious God, though he is one and supremely simple in essence, yet most truly is three in person; and that from the counsel of this ineffable Trinity the Son of God became incarnate for our saving repair, that his Mother remained a virgin, and to contemplate also the other mysteries of Christ; to consider also how terrible is the God *in his counsels over the sons of men,*[98] how much suavity he shows to his elect, and how severe he is toward the reprobate.

118{119}[28]   *My soul has slumbered through heaviness: strengthen me in your words.*

Dormitavit anima mea prae taedio; confirma me in verbis tuis.

118{119}[28] *Dormitavit anima mea prae taedio, my soul has slumbered through heaviness.* To sleep is properly fitting to the lazy, according to this: *Slothfulness casts into a deep sleep.*[99] And again, Solomon says: *How long will you sleep, O sluggard?*[100] Yet to sleep also is fitting for those that are worn out and tired. But the soul is burdened and tired with the troubles of the body because of its various necessities. The soul sleeps with weariness, while it is fatigued by the burdens of the body which influences it to have less affection for spiritual things, and it makes progress with difficulty in such things or it in some fashion

---

98 Ps. 65:5.
99 Prov. 19:15a.
100 Prov. 6:9a.

is disheartened because of the delay of internal consolations: and so it is in need to be strengthened by God. And he prays for this, adding: *confirma me in verbis tuis, strengthen me in your words,* that is, give to me from the reading, hearing, or recollection of sacred Scripture to be strengthened heartily, as I then hear it, read it, or recall: *The sufferings of this time are not worthy to be compared with the glory to come;*[101] and, *Watch, stand fast in the faith, do manfully, and be strengthened;*[102] For according to the Apostle, *All scripture, inspired of God, is profitable to teach, [to reprove, to correct, to instruct in justice,] that the man of God may be perfect, furnished to every good work.*[103] And it is written: *The word of God . . . is a buckler to them that hope in him.*[104]

———————

118{119}[29] *Remove from me the way of iniquity: and out of your law have mercy on me.*

Viam iniquitatis amove a me, et de lege tua miserere mei.

118{119}[29] *Viam iniquitatis, the way of iniquity,* that is, the wrong way, or the preparation, the disposition, or the occasion of sinning; *amove a me, remove from me*: for it is not possible to avoid sin unless one avoids the occasions of sin, which we pray that God remove, anticipating them with his grace and preserving us from all ruin, since we are not able always to avoid them with human power. *Et de lege, and out of your law,* that is, according to the decree of your mercy, for it is a quality proper to you to have mercy and to spare, *miserere mei, have mercy on me,* forgiving sins, and multiplying the gifts of grace in me. Or [we can understand it this way], *out of your law,* that is, in the divine law that is proposed to us, *have mercy,* pardoning that which I have committed or omitted against it.

———————

118{119}[30] *I have chosen the way of truth: your judgments I have not forgotten.*

Viam veritatis elegi; iudicia tua non sum oblitus.

118{119}[31] *I have stuck to your testimonies, O Lord: put me not to shame.*

Adhaesi testimoniis tuis, Domine; noli me confundere.

———————

101 Rom. 8:18.
102 1 Cor. 16:13.
103 2 Tim. 3:16–17. E. N. The part of the verse in brackets replaces the "etc." of Denis.
104 Prov. 30:5.

118{119}[30] *Viam Veritatis, the way of Truth*, that is, the Catholic faith and the just manner of life, *elegi, I have chosen*, holding in contempt my earlier errors and sins. Whence the Apostle said: *For I am delighted with the law of God, according to the inward man.*[105] *Iudicia tua, your judgments*, that is, the just and vindicatory sentences, by which from the beginning of the world you have reprobated and afflicted the unjust but have saved the good: as it was made clear in the flood, in the destruction of the five cities, and the killing of Pharaoh and his people;[106] *non sum oblitus, I have not forgotten*, for their memory inspires a saving fear and strengthens hope in me. 118{119}[31] *Adhaesi testimoniis tuis, Domine; I have stuck to your testimonies, O Lord*, by faith and by works, doing that which I knew would be pleasing to you: for which reason, *noli me confundere, let me not be put to shame*, frustrating my hope, rejecting my prayers, or permitting that I might fall and be found worthy of being confounded.

118{119}[32] *I have run the way of your commandments, when you did enlarge my heart.*

Viam mandatorum tuorum cucurri, cum dilatasti cor meum.

118{119}[32] *Viam, the way*, that is, the operations, *mandatorum tuorum cucurri, of your commandments . . . I have run*, that is, speedily have I fulfilled, ardently have I executed [your commandments], *cum dilatasti cor meum, when you did enlarge my heart*, filling it with a fervent desire, so that the heart opened up to hold fast to all those things that please the beloved. For the heart is spiritually enlarged, exhilarated, and broadened by charity in God and in [the doing of] good works. For nothing is difficult for the lover. And so, such a person runs faster than those merely going or walking in the divine law. And such a person experiences to be true that which is written: *His commandments are not heavy;*[107] and, *My yoke is sweet and my burden light.*[108] When, therefore, we feel ourselves fervent and eager regarding divine things, we ought not to glory vainly in ourselves, but to glory in God, humbly giving thanks for his charity and grace; and let us be cautious and provide against vainglory, the contempt of others, and future ruin.

---

105 Rom. 7:22.
106 Gen. chps. 7, 19; Ex. 14:28. E. N. Denis uses the word *Pentapolis*, the "five cities," referring Sodom, Gomorrah, Bela, Admah, and Zeboim. *See* Gen. 14:8.
107 1 John 5:3b.
108 Matt. 11:30.

PRAYER

R EMOVE US FROM THE WAYS OF INIQUITY, O Lord, and by your gratuitous kindness make that we run with an enlarged heart in the way of your commandments, so that, when we take leave of our body, we might be constituted citizens of the heavenly fatherland.

Iniquitatis vias amove a nobis, Domine, et tuo gratuito munere viam mandatorum tuorum dilatato corde da nos percurrere: ut exuti corpore, per te cives constituamur caelestis patriae.

HE
(PART V)

118{119}[33] *Set before me for a law the way of your justifications, O Lord: and I will always seek after it.*

Legem pone mihi, Domine, viam iustificationum tuarum, et exquiram eam semper.

118{119}[34] *Give me understanding, and I will search your law; and I will keep it with my whole heart.*

Da mihi intellectum, et scrutabor legem tuam, et custodiam illam in toto corde meo.

118{119}[35] *Lead me into the path of your commandments; for this same I have desired.*

Deduc me in semitam mandatorum tuorum, quia ipsam volui.

118{119}[33] *Legem pone mihi, Domine, viam iustificationem tuarum; set before me for a law the way of your justifications,* that is, the divine law set down generally for all men, which is the way of your justification, for by your law we acquire your justification. In a singular way, place this law in my heart, and before the eyes of my mind, so that day and night I might think of it. Now this position is obtained in this way: that God copiously infuses into the soul the light of grace, by which one meditates frequently, easily, and perseveringly in those things that are written in the divine law, both in the old and the new. And so there is added: *et exquiram, and I will seek after,* that is, with great care will I seek after, *eam semper, it always*, persevering in it so long as I exist. 118{119}[34] *Da mihi intellectum, give me understanding*, that is, the gift of the Holy Spirit which is called understanding,[109] or [alternatively, *give me*] *understanding*, that is, actual understanding proceeding from grace; *et scrutabor, and I will search*, that is, I will diligently consider and scrutinize, *legem tuam, your law*, thinking about those things proposed by it as to what needs to be believed, what to be hoped in, what to be loved, what to be feared, what to be done, and what to be cautious of, and what also it says by precept and what by counsel; *et custodiam illam, and I will keep it*, namely, the divine law, *in toto corde meo, with my whole heart*, namely, recalling it, contemplating it, loving it, and carrying it out. 118{119}[35] *Deduc me, lead me*, by the clarity of grace and the direction of angels, *in semita, into the path*, that is, in the process and execution, *mandatorum tuorum, of your commandments*, of your moral commandments (for the ceremonial commandments [of the Jewish law] have ceased), lest I go astray; *quia ipsam volui, for this same have I desired*, that is, because I have desired this path, and so I have done that which is in me, namely, preparing myself by the leading of your grace. It befits you, therefore, that you might hear me and lead me.

118{119}[36] *Incline my heart into your testimonies and not to covetousness.*

Inclina cor meum in testimonia tua, et non in avaritiam.

118{119}[37] *Turn away my eyes that they may not behold vanity: quicken me in your way.*

Averte oculos meos, ne videant vanitatem; in via tua vivifica me.

118{119}[36] *Inclina cor meum in testimonia tua, incline my heart into your testimonies*: that is, by your grace convert the intellect and will of my soul to your words, and begin the good in me, because in accord with a good will, that is, out of your kindness, you are he who works in us, both to will and to advance, according to the Apostle.[110] Also, *you have wrought all our works for us.*[111] *Et non in avaritiam, and not to covetousness*: for they who *will become rich, fall into temptation and into the snare of the devil.*[112] And so incline my heart toward divine things,

---

109 Is. 11:2.
110 *Cf.* Phil. 2:13: *For it is God who works in you, both to will and to accomplish, according to his good will.*
111 Is. 26:12a.
112 1 Tim. 6:9a.

so that I might completely turn away from an inordinate love of earthily things. 118{119}[37] *Averte oculus meos, turn away my eyes,* both my interior and exterior [eyes], *ne videant, that they may not behold* or desire to see *vanitatem, vanity,* that is, the spectacles of the world, the beauty of an elegant woman, etc. the consideration of which causes harm. For thoughtlessness of sight causes harm to a great number of persons, and it disposes one to great ruin.[113] Indeed, *death comes through our windows,*[114] thought is distracted, disordered desires are provoked, and hence affections for various and harmful things are born. For this reason, it is written: *Look not round about you in the ways of the city, ... turn away your face from a woman dressed up ... for many have perished by the beauty of a woman.*[115] And Ezechiel: *Let every man cast away the scandals of his eyes,* says the Lord.[116] *In via tua, in your way,* that is, in the observation of the divine law, *vivifica me, quicken me* with the life of grace so that my works may be meritorious for the life of glory, namely, eternal life.

118{119}[38] *Establish your word to your servant, in your fear.*

Statue servo tuo eloquium tuum in timore tuo.

118{119}[39] *Turn away my reproach, which I have apprehended: for your judgments are delightful.*

Amputa opprobrium meum quod suspicatus sum, quia iudicia tua iucunda.

118{119}[40] *Behold I have longed after your precepts: quicken me in your justice.*

Ecce concupivi mandata tua; in aequitate tua vivifica me.

118{119}[38] *Statue servo tuo eloquium tuum in timore tuo, establish your word to your servant in your fear*: that is, cause your servant reverently

---

113 *E. N.* Denis is referring to the ascetic practice of *custodia oculorum,* the "custody of the eyes." "How many experiences like David's! ... If you guard your sight (*si guardáis la vista*) you will have assured the custody of your heart (*la guarda de vuestro corazón*)." St. Josemaría Escrivá, *Camino,* No. 183 (Leominster: Gracewing, 2002), 80. "To take some sort of care over what we look at is essential if our imaginations are not going to be stored with an army of images that will come back to trouble us sooner or later." Jonathan Robinson, *Spiritual Combat Revisited* (San Francisco: Ignatius Press, 2003), 139–40.

114 Jer. 9:21a.

115 Ecclus. 9:7a, 8a, 9a.

116 Ez. 20:7a.

and fearfully to recall sacred Scripture, not as a result of vain glory, but that by it he may be drawn away from vice, and that he might in all things be governed according to the divine word. **118{119}[39]** *Amputa opprobrium meum quod suspicatus sum,* turn away my reproach, which *I have apprehended*: that is, remove from me all the evil that I have imputed upon others out of mere suspicion, lest I judge someone temerariously;[117] *quia iudicia tua iucunda,* for your judgments are delightful, that is, just, true, and holy, and consequently, they are, by their nature, delightful: indeed, good men are delighted by the judgment by which the perverse are damned; but the elect will be delighted by that judgment which the Lord will render as to them, *Come,* he will say, *blessed of my Father.*[118] **118{119}[40]** *Ecce concupivi mandata tua,* behold I have longed *after your precepts* more than all earthly goods; *in aequitate tua,* in your justice, that is, in a just manner of living, which is called your justice because it is given by you and is acceptable to you, *vivifica me,* quicken me, strengthening grace in my soul, so that it may be always vigilant, living, and agile in the life of honesty, lest that stated in Revelation be said of me: *You have the name of being alive, but you are dead.*[119]

PRAYER

EXPIATED FROM THE FILTH OF OUR SINS, lead us, O Lord, in the paths of your commandments; turn away our hearts from all avarice and the eyes of our hearts from the vanity of harmful pleasures, so that endeavoring to live rightly we might always direct ourselves to you, our Creator.

Expiatos a sordibus peccatorum deduc nos, Domine, in semita mandatorum tuorum; corda nostra ab omni avaritia, et a noxiae delectationis vanitate oculos cordis nostri averte: ut recte vivendi studium semper dirigamus ad te Creatorem nostrum.

---

117 E. N. "[O]ur Lord forbids temerarious judgment (*iudicium temerarium*) which is about the intention of the heart or of other uncertain things." A temerarious or rash judgment occurs "when it lacks the certitude of reason, as when a man forms a judgment on some doubtful or hidden things, and such is called judgment by suspicion or temerarious judgment (*iudicium suspiciosum vel temerarium*). ST IIaIIae, q. 60, art. 2, ad 1 & co.
118 Matt. 25:34.
119 Rev. 3:1b.

VAU

(PART VI)

118{119}[41] *Let your mercy also come upon me, O Lord: your salvation according to your word.*

Et veniat super me misericordia tua, Domine; salutare tuum secundum eloquium tuum.

118{119}[41] *Et veniat super me misericordia tua, Domine; let your mercy also come upon me, O Lord.* According to the holy doctors, the Prophet [David] here speaks in the person of the Gentiles or of all the human race, praying for the coming of Christ and for the redemption effected by him, so that it is [to be understood] in this sense: *Let . . . also come upon me* through the Incarnation *your mercy, O Lord,* that is, your Son, O God the Father, by whom he had compassion upon us, and who is the fountain of all goodness and grace. Whence what is to be understood by this mercy is plainly set forth: *salutare tuum, your salvation,* that is, Christ the Savior: of which we find in Isaiah, *All the ends of the earth shall see the salvation of our God;*[120] *secundum eloquium tuum, according to your word,* that is, [according to the] Christ sent to us, in the way you spoke and promised by the Prophets. Also, each man can individually pray this for himself. *Let your mercy also come upon me, O Lord,* that is, fill me with the effects of your goodness; let *your salvation,* that is, your deliverance, come upon me *according to your word,* by which in Scripture you have promised grace to those who plead to you, saying: *The Father from heaven will give the good Spirit to them that ask him.*[121]

118{119}[42] *So shall I answer a word to them that reproach me; for I have trusted in your words.*[122]

Et respondebo exprobrantibus mihi verbum, quia speravi in sermonibus tuis.

118{119}[42] *Et,* so I, aided by your grace, *respondebo, shall answer,* inspired by the Holy Spirit, those *exprobrantibus mihi, that reproach me,* that is, those that speak opprobriously against me, *verbum, a word, a*

---

120 Is. 52:10b.
121 Luke 11:13b.
122 E. N. I have departed from the Douay-Rheims. I find the translation here lacking in fidelity to the Latin text, and this certainly in the light of Denis's *Commentary.*

good and efficacious [word] as the circumstances might require. For I will respond to demons a word of the heart — denying consent; to heretics, a word of wisdom — defending the faith; to those causing injury, a word of patience — overcoming evil with good;[123] to the detractor, the word of works — living rightly. And so I will fulfill the word of the Apostle: *You may know how you ought to answer every man.*[124] Finally, I shall efficaciously so answer, *quia speravi in sermonibus tuis, for I have trusted in your words,* that is, I have truly believed and hoped to be fulfilled in me that which is said in the Gospel: *It is not you that speak, but the Spirit of your Father that speaks in you;*[125] and again, *I will give you a mouth and wisdom, which all your adversaries shall not be able to resist and gainsay.*[126] Or [we can look at it] thus: *I shall answer a word to them that reproach me* which follows: *for I have trusted in your words:* that is, whatever it is that they reproach me with, I will not care, nor will I contend with words, but I will say to them: "I hope in the words of my God, who predicted that blessed are those who suffer persecution for justice's sake";[127] and, *Vengeance is mine, I will repay.*[128] I will hope, therefore, that the Lord in his time will respond and will judge for me: as it is written: *Say not: I will return evil: wait for the Lord and he will deliver you.*[129]

118{119}[43]   *And take not the word of truth utterly out of my mouth: for in your judgments have I hoped exceedingly.*[130]

Et ne auferas de ore meo verbum veritatis usquequaque, quia in iudiciis tuis supersperavi.

118{119}[44]   *So shall I always keep your law, for ever and ever.*

Et custodiam legem tuam semper, in saeculum et in saeculum saeculi.

118{119}[43] *Et ne auferas de ore meo verbum veritatis usquequaque, and take not the word of truth utterly out of my mouth,* that is, do not take away from me the word of divine praise, of fraternal instruction, of Catholic

---

123 *Cf.* Rom. 12:21.
124 Col. 4:6b.
125 Matt. 10:20.
126 Luke 21:15.
127 *Cf.* Matt. 5:10.
128 Luke 12:19b; Heb. 10:30a.
129 Prov. 20:22.
130 E. N. The Douay-Rheims translates *iudiciis* as "words," and I have changed that to "judgments," an obviously more literal translation.

preaching, or worthy responses [to detractors or unjust interrogators] because of my sins. But you, O Lord, be to me the engine and teaching of my tongue, as it is said in Ecclesiasticus: *The Lord has given me a tongue for my reward;*[131] and through Isaiah: *The Lord has given me a learned tongue, that I should know how to uphold by word him that is weary.*[132] Give to me these things, O Lord, *quia in iudiciis tuis, for in your judgments,* by which you judge justly, and do justly, since you hide the word in this way *from the wise and prudent,* and reveal it *to the little ones;*[133] and also in the *judgments* by which you choose things of the world that are cast aside or abject to confound the strong and the wise;[134] *supersperavi, I have hoped exceedingly,* that is, I have intensely hoped in. My hope is strengthened from such considerations, and, with such thoughts, I cannot possibly despair however low, abject, and insignificant I am. **118{119} [44]** *Et custodiam legem tuam semper, and so shall I always keep your law,* namely, *in saeculum et in saeculum saeculi, for ever and ever,* that is, so long as I live, revolving it in my mind, and fulfilling it through my deeds.

118{119}[45] *And I walked at large: because I have sought after your commandments.*

Et ambulabam in latitudine, quia mandata tua exquisivi.

118{119}[45] *Et ambulabam, and I walked,* that is, I lived a manner of life, *in latitudine, at large* in the love (*caritatis*) of God and of neighbor: which love (*caritas*) is of such breadth that it communicates itself everywhere, never serving itself, but extending even towards one's rivals: for (as the Apostle says) *charity envies not, deals not perversely, . . . is not provoked to anger, and does not seek its own;*[135] *quia mandata tua, because . . . your commandments,* by which you also command us to love our enemies,[136] *exquisivi, I have sought after* to know and to fulfill them. But since Christ said, *strive to enter by the narrow gate;*[137] and, *strait is the way that leads to life:*[138] how is it that someone just can walk at large, especially since *broad is the way that leads to death?*[139] The answer is that the way of

---

131 Ecclus 51:30.
132 Is. 50:4a.
133 Matt. 11:25b.
134 *Cf.* 1 Cor. 1:27.
135 1 Cor. 13:4, 5.
136 Luke 6:27.
137 Luke 13:24a.
138 Matt. 7:14b.
139 Matt. 7:13a.

the Lord leading to life is called narrow and strait, but the way or the gate of perdition, broad and wide because — as the most holy Dionysius, the prince of theologians attests (and also Aristotle says), virtue or good is from an integral cause (*ex integra causa*), namely, with all the concurrent circumstances required for virtue; but sin is the absence of a single circumstance. And therefore there are many ways to sin, to err, and to fail; but this is not so in doing good, which can happen but in one way.[140] For virtue consists of a mean; but sin is a departure from the mean. But because the mean is attained in one way, it is difficult to attain; but many and easy are the ways by which one might depart from the mean: and so it is more easy to sin than to act virtuously, just as it is more easy to miss the target towards which archers aim their arrows than to hit it. But here, the narrowness does not oppose itself to the broad way of love, which makes all narrowness broad, and renders all difficulties as if they were nothing: because nothing disposes one ready and happy to work as love does.[141]

140　E. N. Denis is articulating the classic Christian teaching that an act is good only if it is good in all relevant respects (in all the fonts of morality, *i.e.*, intent, moral object, and circumstances), whereas a defect in any one of these fonts renders the act evil. This teaching is synopsized in the saying: *bonum ex integra causa, malum ex quocumque defectu.* What is true for Aquinas is true for Denis: Aquinas "holds that no human act is morally good (right, in the sense of not wrong) unless it is in line with love of self and neighbor (and thus with respect for the basic aspects of the wellbeing of each and all human beings) not only: (i) in the motives or intentions with which it is chosen, and (ii) in the appropriateness of the circumstances, but also (iii) in its object (more precisely the object, or closest-in intention of the choosing person). This is the primary sense of the axiom he frequently articulates by quoting an old tag: *bonum ex integra causa, malum ex quocumque defectu* (good from an unflawed set of contributing factors, bad from any defect in the set). That is, there is a fundamental asymmetry between moral good and moral evil — a notion very foreign to any version of utilitarian or post-utilitarian consequentialist or 'proportionalist' ethics. John Finnis, "Aquinas's Moral, Political, and Legal Philosophy," Stanford Encyclopedia of Philosophy, https://plato.stanford.edu/entries/aquinas-moral-political/. The reference to Pseudo-Dionysius is to his *Divine Names*, IV, 30 ("Good comes from the one universal Cause, and evil originates in numerous partial deficiencies") *Pseudo-Dionysius: The Complete Works* (New York: Paulist Press 1987), 93 (trans., Colm Luibheid). The reference to Aristotle is to Nicomachean Ethics II, 6: 1106b28–35: "It is possible to fail in many ways, . . . while to succeed is possible only in one way (for which reason also one is easy and other difficult): to miss the mark easy, to hit it difficult; for these reasons also, then, excess and defects are characteristic of vice, and the mean of virtue. For men are good in but one way, but bad in many." *Works of Aristotle* (Oxford: Clarendon Press, 1925), Vol. IX, (trans. W. D. Ross); *See also* ST IaIIae, q. 18, art. 4, ad 3; q. 19, art. 6, ad 1.

141　"Love makes every work appear easy and pleasant, though it be right displeasing of itself." St. John Fisher, "The Wayes to Perfect Religion," *The English Works of John*

118{119}[46] *And I spoke of your testimonies before kings: and I was not ashamed.*

Et loquebar in testimoniis tuis in conspectu regum, et non confundebar.

118{119}[46] *Et loquebar in testimoniis tuis in conspectu regum, et non confundebar; and I spoke of your testimonies before kings: and I was not ashamed.* This verse principally applies to the holy martyrs, of whom Christ says in the Gospel: *You shall be brought before kings and governors for my sake.*[142] These confessed the name, faith, and teachings of Christ before them, and they were not ashamed. Indeed, the adversaries of faith were ashamed, because they were unable to resist the wisdom and the spirit by which the martyrs spoke, as is written about Stephen [the protomartyr].[143] And it was a spectacularly marvelous and entirely more wondrous than any miracle that the delicate virgins and most illustrious youths so constantly and so unsurpassably responded to kings, to judges, to philosophers, and to tyrants, as is manifested of the most blessed Ursula, Barbara, Catherine, Agatha, Agnes and infinite others. We ought also freely to confess Christ before all men,[144] and faithfully disclose his testimony, because he himself said: *He that shall be ashamed of me and of my words, of him the Son of man shall be ashamed when he shall come into his kingdom.*[145]

118{119}[47] *I meditated also on your commandments, which I loved.*

Et meditabar in mandatis tuis, quae dilexi.

118{119}[48] *And I lifted up my hands to your commandments, which I loved: and I was exercised in your justifications.*

Et levavi manus meas ad mandata tua, quae dilexi, et exercebar in iustificationibus tuis.

118{119}[47] *Et meditabar in mandatis tuis quae dilexi, I meditated also on your commandments which I loved.* For one more frequently thinks about those things that one more ardently loves; and a meditation with this form is the fruit of the commandment. 118{119}[48] *Et levavi, and*

Fisher (New York: C. Scribner & Co. 1876, 364 (I have modernized St. John's English).
142 Matt. 10:18a.
143 Acts 6:10: *And they were not able to resist the wisdom and the spirit that spoke through Stephen.*
144 *Cf.* Tob. 12:6: *Bless the God of heaven, give glory to him in the sight of all that live, because he has shown his mercy to you.*
145 Luke 9:26a.

I lifted up, that is, I extended upwards, *manus meas, my hands*, that is, the operative powers, the desires of the heart, and the members of the body, *ad mandata tua quae dilexi, to your commandments which I loved*, so that I might fulfill them by actions: because this meditation without works is not sufficient, if an opportunity for doing work exists;[146] *et exercebar, and I was exercised*, according to the manner just stated, namely meditating, speaking, and doing, *in iustificationibus tuis, in your justifications*, that is, in the divine commandments justifying those who are obedient to them.

PRAYER

ET YOUR MERCY COME UPON US, O LORD, and make us thrive in good hope in you, and grant us vigilance in the double breadth of charity, that we might be devoted to the keeping of your law, and that in it we might always gloriously live.

Veniat super nos misericordia tua, Domine, et spe bona fac nos in te vigere, daque vigilare in geminae caritatis latitudine; et ut in custodia legis tuae devoti simus, semper in ea gloriose vivamus.

ZAIN
(PART VII)

118{119}[49]   *Be mindful of your word to your servant, in which you have given me hope.*

Memor esto verbi tui servo tuo, in quo mihi spem dedisti.

118{119}[50]   *This has comforted me in my humiliation: because your word has enlivened me.*

Haec me consolata est in humilitate mea, quia eloquium tuum vivificavit me.

---

146 E. N. Denis appears to be referring to the fact that affirmative precepts always bind, but do not require performance at all times. In other words, affirmative precepts bind always (*semper*), but not at every instance (*sed non ad semper*), that is, only at appropriate times. This is in marked distinction to negative precepts which bind *semper et ad semper*, always and in every instance. ST IIaIIae, q. 33, art. 2; IaIIae, q. 71, art. 5, ad 3; q. 89, art. 6, ad 3; q. 100, arts. 10 & 12. *See also* St. Thomas's *De Malo*, II, 1 ad 11.

118{119}[49] *Memor esto verbi tui servo, be mindful of your word to your servant:* that is, do as you have spoken, namely that you not desist doing that which you did to others for the salvation of your servant because of our sins. For you have said, O Lord: *Every one that asks, receives: and he that seeks, finds: and to him that knocks, it shall be opened.*[147] You also said: *Blessed are they that have not seen, and have believed;*[148] and elsewhere, *Where I am, there also shall my minister be.*[149] Let all these words be fulfilled in me, and in each of us. *In quo, in which* word *mihi spem dedisti, you have given me hope.* For this word and similar words provide the hope of indulgent mercy, the hope of grace, and the confidence of acquiring glory. This is similar to that which Solomon prayed for: *And now, Lord God of Israel, let your words be established, which you have spoken to your servant David my father;*[150] and *Do as you have spoken, that your name may be magnified.*[151] **118{119}[50]** *Haec, this* hope conceived by the word of God, *me consolata est in humilitate, has comforted me in my humiliation,* that is, in all the oppression and affliction of this present life, and in the humiliation by which I have esteemed myself lowly because of my sins. For out of this hope I exclude desperation and I expect the grace of remission [of my sins], *quia eloquium tuum, because your word* of comfort just spoken about, *vivificavit me, has enlivened me,* that is, it has animated me and inflamed my soul to the good.

118{119}[51] *The proud did iniquitously altogether: but I declined not from your law.*

Superbi inique agebant usquequaque, a lege autem tua non declinavi.

118{119}[51] *Superbi inique agebant usquequaque, the proud did iniquitously altogether,* because in their thinking, speaking, and acting, and by excusing themselves, and corrupting others they have offended God. And so it is written: *The sinner will add sin to sin;*[152] and *The wicked man when he is come into the depth of sins, contemns.*[153] Ecclesiastes also says: *A sinner does evil a*

---

147 Matt. 7:8.
148 John 20:29b.
149 John 12:26a.
150 1 Kings 8:26.
151 2 Sam. 7:25b–26a.
152 Ecclus. 3:29b.
153 Prov. 13:3a.

hundred times, and patiently puts up with it.[154] For sin — especially mortal sin — which is not remitted away by penance drags a person to another by its own weight. Whence the Apostle said: *All things are clean to the clean: but to them that are defiled, and to unbelievers, nothing is clean: but both their mind and their conscience are defiled* . . . since they are *abominable and . . . reprobate.*[155] *A lege autem tua non declinavi, but I have not declined from your law:* either because I have never transgressed it — which befits those who have never sinned mortally — or because for a time and even now I have preserved myself from it — which befits those who have repented [of past mortal sin]. For David speaks in this Psalm of the just man in a general sense, and so not all the words of this Psalm apply to every kind of just man.

118{119}[52] *I remembered, O Lord, your judgments of old: and I was comforted.*

Memor fui iudiciorum tuorum a saeculo, Domine, et consolatus sum.

118{119}[52] *Memor fui iudiciorum tuorum, I remembered . . . your judgments* which were done *a saeculo, of old,* that is, from the origin of the world, *Domine, O Lord,* considering how from the beginning of the world you rejected the rebellious and the proud; but you delivered the meek, the obedient, and the humble as it pertains to eternal life, since for a time you have permitted them to undergo temporal tribulations and die for the cleansing of their faults and the increase of their merits and their reward: for in the manner that your elect are always afflicted in this life, so the reprobate flourish here. *Et consolatus sum, and I was comforted* from this thought, hoping myself to have been chosen to be part of the elect because I have been afflicted by so many trials and temptations.

118{119}[53] *A fainting has taken hold of me, because of the wicked that forsake your law.*

Defectio tenuit me, pro peccatoribus derelinquentibus legem tuam.

118{119}[53] *Defectio tenuit me, a fainting has taken hold of me,* that is, I have been attacked by a great fear, *pro peccatoribus derelinquentibus legem tuam, because of the wicked that forsake your law,* that is, from the

---

154 Eccl. 8:12a. *E. N.* I have departed from the Douay-Rheims, whose translation here is somewhat wooden and obsolete.
155 Tit. 1:15–16.

consideration of perverse men: for since I see them to be similar to me by nature, I greatly fear that I might fall from human weakness into the vices and dangers that I see them to have fallen into. For no matter how much a man is perfect, still he has need to be cautious and fearful, lest he find himself similar in fault with those whom he shares a similar nature. And so Solomon said: *Blessed is the man that is always fearful.*[156] And the Apostle said: *Considering yourself, lest you also be tempted;*[157] and elsewhere, *Wherefore he that thinks himself to stand, let him take heed lest he fall.*[158] Or [an alternative reading is] this: *A fainting,* that is, a falling into a great compassion or sorrow has seized me *because of the wicked that forsake your law* inasmuch as I suffer from their error and blindness, as the Apostle [Paul] said of himself: *I have great sadness, and continual sorrow in my heart...for my brothers,* the Jews.[159] Of this sort of despondence that arises from true charity, Micah says: *Would God I were not a man that has the spirit, and that I rather spoke a lie.*[160] For the piety of a perfect man is so great that it grieves more of another's fault and misery than of his own punishment and injury, as also a most indulgent father grieves for his insane son all the more when he is battered by blows and violence from him.

118{119}[54]   *Your justifications were to me worthy to be sung, in the place of my pilgrimage.*[161]

Cantabiles mihi erant iustificationes tuae in loco peregrinationis meae.

118{119}[55]   *In the night I have remembered your name, O Lord: and have kept your law.*

Memor fui nocte nominis tui, Domine, et custodivi legem tuam.

---

156 Prov. 28:14a.
157 Gal. 6:1b.
158 1 Cor. 10:12.
159 Rom. 9:2–3.
160 Micah 2:11a. *E. N.* In his *Commentary on Micah*, Denis suggests this statement of Micah's may be hyperbole similar to St. Paul's statement in Rom. 9:3 and Moses's statement in Ex. 32:31–32. The point that ought to be considered is "how great the zeal and the fervor of charity was in this holy prophet of fraternal salvation, which preferred absolutely to lack the gift of prophecy, which is a grace freely given, and cannot be cast aside without sin, and to appear a liar in a way, rather than that his people perish." Doctoris Ecstatici D. Dionysii Cartusiani, *Opera Omnia*, Vol. 10 (Montreuil: 1900), 481.
161 *E. N.* I modified the verse from "your justifications were the subject of my song" to "your justifications were to me worthy to be sung."

118{119}[56] *This happened to me: because I sought after your justifications.*
Haec facta est mihi, quia iustificationes tuas exquisivi.

118{119}[54] *Cantabiles mihi, to me worthy to be sung,* indeed always
to be sung and to be carried out with delight, *erant iustificationes tuae,*
were your justifications, that is, the divine gifts by which we are justified by
you, namely, praises of God, the commandments, scourges, and all other
things by which we are salubriously disquieted; *in loco peregrinationis*
meae, in this place of my pilgrimage, that is, in the Church militant, in
this way of exile, in this corruptible body, as is written: *Give praise, O*
daughter of Sion: shout, O Israel: be glad, and rejoice with all your heart,
O daughter of Jerusalem.[162] And the Apostle says [we should be]: *singing*
and making melody in your hearts to the Lord always.[163] **118{119}[55]**
Memor fuit nocte nominis tui, Domine; in the night I have remembered
your name, O Lord: as we have in Lamentations: *Arise, give praise in*
the night, in the beginning of the watches.[164] Or *in the night,* that is, in
the time of adversity and temptation. *Et custodivi legem tuam, and have*
kept your law. For the memory, knowledge, or contemplation of God
without the observance of the law is an empty and formless thing, as
Paul acknowledges of the reprobate: *They profess that they know God:*
but in their works they deny him.[165] **118{119}[56]** *Haec, this* keeping of
the law *facta est mihi, happened to me,* that is, the keeping of the law is
given to me through grace, *quia iustificationes tuas, because . . . your justi-*
fications, that is, precepts, *exquisivi, I sought after,* so that I might fulfill
them. And so the Creator gave me the grace to fulfill them. For, as is
written, *Every one that asks, receives: and he that seeks, finds.*[166]

---

162 Zeph. 3:14. E. N. In his *Commentary on Zephaniah* Denis observes: "*Daughter*
of Sion, that is, the Church militant, standing firm in the contemplation of divine
things," and "*Israel,* that is, the Christian people, who are truly worthy of being
called Israel, that is 'contemplating God with faith,' for Israel is interpreted to mean
'seeing God,'" and "*daughter of Jerusalem,* that is the Church of Christ in peace by
its resting in the contemplation of divine things." As Denis summarizes: "The holy
Prophets frequently call the Christian people or Church of Christ with the name
Sion, Israel, and Jerusalem." Doctoris Ecstatici D. Dionysii Cartusiani, *Opera Omnia,*
Vol. 10 (Montreuil: 1900), 594–95.
163 Eph. 5:19b.
164 Lam. 2:19a.
165 Titus 1:16a.
166 Matt. 7:8a.

PRAYER

O OBTAIN THE HEAVENLY FATHERLAND from this place of pilgrimage, O Lord, your justifications were worthy to be sung by us: may we receive from you the reward of eternal mercy through such a delightful melody.

Pro obtentu caelistis patriae, Domine, iustificationes tuae sint nobis cantabiles in locis peregrinationis nostrae: quibus suaviter modulatis, aeternae misericordiae mercedem a te percipiamus.

HETH
(PART VIII)

118{119}[57] *O Lord, my portion, I have said, I would keep your law.*

Portio mea, Domine, dixi, custodire legem tuam.

118{119}[57] *Portio mea, Domine, dixi custodire legem tuam;* O Lord, my portion, I have said, I would keep your law: that is, O Lord, *I have said,* that is, I have set it upon myself that I would keep your law: that is, the keeping of the divine law is my portion, that is, the good that I have chosen out of all and before all temporal goods, so that while others may chose exterior and sensible goods, I for the better choose to be obedient to you in all things, that is, to serve your law. For the greatest Christian wealth ought to be the divine law, so that he is able to say this: *I preferred her before kingdoms and thrones, and esteemed riches nothing in comparison of her.*[167] No wonder it adds, *Now all good things came to me together with her.*[168] Or [we can see it] thus: O Lord, who is *my portion,* that is the only good I love before all others and which I desire alone to obtain; *I have said,* that is, I have strongly ordained myself towards it, to keep your law, and without which keeping no adult is saved.[169]

---

167 Wis. 7:8.
168 Wis. 7:11a.
169 E. N. As Cardinal Burke succinctly stated it in a speech at the Human Life International World Prayer Congress on October 9, 2010: "Obedience to the demands of the natural law is necessary for salvation, and, therefore, the teaching of the natural law is within the authority of the Magisterium and part of its solemn responsibility... There is no other way to salvation than hearing God's word and putting it into practice with all our being." https://www.catholicculture.org/culture/library/view.cfm?recnum=9437. This is simply a repetition of Papal teaching and the infallible

118{119}[58] *I entreated your face with all my heart: have mercy on me according to your word.*

Deprecatus sum faciem tuam in toto corde meo; miserere mei secundum eloquium tuum.

118{119}[59] *I have thought on my ways: and turned my feet unto your testimonies.*

Cogitavi vias meas, et converti pedes meos in testimonia tua.

118{119}[58] *Deprecatus sum faciem tuam in toto corde meo; I entreated your face with all my heart,* that is, everywhere present and observing all things, or your kindly glance and the assistance of your grace: I prayed for this face of yours as my final end, so that one day I might see it by sight, as also Moses prayed for: *If . . . I have found favor in your sight, show me your face, that I may know you.*[170] Indeed, my beatitude is to be found in this vision. Or, *I entreated your face with all my heart* for that which comes next: *have mercy on me,* bestowing upon me forgiveness and grace, *secundum eloquium tuum, according to your word,* which has said: *If the wicked does penance for all his sins which he has committed . . . I will not remember all his iniquities that he has done.*[171] 118{119}[59] *Cogitavi vias meas, I have thought on my ways,* that is, I have scrutinized my life and all my works, and I have returned thanks to you, O Lord, for your good things, but I have repented of evil. And so *converti pedes meos, I have turned by feet,* that is, my desires, my works, and bodily foothold, *in testimonia tua, unto your testimonies,* that is, in the words of your sacred speech so that I might govern myself in all things according to your precepts, examples, and counsels. Hence we find stated in Haggai: *Set your hearts upon your ways.*[172]

118{119}[60] *I am ready, and am not troubled: that I may keep your commandments.*

Paratus sum, et non sum turbatus, ut custodiam mandata tua.

118{119}[61] *The cords of the wicked have encompassed me: but I have not forgotten your law.*

Funes peccatorum circumplexi sunt me, et legem tuam non sum oblitus.

Magisterium: "For the natural law, too, declares the will of God, and its faithful observance is necessary for men's eternal salvation." Paul VI, *Humanae vitae,* No. 4.umHu

170 Ex. 33:13a.

171 Ez. 18:21–22a.

172 Haggai 1:7.

118{119}[60] *Paratus sum, I am ready* out of a fervent charity, habitual grace, and virtuous habits *et non sum turbatus, and am not troubled* by inordinate passion, *ut custodiam mandata tua, that I might keep your commandments*: for virtuous habits make a man ready to go toward God. For this reason, we read in Jeremiah: *I am not troubled, following you for my pastor.*[173] And the Apostle admonishes: *Whatsoever you do, do it from the heart.*[174] He who is not troubled about many things, but for whom there is only one thing necessary, which thing he seeks, desires, and loves supremely and exclusively is clearly blessed.[175] Of such persons, one can say: 118{119}[61] *Funes peccatorum, the cords of the wicked,* that is, the assaults of the visible and invisible enemies, *circumplexi sunt me, have encompassed me,* since I walk in the midst of snares. For demons and perverse men strive to divert us on all sides from God and have our will conform to theirs. For this reason it is written: *Your adversary the devil, as a roaring lion, goes about seeking whom he may devour: whom you resist, strong in faith, knowing that the same affliction befalls your brothers.*[176] *Et legem tuam non sum oblitus, but I have not forgotten your law,* that is, I have not by any means withdrawn from you because of temptation or adversity, nor have I transgressed your law.

118{119}[62] *I rose at midnight to confess to you; for the judgments of your justification.*[177]

Media nocte surgebam, ad confitendum tibi super iudicia iustificationis tuae.

118{119}[62] *Media nocte surgebam ad confitendum tibi, I rose at midnight to confess to you* with a double confession, namely, of your praise and of my own fault. For while the hour of midnight is more dangerous to those who are customarily sluggish sleepers, to those religious who are accustomed rise up then it is more wholesome.[178] Indeed, at that

---

173 Jer. 17:16.
174 Col. 3:23a.
175 *Cf.* Luke 10:41–42.
176 1 Pet. 5:8–9.
177 *E. N.* I have replaced the Douay-Rheims's "to give praise to" with "to confess to," for as Denis understands this verse, it applies both to the confession of praise and the confession of fault.
178 *E. N.* A typical Carthusian schedule would be to go to bed early (7:30–8:00 p.m.) and wake up at around midnight for Matins and Lauds (in common) between shortly past midnight until about 2:15 or 3:00 a.m., depending upon the length of

time [for the late sleeper], as Ambrose says, the allure of the flesh rages, at that time the mind is drowsy, at that time the tempter stands by and throws a net by which it disturbs the careless mind, at that time he fills the breast of the sleeper with various deceptions.[179] And so this hour provides the greatest occasion for devotion [for the early riser], because at that time the din of external things ceases, and they do not expose the senses of their bodies to images of things as occurs during the day. And so I will rise at midnight to confess to you *super iudicia iustificatio-nes tuae, for the judgments of your justification,* that is, for the judgments of your justice, which you have employed upon me, by which you have justified me, namely, of all the mercy which you have shown me, of the chastisements with which you have afflicted me, and all the other words which from your judgment you have done regarding me.

118{119}[63]   *I am a partaker with all them that fear you, and that keep your commandments.*

Particeps ego sum omnium timentium te, et custodientium mandata tua.

118{119}[63] *Particeps ego sum omnium timentium te, I am a partaker with all them that fear you* with a chaste and filial fear, *et custodientium mandata tua, and that keep your commandments.* For all existing in grace are one in Christ because of the bond of charity by which they are connected, and they seek not their own, but those things of others.[180] And so the merit of one person redounds to the other to the extent they mutually help themselves and exist as one by love. For here they share in the efficacy of mercy, because according to the unity of the head and the members, namely of Christ and Christians, and of the members (that is the faithful) among themselves, the merits of Christ and of the Saints are communicated to and work upon us. For about this mystical participation, communion, and unity of the elect in Christ, the Apostle admonishes: *Let no man seek his own, but that which is another's;*[181] and

---

the office. Following that, the monk will retire to his cell and recite the office of the Blessed Virgin Mary and go to bed. He will then wake up around 6:00 a.m. for individual prayer, and then around 8:00 a.m. go to the church for a conventual Mass.
179 E. N. Denis is referring to St. Ambrose's exposition or homily of Psalm 118 (119), 46, PL 15, 1382. See *Homilies of Saint Ambrose on Psalm 118 (119)* (Dublin: Halcyon Press, 1993) (trans., Íde Ní Riain)
180 *Cf.* 1 Cor. 10:24.
181 *Ibid.*

again, *We, being many, are one bread, one body.*[182] This also Christ prayed for: *I pray . . . Father, that they may all be one, as you, Father, in me, and I in you, . . . that they may be made perfect in one;*[183] and yet again: *Holy Father, keep them in your name whom you have given me, that they may be one, as we also are.*[184]

118{119}[64] *The earth, O Lord, is full of your mercy: teach me your justifications.*

Misericordia tua, Domine, plena est terra; iustificationes tuas doce me.

118{119}[64] *Misericordia tua, Domine, plena est terra; the earth, O Lord, is full of your mercy,* that is, the effects of your divine goodness [fill] wayfaring men, either because they are mercifully converted, or patiently endured, or paternally corrected, or they suffer less than they deserve; and all use the common benefits generally, namely, the gifts of nature; and God offers grace to all, as the Apostle said: *For Christ therefore we are ambassadors, God as it were exhorting by us. For Christ, we beseech you, be reconciled to God.*[185] *Iustificationes tuas, your justifications,* that is, the commandments of life, *doce me, teach me,* so that I might always know them clearly and I might fulfill them more perfectly.

PRAYER

MAKE US PARTAKERS WITH THOSE WHO fear you, O Lord, and grant that we might keep your law with grace; and, in accordance with your mercy, show mercy on those in necessity who seek your face with all their hearts.

Fac nos participes, Domine, timentium te, et da nobis legem tuam in beneplacito custodire; et in necessitatibus in toto corde deprecantes faciem tuam, miserere secundum misericordiam tuam.

---

182 1 Cor. 10:17a.
183 John 1:20–21, 23a.
184 John 17:11.
185 2 Cor. 5:20.

TETH
(PART IX)

118{119}[65]   *You have done well with your servant, O Lord, according to your word.*

Bonitatem fecisti cum servo tuo, Domine, secundum verbum tuum.

118{119}[65] *Bonitatem fecisti cum servo tuo, Domine; you have done well with your servant, O Lord,* that is, you have communicated your goodness to me, giving me piety and grace, the endowments of nature, and the gift of grace, *secundum verbum tuum, according to your word,* that is, as you command us to do. For you tell and command us to do good to others readily and abundantly, in the manner that we read: *Give to every one that asks you.*[186] And in the Acts of the Apostles, Paul says: *You ought.... to remember the word of the Lord Jesus,* who said, *It is a more blessed thing to give rather than to receive.*[187] Or [we can see it thus], *according to your word,* that is, as you have said you would do good to us. For it is written: *The Lord is good to them that hope in him, to the soul that seeks him.*[188]

118{119}[66]   *Teach me goodness and discipline and knowledge; for I have believed your commandments.*

Bonitatem, et disciplinam, et scientiam doce me, quia mandatis tuis credidi.

118{119}[66] *Bonitatem, goodness,* that is, kindliness or mercy, *et disciplinam, and discipline,* that is, the rigor of justice, *et scientiam, and knowledge,* that is, the discretion used in doing good and in discipline, *doce me, teach me,* so that I might efficaciously rule myself or those who are committed to my care, so that my service might be reasonable.[189] These three things are particularly important with respect to prelates and princes. It is not sufficient for them to have one of these without the others, lest kindness or mercy be lax, or justice cruel, or knowledge

---

186 Luke 6:30a.
187 Acts 20:35b.
188 Lam. 3:25.
189 Cf. Rom. 12:1: *I beseech you therefore, brethren, by the mercy of God, that you present your bodies a living sacrifice, holy, pleasing unto God, your reasonable service.*

without works. For the disciplining prelate, kindliness or mercy is necessary or just, and discipline is good: but this cannot be unless done with essential discretion, which discerns when and in what manner it is fitting to use kindliness or mercy and discipline, mixing both with each other according to the true judgment of reason. This goodness also pertains to the ruler, according to this, *The throne of a king is strengthened by clemency*;[190] also justice or discipline, according to this, *The king that judges the poor in truth, his throne shall be established forever.*[191] Also he should regard knowledge most greatly so he might be able to judge between what is true and false, good and evil. Whence the Lord complains in Isaiah: *The shepherds themselves knew no understanding.*[192] And he states through Hosea: *Because you have rejected knowledge, I will reject you, that you shall not do the office of priesthood to me.*[193] For as Christ spoke regarding himself, *If the blind lead the blind, both will fall into the pit.*[194] Here also Moses, suggestive of those who were to preside over and rule others worthily and fittingly, said: *Let me have from among you wise and understanding men, and such whose conversation is approved among your tribes, that I may appoint them your rulers.*[195] This give to me, O Lord, *quia mandatis tuis credidi, for I have believed your commandments*, that is, I consented by doing, and I believed in them not by word or tongue alone, but *in deed and in truth.*[196] For it behooves us, according to the Philosopher [Aristotle], to believe in order to obtain knowledge.[197] Isaiah does not disagree, for he says: *If you will not believe, you shall not understand.*[198] For he who desires to be illumined about divine things must firmly believe.

118{119}[67] *Before I was humbled I offended; therefore have I kept your word.*

Priusquam humiliarer ego deliqui, propterea eloquium tuum custodivi.

---

190 Prov. 20:28b.
191 Prov. 29:14.
192 Is. 56:11a.
193 Hosea 4:6a.
194 Matt. 15:14b.
195 Deut. 1:13.
196 1 John 3:18b.
197 E. N. The reference is to Aristotle, *On Sophistical Refutations* 1.2, 165b3 (δεῖ γὰρ πιστεύειν τὸν μανθάνοντα: "for the learner is obliged to believe"); *see also* St. Thomas Aquinas, *Super Sent.*, lib. 3, d. 25, q. 2, a. 1, qc. 4, s. c. 1.
198 Is. 7:9 (LXX).

118{119}[67] *Priusquam humiliarer, before I was humbled* by chastisements, misfortunes, and adversities, *ego deliqui, I offended.* For many men sin in many ways during a time of prosperity, who, during the time when they are cast down from the state of prosperity and punished by God, back away from evil, are taught by being chastised, and convert to God. And so it adds: *propterea, therefore,* that is, because of this humiliation, *eloquium tuum custodivi, I have kept your word,* obeying from that point on those things you have said. And Jeremiah states: *You have chastised me, and I was instructed.* And elsewhere the Lord says: *I will hedge up your way with thorns, and I will stop it up with a wall.*[199] Therefore, man experiences from this divine correction how good it is to obey the Lord, to which this suitably applies: *Vexation alone shall make you understand what you hear.*[200] Or [alternatively, we can understand it] thus: *Before I was humbled,* that is, before I humbled myself, considering my innumerable miseries, *ego deliqui, I offended,* because pride is the mother of all sin. Whence he who does not humble himself falls into infinite vices. *Therefore,* lest I sin in this way, *your word* in which you say, *Learn from me for I am meek and humble of heart,*[201] *I have kept,* humbling myself: for *pride is hateful before God and men.*[202] For this reason we have contained in Tobit: *Never suffer pride to reign in your mind, or in your words: for from it all perdition took its beginning.*[203]

118{119}[68] *You are good; and in your goodness teach me your justifications.*

Bonus es tu, et in bonitate tua doce me iustificationes tuas.

118{119}[68] *Bonus es tu, you are good* by nature in every way and completely. Whence Scripture affirms: *None is good but God alone.*[204] *Et in bonitate tua, and in your goodness,* that is, in accordance with the fact that you are good and merciful, *doce me iustificationes tuas, teach me your justifications,* that is, your commandments. *Blessed is the man whom you shall instruct:*[205] because *everyone that has heard of the Father, and has learned, comes to* Christ, as he himself said.[206]

---

199 Hosea 2:6a.
200 Is. 28:19b.
201 Matt. 11:29
202 Ecclus. 10:7a.
203 Tob. 4:14.
204 Luke 18:19b.
205 Ps. 93:12a.
206 John 6:45b.

118{119}[69] *The iniquity of the proud has been multiplied over me: but I will seek your commandments with my whole heart.*

Multiplicata est super me iniquitas superborum; ego autem in toto corde meo scrutabor mandata tua.

118{119}[70] *Their heart is curdled like milk: but I have meditated on your law.*

Coagulatum est sicut lac cor eorum; ego vero legem tuam meditatus sum.

118{119}[69] *Multiplicata est super me iniquitas superborum, the iniquity of the proud has been multiplied over me*: that is, proud devils and pretentious men whose father is the devil,[207] in many ways endeavor to lead me to evil, by threatening, by enticing, and persecuting me; *ego autem in todo corde meo scrutabor mandata tua, but I will seek your commandments with my whole heart*, so that I might know what is agreeable to you, to which, the more those urge me more often to evil, the more eagerly I want to please and adhere to you. This does not apply to those who *have no roots*, but fall in the time of temptation.[208] And so Ecclesiasticus teaches: *Be steadfast in the way of the Lord, and in the truth of your judgment.*[209] 118{119}[70] *Coagulatum est sicut lac cor eorum, their heart is curdled like milk*, that is, it is hardened in malice; *ego vero legem tuam meditatus sum, but I have meditated on your law*, which meditation is a shield against the evil of temptation.

118{119}[71] *It is good for me that you have humbled me, that I may learn your justifications.*

Bonum mihi quia humiliasti me: ut discam iustificationes tuas.

118{119}[72] *The law of your mouth is good to me, above thousands of gold and silver.*

Bonum mihi lex oris tui, super millia auri et argenti.

118{119}[71] *Bonum mihi quoniam humiliasti me, it is good for me that you have humbled me* by chastisement and temptation, or by depriving me of worldly honor and glory, or by giving to my soul the virtue of humility, *ut discam iustificationes tuas, so that I may learn your justifications*: which is something the proud man is unable to say, because the Holy Spirit

207 *Cf.* John 9:44a.
208 Luke 8:13.
209 Ecclus 5:12a.

abhors the proud man. **118{119}[71]** *Bonum mihi lex oris tui, the law of your mouth is good to me,* that is, the ten laws of the moral precepts and the evangelical law which Christ himself taught by his mouth, are *super millia auri et argenti, above thousands of gold and silver,* that is, are above all worldly riches. Here a determinate term is placed for an indeterminate term, because the divine law is incomparably better for us than any temporal good, according to this: *The purchasing thereof is better than the merchandise . . . of* gold and silver.[210] For this reason, we are obligated to return the greatest thanks to God that he has bestowed upon us the divine law; and the more gravely we have sinned in transgressing the law, the more thanks we ought to have that we have the law as his most holy gift.

PRAYER

GOD, WHO ARE BY NATURE GOOD, IN your goodness instruct us with heavenly discipline and knowledge; make us to accept your words and faithfully to keep them, to meditate upon and fulfill your law with our whole heart, and to possess always an unblemished heart in your justifications.

Deus, qui naturaliter es bonus, in bonitate tua instrue nos caelesti disciplina et scientia; fac nos accepta eloquia tua fideliter custodire, et toto corde legem tuam meditari et adimplere, et in iustificationibus tuis immaculatum cor semper possidere.

IOD
(PART X)

118{119}[73]   *Your hands have made me and formed me: give me understanding, and I will learn your commandments.*

Manus tuae fecerunt me, et plasmaverunt me; da mihi intellectum, et discam mandata tua.

118{119}[73] *Manus tuae fecerunt me, et plasmaverunt me, your hands have made me and formed me.* These same words are written in the book of Job;[211] and they have this meaning: O sublime and blessed Creator,

---

210 Prov. 3:14.
211 Job 10:8.

incorporeal and uncircumscribable, *manus tuae, your hands*, that is, your power and wisdom, *fecerunt me, made me*, producing my soul from nothing,[212] *et plasmaverunt me, and formed me*, forming my body from a sperm cell. Whence it is said by Job: *Behold God has made me as well as you, and of the same clay I also was formed*.[213] Now as the rational soul is the most noble of all the forms of this world, so the body of humans is more excellent than all mixed and elementary things, and it is allotted a more noble figure — namely an erect one — so as to contemplate the heavens.[214] For matter is proportionate to the form, as potency to act. And so, as the rational soul is contemplative toward heavenly things, so its body is raised toward heaven, in order that the soul through sense of sight might acquire knowledge of heavenly things. *Da mihi intellectum, give me understanding*, that is, intellectual enlightenment *et discam mandata tua, and I will learn your commandments*, so that I might understand them more sincerely, meditate upon them more frequently, and follow them more perfectly. For because whatever I have or whatever I am I have from you, O Lord, so do I bind myself to you; but I am unable to repay you with anything except by loving and honoring you. And so I request understanding in order that I might learn your commandments, because your love demands that I fulfill your commandments, as it is asserted: *And by this we know that we have known him, if we keep his commandments*.[215] One should note also that understanding sometimes is taken to mean the intellectual substance, and sometimes as the intellective power, at times as the habit of natural intellect, other times for the gift

---

212 *E. N.* "The Church teaches that every spiritual soul is created immediately by God — it is not 'produced' by the parents." CCC § 366.

213 Job 33:6.

214 *E. N.* This is a commonplace in pagan and Christian sources. For example, Lactantius (*ca.* 250–*ca.* 325) (citing Ovid, *Metamorphosis*, I, 85), in his *Divine Institutions*, II, 1, states: "God willed that we should look up to heaven, and undoubtedly not without reason. For . . . it is given to us in a peculiar manner to behold the heaven as we stand erect, that we may seek religion there; that since we cannot see God with our eyes, we may with our mind contemplate Him, whose throne is there." And in his *On the Workmanship of God*, chp. 8, Lactantius states: "When, therefore, God had determined of all the animals to make man alone heavenly, and all the rest earthly, He raised him erect to the contemplation of the heaven, and made him a biped, doubtless that he might look to the same quarter from which he derives his origin." "Divine Institutes," *The Ante-Nicene Christian Library* (Edinburgh: T & T Clark, 1871), Vol. 21, 73 (eds., Alexander Roberts, *et al.*) and "On the Workmanship of God," *The Ante-Nicene Christian Library* (Edinburgh: T & T Clark, 1871) (eds. Alexander Roberts, et al.), Vol. 22, 66.

215 1 John 2:3.

of understanding, which is the supernatural intellectual habit infused by the Holy Spirit, and sometimes as the act of intellective potency, or its illustration, and so here it is to be accepted in this [last] way.[216]

118{119}[74] *They that fear you shall see me, and shall be glad: because I have greatly hoped in your words.*

Qui timent te videbunt me, et laetabuntur, quia in verba tua supersperavi.

118{119}[73] *Qui timent te, they that fear you* with a friendly and filial fear, *videbunt me, shall see me*, that is, they will take consideration of my deeds, *et laetabuntur, and shall be glad* in you, rejoicing in my perfection and venerating your majesty. For in the way that perverse men are glad and rejoice with respect to evil things,[217] so the just and those who fear heartily rejoice, out of fraternal charity, in the progress of their neighbor as if it were their own: and they especially are rejoiceful of this, that they see God being honored. For this reason, Paul said: *Charity... rejoices not in iniquity, but rejoices with the truth.*[218] They shall see, therefore, and they shall be glad, and they shall not interpret my deeds wrongly, *quia in verba mea supersperavi, because I have greatly hoped in your words*, that is, I have an exceedingly great hope in the divine word, by which you have promised grace in the present and glory in the future. Whence also the holy Job said: *Although he should kill me, I will trust him.*[219] For we ought in all things to greatly hope in the words of God as most certain that *heaven and earth shall pass, but the words* of the divine law shall persevere.[220]

---

216 E. N. Denis is saying that the prayer of the Psalm is not to obtain "understanding" as an intellectual substance, or "understanding" as the natural power of the intellect (a habit), or even "understanding" as the supernatural gift (also a habit) — all of which the person praying presumably already has since he has right reason and is in a state of grace; rather, it asks for a specific act of intellectual power or illumination of the Holy Spirit's gift of understanding specific to keeping the commandments. In short, one might say it asks for an actual grace that the Holy Spirit's gift of understanding be activated for the specific purpose of understanding and applying the commandments. *See* ST IIaIIae, q. 8, art. 3, co. As Jordan Aumann, O. P., observes: "The actuation of the gifts depends entirely on the Holy Spirit, but the soul can do much to dispose itself, with the help of grace, for that divine movement." Patently, one of those things it can do is to pray for it, as the Psalmist does. *Spiritual Theology* (New York: Continuum, 2006), 253.
217 *Cf.* Prov. 2:14: *Who are glad when they have done evil, and rejoice in most wicked things.*
218 1 Cor. 13:4a, 6.
219 Job 13:15a.
220 Matt. 24:35.

118{119}[75] *I know, O Lord, that your judgments are equity: and in your truth you have humbled me.*

Cognovi, Domine, quia aequitas iudicia tua, et in veritate tua humiliasti me.

118{119}[75] *Cognovi, Domine; I know, O Lord,* from faith and divine revelation, *quia aequitas iudicia tua, that your judgments are equity,* that is, that the divine judgments, namely, the adjudications and remunerations proceeding from divine justice, are exactly just and true, and assert equity more properly than equality, although no wayfarer has the ability to apprehend the rationale and the measure of the justice of this judgment. For this is stated in Revelation: *Yea, O Lord God Almighty, true and just are your judgments;*[221] and in Daniel: *All . . . that you have done to us, you have done in true judgment.*[222] And the Lord said to Job: *Will you make void my judgment: and condemn me, that you may be justified?*[223] *Et in veritate tua, and in your truth,* that is, in consideration of the divine truth, *humiliasti me, you have humbled me,* that is, you have bestowed the humiliation upon me by which I have humbled myself. For we humble ourselves by considering those things that are said in sacred Scripture regarding the divine majesty and human lowliness. Or [we can understand it thus]: *In your truth,* that is, in your justice or in your just judgment, *you have humbled me,* taking me down from a high state, from temporal glory, from false prosperity, as holy Job said: *I that was formerly so wealthy, am all of a sudden broken to pieces.* Therefore, let us not find ourselves impatient or grumbling if we are humbled in this way; let us say with holy Job: *The Lord gave, and the Lord has taken away; as it has pleased the Lord, so is it done. Blessed be the name of the Lord.*[224]

118{119}[76] *O let your mercy be for my comfort, according to your word unto your servant.*

Fiat misericordia tua ut consoletur me, secundum eloquium tuum servo tuo.

118{119}[77] *Let your tender mercies come unto me, and I shall live: for your law is my meditation.*

Veniant mihi miserationes tuae, et vivam, quia lex tua meditatio mea est.

221 Rev. 16:7b.
222 Dan. 3:31.
223 Job 40:3.
224 Job 1:21.

118{119}[76] *Fiat misericordia tua ut consoletur me, O let your mercy be for my comfort*, that is, may the effect of your mercy which you pour out upon me be such that in every adversity I am refreshed by the hope of forgiveness and heavenly beatitude, *secundum eloquium tuum servo tuo, according to your word unto your servant*: that is, your mercy dispensed to me your servant, in the manner that is promised in the Scriptures: that you would have mercy on all those who call upon you. For through Isaiah you say: *Every one that calls upon my name, I have created him for my glory.*[225] You have also promised consolation to the afflicted, saying to the Prophet [Nahum]: *The Lord is good and gives strength in the day of trouble.*[226] And elsewhere: *I am the salvation of the people, . . . in whatever tribulation they shall cry to me, I will hear them.*[227] 118{119}[77] *Veniant mihi miserationes tuae, let your tender mercies come*, that is, the effects of your divine goodness, *et vivam, and I shall live*, with the life of grace in the present and the life of glory in the future; *quia lex tua meditatio mea est, for your law is my meditation*, materially, that is, I meditate on your law, and so thereby I am found worthy of your tender mercies, namely, your indulgence and perseverance.

118{119}[78]   *Let the proud be ashamed, because they have unjustly done wickedness towards me: but I will be employed in your commandments.*

    Confundantur superbi, quia iniuste iniquitatem fecerunt in me; ego autem exercebor in mandatis tuis.

118{119}[79]   *Let them that fear you turn to me and they that know your testimonies.*

    Convertantur mihi timentes te, et qui noverunt testimonia tua.

118{119}[80]   *Let my heart be undefiled in your justifications, that I may not be confounded.*

    Fiat cor meum immaculatum in iustificationibus tuis, ut non confundar.

118{119}[78] *Confundantur superbi, let the proud be ashamed*, that is, let arrogant men be remorseful of their evil deeds, and let them be led in their confusion to repentance; or [alternatively], *Let the proud be ashamed*, that is, let the devil be cast down from heaven because of his pride; *quia iniuste, because . . . unjustly*, that is, with evil intent and without

---

225 Is. 43:7.
226 Nahum 1:7.
227 E. N. This Introit, adapted from Ps. 36:39, is from the 19th Sunday after Pentecost (25th Sunday in Ordinary Time).

me deserving it, *iniquitatem fecerunt me, they have done wickedness towards me*, tempting and persecuting my soul. *Ego autem exercebor in mandatis tuis, but I will be employed in your commandments*, busying myself with them in both mind and by deed, all the more urgently the more unjust my adversaries are against me, since holy and intense exercises, I say, expel the exercises of the enemies. For the operations of one vehemently intent soul pays little or no attention to other things. 118{119}[79] *Convertantur mihi timentes te, let them that fear you turn to me*, that is, let them that fear you with a holy and chaste fear turn towards me so that they might obtain help from me, whereby driven by love they take pity upon the afflicted, as the Apostle writes: Confirm your charity towards them,[228] that is, render aid to the sinner. And let *qui noverunt testimonia tua, they that know your testimonies* turn also to me. 118{119}[80] *Fiat cor meum, let my heart*, that is, my soul, *immaculatum in iustificationibus tuis, be undefiled in your justifications*, that is, your commandments, so that it might observe them perfectly, lest, like a transgressor, it be deformed by the stain of fault, *ut non confundar, that I may not be confounded* by you, O fearsome Judge, being that I am such a neglector and transgressor of the divine law. For as we find contained in the second book of Maccabees, *Acting wickedly against the laws of God, does not pass unpunished.*[229]

Let us sing and utter this entire Psalm, in which the virtues of the just are so diligently enumerated, not in in our own person, but in the person of a just man, so that we can acknowledge what of the perfection of justice is wanting in us; and then let us endeavor to attain it. But for he who is just because he abounds in grace, so that the words of this Psalm are applicable to him, he can proclaim all these words in his own person to the glory of God and the edification of his neighbor, as Paul in is epistles frequently describes his good.

PRAYER

GOD, GIVER OF LIFE, LET YOUR TENDER mercies come upon us so that we might live justly; give us understanding that we might learn your commandments, so that, vigilantly keeping them, we might truly please you.

Vitae dator, Deus, veniant nobis miserationes tuae, ut iuste vivamus; da nobis intellectum ut mandata tua discamus, ut vigilanter observantes tibi veraciter placeamus.

228 *Cf.* 2 Cor. 2:8.
229 2 Macc. 4:17.

CAPH
(PART XI)

118{119}[81] *My soul has failed after your salvation: and in your word
I have very much hoped.*[230]

*Defecit in salutare tuum anima mea, et in verbum tuum
supersperavi.*

118{119}[81] *Defecit in salutare tuum anima mea, my soul has failed after
your salvation.* Up to this point, the Prophet [David] has treated beatitude
as applied to those works of the active life; from this point forward even
up to the end of this Psalm he addresses those things that ought to be
considered in acts of the contemplative life: *Defecit in salutare tuum anima
mea, my soul has failed after your salvation,* that is, in the love and the
contemplation of your salvation, namely, of Christ;[231] or *your salvation,*
that is the eternal salvation promised to us;[232] or of your very self, who
are our most high salvation. This failing can be understood in three ways.
The first way is this: *My soul has failed after your salvation,* that is, my
soul cannot sufficiently and fully love and contemplate your salvation:
because, as the Apostle says, *Eye has not seen, nor ear heard, neither has it
entered into the heart of man, what things God has prepared for them that
love him.*[233] And these goods prepared for us are our eternal deliverance
and salvation. For what else has God prepared for his beloved other than
himself? But especially in this present life no one is able clearly to know
and ardently love God, or eternal life, as God himself is knowable and
lovable. And so *my soul has failed after* the divine *salvation.* The second
explanation is thus: *My soul has failed after your salvation,* that is, before
the high contemplation and most fervent love of your salvation, *my soul
has failed* [or has been withdrawn] from the operations of its sensitive
powers, and it has become bodily weak. For the more pure and sublime the
contemplation will be, and the more the love of God is fervent, the greater
will the natural and sensitive powers be lacking of their acts. Hence, when
a soul comes to rapture or ecstasy, the bodily or the sensitive life is almost
entirely suspended, so that man does not live as man. But some explain

---

230 E. N. The Douay-Rheims has translated *defecit* as "fainted" in this verse, and
as "failed" in verse 2. Denis construes the verses together, so I have replaced "fainted"
with "failed" so that it is consistent with the *Commentary's* argument.
231 Cf. Luke 1:46: *And my spirit has rejoiced in God my Savior.*
232 Cf. Luke 2:20: *Because my eyes have seen your salvation.*
233 1 Cor. 2:9.

it in this way: *My soul has failed after your salvation*, that is, it has failed from overwhelming expectation and delay of the divine salvation or glory, that is, it my soul is crushed, exhausted, and weak with weariness.[234] For as Solomon said: *Hope that is deferred afflicts the soul: desire when it comes is a tree of life.*[235] *Et in verbum tuum*, *and in your word*, by which your promise help and grace in the present, but security and glory in the future, *supersperavi, I have very much hoped*, that is, I am strongly confident in.

118{119}[82]   *My eyes have failed in your word, saying: When will you comfort me?*

Defecerunt oculi mei in eloquium tuum, dicentes: Quando consolaberis me?

118{119}[82] *Defecerunt oculi mei, my eyes have failed*, my interior [eyes have failed], *in eloquium tuum, for your word*, that is, in your words of sacred Scripture, namely in the divine promises and the testimonies and the commandments. And this failure, like the former [in verse 118:81], can be understood in three ways: for we cannot fully comprehend the words of God; and sometimes while contemplating these words the holy soul so fully rapt and suspended toward God fails in its exterior and sensorial reality. And so with exceeding desire to obtain the promises of the divine words, our internal eyes fail for a while, *dicentes, saying* to the Lord: *Quando consolaberis me, when will you comfort me*, giving to me that which I await, namely, the desired presence of your very self and the enjoyment of beatitude? Of this failure of the divine words, Jeremiah says: *There came in my heart as a burning fire shut up in my bones, and I was wearied, not being able to bear it.*[236]

118{119}[83]   *For I am become like a bottle in the frost: I have not forgotten your justifications.*

Quia factus sum sicut uter in pruina; iustificationes tuas non sum oblitus.

---

234 E. N. This sentiment is classically expressed by St. Teresa of Ávila: "¡Ay, qué larga es esta vida! / ¡Qué duros estos destierros! / Esta cárcel y estos hierros / En que está el alma metida! / Sólo esperar la salida / Me causa un dolor tan fiero, / Que muero porque no muero." "Ah, how weary this life! / These exiles so hard! / This jail and these shackles / By which the soul is fettered! / Longing only to go forth / Brings such terrible sorrow, / I die because I do not die." *The Collected Works of St. Teresa of Ávila* (Washington, DC: ICS Publications, 1985), Vol. 3, 375 (trans., Kieran Kavanaugh, O. C. D. and Otilio Rodriguez, O. C. D.).
235 Prov. 13:12.
236 Jer. 20:9b.

Rightly do I require this consolation, **118{119}[83]** *Quia sum sicut uter in pruina, for I am become like a bottle in the frost*: that is, in the manner that a leathern vessel abandoned, shrunk, and permeated or frozen in the snow appears unsuitable for human use, so I am reputed to be entirely worthless and useless in political and human intercourse by worldly men conversant with exterior things. For men who are highly contemplative become in a certain way insensible to outward things, and for this reason they are reputed to be inept and stupid in active and outward things; indeed, sometimes they are simply reputed to be fools by those who are prudent in a worldly sense. Hence we read that the princes who were with Jehu, the son of Nimshi, when they saw one of the sons of the prophets whom Elisha sent so that he might anoint Jehu as king, said: *Why came this mad man to you?*[237] Or [we can understand it] thus: *For I am become like a bottle in the frost*, that is, as a bottle filled with frozen liquor, so am I full with desire for the heavenly fatherland or with the afflictions of this life, and so do I desire to be consoled. *Iustificationes tuas, your justifications*, that is, your commandments, *non sum oblitus, I have not forgotten*. Indeed, it is best to take care to fulfill them: *Fear God, and keep his commandments: for this is all man;*[238] and also that which the Apostle said: *Keep the commandment without spot, blameless, unto the coming of our Lord Jesus Christ.*[239]

118{119}[84]   *How many are the days of your servant? When will you execute judgment on them that persecute me?*

Quot sunt dies servi tui? Quando facies de persequentibus me iudicium?

118{119}[85]   *The wicked have told me fables: but not as your law.*

Narraverunt mihi iniqui fabulationes, sed non ut lex tua.

118{119}[84] *Quot sunt dies servi tui? How many are the days of your servant?* That is, would that this time of exile, during which I am on pilgrimage towards you,[240] come quickly to an end, so that I might not be delayed any longer from heavenly felicity. Paul spoke in this manner: *I desire to be dissolved and to be with Christ.*[241] Whence in an earlier Psalm is said: *I spoke with my tongue: O Lord, make me know my end.*

---

237 2 Kings 9:11.
238 Eccl. 12:13b.
239 1 Tim. 6:14.
240 Cf. 2 Cor. 5:6.
241 Phil. 1:23b.

And what is the number of my days.[242] *Quando facies de persequentibus me iudicium? When will you execute judgment on them that persecute me?* That is, would that the day of final judgment come, when you will justly condemn the devils persecuting me. This day is desired by just and contemplative men, though it is feared by other men. For this reason the Savior said: *When these things begin to come to pass, look up, and lift up your heads,* that is, breathe cheerfully.[243] **118{119}[85]** *Narraverunt mihi iniqui, the wicked have told me,* namely, demons and depraved men, *fabulationes, fables,* that is, false suggestions, perverse arguments, useless sermons; *sed non ut lex tua, but not as your law,* that is, these contrived fables and vain stories spiritually or bodily are not consonant with the divine law. Whence the Apostle [Paul] states: *Avoid foolish and unlearned questions, knowing that they beget strifes.*[244]

118{119}[86] *All your statutes are truth: the wicked have persecuted me: help me.*[245]

> *Omnia mandata tua veritas, iniqui persecuti sunt me, adiuva me.*

118{119}[87] *They very nearly made an end of me upon earth: but I have not forsaken your commandments.*[246]

> *Paulo minus consummaverunt me in terra; ego autem non dereliqui mandata tua.*

118{119}[88] *Quicken me according to your mercy: and I shall keep the testimonies of your mouth.*

> *Secundum misericordiam tuam vivifica me, et custodiam testimonia oris tui.*

118{119}[86] *Omnia mandata tua veritas, all your statutes are truth,* that is, they are so true that they are more appropriately called truth in the abstract, than true in the concrete.[247] *Iniqui, the iniquitous,* heretics,

---

242 Ps. 38:5.
243 Luke 21:28. E. N. Denis says *hilariter respirate,* "breathe cheerfully," perhaps meaning "breathe easily."
244 2 Tim. 2:23.
245 E. N. The Douay-Rheims follows the Sixto-Clementine Vulgate: *inique persecuti sunt me,* "they have persecuted me unjustly." However, Denis's version reads: *iniqui persecuti sunt me,* "the iniquitous have persecuted me." I have followed Denis.
246 E. N. I have departed from the Douay-Rheims's "They had almost made an end of me upon earth."
247 E. N. What Denis is conveying here is that the abstract noun—which identifies the attribute or quality of something—is a better indicator than the concrete

schismatics, false brethren, demons, and infidels, *persecuti sunt me, have persecuted me* with words and blows; *adiuva me, help me*, lest I succumb to them, for I am unable to fight back without your help. **118{119}[87]** *Paulo minus, very nearly*, that is, almost or just about, *consummaverunt me, made an end of me*, that is, perfectly oppressed me or cast me down *in terra, upon earth*: as also the Apostle said: *We were pressed out of measure above our strength;*[248] *ego autem non dereliqui mandata, but I have not forsaken your commandments*, [the obedience] to which you command be undertaken with fortitude and perseverance, saying: *Fear not them that kill the body;*[249] and elsewhere: *Strive for justice for your soul, and even unto death fight for justice;*[250] and *Behold I command you, take courage, and be strong. Fear not and be not dismayed: because the Lord your God is with you.*[251] However much, therefore, the enemy raves and tribulation increases, we ought to recall the divine precepts and not grow faint, as the Apostle admonishes: *Be not wearied ... in your minds.*[252] **118{119}[88]** *Secundum misericordiam tuam vivifica me, quicken me according to your mercy*, increasing the grace in my soul, *et custodiam, and I shall keep* with faith and by works *testimonia oris tui, the testimonies of your mouth*, that is, the words of sacred eloquence, especially the articles of the faith and the precepts of the Decalogue.

PRAYER

THROUGH YOUR BROAD CLEMENCY, O Lord, strengthen our hearts with the love of your most holy name lest we depart from your commandments; quicken us with the work of your mercy so that making headway we might keep the testimonies of your mouth.

Tua, Domine, larga clementia sanctissimi nominis tui amore corda nostra confirma, ne derelinquamus mandata tua; vivificet nos misericordiae tuae opus, ut testimonia oris tui proficiendo custodiamus.

noun — which identifies something as possessing those attributes. So — because God's commandments *are true* simpliciter, intrinsically, rather than merely possessing *truth* accidentally or obliquely — it is more accurately to call them truth rather than merely true.

248 2 Cor. 1:8b.
249 Matt. 10:28a.
250 Ecclus. 4:33a.
251 Joshua 1:9.
252 Heb. 12:3b.

LAMED
(PART XII)

118{119}[89] *Forever, O Lord, your word stands firm in heaven.*

    In aeternum, Domine, verbum tuum permanet in caelo.

118{119}[90] *Your truth unto all generations: you have founded the earth, and it continues.*

    In generationem et generationem veritas tua; fundasti terram, et permanet.

118{119}[89] *In aeternum, Domine, verbum tuum; forever, O Lord, your word,* that is, your command, your illumination, and your work, *permanent in caelo, stands firm in heaven,* that is, in the Church triumphant: because all the holy angels and the blessed obey you at your behest, and unceasingly receive your illumination. Whence we pray daily that your will (that is that your precepts) be done in heaven and on earth,[253] namely, that men might obey you as do the angels. This can also be understood as referring to the Son of God: of whom is written, *In the beginning was the Word.*[254] This Word remained in heaven in eternity, for although he came to men, yet he remained in heaven, indeed he was simultaneously and for a time entirely in the womb of the Virgin and in the bosom of the Father. Because he was standing on earth and talking to Nicodemus, he said: *No man has ascended into heaven, but he that descended from heaven, the Son of man who is in heaven.*[255] **118{119}[90]** *In generationem et generationem, unto all generations,* that is, through all successive generations in the world, *veritas tua, your truth,* that is the Catholic faith, the Christian law, the evangelical doctrine, remains in the Church militant. *Fundasti, you have founded,* that is, you have firmly placed, *terram, the earth* in the middle of the world, *et permanet, and it continues,* as you bring up in Ecclesiastes: *One generation passes away, and another generation comes; but the earth stands forever.*[256] But spiritually, *you have founded the earth,* that is, the Church, in faith and in divine truth, in the manner you stated: *Upon this rock I will build my Church;*[257] and it will remain firm in the faith even until the end of the world.[258]

---

253 Matt. 6:10.
254 John 1:1.
255 John 3:13.
256 Eccl. 1:4.
257 Matt. 16:18.
258 *E. N.* "[T]he Church possesses 'an unconquered stability' and . . . 'built on a rock, she will continue to stand until the end of time.' The Church's indefectibility,

118{119}[91] *By your ordinance the day goes on: for all things serve you.*

Ordinatione tua perseverat dies, quoniam omnia serviunt tibi.

118{119}[91] *Ordinatione tua perseverat dies, by your ordinance the day goes on,* [which day] is caused by the movement and light of the sun. For the higher, lower, and universal times are moderated by the ordinance of your wisdom.[259] For this reason, we have elsewhere: *Thus says the Lord, who gives the sun for the light of the day, the order of the moon and of the stars, for the light of the night;*[260] *Seek him that makes Arcturus, and Orion, and that turns darkness into morning.*[261] Or [we can view it thus], *by your ordinance the day* of created eternity, namely, of the aevum where the saints in the heavenly fatherland enjoy you;[262] or *the* spiritual *day,* that is, the illumination of the blessed [with the light of glory]. *Quoniam omnia serviunt tibi, for all things serve you*: in the way that is stated: *O Lord, Lord, almighty King, for all things are in your power, and there is none that can resist your will.*[263] For there is in all of created nature an obediential potency by which it submits to its Creator in all things.[264]

---

therefore, means that she now is and will always remain the institution of salvation, founded by Christ. This affirms that the Church is essentially unchangeable in her teaching, her constitution, and her liturgy." John A. Hardon, S. J., *Catholic Dictionary* (New York: Image, 1980) (s.v. "indefectibility"), 225–26

259 E. N. In speaking of "higher time" (*tempora superiora*) and "inferior time" (*tempora inferiora*), perhaps Denis is referring to the notions of the Neoplatonist Iamblichus (250–325). Iamblichus distinguished between a higher time which was part of the intelligible world (an ideal time, or form of time) and the lower time which was part of the world of change and of motion. *See* J. J. A. Mooij, *Time and Mind: The History of a Philosophical Problem* (Leiden: Brill, 2005), 62 *ff.* (trans., Peter Mason).

260 Jer. 31:35a.

261 Amos 5:8a. E. N. Arcturus is a large red star, the brightest star in the constellation of Boötes (the Ox-Driver or Herdsman) and the fourth brightest star visible in the northern hemisphere, though it may be a synecdoche for the constellation Ursa Maior (the Great Bear). Orion (named after the famous hunter of Greek mythology) is another bright constellation.

262 E. N. The scholastic theologians commonly distinguished between the divine eternity (*aeternitas*, which has neither beginning or end) and which God alone enjoyed, the heavenly aeviternity (*aeviternitas* or the *aevum*, which has a beginning but no end), which the saints in heaven enjoyed, and mundane time (*tempus*, which has a beginning and end). *See* Henryk Anzulewicz, "*Aeternitas-Aevum-Tempus*: The Concept of Time in the System of Albert the Great," *The Medieval Concept of Time: Studies on the Scholastic Debate and its Reception in Early Modern Philosophy* (Leiden: Brill, 2001) (trans., Martin J. Tracey).

263 Esther 13:9.

264 "Now it must be kept in mind that in the human soul, as in every creature, a double passive power (*potentia passiva*) is to be considered: one in comparison with a natural agent; the other in comparison with the first agent, which can lead any creature to a

But if all things serve God, why is it that men do not serve God? The answer to this question is that all things are said to serve God in this way: that nothing is able to resist the divine ordinances.

———

118{119}[92] *Unless your law had been my meditation, I had then perhaps perished in my abjection.*

Nisi quod lex tua meditatio mea est, tunc forte periissem in humilitate mea.

118{119}[93] *Your justifications I will never forget: for by them you have given me life.*

In aeternum non obliviscar iustificationes tuas, quia in ipsis vivificasti me.

118{119}[92] *Nisi quod lex tua meditatio mea est,* unless your law had been my meditation, that is, unless I would have had the testimony of your laws before my eyes, *tunc forte periissem, I had then perhaps perished,* that is, I would have been vanquished or fallen into despair, *in humilitate mea, in my abjection,* that is, through the tribulation and the temptation that I have suffered, or through reflection by which I considered my imperfection and misery. For unless we partake in tribulation or consideration of this kind, and ponder how great the happiness is of those who suffer for the sake of justice and imitate the path of Christ, and remain unmoved in the face of temptations, and also how great is the mercy of God shown to miserable penitents is, then indeed we might have perished in such abjection. So that I might never perish, therefore, 118{119}[93] *In aeternum non obliviscar iustificationes tuas, your justifications I will never forget,* that is, I will never neglect to recall and to keep the divine commandments; *quia in ipsis vivificasti me, for by them you have given me life* with the life and spiritual progress in the way the Savior says: *If any one love me, he will keep my word, and my Father will love him, and we will come to him, and will make our abode with him.*[265]

———

higher act than a natural agent can lead it, and this is usually called the obediential potency (*potentia obedientiae*) of a creature." ST IIIa, q. 11, art. 1, co. "[T]he supernatural may be called natural to the extent that it is not unnatural. And it is not unnatural, first, because nature, while not aspiring to the supernatural by its own forces, is capable of reaching the supernatural through the influence and operation of another, higher nature. This is obediential potency, which is actuated under the guidance of a higher being to which unreserved obedience is given." Matthias Joseph Scheeben, *Nature and Grace* (Eugene, OR: Wipf & Stock, 2009), 40 (trans., Cyril Vollert, S. J., S. T. D.).
265 John 14:23.

And it is written: *This is the book of the commandments of God, and the law, that is forever: all they that keep it, shall come to life: but they that have forsaken it, to death.*[266]

118{119}[94]   *I am yours, save me: for I have sought your justifications.*

Tuus sum ego; salvum me fac, quoniam iustificationes tuas exquisivi.

118{119}[95]   *The wicked have waited for me to destroy me: but I have understood your testimonies.*

Me exspectaverunt peccatores ut perderent me; testimonia tua intellexi.

118{119}[94] *Tuus sum ego, I am yours* in condition and in worship, in faith and in works, *salvum me fac, save me* in the present by grace and in the future by glory, *quoniam iustificationes tuas exquisivi, for I have sought your justifications,* that is, I have taken care to fulfill your commandments and so, in accordance with your promises, salvation is due to me, because it is written: *But if you will enter into life, keep the commandments;*[267] and again, *Direct your heart into the right way* that you may be saved.[268] **118{119}[95]** *Me exspectaverunt peccatores, the wicked have waited for me,* that is, my visible and invisible enemies [have waited for me], *ut perderent me, to destroy me,* leading my soul to the ruin of sin or my body to death or injury. This is most fittingly applicable to the holy martyrs, whom tyrants waited to kill spiritually or bodily. *Testimonia tua, your testimonies,* that is, the words of the Holy Spirit contained in Scripture, *intellexi, I have understood,* that is, I have clearly examined, considering the deceit of the ungodly, the briefness of this life, and the immensity of future glory: by which thoughts I strongly endured all things, evaded their attacks, or overcame them with patience.

118{119}[96]   *I have seen the end of all consummation: your commandment is exceeding broad.*[269]

Omnis consummationis vidi finem, latum mandatum tuum nimis.

---

266 Baruch 4:1.
267 Matt. 19:17b.
268 Jer. 31:21.
269 E. N. I have departed from the Douay-Rheims translation, which read "I have seen an end to all persecution," with "I have seen the end of all consummation."

118{119}[96] *Omnis consummationis, of all consummation,* that is, to all of human perfection, *vidi, I have seen,* that is, I have given consideration to, *finem, the end:* to which all human virtue should be referred to. Now this end is eternal life, which is the end of every act and virtue. This end can also be said to be charity, because it is the highest virtue, the origin and end of every virtue. For this reason the Apostle [Paul] says: *Love is the fulfilling of the law;*[270] and again, *The end of the commandment is charity.*[271] And so that which follows — *latum mandatum tuum nimis, your commandment is exceeding broad* — expounds upon what was said — *I have seen the end of all consummation* — so that it is understood in this sense: *I have seen the end of all consummation,* indeed, *your commandment is exceeding broad,* that is, I have seen that the precept of charity — which is very wide — is the end and the perfection of the consummation of the universe, for all other precepts are referred to it. The precept of charity is said to be *exceeding broad* also because it is applicable to all men: for it makes us lovers even of our adversaries. Secondly, because it contains virtually all commandments, according to this: *On these two commandments,* namely, the love of God and of neighbor, *depends the whole law and the prophets.*[272] Third, because as we read, *Charity covers all sins.* And wo we can literally expound it thus: *I have seen the end,* that is, the termination, *to all consummation,* that is, to all the possessions of the earth, all temporal ambitions and glory. These things quickly fail us, as we are led to consider by John: *The world passes away, and the concupiscence thereof;*[273] *your commandment is exceeding broad,* that is, lasting throughout eternity and leading to the wide expanse of heaven.

PRAYER

GOD, WHOM ALL CREATED THINGS SERVE, grant us to serve you with perfect faith, hope, and charity so that we do not forget your justifications in eternity, but that by persisting in them through good works we might be given life through your propitiation.

Deus, cui omnis serviunt creata, da nos servire tibi fide, spe, et caritate perfecta: ut in aeternum iustificationes tuas non obliviscamur, sed in ipsis tua propitiatione bonis operibus insistendo vivificemur.

270 Rom. 13:10b.
271 I Tim. 1:5a.
272 Matt. 22:40.
273 1 John 2:17a.

MEM
(PART XIII)

118{119}[97] *O how have I loved your law, O Lord? It is my meditation all the day.*

Quomodo dilexi legem tuam, Domine? Tota die meditatio mea est.

118{119}[97] *Quomodo dilexi lege tuam, Domine? O how have I loved your law, O Lord?* The Prophet [David] asks God, in the person of the Church, how he loves the law. And he himself responds: *Tota die meditatio mea est; it is my meditation all the day.* For he asks and he responds so that all those who hear may be informed. Now, when he asserts himself to meditate on the law of the Lord all the day long, he declares that he most ardently loves God, the degree by which one honors God is the degree that one loves him, in the manner that we have elsewhere [written]: *He that keeps Christ's word, in him the charity of God is perfected.*[274] For that which is loved more is thought about often. He therefore who meditates on the law of the Lord the whole natural day, which includes the night, and which is composed of twenty-four hours, loves it greatly, and consequently also the Legislator, indeed, God. Now how someone is able to meditate on the divine law all day has been frequently explained.

118{119}[98] *Through your commandment, you have made me wiser than my enemies: for it is ever with me.*

Super inimicos meos prudentem me fecisti mandato tuo, quia in aeternum mihi est.

118{119}[99] *I have understood more than all my teachers: because your testimonies are my meditation.*

Super omnes docentes me intellexi, quia testimonia tua meditatio mea est.

118{119}[100] *I have had understanding above ancients: because I have sought your commandments.*

Super senes intellexi, quia mandata tua quaesivi.

118{119}[98] *Super inimicos meos prudentem me fecisti, you have made me wiser than my enemies,* that is, you have made me more prudent and

---

274 2 John 2:5a.

more wise than my enemies, namely the Jews and the infidels — indeed all those rebelling against God: whom *I have hated . . . with a perfect hatred*,[275] not insofar as they are men with the capacity of [eternal] happiness, but insofar as they are disobedient to God and in agreement with the devil; *mandato tuo, through your commandment*: that is, by the fact that by giving me the grace to keep your commandment, you have made me wiser than those who do not observe them. For no man is truly prudent without the keeping of the precepts; and the highest prudence is to serve God. Whence it is written: *Who is a wise man, and endued with knowledge among you? Let him show, by a good conversation, his work in the meekness of wisdom.*[276] Now in this manner you have made me in your commandment, *qui in aeternum mihi est, for it is ever with me*, that is, because I intend perseveringly and constantly to adhere to it. **118{119}[99]** *Super omnes docentes me intellexi, quia testimonia tua meditatio mea est; I have understood more than all my teachers, because your testimonies are my meditation.* He does not here speak of all of his teachers absolutely, because as Christ testified, *The disciple is not above the master;*[277] and it would be presumptuous for a person to prefer himself to his teachers. Therefore, of which teachers does he speak, unless it be of those *who say and do not*,[278] or they who teach philosophical knowledge or worldly prudence? In this regard, he who is obedient to God is more intelligent: for the testimonies of God are his meditation, and he thinks about the divine words in order that he might govern his thoughts, words, and acts according to the teaching and the precepts of Christ. **118{119}[100]** *Super senes intellexi, I have had understanding above ancients*, that is, I was more learned than the ancients, *quia mandata tua quaesivi, because I have sought your commandments* to know them and to fulfill them. From this it is certain that he speaks here of none other than those ancients who did not seek the commandments, who were among those regarding which is stated in Daniel: *Iniquity came out from Babylon from the ancient judges, that seemed to govern the people.*[279]

118{119}[101] *I have restrained my feet from every evil way: that I may keep your words.*

  Ab omni via mala prohibui pedes meos, ut custodiam verba tua.

---

275 Ps. 138:22a.
276 James 3:13.
277 Matt. 10:24a.
278 Matt. 23:3b.
279 Dan. 13:5b.

118{119}[102] *I have not declined from your judgments, because you have set me a law.*

A iudiciis tuis non declinavi, quia tu legem posuisti mihi.

118{119}[101] *Ab omni via mala, from every evil way,* that is, mortal sin, pestiferous doctrine, and other things whose paths lead to eternal death, *prohibui, I have restrained* by the rule of reason, *pedes meo, my feet,* that is, the affections, thoughts, and works, or also the bodily feet, avoiding those places in which I think I would be likely to sin;[280] *ut custodiam verba tua, that I may keep your words,* by which you have commanded me to avoid the ways of evil men. 118{119}[102] *A iudiciis tuis non declinavi, I have not declined from your judgments,* that is, I have not departed from those things that you judge to be good and you approve, *quia tu legem posuisti mihi, because you have set me a law,* that is, the precept of consenting to that which is true and good and resisting that which is evil and false, in the way is written in Ecclesiasticus: *He gave them the law of life for an inheritance* (namely, God gave to men) . . . *and he showed them his justice and judgments, . . . and he said to them: Beware of all iniquity.*[281]

––––––––––

118{119}[103] *How sweet are your words to my palate! More than honey to my mouth.*

Quam dulcia faucibus meis eloquia tua! Super mel ori meo.

118{119}[103] *Quam dulcia faucibus meis eloquia tua! How sweet are your words to my palate!* That is, the divine words are very sweet to the palate of my interior heart, namely, the reason and the will, which relish spiritual sweetness, chew on the food of the soul, and drink heavenly joy. *Super mel ori meo, more than honey to my mouth,* that is, they are sweeter to my internal mouth, namely, to my mind, which brings forth the word of the heart, as honey is to the bodily palate. For the word of God is food for the soul, whose refreshment is sweeter by its very nature than

––––––––––

280 E. N. One has a "moral responsibility of not exposing oneself unnecessarily to occasions of sin. The principles are standard in Catholic moral teaching: 1. No one is obliged to avoid the remote occasions of sin. This is true because the danger of sin is slight and otherwise it would be impossible to live in the world; 2. Everyone is obliged to avoid voluntary proximate occasions of sin, where 'voluntary' means that it can easily be removed or avoided; 3. Anyone in a necessary proximate occasion of sin is obliged to make the occasion remote. . . . What is a proximate danger to sinning can be rendered remote by such means as prayer, the sacraments, and custody of the senses, especially the eyes." John A. Hardon, S. J., *Catholic Dictionary* (New York: Image, 1980), 41–42 (s.v. "avoiding sin").

281 Ecclus.17:9b, 10b, 11b.

all bodily food: although sometimes it appears to us to be the opposite because we see that our appetite is not yet purged from vice and from disordered desires. For this is written about wisdom: *I know that she will communicate to me of her good things, and will be a comfort in my cares and grief. When I go into my house, I shall repose myself with her: for her conversation has no bitterness, nor her company any tediousness, but joy and gladness.*[282] And why should we wonder if sacred doctrine or divine and Christian wisdom is so sweet to a contemplative man, when Aristotle said that philosophy has mixed within it admirable pleasures; and again, that our life, when it engages for a while in such state, is always a life of first principles; moreover, that a contemplative man does not seek external delights, because he is internally filled with speculative delights.[283]

118{119}[104] *By your commandments I have had understanding: therefore have I hated every way of iniquity.*

A mandatis tuis intellexi; propterea odivi omnem viam iniquitatis.

118{119}[104] *A mandatis tuis intellexi, by your commandments I have had understanding,* that is, from the consideration of the precepts I have understood the distance between virtues and vice. Or [we can see it thus], *by your commandments I have had understanding,* that is, true understanding fitted to keeping your commandments: as is written, *Son, if you desire wisdom,* keep the commandments, *and God will give her to you.*[284] Prophetic scripture also says: *Whom shall he teach knowledge? And whom shall he make to understand the hearing?* And he responds to the Prophet [Isaiah]: *Them that are weaned from the milk, that are drawn away from the breasts,* that is, those who reject the pleasures of the flesh and live spiritually and penitentially according to the divine precepts. *Propterea odivi omnem viam iniquitatis, therefore have I hated every way of iniquity:* which, if I did not hate, out of certain knowledge (and not out of ignorance), I would have sinned; and this would befit me: *The servant who knew the will of his lord, . . . and did not do it, he will be beaten with many blows.*[285]

---

282 Wis. 8:9b, 16.
283 E. N. Denis is probably referring to Aristotle's *Nicomachean Ethics. See, e.g.,* X.vii.1–9 (1177a11–1178a1), X.viii.13 (1179a25–28).
284 Ecclus. 1:33a. E. N. The Sixto-Clementine Vulgate reads *conserva iustitiam,* and not *serva mandata,* which is what Denis quotes. Wisdom (*sapientia*) is female gender in Latin, hence it is referred to by a female personal pronoun.
285 Luke 12:47.

PRAYER

LORD, GIVER OF EVERY GOOD, GRANT us to love your holy law, and to submit to it with a mind of watchful meditation; make us to understand your commandments rightly, and with your help prevent our feet from traveling on every evil way of depravity.

Totius boni largitor, Domine, da nobis legem tuam sanctam diligere, et eius meditationi pervigili mente inservire; fac nos mandata tua recte intelligere, atque ab omni via mala te adiuvante nostrae pravitatis pedes prohibere.

NUN
(PART XIV)

118{119}[105] *Your word is a lamp to my feet, and a light to my paths.*

Lucerna pedibus meis verbum tuum, et lumen semitis meis.

118{119}[106] *I have sworn and am determined to keep the judgments of your justice.*

Iuravi et statui custodire iudicia iustitiae tuae.

118{119}[105] *Lucerna pedibus meis verbum tuum, your word is a lamp to my feet*: that is, sacred Scripture is the light of all my understanding and affections and all my works, for it illumines me lest I walk with the darkness of vices; *et,* and this word is *lumen semitis meis, a light to my paths*, that is, it is my directive in the observations of the counsels of Christ: these are called paths because they are the more narrow and shorter ways to come to God than the precepts.[286] This is what Solomon asserts: *The commandment is a lamp, and the law a light, and reproofs*

---

286 "The difference between a counsel and a commandment is that a commandment implies obligation, whereas a counsel is left to the option of the one to whom it is given. Consequently, in the New Law, which is the law of liberty, counsels are added to the commandments, and not in the Old Law, which is the law of bondage. We must therefore understand the commandments of the New Law to have been given about matters that are necessary to gain the end of eternal bliss, to which end the New Law brings us forthwith: but that the counsels are about matters that render the gaining of this end more assured and expeditious." ST IaIIae, q. 108, art. 4, co. (translated by Fathers of the English Dominican Province).

of instruction are the way of life.[287] And elsewhere: *Take hold of the law, walk in the way by its brightness, in the presence of the light thereof.*[288] **118{119}[106]** *Iuravi, I have sworn,* that is, I have irrevocably affirmed, *et statui, and am determined,* that is, I have proposed, *custodire iudicia iustitiae tuae, to keep the judgments of your justice,* that is, the precepts which your justice judges to be right and to be performed. When the matter calls for it, it is lawful to make an oath: indeed, depending upon the circumstances, to swear an oath is an act of virtue which is called *latria;*[289] and so Scripture admits, praises, and rejoices in an oath, according to this, *You shall fear the Lord your God, . . . and you shall swear by his name;*[290] and, *With all their heart they swore, and with all their will they sought him, and they found him.*[291] But that which Christ says in the Gospel — *I say to you not to swear at all* — he does not say preceptively in a strict sense, but that we might not swear without necessity, so that we might avoid occasions of perjury and the use of oaths.

118{119}[107] *I have been humbled, O Lord, exceedingly: quicken me according to your word.*

Humiliatus sum usquequaque, Domine; vivifica me secundum verbum tuum.

118{119}[108] *The free offerings of my mouth make acceptable, O Lord: and teach me your judgments.*

Voluntaria oris mei beneplacita fac, Domine, et iudicia tua doce me.

118{119}[107] *Humiliatus sum usquequaque, I have been humbled exceedingly,* that is, I am greatly afflicted, disheartened, and scorned, or have greatly humbled myself, despising myself because of my negligences and my infinite defects. And so, *Domine, vivifica me secundum verbum tuum; O Lord, quicken me according to your word,* that is, bestow grace upon me so that I might live according to the word of your doctrine. Or [alternatively], *quicken me,* by the infusion of grace, *according to your word,* that is, in accordance to your promises of giving grace to the afflicted and to the humbled. For it is written: *He that has been humbled, shall be*

---

287 Prov. 6:23.
288 Baruch 4:2b.
289 *E. N.* Denis relies on ST IIaIIae, q. 89, in particular arts. 4 and 5.
290 Deut. 6:13b.
291 2 Chr. 15:15.

in glory;[292] and elsewhere: *He will surely have pity on you at the voice of your cry; as soon as he shall hear, he will answer you.*[293] **118{119}[108]** *Voluntaria oris mei, the free offerings of my mouth,* that is, my prayers and all things which I desire, or all things that I freely offer to you, *beneplacita fac, Domine; make acceptable, O Lord,* that is, provide grace to such acts so that they be ordained or presented in a manner pleasing to you. *For we know not what we should pray for as we ought; but the Spirit himself asks for us,* that is, he imparts to us what ought to be asked for.[294] Whence the Apostle prays: *May my God supply all your want, according to his riches . . . in Christ Jesus.*[295] *Et iudicia tua, and your judgments,* that is, the commandments which are approved by you, *doce me, teach me.* Or [alternatively], *teach me your judgments,* that is, give me the grace that I might contemplate the divine judgments through which every person is given what he deserves, so that I know *it is a fearful thing to fall into the hands of the living God.*[296]

118{119}[109] My soul is continually in my hands: and I have not forgotten your law.

Anima mea in manibus meis semper, et legem tuam non sum oblitus.

118{119}[109] *Anima mea in manibus meis semper, my soul is continually in my hands:* that is, because of the snares of the devil, the disordered desires of the flesh, and other impediments of the world and the body by which I am drawn away from God and drawn to vices, I live in a continuous danger of being cut down by sin, and, as a consequence, eternal damnation. For by this statement — that I have my soul in my hands — Scripture indicates something is a clear danger, as when Jonathan said of David: *He put his soul in his hand and slew the Philistine.*[297] And Jephtha said the same thing when returning from the war against the Ammonites.[298] And the witch also said the same to Saul.[299] If, therefore,

---

292 Job 22:29a.
293 Is. 30:19b.
294 Rom. 7:26.
295 Phil. 4:19.
296 Heb. 10:31.
297 1 Sam. 19:5a.
298 Judges 12:3: *When I saw this, I put my soul in my own hands, and passed over against the children of Ammon, and the Lord delivered them into my hands.*
299 1 Sam. 28:21: *Behold your handmaid has obeyed your voice, and I have put my life in my hand.*

our soul is always in our hands, that is, in such danger, it is a wonder how untroubled, light-hearted, care-free we live our lives. And it is truly written: *The heart of the wise is where there is mourning, and the heart of fools where there is mirth.*[300] *Et legem tuam non sum oblitus, and I have not forgotten your law,* but I have kept it by memory and by obedience.

118{119}[110] *Sinners have laid a snare for me: but I have not erred from your precepts.*

Posuerunt peccatores laqueum mihi, et de mandatis tuis non erravi.

118{119}[111] *I have purchased your testimonies for an inheritance forever: because they are a joy to my heart.*

Haereditate acquisivi testimonia tua in aeternum, quia exsultatio cordis mei sunt.

118{119}[110] *Posuerunt peccatores, sinners have laid,* namely, demons and unrighteous men, *laqueum, a snare,* that is, an occasion of ruin and deception, *mihi, for me,* so that they might in some way divert me from the way of God. For the snares by which these [demons and unrighteous men] hope to deceive the incautious are adulation, praise, threats, worldly vanities, temporal riches, and other things by which affections are defiled. *Et de mandatis tuis non erravi, but I have not erred from your precepts:* for I have not consented to their temptations and suggestions, as Solomon warned: *My son, if sinners shall entice you, consent not to them.*[301] **118{119}[111]** *Hereditate, for an inheritance,* that is, as an enduring possession, *aquisivi testimonia tua, I have purchased your testimonies,* that is, the divine precepts, and the other words approved by divine testimony, namely all things stated in sacred Scripture, *in aeternum, forever,* so that I might adhere to them eternally; *quia exsultatio cordis mei sunt, because they are a joy to my heart,* that is, I rejoice more from their possession and knowledge than of all my temporal goods.

118{119}[112] *I have inclined my heart to do your justifications forever, for the reward.*

Inclinavi cor meum ad faciendas iustificationes tuas, in aeternum, propter retributionem.

---

300 Eccl. 7:5.
301 Prov. 1:10.

118{119}[112] *Inclinavi cor meum ad faciendas iustificationes tuas, I have inclined my heart to do your justifications*, that is, whatever commandments or works by which man is justified by you: and this, *in aeternum, forever*, that is, unceasingly as long as I live. For some precepts are also fulfilled in the heavenly fatherland more perfectly than while wayfaring, such as the precept of charity. *Propter retributionem, for the reward*, the eternal [reward], namely, so that I might obtain heavenly happiness. But since it is the work of a hireling when one labors for reward (and not of a son or a friend), in what way does he mean that he had inclined his heart to good works? The answer is that as a purely servile fear merits nothing, so to labor only for reward merits nothing, for both of these [behaviors] proceed from self-love. But in the way that initial fear is meritorious inasmuch as it has some connection to charity, so to labor for reward is meritorious when the ultimate intention is to provide it to the honor of God or God himself, whom one must have as one's principal intent for any act to be meritorious. Finally, in the manner that filial fear most highly pleases God, so to intend to honor God with one's whole mind, and to do good works for a pure love of God is most highly holy and meritorious, because it is caused by the divine love. Nevertheless, such a man implicitly does things for reward, and in a certain manner intends it, not out of self-love, but out of divine love, inasmuch, namely, as God wills that we might do things for the reward of eternal happiness.

PRAYER

O GOD, THE PATH OF RIGHT LIVING AND the splendor of souls, let Christ, your Word, be the lantern for our feet and the light of our paths, so that being led by him, we might through his commandments understand rightly, and always harbor hate toward, and turn away from, every way of iniquity.

Deus, recte viventium semita, et splendor animarum, Verbum tuum Christus sit lucerna pedibus nostris et lumen semitis nostris: ut eius ductu, a mandatis eius recta intelligamus, et omnem viam iniquitatis semper odio habeamus et declinemus.

SAMECH
(PART XV)

118{119}[113] *I have hated the unjust: and have loved your law.*

Iniquos odio habui, et legem tuam dilexi.

118{119}[113] *Iniquos odio habui,* I have hated the unjust, insofar as they are unjust: for such also are hateful to God, according to this, *To God the wicked and his wickedness are hateful alike.* Not, however, that I hate them insofar as they are men, since it is written, *Love your enemies.*[302] But to love, according to the Philosopher [Aristotle], is to wish someone good; but to hate is to wish another evil.[303] And so we should will or desire for the unjust, insofar as they are men, their good, namely, grace now and afterward glory. But we should not desire good to them insofar as they are unjust; for this would be contrary to justice: indeed, we should desire for them the evil of punishment in the present age, or in the future if they do not repent.

Now regarding the hatred of the enemies and the impious, the Jews erred and continue to err, judging according to the law that they might hate the unjust and their enemies, because Moses said: *You shall love your friend as yourself,*[304] and *you shall hate your enemy.*[305] But this is completely false; and the opposite can be proved not only from the canonical scriptures of the Old Testament, but also from the deeds of the ancient Saints. For without doubt David loved Saul, whom he so frequently spared, and whom he so kindly referred to as his father;[306] but he also killed him who claimed (albeit falsely) to have killed Saul.[307] Similarly, he extended his love to Saul's son Ishbaal. For after he died, he told the thieves that had killed him: *When wicked men have slain an innocent man in his own house, upon his bed, shall I not require his blood*

---

302 Matt. 5:44.
303 *E. N.* The reference would appear to be to Aristotle's *Rhetoric:* II.4, 1380b35–1381a6 and 1382a8, and perhaps also his *Nicomachean Ethics,* 1155b32–1156a5.
304 Lev. 19:18b.
305 Matt. 5:43. *E. N.* Leviticus does not have the injunction to hate the enemies, so it appears to have been a popular interpolation. In the *Community Rules* in the Dead Sea Scrolls, the members of the Qumran community are told that they "may love all the sons of light, each according to his lot in God's design, and hate the sons of darkness, each according to his guilt in God's vengeance." I, 10–12. *The Dead Sea Scrolls in English* (Sheffield: Sheffield Academic Press, 1995) (trans., Geza Vermes), 70.
306 1 Sam. 24:12.
307 2 Sam. 1:15.

at your hand, and take you away from the earth?[308] And the same thing applies to many others in the Old Testament. And so Moses said: *You shall not hate your brother in your heart, but reprove him openly, lest you incur sin through him;*[309] and again, *Seek not revenge, nor be mindful of the injury of your citizens.*[310] Solomon also said: *Say not: I will do to him as he has done to me;*[311] and again *When your enemy shall fall, be not glad, and in his ruin let not your heart rejoice.*[312] Holy Job concurs in this, saying: *If I have been glad at the downfall of him that hated me, and have rejoiced that evil had found him.*[313] And also elsewhere we have: *If your enemy be hungry, give him to eat: if he thirst, give him water to drink ... and the Lord will reward you.*[314] And the Apostle puts forth these very words to prove by them that enemies are to be loved.[315]

Et legem tuam dilexi, and I have loved your law, as has just now been said, *above thousands of gold and silver.*[316] For this reason it is written: *We are ready to die rather than to transgress the laws of God, received from our fathers.*[317] If, therefore, I love your law, I will also love those who keep them, namely, the just.

118{119}[114] *You are my helper and my protector: and in your word I have greatly hoped.*

Adiutor et susceptor meus es tu, et in verbum tuum supersperavi.

118{119}[115] *Depart from me, you malignant: and I will search the commandments of my God.*

Declinate a me, maligni, et scrutabor mandata Dei mei.

118{119}[114] *Adiutor meus, my helper,* by cooperating with me with grace, as the Apostle says, *yet not I, but the grace of God with me; et susceptor meus es tu, and my protector are you,* that is, the hearer of my prayers, and my merciful embracer in whom I take refuge: in the manner

---

308 2 Sam. 4:11.
309 Lev. 19:17.
310 Lev. 19:19a.
311 Prov. 24:29a.
312 Prov. 24:17.
313 Job. 31:29. E. N. This is from Job's defense; thus, he is stating that he did not incur the fault of being glad at the downfall of his enemies and happiness at their misfortune.
314 Prov. 25:21–22.
315 Rom. 12:20.
316 Ps. 118:72.
317 2 Macc. 7:2b.

that is testified, *Him that comes to me, I will not cast out;*[318] *et in verbum tuum, and in your word* by which you promised mercy, *superiperavi, I have greatly hoped,* knowing infallibly that what you promise is true. And so, in order that I might deserve this eternal kindness, **118{119} [115]** *Declinate a me, maligni; depart from me, you malignant,* whoever they may be, and depart from me O you vain and evil thoughts, and let nothing approach me by which I might withdraw from God. Now it says that the malignant should depart from him, and not that he be absolutely free from the temptations of the devil and the persecutions of the world, since it is written, *Through many tribulations we must enter into the kingdom of God;*[319] but it says, *depart from me, you malignant,* so as to rouse himself against the malignant, so that one might deny them consent, and he might detest and despise them inasmuch as they are endeavoring to withdraw him from going in the ways of God. *Et scrutabor mandata Dei mei, and I will search the commandments of my God* diligently and humbly, so that I might clearly know them and reverently fulfill them.

118{119}[116] *Uphold me according to your word, and I shall live: and let me not be confounded in my expectation.*

Suscipe me secundum eloquium tuum, et vivam, et non confundas me ab exspectatione mea.

118{119}[117] *Help me, and I shall be saved: and I will meditate always on your justifications.*

Adiuva me, et salvus ero, et meditabor in iustificationibus tuis semper.

118{119}[116] *Suscipe me, uphold me* with your immense arms of kindness, *secundum eloquium tuum, according to your word* by which you said, *Turn to me, . . . and I will turn to you,*[320] *et vivam, and I shall live* by grace much more happily than I would live by nature or the animal principle of life;[321] *et non confundas me, and let me not be confounded,* that is, do not permit me to be confounded, *ab exspectatione mea, in my*

---

318 John 6:37b.

319 Acts 14:21b.

320 Zech. 1:3b.

321 E. N. Denis says that the life of grace (the state of supernature) exceeds the life one would live *per naturam seu animam.* Denis would appear to be using the word *anima* to refer to the animal soul or animal principle of life as distinguished from *animus,* the intellectual or spiritual principle of man.

expectation, that is, from the good that I expect from you, which is grace in the present and eternal beatitude in heaven. Now this expectation is the same as hope, because hope is the certain expectation of future happiness.[322] He prays, therefore, that he might not be frustrated in his hope, but that he may be found worthy to merit the effect and fruit of hope. For the Lord has also promised this in Isaiah, saying: *I am the Lord, for they shall not be confounded that wait for him.*[323] Whence, in the same [book] it states: *The Lord is the God of judgment: blessed are all they that wait for him.*[324] Here we find contained in Ecclesiasticus: *No one has hoped in the Lord, and has been confounded.*[325] **118{119}[117]** *Adiuva me, help me* by unceasing grace, *et salvus ero, and I shall be saved* from all danger. Indeed, *If God be for us, who is against us?*[326] For this reason, holy Job says: *Set me beside you, and let any man's hand fight against me.*[327] For no one has the power to oppose almighty God.[328] And so in the book of Esther it states: *If you determine to save us, we will immediately be set free.*[329] *Et meditabor in iustificationibus tuis, and I will meditate… on your justifications*, that is, on your commandments, *semper, always*, that is, at every appropriate or due time. For it states that the thing will be done always, so that it is never omitted when it ought to be done.

118{119}[118] *You have despised all them that fall off from your judgments; for their thought is unjust.*

Sprevisti omnes discedentes a iudiciis tuis, quia iniusta cogitatio eorum.

118{119}[119] *I have accounted all the sinners of the earth prevaricators: therefore have I loved your testimonies.*

Praevaricantes reputavi omnes peccatores terrae; ideo dilexi testimonia tua.

---

322 E. N. This classic definition of the theological virtue of hope (*spes est certa exspectatio futurae felicitatis*) is found, for example, in Peter Lombard's *Sentences*. *See* III Sent. d. 26, c. 1.

323 Is. 49:23b.

324 Is. 30:18b.

325 Ecclus. 2:11b.

326 Rom. 8:31b.

327 Job 17:3.

328 *Cf.* Gen. 50:19: *Fear not: can we resist the will of God?*

329 Esther 13:9. E. N. Denis's quotation of Esther (*continuo liberemur*) departs from the Sixto-Clementine Vulgate, which reads *non est qui possit tuae resistere voluntati*, "there is none that can resist your will."

118{119}[118] *Sprevisti, you have despised,* O Lord, *omnes discedentes a iudiciis tuis, all them that fall off from your judgments,* that is, all who persevere in evil and do not observe your commandments. For just as God hates them, so he despises them. Whence it is written: *The way of the wicked is an abomination to the Lord.*[330] And again, Wisdom states: *I hate arrogance, and pride, and every wicked way, and a mouth with a double tongue.*[331] *Quia iniusta cogitatio eorum, for their thought is unjust.* For it is contrary to divine justice, according to that in Micah: *Woe to you that devise that which is unprofitable, [and work evil in your beds: in the morning light they execute it,] because their hand is against God.*[332] 118{119}[119] *Praevaricatores, prevaricators,* that is, transgressors of the law of the most High, *reputavi omnes peccatores terrae, I have accounted all the sinners of the earth:* of whom is written: *O Lord . . . all that forsake you shall be confounded: they that depart from you, shall be written in the earth;*[333] *ideo dilexi testimonia tua, therefore I have loved your testimonies* with an interior affection and by faithful execution, lest I should become like them [who forsake you].

118{119}[120] *Pierce you my flesh with your fear: for I am afraid of your judgments.*

Confige timore tuo carnes meas; a iudiciis enim tuis timui.

118{119}[120] *Confige timore tuo carnes meas, pierce you my flesh with your fear,* that is, curb and mortify the carnal movements existing in me with the fear of future judgment and of eternal punishment; *a iudiciis enim tuis timui, for I am afraid of your judgments:* that is, from the consideration of the particular judgment (by which I will be judged by you as soon as I die), and from the consideration also of the last judgment, and because of the judgment done in the past, by which you destroyed lustful and carnal men, such as occurred at the flood, when all flesh had corrupted its way let me be terrified lest I might be condemned.[334] Indeed, these judgments should be extremely feared. Indeed, he who diligently considers them will be seized by a holy fear and will struggle against carnal movements.

---

330 Prov. 15:9a.
331 Prov. 8:13.
332 Micah 2:1. *E. N.* The part in brackets replaces the "etc." of Denis.
333 Jer. 17:13a.
334 Gen. 6:12.

PRAYER

RECEIVE US IN YOUR GRACE, O LORD GOD, and do not confound us from the blessing of eternal salvation which we expect from you; grant, we beseech you, that we might perseveringly meditate in your justifications, and, with your help, makes us depart from this present life with unimpaired faith.

Suscipe nos in gratiam tuam, Domine Deus, et non confundas nos ab aeternae salutis benedictione, quam a te exspectamus; tribue, quaesumus, nos in iustificationibus tuis perseveranter meditari, et te adiuvante, cum integra fide praesenti vita dissolve.

AIN
(PART XVI)

118{119}[121] *I have done judgment and justice: give me not up to them that slander me.*

Feci iudicium et iustitiam, non tradas me calumniantibus me.

118{119}[122] *Uphold your servant unto good: let not the proud calumniate me.*

Suscipe servum tuum in bonum: non calumnientur me superbi.

118{119}[121] *Feci iudicium, I have done judgment,* diligently scrutinizing and judging myself, discerning good from evil, true from false, pure from polluted; or *I have done judgment* to the subjects over whom I have authority; *et iustitiam, and justice,* giving to everyone that which is his and correcting myself justly, venerating God in all things and before all things, and also doing to my neighbor as I would want to be done to me. Before all else, God seeks two things from us, as we find stated in Micah: *I will show you, O man, what is good, and what the Lord requires of you: Verily, to do judgment, [and to love mercy, and to walk solicitous with your God].*[335] *Non tradas me, give me not up,* do not permit me to be given up *calumniantibus me, to them that slander me,* that is, to be under the will and power of those who inflict calumny upon me, seeking to deceive, to infect, and to pervert my soul. Do not, therefore, O Lord, permit me to be overcome or subdued by demons. This is said in Ecclesiasticus: *Sovereign ruler of my life, leave me not to their thoughts*

---

335 Micah 6:8. E. N. The part in brackets replaces Denis's "etc."

and *counsel, etc.,* ... *lest I fall before my adversaries; and give me not over to a shameless* ... *mind.*[336] **118{119}[122]** *Suscipe servum tuum in bonum,* *uphold your servant unto good,* kindly pardoning his imperfections, mercifully accepting his service, and filling him with grace which always causes progress; *non calumnientur me superbi, let not the proud calumniate me,* that is, let the demons in their obstinate pride and men following in their footsteps not find just cause to calumniate me.

118{119}[123] *My eyes have failed after your salvation: and for the word of your justice.*[337]

Oculi mei defecerunt in salutare tuum, et in eloquium iustitiae tuae.

118{119}[124] *Deal with your servant according to your mercy: and teach me your justifications.*

Fac cum servo tuo secundum misericordiam tuam, et iustificationes tuas doce me.

118{119}[125] *I am your servant: give me understanding that I may know your testimonies.*

Servus tuus sum ego, da mihi intellectum, ut sciam testimonia tua.

118{119}[123] *Oculi mei defecerunt in salutare tuum, et in eloquium iustitiae tuae; my eyes have failed after your salvation: and for the word of your justice.* This states [something similar to] what a short time earlier was said and explained in various ways — *My soul has failed after your salvation,* and *My eyes have failed for your word.*[338] For just as the soul, so the inner eyes, which are here being discussed, assert to have failed after the salvation of God: and how it should be understood should be sought there [in the explanation of verses **81** and **82**]. **118{119}[124]** *Fac cum servo tuo, deal with your* servant, namely with me and with any one of the faithful, *secundum misericordiam tuam, according to your* mercy, which truly is immense, and [do not deal with your servant] according to my incalculable malice; but as you perceive my great need, so come to my aid and deign to reveal to me the abyss of your kindness: in the manner that is begged by Daniel: *Put us not to confusion, but deal with us according to your meekness, and according*

---

336 Ecclus. 23:1, 3, 6.
337 *E. N.* I have replaced "fainted" in the Douay-Rheims with "failed," so that it is consistent with verses 119:81 and 119:32.
338 Ps. 119:81a, 82a.

to the multitude of your mercies.[339] *For it is not for our justifications that we present our prayers before your face, but for the multitude of your tender mercies.*[340] *Et iustificationes tuas, and your justifications,* that is, your justifying commandments, *doce me, teach me.* And it befits you, for **118{119}[125]** *Servus tuus sum ego, I am your servant:* and so *da mihi intellectum, give me understanding,* a pure illumination or understanding by divine influence *ut sciam testimonia tua, that I may know your testimonies,* that is, those things to be believed and those things to be done.

118{119}[126] *It is time, O Lord, to do: they have dissipated your law.*

Tempus faciendi, Domine; dissipaverunt legem tuam.

118{119}[127] *Therefore have I loved your commandments above gold and the topaz.*

Ideo dilexi mandata tua super aurum et topazion.

118{119}[128] *Therefore was I directed to all your commandments: I have hated all wicked ways.*

Propterea ad omnia mandata tua dirigebar; omnem viam iniquam odio habui.

118{119}[126] *Tempus faciendi, Domine; it is time, O Lord,* that is, it is the hour that you concede these things to me because of imminent dangers. For *disspaverunt legem tuam, they have dissipated your law:* that is, heretics, perverse teachers, Jews, and other reprobates have perverted the evangelical and divine law, and, to the degree they are able, they have annihilated it, expounding it in a lying fashion, impiously blaspheming, and contumaciously transgressing it. **118{119}[127]** *Ideo dilexi mandata tua, therefore have I loved your commandments:* that is, the more I perceive that your law is dissipated by them, the more ardently I am inflamed with zeal, so that I might restore, confirm, and observe it. Whence I have loved your commandments *super aurum et topazion, above gold and topaz,* that is, more than all gold or that most precious stone with the name topaz. For in this divine law is true wisdom: and so one can most truly say this about the love of the law and of the commandments of God: *It is more precious than all riches; and all the things that are desired are not to be compared with it.*[341] And elsewhere: *The finest gold shall not purchase it, neither shall silver*

---

339 Dan. 3:42.
340 Dan. 9:18b.
341 Prov. 3:15. E. N. I have replaced the feminine pronouns ("wisdom," *sapientia,* has feminine gender in Latin) with neuter gender.

be weighed in exchange for it. It shall not be compared with the dyed colors of India, or with the most precious stone sardonyx, or the sapphire. . . . The topaz of Ethiopia shall not be equal to it.[342] But the topaz is a most precious stone having two colors, namely, of most pure gold and another resplendent with ethereal splendor, and its appearance is most pleasing to the eye. This stone is so expensive that kings judge that there is nothing richer in their treasures. **118{119}[128]** *Propterea,* therefore, namely because of the fact that I loved your commandments, *ad omnia mandata tua dirigebar, I was directed to all your commandments,* with the mind, mouth, and deed, because one cannot observe one law if one neglects another; *omnem viam iniquam, all wicked ways,* that is, all sin, *odio habui, I have hated,* not only because of the sin punishment that follows, but because the deformity of sin, and especially because it is displeasing to the sublime and blessed Creator.

See how most ardent the prayers, how most wholesome the examples, how most perfect the works contained and described in this present Psalm. He, therefore, who possesses these works becomes grateful to God and instructs others. But he who does not have them should be zealous to have them, should be zealous to implement these examples, should be zealous to offer these prayers to the Savior ardently, so that he might receive the grace to live so perfectly, so that all these things might be applicable to him, and he might sing of them in his own person to the glory of God with a joyful and most grateful soul, saying with the holy Apostle: *By the grace of God, I am what I am;*[343] and also with the incomparable and most excellent blessed Virgin: *He that is mighty has done great things to me, and holy is his name.*[344]

PRAYER

RANT TO US, O ALMIGHTY FATHER, THAT we might love your commandments above gold and topaz, and to harbor hate of, and turn away from, all wicked ways: so that defended by your protection we might be delivered from the calumny of the proud.

Dona nobis, omnipotens Pater, mandata tua super aurum et topazion diligere, et omnem viam iniquam odio habere, et ab ea declinare: ut tua protectione defensi, a calumnia superborum valeamus liberari.

342 Job 28:15–16, 19a.
343 1 Cor. 15:10a.
344 Luke 1:49.

PHE
(PART XVII)

118{119}[129]   *Your testimonies are wonderful: therefore my soul has sought them.*

Mirabilia testimonia tua, ideo scrutata est ea anima mea.

118{119}[129] *Mirabilia testimonia tua, your testimonies are wonderful.* As has already been said, the divine law is of two parts, namely the commandments, which pertain to what is to be done, and the testimonies, which pertain to that which is to be believed. Now, however wondrous and marvelous are those things which we are prescribed to do, or the commandments, yet much more marvelous are those things we are ordered to believe. For the moral precepts do not exceed the dictates of natural reason: though, according to some teachers, we are ordered to do some things which exceed natural reason, such as loving one's enemies, and doing good to adversaries.[345] For as it is natural to love the beloved, and to do good to one's benefactor; so does it seem [natural] to have hate toward the hateful, and to pay back evil with evil. Yet those things which are proposed to us as things to be believed completely transcend reason, as would the Trinity of Persons, the Incarnation of the Word, the integrity of the Mother, the existence of Christ under Sacramental form. Since, therefore, so wonderful are your testimonies, O Lord, *ideo scrutata est ea anima mea, therefore my soul has sought them*, desiring and occupying itself to understand them in every way whatsoever. For searching arises out of wonder. Philosophers begin to philosophize from wonder, for when seeing marvelous effects — such as eclipses of the sun, earthquakes, and other such things, and ignorant of the cause — they marvel, and they being to seek their cause. So likewise, the holy doctors inspect sacred Scripture, and, seeing the marvelous testimonies of God in it, they become filled with wonder; and they begin to search for an understanding of them, and through God's enlightenment they make progress, although they are not able to comprehend these things perfectly.

But since Solomon asserts, *As it is not good for a man to eat much honey, so he that is a searcher of majesty, shall be overwhelmed by glory;*[346] and Paul [admonishes], *not to be more wise than it behooves to be wise, but to be wise unto sobriety;*[347] and again, *be not high minded, but fear;*[348] and

---

345 Luke 6:27.
346 Prov. 25:27.
347 Rom. 12:3a.
348 Rom. 11:20b.

again, it is written, *Seek not the things that are too high for you, and search not into things above your ability.*[349] What is it that the Prophet or any just man means when he says he wishes to search, saying, *I will consider the wondrous things of your law;* and *I shall be exercised in your wondrous works,*[350] and now also, *Your testimonies are wonderful, therefore my soul has sought them?* And the answer is that some searching is curious and undaunted as when a man, relying upon his own genius, seeks to understand divine things or to know more than the measure of his capacity. And this [sort of searching] is culpable and is to be avoided. Whence it is said by Ecclesiasticus: *In many of his works be not curious. For it is not necessary for you to see with your eyes those things that are hid.*[351] But another kind of searching is pious and humble, as when a man, relying upon divine help, endeavors to understand divine things so that he might advance in the love of God, so that he might approach, as much as possible, the contemplation of the blessed. And this [sort of searching] is good and holy, and Christ exhorted the Jews to this, saying: *Search the scriptures, ... for the same are they that give testimony of me.*[352] And the most blessed Luke praises the Thessalonians, saying that they daily searched the Scriptures.[353]

***

118{119}[130] *The declaration of your words gives light: and gives understanding to little ones.*

> *Declaratio sermonum tuorum illuminat, et intellectum dat parvulis.*

118{119}[130] *Declaratio sermonum tuorum, the declaration of your words,* that is, the elucidation of sacred Scripture by the infusion of the Holy Spirit or by men divinely made enlightened by others, *illuminat, gives light* to the human mind toward right thinking and just living. For this reason, the Apostle says: *You have known the holy scriptures, which can instruct you.*[354] *Et intellectum, and ... understanding,* that is, a formed and wholesome knowledge, *dat parvulis, gives ... to little ones,* that is, to the humble. For this reason, Christ says: *I confess to you, O Father, Lord of heaven and earth, because you have hidden these things from the wise and prudent, and have revealed them to little ones.*[355] And Wisdom says: *Whosoever is a little one, let him come*

---

349 Ecclus. 3:22a.
350 Ps. 118:18b, 27b.
351 Ecclus. 3:22b–23.
352 John 5:39.
353 *Cf.* Acts 17:11.
354 2 Tim. 3:15a.
355 Luke 10:21.

to me.[356] For the knowledge of the proud is deformed, vain, and damning, since it is not united to charity and a virtuous life.

118{119}[131] *I opened my mouth and panted: because I longed for your commandments.*

Os meum aperui, et attraxi spiritum, quia mandata tua desiderabam.

118{119}[131] *Os meum*, my mouth, [my] bodily [mouth] *aperui*, I opened, praying, singing Psalms, seeking, sighing, *et attraxi spiritum*, and panted, that is, [I have drawn in] air, without which drawing in one is unable to form voice with the mouth. Or [we can understand it] thus: *My mouth*, [my] intellectual [mouth], namely, the intellect, wherein the word of the mind is pronounced, *I have opened*, that is, I have affectionately disposed it to receiving the grace of God, in accordance with this, *She has opened her mouth to wisdom;*[357] *and panted*, that is, by merit of this holy affection or openness, I drank from and received the spirit of wisdom and understanding, indeed, the Holy Spirit, who does not shrink back from descending into the heart that desires his coming. For here the book of Wisdom says: *I wished, and understanding was given me: and I called, and the spirit of wisdom came upon me.*[358] In this way, therefore, I open my mouth and drew in the spirit, *quia mandata tua desiderabam, because I longed for your commandments*, O Lord, with greatest desire, so that I might know them clearly and may observe them always: because not to advance in the way of your commandments is to be found wanting. And by this ardent desire is caused both this openness and double panting: for he who vehemently desires, frequently sighs and groans.

118{119}[132] *Look upon me, and have mercy on me, according to the judgment of them that love your name.*

Aspice in me, et miserere mei, secundum iudicium diligentium nomen tuum.

118{119}[133] *Direct my steps according to your word: and let no iniquity have dominion over me.*

Gressus meos dirige secundum eloquium tuum, et non dominetur mei omnis iniustitia.

---

356 Prov. 9:4a.
357 Prov. 31:26a.
358 Wis. 7:7.

118{119}[132] *Aspice in me, look upon me*, not with the eyes of strict vengeance, but with fatherly kindness, *et miserere mei, and have mercy on me*, giving to me the grace of the most pure contemplation, *secundum iudicium diligentium nomen tuum, according to the judgment of them that love your name*, that is, as those who love you would judge necessary or wholesome for them. Or [we can look at it thus], *according to the judgment of them that love your name*, that is, according to the judgment of your discretion, which you effect in the ones who loved you, those your wisdom judged to be filled with your mercy. Or [yet again, in this way], *according to the judgment of them that love your name*, that is, as you decreed to those who love you to do, to whom you have arranged to give so many and so many different kinds of good things *that eye has not seen, nor ear heard* of such things.[359] 118{119}[133] *Gressus meos, my steps*, that is, my affections, thoughts, words, and deeds, *dirige secundum eloquium tuum, direct... according to your word*, that is, according to the doctrine of sacred Scripture, so that I might observe the commandments, and also fulfil the counsels; *et non dominetur mei omnis iniustitia, and let no iniquity have dominion over me*, that is, let no sin or passion prevail over my reason, lest I be a *servant of sin* and subject to the flesh: indeed, [direct my steps] that I might find repugnant and effectively have dominion over all perverse suggestions and immoderate passions.[360] For this the Lord said: *If you do evil, sin shall forthwith be present at the door; but the lust thereof shall be under you, and you shall have dominion over it.*[361] The reason, therefore, should always have dominion over our sensitive appetites, which are divided into being concupiscible or irascible.[362]

118{119}[134] *Redeem me from the calumnies of men: that I may keep your commandments.*

Redime me a calumniis hominum ut custodiam mandata tua.

---

359 1 Cor. 2:9a.

360 John 8:34b; *cf.* Rom. 8:20.

361 Gen. 4:7b.

362 *E. N.* The passions are divided broadly into the concupiscible — which seek something suitable or flee from something hurtful — and the irascible — which seek to resist that which hinders what is suitable and or might inflict harm. St. Thomas Aquinas identifies six concupiscible passions divided by attraction and repulsion. The six concupiscible passions are love and hatred, desire and aversion, and joy and sadness. The five irascible passions are divided into difficulty of attainment or difficulty in avoidance. These are hope and despair, courage and fear, and anger. Anger has no contrary. ST Ia, q. 81, art. 2, co. IaIIae, q. 23, arts. 1–4.

118{119}[135] *Make your face to shine upon your servant: and teach me your justifications.*

Faciem tuam illumina super servum tuum, et doce me iustificationes tuas.

118{119}[134] *Redime me a calumniis, redeem me from the calumnies,* that is, from the false accusations, *hominum, of men,* of evil men: not, however, that I suffer absolutely no calumny which Christ suffered so often, and whose footsteps we ought to follow; but let me not be overcome by impatience, or murmuring, or to be involved in such; rather, grant that I not pay heed to such, that I not dwell upon them, *ut custodiam mandata tua, that I may keep your commandments* with a quiet and untrammeled heart, and which cannot be kept by impatient and argumentative men. **118{119}[135]** *Faciem tuam illumina super servum tuum, make your face to shine upon your servant,* that is, sign upon us *the light of your countenance,*[363] fill me with your own knowledge, make me for a time to contemplate you solely with faith and grace, and after such time also by sight: because *This is eternal life: that they may know you, the only true God;*[364] *and all are vain in whom there is not the knowledge of God.*[365] *Et doce me iustificationes tuas, and teach me your justifications,* that is, your commandments. He abundantly repeats this, to penetrate his heart toward a most ardent longing and to the necessity of the observing of the precepts! For this reason, it is written: *The things that God has commanded you, think on them always, . . . in unnecessary matters be not over curious.*[366]

118{119}[136] *My eyes have sent forth springs of water: because they have not kept your law.*

Exitus aquarum deduxerunt oculi mei, quia non custodierunt legem tuam.

118{119}[136] *Exitus aquarum, springs of water,* that is rivers of tears or copious tears, *deduxerunt oculi mei, my eyes have sent forth,* [my] exterior [eyes], *quia non custodierunt legem tuam, because they have not kept your law,* that is, because I did not keep the divine law with them, since I used them for vanities, and not for spiritual progress. See this most sacred verse teaches us what we ought to do, namely, that we should

---

363 Ps. 4:7a.
364 John 17:3a.
365 Wis. 13:1a.
366 Ecclus. 3:22b, 24a.

abundantly deplore our sins, suffering most vehemently that we have ever offended God our Creator, who is naturally good and most exceedingly kind. For he who does not lament in this way, so that he can sing this verse as applying to himself, cannot regard himself as efficaciously penitent. Whence Jeremiah exhorts: *Let tears run down like a torrent day and night: give yourself no rest, and let not the apple of your eye cease.*[367]

Finally, which mortal is capable of worthily or completely praising this eight-versed Psalm-section, four of which verses include and contain the most efficacious and completely devout prayers?

PRAYER

SHINE THE FACE OF YOUR MERCY UPON us, O Lord, and teach us to carry out the works of your justifications, so that we might overwhelm the dark haunts of sinners, and that, illuminated by the clarification of your words, we might be shed of these.

Faciem misericordiae tuae illumina super nos, Domine, et doce nos iustificationum tuarum opera peragere: ut qui tenebris peccatorum deprimimur, ab his declaratione sermonum tuorum illuminati exuamur.

SADE
(PART XVIII)

118{119}[137] *You are just, O Lord: and your judgment is right.*

Iustus es, Domine, et rectum iudicium tuum.

118{119}[138] *You have commanded justice your testimonies and your truth exceedingly.*

Mandasti iustitiam testimonia tua et veritatem tuam nimis.

118{119}[137] *Iustus es, Domine, et rectum iudicium tuum;* you are just, O Lord, and your judgment is right. This is what is stated in the book of Wisdom: *You are just, you order all things justly . . . for your power is the beginning of justice.*[368] And elsewhere: *Far from God be wickedness,*

367 Lam. 2:18b.
368 Wis. 12:15a, 16a.

and iniquity from the Almighty; for he will render to a man his work, and according to the ways of everyone he will reward them.[369] **118{119}[138]** *Mandasti iustitiam, you have commanded justice,* namely, *testimonia tua, your testimonies,* that is, to fulfill the commandments. For God commands the faithful to have a righteous manner of life which consists in their observing the divine testimonies. *Et veritatem tuam, and your truth,* that is, the Faith, *nimis, exceedingly* you have commanded that we keep: because a man cannot be saved unless he firmly and unwaveringly keeps every one of the articles of the faith.[370] It is absolutely fitting that we be guided with all reverence by, and also most faithfully believe, such a great Lawgiver and Lord. For this reason, it is written: *Cursed be he that does the work of the Lord deceitfully.*[371]

118{119}[139] *My zeal has made me pine away: because my enemies forgot your words.*

Tabescere me fecit zelus meus, quia obliti sunt verba tua inimici mei.

118{119}[140] *Your word is exceedingly fiery: and your servant has loved it.*[372]

Ignitum eloquium tuum vehementer, et servus tuus dilexit illud.

118{119}[139] *Tabescere me fecit zelus meus, My zeal has made me pine away:* that is, from a great sorrow, the zeal of my soul, which proceeds from divine love, weakens or fades away, *quia obliti sunt verba tua inimici mei, because my enemies forgot your words,* that is, my enemies, who work against the divine precepts and hate God and just men, do not fulfil or believe the divine precepts by engaging in works. This zeal overcame Elijah, who said: *With zeal have I been zealous for the Lord God of hosts.*[373] And so as to any person who loves God with fervor, the more fervent he loves, the more afflicted he is by his being dishonored; and he forms resolve with holy zeal. **118{119}[140]** *Ignitum eloquium tuum vehementer, your word is exceedingly fiery:* that is, the divine sermon, sacred Scripture,

---

369 Job 34:10b–11.
370 E. N. Compare the Athanasian Creed, the *Quicumque vult*: "Whosoever will be saved, before all things it is necessary that he hold the catholic faith. Which faith unless every one do keep whole and undefiled, without doubt he shall perish everlastingly, etc."
371 Jer. 48:10a.
372 E. N. I have replaced "refined" in the Douay-Rheims with "fiery."
373 1 Kings 19:10a.

the word of Christ is very fiery and igniting, since, filled by the fire of the Holy Spirit, every devout mind is set afire with divine love, has his sins burned away, and has his cold heart set ablaze. The word of God is said to be fiery, that is, burning with affection. Because of this Christ said: *I am come to cast fire on the earth; and what will I, but that it be kindled?*[374] This fire was his most ardent preaching, or the grace of the Holy Spirit, as it states in Proverbs: *Every word of God is fire tried.*[375] *Et servus tuus dilexit illud, and your servant has loved it*, that is, the word.

118{119}[141] *I am very young and despised; but I forgot not your justifications.*

Adolescentulus sum ego et contemptus; iustificationes tuas non sum oblitus.

118{119}[141] *Adolescentulus sum ego, I am very young*, that is, recently or newly [young] by grace, as the Apostle warns: *Be renewed in the spirit of your mind.*[376] And again, he says: *The inward man is renewed day by day.*[377] It is written of those persons who have this sort of youth: *Young maidens have loved you.*[378] For he who advances daily is daily renewed, and is made more young. *Et contemptus, and despised.* This refers to what was said above [in verse **118:83**], *I am become like a bottle in the frost.* For the world hates, despises, and persecutes the devout and those dead to the world and vices. For this reason, Christ says: *If you had been of the world, the world would love its own.*[379] Whence the Lord said to Ezechiel: *I have set you for a sign . . . to the house of Israel. . . . Say: I am a sign of things to come to you*[380] And the Apostle: *If I yet pleased men, I should not be the servant of Christ.*[381] See, we are taught from this verse how we should more wholeheartedly rejoice the more we are despised. *Iustificationes tuas non sum oblitus, but I forgot not your justifications*: that is, I will not neglect to fulfill the commandments, nor will I depart from the path of salvation because of

---

374 Luke 12:49.
375 Prov. 30:5a.
376 Eph. 4:23.
377 2 Cor. 4:16b.
378 Songs 1:2b. *E. N.* The "young maidens" referring to souls aspiring union with God.
379 John 15:19a. *E. N.* Christ continues, with even greater relevance to this specific point, "but because you are not of the world, but I have chosen you out of the world, therefore the world hates you."
380 Ez. 12:6b, 11. *E. N.* What Ezechiel was to the Jews, a "portent" or a "sign," *see* Ez. 12:6, 11; 24:24, 27, Christ is to the Christians; accordingly, as Christ was hated, despised, and persecuted, so shall those who follow him be hated, despised, and persecuted.
381 Gal. 1:10b.

the affliction from those who despise me. The most holy Job was a man of this manner, who when he said, *The Lord has tried me as gold that passes through the fire*, he added: *I have not departed from the commandments of his lips, and the words of his mouth I have hid in my bosom.*[382]

118{119}[142] *Your justice is justice for ever: and your law is the truth.*

Iustitia tua, iustitia in aeternum, et lex tua veritas.

118{119}[142] *Iustitia tua, iustitia in aeternum; your justice is justice forever*: for the uncreated justice of God is eternal. Also, the effect of divine justice remains forever with the reprobate. Similarly, justice, that is, the just law and faith of Christ, will never fail during this world; nor will it be succeeded by another law, such as it succeeded the justice of the Old Law, which was not eternal, but ceased when Christ came and suffered. *Et lux tua veritas, and your law is the truth*: because it is precisely true, so it is more fitting to call it truth rather than true. For without any doubt, it is unmixed with any falsity.

118{119}[143] *Trouble and anguish have found me: your commandments are my meditation.*

Tribulatio et angustia invenerunt me; mandata tua meditatio mea est.

118{119}[144] *Your testimonies are justice forever: give me understanding, and I shall live.*

Aequitas testimonia tua in aeternum; intellectum da mihi, et vivam.

118{119}[143] *Tribulatio et angustia, trouble and anguish*, that is, suffering both exterior and interior, *invenerunt me, have found me*: that is, persecution, sluggishness, and temptation have found me during the course of this miserable life, so full of punishments and vices; but what is the remedy in facing so much hardship is added: *mandata tua, meditatio mea est, your commandments are my meditation*, that is, to them is ordered all the efforts and entire occupation of my soul lest because of such adversity I depart from you in any way. This meditation causes constancy in one's spirit. **118{119}[144]** *Aequitas testimonia tua in aeternum, your testimonies are justice forever*: that is, because of their exceeding justice, the words of sacred Scripture are called not only just, but justice forever. Whence

---

382 Job 23:10, 12.

Wisdom said: *All my words are just, there is nothing wicked nor perverse in them.*[383] *Intellectum, understanding,* that is, a supernatural and gracious enlightenment of mind, *da mihi, et vivam; give me ... and I shall live* by grace, by formed faith, by divine charity, and by just activity.

PRAYER

ET AFLAME BY THE FIRE OF YOUR SPIRIT, O Lord, make us your servants love your fiery words, and carry out good works: that along with that same Spirit we might be given the understanding by which we might live forever.

Spiritus tui igne accensos, Domine, ignitum eloquium tuum fac nos servos tuos diligere, et operibus bonis adimplere: ut eodem Spiritu tribuente, intellectum capiamus, quo in aeternum vivamus.

COPH
(PART XIX)

118{119}[145] *I cried with my whole heart, hear me, O Lord: I will seek your justifications.*

Clamavi in toto corde meo: exaudi me, Domine; iustificationes tuas requiram.

118{119}[146] *I cried unto you, save me: that I may keep your commandments.*

Clamavi ad te; salvum me fac, ut custodiam mandata tua.

118{119}[145] *Clamavi in toto corde meo, I cried with my whole heart,* that is, with a heart entirely turned toward you, I do not wander, nor am I divided with the love of temporal things, but am recollected and fixed upon you. This interior outcry of the heart is a vehement desire by which a loving soul tends towards God. Or [we can understand it thus], *I cried* to you, O Lord, by praying to you *with my whole heart,* that is, with all my heart, namely, by the intellect diligently thinking of the meaning of the words and the will ardently desiring that which I need. *Exaudi me, Domine; hear me, O Lord,* begging in this way; *iustificationes tuas requiram, I will seek your justifications:* that is, since you deign to

---

383 Prov. 8:8.

hear me more promptly and completely, I most firmly propose to seek your commandments. **118{119}[146]** *Clamavi ad te, I cried unto you* saying: *Salvum me fac, save me,* removing from me the evil of punishment and of fault, and bestowing upon me the goods of grace and glory, *ut custodiam mandata tua, that I may keep your commandments,* that is, by this deliver me from the evil of present perturbations so that I might always obey you with a quiet and willing heart.

118{119}[147] *I prevented the dawning of the day, and cried: because in your words I very much hoped.*

Praeveni in maturitate, et clamavi: quia in verba tua supersperavi.

118{119}[148] *My eyes to you have prevented the morning: that I might meditate on your words.*

Praevenerunt oculi mei ad te diluculo, ut meditarer eloquia tua.

118{119}[147] *Praeveni, I prevented,* that is, before I passed over unto other things, I came to you, *in maturitate, the dawning of the day* of my senses, namely from orderly deliberation, not in importunate haste, seeking first the kingdom of God and his justice,[384] *et clamavi, and cried* singing or praying with devotion; *quia in verba tua, because in your words,* in which you promised benignant hearing, godly grace, and everlasting glory, *supersperavi, I very much hoped.* **118{119}[148]** *Praevenerunt oculi mei ad te diluculo, my eyes have prevented the morning:* that is, I have directed the eyes of my heart toward you before I might have to turn them to temporal matters, or to have them occupied with exterior things, namely, early, that is, in the morning, and the very beginning of dawn: in the manner that Isaiah says, *In the morning early I will watch for you.*[385]

---

384 *Cf.* Matt. 6:33. E. N. The Latin *maturitate* refers to *maturitas,* "early morning, dawn." "Used only in the phrase *in maturitate* in Ps. 118:147. *Praeveni in maturitate.* I prevented (=anticipated, forestalled) the dawning of the day, *i.e.,* I rose early. 161 (s.v. "maturitas"). *A Dictionary of the Psalter* (New York: Benziger Brothers, 1928) (ed., Dom Matthew Britt, O. S. B.). However, it might also be translated as ripeness, promptness, at the proper time, or in the fullness of time. Contrary to the following verse, Denis does not seem to see the verse as referring to time, but rather more as "matutinal knowledge," which focuses on the Creator, as distinguished from "vespertinal knowledge," which focuses on created things. *See* ST Ia, q. 58, arts. 6, 7. In short, he appears to understand this verse *ontologically* or *intentionally,* whereas the next verse he clearly understands *chronologically.*

385 Is. 36:9.

And in Ecclesiasticus it states of the just man: *He will give his heart to resort early to the Lord that made him, and he will pray in the sight of the most High.*[386] Or [we can look at it thus], *the morning*, that is, the beginning of the spiritual day, namely, your radiant grace in my soul, because without it the brightness of my eyes would be unable to reach or direct itself to you. And so my eyes have been prevented by you, *ut meditarer eloquia tua, that I might meditate on your words*: in which are contained some words pertaining to the contemplation of your majesty, but some words pertaining to the cognizance of my weakness, and some words regarding the knowledge of the commandments: and all these should be meditated upon diligently and constantly.

118{119}[149] *Hear my voice, O Lord, according to your mercy: and quicken me according to your judgment.*

Vocem meam audi secundum misericordiam tuam, Domine, et secundum iudicium tuum vivifica me.

118{119}[149] *Vocem meam, my voice*, that is, my prayer, *audi secundum misericordiam tuam, Domine; hear . . . O Lord, according to your mercy*. Note that he who has set forth [in the earlier verses] that he was adorned with such perfections asks to be heard by the mercy of God, and not according to his own righteousness or merits: so we might advert to the fact that our merits are not sufficient for us, unless the mercy of God provides assistance, overlooking our imperfections, and mercifully saving us. *Et secundum iudicium tuum, and quicken me according to your judgment*, that is, as you see and judge as it becomes you and as I need, as you judge to be good, as your wisdom dictates, *vivifica me, quicken me* with grace, charity, and completed works. For in this place judgment is taken to mean an act existing in him who judges, not in the sense of reprobation, remuneration, or the effects of justice. And so we frequently read the faithful to pray that God might do to him according to his judgment, in the manner that Joab said: *The Lord will do what is good in his sight.*[387]

118{119}[150] *They that persecute me have drawn nigh to iniquity; but they are gone far off from your law.*

Appropinquaverunt persequentes me iniquitati, a lege autem tua longe facti sunt.

---

386 Ecclus. 39:6.
387 2 Sam. 10:12b.

118{119}[151] *You are near, O Lord: and all your ways are truth.*

Prope es tu, Domine, et omnes viae tuae veritas.

118{119}[152] *I have known from the beginning concerning your testimonies: that you have founded them forever.*

Initio cognovi de testimoniis tuis, quia in aeternum fundasti ea.

118{119}[150] *Appropinquaverunt persequentes me iniquitati, they that persecute me have drawn nigh*, that is, they who have behaved iniquitously by persecuting me [have drawn nigh]; *a lege autem tua longe facti sunt, but they are gone far from your law*, that is, their affection and the work they have engaged in greatly contradict the divine law and judge, in that they have maliciously and impiously persecuted the innocent and the just. For a man sins more seriously the greater he distances himself and departs from God and the divine law. For this reason, we find contained in Hosea: *They have forsaken the Lord in not observing his law.*[388] **118{119} [151]** *Prope es tu, Domine; you are near, O Lord*, that is, you assist me by grace and never-failing help, *et omnes viae tuae veritas, and all your ways are truth*, that is, true and just are all your works, words, and commands. For although *all the ways of the Lord are mercy and truth*,[389] nevertheless in some way all his ways are truth, and again all his ways are mercy.[390] For while he justifies a sinner by grace, he is just with respect to his goodness, which is so great, that he is just to it even when he has mercy upon the unworthy. **118{119}[152]** *Initio, from the beginning*, that is, before all things, and at the beginning of my considerations, *cognovi de testimoniis tuis, I have known ... concerning your testimonies*, that is, the words of sacred Scripture, *quia in aeternum fundasti ea, that you have founded them forever*, that is, you have confirmed and established them in such a way that they never prove false, nor will they be annulled by anyone. This is what Christ said: *Heaven and earth shall pass away, but my words shall not pass away.*[391] And Isaiah attests: *The word of our Lord endures forever.*[392]

---

388 Hosea 4:10b.

389 Ps. 24:10a.

390 *E. N.* Denis seems to want to disabuse the reader from thinking that there are two "ways" of the Lord, either the way of "mercy" or the way of "truth" (which he equates with justice), and they are in some way opposed, since he insists that all the "ways" of God are always composed of an admixture, as it were, of both mercy and truth. Thus God remains "true" and "just" even when he pardons the sinner in his "mercy."

391 Luke 21:33.

392 Is. 40:8b.

PRAYER

BE CLOSE TO US, O LORD, AND DRIVE AWAY from us any one approaching or persecuting us in iniquity; save those who cry out to you, so that by you we might securely keep your commandments.

Prope esto nobis, Domine, et appropinquantes et persequentes nos in iniquitate a nobis repelle; ad te nos clamantes salva: ut per te securi custodiamus mandata tua.

RES
(PART XX)

118{119}[153] *See my humiliation and deliver me: for I have not forgotten your law.*

Vide humilitatem meam, et eripe me, quia legem tuam non sum oblitus.

118{119}[154] *Judge my judgment and redeem me: quicken me for your word's sake.*

Iudica iudicium meum, et redime me: propter eloquium tuum vivifica me.

118{119}[153] *Vide humilitatem meam,* see my humiliation, that is, mercifully, O Lord, consider how greatly I am afflicted, I am despised, and how also I humble myself, despise myself, and reprove myself; *et eripe me, and deliver me* from all misery. For it is written: *He who humbles himself shall be exalted.*[393] Job also said: *He that has been humbled, shall be in glory.*[394] Whence it is also said elsewhere: *Humility goes before glory.*[395] *Quia legem tuam non sum oblitus, for I have not forgotten your law,* but I have served it with mind and in deed. **118{119}[154]** *Iudica iudicium meum, judge my judgment,* that is, carry out your sentence upon me, and distinguish and determine my cause which I have against the ungodly who try to distance me from you. Judge, therefore, that my holy angel might protect me, that

393 Luke 14:11b.
394 Job 22:29a.
395 Prov. 15:33b.

[the ungodly] not prevail over him, *et redime me, and redeem me* from all past, present, and future evil. *Propter eloquium tuum vivifica me, quicken me for your word's sake* with the grace of the Holy Spirit. Now this which he says — *for your word's sake* — can be explained in three ways. The first is thus: *for your word's sake,* that is, so that your word where you have promised grace to those who ask for it might be fulfilled, *quicken me.* The second is thus: *for your word's sake,* that is, to the honor of the divine law, that it might be promulgated and observed, *quicken me.* The third is thus: *for your name's sake,* that is, because of your goodness and grace, by which you have deigned to speak to us and to give to us the divine Scripture and law, *quicken me* so that I may not be in mortal sin, of which the Apostle [Paul] says, The widow *that lives in pleasures is dead while she is living;*[396] and Christ in the Gospel: Let the dead bury their dead.[397]

118{119}[155] *Salvation is far from sinners; because they have not sought your justifications.*

Longe a peccatoribus salus, quia iustificationes tuas non exquisierunt.

118{119}[155] *Longe a peccatoribus, far from sinners* who are unrepentant is *salus, salvation,* because they lack grace, God is not with them according to this: *The Lord is far from the wicked;*[398] and again, A *perverse heart is abominable to the Lord;*[399] and elsewhere, Sin makes nations miserable.[400] Now salvation and happiness are the same. Therefore as happiness of life is unitary, but consists dispositively in operations of moral virtue, yet essentially in the contemplation of God through formed faith, so salvation is twofold: and the sinner is as distant from both [works of virtue and contemplation through faith] as he is distant from the virtues. *Quia iustificationes tuas non exquisierunt, because they have not sought your justifications,* that is, they have not sought diligently to fulfill the commandments. Therefore that which was asserted by the Prophet [Zephaniah] applies to them: I *will destroy out of this place....* them that *turn away from following after the Lord, and that have not sought the Lord, nor searched after him.*[401]

---

396 1 Tim. 5:6.
397 Matt. 8:22b.
398 Prov. 15:29a.
399 Prov. 11:20a.
400 Prov. 14:34b.
401 Zeph. 1:4b, 6a.

118{119}[156] *Many, O Lord, are your mercies: quicken me according to your judgment.*

Misericordiae tuae multae, Domine; secundum iudicium tuum vivifica me.

118{119}[156] *Misericordiae tuae multae, Domine; many, O Lord, are your mercies:* that is, the effects of your divine kindness are many and varied, and you are compassionate to us in many ways, indeed, thousands even innumerable are the ways you know to succor the miserable, as it is written: *The mercies of the Lord are that we are not consumed: because his commiserations have not failed.*[402] Or [we can understand it as saying] that the one and simple mercy of God is called in the plural mercies because of the multiplicity of its acts. *Secundum iudicium tuum vivifica me, quicken me according to your judgment.*

118{119}[157] *Many are they that persecute me, and afflict me; but I have not declined from your testimonies.*

Multi qui persequuntur me, et tribulant me; a testimoniis tuis non declinavi.

118{119}[158] *I beheld the transgressors, and I pined away; because they kept not your word.*

Vidi praevaricantes et tabescebam, quia eloquia tua non custodierunt.

118{119}[157] *Multi qui persequuntur me, et tribulant me; many are they that persecute me, and afflict me,* namely, the devil with his angels, the world with its lovers, and the flesh with its disordered desires. Yet it is not for us to despair, because he told Elisha: *Fear not: for there are more with us than with them.*[403] And as Jonathan said: *It is easy for the Lord to save either by many, or by few.*[404] This Christ also says to the elect: *In the world you shall have distress: but have confidence, I have over-come the world.*[405] Finally, according to the Apostle, *For as the sufferings of Christ abound in us: so also by Christ does our comfort abound.*[406] *A testimoniis tuis non declinavi, but I have not declined from your testimonies,* but I have remained faithful in faith and by works. See the constancy!

---

402 Lam. 3:22.
403 2 Kings 6:16.
404 1 Sam. 14:16b.
405 John 16:33.
406 2 Cor. 1:5.

It is a great thing not to give up in adversity. Whence the Lord says: *Be faithful until death: and I will give you the crown of life.*[407] 118{119} [158] *Vidi praevaricantes, et tabescebam, quia eloquia tua non custodierunt; I beheld the transgressors, and I pined away; because they kept not your word.* This is what was stated and expounded upon a short time ago [in verse 139]: *My zeal has made me pine away: because my enemies forgot your words.* They therefore require to be understood in the same sense.

118{119}[159] *Behold I have loved your commandments, O Lord, quicken me in your mercy.*

Vide quoniam mandata tua dilexi, Domine; in misericordia tua vivifica me.

118{119}[159] *Vide quoniam mandata tua dilexi, behold I have loved your commandments*: that is, mercifully attend to, approve, and accept my pious affections. And repay me to the degree you see me to be zealous for you, and love and glorify me, as you have said: *I love them that love me;*[408] and again, *Whosoever shall glorify me, him will I glorify.*[409] *Domine, in misericordia tua vivifica me; Lord, quicken me in your mercy,* giving to me an incessant and evident progress in the spiritual life, so that I might fulfill that of the Apostle: *your profiting is manifest to all;*[410] and, *Neglect not the grace which is . . . given you.*[411]

118{119}[160] *The beginning of your words is truth: all the judgments of your justice are forever.*

Principium verborum tuorum veritas; in aeternum omnia iudicia iustitiae tuae.

118{119}[160] *Principium verborum tuorum veritas, the beginning of your words is truth*: that is, the first thing that is applicable to the sacred speech is truth, because all the words of sacred Scripture are the most pure truth. For this reason, Christ said to his Father: *Your word is truth.*[412] *In aeternum omnia iudicia iustitiae tuae, all the judgments of your justice are forever*: that is, all things your justice approves of, causes, and asserts are eternally just, and remain always. Or [we can understand it]

---

407 Rev. 2:10b.
408 Prov. 8:17a.
409 1 Sam. 2:30b.
410 1 Tim. 4:15b.
411 1 Tim. 4:14a.
412 John 17:17b.

thus: *The beginning*, that is, the origin or cause, *of your words*, that is, of the words of sacred Scripture, is uncreated *truth*, from which proceeds sacred doctrine, and upon which it immediately rests as its unmovable foundation. Because the certitude and the firmness of the evangelical law, indeed, of all the canonical Scriptures, is so great, the Apostle says: *Though we, or an angel from heaven, preach a gospel to you besides that which we have preached to you, let him be anathema.*[413] Indeed, since the Christian faith is directly supported by eternal truth, nothing can be more false than that which is opposed to the blessed faith. *In aeternum omnia iudicia iustitiae tuae, all the judgments or your justice are forever;* that is, the judgment which you render in the last day, whereby you reward each person, will remain without end: for as the Gospel says, *These shall go into everlasting punishment: but the just, into life everlasting.*[414]

PRAYER

SEE THE HUMILIATION OF YOUR PEOPLE, O Lord, and redeem us from all troublesome evil; in your kindliness, quicken us in every good action, so that we might always keep the judgments of your justice.

Vide humilitatem plebis tuae, Domine, et ab omnibus malis obstrepentibus nos redime; vivifica nos pro tua pietate, in omni bona actione, ut semper custodiamus iudicia iustitiae tuae.

SIN

(PART XXI)

118{119}[161] *Princes have persecuted me without cause: and my heart has been in awe of your words.*

> *Principes persecuti sunt me gratis, et a verbis tuis formidavit cor meum.*

118{119}[161] *Principes, princes* of this world, namely, demons who rule over sinners, *persecuti sunt, have persecuted*, that is, have tempted, *me gratis, me without cause*, that is, without consideration to my demerits; or,

---

413 Gal. 1:8.
414 Matt. 25:46.

without cause, that is, in vain because they did not prevail. Or [alternatively we can view it thus]: *Princes*, that is, ungodly men and other men in dominant positions, *have persecuted me without cause*, as is written: *Do not the rich oppress you by might? . . . Do not they blaspheme the good name that is invoked upon you?*[415] But of those invisible princes, who are very powerful and astute, the Apostle says: *Our wrestling is not against flesh and blood; but against principalities and powers, . . . against the spirits of wickedness in the high places.*[416] *Et verbis tuis formidavit cor meum, and my heart has been in awe of your words*, that is, I have feared and trembled not to be disobedient to the words of your commandments. For the greater the persecution, the greater a man can more easily become a transgressor of the divine law: because it is difficult not to fall in adversity. And so during the time of persecution man needs in a special way to have fear lest he sin and abandon the word of God. Indeed, each one of us, however perfect, has to fear, from the words of God, whether he has the Holy Spirit in himself, as the Lord said: *To whom shall I have respect, but to him that is poor and little, and of a contrite spirit, and that trembles at my words?*[417] Or [we can look at it in this manner], *of your words*, by which you threaten very grave torments to those who are overcome, my heart is terrified: and so, I will remain faithful and constant lest I fall into punishment.

118{119}[162] *I will rejoice at your words, as one that has found great spoil.*

Laetabor ego super eloquia tua, sicut qui invenit spolia multa.

118{119}[162] *Laetabor ego super eloquia tua, I will rejoice at your words,* that is, about those things the divine Scriptures give to me and others and which is revealed: as is brought forward by the prophet [Baruch], *We are happy . . . because the things that are pleasing to God, are made known to us.*[418] Or [another interpretation], *I will rejoice at your words,* meditating, contemplating, and observing them. *Sicut qui invenit spolia multa, as one that has found great spoil,* one who, indeed, rejoices greatly. Whence it is said by Jeremiah: *Your word was to me a joy and gladness of my heart.*[419] And Isaiah said: *They shall rejoice before you, as they that rejoice in the harvest, as conquerors rejoice after taking a prey, when they divide the spoils.*[420] In

---

415 James 2:6–7.
416 Eph. 6:12.
417 Is. 66:2b.
418 Baruch 4:4.
419 Jer. 15:16a.
420 Is. 9:3.

both ways ought we to rejoice over the words of God. For the greatest benefit of God is that he illumines the Church with his sacred words; and he who loves God should take delight in his utterances.

118{119}[163] *I have hated and abhorred iniquity; but I have loved your law.*

> *Iniquitatem odio habui, et abominatus sum, legem autem tuam dilexi.*

118{119}[163] *Iniquitatem odio habui et abominatus sum, I have hated and abhorred iniquity.* Some hate iniquity, not because of itself, but because of the punishment which follows upon it. And these are the imperfect. For they undertake good things from a servile fear which is not meritorious, since one is disposed to grace based upon one's fear. But some hate iniquity because of its deformity and disgracefulness. Yet others hate iniquity out of the love of God, namely, because it displeases God and because by it God is dishonored and offended. And this [kind of fear] is more perfect than the second, especially when we read about some Gentiles and infidels that have existed with such great perfections that they hated sin because of its deformity, in the manner that Seneca says: Even though I knew the gods would forgive me, I would not sin because of the very vileness of the sin.[421] Let us therefore endeavor to have the third kind of hate, because this kind of hate is of the friends and sons of God, and it is evidentiary of the sign of grace. For it is the property of friends to will and not will the same things.

118{119}[164] *Seven times a day I have given praise to you, for the judgments of your justice.*

> *Septies in die laudem dixi tibi, super iudicia iustitiae tuae.*

118{119}[164] *Septies in die laudem dixi tibi, seven times a day I have given praise to you,* that is, I have daily praised you at the seven Hours or canonical times, *super iudicia iustitiae tuae, for the judgments of your justice,* that is, of the works, words, commandments, and other matters proceeding from your justice, and judicially approved by you. The Jews did not observe this number literally, because Nehemiah says: *Four times a day and four times at night they confessed and adored the Lord God.*[422]

---

421 *E. N. Quamvis scirem deos mihi ignoscituros, non peccarem propter ipsam vilitatem peccati.* This saying in various forms is often misattributed to Seneca by medieval commentators. It is not found in any of his extant works, however.

422 2 Ezra 9:3.

The Prophet [David] says this, therefore, in the person of the Christian people, who every natural day praise and invoke God.[423]

118{119}[165] *Much peace have they that love your law, and to them there is no stumbling block.*

Pax multa diligentibus legem tuam, et non est illis scandalum.

118{119}[165] *Pax multa, much peace,* that is, internal and bountiful, have *diligentibus, they that love* with deed and in truth *legem tuam, your law.* For he who loves the law of God has everything within himself properly ordered. Now peace is the tranquility of the mind, according to Augustine;[424] but tranquility follows upon order. Therefore, the love of the divine love is the cause of internal peace. And the more we love and observe more perfectly the law of God, the more abundantly will we obtain peace within ourselves, which is something greatly desired by every Christian. For also Christ after the Resurrection greeted his disciples in this manner: *Peace be with you.*[425] And the Apostle also said: *If it be possible, as much as is in you, have peace with all men;*[426] and again, *And the peace of the Lord, which surpasses all understanding, keep your hearts and minds;*[427] and again, *Let the peace of Christ rejoice in your hearts;*[428] and again, *Follow peace with all men, and holiness: without which no man*

---

423 E. N. The "natural day" is the twenty-four hour that includes both night and day. The eight canonical hours are: Matins, Prime, Lauds, Terce, Sext, None, Vespers, and Compline. However, in his counting, Denis is likely collapsing Matins and Lauds which are commonly counted as one hour rather than two.

424 E. N. St. Augustine famously speaks about peace as the "tranquility of order" (*tranquillitas ordinis*). "Peace between man and God is the well-ordered obedience of faith to eternal law. Peace between man and man is well-ordered concord. Domestic peace is the well-ordered concord between those of the family who rule and those who obey. Civil peace is a similar concord among the citizens. The peace of the celestial city is the perfectly ordered and harmonious enjoyment of God, and of one another in God. The peace of all things is the tranquility of order." *De Civ. Dei*, XIX, 13 (English text: *City of God*, Vol. 2 (Edinburgh: T & T Clark, 1871), 320 (trans. Marcus Dods). A sermon attributed to St. Augustine speaks of the "tranquility of the mind" (*tranquillitas mentis*): "The third precept is, *Remember to keep the Sabbath day holy.* In this third precept a certain declaration of emptying out (*vacatio*) is suggested, namely, the rest of the heart, the tranquility of the mind, which a good conscience causes. For there is sanctification, for there is the Spirit of God. And so attend to this emptying out (*vacationem*), that is, rest." *Sermo XXI*, PL 39, 1784.

425 John 20:19, 21, 26.

426 Rom. 12:18.

427 Phil. 4:7. E. N. The editor notes marginally that Denis's text departs from the Scriptural text when it says "the peace of the Lord," instead of "the peace of God."

428 Col. 3:15a.

shall see God.[429] See how frequently our Teacher exhorts us to the keeping of peace. *Et non est illis scandalum, and to them there is no stumbling block,* for, as Jerome says, he who is scandalized is a little one. For it is not the elders that are scandalized.[430] Whence the perfect who efficaciously love God or his law do not partake in scandal either actively or passively, that is, they neither scandalize nor are they scandalized. And if someone were to be scandalized from these things being said and done, this would be the scandal of the Pharisees and the Scribes, or from an infirm scandal.

118{119}[166] *I looked to your salvation, O Lord: and I loved your commandments.*

Exspectabam salutare tuum, Domine, et mandata tua dilexi.

118{119}[167] *My soul has kept your testimonies: and has loved them exceedingly.*

Custodivit anima mea testimonia tua, et dilexit ea vehementer.

118{119}[166] *Exspectabam, I looked* with certain hope and patience *salutare tuum, Domine; to your salvation, O Lord,* that is, salvation from you, a wholesome salvation, a saving grace. For we ought in every adversity to expect the salubrious help of God. Or [we can see it this way], *I looked,* as long as I was and lived in this pilgrimage, *to your salvation, O Lord,* that is, to Christ, the Savior of the world — in the manner that Jacob said, *I will look for your salvation, O Lord;*[431] and Habakkuk, *If it make any delay, wait for it: for it shall surely come, and it shall not be slack.*[432] *Et mandata tua dilexi, and I loved your commandments,* since by keeping them in charity I might be found worthy to receive the salvation of God in the heavenly fatherland which I await. **118{119}[167]** *Custodivit anima mea, my soul has kept* holding fast in the memory and by praiseworthy life *testimonia tua, your testimonies,* that is, the words of sacred Scripture displaying your testimonies in them, which you through many miracles have testified to being true: as is stated of the Apostles, *They preached everywhere, the Lord working withal, and confirming the word with signs that followed.*[433] And the Apostle [Paul] said: *We ought more diligently to*

---

429 Heb. 12:14.
430 E. N. This is a reference to St. Jerome's *Commentary on Matthew* (III, 18, 6). *See also* ST IIaIIae, q. 43, art. 5, s.c.
431 Gen. 49:18.
432 Hab. 2:3b.
433 Mark 16:20.

observe the things we have heard . . . God also bearing them witness by signs, and wonders, and diverse miracles, and distributions of the Holy Spirit.[434] See how inviolate and unshakeable the certitude of the Christian and Catholic faith is. *Et dilexit ea vehementer, and [my soul] has loved them exceedingly,* as it befits ardently to love a great good.

118{119}[168] *I have kept your commandments and your testimonies: because all my ways are in your sight.*

Servavi mandata tua et testimonia tua, quia omnes viae meae in conspectu tuo.

118{119}[168] *Servavi mandata tua, I have kept your commandments* by being obedient to them, *et testimonia tua, and your testimonies* by a formed faith, that is [a faith] united with charity, *quia omnes viae meae in conspectu tuo, because all my ways are in your sight,* that is, all the things that I think, desire, speak, and do: these are all seen and judged by you. For this is what the holy Job said: *Does not God consider my ways, and number all my steps?* And again, *You have sealed up my offenses as it were in a bag;* and also, *You have observed all my paths, and have considered the steps of my feet.*[435] O how great a reason for us to walk before God our judge with solicitude and fear![436] For he who does a forbidden evil in front of the judge has done him a very great injury. In a like manner, we — who know that God perceives all our works — exceedingly dishonor him when we live our lives before him without diligent custody of the heart. And so Boethius says so very well: *Great is the necessity of righteousness laid upon you, if you do not wish to dissimulate, because all you do is done before the eyes of a Judge who sees all things.*[437] Always, therefore, ought we to reflect on the presence of the divine majesty, saying with Elijah, *As the Lord lives, . . . in whose sight I stand today:*[438] and so let us live as if we are immediately to be judged by him. And if we think this way, we shall most assuredly begin to fear God exceedingly, so much so that we will be able to say with blessed Job: *When I consider God I am made*

---

434 Heb. 2:1, 4.
435 Job 31:4; 14:17a; 13:27b.
436 *Cf.* Micah 6:8: *I will show you, O man, what is good, and what the Lord requires of you: Verily, to do judgment, and to love mercy, and to walk solicitous with your God.*
437 E. N. Boethius, *Consolation of Philosophy: Magna est vobis indicta necessitas probatis, si dissmulare non vultis, quoniam omnia agitis ante oculos Iudicis cuncta cernentis.* It is how Boethius ends his reflections.
438 1 Kings 18:15; 17:1.

pensive with fear; and again, *I have always feared God as waves swelling over me, and his weight I was not able to bear.*[439] For this excellent fear makes us avoid sins and observe the commandments, in the way that Solomon confessed: *The fear of the Lord is a fountain of life, to turn aside from the ruin of death.*[440]

PRAYER

ESTOW ETERNAL PEACE, O LORD, UPON us who love your law; may our soul love your testimonies: so let there be no stumbling block before us, but glory and eternal salvation, because we hope in you.

Diligentibus nobis, Domine, legem tuam, pacem largire perpetuam; diligat anima nostra testimonia tua: unde nullum sit nobis scandalum, quod in te speramus, sed gloria et perpetua salus.

TAU
(PART XXII)

118{119}[169] *Let my supplication, O Lord, come near in your sight: give me understanding according to your word.*

Appropinquet deprecatio mea in conspectu tuo, Domine; iuxta eloquium tuum da mihi intellectum.

118{119}[170] *Let my request come in before you; deliver me according to your word.*

Intret postulatio mea in conspectu tuo; secundum eloquium tuum eripe me.

118{119}[169] *Appropinquet deprecatio mea in conspectu tuo, Domine;* let my supplication, O Lord, come near in your sight, that is, let it be pleasing to you, let it not be repulsed by you, but let it obtain the effect of salvation, as is written: *The prayer of him that humbles himself, shall pierce the clouds.*[441] *Iuxta eloquium tuum,* according to your word,

439 Job 23:15b, 31:23.
440 Prov. 14:27.
441 Ecclus. 35:21a.

that is, as you stated and promised in sacred Scripture, you will give understanding to those who ask it of you,[442] *da mihi intellectum, give me understanding,* that is, intellective illumination. For it is written: *If any of you want wisdom, let him ask of God,... and it shall be given him.*[443] And the Apostle [Paul]: *The Lord will give you in all things understanding.*[444] Also, you stated in a Psalm above: *I will give you understanding, and I will instruct you.*[445] Or [we can also see it in this way], *According to your word,* that is, according to the condition and the sublimeness of sacred Scripture, give to me the understanding to comprehend it truthfully, and, since [sacred Scripture] is supernatural and so sublime, confer upon me a heightened capacity of mind and a supernatural illumination. **118{119}[170]** *Intret postulatio mea in conspectu tuo, let my request come in before you,* so that it may be entirely admitted before you, and fulfilled by you. It is customary with sacred Scripture in those matters that concern the affections to repeat frequently the same sense using different words, and in this way ignite and re-ignite, and by such means cause the will to boil fervently in divine love and holy affection. *Secundum eloquium tuum, according to your word,* by which you mercifully promised that you would be the helper to the needy who cried out to you, *eripe me, deliver me* from all danger.

118{119}[171]   *My lips shall utter a hymn, when you shall teach me your justifications.*

   Eructabunt labia mea hymnum, cum docueris me iustificationes tuas.

118{119}[172]   *My tongue shall pronounce your word: because all your commandments are justice.*

   Pronuntiabit lingua mea eloquium tuum, quia omnia mandata tua aequitas.

118{119}[173]   *Let your hand be with me to save me; for I have chosen your precepts.*

   Fiat manus tua ut salvet me, quoniam mandata tua elegi.

---

442 *Cf.* Luke 11:13: *If you then, being evil, know how to give good gifts to your children, how much more will your Father from heaven give the good Spirit to them that ask him?* E. N. The giving of the Spirit includes the gift of understanding. Is. 11:1–2.
443 James 1:5.
444 2 Tim. 2:7b.
445 Ps. 31:8a.

118{119}[171] *Eructabunt labia mea hymnum, my lips shall utter a hymn,* that is, from the interior joy the lips of my mouth pour forth praise and the giving of thanks, *cum docueris me, when you shall teach me* actually *iustificationes tuas, your justifications,* that is, the commandments, so that I might clearly and operatively know them. Then also 118{119} [172] *Pronuntiabit lingua mea eloquium tuum, my tongue shall pronounce your word* by singing the divine praises *quia omnia mandata tua aequitas, because all your commandments are justice,* that is, they are totally just and holy, so that they are better called justice than just.[446] 118{119}[173] *Fiat manus tua, let your hand,* that is, your power, O almighty God, so hold itself forth regarding to me, *ut salvet me, to save me,* freeing my soul from evil, and strengthening it in the good, *quoniam mandata tua elegi, for I have chosen your precepts* to keep them rather than to please men or to serve the world.

118{119}[174] *I have longed for your salvation, O Lord; and your law is my meditation.*

Concupivi salutare tuum, Domine, et lex tua meditatio mea est.

118{119}[175] *My soul shall live and shall praise you: and your judgments shall help me.*

Vivet anima mea, et laudabit te, et iudicia tua adiuvabunt me.

118{119}[174] *Concupivi salutare tuum, Domine; I have longed for your salvation, O Lord,* that is, I have opted to seek the fruits of Christ and his coming. Indeed of this salvation of Christ is written: *The desired of all nations shall come.*[447] Or *I have longed for your salvation,* that is, salvation, or salvific grace, eternal life, and the consummation of glory. *Et lex tua meditatio mea est, and your law is my meditation* objectively, for my thoughts are unceasingly concerned with it and about it. 118{119} [175] *Vivet anima mea, my soul shall live,* as I hope in your goodness, O Lord, by grace in the way, and also by glory in the heavenly fatherland, *et laudabit te, and it shall praise you* here initially and imperfectly, but there in a consummate, full, and eternal way, as it is promised: *Blessed are they that dwell in your house, O Lord: they shall praise you for ever and ever.*[448] *Et iudicia tua, and your judgments,* that is, the considerations of

---

446 *E. N.* They are substantively, essentially, nominatively justice, and not merely accidently, adjectively just.
447 Haggai 2:8a.
448 Ps. 83:5.

your judgments, and the commandments and the divine words by which you justly judge, or the scourges by which in the present you chastise your elect, *adiuvabunt me, shall help me*: that I might obtain from these the help of grace by which I am led to eternal life.

118{119}[176] *I have gone astray like a sheep that is lost: seek your servant, because I have not forgotten your commandments.*

Erravi sicut ovis quae periit; quaere servum tuum, quia mandata tua non sum oblitus.

118{119}[176] *Erravi sicut ovis quae periit, I have gone astray like a sheep that is lost.* Nicolas of Lyra, and some after him, have the opinion that this is not to be understood as referring to an error in behavior or of an error of sin or ignorance, since it follows [with the words], *I have not forgotten your commandments*; but rather [that it refers to] that error that contemplative men who have fled to solitary places, and are judged by worldly men to have erred and have acted foolishly. But because after these words there is immediately added, *because I have not forgotten your commandments*, I judge it better that it ought to be understood of the error of fault and of ignorance. For *in many things* (as acknowledged by James) *we all offend.*[449] And according to the Apostle, *God has concluded all in sin, that he may have mercy on all.*[450] The Prophet [David] speaking in the person of the faithful people, or the righteous man, who sometimes wanders from the way of truth: *Erravi, I have gone astray*, it says, from you, O Lord my God, and from your precepts, following evil, *sicut ovis quae periit, like a sheep that is lost*, because I have left the shepherd, for which reason the wolf had an opportunity to bite. Whence it is written: *All we like sheep have gone astray, everyone has turned aside into his own way.*[451] And so, O Lord, *quaere servum tuum, seek your servant*, that is, from the hands of the wolf or demons deliver me, visit me by grace, and lead me back to the sheepfold of your elect sheep, for whom you laid down your life, *quia mandata tua non sum oblitus, because I have not forgotten your commandments* at the end of the day, although I may have for a time neglected them.

See, we have heard this Psalm which contains a great quantity of words, but which contains a much greater excellence of meaning. In it,

---

449 James 3:2a.

450 Rom. 11:32; Gal. 3:22. E. N. Denis replaces *incredulitate* (unbelief) with *peccato* (sin) in Rom. 11:32, borrowing from Gal. 3:22: *But the scripture hath concluded all under sin (peccato)*.

451 Is. 53:6a.

as by single verses, the soul of the faithful man lovingly and trustingly addresses God; in it the most beneficial examples shine like the stars in the firmament; in it the most affection-filled prayers are recruited; in it we are taught what pertains to a perfect man, which, so long as we see within ourselves the virtues and the holy works which we sing about, we are most grateful to God, and we are all the more humbled the more we are obligated to love and honor God by the amount of gifts we have received. Finally, if we have not yet received these good things, but we are entangled in various vices and imperfections, let us sigh and implore and let us advance to things more perfect (as the Apostle admonishes), lest we become slothful.[452]

PRAYER

O LORD JESUS CHRIST, O GOOD SHEPHERD, who for the redemption of the human race willed to suffer the ignominy of the Cross, seek after us your servants, who like perishing sheep have erred; hold out your hand that it might save us, and restore us to be among the blessed in the glory of your kingdom.

Domine Iesus Christe, Pastor bone, qui pro humani generis
redemptione ignominiam crucis voluisti sustinere, nos
servos tuus, qui sicut oves pereuntes erravimus,
require; fiat manus tua ut salvet nos,
et in gloria regni redde beatos

---

452 *Cf.* Heb. 6:1, 12.

Psalm 119

ARTICLE XXX

EXPLANATION OF THE
ONE HUNDRED AND NINETEENTH PSALM:
AD DOMINUM, CUM TRIBULARER, ETC.
IN MY TROUBLE, I CRIED TO THE LORD, ETC.

119{120}[1] *A gradual canticle. In my trouble I cried to the Lord: and he heard me.*

> *Canticum graduum. Ad Dominum cum tribularer clamavi, et exaudivit me.*

HE TITLE OF THE PSALM NOW BEING explained is: *Canticum graduum, a gradual canticle.* Now this Psalm and the fourteen immediately following this one are called gradual Psalms or canticles because they were sung by the priests or Levites as they ascended into the temple which required climbing fifteen steps.[1] According to Catholic teachers, by this bodily ascension is signified the ascent of virtue in the steps of spiritual building or progress, as has been previously said of the virtuous: *They shall go from virtue to virtue.*[2] For man makes progress in an orderly and step-by-step fashion.[3] The spiritual grades of virtue are touched upon in these Psalms. Of those grades of virtue, the first is to withdraw from the vices of this present

---

1 E. N. The English word "gradual" is derived from the Latin word *gradualis* meaning "having steps," which comes from the Latin *gradus*, which means "a step."

2 Ps. 83:8.

3 E. N. "A virtue-based approach to the moral life regards it as a process of gradual growth and transformation over time.... The 'law of gradualness' refers to the fact that conversion is an ongoing process in the life of a Christian. Individuals ... who are followers of Jesus are called to grow in holiness in the whole of their daily lives ... Of course, living in a fallen world and subject to their own concupiscence, disciples do fail. When they do so, they need to return to God for his gracious mercy made visible in the cross of Christ and accessible in the sacraments of the Church so as to continue to grow in holiness." John S. Grabowski, *Sex and Virtue: An Introduction to Sexual Ethics* (Washington, DC: The Catholic University Press of America, 2003), 162. This "law of gradualness" should be sharply distinguished from a counterfeit double called the "gradualness of the law." See *Familiaris consortio*, No. 34; John Paul II, Homily at the Close of the Sixth Synod of Bishops (Oct. 25, 1980), 8: AAS 72 (1980), 1083.

age and to desire the future age. The sense [or meaning] of this title is: This Psalm is a *gradual canticle* because it was literally sung during the climbing of the temple steps; but spiritually it is called gradual canticle, that is, the exultation of the mind of the spiritual progress of virtue.

The Prophet [David], therefore, speaking in the person of a man desiring to advance spiritually, and beginning his progress from the previously mentioned foundation or the first grade just mentioned, says: **119{120}** [1] *Ad Dominum, cum tribularer, clamavi; in my trouble, I cried to the Lord*: that is, when I was weak in mind or body, when I was tempted by the world, the devil, and the flesh, or when I was direly afflicted in some other way, I invoked God as helper and savior, I took refuge in him, and cried out to him, that is, I spoke with great affection as also he himself advised in a Psalm above, *Call upon me in the day of trouble.*[4] Whence it is also written: *O Lord Almighty, the God of Israel, the soul in anguish, and the troubled spirit cries to you.*[5] Indeed, this is the only and the best solace in every tribulation: to cry out to God, according to this: *For us we have not strength enough, to be able to resist this multitude, which comes violently upon us. But as we know not what to do, we can only turn our eyes to you.*[6] Whence the venerable Sarah greatly afflicted said: *To you, O Lord, I turn my face, to you I direct my eyes.*[7] And the prayer of most holy Esther is in this manner: *O my Lord, who alone are our king, help me a desolate woman, and who have no other helper but you.*[8] So when troubled, cry out to the Lord: and it will not be in vain. For *exaudivit me, he heard me*: in the way it is written: *I am the salvation of the people, says the Lord. From whatever pain they cry unto me, I will hear them.*[9] And [in a Psalm] above, it states: *I am with him in tribulation, I will deliver him, and I will glorify him.*[10] The prophet Jonah sang a verse such as this: *I cried out of my affliction to the Lord, and he heard me.*[11] For the merciful Lord is most at hand during the time of tribulations of his servants, and he undoubtedly hears them at the appropriate time, provided that they cry out perseveringly, and they ask in the name of

---

4 Ps. 49:15a.

5 Baruch 3:1.

6 2 Chr. 20:12.

7 Tob. 3:14.

8 Esther 14:3.

9 E. N. This is actually a quote of an Introit used in the Liturgy which draws perhaps from Psalms 34(35):3 and 36(37):39. The Latin text gives a general reference to the 43rd chapter of Isaiah.

10 Ps. 90:15b.

11 Jonah 2:3a.

Jesus, that is, they beseech those things that are profitable to true salvation. Whence Sarah, that daughter of Raguel, said: *This everyone that worships you is sure of, that his life, if it be under trial, shall be crowned: and if it be under tribulation, it shall be delivered: and if it be under correction, it shall be allowed to come to your mercy.*[12]

119{120}[2]   *O Lord, deliver my soul from wicked lips, and a deceitful tongue.*

Domine, libera animam meam a labiis iniquis et a lingua dolosa.

119{120}[2] *Domine, libera animam meam a labiis iniquis; O Lord, deliver my soul from wicked lips,* that is, from those which utter forth words against me that are evidently malicious, combative, derisive, and detractive, *et a lingua dolosa, and a deceitful tongue,* that is, from those who flattering, and proposing evil things under the guise of good, are endeavoring to divert my soul from God, to detract it from spiritual progress, or in some other way to ensnare me. The faithful man asks to be delivered from this: either that he not suffer all these things, so that he might be more free and more at peace for God: for the Apostle [Paul] also said this, *Pray... that we may be delivered from evil and importunate men;*[13] or that he not be troubled by these things and impeded in good works or handed over to impatience, as the Apostle said: *Be not overcome by evil, but overcome evil by good.*[14]

119{120}[3]   *What shall be given to you, or what shall be added to you, to a deceitful tongue?*

Quid detur tibi, aut quid apponatur tibi ad linguam dolosam?

119{120}[4]   *The sharp arrows of the mighty, with coals that lay waste.*

Sagittae potentis acutae, cum carbonibus desolatoriis.

Now those [verses] which follow can be explained in two ways. First, as the words of the Prophet to the wicked and deceitful; and it would then be [understood] in this sense: 119{120}[3] *Quid detur tibi, aut quid apponatur tibi ad linguam dolosam? What shall be given to you, or what shall be added to you, to a deceitful tongue?* That is, what is the profit

---

12 Tob. 3:31.
13 2 Thess. 3:1a, 2.
14 Rom. 12:21.

to you, O ungodly one, and what is the benefit you seek to obtain that you pronounce such evil and false words against the servant of God? Or [alternatively] thus: *What shall be given you, etc.?* That is, what kind of punishments, how will they be administered, and how often will they be inflicted upon you because of the sins of your words? And the answer is: **119{120}[4]** *Sagittae potentis acutae, the sharp arrows of the mighty,* that is, the punishments of almighty God, which are extremely sharp and afflictive will be rendered against you for your sins, *cum carbonibus desolatoriis, with coals that lay waste,* that is, with the inextinguishable desolatory fire of hell, in which no one is consoled by future liberation, but the desperation is eternal. By *sharp arrows* we understand the punishments of the present which are inflicted upon the ungodly or future punishments other than the punishment of the fires of hell. But by the *coals that lay waste* are signified the punishment of infernal fire, which of all the punishments is the most oppressive.

The second explanation is that they are the words of God or of the Prophet [David] to the virtuous man. And they would then be [understood] in this sense: O faithful man, *what shall be given to you* as help, *or what shall be added to you* as a remedy *to a deceitful tongue* so as to overcome it? It is as if it were saying: What counsels and support can be given to you, that you might arm yourself against and overcome a deceitful tongue? And the answer: *The sharp arrows of the mighty,* that is, in the kindling and penetrative words of almighty God, *with coals that lay waste,* that is, with the examples of those who, after a sinful life, were converted to a religious manner of living you are given arms against deceitful tongues. For the knowledge of the Scriptures, or the words of the Holy Spirit, most mightily prevail against the deceitful tongue, so that we might not become deceitful in speech, nor be deceived by a deceitful tongue, nor be overcome by impatience. For all these things are fulfilled if we weigh how much the divine Scriptures reprove the deceitful tongue. For it is written: *The vessels of the deceitful are most wicked;*[15] and again, *Cursed is the deceitful man;*[16] and yet again, *The bloody and the deceitful man the Lord will abhor.*[17] In Ecclesiasticus also: *He that speaks sophistically, is hateful: he shall be destitute of everything. Grace is not given him from the Lord, for he is deprived of all wisdom.*[18] The words of sacred Scripture are also called sharp arrows because they pierce the souls with

---

15 Is. 32:7a.
16 Mal. 1:14a.
17 Ps. 5:7b.
18 Ecclus 37:23–24.

the wound of charity, they kill sin, and they penetrate the interior of the soul. Whence it is written: *The Lord has made my mouth like a sharp sword,... and has made me as a chosen arrow.*[19] And the Apostle [Paul] said: *The word of God is living and effectual, and more piercing than any two-edged sword; and reaching unto the division of the soul and the spirit.*[20] Of these arrows of Christ it has been earlier stated: *Your arrows are sharp: under you shall people fall, etc.*[21] Finally, the examples of the saints are said to be coals that lay waste, that is, devastating because they invite us to love and imitation, and because, and these devastate, destroy, and expel whatever a demon has been building in us, namely vices and sins.

119{120}[5] *Woe is me, that my sojourning is prolonged! I have dwelt with the inhabitants of Kedar:*

Heu mihi, quia incolatus meus prolongatus est! Habitavi cum habitantibus Cedar:

119{120}[6] *My soul has been long a sojourner.*

Multum incola fuit anima mea.

119{120}[5] *Heu mihi,* woe is me wretched man and pilgrim, *quia incolatus meus,* that my sojourning, that is, my dwelling in this present exile, *prolongatus est,* is prolonged, that is, it seems exceedingly long to me who am aspiring to reach the heavenly fatherland. This is fitting to those who, tired of the present life, hunger with all their desire for the heavenly fatherland, those who can say with the Apostle, *Our conversation is in heaven;*[22] and, *I desire to be dissolved and to be with Christ;*[23] and, *We have not here a lasting city, but we seek one that is to come.*[24] People like this are able to say that which Tobias said: *Now, O Lord, do with me according to your will, and command my spirit to be received in peace: for it is better for me to die, than to live.*[25] The saints of the Old Testament were like this, of whom is said by Paul: *All these died according to faith, not having received the promises, but beholding them afar off, and saluting them, and confessing that they are pilgrims and strangers on the earth.*[26] *Habitavi,* I have dwelt in this exile *cum*

---

19 Is. 49:2.
20 Heb. 4:12a.
21 Ps. 44:6.
22 Phil. 3:20a.
23 Phil. 1:23.
24 Heb. 13:14.
25 Tob. 3:6.
26 Heb. 11:13.

habitantibus Cedar, with the inhabitants of Kedar, that is, with the darkened and blind sinners. For Kedar is interpreted to mean darkness. And Kedar was the son of Ishmael.[27] 119{120}[6] *Multum incola, long a sojourner*, that is, an exile and a pilgrim, *fuit anima mea, my soul has been* during this time. For it lives in a region of dissimilarity, in the prison of death, in burdensome exile hastening toward the heavenly fatherland: from the many things, about which it wanders daily, it sighs for and hurries toward the one highest thing upon which it is perpetually affixed.

119{120}[7]   *With them that hated peace I was peaceable: when I spoke to them they fought against me without cause.*

Cum his qui oderunt pacem eram pacificus; cum loquebar illis, impugnabant me gratis.

119{120}[7] *Cum his qui oderunt pacem, with them that hated peace*, that is, with those who are turbulent and murmurers, and those who are divisive of holy unity, *eram pacificus, I was peaceful*, not arguing, but enduring all things patiently; *cum loquebar illis, when I spoke to them* with charity, reprovingly, reasonably, and modestly, *impugnabant me gratis, they fought against me without cause*, that is, they returned evil against me without just cause: as is set forth with Amos, *They have hated him that rebukes in the gate: and have abhorred him that speaks perfectly.*[28]

ARTICLE XXXI

EXPLANATION OF THE SAME
ONE HUNDRED AND NINETEENTH PSALM OF CHRIST.

NOW SOME EXPOUND UPON THIS PSALM LIT-erally of the Jewish people living during the Babylonian captivity. And although one literally can apply this to this Psalm, yet such an exposition contains little devotion. It is therefore better that it be expounded of Christ, in whose person the Prophet speaks, saying:

119{120}[1]   *In my trouble I cried to the Lord: and he heard me.*

Ad Dominum cum tribularer clamavi, et exaudivit me.

---

27 Gen. 25:13.
28 Amos 5:10.

119{120}[2]   *O Lord, deliver my soul from wicked lips, and a deceitful tongue.*

Domine, libera animam meam a labiis iniquis et a lingua dolosa.

119{120}[1] *Ad Dominum, to the* Lord, that is, to God the Father, *cum tribularer, in my* trouble, that is, at the instance of or when facing the Passion, when I began to feel sorrow and feel fear,[29] when my sweat became as drops of blood flowing unto the earth,[30] *clamavi, I cried out,* saying: *Father, if it be possible, let this chalice pass from me.*[31] Indeed, encountering this agony, I prayed even longer.[32] *Et exaudivit me, and he heard me,* the Father, he to whom I said, *But yet not my will, but yours be done:*[33] this is to be understood as relating to the natural appetite, by which Christ as man dreaded death. This is what the Apostle says: Christ *in the days of his flesh, with a strong cry and tears, offering up prayers and supplications to him that was able to save him from death, was heard for his reverence.*[34] 119{120}[2] *Domine, O Lord* Father, *libera animam mea, deliver my soul,* that is, my very self or my bodily life, *a labiis iniquis, from wicked lips* of the Jews who shouted, *Away with him; away with him, crucify him,*[35] *et a lingua dolosa, and a deceitful tongue* of Judas the traitor, who said: *Whomsoever I shall kiss, that is he; lay hold on him, and lead him away carefully.*[36] Now, Christ asked to be delivered from these things, not so that he not be killed, but so that he not be detained in death.

119{120}[3]   *What shall be given to you, or what shall be added to you, to a deceitful tongue?*

Quid detur tibi, aut quid apponatur tibi ad linguam dolosam?

119{120}[4]   *The sharp arrows of the mighty, with coals that lay waste.*

Sagittae potentis acutae, cum carbonibus desolatoriis.

But what is added next, 119{120}[3] *Quid detur tibi, aut quid apponatur tibi, etc. What shall be given to you, or what shall be added to you, etc.* This

---

29 Mark 14:33.
30 Luke 22:44.
31 Matt. 26:39.
32 Luke 22:43.
33 Luke 22:42.
34 Heb. 5:7.
35 John 19:15a.
36 Mark 14:44b.

can be the word of the Prophet aimed toward the Jewish adversaries of Christ, according to the sense suggested by the prior article. And the response: *Sagittae potentis acutae, etc. The sharp arrows of the mighty, etc.* where the *sharp arrows of the mighty* are understood to refer to the punishments inflicted upon the Jews by the powerful army of the Romans in avenging the blood of Christ. Also, by *coals that lay waste* are understood the burnings by which the Romans lit and burned down the temple and the city of Jerusalem and other cities of Judah along with a great part of the population. Isaiah evidently foretells of this punishment of the Jews when he says, among other things: *They are all the snare of young men, and they are hid in the houses of prisons: they are made to suffer ruin; there is none to deliver them; a spoil, and there is not that says: Restore. Who has given Jacob for a spoil and Israel to robbers? Has not the Lord himself, against whom we have sinned? And they would not walk in his ways. . . . He has burnt him round about, and he knew not; and set him on fire, and he understood not.*[37] These words of the most blessed Isaiah which can be understood as referring to no other oppression of the Jews but for that which they suffered from the Romans, in which even until now they are and burdened with and endure; and yet they do not recognize their sin; and so they do not deserve any pardon.

119{120}[5]   *Woe is me, that my sojourning is prolonged! I have dwelt with the inhabitants of Kedar:*

Heu mihi, quia incolatus meus prolongatus est! Habitavi cum habitantibus Cedar:

119{120}[6]   *My soul has been long a sojourner.*

Multum incola fuit anima mea.

And then Christ existing in a certain way as wayfarer and therefore passible, glorifying yet not glorified, says: **119{120}[5]** *Heu mi, quia incolatus meus prolongatus est; woe is me, that my sojourning is prolonged.* For Christ desired to be delivered from this exile and to return to the heavenly fatherland. For this reason, he said: *O incredulous generation, how long shall I be with you? How long shall I suffer you?*[38] And again: If you loved me, you would indeed be glad, because I go to the Father, that is, you would be rejoicing with me in my rejoicing of my return to the

---

37 Is. 42:22, 24, 25. E. N. Denis's text reads *facti sunt in ruinam*, instead of the Sixto-Clementine's *facti sunt in rapinam*, "they are made a prey."
38 Mark 9:18.

Father. *Habitavi cum habitantibus Cedar, I have dwelt with the inhabitants of Kedar*, that is, with the blind and darkened Jews, among whom I lived for a long time, as I elsewhere said, *Afterwards he was seen upon earth, and conversed with men.*[39] **119{120}[6]** *Multum incola, long a sojourner*, that is, a pilgrim in this world, *fuit anima mea, my soul has been.* For one who lives or passes through an alien land and is separated from and far away from his homeland is called a sojourner. In this manner, Christ was a pilgrim or sojourner in the present life, in the way that Jeremiah said to him: *Why will you be a stranger in the land, and as a wayfaring man turning in to lodge?*[40] Whence also Christ acknowledged: *My kingdom is not of this world.*[41] For although this world is not in a condition that is foreign to Christ for he created it, and *he came unto his own*, yet it is said to be alien, because it was not for him his homeland.

119{120}[7] *With them that hated peace I was peaceable: when I spoke to them they fought against me without cause.*

Cum his qui oderunt pacem eram pacificus; cum loquebar illis, impugnabant me gratis.

119{120}[7] *Cum his qui oderunt pacem, with them that hated peace*, that is, with the Jews who rejected the harmony of fraternal charity, the peace of the evangelical preaching, and the true tranquility of the mind in God and were adverse to me and my disciples, *eram pacificus, I was peaceful*, inflicting upon them no molestation, indeed returning good for evil; *cum loquebar illis, when I spoke to them*, rebuking their evil life, preaching to them the contempt of riches, and the kingdom of God, and telling them that I was the Christ promised to them in the Law, *impugnabant me, they fought against me* with words and blows *gratis, without cause*, saying, *You give testimony of yourself: your testimony is not true;*[42] and one time you attempted to cast me down a cliff,[43] and another time to stone me,[44] and finally you crucified me.[45]

See in this brief and concise Psalm we are taught to begin our spiritual progress step-by-step by withdrawing from our former vices, as

---

39 Baruch 3:38.
40 Jer. 14:8b.
41 John 18:367.
42 John 8:13b.
43 Luke 4:29.
44 John 10:31.
45 Mark 15:25.

the Scriptures exhort: *My son, have you sinned? Do so no more: but for your former sins also pray that they may be forgiven you; flee from sins as from the face of a serpent.*[46] Above all, we are taught to cry out to God in all our tribulations, and to entreat him especially that we might be delivered from wicked lips, both those of others as well as our own, in the manner stated earlier. For *evil communications corrupt good manners,* according to the Apostle.[47] This Psalm also informs us to spurn this present life with all its pomps and glories, to desire with all one's heart the happiness of the heavenly fatherland, and to converse peacefully with turbulent men, because as Christ asserted, *Blessed are the peacemakers, for they shall be called the sons of God.*[48]

PRAYER

EAR THE CRIES OF OUR TRIBULATIONS, O Lord, and grant that we constantly rejoice in your peace, so that we might manfully withstand the haters against peace and those seeking to attack us, and we might triumph over these by the help of your power.

Tribulationum nostrarum clamorem exaudi, Domine, et da nos in pace tua iugiter exsultare: ut contra pacem odientes, nosque impugnare quaerentes, fortiter stemus, et tuae potentiae auxilio de his triumphemus.

46 Ecclus. 21:1–2a.
47 1 Cor. 15:33b.
48 Matt. 5:9.

Psalm 120

ARTICLE XXXII

DECLARATION OF THE
ONE HUNDRED AND TWENTIETH PSALM:
LEVAVI OCULOS MEOS IN MONTES
I HAVE LIFTED UP MY EYES TO THE MOUNTAINS.

120{121}[1] *A gradual canticle. I have lifted up my eyes to the mountains, from whence shall help come to me.*

Canticum graduum. Levavi oculos meos in montes, unde veniet auxilium mihi.

120{121}[2] *My help is from the Lord, who made heaven and earth.*

Auxilium meum a Domino, qui fecit caelum et terram.

THE TITLE OF THE PSALM NOW BEING explained is: *Canticum graduum, a gradual canticle,* the understanding of which is clearly explained in the previous Psalm. Now this is the second gradual Psalm; in this one is treated the second grade of spiritual progress, namely, the imploration of divine help that is most necessary for those forsaking their former way of life.

And so the Prophet [David] in the person of a spiritual man making progress and abandoning his prior sins says: 120{121}[1] *Levavi, I have lifted,* contemplating, praying, singing, loving, *oculos meos, my eyes* especially my intellectual, but also my bodily [eyes], since by the elevation of the exterior vision is raised the interior vison, *in montes, to the mountains,* that is, to the heavens, to the holy angels, to the heavenly citizens. Hence it was said to holy Job: *Turn to some of the saints.*[1] *Unde, from whence,* that is, from what mountains, *veniet, shall* come, I trust, *auxilium mihi, help to me:* for the Creator sends the grace of heavenly help to us by means of the holy angels. For all [angels] (according to the Apostle) are *ministering spirits, sent to minister for them who* receive *the inheritance of salvation.*[2] Yet because this help by the angels is instrumentally and

---

1 Job 5:1.
2 Heb. 1:14.

ministerially [rendered on behalf of God], therefore it adds: 120{121} [2] *Auxilium meum a Domino, qui fecit caelum et terram; my help is from the Lord, who made heaven and earth.*

These [verses] can also be explained otherwise, in this way: *I have lifted my eyes,* [my] interior [eyes], *to the mountains,* that is, to lofty considerations and sublime contemplations. And so I ask: *From whence shall come to me help?* And, instructed by the Holy Spirit, I respond: *My help is from the Lord,* who says: *Destruction is your own, O Israel: your help is only in me.*[3] And elsewhere: *Not with an army, nor by might, but by my spirit, says the Lord.*[4] And so *my help is from the Lord,* not my own particular [god], but the universal [God], who rules all things, he *who made heaven and earth.* But by these places — heaven and earth — should be understood in this place all intermediate things and universal things contained in them. But especially by heaven is to be understood the empyrean heaven, which (according to the Damascene) encompasses visible and invisible things.[5]

120{121}[3]   *May he not suffer your foot to be moved: neither let him slumber that keeps you.*

Non det in commotionem pedem tuum, neque dormitet qui custodit te.

120{121}[4]   *Behold he shall neither slumber nor sleep, that keeps Israel.*

Ecce non dormitabit neque dormiet qui custodit Israel.

Supported, therefore, by trust in this divine help, the faithful man speaks to himself, saying: 120{121}[3] *Non det in commotionem pedem tuum, may he suffer not your foot to be moved,* that is, may God not permit your spiritual progress, the affection of your heart, the steadfastness of your soul to fail, to fall, to go to ruin; *neque dormitet, neither let him slumber,* that is, let him not be found in a tired or a sleepy manner, *qui custodit te,* he *that keeps you,* that is, almighty God, who is the first defender of the elect. And see how the holy man, out of his interior and through the impulse of the

---

3 Hosea 13:9.
4 Zech. 4:6.
5 E. N. Denis is referring to St. John of Damascus (*ca.* 675–749), specifically his *Exposition of the Orthodox Faith,* II, 6: "The heavens are the outer shell which contains both visible and invisible created things. For, enclosed and contained within them are the spiritual powers, which are the angels, and all sensible things." *St. John of Damascus Writings* (New York: Fathers of the Church, Inc., 1958) (trans., Frederic H. Chase, Jr.), 210–11.

Holy Spirit, expresses that he was heard: **120{121}[3]** *Ecce non dormitabit, behold he shall neither slumber,* as if he were tired, *neque dormiet, nor sleep,* as if he were ceasing from outward exertions, *qui custodit, he that keeps* by grace and through the administration of angels *Israel,* that is, the faithful people or any one member of the faithful: because God unceasingly cares for, governs, and protects his elect, according to this, *I am the Lord your God that teach you profitable things, that govern you in the way that you walk.*[6] Now God and the holy angels are said to sleep or to be drowsy in the same manner they are said to be angry or to repent, namely in a manner of similitude, and not according to [strict or literal] truth. God, therefore, is said to sleep while he ceases graciously to render aid.

***

120{121}[5] *The Lord is your keeper, the Lord is your protection over and above your right hand.*[7]

Dominus custodit te, Dominus protectio tua super manum dexteram tuam.

120{121}[6] *The sun shall not burn you by day: nor the moon by night.*

Per diem sol non uret te, neque luna per noctem.

120{121}[5] *Dominus custodit te, the Lord is your keeper,* conserving you in the good and preserving you from evil in this present life of exile. Whence it was said by a holy man: *May you have a good journey, and the Lord be with you in your way, and his angel accompany you.*[8] *Dominus protectio tua, the Lord is your protection,* that is, the cause of your protection or your protector, *super manum dexteram tuam, over and above your right hand,* that is, he is able to protect you more completely and more strongly than your right hand, which customarily defends more strongly. For this reason he says: *I am your protector.*[9] **120{121}[6]** *Per diem sol non uret te, neque luna per noctem; the sun shall not burn you by day: nor the moon by night.* In the way the words time or day and night are used to refer to the things that are done during them — as is contained in the book of Maccabees, *Jonathan saw that the time served him* — so the sun, which ushers in the day and causes it, and the moon, which presides at night, are asserted to effect

---

6 Is. 48:17b.
7 E. N. I have replaced "upon your right hand," with "above and beyond your right hand." This is consistent with the Latin and ties in better with Denis's *Commentary*.
8 Tob. 5:21. E. N. Denis's text replaces "God" with "the Lord," and so departs from the Sixto-Clementine.
9 Gen. 15:1b.

those things that occur during the day or night. In this manner of speaking, some hermit might say to another person: "For forty years the sun has not seen me eating." To which the other responded, "Nor [has it seen] me angry."[10] And in the book of Judges: *The stars remaining in their order and courses, fought against Sisera.*[11] And so [this verse] should be understood in this sense: *The sun shall not burn you by day,* that is, during the day you will not be burned, you will not be destroyed, you will not perish; *nor the moon by night,* that is, during nighttime you will not burn just like you did not during the day. For he whom God keeps and protects is never burned, that is, will never be spiritually consumed with the flames of disordered desire, the fires of impiety, or the ardor of sin. And so it is written: *When you shall walk in the fire, you shall not be burnt, and the flames shall not burn in you.*[12] The Church sings this of some of its holy martyrs, who even though their bodies were set afire, yet they did not [burn] in the sense just stated.

120{121}[7]   *The Lord keep you from all evil: may the Lord keep your soul.*

Dominus custodit te ab omni malo; custodiat animam tuam Dominus.

120{121}[8]   *May the Lord keep your coming in and your going out; from henceforth now and forever.*

Dominus custodiat introitum tuum et exitum tuum, ex hoc nunc et usque in saeculum.

120{121}[7] *Dominus custodit te ab omni malo,* the Lord keep you *from all evil* of mortal sin, but also from the evil of punishment—not that one not suffer [absolutely], since *through many tribulations we must enter into the kingdom of God,*[13] but that one's soul not be harmed by punishment; indeed, by God's ordering, [suffering physical, as distinguished from moral, evil] is indescribably beneficial to a person, for he

---

10 E. N. This is a reference to a story told by Abba Cassian of Abba John, who went to see Abba Paesius, and is found in the Life of the Fathers. "'You have been isolated so long, and cannot easily suffer any trouble from man—tell me, what progress have you made?' And he said: 'From the time I began to be a solitary, the sun has never seen me eating.' And Abba John said to him: 'Nor me angry.'" *Western Asceticism* (Philadelphia: Westminster Press, 1958), 52 (ed. and trans., Owen Chadwick). See *De Vitis Patrum,* V, 24, PL 73, 867.
11 Judges 5:20. E. N. Denis's quotation of this verse uses *demicaverunt* instead of the Sixto-Clementine's *pugnaverunt,* but without significant change in meaning.
12 Is. 43:2b.
13 Acts 14:21b.

merits eternal life by remaining patient through it. And so *the Lord keep you*, O chosen man, *from all evil*: or simply *from all evil*, if you fall into no evil; or *from all evil*, from which you are kept or preserved, so that you may know that it is a gift of God if you avoid some evil. *Custodiat animam tuam Dominus, may the Lord keep your soul*, lest you lose grace, lest the flesh prevail over you, and lest you finally perish. **120{121}[7]** *Dominus custodiat introitum tuum et exitum tuum, ex hoc nunc et usque in saeculum; may the Lord keep your coming in and your going out, from henceforth now and forever*, that is, all your interior and exterior works. Or [alternatively]: *Your coming in*, that is, the manner of your life in this world, by which you proceed in this present place of pilgrimage; *and your going out*, when you will be separated from your body and you will exit the world. Of this coming in and going out the Savior said: *I am the door. By me, if any man enter in, he shall be saved: and he shall go in, and go out, and shall find pastures.*[14]

See we have heard this delightful and doctrinal Psalm, in which we are joyfully recommended to the divine providence. Let us therefore lift up our eyes to the holy angels, most devotedly invoking each of those to whom we are especially committed, so that they never cease favorably to look upon us, to keep custody over us, and to defend us; and let us place all our help in God, saying that which Job did: *Behold there is no help for me in myself.*[15]

PRAYER

GOD, TIRELESS GUARDIAN OF ISRAEL, who neither slumbers nor sleeps, be, O Lord (we beseech you), our constant protection, keeping us from all evil, and ordering our coming into the faith even until our going out from this life forever.

Custos Israel indefessus, qui non dormitas neque dormis,
Deus, sis (quaesumus), Domine, nobis assidua
protectio, custodiens nos ab omni malo, fidei
nostrae introitum et vitae exitum usque
in saeculum disponens.

14 John 10:9.
15 Job 6:13a.

Psalm 121

ARTICLE XXXIII

DECLARATION OF THE
ONE HUNDRED AND TWENTY FIRST PSALM:
LAETATUS SUM IN HIS, ETC.
I REJOICED AT THE THINGS, ETC.

121{122}[1]   *A gradual canticle. I rejoiced at the things that were said to me: We shall go into the house of the Lord.*

Canticum graduum. Laetatus sum in his quae dicta sunt mihi: In domum Domini ibimus.

121{122}[2]   *Our feet were standing in your courts, O Jerusalem.*

Stantes erant pedes nostri in atriis tuis, Ierusalem.

THE TITLE OF THIS PRESENT PSALM IS IN both sense and word the same as the title of the preceding Psalm, namely, *Canticum graduum, a gradual canticle.* And it is apparent that this Psalm literally speaks of the construction of the temple built by Solomon,[1] so that David, knowing the future, began [the Psalm] saying:
121{122}[1] *Laetatus sum in his quae dicta sunt mihi, I rejoiced at the things that were said to me*, by divine revelation and Nathan the prophet.[2] And what these things are, he lays out: *In domum Domini, into the house of the Lord*, that is, in the temple constructed by my son Solomon, *ibimus, we shall go.* But since David did not enter into this house, because he died before its construction, he counts himself as if he is among those who entered in that manner of speaking when something is said to be done by the community because it is done by someone belonging to the community. For we read how David proposed to build a temple for the God of Israel, who sent to him the prophet Nathan, saying by him that he would not himself build that temple, but that his son would.[3]
121{122}[2] *Stantes erant pedes nostri, our feet were standing*, that is, we

---

1 1 Kings chps. 5–7.
2 2 Sam. 7:12–13.
3 2 Sam. 7:1–17.

483

ourselves, the people of God, or the children of Israel, were standing bodily, *in atriis tuis, Ierusalem; in your courts, O Jerusalem*, that is, in the courts of the temple and the city. For the temple of Solomon had many courts:[4] One in which stood the priests and made their offerings; another in which stood and prayed the men of the world; the third was the court of the unclean. Similarly, the city of Jerusalem was enclosed by three walls: and so the city had more than one court.[5] Of which he adds:

121{122}[3] *Jerusalem, which is built as a city, which is compact together.*

Ierusalem, quae aedificatur ut civitas, cuius participatio eius in idipsum.

121{122}[3] *Jerusalem quae aedificatur ut civitas, which is built as a city*, that is, built by Solomon, or rather improved by him by building, so excellently and regally, as befitted the construction of the regal city or the capital of his kingdom; *cuius participatio eius in idipsum, which is compact together*,[6] that is, this city is associated with the temple: for in Hebrew we have, "which is associated together with it." Or [we can look at it thus]: it says, *which is compact together* because of the communion of citizens and the peaceful manner of life, or because of the mutual comfort and decoration of the buildings.

121{122}[4] *For toward there did the tribes go up, the tribes of the Lord: the testimony of Israel, to confess the name of the Lord.*[7]

Illuc enim ascenderunt tribus, tribus Domini, testimonium Israel, ad confitendum nomini Domini.

121{122}[5] *Because there, their seats have sat in judgment, seats upon the house of David.*

Quia illic sederunt sedes in iudicio, sedes super domum David.

---

4 1 Kings 6:36.

5 1 Kings 9:15.

6 E. N. The Douay-Rheims is rather free in its translation of the Latin, which might literally read "whose participation is unto itself (or himself)." I have retained the Douay-Rheims translation here (because it accords with the *Commentary* in this section where Denis relies more on the Hebrew text); however, in the next article (which treats of this Psalm anagogically, I have used the literal translation, "whose participation is unto himself," since Denis speaks there of our participation in God.

7 E. N. I have replaced "praise" (in the Douay-Rheims translation) with "confess" for the Latin *confitendum*. Denis makes clear that the confession here is a confession of praise.

121{122}[4] *Illuc enim, for toward there*, that is, toward that city and the temple constructed in it, *ascenderunt tribus, did the tribes go up*, namely, *tribus Domini, the tribes of the Lord*, that is, the twelve tribes of Israel. These are called the tribes of the Lord because, contrary to the other nations who were all turned towards idols, they worshiped the one true God; *testimonium Israel, the testimony of Israel*, that is, as Jacob, called by the other name Israel,[8] asserted and as God foretold. For the building of the temple was prophesied by Jacob: *How terrible is this place! This is no other but the house of God, and the gate of heaven.*[9] And so they ascended *ad confitendum nomini Domini, to confess the name of the Lord*, that is, so that they might praise God and might recall all the benefits in the temple in the days of solemnity, as is contained in the law of Moses.[10] For they were unable to offer sacrifice except for one place, that is, the constructed temple. 121{122}[5] *Quia illic, because there*, namely in the city and the temple of Jerusalem, *sederunt sedes, their seats have sat*. Here, the container is put in place of that which it contains, so that it [ought to be understood] in this sense, *seats*, that is, those sitting in the judicial seats; *in iudicio, in judgment*, that is, so that they might judge the people. For it pertained to the kings and the chief priests living in Jerusalem to determine doubtful causes and great matters that arose, as is written in Deuteronomy.[11] *Sedes super domum David, seats upon the house of David*, that is, those sitting or presiding sat over the house of David, since they justly judge the people or the family of king David.

121{122}[6] *Pray for the things that are for the peace of Jerusalem: and abundance for them that love you.*

Rogate quae ad pacem sunt Ierusalem, et abundantia diligentibus te.

121{122}[7] *Let peace be in your strength: and abundance in your towers.*

Fiat pax in virtute tua, et abundantia in turribus tuis.

And so the Prophet invites others to pray for the good state of Jerusalem. 121{122}[6] *Rogate, pray*, O children of Israel, to God for those things *quae ad pacem sunt Ierusalem, that are for the peace of Jerusalem*, that is, for the people dwelling in it; *et abundantia, and abundance* of spiritual and temporal goods to be offered up to God *diligentibus te, for them that*

8 Gen. 32:28; 35:10.
9 Gen. 28:17.
10 Deut. 16:16.
11 Deut. 17:8–11.

love you, O Jerusalem, the city of God most high. **121{122}[7]** *Fiat pax in virtute tua, let peace be your strength,* that is, in the strength of your structures, lest an adversary conquer you; *et abundantia, and abundance* of supplies be made, O Jerusalem, *in turribus tuis, in your towers:* in which the custodians of the cities are accustomed to keep watch and store arms.

121{122}[8]   *For the sake of my brethren, and of my neighbors, I spoke peace of you.*

Propter fratres meos et proximos meos, loquebar pacem de te.

121{122}[9]   *Because of the house of the Lord our God, I have sought good things for you.*

Propter domum Domini Dei nostri, quaesivi bona tibi.

121{122}[8] *Propter fratres meo, for the sake of my brethren,* that is, the Jewish kinsmen, *et proximos meos, and of my neighbors,* that is, the other faithful, *loquebar pacem de te, I spoke peace of you,* that is, I have spoken to God in prayer, beseeching him for your peace. For the place or the city is ordered to the people, not the people to the city. And so, one prays for the peace of the city for its people, and not the contrary. But the peace of the place ought greatly to be prayed for so that the worship of God may increase. And so it adds: **121{122}[9]** *Propter domum Domini Dei nostri, because of the house of the Lord our God,* that is, because of the temple or the divine cult to be carried out in it, *quaesivi, I have sought* by praying *bona, good things,* that is, a peaceful state and the abundance of goods, *tibi, for you,* O Jerusalem.

ARTICLE XXXIV

ANAGOGICAL EXPOSITION OF THE SAME ONE HUNDRED AND TWENTY-FIRST PSALM, AND HOW IT CAN BE EXPLAINED ALLEGORICALLY

NOW ADOPTING AN ANAGOGICAL UNDER-standing, the Prophet speaks of the heavenly Jerusalem, of which the Apostle [Paul] says: *That Jerusalem, which is above, is free: which is our mother.*[12] The third gradual Psalm is suitably placed here after the two preceding ones because the first step of internal ascent is to leave the

---

12 Gal. 4:26.

evil and vice of this age; the second is to implore the help of God; the third is to have confidence in arriving to the ultimate end or to eternal life, of which step this Psalm unquestionably handles.

121{122}[1] *A gradual canticle. I rejoiced at the things that were said to me: We shall go into the house of the Lord.*

Canticum graduum. Laetatus sum in his quae dicta sunt mihi: In domum Domini ibimus.

The Prophet [David] speaking in the person of a man who regards all the things of the present life as being of little significance, and who desires with all his heart a heavenly mansion, says: **121{122}[1]** *Laetatus sum, I rejoiced* in the Lord, with spiritual joy, *in his, at the things,* that is, from the consideration of those things, *quae dicta sunt mihi, that were said to me* by the Prophets and the Apostles and their successors, or by the angelic revelation, or by internal inspiration. But what these things that have been said are, it adds: *In domum Domini, into the house of the Lord,* that is, into the Church triumphant, in the fatherland of the blessed, in the kingdom of heaven, *ibimus, we go into,* after dwelling in this life. The Apostle says this to us: *We know, if our earthly house of this habitation be dissolved, that we have a building of God, a house not made with hands, eternal in heaven.*[13] And again: *We, who have believed, shall enter into rest.*[14] Christ also said: *I go to prepare a place for you; and if I shall go, and prepare a place for you, I will come again, and will take you to myself; so that where I am, you also may be.*[15] And again the Lord said: *Behold I create new heavens, and a new earth . . . you shall be glad and rejoice forever in these things, which I create.*[16] Now this which is said — *We shall go into the house of the Lord* — is the word of good hope. For we would not know this with certitude, except that these words are said in the person of the Church.[17] And so, how forcefully, ineffable, and incomparably are we to rejoice of this, that we are going into this house of the Lord, in which

---

13 2 Cor. 5:1.

14 Heb. 4:3a.

15 John 14:2–3.

16 Is. 45:17a, 18a.

17 *E. N.* Absent a special private revelation (such as was given to the penitent thief beside Jesus on the Cross), a person does not have the *certainty of faith* that he is saved, though he may have a well-founded hope and have *moral* certainty of it. DS 1540, 1565 (Council of Trent). Hence, Denis says that this verse — *we shall go into the house of the Lord* — cannot be said absolutely of every single member of the Church militant, although it can be said of the members of the Church triumphant (the elect).

God, sublime and blessed, will be seen face to face without end,[18] in which we will find eternal security and fulness of joy, in which we will be as the angels of God,[19] satisfied in all our longing for good things![20] One who rejoices in carnal things, who is occupied with things of the senses, who does not contemplate heavenly things, who does not serve God in holiness and justice is not worthy to enter into this house,[21] for as it is asserted, *There shall not enter into it anything defiled.*[22]

121{122}[2] *Our feet were standing in your courts, O Jerusalem.*

Stantes erant pedes nostri in atriis tuis, Ierusalem.

Now the sign and the cause of hope, that *we go into the house of the Lord*, is because we already: **121{122}[2]** *Stantes erant pedes nostri, our feet were standing*, that is, our desire and our contemplations, were fixed and stable *in atriis tuis, Ierusalem; in your courts, O Jerusalem*, that is, in the mansions of the heavenly kingdom: so that our manner of life was heavenly, and we ordered all our works toward eternal life,[23] which we desired most highly and as our final end. This is what the Apostle said: *You are come to mount Sion, and to the city of the living God, the heavenly Jerusalem, and to the company of many thousands of angels, and to the church of the firstborn, who are written in the heavens.*[24] And elsewhere also he says: *We all beholding the glory of the Lord with open face, are transformed into the same image from glory to glory.*[25]

121{122}[3] *Jerusalem, which is built as a city, whose participation is unto himself.*[26]

Ierusalem, quae aedificatur ut civitas, cuius participatio eius in idipsum.

121{122}[3] *Jerusalem*, this heavenly one, is that one *quae aedificatur, which is built* every day even until the end of the world from living stones,[27]

---

18 *Cf.* 1 Cor. 13:12.
19 *Cf.* Matt. 22:30.
20 *Cf.* Ps. 102:5a.
21 *Cf.* Luke 1:75.
22 Rev. 21:27a.
23 *Cf.* Phil. 3:20: *But our conversation is in heaven; from whence also we look for the Savior, our Lord Jesus Christ.*
24 Heb. 12:22–23a.
25 2 Cor. 3:18.
26 *E. N.* See footnote 121-6.
27 *Cf.* 1 Pet. 2:5a.

that is, holy souls attaining the heavenly fatherland, *ut civitas, as a city* most high and perfect, in such a way that it befits to build the city of the eternal King. For it is built from precious, polished, rational, and holy stones, namely angels and men, in the manner testified to by Paul: In Christ *all the building, being framed together, grows up into a holy temple in the Lord, in whom you also are built together into an habitation of God in the Spirit.*[28] Now the city is what a unity of citizens is called. Therefore, much more truly is the heavenly Jerusalem called a city than is a dwelling of wayfaring state, given that the heavenly city enjoys far greater harmony than any of those in the wayfaring state. *Cuius participatio eius in idipsum, whose participation is unto himself*: that is, all the citizens of this city participate in the good, because all enjoy the same highest good: some more and some less, according to whether they loved more or less.[29] God, therefore, *is unto himself,* that is, the unvarying and indivisible good of the supernal Jerusalem: *whose participation* — that is, the enjoyment, beatitude, deification in which one participates in the divine goodness — is uniform and eternal, in the way it is written: *This is eternal life: That they may know you, the only true God;*[30] and again, *We shall be like to him: because we shall see him as he is.*[31] Or [alternatively], *whose participation is unto himself,* that is, in the heavenly city the good of all is the good of each one, and vice versa. For since love is diffusive and communicative of itself,[32] and since in the heavenly fatherland there is a most perfect mutual love among all the blessed, so also is there the most blessed communion among each of the blessed. For from the happiness of one, the other rejoices as if it were his own; indeed, everyone wishes joy to everyone, and those who are superior give of their perfections given to them by God to the lower, according to the great Dionysius.[33] Now this is not properly applicable to any individual earthly city.

---

28 Eph. 2:21–22.

29 E. N. *A la tarde de esta vida, te examinarán en el amor; aprende a amar como Dios quiere ser amado, y deja tu condición.* St. John of the Cross, *Avisos y sentencias,* 57. "In the evening of this life, you will be examined on love; learn to love how God wants to be loved, and leave behind your condition." *Cf.* CCC § 1022.

30 John 17:3a.

31 1 John 3:2b.

32 E. N. That being, good, and love is diffusive or communicative of itself is a central principle in St. Thomas's thought. *See, e.g.,* ST Ia, q. 5, art. 4 ad 2; q. 19, art. 2; q. 73, art. 3 ad 2; *De Veritate* 21.1 ad 4. *See also* Bernhard-Thomas Blankenhorn, O. P., "The good as self-diffusive in Thomas Aquinas," *Angelicum,* Vol. 79, No. 4 (2002), 803–37. "Perhaps Thomas' richest text on the good as act and as active is SCG I, 37": "Now, the nature of the good comes from its being something appetible. This is the end, which also moves the agent to act. That is why it is said that the good is diffusive of itself and of being (*bonum esse 'diffusivum sui et esse'*)."

33 E. N. See *The Celestial Hierarchy,* IV, 3 in *Pseudo-Dionysius: The Collected Works* (New York: Paulist Press, 1987), 158 (trans., Colm Luibheid).

121{122}[4]   *For toward there did the tribes go up, the tribes of the Lord: the testimony of Israel, to confess the name of the Lord.*[34]

Illuc enim ascenderunt tribus, tribus Domini, testimonium Israel, ad confitendum nomini Domini.

121{122}[5]   *Because there, their seats have sat in judgment, seats upon the house of David.*

Quia illic sederunt sedes in iudicio, sedes super domum David.

121{122}[4] *Illuc enim, for there,* that is, in the supernal Jerusalem, *ascenderunt, did go up,* with respect to their souls, *tribus, the tribes,* not of any kind, but *tribus Domini, the tribes of the Lord,* that is, the people born of God by grace, namely, all the elect already deceased and purified of all stain. For many of them ascended together with Christ, and others follow in the interim. And they have gone before us so as to prepare for us a place, so that they might pray for us, so that we might imitate their way, as the Apostle warns: *Therefore we also having so great a cloud of witnesses over our head, laying aside every weight and sin which surrounds us, let us run by patience to the fight proposed to us.*[35] *Testimonium Israel, the testimony of Israel:* that is, this ascension is the testimony of Israel, that is, of the faithful people contemplating God. For God told this people that they would ascend up to their heavenly house. Indeed, God promised this to Jacob, as also to Abraham. *Ad confitendum nomini Domini, to confess the name of the Lord,* with the confession of eternal praise, in the manner we read in Revelation: *They rested not day and night, saying: Holy, holy, holy, Lord God Almighty, who was, and who is, and who is to come.*[36]

121{122}[5]   *Because there, their seats have sat in judgment, seats upon the house of David.*

Quia illic sederunt sedes in iudicio, sedes super domum David.

121{122}[5] *Quia illic, because there,* that is, in the heavenly city, *sederunt, they have sat,* sit, and will sit, *sedes, seats,* that is, the holy Apostles and apostolic men in whom God comes to rest by grace. For also the soul of the just man is the seat of uncreated Wisdom, which is God.[37] The seats will be *in iudicio, in judgment,* that is, these [apostles and apostolic men] will sit

---

34 E. N. I have replaced "praise" (in the Douay-Rheims translation) with "confess" for the Latin *confitendum.* Denis makes clear that the confession here is a confession of praise.
35 Heb. 12:1.
36 Rev. 4:8b.
37 *Cf.* Prov. 14:33a: *In the heart of the prudent rests wisdom;* Wis. 7:27: *Wisdom conveys herself into holy souls, she makes the friends of God and prophets.*

in the heavenly kingdom with Christ as they will judge with Christ in the day of judgment, in the manner that it states in the Gospel: *You, who have followed me, in the regeneration, when the Son of man shall sit on the seat of his majesty, you also shall sit on twelve seats judging the twelve tribes of Israel.*[38] Whence, elsewhere it states: *They shall judge nations, and rule over people.*[39] *Sedes super domum David, seats upon the house of David*, that is, over the people of Christ, over whom they were appointed prelates and judges. And so Christ alone will judge in the sense of carrying out his sentences. Now the superlatively most blessed Trinity will judge by authority. Yet the saints and apostolic men — who because they left everything behind and denied themselves for the love of Christ — will judge by approbation and assent.[40]

121{122}[6] *Pray for the things that are for the peace of Jerusalem: and abundance for them that love you.*

Rogate quae ad pacem sunt Ierusalem, et abundantia diligentibus te.

Since, therefore, the beatitude of the supernal city will be so great, O all you faithful, 121{122}[6] *Rogate quae ad pacem sunt Ierusalem, pray for the things that are for the peace of Jerusalem*: that is, invoke God for his goods, namely, for the gifts of the Holy Spirit, by which we might be found worthy to be led to the peace of the heavenly Jerusalem. Thereupon, the Prophet shifts to speak words toward the Church triumphant, saying: *Et abundantia, and abundance* of the divine charisms or spiritual graces given by God as a result of your intercession, *diligentibus te, for them that love you*, that is, to us wayfarers who desire to be led to your fellowship.

121{122}[8] *For the sake of my brethren, and of my neighbors, I spoke peace of you.*[41]

Propter fratres meos et proximos meos, loquebar pacem de te.

121{122}[9] *Because of the house of the Lord our God, I have sought good things for you.*

Propter domum Domini Dei nostri, quaesivi bona tibi.

But because Peter in his epistle says, *as every man has received grace, ministering the same one to another,*[42] therefore: 121{122}[8] *Propter fratres*

---

38 Matt. 19:28.
39 Wis. 3:8a.
40 E. N. ST IIIa (Supp.), q. 89, arts. 1, 3, co.
41 E. N. Denis skips over verse 7 in this section of the Commentary.
42 1 Pet. 4:10a.

meos et proximos meos loquebar pacem de te; for the sake of my brethren, and of my neighbors, I spoke peace of you, that is, I preached to others of your happiness and joy, O supernal Jerusalem, so that I might teach my brothers and my neighbors, that is, the faithful and those close to me, and ignite them with your love so that they might be led to saving union with you or eternal life. **121{122}[9]** *Propter domum Domini Dei nostri, because of the house of the Lord God,* that is, so that in this manner I might edify the Church militant, *quaesivi bona tibi, I have sought good things for you,* that is, to your honor and glory: that is, praying and preaching I have sought spiritual goods for the wayfarers to the glory of the blessed, namely, so that they might be more amply joyful as it relates to accidental reward, with the arriving wayfarers coming to join their fellowship. Or [alternatively], *I have sought good things for you,* the Church triumphant, working for men, so that the number of the elect might be completed, and your walls might be constructed and finished.[43]

ALLEGORICAL EXPOSITION

IN ADDITION, BECAUSE BY JERUSALEM IS SIG-nified allegorically the Church militant, therefore this Psalm can be explained in reference to the Church militant.

> **121{122}[1]** *I rejoiced at the things that were said to me: We shall go into the house of the Lord.*
>
> *Laetatus sum in his quae dicta sunt mihi: In domum Domini ibimus.*
>
> **121{122}[2]** *Our feet were standing in your courts, O Jerusalem.*
>
> *Stantes erant pedes nostri in atriis tuis, Ierusalem.*

And so, the Prophet [David] speaking in the person of the Gentile people, says: **121{122}[1]** *Laetatus sum in his quae dicta sunt mihi, I rejoiced at the things that were said to me* by the Apostles, namely that *in domum Domini, into the house of the Lord,* that is, the Church of Christ, *ibimus, we shall go,* so that we might belong to the society and number of Christians. This is what is recited in the book of Acts. For when Paul responded to

---

43 *E. N.* The reference to the walls of Jerusalem is to Rev. 21:12–20, and brings to mind the 7th or 8th century hymn *Urbs beata Ierusalem: Urbs beata Ierusalem, / dicta pacis visio, / quae construitur in caelo / vivis ex lapidibus, / et angelis coronata / ut sponsata comite.* Blessed city Jerusalem, / Called vision of peace, / Which is built in heaven / from living stones, / and crowned with angels / as a bride adorned for her consort.

the blaspheming Jews he said: *To you it behooved us first to speak the word of God: but because you reject it, and judge yourselves unworthy of eternal life, behold we turn to the Gentiles. For so the Lord has commanded us: I have set you to be the light of the Gentiles; that you may be for salvation unto the utmost part of the earth* (which are the words of God speaking about Christ through Isaiah); [the book of Acts] adds: *And the Gentiles hearing it, were glad, and glorified the word of the Lord,* namely because having been rejected by the Jews, they were able to enlighten them [the Gentiles] in Christ.[44] **121{122}[2]** *Stantes erant, they were standing,* that is, they will be standing: for often the Prophets speak of the future by means of the past because of the certitude of the prophecy; *pedes nostri, our feet* of the body and of the spirit, *in atriis tuis, Ierusalem; in your courts, O Jerusalem,* that is, in the place of the Church. For by courts are meant entrances or places by which one enters into a home. Whence the spiritual courts are faith, hope, and charity, by which we enter into the unity of the Church and the divine worship. And so in spiritual courts stand spiritual feet, namely, good affections and holy thoughts, by which the soul ascends toward God; but in the bodily courts stand bodily feet.

121{122}[3] *Jerusalem, which is built as a city, whose participation is unto itself.*[45]

Ierusalem, quae aedificatur ut civitas, cuius participatio eius in idipsum.

121{122}[4] *For toward there did the tribes go up, the tribes of the Lord: the testimony of Israel, to confess the name of the Lord.*[46]

Illuc enim ascenderunt tribus, tribus Domini, testimonium Israel, ad confitendum nomini Domini.

121{122}[5] *Because there, their seats have sat in judgment, seats upon the house of David.*

Quia illic sederunt sedes in iudicio, sedes super domum David.

121{122}[3] *Jerusalem,* that is, the Church militant, *quae aedificatur, which is built* from the Christian faithful as from living stones,[47] *ut civitas, as a city* of God, because it is the city of the Savior; *cuius participatio eius in idipsum,*

---

44 Acts 13:46–48; Is. 49:6.
45 E. N. See footnote 121-6.
46 E. N. I have replaced "praise" (in the Douay-Rheims translation) with "confess" for the Latin *confitendum.* Denis makes clear that the confession here is a confession of praise.
47 Cf. 1 Pet. 2:5.

whose participation is unto itself, that is, the spiritual goods of this city in some way shared in common: because one member of the faithful imparts to another what he himself has received; indeed, he desires to provide and to aid the other as he does himself, in the manner that the Apostle said: I do not seek *that which is profitable to myself, but to many, that they may be saved;*[48] and elsewhere, *Each one not considering the things that are his own, but those that are other men's.*[49] And is this to be marveled at since the participation in the Church *is unto itself,* as the Apostle affirms, *For you are all one in Christ Jesus?*[50] **121{122}[4]** *Illuc enim, for towards there,* that is, towards the Church militant, *ascenderunt tribus, tribus Domini; did the tribes go up, the tribes of the Lord,* that is the families and the generations of the elect to faith and grace, namely, the Christians: of which is said in Acts: *As many as were ordained to life everlasting, believed.*[51] For Christians move their bodies to assemble at a material church; but to the spiritual Church, that is, the congregation of the faithful or ecclesiastical unity, they assemble with affection, faith and works, believing the same, hoping the same, loving the same, and observing the same precepts. **121{122}[5]** *Quia illic sederunt sedes in iudicio, because there, their seats have sat in judgment.* For judges, both spiritual and secular, are constituted in the Church: and these are the *seats,* that is, sitting in the seats, *super domum David, upon the house of David,* that is, they preside over the people of Christ, who are signified by David.

121{122}[6] *Pray for the things that are for the peace of Jerusalem: and abundance in them that love you.*

Rogate quae ad pacem sunt Ierusalem, et abundantia diligentibus te.

121{122}[6] *Rogate, pray,* O saints in the heavenly fatherland, and all devout wayfarers, *quae ad pacem sunt Ierusalem, for the things that are for the peace of Jerusalem,* that is, procure for the Church by your prayers those things that are needed for spiritual peace and its peaceable state. For this the Apostle prayed for: I desire therefore, *first of all, that ... prayers ... be made for all men, for kings, and for all that are in high station, that we may lead a quiet and a peaceable life in all piety.*[52] *Et abundantia, and abundance* of grace and virtue be, *diligentibus te, in them*

---

48 1 Cor. 10:33.
49 Phil. 2:4.
50 Gal. 3:28b.
51 Acts 13:48b.
52 1 Tim. 2:1–2.

that love you, that is, in all those who have pious and loving zeal for the good state and the spiritual progress of the whole militant Church, such as Paul, who was afflicted by the *solicitude of all the Churches.*[53]

121{122}[8]   *For the sake of my brethren, and of my neighbors, I spoke peace of you.*[54]

Propter fratres meos et proximos meos, loquebar pacem de te.

121{122}[9]   *Because of the house of the Lord our God, I have sought good things for you.*

Propter domum Domini Dei nostri, quaesivi bona tibi.

121{122}[8] *Propter fratres meo et proximos meos, for the sake of my brethren and of my neighbors,* that is, for the salvation and the formation of my brothers and my neighbors, *loquebar, I spoke* in my prayers to God *bona de te, goods of you,* praying to God that he might confer spiritual goods to you.[55] 121{122}[9] *Propter domum Domini Dei nostri, because of the house of the Lord our God,* that is, that the Church of Christ will for a time advance in grace, and after a time will be in glory, *quaesivi bona tibi, I have sought good things for you,* that is, I have labored to acquire the gifts of God for you, O Church of Christ, now in its militant state — as if to say, I have endeavored to help you not because of my own benefit, but for your salvation.

EE, WE HAVE HEARD THIS PSALM DRENCHED with spiritual joy and spiritually gladdening the devout soul, which it befits us to sing with heartfelt rejoicing; one cannot utter the first verse of this Psalm without the fervor of charity and an overabundance of spiritual joy. And because no one except for the lover and observer of charity and peace attains to this heavenly Jerusalem, in which there is ineffable concord and the most abundant of charity, let us endeavor to live and to make progress in the true love of God and neighbor, carefully considering and keeping that which the blessed Apostle said: *I a prisoner in the Lord, beseech you that you walk worthy of the vocation in which you are called, with all humility and mildness, with patience, supporting one another in charity, careful to keep the unity of the Spirit in*

---

53 2 Cor. 11:28b.
54 *E. N.* Denis skips over verse 7 in this section of the Commentary.
55 *E. N.* Denis's text reads *bona,* "goods," and not *pacem,* "peace," though earlier Denis used "peace." The editor notes the discrepancy and attributes it to an alternative reading.

the bond of peace.[56] And in this manner abiding in the Church militant, they will be held to be worthy to enter into the Church triumphant, the heavenly Jerusalem, because they imitated the life of its citizens on earth. For elegantly describing this supernal city, Isaiah in the person of God says: *I will make your visitation peace, and your overseers justice; salvation shall possess your walls. You shall no more have the sun for your light by day, neither shall the brightness of the moon enlighten you; but the Lord shall be unto you for an everlasting light and your God for your glory. And your people shall all be just.*[57] See how appealing and decorous is this city! Let us go and let us arrive to it with the two feet of charity, namely of God and of neighbor. For love—which enters where knowledge stands without, as the venerable Hugh attested—is what moves the foot of the spiritual journey.[58]

PRAYER

LORD, ARTISAN OF ALL EXISTING THINGS, set our feet in your courts, and build within us the supernal Jerusalem; by your power cause us to have continual peace so that we might also always devotedly seek the goods of that city, and, by your aid, we might come upon it.

Omnium exsistentium opifex, Domine, statue pedes nostros in atriis tuis, et aedifica Ierusalem supernam in nobis; fiat nobis pax continua in virtute tua: ut et eiusdem semper civitatis bona devote quaeramus, et te praestante inveniamus.

---

56 Eph. 4:1–3.

57 Is. 60:17b, 18b, 19, 21a.

58 E. N. *quae [dilectio] intrat ubi scientia foris stat.* Denis is referring here to the *Commentary on the Celestial Hierarchy* of Hugh of St. Victor (Book VI, exp. of ch. 7): *Intrat dilectio ubi scientia foris stat.* See St. Thomas, *Super Sent.*, lib. 4 d. 49 q. 1 a. 1 qc. 2 arg. 5. "'*Dilectio supereminet scientiae, et major est intelligentia. Plus enim Deus diligitur quam intelligatur; intrat dilectio ubi scientia foris est.' Ergo beatitudo consistit magis in dilectione quam in cognitione, et in voluntate quam in intellectu.* "Love surpasses knowledge, and is great that understanding. For God is loved more than he is understood; love enters where knowledge is outside.' Therefore, beatitude consists more in love than knowledge, and in will rather than intellect.'"

Psalm 122

ARTICLE XXXV

EXPLANATION OF THE
ONE HUNDRED AND TWENTY-SECOND PSALM:
AD TE LEVAVI OCULOS MEOS.
TO YOU HAVE I LIFTED UP MY EYES.

122{123}[1] *A gradual canticle. To you have I lifted up my eyes, who dwells in heaven.*

Canticum graduum. Ad te levavi oculos meos, qui habitas in caelis.

EFORE THE TITLE OF THIS PSALM NOW BEING addressed is: *Canticum graduum, a gradual canticle,* whose meaning is clear from what has been already said. In this fourth gradual Psalm is addressed the fourth grade of spiritual ascent, which is to have unshakeable confidence in the divine mercy when confronted by all aversities and distress, as Job said: *Although he should kill me, I will trust him.*[1]

The Prophet speaking in the person of a man beset by weighty tribulations, yet also immovably confident of the Lord, says: **122{123}[1]** *Ad te levavi, to you have I lifted up,* believing, hoping, loving, contemplating, patiently enduring, faithfully working, *oculos meos, my eyes,* especially [my] intellectual [eyes], but also [my] bodily [eyes], in the manner that Jeremiah said: *Let us lift up our hearts with our hands,* both material and immaterial, *to the Lord in the heavens;*[2] *qui habitas in caelis, who dwells in heaven.* For the eternal God is without boundary, he cannot be confined by any created being, so that he could in any way be included, or comprehended, or limited; yet he is in all things by essence, presence, and power. But he is especially thought to be and dwell where he has worked more graciously and more evidently; and so he is asserted to be and to dwell especially in the holy angels and devout men. In the heavens, especially in the empyrean heaven, God also dwells, because there he is seen the way he is.[3] But, because all the blessed dwell in a material

---

1 Job 13:15a.
2 Lam. 3:41.
3 1 John 3:2b.

497

heaven,[4] and in this place by the words *who dwells in the heaven* is understood to mean God, it seems to speak of an immaterial heaven, because to dwell in such [and immaterial heaven] is proper to God.

122{123}[2]   *Behold as the eyes of servants are on the hands of their masters, As the eyes of the handmaid are on the hands of her mistress: so are our eyes unto the Lord our God, until he has mercy on us.*

Ecce sicut oculi servorum in manibus dominorum suorum; sicut oculi ancillae in manibus dominae suae: ita oculi nostri ad Dominum Deum nostrum, donec misereatur nostri.

122{123}[2] *Ecce sicut oculi servorum,* behold as the eyes of servants are *in manibus,* on the hands, that is in the power and will, *dominorum suorum, of their masters,* so that they are directed towards them, begging their pardon if they offended them; or a reward, if they have labored; or information, if they are ignorant about what they ought to do. *Sicut oculi ancillae,* as the eyes of the handmaid are *in manibus dominae suae, in the hands of her mistress,* in the manner just stated; *ita oculi nostri,* so are our eyes directed *ad Dominum Deum nostrum, unto the Lord our God,* praying for his help, indulgence, and grace, *donec misereatur nostri, until he has mercy on us,* doing that which we request, or certainly giving us that which he knows will be useful for us. And because so long as we find ourselves in this world we will have need of the mercy of God, so ought we, as long as we live here, unceasingly to direct our eyes to God, especially when we are seriously tempted or afflicted. It should be noted that in this place, this word — *donec, until* — is affirmative and inclusive of all time, such as we find regarding Joseph: *He knew her* (namely, Mary) *not until (donec) she brought forth her firsborn son.*[5] For it is not said that we direct our eyes to the Lord until he has mercy, in the sense that when he is merciful to us we no longer direct ourselves to him.[6]

---

4 E. N. After the final Resurrection, the blessed will be rejoined with their *material* (albeit *glorified* or *spiritual*) bodies, thus inferring that heaven will be in some way material so as to accommodate the material resurrected body. One might also recall that the Lord Jesus is present in heaven with his risen, glorified body, as is the Blessed Virgin Mary. See F. J. Boudreaux, S. J., *The Happiness of Heaven* (London: Burns & Oates, 1881), 58*ff.*

5 Matt. 1:25.

6 E. N. ST IIIa, q. 23, art. 3, ad 3. Relying on St. Jerome (*Adv. Helvidium,* 5, PL 23, 188), St. Thomas Aquinas states: "before (*usque*) or until (*donec*) can be understood in two ways in the Scriptures. For sometimes it means a certain time such as in

122{123}[3] *Have mercy on us, O Lord, have mercy on us: for we are greatly filled with contempt.*

Miserere nostri, Domine, miserere nostri, quia multum repleti sumus despectione.

122{123}[4] *For our soul is greatly filled: a reproach by those in abundance, and contempt to the proud.*

Quia multum repleta est anima nostra opprobrium abundantibus, et despectio superbis.

122{123}[3] *Miserere nostri, Domine;* have mercy on us, O Lord, by taking away the evil of fault and of punishment, *miserere nostri,* have mercy, conferring grace and glory, *quia multum repleti sumus despectione, for we are greatly filled with contempt,* that is, we are greatly despised by sinners. *The simplicity of the just man is laughed to scorn,* as Job said.[7] And Paul says: *We are fools for Christ's sake.*[8] For the elect are derided by the reprobate, the religious by the worldly, the humble by the proud, the needy by the rich. And so it adds: **122{123}[4]** *Quia multum repleta est anima nostra, for our soul is greatly filled* with various miseries, so much so that it is *opprobrium abundantibus, a reproach by those in abundance,* that is, the rich, *et despectio superbis, and contempt to the proud.*

This Psalm instructs us to raise the eyes of our hearts to God in all necessity, and not to desist until we obtain mercy. For *we ought always to pray, and not to faint.*[9] Furthermore, Christ by his example leads us to this trust and holy raising [of the eyes of our heart]. Of him it is written: *Lifting up his eyes to heaven, he said: Father, the hour is come, glorify your Son.*[10] And again: *Jesus lifting up his eyes said: Father, I give you thanks.*[11] Why was this elevation of the bodily eyes necessary for him whose interior eyes incessantly saw God by sight, and whose will always burned evenly with divine love? He therefore did this for no other reason than that we might do the same. He did it so as to show himself to have all things from the Father; but he also did this so that

---

Galatians [3:19] . . . But sometimes it means an indefinite time (*infinitum tempus*) as in the Psalm [122:2], 'So our eyes [are directed] unto the Lord our God until (*donec*) he has mercy on us.' It is not understood from this that after the Lord has shown mercy people no longer turn their eyes to God."

7 Job 12:4b.

8 1 Cor. 4:10a.

9 Luke 18:1b.

10 John 17:1.

11 John 11:41.

we might constantly acknowledge whatever good has taken place in us to be from God, according to this: *A man cannot receive any thing, unless it be given him from heaven.*[12]

PRAYER

WE YOUR SERVANTS LIFT OUR EYES UPWARD to you, O Lord God, who dwell in the heavens; have mercy upon us, and deliver us from the reproach and eternal contempt of the proud.

Nos tui servi oculos nostros ad te levamus, qui habitas in caelestibus, Domine Deus, nostri miserere, et de oprobrio et aeterna superborum eripe despectione.

---

12 John 3:27.

Psalm 123

ARTICLE XXXVI

EXPOSITION OF THE
ONE HUNDRED AND TWENTY-THIRD PSALM:
NISI QUIA DOMINUS ERAT IN NOBIS.
IF IT HAD NOT BEEN THAT THE LORD WAS WITH US.

IN FRONT OF THIS PSALM IS THE SAME TITLE as the preceding Psalm. Now since this Psalm is most fittingly expounded in the person of the martyr already triumphant with Christ or of the other blessed saints in the heavenly fatherland who *through many tribulations* entered into the kingdom of heaven,[1] yet it also can apply to wayfarers who, delivered by God from temptations, passions, and persecutions, return thanks for their deliverance. And this Psalm is rightly placed in the fifth step of spiritual ascent, which is, to ascribe one's deliverance not to one's own strength, but to the grace of God. Whence the Lord in the book of Judges says: *Let not Israel glory against me, and say: I was delivered by my own strength.*[2]

123{124}[1]   *A gradual canticle. If it had not been that the Lord was with us, let Israel now say:*

Canticum graduum. Nisi quia Dominus erat in nobis, dicat nunc Israel,

123{124}[2]   *If it had not been that the Lord was with us, When men rose up against us,*

Nisi quia Dominus erat in nobis: cum exsurgerent homines in nos,

123{124}[3]   *Perhaps they had swallowed us up alive. When their fury was enkindled against us,*

Forte vivos deglutissent nos; cum irasceretur furor eorum in nos,

123{124}[4]   *Perhaps the waters had swallowed us up.*

Forsitan aqua absorbuisset nos.

---

1 Acts 14:21b.
2 Judges 7:2b.

501

Therefore, the Prophet [David] speaking of men or a people delivered from many temptations and dangers, says: 123{124}[1] *Nisi quia Dominus erat in nobis, dicat nunc Israel; if it had not been that the Lord was with us, let Israel now say*: that is, the faithful people, contemplating God faithfully, already professing with a devoted and grateful heart, that if God had not been graciously with us—which is repeated for greater certitude, for a more ample gratitude, for a more fervent exhortation, thereby it adds, 123{124}[2] *nisi quia Dominus erat in nobis, if it had not been that the Lord was with us*, that is, protected us by the grace of his defense; *cum exsurgerent homines, when men rose up*, [men who were] infidels, heretics, tyrants, malicious, *in nos, against us*, that is, opposed to us, bringing against us evils of punishment, and fully determined to lead us to the evils of fault, 123{124}[3] *forte vivos deglutissent nos, perhaps they had swallowed us alive*, that is, so that they might kill us, just as one alive is killed when swallowed by an animal. Now this language properly applies to martyrs, because tyrants tried to lead them to idolatry or the denial of Christ: and if this had been successful, their souls, not their flesh, would have been consumed: and so they would have been swallowed up alive. For though living in the body, they would have been dead in soul; and having the life of nature, they would have lost the life of grace and glory.

Cum irasceretur furor eorum in nos 123{124}[4] *forsitan aqua; when their fury was enkindled* 123{124}[4] *perhaps the waters*, [the waters, that is] of tribulation, that is furious persecutions, *absurbuissent nos, had swallowed us up*, that is, would have prevailed against us so that we would have been dead with sin, consenting to evil or overcome by a want of endurance. For unless God would give patience and constancy, who would have been able to persist unshaken against such tribulations? Whence Moses was told: Do not say *in your heart: My own might, and the strength of my own hand have achieved all these things for me; but remember the Lord your God, that he has given you strength.*[3] Now a great tribulation is signified by water, such as it is here: *[The Lord] will bring upon them the waters of the river strong and many, the king of the Assyrians.*[4] And elsewhere: *Waters have flowed over my head: I said: I am cut off.*[5]

---

3 Deut. 8:17–18a.
4 Is. 8:7a.
5 Lam. 3:54.

123{124}[5] *Our soul has passed through a torrent: perhaps our soul had passed through a water insupportable.*

Torrentem pertransivit anima nostra; forsitan pertransisset anima nostra aquam intolerabilem,

123{124}[6] *Blessed be the Lord, who has not given us to be a prey to their teeth.*

Benedictus Dominus, qui non dedit nos in captionem dentibus eorum.

123{124}[5] *Torrentem, a torrent,* that is, an extensive and great tribulation and temptation, *pertransivit anima nostra, our soul has passed through,* sustaining adversities with equanimity, and not consenting to perverse suggestions; *forsitan pertransisset anima nostra aquam intolerabilem, perhaps our soul had passed through water insupportable*: that is, if the Lord had not rendered help, we would have been pressed down and tempted beyond our strength,[6] and our soul would have been forced to pass through, that is, to suffer, insupportable waters, that is, persecution which we would have been unable to resist. But the Lord, who will not let us suffer temptation beyond our ability, is faithful: indeed, he will bring forth with the temptation a happy result, giving us glory in exchange for the torment.[7] A man could not possibly resist his invisible enemies if the holy angels would not provide help, and God himself or through an angel provides assistance. For of the strength of the devil it is written: *There is no power upon earth that can be compared with him.*[8] For [the devil and his minions] are incomparably more astute, more agile, and more experienced than we are. And so: 123{124}[6] *Benedictus Dominus, blessed be the Lord,* that is, by all he is blessed and praised, and he is eternally blessed, *qui non dedit nos, who has not given us* effectively or permissively *in captionem dentibus eorum, to be a prey to their teeth,* that is, to the cruelty and malignity of the invisible and visible enemies: that is, even though we may be vanquished, afflicted, and killed by them in body, he does not permit us to be captured or to be vanquished by enemies with respect to our soul.

---

6 Cf. 2 Cor. 1:8: *We were pressed out of measure above our strength, so that we were weary even of life.*
7 Cf. 1 Cor. 10:13: *And God is faithful, who will not suffer you to be tempted above that which you are able: but will make also with temptation issue, that you may be able to bear it.*
8 Job 41:24a.

123{124}[7]   *Our soul has been delivered as a sparrow out of the snare of the hunters. The snare is broken, and we are delivered.*[9]

Anima nostra sicut passer erepta est de laqueo venantium; laqueus contritus est, et nos liberati sumus.

123{124}[7] *Anima nostra sicut passer erepta est de laqueo venantium, our soul has been delivered as a sparrow out of the snare of the hunters:* that is, in the manner that a sparrow evades a net stretched out over it lest it be captured; so our soul is delivered by the grace of God from the attacks of the enemies against its salvation, namely, ungodly men and demons; these [enemies] are called hunters because they pursue souls like dogs, so that they might kill, deceive, or bind [the soul] with the fetters of a miserable servitude, and subdue it under the power of the devil. Now that not only a demon, but also a malicious man is called a hunter in this way is clear from what is written: *Everyone hunts his brother to death.*[10] And of the unworthy shepherd we are told by Hosea: *They shall lift up their souls to their iniquity.* But all those things that induce a soul to sin or subject it to the power of the devil are called snares. Whence we find this contained in Hosea: *Hear this, O priests ... because you have been a snare to them whom you should have watched over, and a net spread upon Tabor.*[11] Similarly, the sight of a harlot is a snare of the devil.[12] And regarding avarice, the Apostle says: *They that will become rich, fall into temptation, and into the snare of the devil.*[13] Finally, that all vices can be called snares of the devil is clear by that stated by the Apostle: God may give *them repentance to know the truth, and they may recover themselves from the snares of the devil, by whom they are held captive at his will.*[14] Therefore every temptation, every desire of the flesh, every disordered joy is a snare of the hunter.

---

9 E. N. The translators of the Douay-Rheims translated *venantium* as "of the fowlers" because the context involves sparrows. However, the Latin *venator*, "hunter," is broader than "fowler." Because Denis refers to other scriptures that speak of hunters, I have translated *venantium* as "of the hunters."

10 Micah 7:2b.

11 Hosea 5:1.

12 E. N. Denis says *laqueus diaboli, species meretricis*, "the sight of a harlot is a snare of the devil," which might be a reference to St. Ambrose's *Commentary on the Gospel of Luke*, IV, 10: "The snares which we pass through are many. Snares in the body, in the Law, snares in the parapet of the temple, in the foundation of the walls, set by the devil. Snares in philosophy, snares in desires, for the eye of the harlot is a snare for the sinner, a snare in money, a snare in religion, a snare in zeal for chastity." PL 15, 1615.

13 1 Tim. 6:9a.

14 2 Tim. 2:25b–26.

Laqueus contritus est, the snare is broken, that is, the demon is overcome, consent to sin is negated, adversity is unable to cause harm, *et nos liberati sumus, and we are delivered* from the aforementioned snares. We cannot exclaim this during the course of this life perfectly, because temptation lasts even until the end, indeed it becomes more difficult sometimes at the end of life.[15] When, therefore, do we exclaim this perfectly? Never except for the future life, when we will say with joyful soul that which the Apostle states: *O death, where is your victory? O death, where is your sting?*[16] We can also in a certain manner exclaim this in this life, namely, when we have prevailed over some temptation, or we have evaded some adversity through help of God. For the Apostle also said: *Thanks be to God, who has given us the victory through our Lord Jesus Christ.*[17] And of the destruction of the devil and of his snares, he said: *The God of peace crush Satan under your feet speedily.*[18]

123{124}[8] *Our help is in the name of the Lord, who made heaven and earth.*

Adiutorium nostrum in nomine Domini, qui fecit caelum et terram.

123{124}[8] *Adiutorium nostrum, our help* consists *in nomine Domini, in the name of the Lord,* that is, in the power of the Creator, not in our own strength, because it is written: *Lord . . . you have wrought all our works for us, . . . only in you let us remember your name.*[19] And so, in the Lord is situated our help, *qui fecit caelum et terram, who made heaven and earth.*

This present Psalm teaches us to ascribe every triumph, progress, and grace to God with true humility, to recall devoutly the divine benefits, and to offer up thanks for these to the Lord. Finally, according to Hugh [of Saint-Cher], demons invade men by suggestion, they touch them with evil thoughts, they bite them by depraved delectations, they chew them by deliberation, they swallow them by consent, they pass them through the stomach by deed, and they consume them by habit, and lead them to death by damnation. By these steps one descends into hell.[20]

---

15 E. N. This is suggestive of a saying attributed to St. Augustine: "Persevere even unto the end, because temptation lasts even unto the end." The saying might be derived from his commentary on Psalm 59, 10. PL 36, 721: "Be not overcome; persevere even unto the end," *noli vinci; persevere usque in finem.*

16 1 Cor. 15:55.

17 1 Cor. 15:57.

18 Rom. 16:20a.

19 Is. 26:12–13.

20 E. N. Denis is referring to Hugh of Saint-Cher (*ca.* 1200–1263) and his commentary on this Psalm. Hugonis de Sancto Charo, *In Psalterium Universum Davidis Regis & Prophetae* (Venice: Nicolaum Pezzana 1732), Vol. 2, 326.

PRAYER

GRANT, O LORD, OUR SOULS TO PASS through the torrent of vices, so that the snares of diabolical deceit might be crushed by your strength, and we might be delivered continuously by your help.

Torrentem vitiorum, Domine, fac animam nostram pertransire:
ut tua fortitudine laqueo diabolicae fraudis contrito,
tuo in perpetuum liberemur adiutorio.

Psalm 124

ARTICLE XXXVII

EXPOSITION OF THE
ONE HUNDRED AND TWENTY-FOURTH PSALM:
QUI CONFIDUNT IN DOMINO.
THEY THAT TRUST IN THE LORD.

THE TITLE OF THIS PSALM NOW BEING addressed is: *Canticum graduum, a gradual canticle.* For this Psalm here is the sixth among the gradual Psalms, and it addresses the sixth step of spiritual ascent, which is a certain unshakeable trust in God strengthened by past benefits. For the more frequently one experiences the kindness and the grace of God, that much more certainly is the trust in God established, and so from the awareness of present gifts one has a certain expectation of future ones.

124{125}[1] *A gradual canticle. They that trust in the Lord shall be as mount Sion: he shall not be moved forever that dwells . . .*

Canticum graduum. Qui confidunt in Domino, sicut mons Sion: non commovebitur in aeternum, qui habitat . . .

124{125}[2] *. . . in Jerusalem. Mountains are round about it: so the Lord is round about his people from henceforth now and forever.*

. . . in Ierusalem. Montes in circuitu eius; et Dominus in circuitu populi sui, ex hoc nunc et usque in saeculum.

And so the holy Prophet [David] says: 124{125}[1] *Qui confidunt in Domino, they that trust in the Lord,* not in created, transitory, and vain things, these persons will be and are *sicut mons Sion, as mount Sion:* either by Mount Sion is understood the earthly mountain in which the temple of Solomon was constructed or the contemplative man, who transcends others by the grace of contemplation. For, as the mount in that land was immovable — either because in no manner at all or because only with difficulty was it movable — so those trusting in the Lord, either in no way or with difficulty are moved from the rectitude of faith and righteousness of life. Again, as a contemplative man, who is a mount of contemplation, is made stable by grace, so they that trust in the Lord are strengthened in him by the most certain forbearance of hope. Whence Scripture says: *They that hope in the Lord shall renew their strength, they shall take wings as eagles, . . . they shall walk and not faint.*[1] And again: *The name of the Lord is a strong tower: the just run to it, and shall be saved.*[2]

Non commovebitur in aeternum qui habitat 124{125}[2] *in Ierusalem; he shall not be moved forever that dwells* 124{125}[2] *in Jerusalem.* Jerusalem, that patch of land that was a city in Judea, was often subject to earthquakes and destruction. For it was totally destroyed twice, namely, once by the king of Babylon,[3] and once by Titus, the ruler of the Romans. Frequently, however, it was also destroyed in part; but also its inhabitants were often devasted. The Prophet [David] does not here speak of that [earthly, historical] Jerusalem, therefore, but of the heavenly Jerusalem, whose inhabitants are confirmed in good and in the state of beatitude, and so they are not longer able to be moved. It can also be understood as referring to the Church militant which is called by the name Jerusalem so that it is [to be understood] in this sense: *He shall not be moved forever* from the Catholic faith, from the faithful life, from grace, however long he should spend in the present age, *that dwells in Jerusalem*, that is, in the Church militant, adorned by faith, charity, and grace. Not that such a man cannot possibly sin, or that all in the Church dwell in it in this manner, or that he is one of the elect, or is eternally safe, but this is stated in this manner: to suggest what is fitting to one who dwells in, and is a son of, the Church, or is a just man. For so long as he remains a member and son of the Church, he is defended by Christ; but he is not confirmed in the good of the common law, unless, except during the course of this finite life, or, rather, at its end.[4] Nevertheless some of

---

1 Is. 40:31.

2 Prov. 18:10. *E. N.* Denis ends the quote with "shall be saved," *salvabitur*, departing from the Sixto-Clementine Vulgate, which reads "shall be exalted," *exaltabitur*.

3 2 Kings 25:9–10.

4 *E. N.* Immediately after death the eternal destiny of each separated soul is decided by the just judgment of God. "Each man receives his eternal retribution in his immortal soul at the very moment of his death, in a particular judgment that refers his life to Christ: either entrance into the blessedness of heaven — through a purification or immediately — or immediate and everlasting damnation." CCC §1022. "I ever had believed / That on the moment when the struggling soul / Quitted its mortal case, forthwith it fell / Under the awful Presence of its God, / There to be judged and sent to its own place." St. John Henry Newman, *The Dream of Gerontius* (London: Longmans, Green, and Co. 188), 24.

the saints by a special grace dared to assert in this life that they would never be moved from the state of salvation, in the manner that holy Job said: *Til I die I will not depart from my innocence;*[5] and Paul: *I am sure that neither death, nor life, nor angels, nor principalities, . . . nor any other creature shall be able to separate us from the love of God.*[6]

But the cause of this stability is stated subsequently: *Montes in circuitu eius, mountains are round about it*: that is, the blessed in the heavenly fatherland, namely, the holy angels and the men already saved, are *round about it*, that is, on every side of the heavenly Jerusalem, and so that city is not able to be troubled. Or [we can understand it] thus: *Mountains*, that is, the angels of God, who, because of their nature and excellence of grace are called mountains, are *round about it*, that is, the Church militant, inasmuch as they are ordered and sent to keep custody of men. But lest anyone think that this alone suffices, or places his final hope in them, it adds: *et Dominus in circuitu populi sui, so the Lord is round about his people*, the way the Gospel says, *I will not leave you orphans;*[7] and, *I am with you all days, even to the consummation of the world.*[8] For this reason, it continues: *ex hoc nunc et usque in saeculum, from henceforth now and forever*. In a Psalm above it is stated about the Lord, *A congregation of people shall surround you:*[9] which is explained there;[10] now, however, it says, *the Lord is around his people*: and this is more properly stated than the former. For properly speaking nothing can encircle the immensity and uncircumscribability of God; but God eternal and infinite includes all things, contains, surrounds, preserves all things, and graciously defends his elect.

124{125}[3] *For the Lord will not leave the rod of sinners upon the lot of the just: that the just may not stretch forth their hands to iniquity.*

Quia non relinquet Dominus virgam peccatorum super sortem iustorum; ut non extendant iusti ad iniquitatem manus suas.

124{125}[3] *Quia non relinquet Dominus, for the Lord will not leave* finally *virgam peccatorum, the rod of sinners*, that is, the power, persecution,

---

5 Job 7:4.
6 Rom. 8:38–39.
7 John 14:18.
8 Matt. 28:20b.
9 Ps. 7:8a.
10 *E. N. See Beatus Vir* (Volume I), Article XXIV (Psalm 7:8).

and tyranny of the reprobate, *super sortem, upon the lot,* that is, upon the part *iustorum, of the just,* or over the just, who are *the portion* and *inheritance* of God:[11] and this is the reason, *ut non extendant iusti ad iniquitatem manus suas, that the just may not stretch forth their hands to iniquity,* that is, that they not be overcome and sin. Although God for a time leaves the elect to be afflicted by the perverse so that the elect may be purged and be found worthy of glory, yet he does not abandon them finally, but he eternally saves them. And so while he sees them to be tempted and troubled beyond their strength, and to approach a fall, he immediately comes to the rescue, and does away with the temptation lest the just incur the loss of justice.

124{125}[4] *Do good, O Lord, to those that are good, and to the upright of heart.*

Benefac, Domine, bonis, et rectis corde.

124{125}[5] *But such as turn aside into bonds, the Lord shall lead out with the workers of iniquity: peace upon Israel.*

Declinantes autem in obligationes, adducet Dominus cum operantibus iniquitatem. Pax super Israel.

124{125}[4] *Benefac, Domine, bonis; do good, O Lord to the good,* in deed, *et rectis corde, and to the upright of heart,* that is, in intention, giving to them growth of grace while wayfaring and an abundance of beatitude in the heavenly fatherland. The upright of heart are those who are in harmony with the affection of God and justice, those whose eye is single,[12] those whose intention tends towards God. 124{125}[5] *Declinantes autem, but such as turn aside* from the good and a just life *in obligationes, into bonds,* that is, unto sin, binding a man to punishment, *adducet Dominus, the Lord shall lead out* in the day of judgment to his left, and afterwards or even before, into hell, *cum operantibus iniquitatem, with the workers of iniquity,* that is, with the demons, those whose pride ascends continually,[13] who sinned from the beginning,[14] who when they fell, did not attempt to rise again, but remained obstinate in evil. This

---

11 Ps. 15:5, 6.

12 Cf. Matt. 6:22: *The light of thy body is your eye. If your eye be single, your whole body shall be lightsome.*

13 Ps. 73:23b.

14 Cf. 1 John 3:8a: *He that commits sin is of the devil: for the devil sins from the beginning.*

is what is revealed by the evangelist: *Then he shall say to them also that shall be on his left hand: Depart from me, you cursed, into everlasting fire which was prepared for the devil and his angels.*[15] And elsewhere the Lord said to the unjust: *I will very soon return you a recompense upon your own head.*[16] And it is written: *Behold the day shall come kindled as a furnace: and all the proud, and all that do wickedly shall be stubble: and the day that comes shall set them on fire.*[17] *Pax,* peace true [peace] be *super Israel, upon Israel,* that is, the faithful people, in the way the angels sang: *Glory to God in the highest; and on earth peace to men of good will.*[18] And Christ said: *Peace I leave with you, my peace I give unto you.*[19] Indeed, this peace Isaiah wished for, saying: *Lord, you will give us peace.*[20]

See we have heard this brief and very fruitful Psalm that is joyful and greatly overflowing with meaning: in its beginning we learned how blessed it is to trust in God. Whence also Jeremiah attests: *Blessed be the man that trusts in the Lord;*[21] and Solomon says, *Have confidence in the Lord with all your heart, and lean not upon your own prudence.*[22] This Psalm also teaches us how powerful are the defenders of the Church, namely the angels who are called mountains, who run about the Christians like busy bees, so that they might provide for our salvation, restraining demons, suggesting good things, rejoicing in our progress, praying for us, obtaining grace for us. Whence the Lord through Isaiah bears witness: *Upon your walls, O Jerusalem, I have appointed watchmen all the day, and all the night, they shall never hold their peace.*[23] Above all, this Psalm promises to us that the Lord will not leave the rod of the sinners upon the lot of the just, so that in all afflictions of this kind we can trust at length to be helped by God, and meanwhile let us keep true patience: *for he that perseveres unto the end shall be saved,* as the Savior disclosed.[24]

---

15 Matt. 25:41.
16 Joel 3:4b.
17 Mal. 4:1.
18 Luke 2:14.
19 John 14:27a.
20 Is. 25:12a.
21 Jer. 17:7a.
22 Prov. 3:5.
23 Is. 62:6.
24 Matt. 10:22.

PRAYER

CHRIST, MOUNTAIN OF STRENGTH, support us everywhere (we beseech you) with your assistance, be round about your people, and do not leave the rod of the sinner to dominate over the lot of your servants; do good to us, and grant us times of prosperity and peace.

Mons, Christe, fortitudinis, tuis nos (quaesumus) ubique tuere praesidiis, esto in circuitu populi tui, et non derelinquas virgam peccatorum dominari super sortem famulantium tibi; bene fac nobis, et indulge tempora prosperitatis et pacis.

Psalm 125

ARTICLE XXXVIII

LITERAL AND MYSTICAL EXPOSITION OF THE ONE HUNDRED AND TWENTY-FIFTH PSALM: *IN CONVERTENDO DOMINUS.* WHEN THE LORD BROUGHT BACK.

HE TITLE OF THIS PSALM IS ALSO: *CANTI-cum graduum, a gradual canticle*: because spiritually explained, this Psalm treats of the seventh step of spiritual ascent to God: which step consists in the exultation and act of thanksgiving for the spiritual deliverance from the bonds of sins and servitude to the devil. But, as can be seen from its words, this Psalm is literally written about the return of the Jews from the Babylonian captivity, where they had been for seventy years in the manner that Jeremiah had foretold.[1] And this present Psalm is an act of thanksgiving and of joy of the liberation from such a long captivity. Briefly, therefore, the literal exposition will be touched upon.

125{126}[1] *A gradual canticle. When the Lord brought back the captivity of Sion, we became like men comforted.*

Canticum graduum. In convertendo Dominus captivitatem Sion, facti sumus sicut consolati.

125{126}[2] *Then was our mouth filled with gladness; and our tongue with joy. Then shall they say among the Gentiles: The Lord has done great things for them.*

Tunc repletum est gaudio os nostrum, et lingua nostra exsultatione. Tunc dicent inter gentes: Magnificavit Dominus facere cum eis.

Whence, the Prophet [David] speaking in the person of the people returned from their captivity, says: **125{126}[1]** *In convertendo Dominus captivitatem Sion, when the Lord brought back the captivity of Sion*: that is, when the Lord brought back the Jewish people from captivity, bringing them from Babylon into Judea; *facti sumus, we became*, those returning from there

---

1 Jer. 25:11.

513

[became], *sicut consolati, like men comforted* by the benefit of liberation. As, in this place it signifies not only a similarity, but [the literal] truth, because many rejoiced that they were returning to the place of divine worship, as is clear in the book of Ezra.[2] Now, by Sion is signified the Jewish people because mount Sion was in Jerusalem and it was the place where the temple and the king's place were situated. **125{126}[2]** *Tunc repletum est gaudio os nostrum, et lingua nostra exsultatione; then was our mouth filled with gladness, and our tongue with joy,* that is, we sang the divine praises with a happy mouth and spirit, giving thanks to the Lord. *Tunc dicent inter gentes, then shall they say among the Gentiles,* that is, the subjects of the empire of Cyrus then said: *Magnificavit Dominus facere cum eis, the Lord has done great things for them,* that is, the God of Israel did a marvelous thing for his people: for Cyrus, the king of the Persians, published throughout his whole reign an edict that the Jews were declared free and could return to the land of their fathers.[3] When this was heard, the Gentiles marveled and said that the Lord had done great things for his people, especially because Cyrus in his epistle wrote thus: *The Lord the God of heaven has given to me all the kingdoms of the earth, and he has charged me to build him a house in Jerusalem.*[4] For this reason, some of the Gentiles converted to Judaism.

125{126}[3]   *The Lord has done great things for us: we are become joyful.*
           Magnificavit Dominus facere nobiscum; facti sumus laetantes.

125{126}[4]   *Turn again our captivity, O Lord, as a stream in the south.*
           Converte, Domine, captivitatem nostram, sicut torrens in austro.

Here the Prophet in the person of the Jews adds: **125{126}[3]** *Magnificavit Dominus facere nobiscum, the Lord has done great things for us,* that is, he has done things for us with great graciousness, kindness, and power. Whence Ezra said: *Blessed be the Lord the God of our fathers, who has put this in the king's heart.*[5] *Facti sumus laetantes, we are become joyful* in the Lord because of such great benefits. But because during the time of Ezra in the beginning of this return the people were small in number, and neither the city nor the temple had been repaired, therefore the Prophet prays for the perfect return from the previously-mentioned captivity, adding: **125{126}[4]** *Converte, Domine, captivitatem nostram,*

---

2 Ezra 3:11–13.
3 Ezra 1:1.
4 Ezra 1:2.
5 Ezra 7:27a.

sicut torrens in austro; turn again our captivity, O Lord, as a stream in the south is turned: that is, in the manner that a dried river is filled up again by the blowing of the south wind which causes rain, and so the dried river beds are filled with water; so increase and repair a people of such small numbers, and restore the cities of Judea and the temple.

125{126}[5] *They that sow in tears shall reap in joy.*

Qui seminant in lacrimis, in exsultatione metent.

125{126}[6] *Going they went and wept, casting their seeds.*

Euntes ibant et flebant, mittentes semina sua.

125{126}[7] *But coming they shall come with joyfulness, carrying their sheaves.*

Venientes autem venient cum exsultatione, portantes manipulos suos.

And this is fittingly to be done in this manner, because **125{126} [5]** *Qui seminant in lacrimis, they that sow in tears,* that is, who perform works of penance and pour out tears of compunction and devotion for their past evils, pleading for indulgence, and the grace of future goods, *in exsultatione metent, shall reap in joy,* that is, they will joyfully obtain that which they asked for, and they will receive a glorious reward, according to this: *Blessed are they that mourn: for they shall be comforted.*[6] And the Jews did just this, for **125{126}[6]** *Euntes, going* from Jerusalem and Judea to Babylon, *ibant et flebant, they went and wept* from compunction and the sorrow that they had to relinquish the place of divine worship and that they were forced to enter into a land that was given over to idolatry, *mittentes semina sua, casting their seeds,* that is, doing good works, from which, after an apt time, they obtained the fruit of consolation and of grace. **125{126}[7]** *Venientes autem, but coming* from Babylon to Judea, *venient cum exsultatione, portantes manipulos suos; they shall come with joyfulness, carrying their sheaves,* that is, the fruits of the seeds already discussed.

TROPOLOGICAL EXPOSITION

125{126}[1] *A gradual canticle. When the Lord brought back the captivity of Sion, we became like men comforted.*

Canticum graduum. In convertendo Dominus captivitatem Sion, facti sumus sicut consolati.

---

6 Matt. 5:5.

In addition, this Psalm can be explained mystically of the Church, or of any one member of the faithful, rescued from vices or spiritual Babylon, that is, the confusion of sin. It will [be understood] in this sense: **125{126}** [1] *In convertendo Dominus captivitatem Sion, when the Lord brought back the captivity of Sion*: that is, when the militant Church or any one member of the faithful would convert from a confused life, from mortal sin, from the present misery, to an ordered life, to the state of grace, to the place of glory; *facti sumus sicut consolati, we became like men comforted.* For from such an emphatic conversion every Christian glories. For this reason, the Apostle said: *Great is my confidence for you, great is my glorying for you. I am filled with comfort: I exceedingly abound with joy in all our tribulation.*[7] But especially joyful is the prelate, when those subject to him convert to become better, as in the example of blessed John, who in his epistle professes: *I have no greater grace than this, to hear that my children walk in truth.*[8]

125{126}[2]   *Then was our mouth filled with gladness; and our tongue with joy. Then shall they say among the Gentiles: The Lord has done great things for them.*

Tunc repletum est gaudio os nostrum, et lingua nostra exsultatione. Tunc dicent inter gentes: Magnificavit Dominus facere cum eis.

125{126}[2] *Tunc, then,* that is, upon this conversion from spiritual captivity unto internal consolation, *repletum est gaudio, filled with gladness* with spiritual and joyful praise, *os nostrum, was our mouth* both our mental and bodily [mouth]. For there is a spiritual mouth, intellectual or mental, with which the word of the heart is pronounced, and with which the angels dialogue. Wisdom says of it: *I came out of the mouth of the most High, the firstborn before all creatures.*[9] This mouth is filled with the joy of the Holy Spirit, from the consideration of the grace and the benefits of God. *Et lingua nostra, and our tongue* is filled *exsultatione, with joy,* that is, with vocal praise and exuberant joy. For *out of the abundance of the heart the mouth speaks.*[10] Similarly, the plenitude of interior joy redounds to and appears in the tongue of the body. *Tunc dicent inter gentes: Magnificavit Dominus facere cum eis; then shall they say among the Gentiles: The Lord has done great things for them:* that is, some of the worldly men, or whoever of the

----

7 2 Cor. 7:4.
8 3 John 4.
9 Ecclus. 24:5.
10 Matt. 12:34b.

other people seeing the grace of God bestowed, shall marvel and will say: Great things has God done for them. For frequently, men that are in love with the world, praise in others that which they do not want to imitate; and seeing some convert to Christ, entering the cloister, and quickly being changed, they marvel, and they praise God for his effects, though they do not pray that the same grace be bestowed upon them.

125{126}[3] *The Lord has done great things for us: we are become joyful.*

Magnificavit Dominus facere nobiscum; facti sumus laetantes.

125{126}[4] *Turn again our captivity, O Lord, as a stream in the south.*

Converte, Domine, captivitatem nostram, sicut torrens in austro.

125{126}[3] *Magnificavit Dominus facere nobiscum,* the Lord has done great things for us. This is what the most worthy Virgin said: *He that is mighty, has done great things to me; and holy is his name.*[11] For Christ the Lord has done great things for us, assuming our nature, reversing our first and general captivity, making satisfaction for original sin, conversing among men,[12] unifying us to him by grace, assembling us in the Church, giving us his Body and Blood, sending the Holy Spirit, and bestowing innumerable benefits: and so *facti sumus laetantes, we are become joyful,* both by giving thanks and cheerfully rendering service. For this Judith, an expert on the mercy of God, said: *Praise the Lord our God, who has not forsaken them that hope in him, and by me his handmaid he has fulfilled his mercy.*[13] **125{126} [4]** *Converte, Domine, captivitatem nostrum; turn again our captivity, O Lord:* that is, deliver us from all the corruption of sin because the wounds of the soul infected with original sin into the liberty of the children of God,[14] and remove from us the sins by which we daily are bound and captured; *sicut torrens in austro, as a stream in the south* let us be converted so that we may be filled with the gifts and graces of the Holy Spirit, as a dried stream is filled with the waters of a rainy southern wind.

125{126}[5] *They that sow in tears shall reap in joy.*

Qui seminant in lacrimis, in exsultatione metent.

125{126}[5] *Qui seminant in lacrimis, they that sow in tears,* that is, who for a time exercise themselves in the mourning of penance or the tears

---

11 Luke 1:49.
12 Baruch 3:38.
13 Judith 13:17–18a.
14 *Cf.* Rom. 8:21.

of devotion, who disdain temporal delights, and who minister unto God with contrite and humble hearts: these *in exsultatione metent, shall reap in joy* with the goods of grace in the present and the fruit of glory in the future. *For the fruit of good labors is glorious.*[15] And the Apostle [Paul] said: *He who sows sparingly, shall also reap sparingly: and he who sows in blessings, shall also reap blessings.*[16] For this reason we are encouraged by Jeremiah: *Break up anew your fallow ground, and sow not upon thorns.*[17] There are moreover five kinds of tears. The first kind of tears are for indulgence of one's own fault: and these clean from the filth of sin. The second kind are for the fear of the future judgment and hell: and these are cooled by the ardor of concupiscence and are removed by any kind of sin. The third kind are for having to dwell in the present exile: they give drink to the thirsty soul. The fourth kind are for the defects of the neighbor, and these fatten the mourner. The fifth kind are for the desire of the heavenly fatherland, which make the soul fruitful in all good.

125{126}[6]   *Going they went and wept, casting their seeds.*

Euntes ibant et flebant, mittentes semina sua.

125{126}[7]   *But coming they shall come with joyfulness, carrying their sheaves.*

Venientes autem venient cum exsultatione, portantes mani-pulos suos.

125{126}[6] *Euntes, going* the elect of God while wayfaring in the present life, *ibant, went* by the way of the commandments of the most High, *et flebant, and wept,* according to one of the just-mentioned kinds of weeping, *mittentes semina sua, casting their seeds,* that is, doing meritorious works: which works are called seeds because as fruits are born from seeds, so from good works the fruit of eternal life arises: the infusion of divine consolation. Therefore, they cast their seed, that is, they cast their good works in front of them, gathering up a mass of merits which they hide in Christ, in the way that they are exhorted: *Lay up to yourselves treasures in heaven.*[18] And the Apostle said: Do not fail in doing good; *for in due time we shall reap not failing.*[19] *Venientes autem,*

---

15 Wis. 3:15a.
16 2 Cor. 9:6.
17 Jer. 4:3b.
18 Matt. 6:20a.
19 Gal. 6:9.

but coming to the tribunal of Christ, *venient cum exsultatione, they shall come with joyfulness,* that is, with secure and happy conscience, *portantes manipulos suos, carrying their sheaves,* that is, their virtuous works which they have collected. *For their works follow them.*[20]

We are admonished from this present Psalm to bear in mind our Redemption effected by Christ, and to exult in the Savior because of his benefits by praising, contemplating, and incomparably loving him. And so the text of this Psalm teaches us how to tell the difference between the elect and the reprobate: for the elect walk in the good and make progress weeping; but the reprobate glory in this exile as if it were the heavenly fatherland, and out of the prison of captivity they make for themselves a paradise of pleasure: and so, coming to the judgment of Christ, they come with sorrow, carrying nothing but the writ of their damnation. Whence in the Gospel it is said to them: *Woe . . . to you who have your consolation;*[21] and *Woe to you that now laugh, for you shall morn and weep.*[22] For this Abraham said to the rich man: *Son, remember that you did receive good things in your lifetime, and likewise Lazarus evil things, but now he is comforted; and you are tormented.*[23] Let us despise, therefore, all the pomps, vanities, and glories of this world, and let us repress the desires of the body, and let us occupy ourselves with holy tears, knowing that we cannot now rejoice with the world and afterwards reign with Christ.

PRAYER

CLEANSE US, O LORD, FROM SINS; BUILD for yourself in us a house of your residence, so that you may abide in us and we in you, and when you give to us the sleep of death, we might be heirs of the heavenly kingdom with your beloved.

Expurga nos, Domine, a peccatis; aedifica tibi in nobis domum mansionis: ut tu in nobis, et nos in te manentes, cum dederis nobis somnum mortis, cum dilectis tuis simus heredes regni caelestis.

---

20 Rev. 14:13b.
21 Luke 6:24.
22 Luke 6:25b.
23 Luke 16:25.

ABOUT THE TRANSLATOR

ANDREW M. GREENWELL IS A MARRIED Catholic layman, with three children and four grandchildren. He is a civil trial and appellate lawyer based in Corpus Christi, Texas, who has written articles for Catholic Online and for a number of years wrote a blog on the natural moral law called *Lex Christianorum*. He has translated works from German, Latin, French, and Italian into English. He is a member of the Latin Mass Community at St. John the Baptist Church in Corpus Christi, Texas. Angelico Press is publishing his translations of all of Denis the Carthusian's works on the Mass and the Eucharist.